HAMP

A

HIGHGATE
DIRECTORY
1885-6

London Borough of Camden
Libraries and Arts Department
100 Euston Road London NW1 2AJ

in association with the
Camden History Society

Reprinted December 1985

Printed in Great Britain by
The Garden City Press Limited
Letchworth, Hertfordshire SG6 1JS

ISBN 0 901389 48 X

INTRODUCTION

The first comprehensive Street Directory for Hampstead and Highgate was published in June 1873 by Hutchings & Crowsley of St John's Wood. The 'Buff Book', as it became known from its cover colour, was soon a popular annual guide to the ever-changing inhabitants and tradesmen in the burgeoning suburbs of the Northern Heights.

Publication, which was later taken over by Kelly's Directories, continued every year until 1940 and then became a war-time casualty. Other publishers produced much slimmer directories for Hampstead (and then Camden) after the war but, by 1970, the demand had died and, much to the regret of the local historian, so did the local street directory leaving only the London Post Office Directory.

Not surprisingly, the first section in the directory is devoted to a *Classified List of Tradesmen*, without whose advertisements publication would have been impossible. A more comprehensive list of trades begins on page 263, where you will find such forgotten enterprises as bath-chair hire and Galvano-Electric Baths.

Under *Churches, Chapels, Institutions, etc* come also Mission Rooms, the Salvation Army Barracks in the Vale of Health, Board Schools and British Schools (e.g. at the Baptist Chapel in Heath Street), the Public Library in Stanfield House, the Volunteer Corps and other vanished organisations.

The *Hampstead Streets Directory* proper begins on page 33 and takes us immediately into another world. The first street, Abbey Lane, no longer exists: it has disappeared without trace under the Kilburn Vale Estate. Fortunately, each road name has a note underneath to describe its location. (A map reference is given too and the original map is being republished separately.) Then some of the occupations in Abbey Lane are decidedly unexpected, including cowkeeper, bottler dealer, servants registry office, writer and grainer, and lath render.

Note how other roads have changed character over the past century – all those bootmakers in Back Lane, nursery gardens in Haverstock Hill and Highgate West Hill, a Field Lane Industrial School in Church Row and tea gardens and sweeps in the Vale of Health. The impact of the large, well planned Highgate Cemetery can be seen in the numbers of monumental masons in local streets.

It is a surprise to come across the Eton and Middlesex Cricket Ground in King Henry's Road, the Swiss Cottage Skating Rink in Finchley Road (on the site of Sainsbury's), and the Sailors' Orphan Girls' Home (now Monro House for old people) in Greenhill Road, which is now part of Fitzjohns Avenue. A feature of the area around Highgate Hill was the number of hospitals – the Smallpox Hospital, Holborn Infirmary, St. Pancras Infirmary (all part of the Whittington Hospital since 1949) and a branch of the Hospital for Sick Children.

The changing of street names increased as Hampstead and Highgate became more integrated into London (it was all part of Middlesex until 1889) and as the postal, fire and ambulance services demanded clearer addresses for houses. Many names were changed for this reason in the mid 1930's. The two High Streets became Hampstead High Street and Highgate High Street to distinguish them from all the other High Streets. Both Hampstead and Highgate had streets called The Grove. The latter has kept its name, while the former reluctantly agreed to Hampstead Grove. Note that in the ABC of streets The Grove comes under T, not G. A list of major street changes is given below.

Many streets have been renumbered, some several times, as they filled up with new houses or were redeveloped. Numbers replaced names on most houses by early this century. The need for this is well illustrated here by Broadhurst Gardens, where the builders presumably chose names to attract Continental customers, such as Donauwerth, Blenheim, Ramillies, Oudenarde and Malplaquet.

Only one house has been numbered in Frognal – that newly built by Norman Shaw (see Ellerdale Road) for the popular artist Kate Greenaway. In fact, only the name of her brother, John, is shown here, and the number has since been changed from 50 to 39.

Names of other noted artists and architects pepper these pages: George du Maurier in The Grove (Hampstead), Henry Holiday in Branch Hill (now in Redington Gardens) in a house built by Basil Champneys (see Frognal); Gilbert Scott junior in Church Row, and Bannister Fletcher in Woodchurch Road. Among the literati, you will find Gerald Manley Hopkins and family in Oak Hill Park, A.A. Milne and family in Mortimer Road, and the author of the Eton Boating Song, W.J. Cory, in Heathfield Gardens (now Cannon Place).

Then there are the Farjeons in Adelaide Road, the Harmsworths in Boundary Road, Miss Buss (but not Miss Beale) in King Henry's Road and H.H. Asquith in John Street (now Keats Grove) – and many more of interest.

There is much further London-wide social history to be found in the advertisements. Curiosities include those of hospitals, such as the insipient Hampstead General Hospital and the Royal Free Hospital (then in Grays Inn Road) all urgently appealing for funds to treat the sick. Among the advertisements for patent medicines, Lamplough's Pyretic Saline (a sort of Eno's?) claims to be 'The Great Remedy' for everything from cholera to constipation.

For all of those who are interested in local history or social history, or have puzzled about the history of their houses and been frustrated in their researches these Street Directories are surely the Great Remedy.

Christopher Wade
Malcolm Holmes

STREET NAME CHANGE

HAMPSTEAD

Present name	Old name
Avenue Rd	† Upper Avenue Rd
Belsize Lane	† Belsize Park Terrace
Belsize Rd	† Swiss Terrace
Cannon Place	† Heathfield Gdns
College Cres	† College Terrace & College Villas Rd
Elsworthy Rise	Eton Place
Eton College Rd	College Rd
Fitzjohns Av	† Greenhill Rd
Garnett Rd	Lower Cross Rd
Greencroft Gdns	† Westcroft Rd
Hampstead Grove	The Grove & Grove Cottages
Hampstead High St.	High Street
Harben Rd	Albion Rd
Haverstock Hill	† Haverstock Terrace & Hampstead Green
Heath St. (lower)	† Church Place & Little Church Row
Heath St. (upper)	† Heath Mount
Hermit Place	Abbey Lane
Keats Grove	John Street
Kilburn High Rd	High Rd
Lawn Rd	† Lower Lawn Rd
Lower Merton Rise	Merton Rd
Lyndhurst Terrace	Windsor Terrace
Mount, The	† Silver Street
Mount Square	Golden Square
New End	† Grove Place
North End Way	Hampstead Heath
Oriel Place	Wells Buildings
Parkhill Road	Park Rd
Perrins Lane	Church Lane & Prince Arthur Mews
Pilgrim's Lane	† Worsley Road
Platt's Lane	† West Heath
Primrose Gdns	Stanley Gdns
Priory Terrace	St George's Rd
Rosslyn Hill	† Mansfield Terrace & Rosslyn Cottages, Street & Terrace
Sandy Road	North End
Spaniards End & Rd	Heath End
Springfield Lane	Goldsmith Plac
Tasker Rd	Church Rd
Well Walk	† Foley Avenue
West End Lane	† Providence Pla & West End
Whitestone Lane	Hampstead He
Wildwood Grove & Terrace	North End

HIGHGATE

Present name	Old name
Balmore St	Colva St
Boscastle Rd	Grove Rd
Bredgar Rd	Langdon Rd
Carrol Place	Pleasant Row
Chetwynd Rd	† Carrol Rd
Dartmouth Park Rd	† Dartmouth Rd
Evangelist Rd	St. John the Evangelist R
Fortress Walk	Willow Walk
Gaskell Rd	Grange Rd
Greenwood Place	Prospect Place & Cottages
Highgate High St	High St
Hargrave Park	Hargrave Park
Highgate West Hill	Highgate Rise, South Grov (north part West Hill
Laurier Rd	Lewisham Rd
MacDonald Rd	Brunswick Rd
Park, The	Park House Rd
Shepherds Hill	Shepherds Hill
Spencer Rise	Spencer Rd

† means that only part of a present road has changed its name

Most minor changes not included e.g. Christchurch Road to Christchurch Hill

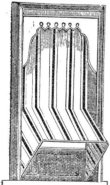

Thirteenth Annual Edition.]　　　　　　　　　　　　　　［*Entered at Stationers' Hall.*

THE

HAMPSTEAD

AND

HIGHGATE

DIRECTORY

("BUFF BOOK")

FOR 1885-6.

THE DISTRICT INCLUDED

EXTENDS FROM JUNCTION ROAD, *EAST*, TO HIGH ROAD, KILBURN,
WEST;　AND FROM FINCHLEY. *NORTH*, TO PRIMROSE HILL,
SOUTH.

THE WORK COMPRISES ALPHABETICAL LISTS OF

STREETS, PRIVATE INHABITANTS, AND TRADESMEN;

LOCAL MEDICAL DIRECTORY, CALENDAR, LOCAL POSTAL GUIDE,
LISTS OF PUBLIC OFFICERS AND OFFICES, CHURCHES, CHAPELS,
INSTITUTIONS, ETC., FIRE AND LIFE ASSURANCE OFFICES,
PRINCIPAL CLUBS AND CLUB-HOUSES, LONDON BANKS
AND BANKERS, AND LONDON HOSPITALS, TABLES OF
WEIGHTS AND MEASURES, AND A READY
RECKONER;

ALSO

A NEW MAP OF THE DISTRICT

Divided into half-mile squares, and giving radius lines from Charing Cross;

AND A

VISITORS' GUIDE

TO PLEASURE AND HEALTH RESORTS.

LONDON: PRINTED AND PUBLISHED BY THE PROPRIETORS,

HUTCHINGS & CROWSLEY, LIMITED.

Chief Office and Works:
35, 37, 39 & 41, HENRY STREET, ST. JOHN'S WOOD, N.W.

Branch Works:
123, FULHAM ROAD, SOUTH KENSINGTON, S.W.

City Office:
IMPERIAL BUILDINGS, LUDGATE CIRCUS, E.C.

Price 1s.; Bound in Cloth, 2s., Net.

GENERAL INDEX.

———o———

CLASSIFIED LIST OF TRADESMEN
AND OTHERS,

WHOSE ADVERTISEMENTS APPEAR IN THIS DIRECTORY.

ADVERTISER.

PAGE

Dalton's Weekly 21 South Lambeth rd. S.W. and 295 Strand W.C. ... ... 260(*b*)

ART NEEDLEWORK AND FANCY WAREHOUSE.

Brooking & Co. 298 High rd. Kilburn N.W.... ... ... 166(*a*)

AUCTIONEERS.

Batcheler, Dalston junction E. 260(*b*)
Dolman & Pearce 62 Haverstock hill N.W. ... ... 32(*d*)
Phillips & Dyer 123 Finchley rd. N.W. ... ... MAP
Salter, Rex & Co. 311 Kentish town rd. N.W. FRONT COVER
Stevens, Finchley Road station N.W. ... ... 222(*c*)

BANK.

Birkbeck 29 & 30 Southampton buildings Chancery lane W.C. 260(*c*)

BICYCLE AND TRICYCLE WORKS.

Petts 2*a* Prince of Wales rd.N.W. MAP

BLIND WORKS.

Mallett 1 Canfield pl. Fitzjohns' parade N.W. ... ... 166(*c*)

BOOKBINDERS.

Hutchings & Crowsley, Limited 35 to 41 Henry st. St. John's wood N.W. & 123 Fulham rd. South Kensington S.W. ... 274

BOOKSELLER, STATIONER, &c.

Phillips 248 High st. Camden town N.W. 271

BOOT AND SHOE MAKER.

Martin 3 Flask walk Hampstead N.W. 271

BREWERS.

PAGE

Collier Bros., *Essex Brewery*, Walthamstow FRONT COVER & 260(*b*)
Lovibond and Son, *Cannon Brewery*, North end Fulham S.W. ... ... 106(*b*)
Michell and Phillips, *Kilburn Brewery*, High rd. Kilburn N.W. ... ... 32(*a*)

BUILDERS & DECORATORS.

Tugwell & Son 4 Belsize cres. N.W. ... ... MAP

BUILDING SOCIETIES.

Birkbeck 29 & 30 Southampton buildings Chancery lane W.C. 260(*c*)
The Imperial Permanent Benefit 40 Chancery lane W.C. ... 260(*a*)
The London Commercial Deposit 15 Lamb's Conduit st. W.C.... 260(*c*)

BUTCHERS.

Barrett 18 Elizabeth ter. Haverstock hill N.W. viii
Pippett 18 Queen's ter. St. John's wood N.W. ... ... 166(*d*)
Randall 93 Haverstock hill N.W. iv

CARPENTERS, BUILDERS, &c.

Perkins 4 New end sq. Hampstead N.W. ... ... 32(*b*)
Thomas 43 Crogsland rd. N.W. 222(*b*)

CARPET BEATERS AND CLEANERS.

Simmons & Tullidge, Latimer rd. Notting hill W. ... ... 260(*b*)
Smith 8 Kingsford st. Gospel oak N.W. ... ... 222(*b*)

CARVER AND GILDER.

Devonald 57 High st. St. John's wood N.W. 8

CHEESEMONGER PORKMAN, AND POULTERER.

Tarrant 3 Queen's ter. St. John's wood N.W. BACK COVER

CHEMISTS.
PAGE
Lamplough 113 Holborn E.C. ... 222(*a*)
McGeorge 346 Essex rd. Islington N. ...   . 222(*d*)

CLOTHIERS & OUTFITTERS.
Charles Baker & Co. 271 & 272 High Holborn W.C., 82 Fleet st. E.C., and 137 & 138 Tottenham court rd. W.
BACK OF BOOK, 24 & 25

CLOTHING STORES.
Southon 131 High rd. Kilburn N.W. ...   . MAP

COCOA MANUFACTURERS.
Epps & Co., Holland st. Blackfriars rd. S.E.   ... FRONT COVER
Schweitzer & Co. 10 Adam st. Strand W.C. Sole proprietors of Cocoatina (guaranteed pure soluble Cocoa)   ...   ... 260(*d*)

COD LIVER OIL.
Möller 43 Snow hill E.C.   ...   248

COOKS & CONFECTIONERS.
Callard & Callard, Queen's ter. St. John's wood N.W.   ...
FRONT COVER & iii
Rieger 20 Elizabeth ter. Belsize park N.W.   ...   . 166(*d*)

CO-OPERATIVE DRUG STORES.
Lewis 2 Fitzjohns' parade South Hampstead N.W. and 22 Great Portland st. W.   ...   ... 32(*b*)

CORN, FLOUR, AND SEED MERCHANTS.
Edwards & Coxwell 88 Haverstock hill N.W.   ...   ... 32(*d*)

COURT HAIRDRESSER.
Martin 1 Dawson ter. Haverstock hill N.W.   ...   ... 222(*c*)

DAIRYMEN.
Beahan 126 Regent's park rd. & 13 Fitzjohns' parade N.W.   vii
Richards 8 Elizabeth ter. Belsize park and 3 Exeter ter. West Hampstead N.W.   ...   iv
Walker 58 Haverstock hill N.W. 166(*a*)

DANCING & CALISTHENICS.
PAGE
Barnett Mrs. 27 Belgrave rd. Abbey rd. N.W.   ...   ... 188(*b*)

DIRECTORY PUBLISHERS.
Hutchings & Crowsley, Limited 35 to 41 Henry st. St. John's wood N.W., & 123 Fulham rd. South Kensington S.W.   ...   4

DISTILLERS AND WINE MERCHANTS.
Pendred Applebee & Co. 107 Hampstead rd. N.W....   ... 260(*a*)

DRAPERS, SILK MERCERS, AND COMPLETE HOUSE FURNISHERS.
Crisp & Co. 67, 69, 71, 73, 75, 79, 81 & 83 Seven Sisters' rd., 135, 136, 137, 138, 139 & 140 Holloway rd., and 1, 1*a*, 2 and 4 Sussex rd. Holloway N.   ...   ii

DYERS AND CLEANERS.
Hannett & Sons 69 Fairfax rd. South Hampstead and 102 High st. St. John's wood N.W.   viii
Hutchins & Co. 4 Belsize park ter. and 29 Park st. Camden town N.W.   v

FILTER MANUFACTURER.
Maignen 32 St. Mary-at-hill E.C.   2

FURNITURE DEPOSITORY.
Bedford Pantechnicon Company, Limited 194 Tottenham court road W.   x

GAS & HOT WATER FITTER.
Peter 11 Upper Belsize ter. N.W. 222(*c*)

GAS, HOT WATER, SANITARY AND ELECTRICAL ENGINEER.
Smith 3 Iverson rd.Kilburn N.W.   15

GAS METER MANUFACTURERS.
Hubbard & Whitbread 10½ Great Percy st. King's cross rd. W.C. 222(*c*)

GOVERNESSES' INSTITUTE.
Praunsmandel 111 Edgware rd. W.   v

LOCAL MEDICAL DIRECTORY,

GIVING the names, qualifications, and legal medical descriptions of *registered* medical men residing within the district embraced by the " Hampstead and Highgate Directory." Every care has been taken to avoid mistake, and it is hoped that this addition to the Directory will prove of public service.

EXPLANATIONS OF ABBREVIATIONS.

BAC. SURG.	Bachelor in Surgery.
F.FAC.PHYS. & SURGS.	Fellow of the Faculty of Physicians and Surgeons.
F.R.C.P.	Fellow of the Royal College of Physicians.
F.R.C.S.	,, ,, ,, Surgeons.
L.A.H.	Licentiate of the Apothecaries' Hall.
L.FAC.P. & S.	,, of the Faculty of Physicians and Surgeons.
L.K.Q.C.P.	,, of the King & Queen's College of Physicians.
L.M.	,, in Midwifery.
L.MED.	,, in Medicine.
L.R.C.P.	,, of the Royal College of Physicians.
L.R.C.S.	,, ,, ,, Surgeons.
L.S.	,, in Surgery.
L.S.A.	,, of the Society of Apothecaries.
M.B.	Bachelor of Medicine.
M.D.	Doctor ,,
M.R.C.P.	Member of the Royal College of Physicians.
M.R.C.S.	,, ,, ,, Surgeons.
MAST. SURG.	Master in Surgery.

Aber., Aberdeen ; Dub., Dublin ; Dur., Durham ; Edin., Edinburgh ; Eng., England ; Glas., Glasgow ; Irel., Ireland ; Lond., London ; St. And., St. Andrew's.

NAME.	ADDRESS.	QUALIFICATIONS.
Alexander Frederick Wm.	94 Belsize rd.	M.R.C.S. Eng., 1881 ; L.R.C.P. Edin., 1883
Alford Frederick Stephen	61 Haverstock hill Hampstead	M.R.C.S. Eng., 1874
Allen J. W.	(Meadow bank) 13 Fairfax rd.	M.R.C.S. Eng., 1885 ; L.S.A. Lond., 1857
Anderson John Ford	28 Buckland cres. Belsize park Hampstead	L.R.C.S. Edin., 1861 ; M.D., Mast. Surg., 1863, Univ. Aber.
Andrew John May	140 Haverstock hill Hampstead	M.R.C.S. Eng., 1855
Andrews James	(Everleigh) 1 Prince Arthur rd.	L.S.A. Lond., M.R.C.S. Eng., 1851 ; M.D. Univ. St. And., 1854
Archer Lewis Hitchin ...	1 Upper Avenue rd. St. John's wood Hampstead	M.R.C.S. Eng., 1851 ; L.S.A. Lond., 1858
Atterbury Walter	(Acacia villa) Oppidans rd. Hampstead	L.S.A. Lond., 1880 ; M.R.C.S. Eng., 1881 ; M.D. R. Univ., Irel., 1883
Battiss W. S.	147 High rd. Kilburn	M.R.C.S. Eng., L.S.A. Lond., 1880
Bennett Deane	1 Haverstock hill Hampstead	L.K.Q.C.P. Irel., 1879

Name.	Address.	Qualifications.
Berry Edward Unwin......	17 Sherriff rd. West Hampstead	L.S.A. Lond., 1833 ; M.R.C.S. Eng., 1842
Biggs John M.	2 Claremont rd. Cricklewood Hampstead	M.R.C.S. Eng., 1878 ; L.S.A9 Lond., L.R.C.P. Lond., 187.,
Bonnor William James ...	43 Upper Park rd. Haverstock hill Hampstead	M.R.C.S. Eng., L.S.A. Lond 1861
Boulting William	The Mount, Heath st. Hampstead	L.R.C.P. Lond., 1877
Bowden William John ...	189 Adelaide rd. South Hampstead	M.R.C.S. Eng., L.S.A. Lond., 1841
Bowman Richard	24 Claremont rd. Kilburn	L.R.C.P., L.R.C.S.Edin.,L.A.H. Dub., 1880
Brinton Roland Danvers	7 College ter. Belsize park Hampstead	M.R.C.S. Eng., L.S.A. Lond., 1882; M.B. Univ. Cam.,1884
Brookfield J. S.	2 Devonshire villas Cricklewood	M.B., Mast. Surg., 1871, M.D. 1873, Univ. Edin.; M.R.C.S. Eng., 1871
Buck Alfred Henry	48 Primrose hill rd. Hampstead	M.R.C.S. Eng., 1867 ; L.R.C.P. Edin., 1868
Buss Howard Decimus ...	37 South hill park............	L.S.A. Lond., 1884
Butt W. F.	(The Bijou) Cricklewood	M.R.C.S. Eng., 1863 ; L.S.A. Lond.,1864; L.R.C.P. Lond., 1870
Calthrop Edward	(The Cheal) Hornsey lane	M.R.C.S. Eng., L.R.C.P. Lond., 1862
Campbell William Fredk.	88 Junction rd.	L.S.A. Lond., 1877 ; L.R.C.P. Edin., L. Fac. Phy. & Surg. Glas., 1878
Castor Richard Henderson	44 Ainger rd.	M.R.C.S.Eng., L.R.C.P. Lond., 1884
Chant Thomas	208 Adelaide rd. South Hampstead	L.S.A. Lond., M.R.C.S. Eng., 1875
ClarkeFencastleG. Barlow	7 Fordwych rd. West Hampstead	L.S.A. Lond., 1881
Clayton Geoffrey Sherborne	11 Fairfax rd. Hampstead	L.S.A. Lond., 1883 ; M.R.C.S. Eng., 1884
Clothier Henry	1 North rd. Highgate	M.R.C.S. Eng., 1865 ; M.B. 1866, M.D., 1869, Univ. Lond.;L.S.A.Lond.,L.R.C.P. Lond., 1866
Collie Alexander	9 South hill park gardens	M.D., Mast. Surg.,1863, Univ. Aber.; L.S.A. Lond., 1867 ; L.R.C.P. Lond., 1876
Collins George William ...	66 Adelaide rd. Hampstead	M.R.C.S. Eng., 1881
Connell Robert	50 Netherwood st.	L.R.C.S. Edin., 1846 ; M.D. Univ. St. And., 1861
Cook Augustus Henry ...	25 Denning rd. Hampstead	M.R.C.S. Eng., L.S.A. Lond., 1881 ; L.R.C.P. Lond., 1884
Cooper Herbert	1 Rosslyn ter. Hampstead	M.R.C.S. Eng., L.S.A. Lond., 1861
Copeland John	78 Alexandra rd. Hampstead	M.R.C.S. Eng., 1859 ; L.R.C.P. Edin., 1860
Cowley Alexander	62 Cromwell avenue.........	M.B.,Mast. Surg.,1881, Univ. Aber.
Cran John	(Netherdale) Broadhurst gardens Hampstead	M.D., 1861, Mast. Surg., 1873, Univ. Aber.
Cree E. H.	2 Pemberton villas St. John's park	M.R.C.S. Eng., 1846 ; M.D. Univ. Edin., 1847 ; L.S.A. Lond., 1836

NAME.	ADDRESS.	QUALIFICATIONS.
Cree Herbert Eustace	2 Pemberton villas, St John's park	L.S.A. Lond., 1882 ; M.R.C.S. Eng., 1883
Cree William Edward	2 Pemberton villas, St. John's park	M.R.C.S. Eng., L.S.A. Lond., 1874 ; L.R.C.P. Lond., 1880
Crowdy F. Hamilton	South grove Highgate......	M.B.,Mast. Surg.,1875, Univ. Edin., L.R.C.S. Edin.,L.S.A. Lond., 1875
Dane Thomas.................	86 Finchley rd.Hampstead	M.R.C.S. Eng., 1860 ; L.S.A. Lond., 1861
Davies W. G.	181 High rd. Kilburn	L.R.C.P. Edin., L.R.C.S. Edin., 1884
Dimsey Edgar Ralph	4 Dartmouth park avenue Hampstead	M.R.C.S.Eng., L.R.C.P. Lond., 1883
Dixon John	(Calverley lodge) Wood ln	L.R.C.P. Edin., 1870 ; M.B., Mast.Surg.,1872,UnivEdin
Duncan Henry Montague	98 Abbey rd. Hampstead...	M.R.C.S. Eng., L.S.A. Lond., 1849 ; M.B. 1857, M.D. 1861, Univ. Lond.
Edwards Edwin Thomas	103 Abbey rd. St. John's wood Hampstead	M.R.C.S. Eng., 1855 ; L.S.A. Lond., 1857
Evans Herbert Norman ...	3 Thurlow rd. Hampstead	M.R.C.S. Eng., 1860 ; M.B. Univ. Oxf., 1862
Evans William Henry......	90 Finchley rd.	M.R.C.S. Eng., 1869 ; L.R.C.P. Edin., 1870
Evershed Arthur	10 Mansfield villas Hampstead	M.R.C.S. Eng., L.S.A. Lond., 1863 ; L., 1867, M., 1875, R.C.P. Lond.
Fletcher George...............	(Soham house) Southgate lane Highgate	M.R.C.S. Eng., L.S.A. Lond., 1872; M.B.,1873, M.D., 1877, Univ. Camb.
Forshall Francis Hyde......	8 Southwood ln. Highgate	M.R.C.S. Eng.,1855 ; L.R.C.P. Lond., 1863
Fox William Symth.........	29 Adamson rd.	L.R.C.P. Edin., L.R.C.S. Irel., 1864
Franklin Jabez Austin.. ...	High st. Hampstead.........	L.S.A. Lond., 1879
Freeman Henry Pettener	34 Priory rd. Kilburn Hampstead	M.R.C.S., Eng., 1842 ; L.S.A. Lond., 1843
Garlick William...............	11 Well rd. Hampstead ...	M., 1837, F., 1854, R.C.S. Eng.; L.S.A. Lond., 1837
Gay John	51 Belsize park Hampstead	M.R.C.S. Eng., 1884
Gervis F. Hendebourck ...	Fellows rd. Haverstock hill Hampstead	M.R.C.S. Eng., L.S.A. Lond., 1863
Goodchild John...............	23 Thurlow rd. Hampstead	L.S.A. Lond., 1842 ; M.R.C.S. Eng.,1846 ; L.R.C.P. Edin., 1859
Goodchild N.	9 Highgate rd.	L.R.C.P. Edin., L.S.A. Lond., 1872
Greaves Frank	50 Junction rd.	M.R.C.S. Eng., L.S.A. Lond., 1872
Grosvenor A. Octavius ...	(The Tower) Priory rd. West Hampstead	M.D. Univ. Edin., M.R.C.S. Eng., 1864
Gwynn Edmund	6 Hampstead hill gardens	M.R.C.S. Eng., L.S.A. Lond. 1861 ; M.D. Univ. St. And. 1862
Hardwicke R. Reece	47 Gascony avenue West Hampstead	M.R.C.S. Eng., 1881
Harris Charles James	11 Kilburn priory Hampstead	M.R.C.S. Eng., L.S.A. Lond., 1865

NAME.	ADDRESS.	QUALIFICATIONS.
Heelas James	50 Primrose hill rd.Hampstead	L.S.A. Lond.,1876; M.B.,Mast. Surg.,1876,M.D.,1879,Univ Aber.
Henderson A. Milne.........	6 Hampstead lane Highgate	M.B., Mast. Surg., 1877, M.D., 1879, Univ. Aber.
Hill Frederic Adolphus ...	76 Abbey rd. St. John's wood Hampstead	M.R.C.S. Eng., 1865 ; L.R.C.P. Lond., 1872
Holman William Henry ...	68 Adelaide rd. South Hampstead	L.S.A. Lond., 1845 ; M.R.C.S. Eng., 1846; M.B. Univ. Lond., 1847
Howell Horace Sydney ...	18 Boundary rd. St. John's wood Hampstead	L.S.A. Lond., 1860 ; M., L.M., 1861, F., 1872, R.C.S. Eng. ; L.R.C.P. Lond., 1861 ; M.D. Univ. St. And., 1862
Hunstone George	177 Belsize rd..................	M.R.C.S. Eng., L.S.A. Lond., 1861
Innes Charles Barclay......	2 Lyndhurst rd.	M.R.C.S. Eng., 1884
Innes F. W., C.B.	2 Lyndhurst rd..............	L.R.C.S. Edin., 1834 ; M.D. Univ. Edin., 1836
Johnston Joseph	24 St. John's wood park Hampstead	M.D. Univ. Edin., 1854 ; L.R.C.S. Edin., 1861
Jones George Thomas	40 Archway rd. Highgate	M., 1849, F.,1869, R.C.S. Eng. ; L.S.A. Lond., 1849
Keele Charles F.	(Clumber house) Shoot-up hill Cricklewood and 120 High rd. Kilburn	M.R.C.S. Eng., L.S.A. Lond., 1860
King Joseph	(Welford house) 13 Arkwright rd. Hampstead	M.R.C.S. Eng., L.S.A. Lond., 1840
Lawrence Lawrie Asher ...	37 Belsize avenue	L.S.A. Lond., 1883 ; M.R.C.S. Eng., 1884
Lawrence Norman Henry	34 Highgate rd.	L.R.C.P., L.R.C.S., Edin., 1881
Mackenzie William Ord ...	37 Belsize park gardens Hampstead	M.D. Univ. Edin., 1837; L.R.C.S. Edin., L. Fac. Phy. & Surg. Glas., 1838
Mackintosh Donald	10 Lancaster rd. Belsize park	L. Fac. Phy. & Surg. Glas., 1830 ; M.D. Univ. Glas., 1841; M.D. Univ. Dur., 1859
McMillan John Furse	161 Adelaide rd.	L.S.A. Lond., 1881 ; M.R.C.S. Eng.,L.R.C.P. Lond., 1882
Marshall Thomas	55 Fortess rd. Highgate ...	M.B. Mast. Surg. Univ. Edin. 1878
Martin Henry Victor	30 Belgrave rd. Abbey rd.	M., 1834, F., 1859, R.C.S. Eng.
Martin John	98 Palmerston rd. Kilburn	L.S.A. Lond., 1857 ; M.R.C.S. Eng., 1860
Maude Arthur..................	5 Bishop wood rd.Highgate	M.R.C.S. Eng., 1882
Maude Frederic	5 Bishop wood rd. Highgate	M.B.,Mast.Surg.,Univ. Aber. 1883
Maynard C. D.	1 Pemberton villas St. John's park	L.R.C.P. Lond., 1869
Miller Andrew	1 Hampstead hill gardens	M.R.C.S. Eng., 1864 ; M.D Univ. Edin., 1866
Milson Richard Henry ...	88 Finchley rd. South Hampstead	M.R.C.S. Eng., L.S.A. Lond. 1860 ; M.D. Univ. Dur. 1878
Monks Frederick Aubin...	(Heath villa) 22 Sherriff rd. and (Buckland house) Fitzjohns' avenue Hampstead	L.S.A. Lond., M.R.C.S. Eng 1871 ; L.R.C.P. Edin., 1878

Name.	Address.	Qualifications.
Morton Thomas	15 Greville rd. Kilburn priory	M.R.C.S. Eng., L.S.A. Lond., 1862; M.B., 1862, M.D., 1865, Univ. Lond.
Moxon Walter	(Northolme) Bishop wood road	M.R.C.S. Eng., 1858; M.B. Univ. Lond., 1859; M.R.C.P. Lond., 1861
Murray Andrew	34 Gayton rd. Hampstead	M.B., Bac. Surg., 1879, M.D., 1883, Univ. Dub.
Neale Richard	60 Boundary rd. South Hampstead	M.R.C.S. Eng., L.S.A. Lond., 1850; M.D. Univ. Lond., 1854
Neatby Thomas	29 Thurlow rd. Hampstead	M.R.C.S. Eng., M.D. Univ. St. And., L.S.A. Lond., 1861
Newby Charles Henry	87 Adelaide rd.	M., 1873, F., 1880, R.C.S. Eng.; L.R.C.P. Lond., 1874
Nicholson Joseph John	162 Adelaide rd. South Hampstead	L.R.C.S., LL.M., K.Q.C.P. Irel., 1877
Oakes Arthur	(Merimbula) 99 Priory rd.	M.R.C.S. Eng., 1853; L.R.C.P. Lond., 1860
Oakley A. R. Hamilton	(Northlands) Bishop wood road	L.R.C.P., L.R.C.S. Edin., 1882
O'Reilly George John	(Rathmore) Archway rd. Highgate	L.R.C.S., LL.M., K.Q.C.P. Irel., 1875
Parker Herbert	Southwood lane Highgate	M.R.C.S. Eng., 1884
Picard P. Kirkpatrick	59 Abbey rd. St. John's wood Hampstead	M.D. Univ. Edin., 1859; M.R.C.S. Eng., 1863
Pidcock George Douglas	52 Downshire hill Hampstead	L.R.C.P., L.R.C.S. Edin., 1878; M.B. Univ. Camb., 1881
Pinches William Hooper	(Grove house) Highgate	L.R.C.P. Edin., M.R.C.S. Eng., 1884
Platt William Henry	(St. James' villa) West end lane	L.R.C.S. Irel., 1863; L.R.C.P. Edin., 1866
Prance Robert Rooke	Greenhill rd. Hampstead	M.R.C.S. Eng., 1849; M.D. Univ. St. And., L.S.A. Lond., 1850
Pritchard Urban	8 Heath rise Willow rd.	L.S.A. Lond., 1868; M.B., Mast. Surg., Univ. Edin.; M.R.C.S. Eng., L.R.C.P. Lond., 1869
Randall John	204 Adelaide rd. South Hampstead	M., 1840, F., 1860, R.C.S. Eng.; L.S.A. Lond., 1841; M.D. Univ. Lond., 1848; M.R.C.P. Edin., 1871
Rawlins William P.	(Gordon ho.) Highgate rd.	M.D. Univ. St. And., M.R.C.S. Eng., L.S.A. Lond., 1862; L.R.C.P. Lond., 1863
Reynolds E. R. B.	(Highcroft) Shepherd's hill rd.	M.R.C.S. Eng., L.S.A. Lond., 1874
Roberts Arthur Henry	(Hillcrest) Greenhill rd. Hampstead	M.R.C.S. Eng., L.R.C.P. Lond., 1883
Roberts John Henry	(Hillcrest) Greenhill rd. Hampstead	M., 1835, F., 1855, R.C.S. Eng.: L.S.A. Lond., 1836
Rose Henry Cooper	Rosslyn hill Hampstead	M.R.C.S. Eng., L.S.A. Lond., 1853; M.D. Univ. St. And., 1854
Sanders James Lewis	38 Junction rd.	M.R.C.S. Eng., 1852
Selous Edric	133 Adelaide rd. South Hampstead	M.R.C.S. Eng., 1858; M.D. Univ. Dur., 1880

Name.	Address.	Qualifications.
Senior Charles	22 Hilgrove rd. South Hampstead	M.L.M., R.C.S. Eng., L.S.A. Lond., 1858
Shaw Alexander	136 Abbey rd. Hampstead	F.R.C.S. Eng., 1843
Shaw John	(Burlington house) 1 Rudall cres. Hampstead	M.R.C.S. Eng., L.S.A. Lond., 1879 ; M.B., 1880, M.D. Univ.Lond.,1881 ; M.R.C.P. Lond., 1882
Shepherd Frederic	33 KingHenry's rd.Hampstead	M., 1855, L.M., R.C.S. Eng., 1856 ; L.R.C.P. Edin., 1860
Silk John F. W.	3 Highgate hill	L.S.A. Lond., 1879 ; M.R.C.S. Eng., 1880
Smith E. Thomas Aydon	10 Alexandra rd.St.John's wood Hampstead	L.S.A. Lond., 1882
Smith John Charles	2 Gascony avenue	L.S.A. Lond., 1883 ; M.R.C.S. Eng., 1884
Smith Richard Thomas	53 Haverstock hill Hampstead	M.R.C.S. Eng., L.S.A. Lond., 1869; M.B., 1870,M.D. Univ. Lond.,1873; M.R.C.P.Lond., 1876
Smyth Luke Dowel	21 Parliament hill rd. Hampstead	M.R.C.S. Eng., 1832 ; L.A.H. Dub., 1833 ; M.D. Univ. Glas., 1836 ; L.S.A. Lond., 1841
Southby Edmund Richd.	101 South hill park Hampstead	M.R.C.S. Eng., 1855
Spreat Frank Arthur	47 Belsize sq.	M.R.C.S. Eng., 1884
Spreat John Henry	47 Belsize sq.	L.S.A. Lond., 1884
Steet George Carrick	130 King Henry's rd. Hampstead	M., 1840, F., 1849, R.C.S. Eng.; L.S.A. Lond., 1840
Stott Thomas Sibley	1 Highgate rd.	M.R.C.S. Eng., 1863
Strange William Heath	2 The Avenue Belsize park Hampstead	M., 1864, L.M., 1865, R.C.S. Eng.; L.S.A. Lond., 1865 ; M.B., Mast. Surg., 1865, M.D. 1866, Univ. Aber.
Strugnell Frederick Wm.	45 Highgate rd.	M.R.C.S. Eng., 1873 ; L.S.A. Lond.,1874; L.R.C.P.Lond., 1875
Sugden Edgar Brewitt	13 Adamson rd.	L.S.A. Lond., 1884
Threadgale Robert Easy	74 High rd.Kilburn Hampstead	L.S.A. Lond., 1862 ; L. Fac. Phy. & Surg. Glas., 1877 ; L.R.C.P. Edin., 1878 ; M.D. Univ. St. And., 1880
Tibbits Herbert	(Burfield ho.) Archway rd.	L.R.C.P. Lond., M.L.M., R.C.S. Eng., L.S.A. Lond., 1865 ; M., 1874, F., 1876, R.C.P. Edin.; M.D. Univ. St. And., 1881
Tilly Alfred	10 Garlinge rd. Hampstead	L.S.A. Lond., 1882
Tuchmann Maro	148Adelaide rdHampstead	M.R.C.S. Eng., 1877
Wake Edward George	(Lewisham ho) Dartmouth hill park Highgate	M.R.C.S. Eng., L.S.A. Lond., 1851 ; M.D. Univ. St. And., 1862
Walford Walter Gilson	49 Finchley new rd.Hampstead	M.R.C.S. Eng., 1861 ; L.R.C.P. Lond., 1862 ; M.D. Univ. Dur., 1881
Walker George S.	(Cavendish house)Cricklewood	M.R.C.S. Eng., 1868
Warn Reuben Thomas	37 Highgate rd. Highgate	M.R.C.S. Eng., L.S.A. Lond., 1862

NAME.	ADDRESS.	QUALIFICATIONS.
Waterhouse Wm. Dakin ...	18 Woodchurch rd. West Hampstead	L.R.C.S. Irel., L. and L.M., K.Q.C.P. Irel., 1881
Watts Fred	31 Highgate rd. Highgate	M.R.C,S. Eng., L.S.A. Lond., 1874 ; L.R.C.P. Lond., 1875
Wells Charles.................	13 College cres. Belsize park Hampstead	L.S.A. Lond., 1878 ; M.D. Q. Univ. Irel., 1880 ; M.R.C.S. Eng., 1881
Westland Albert	17 Belsize pk. Hampstead	M.B.,Mast. Surg., 1875 ; M.D., 1877, Univ. Aber.
Wharton Henry Thornton	39 St. George's rd. Abbey rd. Hampstead	M.R.C.S. Eng., 1875
Willis Arthur Keith.........	(Gascony house) West end lane Hampstead	M.R.C.S. Eng., 1881
Wills Charles James.........	(Broadhurst house)Broadhurst gardens	M., L.M., R.C.S. Eng., 1864 ; L.S.A. Lond., 1873 ; M.B., Mast. Surg., 1865 ; M.D., 1867, Univ. Aber.
Winn James Michell	21 Goldhurst ter.	M.D.Univ.Glas.,1833;M.R.C.P. Lond., 1852
Winter Robert	(Eland ho.) Rosslyn hill Hampstead	M.R.C.S. Eng., 1864

ANNOUNCEMENTS

OF

HOSPITALS AND

INSTITUTIONS.

George Cruikshank

FIELD LANE REFUGES, RAGGED SCHOOLS,
Industrial Homes, Servants' Home, Creche, &c.,
VINE STREET, CLERKENWELL ROAD, E.C.,
AND HAMPSTEAD, N.W.

President : THE RT. HON. THE EARL OF SHAFTESBURY, K.G.
Treasurer : WILFRID A. BEVAN, Esq., 54, Lombard Street, E.C.
Bankers : { Messrs. BARCLAY, BEVAN & Co., 54, Lombard Street, E.C.
{ Messrs. RANSOM & Co., 1, Pall Mall East, S.W.

Maintains and Benefits 2,020 Weekly.

Supported by Voluntary Contributions.
FUNDS URGENTLY NEEDED.

Contributions will be thankfully received by the Treasurer, Bankers,
or by PEREGRINE PLATT, *Secretary.*

FORM OF BEQUEST.

"*I give and bequeath unto the Treasurer for the time being of* 'The FIELD
LANE RAGGED SCHOOLS AND NIGHT REFUGES FOR THE HOMELESS,' Vine
Street, Clerkenwell Road, London, *the sum of* * *, for the use of the said
Charity ; and I direct the said Legacy to be paid, free of Legacy Duty, out of
such part of my Personal Estate as may be legally applied in payment of
Charitable Bequests.*"

* The sum to be expressed in words at length.

[H 2]

[H 3]

Charing Cross Hospital.

THE Council earnestly appeal for substantial assistance The average number of cases treated annually amount to **20,000.** The Hospital is situated in a densely populated and, for the most part, very poor neighbourhood while owing to the crowded character of the surrounding thoroughfares it receives a larger number of street accidents, proportionately, than any other Hospital in London. The annual deficit amounts to £8,000, the reliable income, *including* Annual Subscriptions, being only £4,000, while the expenditure i £12,000.

A Donation of £21, or an Annual Subscription of £3 3s qualifies for a Governorship.

The regulations provide for the acceptance of the proposal c any Benefactor to endow or found and name a Bed by paymen of a benefaction of £1,000, or any number of Beds by a corres ponding larger benefaction.

Donations or Annual Subscriptions will be gratefully receive by Messrs. DRUMMOND, 49, Charing Cross, S.W.; Messrs. COUTT 59, Strand, W.C.; Messrs. HOARE, 37, Fleet Street, E.C.; or b the *Treasurers*, at the Hospital.

ARTHUR E. READE, *Secretary.*

FORM OF BEQUEST.

I give and bequeath to Charing Cross Hospital, ne Charing Cross, Westminster, for the use of that Charity, t sum of

NOTE.—By its Act of Incorporation, this Hospital is entitled to take and hold real property.

"A Home in Sickness."

BOLINGBROKE HOUSE PAY HOSPITAL.

Founded in 1880.

FOUR MILES FROM CHARING CROSS.
FACING WANDSWORTH COMMON.

THIS INSTITUTION offers to sick persons, who are able to pay, wholly or partially, for their support, all the advantages of Hospital treatment and nursing, with, as far as possible, the comfort and privacy of Home.

The funds for its establishment were contributed by those who wished to give people an opportunity of obtaining treatment, during sickness, without their resorting to one of the general Free Hospitals as objects of charity.

Bolingbroke House is a spacious and conveniently arranged mansion, standing in pleasant grounds, on the verge of Wandsworth Common : one of the most beautiful and extensive Commons near London, which is proverbial for its salubrity. The Hospital is within a short distance of Clapham Junction, and is therefore easy of access from almost every point. Baths have been added, and new drainage and other sanitary arrangements have been thoroughly provided.

Patients are admitted on payment of a reasonable proportion of their weekly cost which averages £2 2s., *if they are really unable to pay the whole of that sum.* Each room contains from two to six beds. A private room may be had for £3 3s. weekly. The payment includes charges for Medical Attendance, Board, and Lodging, and must be paid weekly in advance. If desired, the patient's own doctor may attend the case, in which event his fee has to be paid by the patient.

Personal inquiries should be made at Bolingbroke House; but written communications are to be addressed to the Honorary Secretary, J. S. WOOD, Esq., Woodville, Upper Tooting, S.W.

ROYAL FREE HOSPITAL,

GRAY'S INN ROAD, LONDON,

W.C.

THIS HOSPITAL was founded in 1828 on the principle of *free* and unrestricted admission of the Sick Poor; poverty and suffering being the only passports required. Having no endowment, it is ENTIRELY DEPENDENT FOR SUPPORT ON THE SUBSCRIPTIONS OF ITS GOVERNORS AND THE VOLUNTARY DONATIONS AND BEQUESTS OF ITS FRIENDS.

The Hospital, which has recently been entirely rebuilt on the most modern principles of Hospital construction, now contains 150 beds. It admits into its wards about 1,800 poor sick persons annually, besides administering advice and medicine to nearly 30,000 out-patients, who resort to it, not only from the crowded courts and alleys in its immediate neighbourhood, but from all parts of London and the suburban districts. The relief thus afforded is effected at a cost of about £10,000 per annum, while the income of the Charity from annual subscriptions is not more than £1,200; so that the large balance of about £9,000 has to be raised by means of constant APPEALS TO THE PUBLIC BENEVOLENCE.

Punch *thus bears testimony to the good work effected by this Hospital :—*

"THE ROYAL FREE HOSPITAL is not more free than welcome as a charitable helping-place to thousands of our poor. When first it was started, not a Hospital in London was ever freely open—as in Charity all should be, to such sick folk as the Royal Free was founded specially to succour. In this really useful Hospital, so long as there are funds unspent, and sleeping wards unfilled, any poor sick person may come to them and fill them; and they need not lose their little strength by hunting up subscribers to send them 'Open Sesame' in an admission ticket. Think what suffering is succoured by a Charity like this. Think that, but for Heaven's mercy, you yourself, O Crœsus! might haply there become a suppliant. Remember, there's no shamming in the sick ward of a hospital. Shut your hands against sham sick folk as close as you can clinch but be royally free-handed to the Royal Free, and be sure that you do good with every shilling that you give to it."

Subscriptions, Donations, and Legacies are kindly received by the Treasurer, E. MASTERMAN, Esq., 27, Clement's Lane, E.C.; Messrs. BROWN, JANSON & CO.; Messrs. BARCLAY, BEVAN & CO.; Messrs. COUTTS & CO. Messrs. DRUMMOND & CO.; Messrs. HERRIES & CO.; Messrs. PRESCOTT, GROTE & CO.; Messrs. RANSOM & CO.; Messrs. SMITH, PAYNE & SMITHS Messrs. WILLIAMS, DEACON & CO.; and at the Hospital by

JAMES S. BLYTH, *Secretary.*

ST. JOHN'S HOSPITAL FOR SKIN DISEASES,

(Founded 1863,)

LEICESTER SQUARE, W.C., and
MARKHAM SQUARE, CHELSEA, S.W.

Patroness: H.R.H. THE PRINCESS OF WALES.

Patrons:

HIS MAJESTY LEOPOLD II., KING OF THE BELGIANS.

H.R.H. THE DUKE OF CAMBRIDGE, K.G.   H.R.H. PRINCE CHRISTIAN, K.G.

H.R.H. THE GRAND DUKE OF HESSE, K.G.

H.R.H. THE CROWN PRINCE OF GERMANY, K.G.

The following extract from an Appeal for Aid to St. John's Hospital, written by the late Charles Reade, commends the objects of the Institution to all philanthropists :—

"We live, thank God, in a nation whose charity is only bounded by its knowledge.

"The fatal Scurvy, the foul Leprosy, the maddening Eczema, are all skin diseases, and all far more common than supposed. Other skin diseases, less generally known, inflict agony, misery, and shame on many respectable persons, and make their lives a burden.

"In estimating the less fatal diseases of the skin, it must be remembered that the skin covers the whole body, a surface of sixteen or eighteen square feet, and is very sensitive, and that most of its diseases are seen as well as felt, causing the sufferers to be despised or shunned, whereas internal maladies invite the boon of sympathy. As an example, take the fate of domestic servants so afflicted. Their employers dismiss them, however meritorious, and their friends shun them; mental despair too often follows, and they say, with the Patriarch Job, whose bodily afflictions, selected by knowledge and malignity in person, was a disease of the skin, 'My misery is greater than I can bear.'

"Against such a weight of suffering, shame, and sorrow, what is the special provision in our enormous city? I cannot undertake to say positively, but at present I am acquainted only with one small Hospital ;—that ought to be a great one, and will be in a year, if the public pleases. This is ST. JOHN'S HOSPITAL FOR DISEASES OF THE SKIN."

St. John's Hospital admits In-Patients from all parts of the country. The poor are treated *free*, and those who can afford to make a small monthly payment are also received. Last year 86 new In-Patients and 2,728 new Out-Patients were admitted.

Out-Patients are seen at Leicester Square every Week-day (except Saturday) at 2 p.m., and on Monday, Wednesday, and Friday nights at 7 p.m. ; also at Markham Square on Mondays and Thursdays at 10 a.m. Dental Cases are seen at Markham Square on Saturdays at 9 a.m.

Contributions will be gratefully received by Messrs. COUTTS & Co., 59, Strand, W.C., the Bankers ; or at the Hospital, by

ST. VINCENT MERCIER, *Secretary.*

The Oldest Hospital for Consumption and Diseases of the Chest in Europe.

THE ROYAL HOSPITAL
FOR DISEASES OF THE CHEST,
CITY ROAD, LONDON, E.C.

Founded by his late R.H. the Duke of Kent A.D. 1814.
Rebuilt 1863.   New Wing added 1876.   Enlarged 1877

Patron:
HER MAJESTY THE QUEEN.

Vice=Patrons:
H.R.H. the Prince of Wales, K.G., &c.
H.R.H. the Duke of Edinburgh, K.G., &c.
H.R.H. the Duke of Connaught, K.G., &c.
H.R.H. the Duke of Cambridge, K.G., &c.

President:
The Right Hon. the Earl of Shaftesbury, K.G.

Trustees:
The Right Hon. the Lord Wolverton.
The Right Hon. the Lord Charles Bruce, M.P.
Colonel Makins, M.P.
Sir N. M. de Rothschild, Bart., M.P.

Treasurer:
The Hon. Pascoe Charles Glyn, Lombard Street, E.C.

THE central position of this old-established Hospital, the great advantage it provides for the Patients, and the benefits it has dispensed for more than *half a century*, enable the Council to commend its claim for increased support to all who sympathise with sorrow and suffering.

The Wards for In-patients are constantly full, whilst from 1,000 to 2,000 Out-patients are under treatment every week. *Funds are very urgently required.*

Annual Subscribers of £3 3s., and Donors of £31 10s., are entitled to recommend one In-patient and four or eight Out-patients per annum.

Annual Subscribers of £1 1s., and Donors of £10 10s., are entitled to recommend six Out-patients per annum.

Secretary, LOWTHER KEMP.

FORM OF BEQUEST.

'I give and bequeath to the Treasurer for the time being of THE ROYAL HOSPITAL FOR DISEASES OF THE CHEST, CITY ROAD, LONDON, the sum of *
to be applied in and towards carrying on the charitable objects of the Institution: the said sum of *   to be paid free of Legacy Duty, out of such part of my personal estate as I may lawfully bequeath to the purposes of the said Institution, and I direct that the receipt of the Treasurer for the time being shall be a sufficient discharge to my executors for the same.'

* *The sum to be expressed in words at length.*

METROPOLITAN
Drinking Fountain & Cattle Trough
ASSOCIATION.

SUPPORTED ENTIRELY BY VOLUNTARY CONTRIBUTIONS.

Offices: Victoria House, 111, Victoria Street, Westminster, S.W.

President—HIS GRACE THE DUKE OF WESTMINSTER, K.G., &c., &c.
Chairman of Committee and Treasurer—JOSEPH FRY, Esq.

THIS IS THE ONLY AGENCY FOR PROVIDING

FREE SUPPLIES OF WATER FOR MAN AND BEAST IN THE STREETS OF LONDON,

And the relief it affords to human beings and dumb animals is incalculable.

The total number of Troughs and Fountains now erected, and at work in the Metropolis, is as follows:—**566 Troughs** for animals, and **557 Fountains** for human beings, at which multitudes of men, women, and children, horses, oxen, sheep, and dogs, quench their thirst daily, amounting in the aggregate to probably not less than the enormous total of **250,000,000** drinkers in a year.

The Committee earnestly solicit liberal contributions to enable them to sustain and extend this simple scheme for the amelioration of animal suffering, and the promotion of habits of temperance amongst our itinerant and working population.

Annual Subscriptions and Donations will be thankfully received by the Bankers, Messrs. RANSOM, BOUVERIE & CO.; Messrs. BARCLAY, BEVAN & CO.; or by the Secretary, at the Office.

M. W. MILTON, *Secretary.*

FORM OF BEQUEST.

" *I give and bequeath the sum of   , to be paid out of such parts of my personal estate as can be lawfully applied for that purpose, unto the Treasurer for the time being of a Society called or known by the name of* THE METROPOLITAN DRINKING FOUNTAIN AND CATTLE TROUGH ASSOCIATION, *to be at the disposal of the Committee for the time being of the said Society.*"

[H 9]

ASSOCIATION FOR PROMOTING
𝕿𝖍𝖊 𝕲𝖊𝖓𝖊𝖗𝖆𝖑 𝖂𝖊𝖑𝖋𝖆𝖗𝖊 𝖔𝖋 𝖙𝖍𝖊 𝕭𝖑𝖎𝖓𝖉
28, BERNERS STREET, W.

Patrons—HER MAJESTY THE QUEEN.   H.R.H. THE PRINCE OF WALES, K.G.
H.R.H. THE PRINCE CHRISTIAN, K.G.   H.S.H. THE DUKE OF TECK, G.C.B.

President—THE ARCHBISHOP OF CANTERBURY.
Vice-President—F. GREEN, Esq.   *Lady-President*—Miss GILBERT.
Treasurer—W. S. DEACON, Esq.   *Secretary*—Col. H. LEWIS.

This Association, the parent of all for employing the Adult Blind, was founded in 1856, b
Miss GILBERT (herself blind), daughter of Bishop Gilbert, of Chichester, for the special purpose
of teaching trades to the adult blind, of giving them employment in the workshops of th
Association and at their own homes, of providing them with material, and of ensuring a marke
for the sale of their work through its retail shop.

Ninety-one men and women are now employed in the workshops and at their own houses, an
27 others are receiving small pensions. Many women and children are dependent on these Blin
for support. The industrial arts carried on are the manufacture of Brushes, Brooms, Baske
Mats, and Rugs, Firewood chopping and tying by the men; and of Brushes, Baskets, Chair-canin
Sash-line making, and Fancy Woolwork making by the women. It is hoped to introduce oth
trades. As these articles are equal in make and quality to those produced by sighted workers, th
Committee would urge upon all interested in the welfare of the Blind to purchase them of th
Association, and they will thus contribute towards allowing a large number of those sadl
afflicted persons to be employed regularly. An increase in the custom of hotels and other lar
establishments, as well as of private households, is earnestly solicited.

**A great many Blind are applying for admission, and cannot be taken on
for want of funds.**

The Committee gladly invite inspection of the premises, where some of the Blind may t
seen at work.

Contributions in aid of this Charity are earnestly needed for current expenses, and also t
enable the Association to obtain what is most essential for carrying on trade—a working capita

SUBSCRIPTIONS and DONATIONS will be thankfully received by Miss GILBERT, 5, Stanhop
Place, Hyde Park, W.; by the following Bankers—Messrs. WILLIAMS, DEACON & CO., 20, Birch
Lane, E.C.; Messrs. DRUMMOND & CO., 49, Charing Cross, S.W., and by Sir SAMUEL SCOT
Bart., & CO., 1, Cavendish Square, W.; by the Secretary, Col. H. LEWIS, at the Associatio
28, Berners Street, W.

For Price Lists and information apply to the Manager, Mr. JENNINGS.

SIX HUNDRED ORPHANS.

ORPHAN WORKING SCHOOL
(FOUNDED 1758),
HAVERSTOCK HILL, N.W.

President: H.R.H. THE DUKE OF CAMBRIDGE, K.G.
Treasurer: SIR WILLIAM McARTHUR, K.C.M.G., M.P.
Sub=Treasurer: WILLIAM HOLT, ESQ., V.P.

THE ORPHAN WORKING SCHOOL is a NATIONAL INSTITUTION.
THE ORPHAN WORKING SCHOOL is One Hundred and Twenty-six Years Old.
THE ORPHAN WORKING SCHOOL supports 420 Orphans at Haverstock Hill, London.
THE ORPHAN WORKING SCHOOL supports 180 Infant Orphans at Alexandra Orphanage, Hornsey
THE ORPHAN WORKING SCHOOL has trained over 4,000 Children.   [Rise.
THE ORPHAN WORKING SCHOOL is supported by Voluntary Contributions, and needs about
THE ORPHAN WORKING SCHOOL is now in urgent need of Funds.   [£17,000 a year.

ALEXANDRA ORPHANAGE
(FOUNDED 1864),
JUNIOR BRANCH OF THE ORPHAN WORKING SCHOOL, HORNSEY RISE.
Contributions earnestly solicited and thankfully received.

CONVALESCENT HOME, MARGATE,
FOR CONVALESCENT CHILDREN OF THE ORPHAN WORKING SCHOOL.
Contributions will be thankfully received.

	£ s. d.			£ s. d.
Annual Subscription for One Vote ...	0 10 6	Life Donation for One Vote ...	...	5 5 0
Annual Subscription for Two Votes ...	1 1 0	Life Donation for Two Votes ...	...	10 0 0

OFFICES : 73, CHEAPSIDE, E.C.   JONADAB FINCH, SECRETARY.

PRIVILEGES OF EXECUTORS.
"*That in respect of every Bequest made to this Charity, the Executors shall be entitled to Two Life Votes for every Fifty Pounds received.*"

SPECIAL NOTICE.
Those friends who may determine to bequeath legacies to either of the above Institutions are particularly requested to adhere as closely as practicable to the "Form of Bequest" below, to prevent the possibility of confusion with other Institutions.

FORM OF BEQUEST.
The following Form of Bequest is respectfully offered to those Friends who may thus desire to promote the interest of this important Charity.

"I give and bequeath unto the Treasurer, for the time being, of the Corporation of the ORPHAN WORKING SCHOOL, in Maitland Park, Haverstock Hill, near Hampstead, formerly in the City Road, with which are amalgamated the Alexandra Orphanage (Hornsey Rise), and the Convalescent Home (Harold Road, Margate), the sum of   to be applied towards the general purposes of the said Institution. And I direct the said last-mentioned Legacy to be paid exclusively out of such part of my Personal Estate as may be legally applied in payment of Charitable Legacies."

If the Testator wishes the Charity to receive the Legacy free from duty, he will please add:—
" And I direct the last-mentioned Legacy to be paid free from Legacy Duty, which I direct to be paid out of the same fund."

Gifts by will, of land, tenements or leaseholds, or of money charged on, or secured by mortgage of, or to be laid out in, or to arise from the sale of such property, are void if designed for charitable purposes ; but money, stock, or other personal property, if not directed to be laid out in land, may be bequeathed to charitable objects.

N.B.—All wills made subsequently to the 1st day of January, 1838, or any alteration thereafter made in a prior will, must be in writing, and signed at the foot or end by the Testator, or some person at his or her direction, and in his or her presence ; in the presence of at least two persons present at the same time, who must subscribe their names as witnesses in the presence of the Testator, and of each other.

[H 11]

Licensed Victuallers' School,
KENNINGTON LANE, LAMBETH.

Established 1803. *Enfranchised 1857.*

Patrons: Her MAJESTY the QUEEN & H.R.H. The PRINCE of WALES.

THIS Institution clothes, maintains, and educates upwards of 200 Children of deceased or distressed Licensed Victuallers, at a cost of nearly £7,000 per annum.

From its commencement no fewer than 2,281 Children have been admitted, and many of them are now occupying good positions in life, entirely owing to the liberal education and careful training they have received within its walls.

Duly qualified Children are eligible for admission from 7 to 12 years of age; Boys remain in the School until they attain 14, Girls until 15 years of age.

The Elections generally take place in March every year, at the School House, Kennington Lane. Applications to place the names of Children on the list of Candidates being received until the 31st December.

The scale upon which the School is now maintained requires increased exertions in order to provide for current expenditure, and Subscriptions are earnestly solicited to assist the Governor and Committee in meeting the increasing demands made upon the Charity.

Gentlemen's Life Subscription	... ...	£10 10 0	... 4 Votes.
Lady's Life Subscription	... ...	5 5 0	... 2 Votes.
Annual Subscription	... ...	1 1 0	... 1 Vote.

Subscriptions and Donations will be very thankfully received at the Offices of the Institution, 127, Fleet Street, London; or by the Bankers, Messrs. Goslings & Sharpe, 19, Fleet Street, London.

WILLIAM LLOYD, *Governor.*
EDWARD GRIMWOOD, *Secretary.*

Licensed Victuallers' Asylum,
ASYLUM ROAD, OLD KENT ROAD, S.E.
A HOME FOR NECESSITOUS MEMBERS OF THE TRADE.

Founded 1827. *Incorporated by Royal Charter 1842.*

Patron: H.R.H. THE PRINCE OF WALES.

THIS Institution consists of **170** separate Houses, Chapel, Chaplain's residence, Board and Court room, Library, &c., and is the largest establishment as Almshouses in existence.

The Annual Expenses exceed £8,000, towards raising which support is much needed.

Many of the recipients of the Charity have enjoyed a happy home in the Asylum for a quarter of a century, and received in weekly allowances during that period as much as £500, besides coals, medical and nurse attendance, &c.

Life Donors of Ten Guineas receive at every Election of Inmates				4 Votes.
„ Five Guineas	„	„	„	2 Votes.
Annual Subscribers of One Guinea	„	„	„	1 Vote.

DAVID HUTT, *Chairman.*   ALFRED L. ANNETT, *Secretary.*

Offices: 17, NEW BRIDGE STREET, E.C.

Royal Alfred Aged Merchant Seamen's Institution,

THE HOME,
Belvedere, Kent.

FOUNDED 1867.

PENSIONERS
at all Ports
of the United Kingdom.

Annual Disbursements, £6,000. Annual Subscriptions, £1,800.
Number of Inmates, 100; Out-Pensioners, 175.

Patron: REAR-ADMIRAL H.R.H. THE DUKE OF EDINBURGH, K.G.

Chairman: CAPT. HON. FRANCIS MAUDE, R.N.
Deputy-Chairman: CAPT. DAVID MAINLAND.

THE OBJECT OF THIS CHARITY
IS
To Give a HOME or a PENSION to the MERCHANT SAILOR when Old, Destitute, and Friendless.

677 Old Sailors, out of 1,400 Applicants, have enjoyed the benefits of this Charity; but, from want of funds, the Committee are unable to admit hundreds of necessitous and worthy Candidates, who, for 40 years, have been at Sea as Seaman, Mate, or Master.

The Home is capable of receiving 100 more Inmates, and the Out-Pension List is limited by want of Funds alone.

Elections take place half-yearly—20 only out of 120 Candidates can succeed. The Workhouse is the dreaded resort of many unsuccessful Candidates.

Donations and Subscriptions are **urgently needed** and will be gratefully received.

Bankers: Messrs. WILLIAMS, DEACON & Co.

W. E. DENNY, *Secretary.*

Office: 58, FENCHURCH STREET, E.C.

[H 13]

CHURCH OF ENGLAND
Scripture Readers' Association.
INSTITUTED 1844.

Patron: HIS GRACE THE LORD ARCHBISHOP OF CANTERBURY.
Vice-President: THE EARL OF SHAFTESBURY, K.G.
Treasurer: SIR WALTER R. FARQUHAR, Bart.

THIS Society is employing 120 approved and godly men as Scripture Readers, under the direction of the metropolitan parochial Clergy, who visit the poor from house to house, reading to them the Word of God, and directing them to the **Saviour.**

The Committee are constrained to plead very earnestly for liberal and continued help in order to maintain the present staff of Readers labouring in poor and crowded parishes, with an aggregate population of **nearly a million** souls; and to enable the Association to extend its operations.

Donations and Subscriptions will be thankfully received at the Offices of the Association.

T. MARTIN TILBY, *Lay Secretary.*

Offices: 56, HAYMARKET, S.W.

MOUNT HERMON GIRLS' ORPHAN HOMES,
47, 49 & 55, CAMBRIDGE ROAD, KILBURN, N.W.,
AND
"PRAISE COTTAGE," MILL LANE, WEST HAMPSTEAD, N.W.

Instituted 1864.

DESTITUTE ORPHANS are admitted **Free**, whenever there is a vacancy and funds permit.

The Work is Protestant and undenominational. The children are brought up "in the nurture and admonition of the Lord."

The Homes are conducted on the family system (receive children without election), and are supported by Free-will Offerings, sent in answer to prayer.

One Hundred and Twelve Orphans are now maintained and educated.

To any Guardian wishing to support an Orphan in the Home, the cost is £14 per year. We hope to enlarge the accommodation as soon as the means are provided.

All communications to be sent to MISS M. A. COLE,

Mount Hermon Orphanage, Kilburn, N.W.

FORM OF LEGACY.
" *I give and bequeath to the Treasurer for the time being of* MOUNT HERMON GIRLS' ORPHAN HOMES, *established at Cambridge Road, Kilburn, London, N.W., to be applied to, in, and towards carrying on the Charitable objects of that Institution, the sum of* [expressed in words at length], *to be paid, free of Legacy Duty, out of such part of my personal estate as may by law be bequeathed for charitable purposes.*"

LONDON FEVER HOSPITAL,

LIVERPOOL ROAD, ISLINGTON, N.

ESTABLISHED 1802.

Patron—**H.R.H. THE PRINCE OF WALES.**   President—**THE EARL OF DEVON.**

Treasurer—R. N. FOWLER, ESQ., M.P., Alderman (The Lord Mayor).
Hon. Secretary—M. D. CHALMERS, Esq., 11, New Court, Lincoln's Inn, W.C.
Secretary—E. BURN-CALLANDER, Esq., at the Hospital.

THERE IS NO ENDOWMENT.

THE LONDON FEVER HOSPITAL is the only Hospital in London for the special treatment and prevention of infectious fevers in the case of persons who are not paupers.

SPECIAL PRIVILEGES TO GOVERNORS.

Governors have the privilege of Free Admission for their own domestic servants.

An Annual Subscriber of £1 1s., after the second payment, or a Donor of £10 10s., in one sum, becomes a Governor.

Firms subscribing £5 5s. annually may send gratis to the Hospital two persons in their employ, and one more for every extra £2 2s. Clubs and Hotels subscribing £2 2s. annually may send one employé free of cost.

Admission to General Wards, £3 3s.—(Average stay in Hospital six weeks.) There is private accommodation for those who may require it at £3 3s. per week.

928 PATIENTS WERE ADMITTED LAST YEAR.

FUNDS are most URGENTLY NEEDED, not only to carry on this most useful work, but to enable the Committee to build extra accommodation suitable to the requirements—medically and otherwise—of the present day.

The Surgical Aid Society.

Office—SALISBURY SQUARE, FLEET STREET, E.C.

President—*THE RIGHT HON. THE EARL OF SHAFTESBURY, K.G.*

THE SOCIETY was established in 1862, to supply Trusses, Elastic Stockings, Crutches, Artificial Limbs, &c., and every other description of mechanical support, to the poor, without limit as to locality or disease.

WATER-BEDS AND INVALID CHAIRS ARE LENT TO THE AFFLICTED UPON THE RECOMMENDATION OF SUBSCRIBERS.

60,500 APPLIANCES HAVE ALREADY BEEN SUPPLIED.

Annual Subscription of £0 10 6 ⎫ Entitles to Two Recommendations
Life Subscription of ...   5 5 0 ⎭   per annum.

SUBSCRIPTIONS and DONATIONS will be thankfully received by the Bankers, Messrs. BARCLAY & Co., Lombard Street; or at the Offices of the Society, by

WILLIAM TRESIDDER, Secretary.

[H 15]

RESCUE SOCIETY,

CITY OF LONDON HOSPITAL

FOR

DISEASES OF THE CHEST,

Victoria Park, E.

Patron : HER MAJESTY THE QUEEN
President : H.R.H. THE DUKE OF CONNAUGHT, K.G.

The Hospital contains 164 beds, and affords relief to the Poor and Working Classes afflicted with Consumption and Diseases of the Chest (including Heart Disease). The annual expenditure is more than £10,000, and the reliable income is less than £3,000. The Institution has *No Endowment whatever*, and the support of the public is therefore earnestly solicited to sustain its operations.

In-Patients under treatment, 1883 - - - **998**
Out-Patients ,, ,, - - - **16,489**

T. STORRAR-SMITH, *Secretary.*

Office, 24, FINSBURY CIRCUS, E.C.

THE NEW HOSPITAL FOR WOMEN,

222, MARYLEBONE ROAD.

THE PHYSICIANS ARE WOMEN.

Treasurer : MRS. WESTLAKE, River House, Chelsea Embankment.
Hon. Secretary : MISS VINCENT, 5, Upper Porchester Street.

Physicians :

MRS. ANDERSON, M.D.   MRS. ATKINS, M.D.   MRS. MARSHALL, M.D.
And MRS. DE LA CHEROIS. L.K.Q.C.P.I.

Assistant Physician : MISS HELEN PRIDEAUX, M.B. Lond.
Assisted by a Consulting Staff of Physicians and Surgeons.

THIS Hospital was established to enable women to be attended by FULLY QUALIFIED DOCTORS of their own sex. Twenty-six beds are made up; in 1883 there were 223 In-Patients, and 13,598 visits were made by Out-Patients. In-Patients pay a weekly sum according to their means, Out-Patients a fixed sum.

Visitors are invited to see the Hospital every afternoon between 2 and 4 o'clock.

THE HOSPITAL BEING UNENDOWED
DONATIONS AND SUBSCRIPTIONS ARE EARNESTLY SOLICITED.
Bankers: BANK OF ENGLAND, Burlington Gardens.

FRANCES A. HUNT, *Secretary.*

[H 18]

HOME FOR INCURABLE CHILDREN,

2 (LATE 33), MAIDA VALE, LONDON, W.

President:

H.R.H. THE DUKE OF CONNAUGHT AND STRATHEARN, K.G.

Treasurer:

EDWARD GRIFFITHS SYMS, Esq., 56, Elsham Road, Kensington, W.

·This Institution, founded in 1875, was the first of its kind in the metropolis, and, it is believed, in the United Kingdom. It is still nearly the only one, devoted *exclusively* to the object of providing for the care, maintenance, and medical treatment of children, up to the age of 16, suffering from chronic or incurable complaints of an aggravated character. It combines, as is essential for such cases, the advantages of a Home and a Hospital.

Seventy-seven children have already been admitted, and 29 are at present under treatment. The recent opening of a New Ward affords accommodation for 30 patients in the Home; and the Committee earnestly appeal to all, who can feel for the sufferings of children, to assist in carrying on and extending the good work by becoming Annual Subscribers to the Institution.

A small weekly payment is required with each child.

Visiting Hours: 3 to 5 p.m. daily.

N.B.—Cheques should be crossed to Messrs. HOARE, and Money Orders made payable to the Treasurer, at the Post Office, Charing Cross, W.C.

By order, L. S. LLOYD, *Hon. Sec.*

LONDON
HOMŒOPATHIC HOSPITAL

AND MEDICAL SCHOOL,

GREAT ORMOND STREET, BLOOMSBURY.

Patron: HER ROYAL HIGHNESS THE DUCHESS OF CAMBRIDGE.

Vice=Patron: THE DUKE OF BEAUFORT, K.G.

President: THE EARL CAIRNS, P.C.   **Chairman:** THE LORD EBURY, P.C.

Treasurer: MAJOR W. VAUGHAN MORGAN, 5, Boltons, S.W.

THE Hospital is supported by Voluntary Contributions. The total number of Patients treated since the opening of the Hospital approaches 200,000. Accidents and urgent cases are received at all times. It has accommodation for 70 In-Patients, and receives about 500 annually. The number of Out-Patients treated every year is about 7,000. A Training Institute for Nurses is maintained, and trained Nurses are sent out to nurse invalids at their residences.

FUNDS ARE URGENTLY NEEDED.

G. A. CROSS, *Secretary.*

West End Hospital

FOR DISEASES OF THE NERVOUS SYSTEM, PARALYSIS, AND EPILEPSY,

AND ESPECIALLY

For the Indoor Treatment of Young Paralysed Children,

73, WELBECK STREET, CAVENDISH SQUARE, W.

Instituted 1878.

Under the especial Patronage of

HER ROYAL HIGHNESS THE PRINCESS OF WALES.

President:

HIS GRACE THE DUKE OF PORTLAND.

OPEN at 6 p.m. on Friday evenings; and at 1.30 upon other week-days, Saturdays excepted. A separate waiting room is provided for those who, while unable to afford physicians' customary fees, are yet able to pay 5s. weekly towards the expenses of the Hospital. Other patients contribute according to their means.

Form of FREE treatment for INDIGENT poor to be had on application.

There is a Special Ward for the treatment of Paralysis and Epilepsy in Little Children.

N.B.—Annual Subscriptions are most earnestly solicited. Donations towards erecting New Wards for Adult patients seeking admission urgently needed.

FRANK IAGO, *Secretary.*

NATIONAL DENTAL HOSPITAL,

149, GREAT PORTLAND STREET, W.

Open daily from 9 to 11 a.m.

President: THE RIGHT HON. LORD VISCOUNT ENFIELD.

"Teeth are a trouble when they are coming, a trouble when they are here, and a trouble when they are gone."

A CYNIC.

OVER 27,000 cases were attended to at the above Hospital during 1883 (including 4,770 teeth *saved* by stopping), and the average *yearly increase* in the number of cases is 3,000.

Funds are needed most urgently to meet the expenses of this increase.

All persons unable to pay a registered practitioner for advice are eligible as patients, but are expected to contribute according to their means.

ARTHUR G. KLUGH, *Secretary.*

[H 20]

Hospital for Consumption
AND
DISEASES OF THE CHEST,
MOUNT ✦ VERNON, ✦ HAMPSTEAD.

Out-Patients' Department & Office : 216, TOTTENHAM COURT ROAD, W.

Patients are admitted from all parts of the Kingdom.

A few Wards have been furnished for Patients who are able to pay for their own maintenance.

THE NORTH LONDON CONSUMPTION HOSPITAL

Has special claims on the public. It has verified the correctness of the opinion now generally received, that a dry bracing air, such as that of Hampstead, proves more beneficial, both as to recovery in less advanced disease, and alleviation in the later stages of Consumption, than the warmer and softer air which was formerly so universally recommended.

The Committee desire to bring under the notice of the public the urgent need of funds to enable them to finish building the New Hospital, one-third of which has been completed and furnished for the accommodation of Patients.

C. A. R. HOARE, *Treasurer*, Messrs. C. Hoare & Co., 37, Fleet Street.

LIONEL F. HILL, M.A., *Secretary*, 216, Tottenham Court Road, W.

The Royal Ear Hospital,
FRITH STREET, SOHO SQUARE (formerly in Dean Street).

Patron : HER MAJESTY THE QUEEN.

President : HIS GRACE THE DUKE OF BUCCLEUCH, K.G.

Treasurer : J. CARR, Esq., 40, Bloomsbury Square.

Surgeons : { URBAN PRITCHARD, M.D., F.R.C.S., 3, George St., Hanover Sq.
{ FARQUHAR MATHESON, M.B., C.M., 11, Soho Square, W.

The Royal Ear Hospital was founded in 1816 for the treatment of Deafness and all forms of Ear Diseases. Since the foundation of this Institution upwards of 100,000 Patients have been treated within its walls.

The Hospital contains Wards for Male and Female Patients, and a Special Ward for Children.

Out-Patients are admitted on

Mondays and Saturdays, **Tuesdays and Fridays,**
3 to 5 p.m. **9 to 12 a.m.**

In-Patients daily by previous application to the Secretary.

The necessitous Poor are admitted without Letters of Recommendation.

Donations and Subscriptions (a Donation of £10 10s. confers the privilege of Life Governor) are earnestly solicited, and will be gratefully received by the TREASURER ; the AGRA BANK ; or by

M. C. PUDDY, *Secretary.*

THE RULES FOR ADMISSION OF PATIENTS MAY BE HAD ON APPLICATION TO THE SECRETARY.

HOSPITAL FOR CONSUMPTION
And DISEASES of the CHEST, BROMPTON.

FOUNDED 1841.   INCORPORATED BY ACT OF PARLIAMENT.

FUNDS are URGENTLY REQUIRED for the SUPPORT of this CHARITY, and especially for the MAINTENANCE of the NEW EXTENSION BUILDING, which contains 137 Additional Beds, entailing an EXTRA EXPENDITURE of SEVERAL THOUSANDS a year.

This Hospital is almost entirely dependent on Voluntary Contributions.

NEW ANNUAL SUBSCRIPTIONS as well as DONATIONS are very earnestly solicited.

Bankers: Messrs. WILLIAMS, DEACON & Co., 20, Birchin Lane.

HENRY DOBBIN, *Secretary.*

The Hospital for Diseases of the Skin,
BLACKFRIARS.

Patroness: H.R.H. THE PRINCESS OF WALES.

President : R. N. FOWLER, Esq., M.P.

Chairman : COL. THE HON. PAUL METHUEN, C.B.

Treasurer : JOSEPH GURNEY BARCLAY, Esq.

THIS Hospital was established in 1841, being the first and, for many years, the only Institution in the Kingdom for the special treatment of cutaneous diseases.

From **500** to **700** Patients receive treatment every week, the total number relieved amounting to **281,737.**

FUNDS ARE URGENTLY REQUIRED

in order to continue and extend the benefits of the Hospital, and Annual Subscriptions are particularly needed, the income falling considerably short of the expenditure.

There is a deficiency of £1,000 which the Committee are most anxious to make up, and towards which they invite Special Donations.

Contributions will be thankfully received by the Bankers, Messrs. BARCLAY, BEVAN & Co., 54, Lombard Street, E.C., and at the Hospital, 52, Stamford Street, S.E., by   SAMUEL HAYMAN, *Secretary.*

[H 22]

HOMES FOR LITTLE BOYS,
FARNINGHAM AND SWANLEY.

Patrons: **THEIR ROYAL HIGHNESSES THE PRINCE AND PRINCESS OF WALES.**
President: THE EARL OF ABERDEEN.
Treasurer: W. H. WILLANS, ESQ., 3, Copthall Buildings, E.C.
Bankers: MESSRS. SMITH, PAYNE & SMITHS, 1, Lombard Street, E.C.

THE Cottage Homes at Farningham are for **300** Little Boys, who are homeless, or in danger of falling into crime. They are clothed, fed, educated, and taught a trade, and then sent out into the world to earn an honest livelihood.

The new Orphan Homes at Swanley are for **200** Fatherless Boys, who are wholly maintained and educated, and receive technical instruction to fit them for a working life.

FUNDS ARE URGENTLY NEEDED,

And the Committee very earnestly appeal for Donations, Annual Subscriptions, Congregational Collections, and Bequests, to enable them to carry on this Christian work.

Offices: LUDGATE CIRCUS.   A. O. CHARLES, *Secretary.*

The ROYAL WESTMINSTER OPHTHALMIC HOSPITAL,
19, KING WILLIAM STREET, WEST STRAND, W.C.

Founded in 1816, by the late G. J. GUTHRIE, Esq., F.R.S., for the Relief of Indigent Persons afflicted with Diseases of the Eye.

ENTIRELY SUPPORTED BY VOLUNTARY CONTRIBUTIONS.

Patrons: { HER MOST GRACIOUS MAJESTY THE QUEEN.
H.R.H. THE PRINCE OF WALES, K.G., &c.,

Chairman: SIR RUTHERFORD ALCOCK, K.C.B.
Treasurer: ADMIRAL LEVESON E. H. SOMERSET.
Bankers: Messrs. COUTTS & Co., Strand; Messrs. DRUMMOND, Charing Cross.

THIS HOSPITAL receives the Destitute Poor on their own application, *without* Letters of Recommendation, and was the first to inaugurate this system of *true* Charity. It has Thirteen Wards, capable of accommodating Fifty In-Patients, but from want of funds only Twelve Beds can at present be maintained.

The decease of a large number of Old Subscribers has caused so great a diminution in the income of this much-needed Charity, that the Committee earnestly APPEAL TO THE BENEVOLENT for ANNUAL SUBSCRIPTIONS, so that as many of the numerous afflicted poor, constantly seeking admission, may be received as the Wards of the Hospital are capable of accommodating.

SUBSCRIPTIONS and DONATIONS will be thankfully received by the Bankers, or at the Hospital by   T. BEATTIE-CAMPBELL, *Secretary.*

FORM OF BEQUEST.
"I give and bequeath to the Treasurer for the time being, of the ROYAL WESTMINSTER OPHTHALMIC HOSPITAL the sum of * *to be applied to the general purposes of the said Hospital, and I desire that the said sum be paid, free of Legacy Duty, out of such part of my Personal Estate as I may lawfully devise to charitable uses."*

* The sum to be expressed in words at length.

SEAMEN'S HOSPITAL SOCIETY,
(Late "Dreadnought,")
GREENWICH, S.E.
Dispensary for Out-Patients:—Well Street, London Docks.
(Established on board the "Grampus," 1821.   Removed on shore from the "Dreadnought," 1870.
Incorporated by Act of Parliament, 1833.)

FREE TO SICK SEAMEN OF ALL NATIONS.
No admission ticket, or letters of recommendation, or voting of any sort required
SUPPORTED BY VOLUNTARY CONTRIBUTIONS.
Patron : HER MAJESTY THE QUEEN.   *Vice-Patron :* H.R.H. THE PRINCE OF WALES, K.G.
President : VICE-ADMIRAL H.R.H. THE DUKE OF EDINBURGH, K.G.
Treasurer : JOHN DEACON, Esq., 20, Birchin Lane, London, E.C.
Secretary : W. T. EVANS, Esq., Seamen's Hospital, Greenwich, S.E.

THE Committee earnestly solicit support on behalf of this universal Charity, than
which there is not a more noble or a more useful philanthropic Institution in th
world.   It gives free relief to all Sailors, without regard to race, nationality, or creed
In confidence of being relieved, sick seamen travel to it from the most distant parts o
the kingdom, and find at once a home and a welcome.   Safely harboured there, the
sailor receives medical aid, skilled nursing, convalescent treatment, and all thing
necessary to make him speedily able to rejoin his ship and to again maintain himself
There is also reason to hope that the sick seamen become better men by the religiou
instruction and regular habits which they acquire during their stay in the Hospital.

Since the Hospital was first opened in 1821, upwards of 250,000 sick seamen of al
nations have been relieved, from no less than 42 different countries.   During 1883 th
average number of patients was higher than it ever was before in any one year, havin
been 8,322 as compared with 5,098, the average of the preceding ten years ; while ther
were more patients in the Hospital than there had been since 1854, the year of the las
cholera epidemic.

Under the following exceptional circumstances the Committee URGENTLY APPEA
for additional help.   The Sanitary arrangements of the Hospital (built in 1763) ar
found to be such as are not consistent with the requirements of the present day, and
are reported to be in a state that "nothing short of an entire re-construction of th
system of drainage will place the Hospital in a safe sanitary condition."   In the fac
of so strong a statement, the Committee feel the heavy responsibility which would b
attached to them should any preventible illness break out owing to want of caution o
their part, and they have resolved that these alterations should be carried out forth
with.   The Admiralty, as landlords, undertake to contribute £1,500 towards the cos
which is, however, estimated to be £7,370, and this leaves £5,870 to be provide
by the Committee.

Heavy structural alterations being involved by these drainage works, the Committe
avail themselves of the opportunity, long sought, to build a New Chapel.   To provid
sufficient and proper accommodation in this respect will involve a further cost o
£1,281, and consequently the Committee must be prepared with no less a sum
than £7,151, in addition to that required for their ordinary annual expenditure.

The Hospital is held under six months' notice from the Admiralty, and consequentl
the reserve funds are not more than sufficient to build and equip a New Hospita
should it at any time be necessary to do so ; the Committee, therefore, are very loth t
draw upon their investments, and they earnestly appeal to the public to assist them i
their efforts to raise a special Building Fund.

Contributions and new Annual Subscriptions will be thankfully received by the Bankers, Messr
WILLIAMS, DEACON & CO., 20, Birchin Lane, London, E.C. ; or by the Secretary, at the Hospita
Greenwich, S.E., by whom any information desired will be gladly afforded.

FORMS OF BEQUEST.
A. — FORM OF GIFT BY WILL OF LANDS, &c.
I give and devise to the SEAMEN'S HOSPITAL SOCIETY *All that, &c.* [describing the lands, house
rents, or other property], *for the use of the said Society.*
B. — FORM OF BEQUEST OF MONEY, &c.
I bequeath to the SEAMEN'S HOSPITAL SOCIETY *the sum of £   for the use of the sai
Society, to be paid free from Legacy Duty ; and I declare that the receipt of the Treasurer for the tim
being of the said Society shall be sufficient discharge for the same.*
N.B.—By a clause in its Act of Parliament (3° GUL. IV., cap. 9) the Society is empowered to receiv
any Moneys, Messuages, Lands, Tenements, Rents, Annuities, &c., whatsoever, not exceeding th
value of £12,000 per annum, in addition to any sums of Money to any amount, and any Good
Ships, &c., of whatever value, which may be given or bequeathed to it from time to time.

THE IMPERIAL SANITARY STEAM
LAUNDRY & CLEANING WORKS,

INGESTRE ROAD, DARTMOUTH PARK.
Near HIGHGATE, N.W.

By Appointment { INTERNATIONAL FISHERIES EXHIBITION, 1883.
to the { INTERNATIONAL HEALTH EXHIBITION, 1884.

M. A. BALDWIN & Co., Proprietors.

THE above Laundry is situated in the most healthy suburb of London; and being fitted with all the modern improvements in sanitation, renders it an establishment calculated to supply a great public want.

VANS COLLECT AND DELIVER TO ALL PARTS OF LONDON.
ON COUNTRY ORDERS CARRIAGE PAID ONE WAY.

DYEING and **CLEANING DEPARTMENT.**	Curtains, Chintzes, and Cretonnes Cleaned and Dyed on the shortest notice. Muslin and Lace Curtains Cleaned, 1s. per pair. Ball Dresses, Opera Cloaks, Fancy and other Costumes Cleaned without unpicking, by our new process of Chemical Cleaning.
CARPET BEATING DEPARTMENT.	Carpets Beaten by Patent Machinery, which far supersedes the old-fashioned way of hand beating.

A competent person will wait upon intending customers, if required.
Lists of Prices and further information can be obtained upon application to the Manager, as above.

PRINCIPAL CLUBS AND CLUB-HOUSES.

NAME OF CLUB.	Established.	CLUB-HOUSE.	REMARKS.
Albemarle	1875	25 Albemarle st.	Ladies and gentlemen
Alexandra	1884	33 Old Bond st.	Ladies
Alpine	1857	8 St. Martin's pl.	Intrstd.in mountain explortn.
Army and Navy	1838	36 Pall mall	Officers of Army and Navy
Arthur's	1765	69 St. James's st.	Social
Arts	1863	17 Hanover sq.	Art, literature and science
Arundel	1860	12 Salisbury st. W.C.	Literary and artistic
Athenæum	1824	107 Pall mall	Scientific and literary
Bachelors'	1881	8 Hamilton pl. W.	Social ; ladies adm. as visitors
Badminton	1876	100 Piccadilly	Sporting and coaching club
Beaconsfield	1879	68 Pall mall	Conservative
Boodle's	1762	28 St. James's st.	Social
Brooks's	1764	St. James's st.	Liberal. Social
Burlington	1866	17 Savile row	Amateur artists & cllctrs.of art
Carlton	1832	94 Pall mall	Conservative
City Carlton	1868	St. Swithin's lane	Conservative
City Liberal	1874	Walbrook	Liberal
City of London	1832	19 Old Broad st. E.C.	Merchants, bankers, &c,
Cocoa Tree	1746	64 St. James's st.	Social
Conservative	1840	74 St. James's st.	Strictly Conservative
Crichton	1871	3 and 4 Adelphi ter.	Artistic,scientific and literary
Devonshire	1875	50 St. James's st.	Liberal
East India United Service	1847	14 St. James's sq.	Officers of East India (Civil & Military)Services,& Officers of H.M. Army & Navy
Eclectic	1860	30 Charles st. Mayfair	Social
Empire	1881	4 Grafton st. Piccadilly	Brit. Empire Home & Abroad
Farmers'	1843	Inns of Court hotel	Agricultural and social
Garrick	1831	13 Garrick st. Cov. Gar.	Theatrical, literary, &c.
German Athenæum	1869	93 Mortimer st. W.	Literary, artistic and social
Grafton	1863	10 Grafton st. W.	The first Gridiron club
Green Room	1877	20 Bedford st. Cov. Gar.	Dramatic, artistic, &c.
Gresham	1843	1 Gresham pl. E.C.	Merchants, bankers, &c.
Guards	1813	70 Pall mall	Officers of 3 regts. of Guards
Gun Club	1861	Wood lane Notting hill	Pigeon shooting
Hanover Square	1875	4 Hanover sq. W.	Social
Hogarth	1870	27 Albemarle st. W.	Artistic and social
Hurlingham	1869	Fulham S.W.	Polo, and pigeon shooting
Isthmian	1882	12 Grafton st. W.	Uvs.Pblc. Schls. Army & Nvy.
Junior Army & Navy	1869	10 St. James's st.	Officers of Army, Navy & Mar
Junior Athenæum	1864	116 Piccadilly	Scientific and literary
Junior Carlton	1864	Pall mall	Strictly Conservative
Junior Garrick	1867	1a Adelphi ter.	Social and dramatic
Junior Oxf. & Cam.	1878	7 St. James's sq.	Members of either University
Junior United Serv.	1827	Charles st. St. James's	Army,Navy,Marines & Militia
Kennel	1874	6 Cleveland row S.W.	For improving breed of dogs
Law Society	1832	103 Chancery lane	Members of the Incorporated [Law Society

NAME OF CLUB.	Established.	CLUB-HOUSE.	REMARKS.
Marlborough	1869	52 Pall mall S.W.	Social
Military and Royal Naval	1881	16 Albemarle st. W.	For Young Officers on first joining the Service
National	1845	1 Whitehall gardens......	Church of England
Naval and Military	1862	94 Piccadilly	Army, Navy and Marines
New Athenæum	1878	26 Suffolk st. S.W.........	Social and literary
New Thames Yacht	1868	Caledonian Hotel, Adelphi, and Gravesend	Yacht owners & their friends
New United Service	1880	8 Park pl. St. James's ...	Officers of the Army, Navy and Auxiliary Forces
New University	1863	57 St. James's st.	Members of Oxfd. & Cmbdge.
Oriental.................	1824	18 Hanover sq. W..........	Eastern Empire & travellers
Orleans	1877	29 King st. St. James's...	J. W. Knaggs, secretary
Oxford & Cambridge	1830	71 Pall mall	Members of the Universities
Pall Mall	1870	7 Waterloo pl...............	Non-political
Portland	1816	1 Stratford pl. Oxford st.	Non-political
Prince's Racquet ...	1853	Hans pl.	For practice of these games
Raleigh	1858	16 Regent st. S.W.........	Social
Reform	1834	104 Pall mall S.W.........	Strictly Liberal
Regency	1879	23 Albemarle st. W.	Literary, artistic and musical
Road	1874	4 Park pl. St. James's ...	Coaching and sport
Royal Canoe	1866	11 Buckingham st. W.C.	To promote canoeing
Royal London Yacht	1838	22 Regent st. W............	Yacht owners & gents.of pstn
Royal Thames Yacht	1823	7 Albemarle st. W.	Yacht owners & gents. of pstn
Russell Whist	1870	55 Great Coram st. W.C.	Whist, literary and social
St. George's	1875	2 Savile row W.	Roman Catholics. Social
St. George's Chess...	1826	47 Albemarle st. W.	For cultivation of chess
St. James's	1857	106 Piccadilly	Diplomatic
St. James's Whist ...	1883	87 St. James's st.	Members of the principal London Clubs
St. Stephen's	1870	1 Bridge st. Westminster	Conservative
Salisbury	1880	10 St. James's sq.	Ladies admitted as visitors
Savage	1857	Savoy pl. W.C.	Literary, art, drama, science
Savile...................	1868	107 Piccadilly	Social
Scandinavian	1875	80 Strand W.C.	For Scandinavian languages
Science	1874	4 Savile row W.	Strictly scientific
Scottish.................	1879	39 Dover st. W.	Social. Non-political
Thatched House......	1865	86 St. James's st.	Non-political
Travellers'	1819	106 Pall mall	Travellers
Turf	1868	47 Clarges st. Piccadilly	Sporting and social
Union....................	1822	Trafalgar sq.	Social. Non-political
United Service	1815	116 Pall mall	For senior officers only
United University...	1822	1 Suffolk st.	Mmbrs. of Oxfd. & Cam.Univ
United Whist	1876	4 Waterloo pl.	Mmbrs. of prinpl. Lndn. club.
Untd.& Public Schls.	1877	5 Park pl. St. James's ...	Mbrs.Oxfd. & Cam. & Pbl.Schs
Verulam	1875	54 St. James's st.	Social. Non-political
Victoria.................	1865	18 Wellington st. W.C....	Sporting
Volunteer Service ...	1882	32 Dover st. W.	Gentlemen of the Yeomanry and Volunteers
Wanderers'	1874	9 Pall mall	Social. Non-political
Whitehall...............	1866	47 Parliament st.	Social
White's	1730	37 St. James's st.	Social. Non-political
Windham	1828	11 St. James's sq.	Social

LONDON BANKS AND BANKERS.

AGRA BANK, LMTD. 35 Nicholas lane E.C.

ALEXANDERS & Co. 24 Lombard st. E.C.

ALLIANCE BANK, LIMITED, Bartholomew lane E.C. Branch Offices:—88 and 90 Kensington High st. W.; 239 Regent st. W.; and 176 High st. Camden town N.W.

ANGLO-AUSTRIAN BANK 31 Lombard st.

ANGLO-CALIFORNIAN BANK, LIMITED 3 Angel court E.C.

ANGLO-EGYPTIAN BANK, LIMITED 27 Clement's lane E.C.

ANGLO-FOREIGN BANKING Co., LMTD. 2 Bishopsgate st. within E.C.

ANGLO-FRENCH UNION BANK, LIMITED 43 New Broad st. E.C.

ANGLO-ITALIAN BANK, LIMITED 9 St. Helen's pl. E.C.

ANGLO-PERUVIAN BANK, LIMITED 5 Copthall buildings E.C.

ANGLO-UNIVERSAL BANK, LIMITED 41 to 43 Coleman st. E.C.

AUSTRALIAN JOINT STOCK BANK 2 King William st. E.C.

BANK OF AFRICA, LIMITED 25 Abchurch lane E.C.

BANK OF AUSTRALASIA 4 Threadneedle st

BANK OF BRITISH COLUMBIA 28 Cornhill E.C.

BANK OF BRITISH NORTH AMERICA 3 Clement's lane E.C.

BANK OF CONSTANTINOPLE 19 Great Winchester st. E.C.

BANK OF EGYPT 26 Old Broad st. E.C.

BANK OF ENGLAND Threadneedle st. E.C Branch Offices:—1 Burlington gardens W., and New Law Courts W.C.

BANK OF MONTREAL 9 Birchin lane E.C.

BANK OF NEW SOUTH WALES 64 Old Broad st. E.C.

BANK OF NEW ZEALAND 1 Queen Victoria st. E.C.

BANK OF ROUMANIA 15 Moorgate st. E.C

BANK OF SCOTLAND 43 Lothbury E.C.

BANK OF SOUTH AUSTRALIA 31 Lombard st. E.C.

BANK OF VICTORIA 28 Clement's ln. E.C.

BANQUE COMMERCIALE AGRICOLE 5 Bartholomew lane E.C.

BARCLAY, BEVAN, TRITTON & Co. 54 Lombard st. E.C.

BARING BROTHERS & Co. 8 Bishopsgate st. within E.C.

BAUM BROTHERS 46 Regent st. S.W.

BIGGERSTAFF W. & J. 63 West Smithfield E.C. Branch Offices:—6 Bank buildings, Metropolitan Cattle Market N.; and Foreign Cattle Market, Deptford S.E.

BIRKBECK BANK 29 & 30 Southampton buildings, Chancery lane E.C.

BLYDENSTEIN, BENJAMIN WILLIAM & Co. 55 Threadneedle st. E.C.

BOSANQUET, SALT & Co. 73 Lombard st.

BRITISH LINEN Co. 41 Lombard st. E.C.

BROOKS & Co. 81 Lombard st. E.C.

BROWN, JANSON & Co. 32 Abchurch lane

BROWN JOHN & Co. 25 Abchurch lane E.C

CAPITAL & COUNTIES BANK, LIMITED 39 Threadneedle st. E.C. Branch Offices:—25 Ludgate hill E.C.; 68 Oxford st. W.; 195 Edgware rd. W.; and 1 Long acre W.

CENTRAL BANK OF LONDON, LIMITED 52 Cornhill E.C. Branch Offices:—Blackfriars rd. (corner of Stamford st.) S.E.; Goswell rd. (corner of Clerkenwell rd.) E.C.; 91 Newgate st. E.C.; 31 High st. Shoreditch E.; Tooley st. (corner of Bermondsey st.) S.E.; and 110 High st. Whitechapel E.

CHARTERED BANK OF INDIA, AUSTRALIA, AND CHINA, Hatton court Threadneedle st. E.C.

CHARTERED MERCANTILE BANK OF INDIA, LONDON & CHINA 65 Old Broad st. E.C.

CHEQUE BANK 124 Cannon st. E.C. Branch Office:—20 Cockspur st. S.W.

CHILD & Co. 1 Fleet st. Temple Bar E.C.

CITY BANK, LIMITED 5 Threadneedle st. E.C. Branch Offices:—34 Old Bond st. W.; 159 Tottenham court rd. W.C.; 81 Ludgate hill E.C.; 221 Edgware rd. W.; 6 & 7 Lowndes ter. Knightsbridge S.W.; 34 Holborn Viaduct E.C.; and Aldgate bldns. E.C.: and Gt. Eastern st. E.

CLYDESDALE BANK, LIMITED 30 Lombard st. E.C.

COCKS, BIDDULPH & Co. 43 Charing cross

COLONIAL BANK 13 Bishopsgate st. within E.C.

COLONIAL BANK OF NEW ZEALAND 13 Moorgate st. E.C.

COMMERCIAL BANK OF ALEXANDRIA, LIMITED 2 Moorgate st. E.C.

COMMERCIAL BANK OF AUSTRALIA, LIMITED 67 Cornhill E.C.

COMMERCIAL BANK OF SYDNEY, LMTD. 39 Lombard st. E.C.

COMMERCIAL UNION BANK, LIMITED 88 Bishopsgate st. within E.C.

COMPTOIR D'ESCOMPTE DE PARIS 52 Threadneedle st. E.C.

CONSOLIDATED BANK, LIMITED 52 Threadneedle st. E.C. Branch Office:—450 West Strand, Charing cross W.C.

CONTINENTAL BANK AND EXCHANGE, ALEXANDER BROWN AND CO. 79 Lombard st.

COUTTS & Co. 57 to 59 Strand W.C.

COX & Co., 1 & 2 Craig's court Charing cross S.W.

CREDIT LYONNAIS 40 Lombard st. E.C.

CUNLIFFE, ROGER, SONS & Co. 6 Princes st. E.C.

DELHI AND LONDON BANK, LIMITED, Royal Bank buildings, 123 Bishopsgate st. within E.C.

DIMSDALE, FOWLER & Co. 50 Cornhill

DOBREE SAMUEL & SONS 6 Tokenhouse yard E.C.

DRUMMOND, MESSRS., 49 Charing cross

ENGLISH BANK OF RIO DE JANEIRO, LIMITED 13 St. Helen's pl. E.C.

ENGLISH BANK OF THE RIVER PLATE, LIMITED 8 Old Jewry E.C.

ENGLISH BANK OF SPAIN, LIMITED 36 Lombard st. E.C.

ENGLISH, SCOTTISH AND AUSTRALIAN BANK 73 Cornhill E.C.

FULLER, BANBURY & Co. 77 Lombard st.

GERMAN BANK OF LONDON, LIMITED, Bartholomew house E.C.

GILLETT BROS. & Co. 72 Lombard st. E.C.

GLYN, MILLS, CURRIE & Co. 67 Lombard st. E.C.

GOSLINGS & SHARPE 19 Fleet st. E.C.

GRINDLAY & Co. 55 Parliament st. S.W.

HERRIES, FARQUHAR & Co. 16 St. James's st. S.W.

HICKIE, BORMAN & Co. 14 Waterloo pl.

HILL & SONS 17 West Smithfield E.C.; 2 Bank buildings, Metropolitan Cattle Market N.; & Foreign Cattle Market, Deptford S.E.

HOARES & Co. 37 Fleet st. E.C.

HOLT, VESEY & Co. 17 Whitehall pl. S.W.

HONGKONG AND SHANGHAI BANKING CORPORATION 31 Lombard st. E.C.

HOPKINSON & SONS 3 Regent st. S.W.

IMPERIAL BANK, LIMITED 6 Lothbury E.C. Branch Offices :—1 Sydney pl. Onslow sq. S.W.; and 10 Victoria mansions, Westminster S.W.

IMPERIAL OTTOMAN BANK 26 Throgmorton st. E.C.

INTERNATIONAL BANK OF LONDON, LIMITED 113 Cannon st. E.C.

IONIAN BANK 31 Finsbury circus E.C.

KING HENRY S. & Co. 45 Pall mall S.W.; and 65 Cornhill E.C.

LACY, HARTLAND, WOODBRIDGE AND Co. 60 West Smithfield E.C. Branch Offices:—8 Bank buildings, Metropolitan Cattle Market N.; Bank buildings, Deptford Dockyard S.E.; and 98 Jamaica rd. Bermondsey S.E.

LAND MORTGAGE BANK OF INDIA, LIMITED 4 East India avenue E.C.

LAND MORTGAGE BANK OF VICTORIA, LIMITED 17 King's Arms yard E.C.

LLOYDS, BARNETTS, AND BOSANQUET'S BANK, LIMITED 62 Lombard st. E.C.

LONDON AND COUNTY BANKING CO., LIMITED 21 Lombard st. E.C. Branch Offices :—3 Albert gate, Knightsbridge S.W.; 134 Aldersgate st. E.C.; 1 Amhurst rd. Hackney E.; 21 Hanover sq. W.; 1 Connaught st. Edgware rd W.; 4 and 5 Upper st. Islington N. 34 High st. Borough S.E.; Sussex pl Queen's gate S.W.; 67 Kensington High st. W.; 181 & 182 High st. Shoreditch E. 74 and 76 Westbourne grove W.; Henrietta st. Covent garden W.C. 324 & 325 High Holborn W.C.; 165 Westminster bridge rd. S.E.; Deptford broadway S.E.; 680 Commercial rd east E.; 18 Newington Butts S.E.; Victoria st. S.W.; 266 & 268 Pentonville rd. King's Cross ; 369 Brixton rd S.W.; 87 High st. Kingsland E. Church st. Greenwich S.E. ; Tranquil vale Blackheath S.E.; 12 King st west Hammersmith W.; 5 Neeld ter Harrow rd. W.; 4 Bank buildings Westow hill, Norwood S.E.; 111 New Oxford st. W.C.; Stratford broadway E.; Powis st. Woolwich S.E.; and 4 The Mall Ealing

LONDON AND HANSEATIC BANK, LIMITED 27 Lombard st. E.C.

LONDON & NORTH-WESTERN DISTRICT BANK, LIMITED, Dashwood house New Broad st. E.C.

LONDON AND PROVINCIAL BANK, LIMITED 7 Bank buildings E.C. Branch Offices :—163 Edgware rd. W.; Sussex pl. South Kensington W.; 95 High st. Lewisham S.E.; Bank buildings Blackheath Village S.E.; Anerley S.E.; 163 High st. Stoke Newington N.; Walham green S.W.; Stratford E. 1 Kingsland High st. E.; Barking rd Canning town E.; Beckenham, Richmond, Surbiton, Sutton, Tottenham Twickenham, Woolwich, Enfield Walthamstow, and The Triangle Hackney E.

LONDON AND RIVER PLATE BANK LIMITED 52 Moorgate st. E.C.

LONDON AND SAN FRANCISCO BANK LIMITED 22 Old Broad st. E.C.

LONDON AND SOUTH-WESTERN BANK LIMITED 7 Fenchurch st. E.C. Branch Offices:—27 Regent st. W.; Clapham common S.W.; 275 Brixton rd. S.W. 451 Brixton rd. S.W.; High rd. Balham S.W.; 6 Bank buildings, Wandsworth S.W.; Broadway, Lower Tooting S.W.; 127 Upper Richmond rd Putney S.W.; The Broadway, Wimbledon S.W.; Bank buildings Sydenham S.E.; 435 Norwood rd. Lower Norwood S.E.; Westow hill Nor wood S.E.; High st. Forest hill S.E. Streatham rd. Streatham S.E.; 256 Camberwell rd. S.E.; 67 & 68 Park st. Camden town N.W.; 82 Finsbury pavement E.C.; 6 Sutherland garden Harrow rd. W.; 403 Holloway rd. N

228 Kentish town rd. N.W.; 137 Ladbroke grove Notting hill W.; High st. Peckham S.E.; Wellington rd. St. John's wood N.W.; Acton W.; 135 Anerley rd. S.E.; Battersea park rd. S.W.; 159 Old Kent rd. S.E.; 90 & 92 Bow rd. E.; Croydon S.E.; Ealing W.; Hampstead N.W.; Highgate N.; Bank buildings Kilburn N.W.; Hendon N.W.; Shepherd's bush W.; Stepney E.; Chiswick and Turnham green W.; 202 Fulham rd. West Brompton S.W.; Addiscombe S.E.; 3 Garfield ter.; Clapham junction S.W.; Finsbury park N.; South Norwood S.E.; Forest gate E.; and Poplar E.

LONDON AND WESTMINSTER BANK, LIMITED 41 Lothbury E.C. Branch Offices :—1 St. James's sq. S.W.; 214 High Holborn W.C.; 6 High st. Borough S.E.; 130 to 132 High st. Whitechapel E.; 4 Stratford pl. Oxford st. W.; 217 Strand W.C.; 91 Westminster bridge rd. S.E.; 1 Brompton sq. S.W.; and Victoria st. Westminster

LONDON BANKING ASSOCIATION, LIMITED 57 Old Broad st. E.C.

LONDON BANK OF MEXICO & SOUTH AMERICA, LIMITED 144 Leadenhall st.

LONDON AND YORKSHIRE BANK, LIMITED, Drapers' gardens E.C.

LONDON CHARTERED BANK OF AUSTRALIA 88 Cannon st. E.C.

LONDON JOINT STOCK BANK, LIMITED 5 Princes st. E.C. Branch Offices :— 69 Pall mall S.W.; 123 Chancery lane E.C.; Charterhouse st. E.C.; Metropolitan Cattle Market N.; and Foreign Cattle Market, Deptford S.E.; 28 Borough High st. S.E.; 2 Craven rd. Bayswater W.; & 11 Gt. Tower st. E.C.

LONDON TRADING BANK, LIMITED 1 West st. Moorgate E.C.

McCULLOCH & CO. 75 Lombard st. E.C.

McGRIGOR SIR C R. & CO. 25 Charles st. St. James's S.W.

MARTIN & CO. 68 Lombard st. E.C.

MERCANTILE BANK OF SYDNEY 158 Leadenhall st. E.C.

MERCANTILE BANK OF THE RIVER PLATE, LIMITED 5 Copthall buildings E.C.

MERCANTILE INTERNATIONAL BANK, LIMITED 5 Copthall buildings E.C.

MERCHANT BANKING COMPANY OF LONDON, LIMITED 112 Cannon st. E.C.

MORGAN J. S. & C. 22 Old Broad st. E.C.

NATIONAL BANK, LIMITED 13 Old Broad st. E.C. Branch Offices :—68 Gloucester gardens W.; 9 Charing cross S.W.; 189 High st. Camden town

N.W.; 286 Pentonville rd. N.; 158 High st. Notting hill W.; 21 Grosvenor gardens S.W.; 276 Oxford st.W.; 361 Goswell rd. E.C.; 2 Elgin villas Elgin rd. W.; St. Mary's rd. Harlesden N.W.; &c.

NATIONAL BANK OF SCOTLAND 37 Nicholas lane E.C.

NATIONAL PROVINCIAL BANK OF ENGLAND, LIMITED 112 Bishopsgate st. within, E.C. Branch Offices: — 212 Piccadilly W.; 53 Baker st. W.; 218 Upper st. Islington N.; Carey st. Lincoln's inn E.C.; & 88 Cromwell rd. S.W.

NEW LONDON AND BRAZILIAN BANK, LIMITED 2 Old Broad st. E.C.

NEW ORIENTAL BANK CORPORATION, LIMITED 40 Threadneedle st. E.C.

PRAEDS & CO. 189 Fleet st. E.C.

PRESCOTT & Co. 62 Threadneedle st. E.C.

PROVINCIAL BANK OF IRELAND, LMTD. 8 Throgmorton avenue E.C.

QUEENSLAND NATIONAL BANK, LMTD. 29 Lombard st. E.C.

RANSOM, BOUVERIE & Co. 1 Pall mall east S.W.

RICHARDSON & CO. 13 Pall mall S.W.

ROBARTS, LUBBOCK & Co. 15 Lombard st. E.C.

ROTHSCHILD & SONS, New court, St. Swithin's lane E.C.

ROYAL BANK OF SCOTLAND 123 Bishopsgate st. within E.C.

ROYAL EXCHANGE BANK, LIMITED 75 Cornhill E.C.

SAMUEL MONTAGU & Co. 60 Old Broad st. E.C.

SCOTT SIR SAMUEL, BART. & Co. 1 Cavendish sq. W.

SMITH, PAYNE & SMITHS 1 Lombard st.

STANDARD BANK OF SOUTH AFRICA, LIMITED 10 Clement's lane

TWINING R. & Co. 215 Strand W.C.

UNION BANK OF AUSTRALIA, LIMITED 1 Bank buildings E.C.

UNION BANK OF LONDON, LIMITED 2 Princes st. E.C. Branch Offices:—66 Charing cross S.W.; 14 Argyll pl. Regent st. W.; Bishop's rd. Bayswater W.; Holborn circus E.C.; and Chancery lane E.C.

UNION BANK OF SCOTLAND 62 Cornhill

UNION BANK OF SPAIN AND ENGLAND, LIMITED 21 Old Broad st. E.C.

WEST LONDON COMMERCIAL BANK, LIMITED 34 Sloane sq. Chelsea S.W. Branch Offices :—1 Victoria rd. Battersea S.W.; 183 Earl's court rd. S.W.; and 214 Upper Kennington lane S.E.;

WESTERN AUSTRALIAN BANK, London agency 31 Lombard st. E.C.

WILLIAMS, DEACON, THORNTON & CO. 20 Birchin lane E.C.

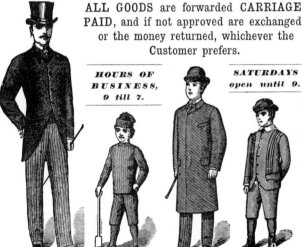

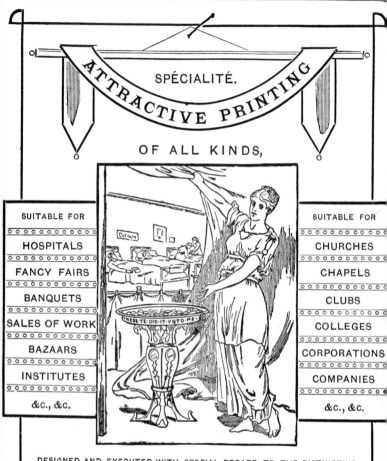

SPÉCIALITÉ.

ATTRACTIVE PRINTING

OF ALL KINDS,

SUITABLE FOR

HOSPITALS

FANCY FAIRS

BANQUETS

SALES OF WORK

BAZAARS

INSTITUTES

&c., &c.

SUITABLE FOR

CHURCHES

CHAPELS

CLUBS

COLLEGES

CORPORATIONS

COMPANIES

&c., &c.

DESIGNED AND EXECUTED WITH SPECIAL REGARD TO THE DISTINCTIVE
CHARACTER AND REQUIREMENTS OF PUBLIC AND
CORPORATE BODIES BY

HUTCHINGS & CROWSLEY,

LIMITED,

ST. JOHN'S WOOD, LONDON, N.W.

CHURCHES, CHAPELS, INSTITUTIONS, ETC.

———o———

Any Church, Chapel, or Institution omitted from the following list, or any error therein, will be corrected in the next edition, on information of the same being sent to the Publishers.

———o———

CHURCH OF ENGLAND.
Hampstead.

All Saints, Child's hill, Finchley new rd.; Rev. John H. Clay, M.A., vicar; Rev. H. L. Dixon, B.A., curate. Services, Sunday 11 a.m. and 7 p.m.; Thursday 7.30 p.m.; Holy Communion first Sunday after Morning Service; second and fourth 8 a.m.; third after Evening Service; Wednesday 11 a.m.

All Souls', Loudoun rd. St. John's wood; Rev. Henry R. Wadmore, M.A., vicar; Rev. F. J. Wrottesley, B.A., curate. Services, Sunday (Holy Communion) 8 a.m., 11 a.m., and 7 p.m.; Saints' Days 11 a.m. and 5 p.m.

Christ Church, Hampstead sq.; Rev. E. H. Bickersteth, M.A., vicar; Rev. W. H. Coates and Rev. J. G. Kitchen, M.A., curates. Services, Sunday (Holy Communion) 8 a.m., 11 a.m., 3.30 and 7 p.m.; Wednesday and Friday 12 noon; Daily 7.30 a.m. and 5.30 p.m. (except Wednesday 7.30 p.m.)

Emmanuel Church, West end; Rev. E. Davys, M.A., curate in charge. Services, Sunday 11 a.m. and 7 p.m.; Holy Communion first after Morning Service, third after Evening Service; Thursday 7.30 p.m.

St. Cuthbert's, Fordwych rd. West Hampstead; Rev. W. J. Watkins, London Diocesan Home Missionary in charge (incumbent designate). Services, Sunday 11 a.m. and 7 p.m.; Children's Service last Sunday in month 3 p.m.; Wednesday 7.30 p.m.

St. John's Episcopal Chapel, Downshire hill; Rev. Gilbert Karney, M.A., minister. Services, Sunday 11 a.m. and 7 p.m.; Friday 7.30 p.m.

St. John's, Church row; Rev. S. B. Burnaby, M.A., vicar; Rev. M. G. Tracy, M.A., curate. Services, Sunday 11 a.m., 3.30 and 7 p.m.; Holy Days and Wednesdays 11 a.m.; Friday 11 a.m. and 7 p.m.; Daily in Lent and Advent) 5.30 p.m.; Holy Communion, first and third Sunday after Morning Service, second and fifth 8.30 a.m., fourth after Evening Service

St. Mary the Virgin, Primrose hill; Rev. C. J. Fuller, M.A., incumbent; Rev. C. W. H. Baker, B.A., curate. Services, Sunday (Holy Communion) 7.30 and 9.45 a.m., 11.15 a.m., 3.30 and 7 p.m.; Wednesday and Friday 10 a.m.; Daily (Holy Communion) 7.30 and 10 a.m. and 5 p.m. (except Wednesday and Friday at 8 p.m.); Holy Days Holy Communion 7.30 a.m.

St. Mary's, Priory rd. Kilburn; Rev. John Robertson, M.A., vicar; Rev. E. N. Coulthard, M.A., curate. Services, Sunday 11 a.m., 3.15 and 7 p.m.; Holy Communion 1st and 3rd Sundays after Morning Service, 2nd 8.30 a.m., 4th after Evening Service, 5th at 4 p.m.; Wednesday 8 p.m., Friday 12 noon

St. Paul's, Avenue rd. St. John's wood; Rev. J. W. Bennett, M.A., vicar; Rev. A. J. Knight, curate. Services, Sunday 11 a.m., 3.30 and 7 p.m.; Holy Communion 8 a.m. and at midday on the 1st and 3rd Sundays in month. Daily 8.30 a.m. and 5 p.m.; Wednesday and Friday 12 noon

St. Peter's, Belsize sq.; Rev. Francis W. Tremlett, D.C.L., vicar, and Rev. W. H. Hewlett-Cooper, M.A., curate. Services, Sunday 11 a.m. and 7 p.m.; Children's Service and Bible Class on alternate Sundays 3.15 p.m.; Wednesday and Friday 10.30 a.m.; Daily in Lent and Advent at 10.30 a.m.

St. Saviour's, Eton rd. Haverstock hill;
Rev. Gerard A. Herklots, M.A., vicar;
Rev. J. Christian Hose, B.A., curate.
Services, Sunday 8 a.m. (Holy Com-
munion), 11 a.m., 3.30 and 7 p.m.;
Wednesday and Friday 12 noon;
Holy Days 8 a.m. (Holy Communion),
11 a.m. and 5 p.m.

St. Silas' Mission Church, Whitefield st.;
Rev. P. R. Mahony, L.D.H.M. Services,
Sunday 11 a.m. and 7 p.m.; 3rd
Sunday Children's Service at 3 p.m.;
Tuesday and Thursday 8 p.m.

St. Stephen's, Hampstead green; Rev.
Joshua Kirkman, M.A., vicar; Rev.
Richard Thornber, B.A., curate. Services, Sunday 11 a.m., 4 and 7 p.m.;
2nd Sunday Children's Service at 3.30
p.m.; Holy Communion 1st Sunday
after Morning Service, 3rd after Evening Service, 2nd, 4th and 5th at 8.15
a.m.

Trinity Church, Hampstead; Rev. Henry
Sharpe, B.D., vicar; Rev. S. A. Boyd,
M.A., curate. Services, Sunday 11
a.m. and 7 p.m.; second Sunday in
the month (for the Young) 3 p.m.;
Holy Communion first Sunday after
Morning Service, third Sunday after
Evening Service and on special occa-
sions; Wednesday 7.30 p.m.; Friday
12 noon during Lent

Highgate.

All Saints' Church, Church rd.; Rev.
Edgar Smith, B.A., vicar; Rev. W.
M. H. Church and H. R. Cooper Smith.
curates. Services, Sunday 8 a.m.
(Holy Communion),11 a.m.and 7 p.m.;
Tuesday and Thursday 7 a.m. (Holy
Communion); Wednesday, Friday and
Holy Days 7.30 a.m. (Holy Com-
munion) and 8 p.m.; Daily 7.45 a.m.
and 5.30 p.m.

Kentish Town Parish Church, Highgate
rd.; Rev. J. C. Cowd, M.A., vicar;
Rev. J. S. Skinner, B.A., Rev. A. Allen,
M.A., curates. Services, Sunday 8 a.m.
(Holy Communion) and first and
third Sunday after Morning Service,
11 a.m., 3.30 and 7 p.m.; Wednesday,
Friday, and Saints' Days 11 a.m.;
Thursday 8 p.m.

St. Anne's, Highgate rise; Rev. Charles
Tabor Ackland, M.A., vicar; Rev.
J. D. K. Mahomed, B.A., curate. Ser-

vices, Sunday 8.30 11 a.m., 4.30 and
p.m.; Saints' Days 10.30 a.m. an
5.30 p.m.; Wednesday and Frida
and daily during Lent and Advent
10.30 a.m. and 5.30 p.m.

St. Augustine's, Archway rd.; Rev
Edgar Smith, vicar. Services, Sun
day 8 (Holy Communion) and 1
a.m., 3.30 and 7 p.m.; Wednesday
10.30 a.m. and 8 p.m.; Holy Day
Holy Communion 7 a.m.

St. Mary, Brookfield, Dartmouth par
hill; Rev. D. J. Twemlow-Cooke, M.A.
vicar; Rev. F. C. Skey, M.A., curate
Services, Sunday 11 a.m. and 7 p.m.
Holy Communion 8 a.m., and afte
Matins; Wednesday 8 p.m., and
Friday 7.30 p.m.; Saints' Days Hol
Communion 8 a.m. and Evensong
5 p.m.

St. Michael's, South grove; Rev. Danie
Trinder, M.A., vicar; Rev. C.W.Kirkby
curate. Services, Sunday 8 a.m. (Holy
Communion) also first and third Sun
days after Morning Service; 11 a.m.
3.45 p.m. (Litany and Sermon) and
7 p.m.; Daily 10 a.m. and 5 p.m.

St. Peter's, Langdon rd. Dartmouth
park hill; Rev. John Francis Osborne
M.A., vicar; Rev. W. L. Payne, curate
Services, Sunday 11 a.m. and 7 p.m
first Sunday 3.15 p.m.; Wednesday
p.m. Holy Communion every Sunday
Whittington College Chapel, Archway
rd.; Rev. R. A. Currey, M.A., chaplain

BAPTIST CHAPELS.
Hampstead.

Brondesbury, High rd. Kilburn, corner
of Iverson rd.; Rev. J. C. Thompson
minister. Services, Sunday 11 a.m.
7 p.m.; Thursday 7.30 p.m.

Child's hill; Rev. W. Rickard, minister
Services, Sunday 11 a.m., 6.30 p.m.
Thursday 8 p.m.; Monday (Praye
Meeting) 8 p.m.

Ebenezer Chapel, Kilburn vale. Services
Sunday 11 a.m., 6.30 p.m.; Friday
7.30 p.m.

Ebenezer Chapel, New end; Rev. Jame
Foreman, pastor. Services, Sunday
11 a.m., 6.30 p.m.; Wednesday 7.30
p.m.

Heath st.; Rev. W. Brock, ministe
Services, Sunday 11 a.m., 6.30 p.m.
Wednesday 7.30 p.m.

New End Baptist Chapel

Highgate.

Highgate, Southwood lane; Rev. John H. Barnard, minister. Services, Sunday 11 a.m. and 7 p.m.

Highgate rd.; Rev. James Stephens, M.A., minister. Services, Sunday 11 a.m., 7 p.m. ; Wednesday 7.30 p.m.

CATHOLIC APOSTOLIC.
Hampstead.

Abbey house, Springfield villas Kilburn ; ministers various

Highgate.

Gordon house rd., Highgate rd.

CONGREGATIONAL CHAPELS.
Hampstead.

Greville pl., Kilburn ; Rev. G. Stewart, minister. Services, Sunday 11 a.m., 7 p.m. ; Wednesday 7.30 p.m.

Haverstock Chapel, Maitland park Haverstock hill; Rev. John Nunn, minister. Services, Sunday 11 a.m., 7 p.m. ; Wednesday 7.30 p.m.

Lyndhurst rd.; Robert F. Horton, M.A., Fellow of New Coll. Oxford, minister. Services, Sunday 11 a.m., 7 p.m. ; Thursday 7.45 p.m.

New College Chapel, Upper Avenue rd. St. John's wood; Rev. Johnson Barker, B.A.,LL.B., minister. Services, Sunday 11 a.m., 7 p.m. ; Wednesday, 7.30 p.m.

Highgate.

Junction rd. Upper Holloway ; Rev. W. J. Craig, F.R.G.S., minister. Services, Sunday 11 a.m., 7 p.m. ; Thursday 7.30 p.m.

South grove, Highgate; Rev. J. M. Gibbon, minister. Services, Sunday 11 a.m., 6.30 p.m. ; Wednesday 7 p.m.

PRESBYTERIAN.
Hampstead.

Oxendon Church, Haverstock hill, near Prince of Wales rd. Services, Sunday 11 a.m., 7 p.m. ; Wednesday 7.30 p.m.

Trinity Church, High st. ; Rev. John Matheson,M.A.,minister 8 Thurlow rd. Services, Sunday 11 a.m., 6.30. p.m. ; Wednesday 7.30 p.m.

PRIMITIVE METHODIST CHAPEL.
Hampstead.

Little Church row; ministers various. Services, Sunday 11 a.m., 6.30 p.m. ; Tuesday 7 p.m.; Friday (Prayer Meeting) 7.30 p.m.

ROMAN CATHOLIC.
Hampstead.

Church of the Sacred Heart, Quex rd.; Rev. Father Charles Cox, superior, Rev. W. Ring and Rev. P. O'Donnell. Services, Sunday, Mass 8, 9, 10 and 11 a.m. ; Benediction 3.30 p.m. ; Vespers and Sermon 7 p.m. ; Daily Mass 7 and 8 a.m. ; Thursday, Benediction 8 p.m. ; Holy Days 7, 8 and 10 a.m. and 8 p.m.

Convent of the Sisters of Providence 198 Haverstock hill ; Sister Adeline, lady superior

St. Mary's,Holly pl.; The Very Rev.Canon Arthur Dillon Purcell, M.R. Services, Sunday, Mass 8 and 11 a.m. ; with Sermon, Compline, and Benediction 4 p.m. ; Week days 8 a.m. ; Friday 8 p.m.

Highgate.

Church of Our Lady, Help of Christians, Fortess rd. Kentish town ; Rev. James Connolly,M.R. Services, Sunday, Mass 8, 10 and 11 a.m. ; Catechism 3 p.m. ; Vespers, Sermon and Benediction 7 p.m.; Week days Mass 8 a.m. ; Wednesday and Friday Service 7.30 p.m.

Convent of La Sainte Union des Sacrés Cœurs, Highgate rd. ; Madame Copin, supéricure

Convent of the Sisters of Providence (Bartram) Haverstock hill

La Sainte Union des Sacrés Cœurs 201 Junction rd.

St. Joseph's Retreat, Upper Whittington pl. Highgate hill; Rev. Father Gregory O'Callagan, rector

UNITARIAN CHAPEL.
Hampstead.

Rosslyn hill Pilgrim's lane, Hampstead ; Rev. Dr. Thomas Sadler, minister. Services, Sunday 11.30 a.m., 7 p.m.

WESLEYAN CHAPELS.
Hampstead.

Finchley rd. Child's hill. Services, Sunday 11 a.m., 6.30 p.m. ; Wednesday 7.30 p m. ; Tuesday 7 p.m.

Fleet rd. Gospel oak. Services, Sunday 11 a.m., 6.30 p.m.; alternate Tuesdays 7.30 p.m.

Prince Arthur rd. ; Rev. Joseph Dixon, minister. Services, Sunday 11 a.m., 6.30 p.m. ; Thursday 7.30 p.m.

Quex rd. Kilburn ; Rev. T.Chope, superintendent minister. Services, Sunday 11 a.m., 6.30 p.m.; Tuesday 8 p.m. ; Prayer Meetings, Sunday 7 a.m.; Friday 7.30 p.m.

Highgate.

Archway rd.; Rev. J. Pearson, minister. Services, Sunday 11 a.m., 6.30 p.m. ; Wednesday 7.30 p.m.

MISSION ROOMS.
Hampstead.

Christ Church Mission Rooms,Lutton ter.

Palmerston Blue Ribbon Mission Room 41 Palmerston rd.

St. Cuthbert's Parish Room 9 Ariel st.

St. Mary's Mission Buildings, Netherwood st.; Rev. W. Kerr Smith, M.A., minister in charge. Services, Sunday 11 a.m., 7 p.m.

St. Peter's Mission Room, Cricklewood lane

St. Saviour's Mission Room, Fleet rd. South Hampstead ; Mr.Charles Mackeson, reader. Services, Sunday 11.30 a.m.; 7 p.m. ; first Sunday 4 p.m. (for men only); Communicants' Meeting, last Sunday 4 p.m.

Salvation Army Barracks,Vale of Health.

Highgate.

All Saints, North hill ; Miss Mary Hughes, lady superintendent

Bartholomew ter. North hill

Forest grove

Highgate New town

North hill

St. Anne's, Raydon st.

St. Benet and All Saints' Mission Room 9 Dartmouth park hill

Southwood lane

51 Vorley rd.

PUBLIC SCHOOLS.
Hampstead.

All Souls' Schools, North end rd. Belsize rd.

Board Schools—
Blenheim pl.
Burghley rd.
Haverstock hill
Netherwood st.
British Schools, Heath st.; W. H. Davie master
Child's Hill Chapel School, The Mea Child's hill
Christ Church Schools, Hampstead sq.
National Schools, Child's hill
North End Infant School ; Miss Stowel mistress
Rosslyn Hill British School, Willoughb road
St. Domenic's School, Mutrix rd.
St. Mary's Catholic School 4 Holly pl. Miss Plummer, mistress
St. Mary's Convent Boarding School
St. Mary's Convent Girls' and Boy Schools 101 Haverstock hill
St. Mary's Schools, West end lane, Ki burn
St. Paul's Schools, Winchester rd.
St. Saviour's School, Fleet rd.
St. Stephen's Infant School, South en green
St. Stephen's Schools, Downshire hill

Highgate.

Highgate Board Schools, North hill
Highgate National Schools, North rd.
St. Ann's Schools, Brookfield, Highga New town
St. Joseph's Catholic Schools, Upp Whittington pl. Highgate hill; Patric O'Loughlin, master ; Madame Alba mistress
Sir Roger Cholmeley's School, Nort rd.; Charles McDowall, M.A., D.D head master

THEOLOGICAL COLLEGE
(Congregational).

New College, Finchley new rd. ; Re Professor Samuel Newth, M.A., D.D principal ; Rev. Wm. Farrer, LL.B., se

BENEVOLENT INSTITUTIONS.
Hampstead.

Charity Organisation Society 56 Gayto rd. ; Henry Toynbee, secretary
Convent of the Sisters of Hope fc Nursing the Sick (Hope house) Que road

Cottage Home for Destitute Orphan Girls, Mill lane ; Miss M. A. Cole, superintendent

Countess of Ducie's Home for Ladies (Evenlode house) 24 Parliament hill rd

Female Servants' Home 28 Church row ; Miss Dale, matron

Field Lane Certified Industrial School for Boys, West end ; George Thomas Peall, superintendent

Field Lane Certified Industrial School for Girls 9 Church row ; Mrs. Nyren, matron

Hampstead Home Hospital and Nursing Institute 3 and 4 Parliament hill rd. ; Miss Macnicoll, matron ; R. A. Owthwaite, honorary secretary

Hampstead Reformatory School for Girls (Heathfield house) East Heath rd. ; Miss Christian Nicoll, lady superintendent

Home for Blind Children, Goldsmith's pl. Kilburn ; Miss Wooderidge, matron

Home for Invalid Orphan Children 8 Tremlett grove ; Miss Spillett, matron

Metropolitan Association for Befriending Young Servants 1 Greville rd.

Mildmay Mission to the Jews Convalescent Home 50 Langdon park rd.

Orphan Working School, Maitland park Haverstock hill ; Jonadab Finch, secretary ; Wm. Smith, master; Miss Haynes, mistress ; Miss C. Bounds, matron

Sailors' Orphan Girls' Home, Greenhill rd. ; Mrs. Maria Smart, matron

St. John's Ambulance Station (No. 9 District), Greville rd. Kilburn

St. Vincent's Orphanage 4 Holly pl. Hampstead ; Canon Purcell, superior

School for the Blind, Upper Avenue rd. ; Mrs. Legge, matron

Society for Organising Charitable Relief and Repressing Mendicity ; Office, Church lane ; Robert Frisby, agent

Soldiers' Daughters' Home, Rosslyn hill ; C. R. Lowe, sec. ; Miss Bartlett, matron

The Orphanage 2 Gayton rd. ; Miss McInnes

Highgate.

Girls' Friendly Society 2 Southwood ter.; Miss Lacy, matron

London Diocesan Penitentiary, North hill ; Rev. J. H. Amps

Miss Giniver's Infants' Orphan Home 8 Tremlett grove ; Miss Tiffin, matron

Society for Organising Charitable Relief and Repressing Mendicity ; Office for North St. Pancras and Highgate Committee 120 Highgate rd.; William Legg & A. N. Butt, hon. secs.; George Harris, agent

Sir Richard Whittington's College, Archway rd. (founded at College hill, London, 1425, removed to Highgate, 1820) ; Rev. R. A. Currey, M.A., chaplain ; Miss A. Mackenzie, matron

Southwood Lane Almshouses, Southwood lane

BUILDING SOCIETIES.

Abbey Road and St. John's Wood Permanent Building Society 45 Fordwych rd. Kilburn ; Gilbert Lane, sec.

Hampstead (725th) Starr - Bowkett Building Society 66 Fleet rd. ; W. H. Pearson, secretary

CHRISTIAN ASSOCIATIONS.

St. Peter's Home and Sisterhood, Mortimer rd.

Sisters of Providence of the Immaculate Conception, Middle Class Boarding School and Orphanage (Bartram), Hampstead green ; Sister Marie Isabelle, superioress

Young Men's Christian Association, Hampstead Branch 31 High st. ; J. H. Swinburn, secretary

Young Men's Christian Association, Greville rd. Kilburn

HOSPITALS & DISPENSARIES.
Hampstead.

North London Hospital for Consumption and Diseases of the Chest, Mount Vernon

Consulting Physician.

Dudley J.G.,M.A.. M.D. CANTAB.,M.R.C.P. LOND.

Physicians.

Tims Godwin W., M.D., M.R.C.P.
Evershed A., M.R.C.P.
Haward Edwin, M.D., M.R.C.P.
Shaw John, M.D., M.R.C.P.
O'Connor Bernard, M.D., M.R.C.P.
Pidcock G. Douglas, B.A., M.D., CANTAB.
Taylor Seymour, M.D., M.R.C.P.

Assistant Physicians.

Cassidy Joseph Lemont, M.D.
Squire J. Edward, M.D., M.R.C.P.
Boulting W., L.R.C.P.

Consulting Surgeons.

Lister Sir Joseph, bart., B.A., M.B., F.R.C.S.

Smith Henry, F.R.C.S.

House Physician—Dr. C. C. Caleb

Secretary—Lionel F. Hill, M.A.

Matron—Miss Blaxland

Patients are seen daily at the Out-Patients' Department 216 Tottenham court rd. at 1 o'clock, and at the Hospital, Mount Vernon, on Tuesdays at 10.30 o'clock. The secretary can be seen daily at the Hospital before 10 o'clock, and afterwards at the office

Child's Hill Provident Dispensary 1 Ridge ter.

Dispensary, Robert Connell, M.D. 50 Netherwood st.

Hampstead Provident Dispensary 13 & 14 New end; Wm. Henry Cook, M.D., W. Boulting, L.R.C.P., Douglas G. Pidcock, M.D., W. Heath Strange, M.D.; J. Fenn, secretary

Kilburn Provident Medical Institute 1 Greville rd.; T. Millachip, secretary

North-West London Hospital, Kentish town rd.; Miss O. Learmouth, hon. sec.

South Hampstead Private Hospital, Invalid Home and Nursing Institution (Erskine lodge) 50 Primrose hill rd.

Highgate.

Highgate Dispensary (Rock house) Pond sq. High st.; Dr. Clothier and Dr. Forshall

Holborn Union Infirmary, Archway rd.

Hospital for Sick Children, in connection with Great Ormond st. (Cromwell house) The Bank, High st.; Miss Laishley. lady superintendent; S. Whitford, secretary

St. Pancras Infirmary, Dartmouth park hill; Dr. McCann, medical superintendent

Small Pox Hospital, Dartmouth park hill; Dr. Goude, superintendent; Miss Crockett, matron

SOCIETIES, HALLS, &c.
Hampstead.

Brondesbury Hall and Sunday School 9 and 11 Iverson rd.

Hampstead Liberal Club 1 Downshire hill; R. S. Fraser and John Lea, honorary secretaries

Hampstead Naturalists' Club, Rosslyn hill Schoolroom, Willoughby rd.; C. H. Watkins, honorary secretary

Hampstead Public Library and Reading Rooms 68 High st.; Miss Marshall, honorary secretary

Hampstead Public Library (Cavendish house) High st.; Miss Field, hon. sec.

Public Library and Literary Institute (Stanfield house) Prince Arthur rd.; A. Wilson, honorary treasurer

St. Thomas's Hall 197 Belsize rd. Kilburn

South Hampstead Working Men's Club 54 Fleet rd. Open daily from 12 to 2 and 6 to 10.30 p.m.; on Saturdays 12 noon to 10.30 p.m.; W. R. Dockrell and W. A. Marsh, hon. secretaries

United Band of Hope 22 Gayton rd.; Robert D. B. McQueen, secretaries

Highgate.

Girls' Friendly Society 2 Southwood ter.; Mrs. Mitchell, matron

Highgate, Hornsey & Stoke Newington Building Societies 6 High st.; E. Mote, secretary

Literary & Scientific Institution, South grove; John H. Lloyd, hon. sec.; J. Drummond, assistant librarian

Reading Rooms, Southwood lane

Temperance Society and Band of Hope; Rev. Josiah Viney, president

SAVINGS BANK.
Hampstead.

Penny Bank 1 Wells buildings High st., open on Saturday evenings 7 to 8

VOLUNTEER CORPS.
Hampstead.

3rd Middlesex A & B Companies Head quarters, High st., Hampstead C. G. Toller, captain commanding F. Lawler, sergeant-instructor

Highgate.

3rd Middlesex D Company, Head quarters, Northbrook hall; Benjamin G. Lake, captain

Kilburn.

London Artillery Brigade, No. 10 Battery 297 High rd.

[1]

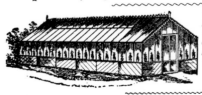

[4]

THE HAMPSTEAD
STREETS DIRECTORY.

ABBEY LANE,
Kilburn.
From 16 West end lane to St. George's ter.

G 5   **4**

LEFT SIDE.
Abbey Cottages.

2 Warden R., jobbing gardener
2a Baldwin Henry
3 Streeter H., writer and grainer
4 Le Franc A., builder
5 Palmer Thos., cowkpr.
6 Dolleymore John, sen. (Fern cottage)
— *Priory mews*

RIGHT SIDE.
Abbey Lane.

2 Billingham Mrs.,dressmaker
  The Kilburn Wholesale Glass Depôt, L. A. Georges & Co. (close to the Town hall)
7 Miles J.
8 Neal Alfred, wardrobe dealer
0 Le Franc Arthur, builder and decorator

11 Mildenhall Joseph, bootmaker
12 Hoggett Mrs., servants' registry office
13 Miller Henry, bottle dealer
13 Bowden Bros.,lathrndrs

ABBEY ROAD,
Kilburn.
Continuation of Abbey rd. St. John's Wood.

G 5   **4**

LEFT SIDE.
119 Woodley John
— *Belsize rd.*
121 *The Princess of Wales,* Benjamin Hayden
123 Heather James
125 Bellamè George T.
127 Trim William
129 Sillett Mrs.
131 Cook Mrs. Mary Elizabeth
133 Harnett Mrs. A. H.
135 Moutrie Mrs. Fredk.
137 Redmond Francis
139 Wardroper Frederick
141 Grave Miss, kindergarten school
143 Cronin Walter Daniel

— *St. George's rd.*
— *Priory rd.*
145 Bentwitch Herbert, LL.B., solicitor (The Limes)
147 Crossley Mrs. A. M.
149 Dobson Thomas Wm.
151 Keysell Miss
153 Sichel Gustave

RIGHT SIDE.
102 Wigley Mrs.
104 Alexander Mrs.
106 Shaw Henry Scott
108 Watson Mrs.
110 Strickland Alfred
112 Bamberger Stanley
114 Jarvis Thomas
116 Hodgson James
118 Roberts Mrs.
120 Rathbone Mrs.
122 Dixon Arthur Wm.
124 Tweedie Robert
126 Shuter Miss
128 Moore Mrs.
134 Wheeler Chas. Molard (St. Mary's lodge)
   ST. MARY'S CHURCH
— *Priory rd.*
136 Shaw Alexander
140 Burleigh Joseph
142 Leonard John William

ABBEY RD.—*continued*

144 Wilkey Charles Edwd.
146 Brenier George
148 Chesterman Mrs. Eliz.
    (Finedon villa)
150 Wynn Mrs. M. A.
    (Coleby lodge)
152 Freeman F.T.(Abbey-
    field)
152 Freeman Chas. Hard-
    castle (Abbeyfield)

ABBEY ROAD,
St. John's Wood.
From Belgrave rd. to
North-Western Railway.
G 6   **3 and 4**
LEFT SIDE. *(Ward 4)*

61*a* Storey John, fruiterer
61*a* Hyde George, chsmngr.
61*b* Curryer William Ben-
    jamin, jeweller
    —*Belgrave rd.*
63 *The Belgrave Hotel,*
    Mrs. M. E. Wheeler
65 Martin B., ironmonger
67 Bourne & Co., book-
    sellers and stationers
69 Myring Jacob, builder
71 Jones Brothers, drapers
73 Poole Charles, cheese-
    monger
75 Cridlan Thos., butcher
77 Harland Bros., grocers
    and wine merchants
79 Warren George Robert,
    chemist
81 Payne Thomas, baker
    and confectioner
    —*Boundary rd.*
83 *The Victoria Tavern,*
    Miss A. E. White
85 Hows T. and Co., corn
    dealers
87 Thwaites Geo., oilman
87 Walker William, ani-
    mal doctor
89 Minter George, ward-
    robe dealer
91 Balfour James, baker
    —*Alexandra mews*
93 Lawson Archd. Scott
95 Davy Edward Monta-
    gue, M.R.C.V.S.L., vete-
    rinary surgeon
97 Richards Percy
101 Womack John (Suth-
    erland house)

—*Holtham rd.*
103 Edwards Edwin Thos.,
    M.R.C.S., surgeon-
    dentist
105 Andrade Samuel Da
    Costa
107 Easton Mrs. M. A.
109 Beck Mrs. M. A.
    —*Alexandra rd.*
111 Fell Miss, ladies'
    school (St. Hilda's
    college)
113 Dobson Mrs. Mary
117 Hill Arthur
RIGHT SIDE. *(Ward 3)*
62 Frazer Thomas Henry
64 Griffin Frederick
66 Punch John
68 Womack James
    —*Springfield rd.*
70 Jacob Mrs.
72 Evans Frederick
74 Gibbs Nathaniel B.
76 Hill Fredk. A., surgeon,
    M.D. (Oxford house)
    —*Boundary rd.*
78 Turner Barrow
82 Baxter William (Cam-
    bridge house)
84 Harris Mrs. R.
86 Williams John
90 Walker John George
    —*Alexandra rd.*
94 Vokins Mrs. Mary
    (Hereford villa)
96 Goddard Philip
98 Duncan Dr. Henry
    Montague, surgeon

ABBOTT'S ROAD,
Kilburn.
From 39 Priory rd. to
West end lane.
G 5   **4**
1 Pedlar Mrs.
2 Duncan George F.
3 Sweeting Mrs.
4 Collmann L.
5 Jennings Mrs.
7 Ellis Ralph Arthur
    Frederick William

ACOL ROAD,
Kilburn.
From 69 Priory rd. to
West end lane.
G 5   **4**
LEFT SIDE.
1 Scott Alexander

2 Muriel Robert (Wara-
    tah house)
3 Woolf Mortimer
4 Corsbie George W. R.
    (Broxbourne)
5 Slaughter W. E.
6 Carter Robert (Ivy ho.)
7 Drysdale Mrs. (Kings-
    ton)
8 Spence James
    —*Wavel mews*
9 Chesterman C. F. (Sta-
    lisfield house)
RIGHT SIDE.
Twinberrow James K.
    (Madresfield)
Trehern C. M. (Good-
    lands)
Gray John Selby (Stone-
    leigh)
Greenwood Wm. (The
    Beeches)
McLeod Hugh Eneva
    (Morville)
Baird Sydney (Long-
    wood)
Lockett Anthony Jsph.
    F. (Ethandene)
Vaile Thos. H.(Meadow
    ville)
Plomer J. D. (Chester-
    ton)
Hall Walter (Clair-
    ville)
Johnston Mrs.(Verona)
James Edwin (Grosve-
    nor house)
Mahler Adolph(Berkel-
    hurst)
Austin J.V.(Swincote)

ADAMSON ROAD,
South Hampstead.
From Winchester rd. to
Lancaster rd.
F 7   **2**
LEFT SIDE.
1 Montefiore Alexr. I
    (Frankfort house)
3 Trier Moritz (Tredega
    house)
7 Frankel Sigismund
9 Riethmuller Chrstophr
    J. (Fairleigh house)
11 Marsden R.
13 Sugden Mrs. (Roxford
    house)

15 Cohen Edward (Stanmore house)
19 Gough C. H.
23 Goldsmidt Edward
25 Johnson Mrs. H. H.
27 Belton Bernard Jsph.
29 Fox Dr. Wm. Smith
31 Haswell Admiral Wm. Henry
33 Burrell Charles E.
35 Hepburn Mrs.
37 Starling Robert Barker
   RIGHT SIDE.
   Childs Augustus B. (Galeton house)
2 Beeton Hy. Coppinger
4 Gibson Rev. R. B.,M.A.
6 Colt Frederick Hoare
8 Bennett Rev. John W.
10 Cohen Albert
14 East Alfred
16 Morris James A.
20 Gottschalk Gustave
26 Hewitt William
28 McLeod Maj. Wm. Sim

ADELAIDE ROAD.
From Haverstock hill to Finchley rd.
G 7   2 & 3
RIGHT SIDE.   *(Ward 2)*
2 Hurlstone Mrs. Ann H.
4 Shapley Edwin
6 Savory Richard
8 Grimaldi Madame
10 Cowderoy R.
12 Norman John
16 O'Keeffe Mrs.
20 Lindoe Captain
22 Lowther Mrs.
24 Rogers Louis
26 Wass Mrs. S. E.
28 Harris William
30 Hamshaw Thos. Philip
32 Mackenzie Mrs. Sarah
34 Batley Henry Gurson
36 Plumpton Robert
38 Hort Mrs. Mary
40 Masters Mrs. Jane M.
42 Frost Mrs. Hannah
44 Mousley John Parkes
46 Gillott John Robert
48 Hyde Arthur
50 Watts Mrs.
52 Fife Mrs.
54 Cornish Henry
56 Macmin John

58 Pile J.
62 Sumner Miss
64 English Walter
66 Collins Mrs. Jane
66 Collins George William, surgeon
— Eton rd. & Fellows rd.
68 Holman Wm. Henry, M.B., physician
72 Alexander James
74 Randegger Guiseppe
76 Burton Walter Hally
78 Watson John
80 Isitt Frederick Thomas
86 Burr John, artist(Warwick house)
88 Dunn Richard
90 Catterson John Josias (Athol house)
— Primrose hill rd.
92 Millington Robert
94 Clarke Mrs. G. M.
96 Hitchcock Charles
98 Gibbon Mrs.
100 Roe Mrs. Freeman
100 Roe Misses, ladies' school
102 Alexander Mrs.
104 Trimmer Mrs. Wm.
106 Bertram Julius, solctr.
108 Fabian Henry
112 Riess Mrs. H.
114 Falkenburg Louis
116 Stanley Miss
118 Sturgess John, artist
120 Ricks James, artist
122 Westbury Mrs. Ruth
124 Daniell Lieut- Col. J. Townshend
126 Macirone George A.
132 Strafford Miss
134 Walters Geo.Stanfield
136 Rose Charles
138 Shepherd F. W.
140 Hodge James
142 Dare William Henry, boys' school
144 Le Jeune Henry
— Merton rd.
146 Linsell Alfred William
148 Tuchmann Dr. Maro, surgeon
150 Hoets John William Van Rees
152 Cooke Mrs. Harriet
154 Williams Mrs.Hannah, ladies' school

158 Wulfson Miss Johana
162 Nicholson Mrs.
164 Ford Edward
166 Bauer Victor
168 Vernon Mrs. Annie
170 Laing Misses
172 Watson Napoleon F.
174 Peile James Kenyon
176 Rosenheim Thordor
178 Holborn Robert
180 Doggett Richard
182 Carlyle Mrs. Robert
184 Rosenheim Max
186 Lyndon Mrs.Elizabeth
190 Johnson Mrs. E. R., preparatory school
192 Oldrey Edmund Page
196 Edwards Charles Hy.
198 Brandon Miss
200 Hill Mrs.
202 Boyes John Henshall
204 Randall John, M.D.
206 Emes Miss
208 Chant Thomas
210 Comins W. W.
212 Johns Charles Fredk.
— Winchester rd.
214 Cale William, florist
   NEW COLLEGE CHAPL.
— Upper Avenue rd.
   Brace J., nurseryman
   Met. Fire Brigade Stn.;
   Richard Percival, engineer
LEFT SIDE.   *(Ward 3)*
1 Dickson D. M. & Sons, butchers
1 *The Adelaide Tavern*, Frederick Vinall
3 Ballinger Wm., builder
5 Holland Sidney
7 Young Colin
11 Carter Miss
13 Farjeon B. L.
15 May Frederick
17 Lucas Misses
— Bridge rd.
19 I'Anson Charles
21 Harding R. B.
23 Cheshire Miss, professor of music
25 Fletcher S.
29 Brinsmead Edgar Wm.
31 Flugel Adolph
33 Hitchcox Matthew Hy.
35 Harper George Povey, M.A.

ADELAIDE RD.—*contind.*
37 Hensman Mrs.
41 Coish Frederick John, surgeon-dentist
43 Miller Mrs. Alice
45 Thwaites Otho
47 Mayall John
49 Profaze George
51 Hammond George
53 Gaskell William
57 Sulley Joseph
59 Halle S. B.
61 Wilkinson Miss
63 Reid Mrs.
65 Jackson Mrs. E. J.
67 Lunn Henry Charles
69 March William
73 Westlake Mrs.
75 Harben Miss
77 Towers George
79 Buist John
81 Cook Frederick
83 Dowling Mrs. Sarah Edith
85 Pratt Mrs.
87 Newby Mrs.
89 Stewart Miss Susan
91 Hailstone Robert Henry
93 Neison F. G. P.
95 Burroughs Colman
97 Hawksley Thomas P.
99 Arrowsmith Rev. Wm. Robson, M.A.
101 Clark Adolphus
103 Dalgleish William
105 Cassal Charles, professor of languages
109 Obicini George Wm.
111 Gould Abrahm.,F.R.G.S
113 Elliott Wm. Timbrell, solicitor
——*Primrose hill rd.*
117 Cathcart Mrs., ladies' school
117 Cathcart Percy
119 Dare Mrs. L. A.
121 Fraser William John
123 Robertson Rev. John. LL.D. (Upton school)
125 Holt Frederick
127 Hassell Henry Joseph
129 Palmer John Ogilvie
133 Selous Edric, M.D.
135 Wilson Edward Jas.
137 Port Charles Thomas
139 Gard W. G. Snowdon, LL.B.

141 Farmery Mrs.
——*Eton pl.*
143 *The Eton Hotel*, Alfd. Barker
145 Dey Robert
147 Lewis James
149 Russell William
151 Neame Norman
153 Archer Reuben
155 Marks Alfred
159 Britain John
161 McMillan John, barrister-at-law
163 Cuming Mrs.Elizabeth
——*Merton rd.*
165 Poulter Rev. James, M.A.
165 Poulter ReginaldClifford, B.A.
167 Tansley George
169 Pickworth George
171 Smithers F. A.
173 Bartlett Charles Thos.
175 Cooper William Wellington
177 Rossi Alexander M.
179 De Berg Adolphous
181 Hadenfelt Rubert
183 Davies Frederick
185 Towle Edward
189 Bowden William John, M.D.
191 Morgan Mrs.
193 Gahagan Edwin C.
195 Rosenheim William
197 Metzger Samuel
——*King's College rd.*
199 Metcalfe Mrs.
201 Knox Mrs.
203 Atherton Mdme. Lucquet, professor of dancing
205 Loewenthal Adolph Ferdinand
207 Augener George
209 Browning George
211 Eley Mrs.
——*Harley rd.*

AGINCOURT RD.
From Fleet rd.
E S   2
LEFT SIDE.
Board School
RIGHT SIDE.
GOSPEL OAK WESLEYAN CHAPEL

AINGER ROAD.
From King Henry's rd.
to Primrose hill rd.
G S   3
1 Escott C., builder and house decorator
2 Ruegenn Henry J., greengrocer
3 Richards Mrs.
4 Timms W. R.
5 Evans Frederick, tailor
6 Hazell Miss,dressmaker
7 Fooks George Harris, bandmaster
8 Holgate Wm., mineral water manufacturer
9 Kearney J. Esmonde
10 Coote F. R., solicitor
11 Nevill Miss
11 Sharples R. H.
12 Oldaker Miss
13 Chamberlain Thomas
14 Hume Rev. Charles
15 Waugh Edgar Weller
16 Frost R.
19 Moody Joseph
21 Eddowes John
22 McCoy Frederick
23 Such Edwin C., MUS. BAC. CANTAB.
24 Ramsbotham James
25 Bonifint Warren Henry
26 Richards John Wm.
27 Hobson Ernest E.
28 Johnson Rev. E., M.A.
29 Bird Charles E.(Ainger house)
——*Ainger mews*
——*Primrose hill rd.*
——*Oppidans mews*
30 Longman Henry
32 Hillman Samuel
33 Burgess Charles Henry
34 Beecham Miss
35 Morson Thomas Pierre
36 Mackay James H.
38 Maas Hugh Max
39 Hills Walter
40 Trinks Carl Heinrich
41 Alliston George Thos.
42 Cumberland E. B.
43 Ramsbotham P. B.
44 Castor Mrs.
45 Davies Commander Robert Watts, R.N.
——*Oppidans rd.*

46 Bradford Mrs. W. E.
   (Ludlow house)
47 Frodsham J.
48 Dyer Mrs. Henry
49 Jervis Mrs.
50 Rutland Alfred
51 Adams George
52 Haskew Edward
53 Inglis Thos. Stewart
54 Nott Alfred
55 Smith G.
56 Greenwood Mrs.
57 Ferguson Robert

ALBION ROAD,
Belsize Road.
From Hilgrove rd. to
Fairfax rd.
F 6   3

RIGHT SIDE.
2 Vander Weyde Henry
   (Hawthorne lodge)
4 Harvey J. W. (Wood-
   stock house)
6 Hallowes Alexander
8 Benito D.
10 Taylor Charles
12 Evans John Edward
14 Deane Mrs. Ellen
16 Shaw Mrs. Elizabeth
18 Griffiths George
20 Mason J. W.
22 Bird Mrs.
24 Silver Mrs.
26 Underwood Mrs.
28 Burn Mrs.
⸻*Belsize rd.*
30 Keele Edward Rush-
   worth
32 Arnett Charles
34 Neuman Jacob Elias
36 Miéville Frederick
38 Batley Richard
40 Whetham Charles
   Langley
42 Ince Edward Brett
44 Crossley Charles Richd.
46 Mills Henry
48 Wildy Arthur
LEFT SIDE.
1 Dixon Mrs.
3 Willis Mrs. Eleanor
5 Powell William Henry
   Wadham
7 Wells John
9 Herrmann Adolphus
11 Spink John

⸻*Belsize rd.*
13 Fisher Mrs.
15 Wickes T. H., engineer
17 Martin George
19 Berridge Frederic
21 Pearce James Horne
23 Doucet Mrs.
25 Taylor Enoch
27 Liberty John Barnes

Albion Terrace,
see Child's hill lane.

**ALEXANDRA
MEWS.**
From 91 Abbey rd.
G 5   4
5 Marchant William, cab
   proprietor
8 and 9 Davy Edward
   Montague, M.R.C.V.S.
16 Newman T., sweep

ALEXANDRA RD.,
St. John's Wood.
From Hilgrove rd. to
Kilburn.
[*From Hilgrove rd. to*
Abbey rd. Ward 3. From
Abbey rd. to the end
Ward 4.]
G 6   3 & 4
LEFT SIDE.
1 Hernoux Charles
3 Tayler Edward
7 Robson Miss
9 Ferguson Donald
11 Allen Charles John
13 Speer Dr. Stanhope
   Templeman
13 Speer Charlton Tem-
   pleman
15 Lawson Mrs. Ellen
17 Robins Julian
19 Hortin John H.
⸻*Loudoun rd.*
21 *The Alexandra Hotel,*
   Charles John Coles
23 Pitzschke Mrs.
25 Gray Mrs.
27 Shaw Henry Wright
29 King David
31 Cracknell Mrs. E.,
   dressmaker
33 Schnegelsberg Herr W.,
   professor of music
35 Billing Eardley

37 Rollason Mrs.
39 Smyth Mrs.
39 Smyth Miss, teacher
   of music
41 Marshall William Wier
43 Burchatt Thomas Jas.
45 Joyce Henry
47 Buxton Dr. David
49 Staines Mrs.
51 Kellow Fredk. Chester-
   field
53 Freeman Rev. Fredk.
   John, M.A.
55 Perrin Rowland Neate
57 Carey Miss
59 Cuff Misses
61 Klugh Arthur G.
65 Meadmore Robert
67 Morel-LadeuilLeonard,
   sculptor
69 Wynne Henry Lifton
71 Bindon Mrs.
73 Green Mrs.
75 Jacobs Angelo
77 Harland Leonard
79 Robins Edmund
83 Story Henry John
85 Field Edward
87 Raphael Alfred
89 Hughes William
91 Harding Major Chas.
93 Slade John
95 Addison Miss
97 Brown Alfred
99 Coote George John
101 Desaxe Morris
103 Savill Alfred
105 Spencer William
107 Oliver David
109 Curtis Mrs. Mary
111 Pratt Misses, ladies'
   school (Lorne house)
115 Viret Benjamin Pope
117 Watt Alex. Pollock
119 Lott Fdk. Tully, artist
123 Sonnenthal Richard
125 Haines Edwd. Walter,
   solicitor
⸻*Abbey rd.*
127 Sampson Samuel
137 Riddell R. Alfred
139 Gibbs Joseph Melton
⸻*Bolton rd.*
139a Orchard John (Sand-
   ringham house)
⸻*Mortimer cres.*
141 Lewis M. H.

ALEXANDRA RD.—*cntnd.*
143 Meredith Herbert J.
RIGHT SIDE.
2 Shepherd Charles
4 Curtis Thomas
6 Cooper Frederick Eastman
8 Cowper Mrs.
10 Smith Rev. J. S. T. W.
10 Smith E. T. Aydon, L.S.A.
12 Davies Mark
14 Mackie Edward
16 Hunter Leslie
18 Bluck Mrs. Mary Ann
— *Loudoun rd.*
28 Bishop Mrs.
30 Purney Henry
34 Morison Mrs.
38 Menzies Sutherland
40 Platt Mrs.
42 Cossart John
44 Strickland William Charles
48 Elliott Mrs.
50 Dart Joseph H.
54 Lucas Mrs. Emily
56 Reid Mrs.
58 Jarvis Miss A. M.
60 Mackway Richard Wm., professor of singing
64 Turner Robt. Drysdale, F.G.S.
66 Saunders Henry
68 Freeman Hy. Golding
70 Chittenden Charles
72 Risdon Misses
74 Andrews Misses
76 Gardner Miss
78 Copeland Jno.,L.R.C.P.E. surgeon
78 Bate Frederick, dental surgeon
80 Legg Henry Simpson
82 Moore Thomas
84 Phillips Henry
86 Hess Frederick
88 Ring Max
90 Rogers Henry
92 Whitehead Thos. Jas.
94 Heddle John
96 Neighbour Henry
100 Geesin Mrs.
104 Buist Robert Gray
106 Box Joseph
108 Hanes John
110 Tuteur Max

112 Lucas Stanley
114 Kinsey Mrs.
114 Peile Miss
116 Kirkman Misses, ladies' school
118 Davis George
120 Collins Captain John Stratford
122 Patten Robert John
126 Scaife John
128 Freeland Mrs.
130 Tompkins Henry, C.E.
132 Brown Mrs.
134 Anchor Richard
136 Green Miss
138 Auerbach Emil
— *Abbey rd.*
140 Hawkes Wm. Henry
144 Henderson Arthur Edward
146 Starling Matthew Henry
148 Mason Mrs. Sarah (Denmark house)
150 Marks Geo. Samuel
152 Kimber Thomas
154 Stiffe J. G.
156 Holmes William
158 Solomon Aaron
160 Croft Adolphus
162 Davies Robert Fredk.
164 Hurditch Chas.Russell
166 Penny J. S.
170 Roberts John
172 Baker Frederick John
174 Imperiali W. G.
180 Stephens Charles Viret
182 Donagan Richard
184 Blundell Miss
188 Peake George
190 *Office of the Evangelistic Mission;* C. Russell Hurditch
192 Kennedy C. N., artist

Alfred Terrace,
see Back lane.

ALFRED TERRACE MEWS.
E 6
From 9 Alfred ter. Back lane Heath st.

Fowler & Son, general wheelwrights

Ambridge Cottages,
see North end.

Arch Place,
see Back lane.

Ardwick Terrace,
see Finchley rd. Child's hill.

ARIEL STREET, *Kilburn.*
From 75 Iverson rd.
F 4
LEFT SIDE.
1 Hanson Samuel H.
2 Harris Mrs.
3 Atkins Mrs.
4 Kenchington Mrs.
5 Vant Fredk. Augustus
6 Young Henry Tom builder
7 Knight Mrs. E.
— *Loveridge rd.*
9 Downton Frederick
9 *St. Cuthbert's Parish Room*
10 Bellamy W.
11 Gibbons John
11 Vanse F., tailor
12 Smith John
13 Fairer Alfred Richard
14 Smith Alexander
15 Chrisp Joseph
16 Coulter Mrs. Ann general shop
RIGHT SIDE.
Spencer Terrace.
1 Broad Stephen
2 Mann Fredk. William
4 Glandt Reynold
5 Newport George
6 Davies John
7 Whitaker Thomas
8 Reeve Samuel
9 Fuller Thomas
11 Frost William Henry
11 Frost Miss, dressmaker
11 Johnson Miss Kate R.A.M., teacher of music

ARKWRIGHT RD.
From Greenhill rd. to Finchley rd.
E 6
LEFT SIDE.
1 Green Theodore, architect (Leyland)

3 Piper Misses (Norton lodge)
3 Bowring Miss Edith A. (Norton lodge)
5 Kilburn Charles (Alvaston)
7 Collett Mrs. (Laurifer)
11 Mannering Edward Hill (Hill side)
13 King Joseph (Welford house)
15 Dawson Miss Mary
17 Hawes F. Sutton (Rawdon)
19 Coles Oakley (Inglesant)
21 Farniloe Thomas M.

⌐*Frognal*
Cow John (Montredon)
Hopton Captain Chas. (Rosland)

RIGHT SIDE.
2 Stuart John Edward (Fairview)
4 Essex Alfred (Dinas)
6 Dawson Miss Ann
8 Cunningham Percy Burdett (Beaulieu)
10 Huntington Frns. Hy. (Abbeville house)
⌐*Ellerdale rd.*
12 Alexander James (Avening house)
⌐*Frognal*
Hackworth Richard (Brightside)
Lupton T. (Woodside)
Miller Adam (Deanshurst)
Thornton G. (Sedgemoor)
Hine R. G., artist
Farrer Rev. W., LL.B. (Oakleigh)
Warburg Edward (Elling lodge)

ASH GROVE,
Kilburn.
From 1 Ash terrace Cricklewood.
D 5
LEFT SIDE.
1 Smith Reuben, builder
3 Mackley Robert
7 Yerbury Francis Wm.
9 Guthrie Charles I.

---

11 Brient William
13 Nallorie William
15 Fowler Mrs. Helen
17 Stevens Thomas
RIGHT SIDE.
2 Evans George
4 Escott Mrs.
6 Painter William
8 Moysey Mrs.
10 Kirman F.
12 Davis P. D. R.
14 Campbell R. B.
16 Shelton John

Ash Terrace,
see Cricklewood.

AVENUE ROAD,
Regent's Park.
From The Parish Boundary to Adelaide rd.
G 7   **3**
LEFT SIDE.
63 Jenkins George Thos., barrister-at-law
⌐*Norfolk rd.*
67 Walther Philip
69 Feis Jacob
71 Muncey Luke
⌐*Queen's rd.*
73 McLaren James
75 Palmer Miss, ladies' school
79 Coates Joseph
81 Lumley Henry Robert
83 Metzler Mrs. (Stanmore house)
85 Burke Mrs.
87 Staples John, F.S.A.
ST. PAUL'S CHURCH
89 Pohler Miss M. (University college for ladies)
RIGHT SIDE.
Neck Chas. (The Elms)
ST. STEPHEN'S CHCH.
24 Johnson Mrs.
26 Kelly Edward
28 Behrens Miss
30 Young James (Venetian villa)
32 Perry Rt. Rev. Bishop, D.D.
34 Browne Hy. Doughty (West lodge)
⌐*Regent's mews*
36 Roscoe William

---

38 Davis Benn
40 Squire Peter Wyatt
42 Fitzgerald Mrs. Samuel
44 Warmuth Edmund
46 Gooch Walter
48 Poole Miss
50 Kinnaird Hon. Miss Olivia
52 Bradford Nicholas (Undercleave)
54 Brown Joseph
56 Attenborough Robert
58 Wainewright Robert Arnold
60 Hall Robert Gresly
62 Goodall Frederick (Rosenstead)
66 Hall John Vine
70 De Hamel Felix John
72 Levy Lionel
74 Quincey Miss
76 De Quincey Roger
78 Bentley Alfred
80 Wood Charles William
82 Ochs Sigismund
84 Woollams Mrs. Elizbth.
86 Corey William

Avenue Villas,
see Child's hill.

BACK LANE.
From Heath st. to Flask walk.
E 6   **1**
RIGHT SIDE.
Arch Place.
1 Ruff Geo., bootmaker
2 Cordell James
3 Ringe F.
4 Brett William
5 & 5a Satterthwaite Robt., bootmaker
Keil's Cottages.
2 Cresswell Wm., cutler
Back Lane.
1 Franklin William
3 Roberts W. George

LEFT SIDE.
Alfred Terrace.
1 Rutland Joseph
2 Slight Geo., bootmaker
3 Beer Philip
4 Taylor Mrs. Sarah
5 Hatch George
6 Leach William
7 Birch Thos., bricklaye

BACK LANE—*continued*
8 Gilbert William
9 Symes William, boot & shoe maker
10 Keep Charles
11 Hill Edward

Baker's Row.
From 59 High st.
E 6   *1*

Bartram Terrace,
see Fleet rd.

Beaconsfield Terrace,
see High rd. Kilburn.

BELGRAVE GDNS.,
St. John's Wood.
From Belgrave rd.
H 5   *4*
1 & 2 Ward William
3 Rasey Henry
Webb Thos., gardener (Belgrave lodge)
4 Hillier William
5 Strudwick W.
6 Hardwick H.
Phillips — (Belgrave cottage)

BELGRAVE ROAD,
St. John's Wood.
From Abbey rd. to Bolton road.
G 6   *4*
2 Sercombe Edward, cabinet maker
6 Phillips Philip
7 Dawson Mrs.
8 Moon P.
9 Daw John M.
10 Franklin William
11 Atkinson Mrs.
12 Dow Alexander
14 Bishop Major Luke
15 Crompton William
16 Webber John
18 Whitaker John L.
19 Durrant Mrs.
20 Vernon Arthur
21 Brown Henry
— *Belgrave gardens*
26 Lee Jacob, tailor
27 Barnett Mrs. George, professor of dancing
28 Beedle Joseph

29 Price Miss
31 Wilkinson Alexander
32 May William
33 Brewer Mrs.
34 Dunn George
35 Longman Miss
36 Fry Robert
37 Monk Thomas
38 Gammie John
39 Cracknell Mrs. Anne
40 Hughes H., boot and shoe maker
41 Turner & Co., dressmakers

BELL TERRACE,
Kilburn.
From High rd.
G 5   *4*
1 & 2 Roper William, draper
3 & 5 Cayford Walter W., wardrobe dealer
4 Pippett Stephen, wardrobe dealer
Goldsmith's Gardens.
1 Frost George
2 Pepper A., sweep and carpet beater

Belmont,
see Finchley new rd.

BELSIZE AVENUE.
From Belsize park to Haverstock hill.
F 7   *2*
LEFT SIDE.
1 Humphreys Richard
3 Barker Rev. J., LL.B.
5 Taylor C. L.
7 Sinclair Joseph
9 Carter G. R.
11 King William
13 Marshall Julian
15 Buttery John
17 Balmain James F.
19 Behrend David
21 Miley Miles
23 Wilson Miss
25 Davenport-Hill Misses
27 Pollak Hermann
29 Light Charles
31 Clarke Henry
33 Lewenz Iwan
35 Larkworthy Falconer
37 Lawrence J. M.

39 Carey Edward Fricker
41 Swann Henry Thomas
43 Marsden Montague M.
45 Joshua Philip
47 Hill Thomas
49 Barchewitz von Josephi Hermann L. R.
51 Clulow George
53 Hadrill Henry John
55 Sandilands George M.
57 Hilton Miss, ladies' school
59 Putney Samuel
61 Beale Mrs. M.
63 Wason Eugene
RIGHT SIDE.
2 Strange W. Heath, M.D.
4 Deans Charles
6 Auld Miss
8 Trail Mrs.
10 Reynolds Miss
12 Karney Rev. Gilbert, M.A.
14 Canney Mrs.
16 Stephenson George
20 Hirschel Arthur F.

BELSIZE CRES,
From Belsize park ter.
F 7   *1*
LEFT SIDE.
1a Szezepkowski G., dressmaker
1a Andrew J., harness mkr.
1 Burdett Wm., jobmstr.
3 WOOD THOMAS, florist and seedsman
5 Pollard Lieutenant G. N. A., R.N.
7 Abram Edward
9 Roche Miss
11 Hopkinson Mrs.
13 Simon Charles M.
15 Mayd Mrs.
21 Wood H. K.
25 Boldero Mrs.
27 Taylor Richard, artist
29 Shaw Charles
— *Lyndhurst gardens*
RIGHT SIDE.
2 & 2a Withers H. R..drpr
4 TUGWELL T. B. & SON, builders
8 Walker A. C.
12 Williams W. H.
14 Davidson Rev. Samuel D.D., LL.D.

16 Ferguson Thomas
18 Gorton J. E.
20 Roy James W.
22 Schöller William F. P.
    WOOD THOMAS,
    nursery grounds

BELSIZE LANE.
From Haverstock hill to
Belsize park.
E 7   **1 & 2**
    Hill Mrs. Charles (Ivy
      bank)
    Shine J. L. (Belsize
      cottage)
    NewtonArthur(Belsize
      court)
    Rosslyn Gardens.
1 Reade Mrs.

BELSIZE PARK.
From College cres. to
Belsize avenue.
F 7   **2**
1 Benson Alfred
2 Bear J. P.
3 Jackson John
4 Harton William Henry
5 Macdonald Murdoch
6 Redman Mrs. J.
7 Abrahams Hyman A.
8 Puzey Mrs.
   ⊏*Belsize sq.*
    St. Peter's Church
9 Turnbull Edward
10 Hawkins John
11 Carlebach Rudolf
12 Landeshut S. M.
13 Klaftenberger A. Augustus
14 Pugh Mrs.
15 Gribble William
16 Hammack H. Laurence
17 Westland Albert, M.D.
18 Loveland Mrs.
19 Ridley John
20 Rosenwald Edward
21 Isaacs Joseph
22 Lamb Alfred
23 Champion Wm. Smith
24 Klein William
25 Byas Edward H.
26 Barry Mrs. Dykes
26 Barry Charles J.
27 Isaacs Henry A.
28 Lacy Charles James
29 Tuckman Charles

30 Stewart Horatio
31 Baker James Wood
32 Huggins John Fredk.
33 Rowlands Wm. Bowen,
     Q.C., J.P.
34 Defries Coleman
35 Watts William M.
36 Dünkelsbühler Anton
37 Marcus Moses
38 Jukes Miles P.
39 Drysdale Mrs. A. D.
40 Bell Charles, architect
41 Canti George F.
42 Shirreff William Moore
43 Kahn Benedict
44 Steel Thomas
45 Drucker Charles
46 Pigeon Henry, jun.
47 Dick Allan B.
49 Daniels Baker
50 Newton H. Cecil
51 Gay John
53 Neate John
54 Halpin Colonel George
55 Greaves Charles Haslehurst
56 Sandilands Mrs.
57 A'Deane John
58 Hill John
59 Somers John B. S.
60 Howard Daniel
61 McLean Thomas M.
62 Smith John
63 Raikes Mrs.
64 Brown G. W
65 Stutely Miss
66 Garrett James
67 Bush Rev. Robert
     Wheler, M.A., F.R.G.S.
    Wright Mrs., ladies'
     school (Blythswood
     house)
    Wright T. H. (Blythswood house)

BELSIZE ROAD,
Hampstead.
From 6 Swiss ter. Finchley
rd. to Abbey rd.
G 6   **3 & 4**
[*Nos. 2 to 44 Right side*
and Nos. 1 to 39 Left side
Ward 3. Nos. 46 to 100
Right side and Nos. 41 to
129 Left side Ward 4.]
    RIGHT SIDE.
2 Whitaker William

⊏*Albion rd.*
8 Mossman David, artist
10 Fisher William
12 Clark Isaac John
14 Davidson William
16 Staples John
18 Reed Frank
20 Stephens William
22 Sutton Mrs. Sarah
24 Weekes Mrs.
26 Cutforth Miss
28 Nicholl William
30 Gibbs Miss
32 New Miss
36 Farrer Miss
38 Carmichael Mrs.
40 Stovell Frederick
42 Findlay William L.
44 Chamberlain Vincent I.
⊏*Fairfax rd. and mews,*
    & Fairhazel gardens
46 Bull Miss
48 Fuller Mrs. A. C.
50 Wortham Frederick
50 Johnson Walter, dntst.
52 Tweddle Linton Stwrt.
54 Jolly George, builder
58 Smith Mrs. Jane
60 Dean Miss
62 Trobridge Lewis
64 Oliver Mrs.
66 Roberts Arthur, veterinary surgeon
68 Birch Mrs. Eliza
70 Weldon Mrs.
70 Weldon Miss, dress &
     mantle maker
72 Taylor Mrs. A.M., kindergarten
76 Howlett Samuel P.
78 Menham John Joseph
80 Whitworth Mrs.
84 Beak Miss M.
86 Pearce Mrs., dressmaker
88 Lawrence George W.
90 Isaac R. C.
92 Ogbourne Mrs.
92 Ogbourne Frank, professor of music
94 Alexander M.
96 Perry Mrs.
98 Plumer Mrs.
100 Oliver John
102 Clark Wm. Newman P.
104 Berliner Isidore
106 Atchison Charles
108 Strong Leonard Ernest

BELSIZE RD.—*continued*
110 Holdsworth Joseph
112 Towler Charles
114 Batten John
116 Ritchie Miss
120 Norman Miss
122 Jeffs Mrs.
124 Lawton Mrs. Sarah
126 Bailey Frederick
126 Roberts Miss
128 Chaudoux Emile
130 Treffry Miss
134 Brown Hy. Duncan
136 Winbolt Mrs., dressmaker
138 Endean Miss, dress and mantle maker
138 Malkin Miss, R.A.M., professor of music
140 Worsop Mrs. Louisa
142 Cooper Mrs. E.
144 Hamilton Mrs.
146 Hodges H. V.
148 Martin Miss
150 Grasemann Carl
152 Imbert Eugene Louis
156 Holland Edward
158 Preston Alfred Chas.
160 Elliott Jas. Wm. & Mrs., professors of music
162 Godwin Henry
164 Cohn Martin Albert
166 Scott James
168 Wainwright Richard
170 Kalterthaler Julius
172 Render Frederick
176 Howden Henry James
178 Middleton Francis
180 Wright Edward
182 Clayton James Wm.
184 Rawlings Mrs. James
186 Stainton Mrs. Sarah Sophia
188 Rogers Mrs. Ann
190 Wright John Lawrence
192 *A C A D E M Y O F MUSIC;* Alfred & Walter Laubach
LEFT SIDE.
1 Fox George
3 Klug Oscar
5 Robinson Mrs. Louisa
⌐*Albion rd.*
7 Mather Miss
11 Foster Major Kingsley
13 Jones Edward Chester, barrister-at-law

15 Fletcher George A. B.
17 Nolloth Mrs. H. C.
19 Tebbut Mrs.
21 Hudson Miss M. A.
23 Wyon Mrs.
25 Meyerstein Emil
27 Bramston Mrs. Amla.A.
29 Carter James
31 Churchill Miss
33 Liggins Henry Joseph
35 Hudson Alfred
37 Sauerbrey Herr E.
39 Johnson Mrs.
⌐*Hilgrove rd. and Loudoun rd.*
41 Turner William Coham
43 Elliot Frederick
45 Cuff William Symes
47 Hollick Frank
49 Colnett Mrs.
51 Gwyn Walter
53 Hennis Capt. William
55 Smith Charles Lacey
57 Parry Mrs. D.
59 Danskin David
61 Mason Henry
63 Hewlings Stuart
65 Bird George King
67 Barrett Frdk. George, nurseryman (Belsize nursery)
71 Colling William Bunn
73 Solomons N.
77 Kellow Frank
79 Pierres Paul
81 Durham C.
83 Lockhart Miss
85 Wardroper Henry
87 Sharpe Arthur, professor of music
89 Lamb Robert
91 Hunter Mrs. Jane
93 Lenton James
95 Evans John Meredith
97 Bullock Mrs. (Vernon cottage)
103 Smith Mrs. George
105 Reynolds Wm. Patrick
107 Fryer George Henry
109 Barnes Edwin, professor of music
111 Fleming John
113 Hunter Peter
115 Baker Mrs. William
117 Corner Wltr. William
121 Paiba Samuel
123 Moore Philip

125 Barrett John Thomas Cresswell
127 Way Mrs.
129 Richardson James
⌐*Abbey rd.*

BELSIZE ROAD,
Kilburn.
G 5   **4**
From Abbey rd. to High road.
RIGHT SIDE.
Lines A. & E., livery stables (Albert yard)
194 Sargeant William D., draper
196 Atkinson John George, pharmaceutical chemist; post and telegraph office
198 Wiggins Fred., builder
200 Dearlove Mrs., fancy repository
202 Rasey Henry, baker
202 Hall Mrs., dressmaker
204 Piggott George, fruitr.
206 Nurse H., stationer
210 Stedman John, corn merchant
212 Jones Saml., watchmkr
214 Summerbell E., dairy
216 Mansfield J., florist
218 Jacoby Fredk., oilman
220 Gilling Wm., fruiterer
⌐*St. George's rd.*
226 Toombs Joseph
⌐*Priory rd.*
228 Sowden Mrs. A. M., baker
230 Palmer William, dairy
232 Redding Fredk. Chas., cheesemonger
234 Dainton Saml. Joseph, builder & decorator
236 Saunders William, stationer & newsagent
238 Bowen John T., chmst.
240 Knowles Jas., builder
242 Fazan William Slater, butcher
246 & 248 Bate & Walter, tea dealers
248 Walter Charles
250 *The Priory Tavern,* S. S. Death
⌐*Abbey lane*
⌐*Kilburn vale*

Barnes R. C., furniture depository (Town hall chambers)

Kilburn Town Hall Co., Limited ; Arthur H. Ayres, secretary

Kilburn House, Land, and Investment Co., Limited

258 Wallas&Jesser,wholesale ironmongers

Post Office District Sorting Office

270a Eede S., hairdresser

272 Shropp John, watchmaker and jeweller

274 Watkins James George coffee & dining rms.

LEFT SIDE.

131 Back Wltr. H.,builder
133 Tanner Nathaniel
133 Scarsbrook F.
135 Mitchell John G.
135 Gross Mrs., certified nurse
137 Wardle Thos., decrtr.
139 Tanner Chas.,carpntr.
141 Learwood George
143 Taylor Mrs.
145 Goodchild Edward
147 Stevens John
149 Ovenden Mrs.
151 Shone William
153 Heaverman Edward
155 Coomber Mrs., dressmaker
159 Newbery W. H.
161 Green Henry
163 Williams Charles
163 Sargent Mrs., dressmaker
163 Redge Mrs., feather cleaner
165 Wilson Frederick
165 Love Mrs.,dressmaker
167 Anstead Mrs., dressmaker
167 Anstead J. W.
167 Read Mrs.
169 King H. H.
171 Harrison John
171 Woodrow Miss M., dressmaker
173 Gardner Charles
175 Wilson H.,bootmaker
179 Back Mrs.
181 Weedon Misses

183 Dolleymore Edwin
185 Trotter James Charles (Kimcote)
187 Duplantier Emile
189 Smallman J. T. Bruce
193 Tawse George
195 Atkinson George, gas & hot water engineer
197 *St. Thomas's Hall*
Springfield villas
199 Barnes R.C., furniture and van office
203 Moore Henry, coffee and dining rooms
205 Ivens W., hairdresser
207 Giles W., greengrocer
209 Pegler Enoch, oil and colourman
211 Barrat T., dyer
213 *Victoria Wine Co.*
215 Kent R. Howard, draper and outfitter
217 Atkinson George, gasfitter
219 Funnell John, bootmaker
221 Coston James
London and North-Western Railway Station

BELSIZE SQUARE.
F 7   **2**

3 Harris Miss
5 Tremellen John
7 Huggins Mrs.
8 Marsden P. Montague
13 Krohn Nicholas
15 Butterworth Rev. J. H.
16 Davies Rev. John, M.A.
17 Roberts Henry
18 Corbett Arthur John
19 MacDonnell J. R., barrister
20 Wornum Mrs.
20 Wornum George Porter, surgeon
21 Green Thomas Allen
22 Halpin Rev. Robert Crawford
Tremlett Rev. F. W., D.C.L.(The Parsonage)
23 Jenour Harry James
24 Leach Rev. William James John
25 Johnstone Mrs.
26 Webb James

27 Marcus Richard
30 Spink Peter
31 Chettle Misses
33 Macdonald William
34 Taylor William George
35 Kelly Henry
36 Brown Samuel Simmons
37 Hillhouse Mrs.
39 Malden Mrs.
39 Mayne Robert Dawson
40 Bateman E.
41 Buxton Mrs.
42 Beeton Henry Ramie
43 White Robert
44 Quin George
45 Goldsmith Walter Chas.
46 Simon Herman
47 Spreat John Henry
48 Day R. E.
49 Simpson G. P.
50 Schuster Felix Otto

BELSIZE TERRACE
In Belsize lane.
F 6   **2**

1 Godwin Rev. J. H.
2 Swan Robert
3 Olney Allen Mrs.
4 Warner Sydney Gates
5 Bouverie Mrs.
6 Svendson Olaf
8 Hemming Mrs.
Daleham gardens

BELSIZE PK.GDNS.
From Belsize park.
F 7   **2**

RIGHT SIDE.

1 Hilhouse Charles
5 *Belsize College of Music;* George Mount, principal
9 Bruty William John
11 Falconer Mrs.
13 Hill Mrs.
15 Lankester Fredk. Wm.
17 Lee J. M.
19 James Mrs.
21 Weatherall Henry
23 Barker Misses
25 Dyson William
27 Haigh Mrs. James
29 De Paula Rudolph
31 Fuller Alfred
33 Dalziel Edward
35 Hecht Max

BELSIZE PK.GDNS.—*cntd.*
37 Mackenzie Wm.O.,M.D.
39 Hitchcock William
43 Tagert & Turner Misses (Belsize college)
45 Venning Walter Chas.
47 Crosley Lady
49 Urwick Rev. William
51 Scott William R.
53 Knox Miss
55 Fischel Leopold
57 Stutfield William
59 Llewellyn Mrs.
61 Bird Arthur
63 Fernan George
65 Kottgen Walther
67 Smith Thomas Elliot
69 Wolff S.
71 Gray Samuel Octavius
73 Hunter Mrs.
75 Chitty Mrs.
77 Loch Mrs. George
79 Addison William
— *Lancaster rd.*
Anderson John E.,nurseryman
— *Eton avenue*
LEFT SIDE.
Jourdan F.(Avenue ho)
2 Mawe Mrs.
4 Osborne Mrs.
6 Agnew Maj.-Gen. Wm
8 Crigan Capt.Chas.A.R.
10 Rogers Miss
12 Paiba John P.
14 Maslen Mrs. & Misses, ladies' college
16 Wright James
18 Ward John Inett
22 Raphael Charles
24 Bingham Thomas
26 Schmitz Leonard,LL.D., F.R.S.E.
28 Krohn William
30 Poulett Earl
32 Collier Mrs. V. J.
34 Raffles William Winter
36 Dalziel Mrs.
38 Howard William
40 Everard Miss
42 Karberg Peter
44 Du Bois Misses
46 & 48 *Manor Mansions*
50 Oesterlie Emil
52 Routledge Lieut.-Col. Robert
54 Ernsthausen Oscar Von

56 Sargant Mrs. Henry
58 Levis Julius
60 Harris Henry (The Bandalls)
62 Moore William B.
— *Haverstock ter.*
64 Richardson William
66 Shuter William
— *Stanley gardens*
68 Des Ruffiéres Mrs.
70 Smith Charles
72 Anderson J.
74 Pinto-Leite Madame
76 Callard Daniel James
80 Schmedes Otto
82 Miles William
86 Walford Cornelius
88 Terrero Maximo
90 Agues Edward
92 Jacob Misses
116 Buckingham Mrs. E.
118 Turnbull Alexander
120 Simpson John, collegiate school
122a Pearn Fred., saddler
The Washington Hotel, F. H. Price

BELSIZE PK. MWS.
Belsize park ter.
F 7   **2**
16 Mildon Richard, veterinary forge
17 Walker W., rag & metal merchant

BELSIZE PK. TER.,
South Hampstead.
F 7   **1**
Trinity Church Parochial Rooms
1a Schaper John, hairdresser
1 Zahringer P., watchmaker and jeweller
2 Johnson J., tailor
3 Mayes George, hosier and outfitter
4 Hutchins L. & Co., dyers & cleaners ; and 29 Park st.Camden tn.
5 *Belsize Provision Strs.,* John Dudman
6 Cooper & Co., dairy
7 Murdoch M. J., statnr.
8 Boggis E., greengrocer

9 Withers H. R., draper
— *Belsize cres.*
10 Collins William, confectioner ; post office
11 Moore & Sons, house, land and estate agents
12 Burbidge Wm., china and glass warehouse
13 Hall C. H., jeweller
14 Noolfrey A., coffee rooms
— *Belsize park mews*
14a Wilson and Dickens, sweeps
15 Alderson M., chimney sweep & carpet beater
— *William's mews*
16 Coward Mrs.,chaircanr.
17 Snow G., builder
18a Wildy George, builder
18 Wilson Henry, stores
20 Heels W.,greengrocer

BELSIZE RD. MEWS.
From Swiss ter.
G 6   **3**
1 Evans Charles,turncock
1 Butler Jas., turncock

BENHAM'S PLACE.
From Holly pl.
E 6   **1**
1 Salter Richard
2 Money Daniel G.
3 Weedon W. T.
4 Thorpe Edward
5 Hurlock Edward
6 Tongue William
7 Franklin Henry
8 Manning Thomas
9 Speight William

BIRCHINGTON RD.,
Kilburn.
From West end lane.
G 5   **4**
RIGHT SIDE.
2 Lane John (Birchington cottage)
4 Palmer Miss (Somerset villa)
6 Tremlett T. D. (Stanmore villa)
8 Brewer Frederick
10 Gurney Mrs.
12 Hart Henry
14 Hodgkinson William

16 Colles William Morris, barrister-at-law
Mutrix rd.
18 Marks C. S.
20 Richards Charles, military tutor
24 Rayner W. S. G.
26 Elliott Ernest B.
28 Smith Sydney, professor of music (Dorchester house)
30 Hatton Ernest
32 Mansbridge Josiah
34 Elliott W. W.
36 Hyams Henry Hart
42 Davis Simon
    Yerbury F. W., builder
LEFT SIDE.
1 Hoskyn Mrs. (Withnoe cottage)
3 Winchester William (Durham villa)
5 Rhind James
7 Wilson F. F.
9 Carter Charles (St. Austin's)
Mutrix rd.
11 Spence Miss
13 Denniston Mrs. Janet
15 Young Morgan Henry
17 Adams Rev. Dr.
19 Carthew Mrs.
21 Monti Francis
23 Radermacher Chas. J.
27 Gow Charles
29 Cadby Miss, preparatory school
31 Southgate Mrs. Sarah
33 Scarlett John
Colla's mews
Edgware rd.

BOLTON ROAD,
St. John's Wood.
From 19 Greville pl. to Alexandra rd.
G 5   **4**
LEFT SIDE.
1 Smith Charles
2 Wallman Charles
2 Wallman Mrs., drssmkr.
3 Wilson Mrs.
5 Handcock Richard
6 Oakes Mrs.
8 Ellis George
10 Saunders William
12 Wardle Jas., ho.decortr.

14 Winter Ernest, professor of music
16 Moses Mrs.
18 Wardle John
18 Wardle Mrs., dressmkr.
22 Frenché Andrew, teacher of languages
26 Hodgson Mrs.
30 Wood John
34 Cronk Thomas, builder
36 Braden Henry
38 Mourant John
42 Ford James
44 Billing E. J.
46 Chadwick Jno. Oldfield. accountant
50 Bishop Miss
RIGHT SIDE.
9a Lush S. B. and Co., Limited, dyers
10a Langridge Geo., builder
9 Thomas Joseph, waiter
11 Hanson James Joseph
15 Bush H. J.
25 Sinclair Misses
31 *The Albert Edward*, W. C. Ginder
Holtham rd.
33 Hayward Wm., school
35 Brooke W. H.
37 Stengel Charles, professor of languages
41 Grimes William

Boundary Mews,
see Boundary rd.

BOUNDARY ROAD,
St. John's Wood.
From 14 St. John's wood park to Greville pl. Kilburn.
G 6   **3 & 4**
[*Finchley rd. to Abbey rd. Ward. 3. Abbey rd. to Greville pl. Ward 4.*]
RIGHT SIDE.
2 Edmondson Thomas (Boundary house)
Finchley rd.
4 Symonds Mrs.
6 Offord Joseph
8 Mathews Francis Claughton
12 Ledsam Mrs. M. V.
14 Manning Edward Thos.
16 Wilson Miss

18 Howell Horace Sydney, M.D., F.R.C.S.
Loudoun rd.
20 Chapman Joseph John, pharmaceutical chmst
22 Stone Richard, stationer; post office
24 Marks John, fruiterer
24 Marks Mrs., registry office for servants
26 Hewett Chas., butcher
28 Field Miss R.. draper
28 Kitchener Miss, ladies' school
30 Clisby John, fishmonger
32 Bulford T., oilman
34 Barrett Jas., confectnr.
Boundary Mews.
2 Laycock John Spencer, builder
Boundary Road.
36 *The Prince Arthur*, Mrs. Mary Ann Clegg
38a Bartlett and Hawkins, builders & undertkrs.
38 Wright Mrs.
40 Moseley Abraham
42 Hume Major Alexander
44 Franck Mrs.
46 Fox Mrs. Mary
48 Radford John Emanuel
50 Ross Edward
52 Smallfield Frederick
54 Cobb Thomas
56 Marshall Wm. Henry
58 Brooks Charles William
60 Neale Richard, M.D.
62 Bennett William
64 Bruce George Barclay
66 Melbourn Herbert
68 Hoyte Wm. Stephenson, professor of music
70 Eadie Henry Alexander
72 Starkey William John
74 Hughes Reginald
76 Scott Matthew Richard
78 West Mrs. Clifton
80 Oldershaw Augustus Piggott
82 Hollebone Henry
84 Very John
88 Sonnenthal George
90 Conrath Fredk. John
92 Bedford John
94 Harmsworth Alfd., bar.
96 Budd Miss, preparatory school
Abbey rd.

BOUNDARY RD.—contind.
98 Cronk George, baker
   and confectioner
102 Steeden Daniel,green-
    grocer
104 Martin Hy., bootmkr.
106 & 108 Baxter James,
    grocer; post office
110 Whittlesey William
    Crowden, butcher
112 Shilston William Geo.,
    cheesemonger
114 De Coster & Co., drprs.
116 Mercer A.,upholsterer
    and cabinetmaker
118 Jacoby Fredk.,oilman
120 Gill John, plumber
122 Victoria Wine Co.
124 Firminger Amos,bldr.
126 Cornwell C. and E.,
    grocers
128 Landrebe Adam,dairy
130 Dunham William Hy.,
    china & glass dealer
132 Challenger M. C.,
    stationer
   LEFT SIDE.
1 John Hillary(Glouces-
   ter cottage)
3 Whitfield Thos. (Essex
   lodge)
   —Marlborough hill
7 Thomas Frank
9 Palmer Wm.(Alhambra
   villa)
11 James Mrs.
   —Loudoun rd.
13 Hardy Albert, artist
   (Inez villa)
15 Chadd Mrs. C.
17 Jetley Victor
19 Cocks Stroud Lincoln
21 Foster Joseph
23 Goodwyn Charles
25 Wilson Stephen Barton
27 Robinson James
29 Harris Walter
31 Lockwood Francis Day
35 Sharp John William
37 Champion James
39 Pearson G. (Lincoln
   house)
41 Francis George Bishop
43 Parkins William
45 Beesley Misses, ladies'
   school
47 Southey Mrs. Lucy

51 Parry Miss
53 Pearce William
55 Batsford Bradley Thos.
57 Gale Miss
61 Agabeg Aviet
63 Carnegie Alexander
65 Browne Miss
67 Baumer Edward
69 Rossner Henry
71 Heuland Mrs.
79 Dulcken Henry, PH.D.
   (Arundel house)
   —Abbey rd.
81 Houghton Frank,cheese
   monger
83 Cartridge James, book-
   seller stationer
85 Savage & Son, dyers
87 Taplin Thomas, toy
   dealer
89 Randall Fredk., fruit-
   erer and greengrocer
91 Griggs John, tobccnst.
93 Streeter S. A., oil and
   colourman
95 Draper Arthur S., ironmonger
97 Badger William,artists'
   colourman
101 Le Dong Henri, hair-
    dresser
103 Setterington Joseph,
    florist
105 Timms Hy.,bootmaker
107 Wilson Joseph, fish-
    monger & poulterer
111 Goodenough Thomas,
    dairy
113 King Mrs. H.,milliner
    and dressmaker
115 Masters Richd., coffee
    rooms

Bradley's Buildings
From 56 High st.
E 6.   1

BRANCH HILL.
From Holly bush hill to
West heath.
D 6   1
Branch Hill Park.
Holiday Henry (Oak
Tree house)
Branch Hill.
Charles Mrs. (Combe
Edge)

Smith Basil Woodd
   (Branch hill lodge)
Schwann Fredk. Sigis-
   mund(West heath lo.)
Hett Henry (Oakhurst)
Higginbotham Misses
   (The Glade)
The Chestnuts.
1 Scott Russell
2 Jevons Mrs. W.Stanley
   Branch Hill.
Pownceby Saml. (Fern
   bank)
Hale Miss
Carter Misses (Sand-
   field lodge)
Barber Mrs. (The
   Grange)
Branch Hill Side.
1 Miller Mrs.
2 Monro Miss Charlotte C.
5 Isaacson Wotton Ward

Branch Hill Park and Side,
see Branch hill.

BRIDGE ROAD,
Chalk Farm.
From 17 Adelaide rd.
F 8   3
Seymour James, florist
1 Dickinson Dr., homœo-
   pathic physician
2 Quick Mrs.

Britannia Villas,
see John st.

BROADHURST GARDENS.
From Finchley new rd.
to West end lane.
RIGHT SIDE.
F 6   4
4 Landau Max
6 Anstie Mrs. F. E.
8 Jennings Rev. Na-
   thaniel, M.A.
10 Gardner Robert
12 Watts Henry William
14 Wyon Allan
15 Gairdner Mrs.
17 Baines Frederick E.

21 Baldwin Christopher George
23 Charles Mrs.
25 Andrews John
  Cran John, M.D. (Netherdale)
⌐*Canfield gardens*
  Hayes H. B. (The Grange)
  Sanders Miss (Westbury)
  Watson Henry (Redholme)
  Tonneau Joseph (Roucourt)
Burlington House.
  Faulding A. J.
  Field Mrs.
  Best Mrs.
  Burckhardt Dr. Wm., secretary to Swiss consulate
Broadhurst Gardens.
  Maynard Miss (West lodge)
Clyde House.
  Evens Richd. Underhay
  Gibson Alfred
  Sayers William
  Sevier James Henry
  Hilton Robert
Broadhurst Gardens.
  Atterbury J. H. (Melcombe house)
  Folkard Misses (Chigwell house)
35 Turner William
33 Edwards Hy. (Norma cottage)
31 Willett Henry Jasper
29 Moulin —
27 Sims Mrs. (Broadhurst villa)
25 Halls Mrs.
23 Barnard Peter
21 Coldwell W.G.,archtct.
19 Camp Jas.,greengrocer
15 Provost Eugène, hairdresser
13 Harrington W.E.,bootmaker
11 Millson S., draper
5 Belcher J.S.,corn dealer
1 & 3 Cornick Henry, ironmonger
   LEFT SIDE.
  Bach Julius Otto (Donauwerth)

11 Lewis Mrs. (Oudenarde)
  Cohen Miss(Bouchain)
  Tatham Miss (Arleux)
17 Brown Oswald (Malplacquet)
  Ries Louis(Tirlemont)
  Marcus C. (Blenheim)
  Dodd Rev. F. W. (Ramillies)
  Wills Charles, M.D. (Broadhurst house)
⌐*Canfield gardens*
  Stoddart Charles (Dettingen)
  Dinham C. (Louvain)
  King Haynes, artist (The Ingle)
  Brightman Mrs.(Braine l'allend)
  Storey George Adolphus (Hougoumont)
115 *Jersey Farm Dairy*, G. Hopkins
119 Adams H.H.,stationer
119 Jones William
121 Lopez G. & Co., wine merchants
123 Ward L.,dining rooms
125 Hickley T. H., statnr.
4 Cox S., florist
2 Bate Thomas (Falcon works)

BUCKLAND CRES.,
Belsize Park.
F 7   **2**
1 Edwards RobertClarke
2 Askin Francis
3 Freeth ColonelWilliam
4 Freeth Charles
5 Fidler William
6 Heal Harris
7 Stott John, F.I.A., F.S.S.
8 Stern Ferdinand
9 Walker W. J. R.
10 Wharton James
11 Morgan Robert
12 Lawry William
13 Ross Hamilton
14 Nichol Donald
15 Jeanes John
16 Skilbeck John
17 Flavell Mrs.
18 Loader R. C.
19 Zingler Maximilian
20 Stephens Alexander

21 Wells Rev. Edward
22 Palfreman F. H.
23 Strauss Otto
24 Burton Frdk. Thomas
25 Birch Mrs. C. F.
26 Gutteman Augustus
28 Anderson John Ford, M.D.

BUCKLAND VILS.,
Belsize Park.
F 7   **2**
1 Hewlett George (Buckland lodge)
2 Staples Henry
3 Marx Hermann
4 Begg David Gray
5 Winter Emil
6 Playne Mrs.
7 Gardiner J. T. (Belsize school)
7 James Miss (Belsize school)
8 Field Abraham
9 Goddard J. L.,barrister
10 Phillips George
11 Flachfeld Julius
12 Snellgrove Frederick
13 Bergmans Mrs.
14 Moon James

Burgess Hill,
see Finchley new rd.

CANFIELD GDNS.
From 1 Fitzjohns' parade Finchley new rd.
F 6   **4**
   LEFT SIDE.
⌐*Broadhurst gardens*
   RIGHT SIDE.
2 *Canfield house*
  Dixon J. M.
  Applin B. A.
  Holcombe W.
⌐*Canfield pl.*
4 TREVERS TREVERS auctioneer and estate agent
6 Taylor Thomas Bennett, cigar stores
6 *Canfield residence*
  Brockman Frederick
  Brown Mrs.
8 Estcourt Ernest, bldr.

CANFIELD GDNS.—*cntnd.*
8 Harrison Miss (Arrandale)
⊏*Broadhurst gardens*

CANFIELD GDNS.,
Kilburn.
From 86 Priory rd.
F 5   *4*
LEFT SIDE.
1 Carlton Thomas William, M.I.M.E.
RIGHT SIDE.
2 Andrews R. L.
4 St. John Lieut. St. Andrew

CANFIELD PLACE.
From Canfield gardens.
F 6   *4*
1 Hart Frederick, coffee and dining rooms
1 Mallett Henry, window blind manufacturer
2 Bryant Charles, chimney sweep

CANNON PLACE.
From Christ Church.
D 6   *1*
1 Smith Miss
2 Phillips Francis Medland
3 Kilburn Henry Ward
4 Norman John Henry
Head Rev. Geo. Fredk. (Christ Church vicrg.)
Marshall James (Cannon hall)
⊏*Squire's mount*

CARLINGFORD RD.
From Worsley rd.
E 7   *1*
LEFT SIDE.
Dale John (Holmside)
4 Swinburn F.
5 Walker Mrs. G. F.
6 Eisdell J. A.
7 Roden Miss
8 Currie Mrs. William C.
Macarthur RobertJohn (Glenlyon)
13 Lockwood John Maitland
12 Davidson Alexander Harvey

11 Kinder Charles
9 Rees Miss E. E.
Palmer W.J.(Caerluel)
5 Gairdner James
17 FitzGerald William
18 Watson Edward
RIGHT SIDE.
2 Duncan Rev. Henry
3 Andresen Gustav Adolph
Meyrick J. C. (Mountfield)
Cook Mrs. Bickersteth (Clover-lea)
Smith George Albert (Lennyfield)
Jelley Miss Marion (Summerfield)
Shepherd Mrs. (Burfield)
WearJonathan(Swanscombe)
Baynes Lister (Silverdale)

Castle Terrace,
see Child's hill lane.

Cavendish Terrace,
see Cricklewood.

Cedar Terrace,
see Willoughby rd.

Cedar Villas,
see Mill lane.

Chalcot Gardens,
see England's lane.

CHILD'S HILL,
Kilburn.
From Cricklewood lane.
D 5
LEFT SIDE.
Saunders Cottages.
1 SimmondsAlfred,lndy.
3 Milton William
3 Matthews John
3 Thorne William
4 CulverhouseJohn,lndy.
The Village.
30 & 31 Wise Samuel, laundry
29 Sharpe Charles
28 Russell Jsph., laundry
27 Cook Mrs., laundress

26 Hickman Miss
25 English John
24 SwinneyChas.,gasfitter
Windsor Cottages.
2 Dadswell E. D.
1 Arkel Frederick
The Village.
22 May Joshua, beer retlr.
21 Sands Richard
20 Howard Wm. (Bloomfield cottage)
19 Windsor Thos., florist
17 & 18 Gwynn Francis, laundry
16 Gibson Thos., painter
15 Chambers Mrs., lndry.
14 Rogers John, laundry
13 Hilder Mrs., laundress
12 Norman Hy., laundry
11 Woodyear Samuel
10 East Thomas
9 Wainwright Mrs.
8 BrackleyJohn,carpntr.
7 Whale Geo., gardener
6 Holdman Mrs.
5 Harvey George
4 Warr Mrs.
4 Cooper Mrs.
4 Gay John
3 Hazell Mark
2 Adams John
1 HipwellMrs.,laundress
The Red Lion, Richard Windsor
Granville Houses.
2 Rogers Alexander, greengrocer
1 Wardley Alfred, provision dealer
RIGHT SIDE.
Avenue Villas.
1 Ashcombe James
2 Smith Richard
3 Faithorn George
4 Bolford Alfred
5 Steinberg Nicholas
6 Webb Alfred
⊏*The Avenue*
7 RainsfordJohnMcLeod (The Retreat)
8 Duppuy Mrs. Eliza
9 Bridgman Alfd. Ernest
10 Maples —
12 Hammond Mrs. R.
13 Elisha James
14 Kennedy Edward
15 Strong William

17 Bursill Charles John
18 Alberga Eugene
19 Neate George
20 Watson Isaac
21 Henry Alfred, F.C.A.
22 Curtis Henry
23 Morley William
24 Flint James
25 Young David
26 Mayer John
27 Embury Arthur, artist
28 Buck George Henry
ALL SAINTS' CHURCH
National Schools
⊏*Church walk*

Ridge Terrace.
6 McCullumGeorge, fishmonger
5 Dunn George, grocer
4 Crowe Miss, confectnr.
4 Crowe John, undertkr.
3 WardleyAlfred, draper
2 WardleyAlfd.,irnmngr.
1 *Child's Hill Provident Dispensary*

High Street.
1 Garwood Wm., oilman
1 DavisEdward,grngrcr.
2 Watson A. J., chemist
2 Philpott Thos.,butcher
3 Thomas Joseph, boot and clothing stores
4 Mole Alfred, tobccnst.
5 Randle Thos., bootmkr.
⊏*The Ridge*
⊏*Finchley rd.*

Child's Hill Cottages,
see Child's hill lane.

CHILD'S HILL LN.
From Finchley rd. to Platt's lane.
D 5   **1**
RIGHT SIDE.
Norfolk Place.
1 Frost Wm., stationer ; post office
2 Bell Fredk.,blacksmith
⊏*Grafton ter.*
Child's Hill Cottages.
1 Russell Thomas
2 McLaughlin Henry
3 Russell William
4 Russell Mrs., laundress
5 Windsor James

Child's Hill Lane.
Hayward James (Clayton cottage)
⊏*Ebenezer rd.*
Hermitage Villas.
9 James David
8 Hasloch Charles
7 Weygang William
6 Greenwood W. O.
5 Lazenby Rev. Albert
4 Russell Robert
3 Pritchard Stephen
Child's Hill Lane.
Fox Mrs. Tilbury (The Hermitage)
LEFT SIDE.
Castle Terrace.
4 Lunnon William
3 Blake Thomas, laundry
2 Taylor William, sweets shop
1 Wallington Isaac
Albion Terrace.
9 Bloxam Alfred, dairy
8 Gardner A., draper
7 Challis Thos., gardener
6 CookEdward,upholstr.
5 Dudley Mrs., laundress
4 Holloway Wm., decrtr.
3 Pepler Mrs.
2 Schroeder Alfred
1 Mayer John

CHRISTCHURCH PASSAGE.
From Hampstead sq.
D 6   **1**
Alvey Mrs. (Myrtle cottage)
Spiers Edward (West view house)
Martin W. (Grove cottage)
Capes Rev. J. M., M.A. (Grove house)
Capes Alfred, architect (Grove house)
⊏*New end*

CHRISTCHURCH ROAD.
From Christ Church to Willow rd.
D 6   **1**
LEFT SIDE.
Canney Charles R. (Camden cottage)

Davey John (Grove cottage)
⊏*Well rd.*
Orrinsmith Harvey (Sunny bank)
Moir Robert Mortimer (Bank side)
WeissMrs.(Birch bank)
Durrant Mrs. (Sunny bank)
King John Webb (Chesils)
⊏*Well walk*
SlackJames,contractor
Willow Place.
1 Pearce Henry
2 Pearce Mrs.
3 Pearce John
4 Abel Matthew, laundry
4 Abel J., carpenter
RIGHT SIDE.
CHRIST CHURCH
⊏*Grove pl.*
Low Thomas Henry (Wellmount)
⊏*Well rd.*
⊏*Well walk*
1 Everett John
2 Stamp Miss
3 Sutcliffe John
4 Belford G.
5 Hillyard Rev. George
6 Chomel Mrs.
8 Austin Mrs.
9 Young Mrs.
10 Phillips Jno.W., solctr.
11 Burt Miss
12 White Miss
13 Jarvis Mrs.
14 Batty Miss
15 Orrin Herbert
16 Mummery Rev. Isaac Vale
17 Thomas Miss, preparatory classes
18 Hipwood Mrs.
19 Dun Alexr. Campbell
20 Jones Mrs.
21 Mearns Misses

CHURCH LANE.
From 76 High st.to Church row.
E 6   **1**
RIGHT SIDE.
Harris John (Farley cottage)

CHURCH LANE—*contind.*
Baxter Benjamin A., carpenter
1 Joiner Joseph, bottle merchant
2 Neal Joseph
3 Satterthwaite Mrs.
4 Fletcher Mrs.
5 Slann Francis John, plumber
6 Simmonds W., chair caner
7 Chettleborough Mrs.
8 Bethel Francis
9 Andrews Jas., bootmkr.
10 Hayes William
    LEFT SIDE.
Watts W. H., builder
Paxon's Cottages.
3 Oakley G., painter
2 Crowson Thos. Henry
1 Morgan Henry
    Church Lane.
15 Perry Thos., dairyman
16 Summerfield William
17 Wilkins Wm., gardnr.

CHURCH PLACE.
From Church lane to Little Church row.
E 6   1
1 Wilkins C., bootmaker
1a Challis Mrs., confectnr.
1b Brown Chas., mineral water manufacturer
2 Culverhouse George, jobmaster
—*Perrins court*
2 Thomas W. I., dairy
4 Hannington Mrs., green grocer
    Oriel Cottages.
1 Griswood Richard
4 Parker G., gardener

CHURCH ROAD.
From 54 Park rd.
F 8   2
    The Mall.
1 Wilson George, artist
2 Morgan Walter, artist
3 Morris William Bright, artist
5 I'Anson Charles, artist
5 Scott John, artist
6 Titcombe —, artist
7 Conquest Alfred, artist

    Church Road
1 Tongue Mrs. A.
2 O'Neill William
3 Bodkin Peter

CHURCH ROW.
From High st.
E 6   1
1 Jelliman Miss
2 Davenport Mrs.
3 Langmead Miss
4 Sparkes William
5 Edwards Francis
6 Poole Frederick
7 Priddle William
8 Smith Miss
9 *Field Lane Certified Industrial School for Girls;* Mrs. Nyren, matron
10 Harrison R. W.
11 Puddifoot Mrs.
12 Vansittart-Neale Edw.
    ST. JOHN'S PARISH CHURCH
16 Scott William Booth
17 Silk William
18 Osmaston F. P.
19 Howse Gerald
20 Garner Thomas
21 Matheson Ewing
22 Brown George
23 Peabody Thomas
24 Bodley George Fredk.
25 Gillies Miss Margaret
26 Scott Geo. Gilbert, F.S.A
27 Thompson James
28 *Female Servants' Home;* Miss Dale, matron

CHURCH WALK,
    Child's Hill.
From Finchley rd. to Cricklewood lane.
D 5
Clay Rev. J. H. (The Vicarage)
ALL SAINTS' CHURCH
School House, William Harvey, master; Miss Whitley, mistress

CLAREMONT RD.,
    Kilburn Lane.
From Cricklewood Station, Cricklewood lane.
E 3   4
1 Wilkes John Staley (Staley house)

2 Poole Daniel George
2 Biggs J. M., L.R.C.P.L.
3 Bratzali N.
4 Bays Samuel
5 Smith George William
6 Woodward Robert
7 Richards Mrs. (Grange villa)
8 Shortis Miss
9 Robinson John R.
10 Tompkins Mrs. E., ladies' school
11 Walker Thos., builder
12 Evans John Houghton
15 Foster Andrew
16 Forman Arthur
17 Knight Alfred H.
18 Walker R. W.
19 Sjolander C. V.
24 Bowman Richard, M.D.
25 Van Wyk W.
26 Knight Henry
27 Yeatman Miss, professor of music
28 Rumsey A. A.

Claremont Terrace,
see Heath st.

Claremont Villas,
see The Ridge.

CLEVE ROAD,
    Kilburn.
From West end lane to Priory rd.
F 5   4
    LEFT SIDE.
Price Harry (Uplands)
Boyd J. P. (Woodcote)
Walter Jacob (Mablethorpe)
    RIGHT SIDE.
15 Gibson Rev. Dr. John Monroe
Gibson Jaspar (Stonecroft)
Herapath Edwin John (Oakhurst)
Stuart Charles, artist (Hermitage)

Clock Terrace,
see Cricklewood.

COLERIDGE GDNS.
From Fairhazel gardens.
G 6   **4**
1 Basham T., genl. shop
2 Neal James, marine
   store dealer

COLLA'S MEWS,
Kilburn.
From 33 Birchington rd.
G 5   **4**
2 Simkins A., bootmaker
4 Aedy Wm., cab prprtr.
12 Pardoe & Sons, iron-
   mongers
12 Rogers R., tin plate
   worker
7 Cook James, carpenter

COLLEGE CRES.,
Belsize Park.
From Finchley rd.
F 6   **2**
3 Carpenter Miss
4 Murtagh Mrs. Emma
5 Bazin Mrs.
7 Anson Adml. Talavera
   Vernon
8 Tarbox Edward
9 Ness Alexander
10 Chambers John
11 Batty Col. George M.
12 Osborne Captain
13 Wells Chas., M.D., surg.

COLLEGE ROAD,
Haverstock Hill.
From 2 Adelaide rd.
F 8   **2**
Hamilton Wm. D., F.S.A.
   (Beaumont cottage)
Uubelen M. (Percy
   cottage)

COLLEGE TER.,
Belsize Park.
From College cres.
F 6   **2**
2 De Martino Edouardo
3 Smith Misses
4 Scratchley Arthur
5 Andrews Mrs.
6 Ford Rev. Joseph
7 Brinton Mrs. Mary
8 Fowke Francis
9 Mills Mrs. Sarah
10 Baily Alfred Head

Belsize park
11 Ross Miss H. R.
12 Leslie Henry John
   (Homelea)
13 Russell Joseph
14 Farmiloe G., jun.
   (Campbell house)

COLLEGE VILLAS ROAD,
Belsize Park.
From Finchley new rd.
F 6   **2**
   Palmer Samuel (North-
   court)
1 Johnston Alexander
2 Burnett John R. F.
3 Tucker George
3 Tucker Mrs.
4 Glover William B.
6 Billing Charles Eardley
7 Fuller Miss Mary, kin-
   dergarten school

CRESSY ROAD.
E 8   **2**
   From Fleet rd.
3 Burden Henry Charles
   *Hampstead Model
   Steam Laundry, Lmtd*

CRICKLEWOOD.
*Continuation of High rd.
Kilburn.*
F 4 and E 3   **4**
   LEFT SIDE.
   Walker George S., sur-
   geon (Cavendish ho.)
Devonshire Villas.
1 Cohen Henry
2 Brookfield J. S., M.D.
3 Sexton R.
4 Beardall Robert
5 Carter William
6 Tildesley David
7 Luxton Mrs., ladies'
   school
   *Kilburn and Brondes-
   bury Station, Metro-
   politan Railway*
Christchurch rd.
Exeter rd.
   Beckington W. (Bron-
   desbury nursery)
   Unwin Thos. (Geneva
   house)
   Cossey Wm. (Leigh ho.)

Shoot-up Hill.
Wright A., dentist
   (Ravena lodge)
Connett George Alfred
   (Bickleigh lodge)
Bowling C. R. (Glad-
   wyn)
Keele Charles F., sur-
   geon (Clumber house)
Marrian Miss (Blake-
   more house)
Dadson J. T. (Melrose)
Cooper Fredk. (Edin-
   burgh)
Negretti Mrs. (Berke-
   ley lodge)
Verey George (Holmby
   grange)
Colman Jeremiah (Clif-
   ton house)
Turner John (Beech
   Holme)
Garcia Rodriguez (Mon
   Abri)
Hodgson Chas. (Glynd-
   hurst)
List Wm. (Eversfield)
Nibblett Fredk. (Long-
   thorpe)
Young Robert (Thorn-
   bank)
Bates R. & A., *Kilburn
   Flour Mills*
Hill Side.
6 Callard Thomas Karr
5 Hawes James
4 Harrison William
3 Roberts Charles Lewis
2 Glyn Richard Henry
1 Reeve E. J.
Cricklewood.
Gladman Geo. (Ivy lo.)
Webb Chas., horse dlr.
   (Wyndham house)
Butt W. F., M.D. (The
   Bijou)
Beard Thomas (Marlow
   cottage)
Roberts Mrs. (The
   Cottage)
Walm lane
Roberts Mrs. (Crickle-
   wood lodge)
Allingham Theodore
   Frdk. (Hawthorn lo.)
Keighley Edwn Holmes
   (Hope villa)

wife Eliza Fisher = Sister to Am 2nd wife of William WHARTON

CRICKLEWOOD—*contind.*
Hatherley John (Clifton cottage)
Bunce William (Prospect cottage)
Prior Samuel, rustic worker (Laurel cott.)
Lisney T.. farrier
Lougher Mrs.,genl.shop
Lougher Edwin, lndry.
The Windmill, William Meager
Hetherington J., jobmaster (The Slade)
Taylor Frederick
Howard George (Oaklands)
Soulby Anthony Morland (Winton lodge)
Goldsmith Alfd. (Richmond villa)

Clock Terrace.
3 Lane Thos.,estate agnt.
3 Lane J. A., builder
6 Clarke Herbert, grocer
7 Longland Thomas, butcher
8 *Clock Farm Dairy,* and at Child's hill ; Alfrd. Bloxam,prprtr.
RIGHT SIDE.
Burrage, Tompkins & Co., timber merchants

Maygrove rd.
Helffenstein Harry (Rhine villa)
Phipps Mrs. (Surrey house)
Curtis Henry (Linden villa)
Seaton Frederick (Garlinge house)

Garlinge rd.
Wartenberg S. (Montague house)
Acworth Joseph W. (Sheldmont house)
Prendergast Edwin (Strathmore)
Helffenstein Henrich Christian (Aberglaslyn)
Michell Richard C. (Oakfield)
Greenway W.(The Firs)
Shipway Major Robert William (Eversholt)

Allen Mrs. Elizabeth (Kingsgate)
Davidson Mrs. P. (Arden lodge)
Cannon Charles(Tan-y-Bryn)
Marsh Wm. (Ravensthorpe)
Macpherson Robert (Thorncliff)
Oliver David (Fernbank)
France Miss (Westhaven)
Reece J. (Westhaven)
Terry E. (Norfolk vil.)
Cayford Ebenezer (Home villa)
Harris F. W. (Hill top villa)
Smith Alfd.(Belle Vue)
Bates Mrs.(Elm lodge)
Mill lane
Royle Henry William (The Mount)
Sonnenberg Charles (Ovingdean)
Garle Mrs. (Winterdyne)
Garle Acton(Elmstead)
Ellaby Thomas (The Elms)

Ash Terrace.
4 Beckensall R. W., insurance agent
4 Beckensall Miss Emily S., milliner
3 Auger Matthew, bootmaker
2 Morris O., stationer
1 Turner J., tobacconist
Ash grove

Oakland Terrace.
10 Capham George
9 Child James Robert
8 Vincent Mrs.
7 Birch John H.
6 Bienvenue Wm.Henry
5 Matthews Philip
4 Boon Charles Edward
3 Wilkinson G.
2 Wilcox John
1 Welch Amos
Grove rd.

Yew Terrace.
5 Simmons G., grocer
4 Satterley W. J.,butcher

3 Taggett C.M.,dairyman
2 Stimson S.,greengrocer
1 Walker Wm.,coffee rms.
Cricklewood.
The Crown, William Oliver
Roper W.(Cricklewood house)
Cricklewood lane
Willing James, jun. (Rock hall)
Bates Robert (Elm lo.)
Kellow W.(Woodbrook house)
Readman Joseph (Ormond house)
Kemp Geo.(Sudley ho.)
Hewlett Mrs. (Batsford house)

Rockhall Terrace.
1 Dunham Miss Maria
2 Chapman Henry
3 Page William Augustus
4 Folkard Richard
6 Redford Geo., F.R.C.S.
7 Roberts Mrs.
8 Pitcher Major D. J.
9 Edgar Mrs.
10 Corfe Mrs.

Midland Cottages.
1 & 2 Bloxham T. Say
3 Patrick Arthur
4 Addy Samuel John
5 Coates Herbert
6 Monk Thomas
7 Hopkins David
8 Lake Frederick
9 Diplock Albert
10 Smith Thomas
11 Draper David
12 Cox Edwin
13 Fletcher Henry
14 Gurden Benjamin
15 Allen John
16 Roper John
17 Smith T.
18 Whiting William
19 Randell Richard
20 Williams Charles
21 Dawes Henry
22 Buckingham Andrew
23 Wheatley Frederick
24 Morris FrederickChas.
25 Chapman Arthur
26 Warren James Thomas
27 Griffin Richard B.
28 Mason John

29 Woodley Thomas
30 Lamb Jacob
31 Edwards Frederick
32 Mantell Henry
33 Anderson William
34 Whitmore William
35 Cox John
36 Lowe George
37 Martin Edward
38 Yates George
39 Pedley William
40 Pearce Henry

CRICKLEWOOD LANE,

D 4   *Cricklewood.*

LEFT SIDE.
Lockhart & Co., coal and coke merchants
Rickett J. C., coal and coke merchant
Knowles John, lime and cement merchant
Finch Alfred (Rockhall cottage)
Midland Railway, Cricklewood Station

⸺*Claremont rd.*

Westcroft Villas.
1 Hammond R. C. (Stourcliffe house)
2 Lovely G. M.
3 Hart Mrs.
4 Read Charles A. (Roselands)
5 Owen Thomas

Cricklewood Lane.
Church of England Temperance Society Coffee Hut; Robert Rogers, hut keeper
St. Peter's Mission Room
Reynolds Mrs. (Providence cottage)

Provident Place.
1 Tyrrell Wltr., gardener
2 Cooper Joseph

Cricklewood Terrace.
1 Cleaver William
2 Stacey Bartholomew
3 Button James
4 Austen Edmund
5 Butterfield John
6 Trevillian Miss, lndrss.
7 Roberts Mrs.
8 Sawyer James

9 Bradbury John
10 Gilbey Daniel
11 Walters William
12 Bridgeland Mrs. M., laundress
13 Dean Samuel
14 Stacey Albert
15 Nicholson J. C.
16 Rix Misses, dressmkrs.
16 Ward Mrs. R., nurse
17 Cole Henry, coffee and dining rooms
18 White William, grocer
19 Martin Edwd.,grngrcr.
20 *Cricklewood Tavern.* Mrs. Caroline Shirley

Cricklewood Lane.
Patent Pyramid Night Light Works; Samuel Clarke, patentee

⸺*Child's hill*

RIGHT SIDE.
Burfield James (The Cottage)

⸺*Elm grove*

8 Oliver William
Englefield Mrs. (Homeleigh)
Budden Herbert (Cleveland cottage)
Chapman W. H. (Oakhurst)

⸺*Oak grove*

4 Pfeiffer R. W.
2 Gilbert George Henry
1 Addy W. F.

Station Villas.
12 Cheshir Charles
11 Brooke Edwin (Kirkby villa)
10 Hedges Francis
9 Bousfield Wm., M.A., barrister (Westbury villa)
8 Davies Richard
7 Thunder C.

⸺*Lichfield rd.*

6 Chard George
5 Hurst J. B.
4 Halse William
3 Spurrell Mrs. S.
2 Flint Frederick
1 Fishburn Miss

Cricklewood Lane.
The Andover & Weyhill Horse Co., Lmtd.; Hny. Newman, mngr.

Wardle Robert (The Lodge)
Francis James, sweep (The Cottage)

The Cottages.
1 Mitchell John, upholsterer
2 Leek Henry
3 Harris James
4 Skinner Mrs.
5 Byrnard Herbert

Granville Terrace.
1 Dewick George
2 Clouser Mrs.
3 Sinfield Joseph
4 Tutton William
5 Crocker John
9 & 10 Hopcroft Henry, grocer
11 Brown Miss Emma, tobacconist
12 Windsor J., dairy
13 Jones W. Joseph, bootmaker
14 Watts Saml., dairyman
15 Wilson J. P., chemist
16 Lenny William, tailor
17 Lea Edward, grngrcr.

⸺*Granville mews*

18 Weller D., vet. forge
18 Snowball Jsph., draper
19 Crease Wm., butcher
20 Clarke J. Melville, baker
21 Pedder Henry
22 Hosking Robert
23 Weller Daniel
24 Richards George Chas.

Cricklewood Terrace,
see Cricklewood lane.

CROSSFIELD ROAD
From Belsize sq.

F 7   **2**
1 Herzberg Bernard
2 Boyd Rev. Sydney A., M.A., B.C.L.
4 Boyd Phillip
6 Malden Mrs.
7 Douthwaite Mrs.
8 Perrins Mrs. T. H.
9 Gieseler Misses
11 Pittman Miss
13 Pitt John Wolley
14 McEntee W. C.
15 Wood Thomas

CROSSFIELD RD.—contnd.
16 Carpenter Robert S.
17 Bence Henry Robert
18 Ford Colonel Arthur
19 Heideman Percy Frncs.
20 Lewel William
21 Brewer Henry
22 Gregory Henry

DALEHAM GDNS.
F 6   1

LEFT SIDE.
1 Franks Mrs. (St. Aubyn's)
3 Surtees Robt. W. (Campvale)
5 Breslauer Louis (Glenville)
7 Weir John Alexander
9 Deschamps C. W.
11 Austin J. G.
13 Henshaw John
15 Sheffield Frank (Palaspai)
17 Berrey Miss Caroline
19 Hodgskin Mrs.
21 Parker Rev. Dr. Joseph, D.D. (Tynehome)
23 Sercombe Mrs. Louisa
25 Brocheton E. (Rose bank)
27 Clarke Samuel
29 Blake Dr. Edward
RIGHT SIDE.
2 Bloxam Alfred (The Corner house)
4 Geare William A. (Southbrook)
6 Donaldson Andrew B., artist (Devereux ho.)
8 Adelmann G. (Ballin-Collig)
10 Walls Mrs.
12 Schleasser Ernest
14 Leatham Charles
16 Porter E. R. (Hesket)
18 Foster G. Carey
20 Mays J. A.
22 Whitworth Benjamin, M.P.
24 Pye W. A.
26 Edwards Mrs.
28 Kilpatrick W. (Closeburn)

Dawson Terrace,
see Haverstock hill.

DENINGTON PARK,
Kilburn.
From West end lane.
F 5   4

LEFT SIDE.
1 Douglas-Hamilton Major-General (Langdale house)
3 Baird Mrs. (St. Aidans)
—*Kingdon rd.*
5 Potter Henry (Little Dene)
7 Brightman F. W.
9 Leakey James
RIGHT SIDE.
—*Holmdale rd.*
Davys Rev. E.
Millington Misses (St. Ambrose)
Pearse Alfred, artist (Thauehurst)

DENNING ROAD.
From Willoughby rd.
E 7   1

LEFT SIDE.
1 West Mrs. (Maythorne)
3 Robinson Major-Genl. Charles Gilbert, R.A.
5 Hyndman Mrs.
7 Child Robert Carlyle
9 Cox Mrs.
11 Dixon Mrs.
13 Concannon Michael
15 Thomas Rev. J. Davies (Ingleside)
17 Gass Mrs. (Ravenscourt)
19 Boocock John (Wyldecroft)
21 Haynes William (Hartsfield)
23 Bonney Rev. Prof. T. G.
25 Cook A. H., M.R.C.S., L.R.C.P., L.S.A., surgeon
Copestick F. D. Rees (Calton house)
34 Chisolm Mrs.
35 Lawford John Lindsay
45 Osbaldeston Mrs. Martha
47 Rock E. G.
49 Coutant Madame
49 Alison Miss
RIGHT SIDE.
2 Earl Alfred William (Denning house)

4 Legg Charles
6 Fell John Corry
8 Rogers James
10 Binnington F., house agent (Hilldrop ho.)
12 McOscar Mrs. John
14 Cowley Mrs. Catherine
14 Cowley Arthur
16 Christie Rev. Geo. Alex.
18 Calkin Percy R.
20 Lardelli Thos. Francis
40 Carter Henry
42 Baker Miss Amy

DEVONSHIRE PL.
From Finchley rd. Child's hill.
E 5   1

1 Batho Thomas William
2 Challice George
3 Adams Mrs.
4 Perry George
5 Messam Thomas
6 Capp George
7 Lammas Randal
8 Butler Cornelius, smith
9 Fry Thomas
10 Haylesbury Henry
11 Fletcher Richard
12 Brown George
13 Paul Thomas
14 Albon Mrs.
16 Simper George
17 Potter Abraham
19 Robins Charles H.
20 Clarke Edward
21 Brooks James
22 Woolford Thomas
23 Lawrence Mrs.
24 Reeman Alfred
25 Stedall Henry

Devonshire Villas,
see Cricklewood.

DOWNSHIRE HILL
From Rosslyn hill to South end rd.
E 7

1 Messenger H. Williams surgeon-dentist
1 *Hampstead Libera Club ;* R. S. Frase and John Lea, secs.
2 Trinder Thomas, riding master
3 Evans John Lane

4 Toplis Thomas James
5 Young Mrs.
6 Moore Temple
7 Adamson Mrs. Ellen
8 Lewes Mrs.
9 MullerJno.(Manor ho.)
10 Burn Miss
11 Vaughan-Jones Major
12 ElliottAlfredHarraden (Warwick house)
13 Bertiole F.
13aRait Logan (Glou- cester house)
14 Hollobon Mrs. (Bel- grave house)
St. Stephen's Schools; John Collins, master ; Mrs. C. E. Atkins, mistress
15 Tasker Elijah, stone merchant (St. Mary's cottage)
16&17 Woodman Cornelius
18 Mallard Alexander
19 Disney Mrs. E.
20 Osmond George(Berke- ley cottage)
21 Smith George Edward
22 Roff Walter William
23 Gude Joseph
24 Humphrey Mrs.
25 Kay Allan William
26 Page Robert
27 Welton Charles
28 Warner Miss M. A.
29 Perkins Mrs. M. A.
30 Shepherd Wm. Robert
31 Whatley Thos., dairy- man
The Freemasons' Arms, Rowland Hill
Hill William, carriage proprietor; licensed to let on hire dog carts, pony chaises, light spring carts, and tri- cycles
South end rd.
4 Foster John (Dean's cottage)
5 Coates Joseph(Victoria cottage)
6 Timms John
6 Timms Mrs.,ladies'schl.
7 Arscott William (Nor- folk cottage)
8 Ewell Miss Louisa

39 Greig William James, solicitor (Blenheim cottage)
40 Blunt A. W.
41 Wash Henry
42 Willmott William
43 Stevenson Edmond
44 Wakefield John
45 Skeel William
ST. JOHN'S CHAPEL
John st.
46 Hankin C., builder
47 Latham Mrs.
48 Greaves William
49 Light Mrs. F.
50 SatchellThomas(Down shire hill house)
52 Pidcock G. Douglas, M.A., M.D.

DUNBOYNE ST.
From 25 Southampton rd.
E 8   **2**
8aJoslin Arthur
9aClayden William
9 Atkins Thomas
10 Russell John
11 Hester William
12 Ransley Alfred
16 Brett James

DYNHAM ROAD,
Kilburn.
From West end lane.
G 5   **4**
LEFT SIDE.
2 Sherbrooke W.
6 Corani H.
8 Spencer Mrs.
10 Jennings W.
12 Henness Mrs.
RIGHT SIDE.
1 Kingdon Miss
3 Baker Mrs. (Longleat house)
5 Antram Rev. R (Or- chardleigh house)

EAST HEATH ROAD
From Heath st.
D 6   **1**
RIGHT SIDE.
Holford rd.
Hampstead Reforma- tory School for Girls; Miss Nicoll, lady suprintendnt. (Heath- field house)

PoulterThomas(Clifton lodge)
Millar H. E. (Heath- down)
Squire's mount
Portland Villas.
2 Edis Robert
1 Saunders C. D.
Heath Cottages.
2 Holland Thomas
1 Humphreys Frederick
Squire's mount
Gotto Edw.(The Logs)
Well rd.
Toller Mrs. C.
Well walk
Christian Ewan (Thwaite head)
Hewson Mrs. (Esk haven)
Cash Mrs. (Banks hill)
Nash Frederick(Beech- croft)
Straube Albert (Fern bank)
PowellR.L.(Heylands)
Riley Edward (South heath)
Millar Miss (South heath)
Hughes Henry Clifford (Heath side)
LevyHenry(Heathfern lodge)
Christchurch rd.
South end rd.
LEFT SIDE.
2 White Miss
1 Ashdown Edwin
Vale of Health
Field Walter (The Pryors)

EBENEZER ROAD,
Kilburn.
From Child's hill lane.
D 5
1 Larner John
2 Andrews Jabez
3 Etheridge Henry
4 Barrett William
5 Peters Simon
6 Castle James
7 McGregor William
8 Ludgate James

Edward Terrace,
see Providence pl. Kilburn.

ELDON ROAD.

From Lyndhurst rd. to Thurlow rd.

E 7   *1*

2 Ford Everard Allen
3 Martineau Basil
4 Curtis Mrs. S. Stuart
5 Martineau Russell
6 Rapp Eugene
7 Preston Stanton Wm.
8 Mitton Edgar W.
9 Sanderson James
10 Rayson James B.
11 Lister Henry

Elizabeth Mews,

in rear of Elizabeth ter.

Elizabeth Terrace,

see England's lane.

ELLERDALE RD.

From Greenhill rd.

E 6   *1*

RIGHT SIDE.
6 Shaw Richard Norman,
    R.A., architect
8 Spalding Hy.,A.R.I.B.A.
    (Meadow bank)
10 Vizard Philip Edward
    (Fernlea)
10 Lovell Miss (Fernlea)
12 Reid Charles T. (Twy-
    fordbury)
14 Sharman Mrs. Eric R.
    (Ellel house)
16 Brock Rev. Wm. (Rose
    Lea)
20 Robertson Jas.(Haugh-
    ton lodge)
22 Duncan Miss(Dunelm)
24 Duncan J.H.(Briarlea)
26 Mulholland William
    (Glenside)
LEFT SIDE.
1 Powell James (Cromer
    Lea)
3 Startin Charles (Fair-
    light)
5 Price Ramsden
7 Matheson Miss Isabella
    (Reay lodge)
9 Duncan Wm. Wallace
    (Fern bank)

Elm Cottages and Villas,

see Elm row.

ELM GROVE,

E 3   *Kilburn.*

From Cricklewood lane.

LEFT SIDE.
1 Luckhurst D. J.
3 Walliker E. H. J.
5 Bowles G.
7 Hayhoe R. H.
9 Rex C. W.
11 Hodge Thomas R.
13 Holden A. E.
15 Fouracres Mrs.
17 Gripper F. F.
25 Hendricks Philip
27 Skinner Arthur
29 Sumpter G. J.
31 Avery J.
35 Milne David
RIGHT SIDE.
2 Bradbury J.
4 Sims William John
6 Mason Henry W., gen-
    eral draughtsman
8 Johnson James
10 Aggleton Mrs.
12 Path Mrs.
   Yew grove
   Ash grove

ELM ROW.

From 31 Heath st.

E 6   *1*

Elm Villas.
2 Shave E. S.
1 Ives James T. B.
Elm Cottages.
1 Clarke G.
2 & 3 McDonald John
Elm Row.
2 Hughes T. J.
3 Dalton John

ELM TERRACE,

Kilburn.

From Child's hill lane.

D 5

1 Murden Mrs., laundry
2 Horn Benjamin
3 Noah Mrs. Mary,
    laundress
4 Chamberlain William
5 Smith William
6 Hawes Robert

7 James Thomas
8 Mulley Searles shoe
    maker
9 Baxter John Richard
    sweep
9aStout Henry John
    carpenter
    Cousins Mrs. (Elm ter
    archway)
10aPocock George
10aAmbrose Chas., painte:
10 Hunt Richard, provi-
    sion dealer
11 Etheridge Timothy
    blacksmith
   Finchley rd.

Elm Villas,

see Elm row.

ELSWORTHY RD.

From Primrose hill rd.

G 7

LEFT SIDE.
Evans John Henr;
    (Fairlight villa)
Phillips Samuel (Glen
    hurst)
5 Shipwright Thomas
7 Walker Mrs. (Ravens
    downe)
9 Smyth Archibald J.
11 Blackborn Edward
13 Tapson Robt.(Montem
15 Main Rev. Thos. John
    M.A.
17 Goldstein Hy. (Caris
    brook)
    Price-Williams Mr:
    (Northbrow)
    Viner Lewis (Spring
    field)
23 Neele George Potte
    (Sunny bank)
   Elsworthy ter.
    Farrer Thomas Chas
    artist (Queen Ann
    house)
RIGHT SIDE.
2 Kay Thos. (Newlands
4 Nowers J. E. L. (Nes
    bank)
6 Walker Mrs.
8 Anderson Miss
    Spooner Mrs. (Sunny
    side)
12 Jones G. F.

4 Pile C. H.
6 Fellowes Mrs.
8 Blaiklock FrankEdwd.
0 Waterlow Charles
8 Matthew Mrs.
8 Vert Narciso
0 Hughes William
2 Barton V. J.
4 Ridgway Mrs. (Dyke house)
6 Walker Miss
8 Jaggars Henry Edwin
0 Adrian Mrs. (Mayfield)

ELSWORTHY TER.
From Elsworthy rd.
7   **3**
1 Rost Dr.R., PH.D.,LL.D.
2 Cruckshank William
3 Schoell Rev. Carl,PH.D
4 Black Mrs.
5 Walton R.
6 Snudden William L.
7 Barber Joseph V.
9 Maclean Charles
0 Hill Henry
1 Walker James
4 Walton Thomas
5 Capstick Mrs.

ENGLAND'S LANE.
From Belsize park gardens to Haverstock hill.
8   **2**
LEFT SIDE.
Elizabeth Terrace.
1 The Washington Hotel, F. H. Price
2 SEARLE WILLIAM, poulterer & chsmngr. Alderney fresh butter received daily
3 Parnell Wm., grocer
4 Hendrick Chas., baker
5 Brown J. A., milliner
6 Randall T. G., butcher
7 Lee HenryW.,fruiterer
8 GiddenW.&H.,saddlers
9 Selway H. J., fishmngr.
0 Moore G. Willis, china and glass stores
1 Stubbs John, stationer
2 Owen R. & Co., wine & spirit merchants
=*Stanley gardens*
3 *Victoria Wine Co.*
4 Brown J. A., draper

16 Bardill H., oilman
17 Cox Charles, fruiterer and greengrocer
18 Barrett Fredk.,butcher
19 Allen J. W., chemist
20 Rieger H., baker and confectioner
21 Ward William, tobacconist
22 Prior Misses H. and C., fancy repository
23 Potter Henry, china & glass dealer
England's Lane.
St. Mary's Convent, young ladies' school (Gifford lodge)
RIGHT SIDE.
1 Allchin Alfd., chemist
2 FerrisEdwd. C., watchmaker and jeweller
3 White William, fruiterer
4 Pugh John, builder
5 Littlewood Wm., ironmonger
6 Tolhurst Mrs., dressmaker
7 Edwards Henry, corn merchant
7 Edwards H., servants' registry
8 Richards James, dairy
Spencer Sydney,school (Chalcots)
Chalcot Gardens.
14 Conor Captain
13 Montbard Georges
12 Wetherbee G. F.
11 Davison Mrs.
10 Hayman Mrs.
9 Boyle William
8 Dale Hylton William
7 Ellis Henry
6 Hickson Mrs.
5 Whitcher John, F.S.S.
4 Toms Edmund
3 Carlyle A., B.A.
2 Bath John
1 Johnson Mrs.
England's Lane.
Schoell Carl (Homeside)
WalkerFrancis(Wychcombe villa)
Wychcombe Studios.
1 Barclay Edgar, artist

2 Overend W. H.
3 Burr Alexander, artist
4 North J. W.

ERSKINE ROAD,
Primrose Hill.
From 91 Regent's park rd. to Ainger rd.
G 8   **3**
1 LangtonJ.,chmny.clnr.
=*Erskine mews*
3 Richards G., marine store dealer
4 Kirby F., bootmaker
Hindley & Son, cabinet makers

ETON PLACE.
From 143 Adelaide rd.
G 7   **3**
1 Saich H., carpenter
Wiffen George, livery stables
2 Ingram Mrs., plumber
Kemp William (King Henry's nursery)

ETON ROAD,
Haverstock Hill.
From No. 61 to Fellows rd.
F 8   **2**
North-London High School for Boys ; Septimus Payne, F.R.G.S., M.S.A., head master (Wellington house)
ST. SAVIOUR'SCHURCH
1 Oxley Robert
2 Danson William
=*Eton villas*
Herklots Rev. Gerard Andreas, M.A. (St. Saviour's vicarage)
3 Nelson Miss, M.C.P.
4 Johnston Rev. Robert
4 Bain George
5 Woollcombe Richard, solicitor
6 Blaiklock Reginald
7 Wolff Rudolph
8 Kennedy John
9 Ross D. A. McBean
11 Model Albert
12 Styer Walter
13 King Mrs. A.
14 Fletcher Mrs.

ETON RD.—*continued*
15 Ash Claudius James
16 Alexander John
    August Mrs. (Eton
    nursery)

ETON VILLAS,
Haverstock Hill.
From Eton rd.
F 8   **2**
1 Hooper Miss
2 Davison Robert
3 Hall William
4 Read Miss
5 Adam John Booth
6 Goodchild Miss
7 Hanhart Nicholas
8 Pearpoint Alfred Henry
9 West John Thomas H.
13 Brown Walter Henry
15 Wallace Alexander
16 Burnet William Cadell
17 Weanhausen David
18 Wich Frederick G.
19 Brinsmead Thomas
20 Colman Miss

Exeter Road,
F 4   *Cricklewood.*

Exeter Terrace,
see West end lane.

FAIRFAX MEWS.
From 59 Fairfax rd.
G 6   **4**
2 Buckingham Jas., dairy
7 Moy & Arnold, farriers
14 to 18 Baines Thomas,
    printer
27 Burdett Wm., lvry. stbls.

FAIRFAX ROAD,
Finchley Road.
From 72 Finchley new rd.
to Belsize rd.
G 6   **3 & 4**
RIGHT SIDE. (*Ward 4*)
1 Edmunds Alfred Sayres
5 Hogg Robert Thomas
7 Verity Geo. Hamilton
9 Coyte George
11 Clayton John Richard
    (Broomfield house)
13 Allen John Wm., surgn.
15 Wadmore Rev. Henry
    Robinson, M.A.
17 White Thomas Jennings

19 Fuller Mrs. H. H.
21 Gordon Rev. John B.,
    M.A.
23 Fripp George Arthur
25 Danvers Mrs.
29 Marlow Henry
31 Cobb Mrs. Lucy
33 Kirkpatrick Mrs.
35 Yeo Robert, estate office
37 Summerfield Mrs. dress
    maker
37 Steer Charles, upholstr.
39 Lang John, bazaar
41 Barrett Thomas Albert,
    corn merchant
43 Osborne O. H., cheese-
    monger
43 Thatcher Thomas
45 Wain James J. & Co.,
    wine merchants
47 ALDRIDGE A. C.,
    draper
49 Wain Jas.J.& Co.,grcrs.
51 Vooght Wm.J.,chemist
53 *Fine Art Emporium*,
    K. Moss
55 Mizen Robert Henry,
    baker & confectioner
57 Pincham Seymour,
    fruiterer
59 Eveleigh George Henry,
    builder
59 Eveleigh Miss, professor
    of music
61 Yeo John, fishmonger
61 Woodward Mrs., ladies'
    nurse
63 ANDREWS G. N.,
    draper, hosier & glover
65 Mason Mrs. F.C., berlin
    fancy repository
67 Hartstone Thomas, hair-
    dresser and perfumer
69 Hannett A. H. & Sons,
    dyers
71 Austin John
71 Abercrombie William,
    bootmaker
73 Jarvis William, tailor
75 Vickers V., music
    library
75 Vickers Miss A., drsmkr.
79 Lines Edward, stationr.
    Office of the South
    Hampstead Observer
81 Kite S., ironmonger
83 Simpson W., cheesmng.

85 Isaac Edwin Joh
    builder & decorator
87 Coles Alexdr., butche
89 Klosz & Clarke, groce
91 Buckingham Jas., dair
93 Maitland David, bake
    post office
95 *The Britannia*, Joh
    Stokes
LEFT SIDE. (*Ward*)
2 Hadow Miss
4 Cope Arthur
    Albion rd.
6 Meakin Miss
8 Luck Michael
10 Barratt Samuel
12 Nevill Henry
14 Putz Joseph Francis
16 Mott Alfred
18 Lowe Chas.Hy.,surv
20 Tweddell Mrs.
22 Hart Robt. Washingt
24 Stevenson Frederick
26 Ruddick David
28 Woodman Miss, ladi
    school
34 Hemming Miss
36 Staines Edward
38 Pontis W. J.
38 Carr Miss

FAIRHAZEL GDN
Kilburn.
From 100 Priory rd.
G 5
1 Suarez F.

FAIRHAZEL GDN
Hampstead.
From Belsize rd.
G 6
RIGHT SIDE.
2 Timms Wm. Richar
    bootmaker
4 Radbourne Mrs.
    Fairfax mews
6 Atkins Henry
6 Atkins Miss, dressml
8 Williams George
    All Souls' Schools
10a Bradman R., fruiter
12 Manvell T. W., butch
    Goldhurst rd.
LEFT SIDE.
Basham Thomas, bo
    maker
1 Newstead J., sweep

3 Cowie David, boot-maker
Coleridge gardens
7 Rowe Joseph, baker and confectioner
9 Dimond Wm., oilman
11 Dimond Wm., cheesemonger
13 *Belsize Park Laundry Co., Limited*
Goldhurst rd.
15 Leon Leonard (Hazel house)

FELLOWS ROAD.
From 66 Adelaide rd.
F 7   **2**

LEFT SIDE.
1 Gervis Fredk. H., surg.
1 Gervis & Alford, surgns.
3 Bates Mrs. B. M.
5 Lloyd Edmund
7 Robinson Josiah
9 Edwards Mrs. Hannah
11 Laws James, architect
11 Laws Mrs. Jane
13 Browne Mrs.
15 Arnold Fred. Hudson
17 Busby Robert
19 Cowan Walter
21 Hornblower Jethro
23 Strauss Mrs. Seigfried
25 Styer William
27 Hawkins C. Thomas
Primrose hill rd.
29 Gordon Mrs. (Aboyne house)
31 Leonie Bernhardt
33 Bradshaw Henry
35 Crouch Charles
37 Hirsch Adolph
39 Hume John
41 Gush Mrs. William F.
43 Gibson Mrs.
45 Francis Mrs. L. C.
47 Schönberg D. Louis
49 Ford Wharton
51 Jourdain Neville
53 Mackeson Charles
55 Paterson Edward Alex.
57 Bartlett Thomas Henry
59 Faber Louis C.
61 Mannering Walter
63 Evans Mrs.
65 Voight L. R.
67 Clark Mrs. Sarah
69 Parker Frank Rowley

71 Grissell Mrs. M.
75 Biddle Arthur Cuming
77 Marriott Frederick
79 Hodge William Furber
81 Dobree George
Merton rd.
83 Porteous Lieut.-Col. Charles A.
85 Cahn Victor
87 Finch Arthur John
89 Cooper Henry James
91 George Edwin Herbert
93 Aspland Mrs.
95 Wood John
97 Whitfield Miss
101 Hall George
King's college rd.
125 Louis S.
127 Bensley Surg.-Major E. C.
133 James Christopher
135 Christie Duncan
139 Fryer Christopher
141 Reed Rev. A. (Ellenslea)
143 Young David
145 Clayton John Essex
151 Jamieson Miss J. S.
153 Hadfield Chas. Alfred
155 Ball H. A.
155 Giovana Mdme. Marie
157 McDowell Hy., artist
Winchester rd.
RIGHT SIDE.
2 Harben H. (Seaford lo.)
Steele's rd.
4 Bond Edward Philip
8 Hibberd H. C.
10 Harrod Mrs., ladies college
12 Smith Vernon
16 Blumenthal Mrs. E.
18 Strauss Max
24 Deed Martin
Primrose hill rd.
26 Preston Alfred
28 Leutner Albert
30 Shaw Mrs. R. H.
32 Brewster Edwin Fredk
34 Earl Thomas H.
36 Freeman Mrs.
38 Wellington James
44 Heydemann Paul
48 Fyfe James
50 Cox Cornelius
52 Judd Bertram Geo. S.
54 Maxton Mrs. M.

56 Edwards Henry Edwrd.
58 Ballance Mrs.
60 Videcoq A.
62 Haward Frederick
64 Van Praagh Isaac
66 Goslett Wm. Maynard
68 Harben Hy. Andrade
70 Cadman Lieut.-Colonel William E.
72 Hirsch Bernhard Chas.
Merton rd.
74 Syer John (Atherstone house)
76 Hudson J. W.
78 Maas H.
80 Rosenbaum Martin
82 Bayes Alfred Walter, artist
84 Aumonier J.
86 Gotch Thomas
88 Mannooch Alfred
96 Brown Gordon
98 Bodkin E. F.
102 Coke Alfred
King's college rd.
112 Park D. F.
128 Perram Rev. G. J.
132 Knox G. Walter
136 Corpe Sandenson, solicitor
138 Marshall Rev. James
140 Scott Miss
142 Child John
146 Roberts Jno. Robinson
Winchester rd.

FINCHLEY ROAD.
From Boundary rd. to the "Swiss Cottage."
G 6   **3**

RIGHT SIDE.
64 Jobson William Watson
66 Rutt Henry
66 Lister Mrs. Daniel
68 Gilbert Alfred
70 Falcke B.
70 Falcke Philip
72 Magnus Samuel
74 Reynolds Mrs. Fanny
76 Nicholson Daniel
78 Dever Henry
80 Hopkins Arthur
82 Riviere Briton, R.A.
Adelaide rd.
84 Rees John
86 Dane Thomas, surgeon
88 Milson Rchd. Hy., M.D.

FINCHLEY RD.—*contind.*

90 Evans William Henry, surgeon
92 Matthew John Wm.
94 Cooper John Foster
96 Merriman T. Mark, solicitor
   The Swiss Cottage, Alfred Savigear & Son
   Burdett William, jobmaster
   Brandon J. (Swiss cottage dairy)
   Upper Avenue rd.
   College crcs.
   LEFT SIDE.
77 Chatfield Rowland
79 Greenfield Harvey
81 Hands Mrs. Jane
83 Allen Mrs.
85 White Chas. Stewart
87 James William
89 Barnes Mrs.
91 Galbraith William R.
93 Daniell Afd.Bainbridge
97 *The High School for Boys ;* Dr. W. Brackebusch, head master
   Hilgrove rd.
99 Sinclair Frederick
101 Prince Julius
103 Blow Mrs. Emma
105 Chadwick Richard
107 Boys Chas. Octavius
107 Boys Miss
109 Bennett Joseph
111 Gullick Thomas
113 Swears Jas. Frederick
115 West Henry, stationer
115 Cuffley A., carver and gilder
116 Robertson Henry S., ladies' outfitter
117 Penhey Robert, fancy draper (Swiss lodge)
119 Lamb J. M., ironmonger
121*a* Saward Hy.,umbrella maker
121 Cale W., nurseryman and florist
123 Phillips H.,auctioneer and estate agent
125 Findlay Jas., cnfctnr.
   Metropolitan Railway Swiss Cottage Station
   Swiss ter.

FINCHLEY ROAD,
Child's Hill.
From Platt's lane Hampstead to The Castle.
   D 5
   LEFT SIDE.
   Burgess Hill.
   Haysman Jas. (Anglo-French college)
   Burgess Miss
   C h a m b e r s Thomas (Stratheden)
   Brown Clifton (Mayfield lodge)
   Scott Frank (Woodville house)
   Gascoine William(Melton house)
   Finchley Road.
   Russell Mrs. J. M. (Lyndale)
   Southwell Chas. (Gurrey lodge)
   Garfield Terrace.
4 Smeys William G., bootmaker
3 Hinton Mrs.,ladies'and children's outfitter
3 Hinton Henry
2 Peover George, dealer in curiosities
1 *Garfield Coffee Palace*
   Prospect rd.
   Finchley Road.
   Cox James,tobacconist
   Morse John, school (Somerville house)
   Private rd.
   Biggs J. M., surgeon
   Child's hill or Cricklewood lane
   RIGHT SIDE.
   Pattison rd.
   WESLEYAN METHODIST CHAPEL
   Devonshire pl.
   Ardwick Terrace.
5 Batho T. A. & Son, builders
4 Thomas Charles, greengrocer
3 Wreford Wm., butcher
2 Clark James, baker
1 Elliott Edward, grocer
   Child's hill lane
   Finchley Road.
   The Castle,Mrs. Randle

FINCHLEY NEW ROAD.
From Swiss Cottage to Platt's lane.
   F 6   **1, 2, 3 & 4**
   [*Left side Nos. 47 to 71 Ward 3 remainder, Ward 4. Right side in Ward 1.*]
   LEFT SIDE.
   Swiss Cottage Coffee Stall ; Mrs. Pitts, manageress
47 Boden Joshua Wigley
48 *London and South Western Bank, Lmtd.* (new premises)
48*a* Sangster A., chemist
48*a* Martin A.
49 Walford Walter Gilson M.D.
51 Phillips Walter
53 Kingston Wm. Biddy
55 Hetley James H.(Peterborough lodge)
57 Gonner Peter
59 Deed John Simpson
61 Henderson Richard
63 Spicer Misses
65 GoleRussell(TheFerns)
66 Mapleson Col. Henry (Hawthorne lodge)
67 Ridpath Edward
68 Biddle Frank H.
68 Biddle Mrs. Daniel
69 Reinhold Henry
70 Young Major.-Gen. R.
71 Turner Huy.(Blenheim lodge)
   Fairfax rd.
72 Cherer Mrs.(Newton lo)
73 Blyth Edmund Kell
74 Mummery Mrs. (Newton villa)
75 Harben Charles Henry (Highfield)
   Swiss Cottage Skating Rink ; J. Freeman, manager
   Goldhurst ter.
   Broadhurst gardens
   Fitzjohns' Parade.
15 *HARROW MUSIC SCHOOL ;* Misses Fox&Frost,principal
15 Bowdich John
15 Emanuel —

4 Farebrother, Ellis, Clark & Co., auctnrs.
3 Beahan M., dairy
3 Wills C. A., professor of music
2 *Victoria Wine Co.*
1 Munday Mrs., milliner
0 Butcher William H., builder, house agent, and undertaker
6 Farley H. A., stationer
5 Wharton and Turner, boot manufacturers
4 Troughton E. A., ladies' and children's outfitter
3 Davies Arthur, watchmaker and jeweller
2 Lewis H. J., chemist
1 Findlay J., confectnr.; post office
— *Canfield gardens*
Metropolitan Railway Finchley Road Station
Stevens Walter G., auctioneer
Booth Brothers, coal merchants
Boam Thomas & Co., coal merchants
Bacon & Co., lime, cement & brick mers.
Midland Railway Stn.
— *Lithos rd.*
L. & N. W. Railway Stn.
Mills J., coal merchant
Scoles Albert, lime and brick merchant
Hewett George, lime and brick merchant
Forsyth James, monumental sculptor (Ednam house)
Tasker Francis (Hedge Bank)
— *West end lane*
Stammers Rev. F. H., M.A. (Wellesley house)
— *Weech rd.*
— *Fortune green rd.*
RIGHT SIDE.
New College
Newth Rev. Prof. Saml., M.A., D.D.
— *College villas rd.*
The North Star, Lewis Ascott

Belmont.
4 Jacobs Henry
3 Clarke W. G.
2 Layland H.
1 Langley Miss
Finchley New Road.
TRINITY CHURCH
Sharpe Rev. Henry (Trinity lodge)
Dow Mrs. (Aberfeldie)
— *Netherall ter.*
— *Frognal*
— *Arkwright rd.*
Robson Thomas (Uphill house)
— *Oak hill park*
— *Fortune green lane*
New West End.
Kerswell Frederick Bartlett (Fern Combe)
2 Phillips Mrs.
3 Brand Charles (Holly lodge)
4 Punnett John
6 Negretti Henry Paul Joseph (Dovedale)
Finchley Road.
Cannon Misses (Kidderpore hall)
— *Platt's lane*

FITZJOHNS' AVNE.
From College ter. to Greenhill rd.
F 6   1
LEFT SIDE.
— *Maresfield gardens*
1 Gavan Alexander
3 Lewis I. (Hyme house)
5 Taylor John Mann (Norheads)
7 Tulloch James (Stambridge house)
9 Mason George H. (St. Dunstan's)
11 Feldenheimer Ferdinand (Eudora house)
13 Eberhart Chas. Leopold (Thuringia house)
15 Malcolm William (Birnam house)
17 Ince Francis, solicitor (St. Fagan's)
19 Carpenter Rev. J. E.
19 Buckton Mrs. (Leathes house)
21 Hay Alexander (Nettlestone)

23 Turnbull Chas. (Cotswold)
25 Coller Richard (Albemarle)
27 Hengler Chas. (Cambridge house)
29 Rider William (Kenwyn)
31 Miller Mrs. (St. Aidans)
33 Slade George Penkivel (Kanimbla)
35 Halliday J. (Bowerhayes)
37 Clarke John Moir, of Garthdee (Kinchyle)
— *Nutley ter.*
Kelly H. & E., estate office
47 Casella Louis Marino (Beauchêne)
49 Uzielli Theodore (Hillside)
51 Mansergh J. (Lune Lea)
53 Meyer Hartwig (Silcote)
55 Baxter Herbert Fleming (The Tower)
59 Ashton Jonas, M.A. (Raithby)
61 Long Edwin, R.A. (Kelston)
— *Netherhall ter.*
63 Lewis John (The Turrets)
65 Lawford Rowland
67 Roberts F. B.
69 Wild C. Kemp (Thornlea)
71 Odgers W. Blake (Sairle house)
RIGHT SIDE.
2 Pettie John (The Lothians)
4 Elgood George J. (Branksome)
6 Holl Frank, R.A. (The Three Gables)
8 Snow Henry. (Fernleigh)
10 Morell Dr. (Clevelands)
12 Fairfax Mrs. Charles (Mayfield)
14 Cole Chas. (Tregenna)
16 Tyer Edwd. (Horneck)
18 Bird William (Grosvenor lodge)

FITZJOHNS' AVNE.—*cntd.*

20 Brown Harold (Howe-foot)
22 Snowden Joseph (Ab-botsford)
24 Harraden Samuel (Homeside)
26 Green George Sangster (Stafford house)
28 Bowen G. D. (St. Winifred's)
30 Morison James Cotter (Clairvaux)
32 Carvalho R. N. (Lam-orna)
36 Cuff C. R. (Lavant house)
38 Farmiloe J.(Montrose)
40 Hornor Allan M.
42 Harris Richard
44 Barton C. A. (Nutley)
Nutley gardens
50 Woodall Corbet, C.E.
52 Johnson David (Cre-mona)
54 Drummond Captain Alfred M.
56 Lewis Robert (Heath-cote)
60 Dakin T. B.
62 Rosenheim H. (High-field house)
64 Channell Arthur (Whit-well house)
66 Spiller William
Daleham gardens
Lyndhurst rd.
68 Dockrell William R. (The Conduit Lodge) Chamberlain E., nur-seryman and florist

Fitzjohns' Mansions,
see Netherhall ter.

Fitzjohns' Parade,
see Finchley new rd.

FLASK COTTAGES.
From 67 Flask walk.
E 6   *1*
1 Dyter John
2 Saggs Frederick
3 Brumby Geo., coal dlr.

FLASK WALK.
From 42 High st.
E 6   *1*

RIGHT SIDE.
2 Harrison Joseph,btchr.
4 Rosbrook John, boot and shoe maker
6 & 8 Martin G. J.,cheese-monger
10 Davies Stephen, baker
12 Jordan Edwd., tbccnst.
The Flask Tavern, Jas. Joseph Freeman
16 Bradbury George, zinc worker
18 Titchener Jsph., grocer
20 Watt Alexander
22 Smith Charles
24 Norris E.
26 Newson George
28 Jones George
30 Styche Miss E.
32 Woodward J.
34 Starling Frederick
36 Hayter William
38 Hepburn D.,bootmaker
40 AdamsW.J.N.,carpntr.
42 Holder John
44 Ringe Charles
46 Sheffield John,carpntr.
48 Jennings Charles Hy.
50 Curtis Mrs., laundress
56 Putt Mrs., grocer
Bryan Benjamin (Lau-der cottage)
LEFT SIDE.
1 Johnson John, oilman
3 MARTIN THOMAS, bootmaker, leather & grindery warehouse
5 Briggs Mrs., hairdrsr.
7 Holmes H., fishmonger
9 Frampton William, greengrocer
11 & 13 Sharpe C. & J., bottle merchants
15 Anderson Chas. Fredk., hairdresser
17 Cheshire Richard
19 Woods Arthur
21 Darling Alfred, police inspector
23 Lowe Thomas
25 Stedall Thomas James
27 Slight Mrs.
29 Hawker Alfred Chris., decorator

31 Hilderley George
33 Grey Henry, builder and contractor
35 Herbert Mrs.
37 Jenkinson Daniel
39 Dowse John
41 Davey Horace
43 Lilley Thomas A.
45 Cooper Edward
47 Frisby Robert, jun.
49 Laspee Arthur de
51 Hawkins Charles
Lutton ter.
53 Bowen James
55 Vine Thomas William
57 Peall John
59 Pope Joseph
61 Donelan James
63 Horne James
65 Bingham Mrs. R.
67 Bridges Frank
Murray pl.
Flask cottages
Wetherall pl.
69 Lovell Mrs. Peter
71 Ray Miss (Mount cott Stubbings Frederick (Catherine cottage)

FLEET MEWS.
From Upper Park ter.
E 8
Cripps Mrs. A., lndrs
Mitchell Geo.,vet. frg
Paul William, sweep

FLEET ROAD.
From Southampton rd. t *South end green.*
E 7
1bFarley James, grocer
1aHayslep Mrs.M.,tbcns
2aSleven James P.,watch maker and jeweller
3a *Duckett Farm Dair Co.;* John Saunder manager
4aEddy G., builder
South Hampstea Working Men's Clu and Institute; Roberts, hon. sec.
St. Saviour's Schools Mission Rooms; Cha Mackeson, lay read
Park rd.
1 Fairchild Geo., groce

2 Raby Edmund, cnfctnr.
3 Rudkin Henry, builder
3 Rudkin Mrs. F. M.,
  newsagnt. & tobccnst.
4 Hook Wm., coff. rooms
5 Tailby George, butcher
6 Moore Edwin, bootmkr.
8 Hobbs William Henry,
  estate & house agent
9 Mott William
0 Salter Mrs. Emma,
  dressmaker
0 Staniforth B., slater
1 Lynch Richd., gasfitter
2 Briggs Amos
3 Green Joseph, wood
  turner
6 Hall Charles, plasterer
0 Vinall Mrs. Elizabeth
  (Fleet laundry)
1 Green Edwin, acount-
  ant and debt collector
3 Hawes George
4 Chapman Edwd., baker
  and grocer
Upper Park rd.
Lower Lawn rd.
  The Stag, Henry Coffin
Bartra*w* Terrace.
3 Stewart & Sons, book-
  sellers and stationers
Cressy rd.
1 Barnden   Cornelius,
  greengrocer
Fleet Road.
5 Aynscombe Bros., grcrs.
  and provision dealers
6 Crudginton Wm. Jno.
7 Crudginton John
8 German George
9 Almond Thomas
0 Whittle Mrs. Sarah
1 Williams Geo. Lwrnce
2 Hunt —
3 Hewat Mrs.
4 Watson George
5 Jones Samuel
6 Jones Albert, fishmngr.
8 Hodge Onslow
9 Vincent William
0 Pryor William
1 Randall D. H.
2 Tucker Joseph
3 Drinkwater Edwd. Frs.
4 Pratt James
5 Hook William
6 Gunby Henry John

47 Hook William
48 Clark Jno., insrnce.agnt
49 Farmer Mrs. Mary
49 Melleney Miss, dress-
   maker
50 Preston Frederick, hairdresser
51 Moule George
52 Stalder Thomas
53 Bowman George, beer
   retailer
54 Pearce James
55 Snow & Collins, con-
   fectioners
56 Plumer William
57 Gale Mrs. Sarah
58 Butcher Isaac
60 Bateman & Mead, green-
   grocers
61 Simons William Thos.
   John
62 Burd Thomas Charles
63 Bradberry Jsph., cheesemonger
64 Hamilton Wm., baker
65 Astrope John Charles,
   oilman
66 *The Hampstead Trad-
   ing Bank, Limited ;*
   J. Burman Rosevear,
   secretary
66 *The Hampstead 725th
   Starr-Bowkett Build-
   ing Society ;* W. H.
   Pearson, secretary
66 *The Fire Fly Coffee
   Tavern*
66 *The Hampstead Life,
   Fire & Accident In-
   surance Offices ;* J.
   Burman Rosevear,
   manager

FOLEY AVENUE.
From 15 Well walk.
D 7   **1**
2 Wilkinson Joseph
4 Peddar S. H.

FORDWYCH ROAD,
Kilburn.
From Maygrove rd.
F 4   **4**
RIGHT SIDE.
1 *West Middlesex Water
  Works ;*   Cornelius
  Robert Cleverly, in-
  spector

3 Nugent James Spencer
5 Turnbull George C.
7 Clarke F. G. B., M.D.
9 Henry Michael
11 Spyers Arthur
13 Salmon Mrs.
15 Gerds C.
17 Compton James
19 Watkins Rev. W. J.
21 Ritson Hugh Daniel
23 Ebsworth Robert M.
25 St. Stephens Ragnar
27 Coulthard Christopher
29 Cuming Captain Fred-
   erick George
31 Elliott Edward
33 Wright Charles Edwd.
35 Wood W. G.
37 King W. H.
39 Theakstone Fawding-
   ton)
41 Parnell Joshua, builder
43 Hutchinson   William
   Hunter
45 Lane Gilbert (Holling-
   ton)
45 *Abbey Road and St.
   John's Wood Perma-
   nent Building Socty.;*
   Gilbert Lane, sec.
   ST. CUTHBERT'S CH.
   LEFT SIDE.
2 Milton John
4 Stainer Alfred
6 Pott Charles
8 Smith Fullarton (Fern
  lea)
10 Spratt Mrs. (Castelnau
   lodge)
12 Bowerbank John A.,
   solicitor
Garlinge rd.

FORTUNE GREEN,
Kilburn.
*From West end to
Finchley rd.*
E 5   **4**
LEFT SIDE.
Notman Capt. Henry
W. (Cholmley lodge)
1 Stevens George
2 Fox Alfred, labourer
3 Barber Wm., plasterer
4 *The Prince of Wales,*
  John Coles
5 Howlett Robt., gardnr.

FORTUNE GREEN—*contd.*
6 Butler Mrs.
7 Mitchell Henry
8 Gibbons Charles
9 Judge John
Hampstead Cemetery ;
W. D. Cochrane,
superintendent
RIGHT SIDE.
Thistlewaite Frederick
(The Cottage)
Underwood & Sons,
cemetery masons and
monumental sculptrs.

FROGNAL.

*From Finchley rd. to
Branch hill.*

E 6   *1*
LEFT SIDE.
⎯*Arkwright rd.*
50 Greenaway Alfred John
Fletcher Mrs. Robert
(St. Nicholas)
Tate Edwin (Frog-
nal priory)
Champneys Mrs.
(Priory hill)
Powell Thos. Edmund
(Priory end)
Smith James (Manor
cottage)
Tagart Misses (Manor
lodge)
Champneys Basil
(Manor farm)
Hooper George (Hart-
lands)
⎯*West end lane*
Anderson James (Frog-
nal park)
Prance Reginald Heber
Anderson William D.
(The Ferns)
Husband Mrs. T. (Manor
house)
⎯*Reddington rd.*
Read William T. (Holly
Bank)
⎯*Oak hill park*
Burnett Frank (The
Oaks)
Devitt Henry (Bay
tree lodge)
Rowe Mrs. (Frognal
house*)*

Weir Mrs. (Upper Frog-
nal lodge)
Lea George Harris
(Montagu grove)
Inman Mrs. (Frognal
rise)
RIGHT SIDE.
⎯*Arkwright rd.*
Pfeil Frederick John
(Priory lodge)
Scripps Mrs. (Frognal
cottage)
Sulivan Miss (The Man-
sion)
Leach Nomy (Florence
cottage)
Swords Thos. (Jasmine
house)
Bremner Thomas, jun.
(Acacia)
Reid Thomas (Plas
Gwyn)
Raven Miss J. A. (Grove
cottage)
⎯*Mount Vernon*

GAINSBOROUGH GARDENS.

D 7
From Well walk.
Timewell Henry Borne

GARDNOR ROAD.

From New end sq.
E 6   *1*
Dennis John (Gardnor
house)
1 Ellis Alexander H. B.
2 Cullis William
3 Hurst Mrs.
4 Curtis George
5 Pearce George
6 Stanlake Robert
7 Hooton Richard
8 Arscott George
9 Found Nthnl., carpntr.
10 Howard John Henry
11 Faulkner E.
12 Baker Moses
13 McGennes Francis
13a Jolly Charles
13b Plum Charles
13c Morgan Charles Henry
14 Carter Mrs. Ellen
15 Myson John
16 Rumbold Richard
17 Bradbury John

18 Spiring Wm. Sainsbury
19 Tyler Henry
20 Andrews Jas., bootmkr.

Garfield Terrace,

*see Finchley rd. Child's
hill.*

GARLINGE ROAD,
Kilburn.
From High rd.
F 4   *4*
LEFT SIDE.
1 McGowan H., builder
3 Speyer S. (Belsize lo.)
5 Edwards W. S. (Ar-
denlea)
7 Hartley Thomas P.
(Uffcalme)
RIGHT SIDE.
2 Anderson Mrs. (Wind-
sor house)
4 Debenham S. J., solctr.
(Holmstadt)
6 Cox Leonard P. (Buck-
ingham house)
8 Isaac Arthur B. (Os-
borne house)
10 Tilly A., L.S.A., surgeon
(Marlborough house)
12 Pratt Mrs. (Clarence
house)

GASCONY AVENUE
Kilburn.
*From 218 High rd. to
West end lane.*
G 5   *4*
RIGHT SIDE.
2 Smith John Charles,
surgeon
4 Claxton Alfred
6 Pavitt Mrs.
8 Piper Mrs.
10 Schuler Mrs. Leon
14 Sitford William John
16 Tofts Rev. Francis
18 Hunt —
34 Bond R.
36 Machell L., bootmakr.
42 Beaton Mrs.
44 Walker Mrs.
⎯*Kingsgate rd.*
St. Ann's Terrace.
8 Tice Mrs.

7 Banford William
6 Hayes Gwyn Clifford
5 Carisbrick Mrs.
4 Allen Charles
3 Clark Mrs.
2 Allen J. E.
1 Lancaster John
══Smyrna rd.

Gascony Avenue.

WalkerMrs.(Ashleigh)
Lowrie Mrs. W. (Maisonnette)
Searle Miss (Glastonbury house)
Wessels Mrs. (Bremen house)

LEFT SIDE.

1 Scott James
3 Thompson Rev. John Charles
5 Watson Mrs. G.
7 Taplin Mrs.
9 Heilbron Selim
11 Rogers Mrs.
13 Allum Francis Henry
15 Blanchard J. J. W.
17 Prichard Richd.Russell
19 Moore Mrs.
21 Rogers John
23 Hills Charles
27 Handford Ebenezer
29 Moxon Henry, architect and surveyor
31 Gerbert R.
33 Jolly Mrs., dressmaker
35 Rowsell H.
37 Reinganum Victor
39 Nathan Lewis
41 Gregory Miss Teresa
43 Moss Miles
45 Rolfe H.
47 Denton George
47 Hardwicke R. R., surg.
══Kingsgate rd.
Cotter Miss (Park ho.)
Daly Miss (Ethel ho.)
Crumplen Benjamin (Allerton)
Dherang George (Espérance)

Springfield.

1 Redhead Alfred
2 Fryer Miss
3 Walton W. G.
4 Fletcher Thomas
5 Adeney A. W.

GAYTON CRES.
From Gayton rd. to Willow rd.

E 6   1

1 Leach Miss
2 Lalor Miss
2 Banks Miss
3 Holford Mrs. J. H.
5 Dashwood Lady
6 Atkinson Miss
7 Hyslop W. J.
8 Mayor Miss
9 Tyson Mrs.
10 Stewart John
11 Cox E. W.
12 Besant Walter
13 Phillips John
14 Dibdin Lewis Tona, barrister

GAYTON ROAD.
From High st. to Willow road.

E 6   1

1 Willis James
2 *The Orphanage ;* Miss McInnes
3 Clowser Richard
4 Acret J. M. & C. H. J., dental surgeons
5 Cross John
6 Walker George P., gardener
7 Clarke Mrs. W.
8 Coombes Charles
9 Till William, builder
10 Cooper Mrs. J.,M.R.C.P. (Hampstead High school)
11 Hamilton Thomas
12 England George
14 Donnoven Miss
15 Ware Mrs. Robert
16 & 17 Crawley Joseph
18 Paterson Mrs. A. H.
19 Vincent Dr. Charles, professor of music
20 Rice Henry John
21 & 22 Marshall W. R. (Crescent house schl.)
23 Beach Benjamin
24 Osborn George
25 DrewryMrs.H. Stewart
26 Dibb Mrs. Ashton
27 Potter George
28 Sherratt Thomas
29 Wills William

30 Russell Charles
31 Coit Mrs.
32 Clarkson William Hill
33 James Miss
34 Murray Andrew, M.D.
35 Comyn Miss
36 Simpson Thomas
38 Anderson John E. (Hampstead nursery)
══Gayton cres.
39 Hudson Mrs. (Delmar house)
39 Hudson Misses, ladies' school(Delmar house)
40 Hudson Misses, boys' preparatory school
41 Cann Alfred Henry .
42 Capp Joseph
43 Webb Thomas
44 Simmonds Mrs. Ann
45 Pease William
47 Plaster Mrs. Emma
50 Jones Misses,dressmks.
51 Holmes Henry
52 Smith Joseph
53 GardinerMiss,drssmkr.
54 Foskett George
55 Payne Miss, dressmkr.
56 Thompson William
56 *Charity Organization Society ;* Hy.Toynbee, secretary
57 Snodgrass Misses E. and F., dressmakers
58 Pearce William
59 Brookson Charles
60 Rider W. R.
60 Adams T., undertaker
61 RichardsonJ.T., manufacturing ironmonger and sanitary engineer
62 Kay Miss, stationer

Gipsy Lane,
West Hampstead,
now numbered Broadhurst gardens.

GOLDEN SQUARE.
From Heath st.

E 6   1

2 Busby Mrs.
1aChester Daniel
2aHawkins James
3aCook William
4 Caraher Henry
5 Hays Christopher

GOLDEN SQ.—*continued*
6a Bass Alfred
1 Wiltshire George
2 Hunt William
3 Clarke Eli
5a and 6 Casey Daniel
7 Gilbert George
8 Eaton Mrs., laundry

GOLDEN YARD.
Between Holly mount and
57 Heath st.
E 6   **1**
   Hadrill George
2 Warne Mrs.
3 Dale Mrs.
5 Quinton James
6 Tink James
7 Hall John

Golder's Hill Cottages and Terrace,
see North end.

GOLDHURST TER.
From Finchley rd. to
Priory rd.
F 6   **4**
   LEFT SIDE.
30 Williams Joseph Crew
    (Wimborne house)
29 Fox Miss
28 Mohr Mrs. (Brightholme)
27 Geary Thomas
26 Groves Edward (Walmer house)
25 Reid Mrs.
24 Knight John
23 Francis Reginald
21 Winn Jas. Michell, M.D.
20 Smith Mrs.
7 Burnett Mrs. Frances
6 Borrow William Henry
4 Stott Mrs.
3 Borthwick Francis
2 Woodcock Mrs.
1 Kellond Charles A.
  Fairhazel gardens
1 Walton Miss
2 Harrison J.
3 Wrottesley Rev. Francs. John, B.A.
4 Cave Frederick
5 Nisbet James
6 Thies Conrad
7 Makie Mrs.

8 Gillington John
9 Hockley Anthony
10 Mitchell Robert
11 Forster Mrs.
12 Home George
13 Jacob Samuel
14 Nutt W. R.
15 Smith Alfred
17 Horrocks F. J.
18 Lanza Madame Laura
19 Holden A. W.
20 Cornwell Mrs.
   RIGHT SIDE.
66 Thompson John
65 King Rev. Richd., M.A.
66 Hanbury Mrs.
63 Almore F.
62 Matthews William
61 Groom George
    Wyatt Vitruvius(Ivor)
    Revell Col. Blackett
    (Shirland lodge)

GOLDSMITH PL.,
Kilburn.
From 36 High rd.
G 5   **4**
1 and 2 Hunt Mrs., shirt and collar dresser
1a Marsh Miss, grocer
5 Woodland John, genl. shop
   Home for Blind Children; Miss Wooderidge, matron
7 Brown Mrs. T. H.
  Springfield gardens
8 Newman J.
9 Murch P.
9 Murch Mrs., wardrobe dealer

Goldsmith's Gardens,
see Bell ter.

GRAFTON TER.
From Child's hill lane.
D 5
1 Burton Benjamin
2 Bartrum T.
3 Weston Alfred
4 Hannell Henry
5 and 6 Jenkins Charles
7 Webb William Robert
8 Green David

Granville Houses,
see Child's hill.

Granville Ter.,
see Cricklewood lane.

GREENHILL.
From Rosslyn hill to
High st.
E 6   **1**
   Griffiths H.J.(Belmont)
   Platt Jas. (Rookwood)
   WESLEYAN CHAPEL
  Prince Arthur rd.

GREENHILL ROAD.
From Church row to
Fitzjohns' avenue.
E 6   **1**
   RIGHT SIDE.
   Brackenbury Capt. E. F. (Lincoln house)
   Williams Thos. (Yarth house)
   Mure Arthur (Hill ho.)
   Dalziel George(Wooler house)
  Ellerdale rd.
   Sherman R. Tatham (St. John's)
   Haynes George (Kenmore)
   Johnston Charles(West view)
   Cocks Robert Macfarlane (Jesmond)
   Prance Robert Rooke, M.D. (Rookeslea)
  Prince Arthur rd.
   Watkins Charles A. (Rosemont)
  Arkwright rd.
   Lyon Benjamin Abbott (Uplands)
   Bompas Henry M., Q.C. (Abingdon house)
   LEFT SIDE.
   Sailors' Orphan Girls' Home; Mrs. Smart, matron
   Watts Husin William (The Hive)
   Sewell Charles John (Birnam villa)
   Burdon-Sanderson Miss (Branksome)
   Roberts John Henry, F.R.C.S. (Hill crest)

Beard Miss M. L. (1 Greenhill villas)
Baynes Mrs. (Mount view)
Beard Miss C. (Mount view)
Prince Arthur rd.
Brooks Henry (Mount grove)

GREVILLE ROAD,
St. John's Wood.
G 5   4

LEFT SIDE.
1 *Kilburn Provident Medical Institute;* T. Millachip, secretary
1 *St. John's Ambulance Station, No. 9 District*
1 *Parish of St. John's, Hampstead, Public Vaccination Station*
1 *Young Men's Christian Association*
1 *Metropolian Association for Befriending Young Servants*
Manchester mews
3 Wroughton Mrs. Genl.
5 Wills Peter
7 Meyers Michael
9 Hamilton Miss
11 Kneller G. H.
13 Burford H. T. B., M.D.
Goldsmith pl.
15 Morton Thomas, M.D.
15 Morton&Willis, surgns.
15 Willis A. K.
17 Cooke James
19 Davis N. Newnhan
21 *North Western College;* J. R. Waddelow, B.A. OXON.
21 Waddelow W.
25 Lindsay William Hy.
27 Turner Mrs.
29 Atchison William (Elm bank)
31 Withers Alfred
33 Hodgson A. (Greville lodge)
Mortimer rd.
35 Gibbs Jas.(Howard lo.)
37 Russell Miss
Greville pl.
39 Perry & Co., jobmasters
Clifton hill

RIGHT SIDE.
6 Evill Edward
8 Willey Mrs.
10 Filton Walter
12 Somervail Mrs. C. R.
14 Levy David
16 Carr Mrs.
18 Jacobs Harry
20 Coleman Mrs.
22 Skeels Thomas
24 Weber Otto
26 Nash C.

GROVE COTTAGES.
From The Grove.
D 6   1
1 Batchelor R., locksmith
2 Chadd Mrs., laundress
3 Holmes Mrs., laundress
4 Brown Thomas
5 Taylor George
6 Dickens Mrs., laundress

GROVE PLACE.
From New end.
D 6   1
Cracknell Harry (Trellis cottage)
1 Charsley J., plumber
2 Brown John
3 Carter David
4 Roach William
5 Guy George, turncock
6 Dodd Thomas
Christchurch rd.

Grove Road.
From 1 Oakland ter. Cricklewood.

Grove Terrace,
see New end.

HAMPSTEAD GRN.
From Haverstock hill to Pond st.
E 7   2
St. Stephen's Church
Roper Frank
Mitchell Alexander D. (Tensleys)
Jennings F. T.
Maas Edward (Kenmore house)

Wilmer Miss C. (Elm tree house)
Lavington Ferres Wm. (Belgrave cottage)
8 Fellows Frank P.
7 Bradshaw Miss
6 Willis Mrs.
5 Myers George H.
4 Davies Alfred (Heathhurst)
3 King H. (Leverton house)
2 Way Thomas (Benthall house)

HAMPSTEAD HEATH.
D 6   1
Lavender Mrs. (Heath view)
Jack Straw's Castle, John Lane
Wright Mrs. H. (The Heath)
Spaniards Road.
Hodgson Mrs. (The Elms)
Hampstead Heath.
Bagehot Edward (Fern cottage)
Case Mrs.(Heath brow)
MacInnes Miss (Fern lodge)
Matheson H. (Heathlands)
Powell George Holt (Cedar lawn)
Hoare Francis (The Hill)
Farmer John S. (Heath lodge)
Owen-Jones Mrs. (Northcote house)
Lister Miss
East Heath rd.
Holford rd.
Barnett Rev. S. A., M.A. (Harrow lodge)
Marshall John T. (Hurst lodge)
Barratt Thomas J.
Nugent Charles Edward (Ludlow cottage)
Rodick Miss Janet P. (Gangmoor)

HAMPSTEAD SQ.
Near Christ Church.
D 6   *1*
1 Hall Rev. Newman
(The Ivy house)
2 Evans M. H.
4 Barter James
5 Broom William
9 Wiltshire Richard, carpenter
9 Wiltshire William, house decorator
8 Faulkner Mrs., laundrs.
7 Vine William, gardener
Lane Samuel A. (Vine house)
CHRIST CHURCH
Christ Church Schools
Kennedy Alex. B. W. (Lawn house)

HAMPSTEAD HILL GARDENS.
From Rosslyn hill.
E 7   *1*
1 Miller Andrew, M.D. (Blair-hyrne)
2 Parker Henry Watson
3 Evans Richard H.
4 Gordon Alexander
5 Brooks Henry J.
6 Gwynn Edmund, M.D., surgeon
7 Henderson Mrs. James
8 Pritchard Andrew Goring
9 Thompson Henry
10 Hibbert Arthur
11 Prentice Ridley
12 Gatliff Charles
Bell Geo. (Bramerton)
Holme Chas. (Hill side)
Green Charles (Charle-cote)
Lee H. J. B. (Sunnycote)
Spiller William Hutchinson (Fairlight)
Smith Benjamin Franklin (Holme house)
Collier T. (Etherow)
Garden Chas. (Aspens)
Merrick Wm (Wycliffe)
Selfe Thomas Vanderhorst (Thistleboon)
40 Despard Major W.
41 Jamieson Henry

42 Edwards Fredc. Yeats (Cromwell house)
43 Smith Mrs. Edward (Fairfield house)
43a Fripp Alfred D.
44 Leake T. W., pharmaceutical chemist
45 Hughes W. H., bootmkr.
46 Fox H., butcher
47 BRUMBRIDGE JAS., dairyman
48 Nicholls Henry, plumbr
49 *The Roebuck Hotel*, G. F. Dettmer

HARLEY ROAD.
From 211 Adelaide rd.
G 7   *3*
RIGHT SIDE.
2 Marshall Charles E.
4 Meeson Alfred
6 Dickens H. P. T.
8 Obermayer A. J.
10 Fase Berkeley William
12 Sullivan John
18 Calkin J. W. A.
20 Perino Joseph
22 Row Rev. Prebendary C. A., M.A.
24 Telfer Mrs.
LEFT SIDE.
1 Bacon Mrs. J. L.
3 Clark Melville
5 Watson George
New Eton & Middlesex Cricket Ground; J. H. Hanson, proprietor

HAVERSTOCK HILL
From Chalk Farm Station to Rosslyn hill.
F 8   *2*
LEFT SIDE.
Dickson & Son, btchrs.
The Adelaide Hotel, Frederick Vinall
Adelaide rd.
Bennett Deane, physician (Eton villa)
3 Triems Miss
5 Humphreyson John
7 Russell Mrs. Edwin
9 Frank Gustav
11 Carman Henry
13 Borrajo Edward M.
17 Blackley C. A.

19 Wedderburn Mrs.
21 Holmes Miss
23 Lawless Albt. Anthony
25 Gill Francis
27 Thompson Mrs.
29 Dean George Henry
31 Reading Miss
33 Pettitt Henry
35 Freeman Jno. (Higham house)
37 Barker Frank William Sizer (Florence ho.)
39 Holmes Misses, Queen's college for ladies (Bellefield house)
41 Kerslake John
43 Parker Reginald Amphlett, solicitor
45 Pritchard William
47 Burgess Miss C. E. college for ladies
49 Birley Samuel, M.D.
51 Pede Thomas (Belgrave house)
53 Smith Richard T., M.D.
57 Laing Mrs. David
59 Phillips Arthur
Eton rd.
61 Alford Fredk. Stephen S., F.R.C.S., L.A.S., surg.
61 Gervis & Alford, surgns.
63 Newton William
65 Bedingfield J. (Richmond villa)
67 Banford James Wm. (Cambridge villa)
69 Holcombe Joseph
71 Woodthorpe Mrs.
73 Wright Mrs., ladies' & children's outfitter
75 Harper Edwin H., music warehouse
77 Marks & Co., dyers
79 Barton Mrs., fancy repository
79 Boodle Mrs.
79 Lee Nelson J., surveyor of taxes
81 Neame Norman, grocer; post office
Steele's rd.
83 Staples Geo. R., draper
85 Stansfield R., M.P.S., dispensing chemist
87 Gudgeon Robt., fancy draper
89 Sharp Benj., fruiterer

91 Smith Edward, cheese-
    monger
93 Randall T. G., butcher
95 Phipps W., fishmonger
97 *The Sir Richard Steele*,
    Henry Clifford
    Steele's Studios.
1 Robertson H. R., artist
1a Whalley Adolphus J.
2 Green Aveling, artist
3 Stretch Matthew, artist
4 Hetherington Ivystan,
    artist
    Haverstock Hill.
99 Bellamy Thos. (Wych-
    combe)
=*England lane leading
    to Elizabeth ter.*
101 St. Mary's Convent
    Girls' & Boys' Schools
103 Angus John
105 Martin Mrs.
109 Sheppard Vincent
    (Chesnut lodge)
    Babidge Richd., wheel-
    wright (Cricket cot.)
113 WOOD RICHARD J.
    (Haverstock hill and
    Bedford nurseries)
115 Allchin Sidney (Man-
    sel cottage)
117 Wood R. J.
117a Wordley Jas. (High-
    field)
119 Aspinall Wm. (Wood-
    stock)
121 Brooks Benjamin
123 Parnell Wm. (Spen-
    cer villa)
125 Booth Allen
133 Russell John, nursery
135 Trudgett Henry Wm.,
    jobmaster
143 Cordery Mrs.
147 Blackstone E.
149 Lescher F. Harwood
    (Oak lodge)
151 Maple J. (Bedford lo.)
=*Haverstock ter.*
153 Mitford Robert Henry
155 Goodman Thomas
    Warner
157 Kent William
159 Ward Charles A.
161 Harrison Miss Lucy
    Woodd Robt. Ballard
    (Woodlands)

Binny Wm. (Hillfield)
Hampstead Vestry Hall
=*Belsize avenue*
=*Ornan rd.*
Hill Mrs. C. (Ivy bank)
    RIGHT SIDE.
2 Reynolds Joseph, beer
    retailer
4 Wells William, port-
    manteau maker
6 Cotterell Henry L.,
    coffee rooms
8 Day William Henry,
    fancy draper
10 Tremari & Camoccio,
    confectioners
12 Weaver George, tobac-
    conist
14 Bacon E., umbrla. mkr.
16 Cork W. J., fruiterer
18 Salter Henry Williams,
    watchmaker
18a Fry E. A., oilman
20 Harding Richard, buil-
    der, decorator, under-
    taker, and valuer
22a Lambden Edward
24 Ward John Charles
    (The Retreat)
28 Read W. de Courtney
    Board School
30 Glover Miss C.
32 Blackborn Mrs.
34 Osborn Mrs. Sarah
    (Holly lodge)
36 Lawrence J. E.
38 Ravenscroft Horatio
40 Talbot Charles (Alton
    lodge)
44 Cart Rev. H., B.A.
46 Debenham William E.,
    photographer (Mas-
    singham house)
48 Harley Thomas, M.D.
    surgeon (The Lawn)
50 West & Boreham, bldrs.
50a Brodie Miss, kinder-
    garten
52 Massingham William
54 Capleton —
56 Pugh John O. (Vincent
    villa)
56a Dean Geo. Henry, court
    dressmaker
60 Wright W. J. (Augusta
    villa)
62a Wiggins Wm., cnfctnr.

62 Patterson Mountain,
    surgeon-dentist (Mars-
    den villa)
62 DOLMAN & PEARCE,
    auctioneers
=*Prince of Wales rd.*
=*Queen's cres.*
=*Maitland park rd. and
    villas*
    Orphan Working Schl.
    CONGREGATIONAL
    CHAPEL
    OXENDEN PRESBYTE-
    RIAN CHURCH
74 Cant Benjamin (Holly-
    well house)
76 Cutts Rev. Edward L.,
    D.D. (Holy Trinity vic-
    arage)
    Dawson Terrace.
1 Martin F., coiffeur
2 Upton K., W. and M.,
    milliners
3 Birkett A., dyer and
    cleaner
4 Forster F. A., A.P.S.,
    chemist
5 Galer Miss, servants'
    registry
    Haverstock Hill.
82 Hutchings T. P., boot-
    maker (Forres house)
84 Gaillard Frank & Co.,
    wine merchants
84 "Nth. Western Gazette"
    Office, M. Smyth
84 Smyth Misses, milliners
    and dressmakers
86 French Joseph, cnfctnr.
88 Edwards & Coxwell,
    corn merchants
90 Smith James, baker &
    confectioner
92 Fowler Bros., stationers
94 *The Load of Hay*,
    William Thos. Marsh
96 Monro George
98 Stroh Augustus
100 Ball Walter Frederick
102 Houghton George
    (Selborne house)
104 Oetzmann John
108 Gundry Joseph
110 Blythe James Nisbit
=*Park rd.*
112 Barham George (Dane-
    hurst)

HAVERSTOCK HILL—*cntd*
114 Hill Mrs.
116 Paris Thomas Ruffle
118 Barnes Mrs.
120 Tuchmann Leo
122 Read John Walter
124 Niemann F. G. B.
126 Wood R. J. (Bedford nursery)
128 Gloag J. R.
130 Stock Eugene
132 Wœrn Lieut. Carl
134 Carter John, jun. (Oakwood house)
136 Cooke John
138 Fry Danby Palmer
140 Andrew John May, M.D.,M.R.C.S.E., surg.
148 Ashworth Mrs. (Crown lodge)
150 Burford &Son, builders (Crown cottage)
152 Paveley F. E., cheesemonger (Dorset ho.)
154 *The Haverstock Hotel*, A. Blackmore
⸺ *Upper Park rd.*
⸺ *Lawn rd.*
156 Scott Mrs.
158 Mallet Rev. Henry F., M.A. (Thanet house)
160 Harcourt Rbt. (Stanley house)
162 Le Riche Edward William (Ormesby ho.)
164 Lyon George
166 Lawrence Mrs. E.
168 Weight James
170 Beach George
172 Lund William Thomas Bullen
174 Birch Thos. (Sycamore house)
176 Baily Walter (Auchmore)
178 Bonacina Ludovico
180 Beeton Mrs.
182 Bagshawe Wm. H. G., Q.C., barrister
184 Haines Fredk., F.S.A. (Boreham house)
186 Perry Joseph J. (Silverholme)
188 & 192 Chamberlain Edmund (Haverstock hill nursery)
Morley Robt. (Studio)

194 Cotton Mrs.
196 Orton William
198 *The Convent of the Sisters of Providence;* Sister Adeline, lady superior
200 *Hampstead Branch Post and Telegraph Office*
202 Taylor Mrs. E., dairy
204 Walton T., analytical chemist
206 Carter Ernest, fancy repository
208 Ross Miss, haberdasher
210 *The George Inn*, H. P. Godsel
210 Trudgett Henry Wm., livery stables
Convent of the Sisters of Providence (Bartram)

HAVERSTOCK TER.
From 151 Haverstock hill.
F 7   2
1 Duncan —
2 Kett Rev. C. W., M.A.
3 Quaritch Bernard
4 Kelly John
5 Gow Mrs. Mary Owen
6 Brooks Arthur
7. Stone Simeon (The Hollies)
Wilson Miss (Gilling lodge)

Heath Cottages,
see East Heath rd.

HEATH END,
Hampstead Heath.
D 6   1
Peache Rev. Alfred (The Firs)
Stedall Henry (Heath end)
The Spaniards' Hotel, W. J. Hudson

HEATH MOUNT.
From 37 Heath st.
D 6   1
Hayter John, bath chair proprietor
Simmonds Mrs.
1 Watts Mrs.

2 Clayton William
3 Weir James
4 Brough Wm. Stanley
Walker Rev. Clemen
Frank, M.A. OXON (Heath mount)

Heath Rise,
see Willow rd.

HEATH STREET.
From High st. to the Heath
D 6   3
1 Courtney George H. bootmaker
2 Humphrey C. E., ward robe dealer
3 May Henry, fruiterer
4 & 5 James John G. draper
6 Nockells W., fishmngr
7 Lauezzari Friedrich tobacconist
8 TOOLEY T., job master (established 1835)
9 Humphreys Frederick corn dealer
11 Jones Albert, ironmngr
⸺ *Back lane*
12 Oxford E. W., fishmonger
13 *The Horse and Groom* Thomas Davidge
14 Gardner George, tailo
15 Edge Frank, tobaccnst
16 Pritchard Geo., builde
17 Street Geo., cowkeepe
18 Whitehorn Thomas watchmaker
19 Ritchie Mrs.H., milline
20 Woodward J., farrier
21 Bridgman Edwd., boot maker
HEATH ST. CHAPEL
Heath Street British Schools
Claremont Terrace.
1 Symmons Miss
1 Lea G. H.
1 Lea John
2 Ware Richard
3 Russell W. J.
Heath Street.
24 Pritchard J., cowkeepe
25 Thompson Francis

26 Maxwell James Laidlaw, M.D.
27 Reid Miss
28a Hawkins Henry, confectioner
28 Batchelor John
29 Foster George, chemist
— *New end*
30 Archer James, baker and confectioner
Express Dairy Company (Limited)
— *Elm row*
31 Groom John
32 Hammond Edgar, btchr
33 Hammond Miss H., fancy draper
34 Borley Alfred, grocer
Jones John P., gardener (Mansfield cottage)
Pattison John (Stamford lodge)
Jones Mrs. (Northcote house)
— *Heath mount*
37 Smith A., grocer
38 Kessels F., dining rms.
39 Jackson J.
40 Lansdown B., fruiterer
43 Davey F., sweets dealer
44 Arnold James J., newsagent
45 *The Coach and Horses*, R. P. Ware
46 Bohlich Adam, tailor
47 Wiltshire Wm., builder and decorator
48 BOWEN ALFRED WALTER, photographer
Baker D., jobmaster
— *The Mount*
57 & 70 Roff & Son, bldrs., plumbers & decorators
58a Davies C. & J., bakers
58 Harris Frederick Wltr., bootmaker
59 Forster James, oilman
60 Ruth E., watchmaker
61 *The Nag's Head*, John Hawkins
62 Dalley John, carver and gilder
63 Burr Mrs. Sarah Ann, tobacconist
Peters Joseph (Prospect cottage)

Messinger J. H. (Prospect house)
64 Staines & Son, china and glass dealers
65 Goord C. W., fancy repository
66a Moseley Wm., upholstr.
66 Poole Frederick, furniture warehouse
67 *Blue Ribbon Coffee Palace*, Welch and Thorpe
68 Buckle Geo., fruiterer and greengrocer
69 Stanley W., confectnr.
69 Pottle Miss, dressmaker
69a Shave E. H., veterinary surgeon
71 Crowe Jno., undertaker
73 *Fire Brigade Station*; Jas. Pearse, engineer

Heath Villas,
see Vale of Health.

HEATHFIELD GARDENS.
From Squire's mount.
D 6   **1**
1 Cory William
3 Risk Bouverie
4 Kitchin Rev. James George, M.A.
5 Robertson John
6 Matheson Thomas
7 Hutton J. Edward
8 Turner Rev. Frdk. Storrs
9 Short Frederick George
10 Griffith D. C.
Hardcastle J. (Beechenden)
Stacey W. S. (Hillcote)
— *Holford rd.*
— *Hampstead sq.*

HEMSTALL ROAD,
Kilburn.
From Palmerston rd.
F 5   **4**
LEFT SIDE.
1 Howell Mrs., laundress
1 Howell Joshua
2 Harrison Chas., turner
— *Lowfield rd.*
4 Keele Charles
5 Green Geo., bricklayer
Lansdowne Terrace.
22 Hutchinson R. M.

20 Milde Frederick
18 Rush Arthur (Springfield house)
16 Guterbock George
12 Westlake Mrs.
10 Lindsay Mrs.
8 Wadd H. C.
2 Miller Arthur (Carrell house)
— *Hilltop rd.*
RIGHT SIDE.
Walden Edward, provision dealer (Kingsgate house)
— *Kingsgate rd.*
Trussell William, baker
2a Rolfe William, grocer
6 Rudderham Mrs., laundress
Allen J., builder (The Limes)

Hermitage Villas,
see Child's hill lane.

HIGH ROAD,
Kilburn.
From Maida vale to Cricklewood.
G 5   **4**
RIGHT SIDE.
(*Hampstead Parish.*)
2 Goubest J. B., nurseryman
4 *The Granaries Co.*
6 Marden Henry, draper
8 *KILBURN SUPPLY STORES*; china, glass, and general furnishing ironmongry; Asher Jacobs, proprietor
10 Fisher Charles, draper
— *Greville rd.*
12 FARMER LEOPOLD, auctioneer and estate agent
12 Foster J. O., water rate collector
14 *The Atlas Sewing Machine Company*
16 ADDISON T., milliner
18 Heighton Bros., furnishing ironmongers
20 Allen Charles Bowen, pharmaceutical chmst.
22 Ingram Algernon, glass and china warehouse

HIGH RD.—*continued*

24 Cooper W. J., butcher
26 Purchas James, grocer
28 & 30 Tompson Bros., drapers and milliners
32 Flower Clare, carver and gilder
34 *Red Lion*, John Ellis
36a & 36 Roper William, general draper
  Goldsmith pl.
38 *The Bell*, Wm. Harwood
40 Roper William (Kilburn Bon Marché)
  Belsize rd.
42 *London & South Western Bank, Limited;* W. H. Williams, manager
44 Pook Geo., bootmaker
46 Hollidge J.E., tobccnst.
46 Spenser Whatley and Underhill, coal mers.
46 Bate John, agent
48 Alp Robert
52 Oldrey H. B., builder
54 BATE THOMAS AND CO., auctioneers
56 *Kilburn Branch Post and Telegraph Office*
58 Bate Walter, grocer
60 Marks L. & Co., fruitrs. and greengrocers
62 Donner Joseph, draper
64 Herbert G. & Co., bootmakers
66 Matthews E. and C., hosiers and hatters
68 Evans Thomas, draper
70 Barron H., sanitary engineer
72 Vere William, builder
  West end lane
74 Threadgale Robert Easy M.D., surgeon
76 Chambers M. and E., dyers
78 Barratt Wm., butcher
80 Stamp Chas., cheesemonger
82 Stamp Mrs., milliner
84 Foster George, gentlemen's outfitter (Cromer house)
  Harrison Mrs. L. (St. Margaret's lodge)
90 Pardoe & Sons, ironmongers

92 Deans R. G., ham and beef dealer
94 Smith Wm., confectnr.
96 Robertson Bros., boot and shoe makers
98 Holman John, tailor
100 Thorne & Co., fancy drapers
102 Star & Co., mantle warehouse
104 Hatton Francis, stationer
  Birchington rd.
106 BAKER JOSHUA & WILKINSON (late Baker & Sons, of Kilburn) auctioneers; and at St. Stephen's chambers, Telegraph st. E.C.
108 Harding Edward, upholsterer
110 Slow Benjamin, oil and colourman
112 Braddish Angelo, bootmaker
114 Hardyment A.F., china and glass warehouse
116 Grover James, coffee and dining rooms
118 Wilson Robert, grocer
120 Adams Hy., chsmngr.
122 Vallis George, fruiteer
124 Rayner W.M., tbccnst.
126 Lee & Son, oyster bar
  Quex rd.
128 *First Clothing Hall Co. (The)*, merchant tailors and boys' outfitters
128 Pugh H.
130 Keele & Co., chemists
130 Keele C. F., surgeon
132 Chappell David, baker
134 Barter Wm., stationer
134 Smyth Misses E. & S., dressmakers
136 Thompson Arthur G., fancy draper
138 Rogers Wm., bootmkr.
140 Sweet & Co., tobccnsts.
142 Lindsay Bros., general salesmen
144 Taylor Edwd., herblst.
144 Yerbury F. W., tailor
146 Ticehurst A., baby-linen warehouse
148 Smith Fredck., florist

150 Bennett J., draper
152 Graham and Graham, tea dealers
154 Clements J. E., fancy draper
156 Yerbury R. A., bookseller and stationer
158 Yerbury R. A., builder
160 Moss W. Charles, coach-bldr. (Clarence ho.)
162 Price Sidney, dairy
164 King Mrs. E. J., beer retailer
166 King Mrs. E. J., cheesemonger
168 Churchill E. A., btchr.
170 Williams Charles
170 Matthews W.A., blind-maker
172 Borasch H., hairdrssr.
174 Halls W. H., fruiterer
176 Broughton James D., fishmonger
178 Smith A. J. and Co., wine merchants
180 Joel C., portmanteau maker
182 Warr & Son, tailors
184 Barratt Wm., butcher
186 Williams William, mantle warehouse
206 Cosser Mason, toy warehouse
208 Ladbury Mrs., milliner
210 Leach Fredck., watchmaker
  Eresby rd.
212 Curram J., baker and confectioner
214 & 216 Kemp J., draper
218 Griffiths Thos., dairy
  Gascony avenue
220 Burkett Thos., butcher
222 Blake & Co., grocers
224 Ravenhill W.J., statnr.
226 Segar & Co., irnmngrs.
228 Arnold Geo., pwnbrkr.
230 Broughton James D., cheesemonger
232 Stray & Sons, btmkrs.
  Messina avenue
234 Peters Mrs. (The Grange)
236 Figden J.F., corn mer.
238 Goss Geo., confectnr.
240 Page Jsph., bootmaker
240 Callon J., jun., hairdsr.

44 Roberts Bros., butchers
48 Williamson C., cheese-
    monger
50 Isitt Levi, wardrobe
    dealer
52 Barnes Isaac, builder
54 Hewing Wm., beer rtlr.
56 Jones Jas., builder, &c.
56 Williams Thomas, um-
    brella maker
58 Yates Robert, butcher
64 Rawlins G.T., gasfitter
66 Thick H. G.
68 Pickett George J.
70 Ralph James
72 *The Black Lion*, John
    Smalley
74 Watkins D., vet. forge
76 Hoare Henry A., boot-
    maker
78 Mable & Co., frtnr. dlrs.
80 Norman W.. coffee and
    dining rooms
82 Matthews E., tobccnst.
88 and 300 Bowling and
    Thomas, drapers
90 Pierce B. S., fishmngr.
92 Taylor Charles, cheese-
    monger
94 Van Praag A. & Son,
    novelty stores
94 Van Praag Alexander,
    tobacconist
96 Ginger Alfred, pork
    butcher
98 Brooking & Co., fancy
    repository
02 Cohen & Co., fruiterers
    and greengrocers
04 Turner & Wharton,
    boot factors
06 Walton, Hassell & Port,
    italian warehsemen.
═*Palmerston rd.*
08 *The Palmerston Hotel*,
    George Shield
10 Pollard Henry John,
    grocer
12 Crockett Thomas Wm.,
    stationer
14 Van Camp E., builder
14 Stephens Mrs., dress-
    maker
16 Tebbutt Edwin, chmst.
═*Netherwood st.*
18 White Gordon A., baker
    and confectioner

320 Snoxall W.W., corn dlr.
322 Woods E., grocer
324 Leake Miss, draper
326 Marsh H., greengrocer
330 Davey R. A. & Co.,
    tobacconists
332 Southcott R., draper &
    milliner
334 Anthony Bros., cheese-
    mongers
336 Mott J. & Co., dairy
338 *London & Provincial
    Furnishing Co.*
═*Iverson rd.*
BAPTIST CHAPEL
340 Brett R., greengrocer
342 Bateman T. H., phar-
    maceutical chemist
344 Treasure H. I. & Co.,
    house agents
348 Wright E.K., cnfectnr.
350 Turner Charles, provi-
    sion stores
352 Kettelwell Mrs., fancy
    draper
354 Stephenson J. P., con-
    fectioner
═*Loveridge rd.*
366 Ellis C. & Son, estate
    agents
LEFT SIDE.
(*Paddington Parish.*)
1 *The Queen's Arms*, T.
    H. P. Hartley
3 Coulton H.H., corn mer.
5 Ford & Sons, printers
7 Stanfield R., turncock
9 Manning G. J., builder
11 & 13 *Police Station*
15 Parsons Mrs., paper
    costumier
17 Norley Geo., bootmkr.
19 Cox John, confectioner
21 Carter A.W., watchmkr.
21a Buckfield J., the old
    established umbrella
    manufacturer ; all re-
    pairs done
23 Norman Jno., bootmkr.
23a Frost D. W., tailor
═*Bridge st.*
25 Bartlett Wm., bootmkr.
27 Sparks Francis, tbccnst.
29 Britnell George, cheese-
    monger
29a Fehrenbach E., watch-
    maker

31 *West London Dairy
    Society;* Robert
    Hornby, managing
    director
33 Mudie Peter, fishmngr.
35 Ford William, ham &
    beef warehouse
37 Symonds John, harness
    maker
39 *Herington's Servants'
    Registry*
39a Gearing H.W., confctnr.
41 Carpenter Thos. Wood,
    baker and confec-
    tioner ; post office
43 Phillips Alfred, piano-
    forte & music wareho.
45 Goodman Chas., grocer
47 Prockter & Son, wine
    and spirit merchants
49 Churchill E.A., butcher
51 Thompson E. W., pawn-
    broker
53 STEWART JAMES,
    silk mercer ; and at 8
    Cambridge rd. Kilburn
55 Mash G., greengrocer
57 Woolfe B. J., grocer
59 *Aërated Bread Com-
    pany, Limited*
61 Houghton F. & Son,
    cheesemongers
63 *Anchor Coffee Tavern*
69 May George, bookseller
71 *Tyne Main Coal Co.*
71 Perraton A., tbccnist.
73 Haynes Samuel & Son,
    ironmongers & smiths
75 Coombes Malachi, sad-
    dler & harness maker
77 *The Volunteer Hotel*,
    J. Pinn
═*Brondesbury villas*
79 Horn F., baker and con-
    fectioner
81 Brown Chas., undertkr.
83 Connell F. H., watch-
    maker and jeweller
85 Purchas Mrs. M. A., gro-
    cer & wine merchant
87 Withers Frederick, fur-
    niture dealer
89 Wilson Misses, book-
    sellers and stationers
91 Hawkins W. M., general
    draper
93 Cooper Bros., oilmen

HIGH RD.—*continued*
95 & 97 Stone Alfred, pawn-broker and furniture dealer
99 Gianella Joseph, café
101 Kelly R., bazaar
◄*Brondesbury rd.*
103 Spells W. E., general draper
107 Stevens Henry, boot & shoe warehouse
109 Cosway and Rutter, chemists
111 Sears Henry W., draper and mercer
113 Walton George, green-grocer
115 Poole J., hairdresser
117 BURBIDGE BROS., wine and spirit mer.
◄*Kilburn sq.*
119 Braun Hy. C., dentist
121 Edwards Peter, florist
125 *The Cock Tavern*, Acton Phillips
125a HEALEY E J., ale stores
127 Watkins D., veterinary shoeing forge
Kilburn National Schls.
◄*Victoria rd.*
131 Southon W., clothier
133 Rogers T. H., boot-maker
137 Tebboth William, zinc worker
139 Bowles George, baker
◄*Glengall rd.*
141 Davies & Evans, oil-men
143 Bridges Mrs., tbccnst.
147 Battiss W., M.R.C.S. ENG., L.S.A., LOND.
153 Stephens P., bedding manufacturer
◄*Priory park rd.*
155 *The Earl Derby*, A. F. Austin
157 Lowmass Henry, con-fectioner
159 Herbstritt Geo, watch-maker
159a Cremer G., ladies' out-fitter
161 Bowen J., photogphr.
161 Phipps Thos. Joseph, watchmkr. & jeweller

163 Egan J. G., builder
◄*The Terrace*
165 Green and Co., blind makers
167 Baker Joshua (Elm lo)
181 Davies W. G., surgeon
183 Fisk W. J. & E. C., dentists
185 Bounford Isaac
187 Catesby E., furntr. dlr.
189 Lambert Jas., oilmn.
191 Stiff Edward, draper
193 Meredith John F., sta-tioner
195 Bevan Wm., chemist
197 Lambert Jas., grocer
199 Bailey Daniel, butcher
201 Staples Arthur H., car-ver and gilder
203 Bond and Son, corn merchants
203 Tilley Samuel, solicitor
205 *The Victoria Tavern*, Hopton Holliman
◄*Willesden lane*
263 Crook James, under-taker
265 Vassie Mrs.
267 Fraser A., saddler and harness maker
269 Reed J., tailor
271 Millard James, grocer and dairyman
     Crook Charles Wm., jobmaster
275 ENDERSON & BROMLEY, decora-tors
277 Bradley Guss Alfred, ladder maker
279 & 281 Williams Am-brose, timber mer-chant (Elmtree yard)
285 Stracey R. G., coffee rooms
287 Werren and Trow-bridge, grocers
289 & 291 Michell and Phillips, brewers and maltsters (Kilburn brewery)
291 Stone C. W.
297 *Offices of Willesden Local Board*, Samuel Tilley, clerk ; O. Claude Robson, sur-veyor (Hampton ho.)

297 *London Artiller Brigade, No. 10 Ba tery*
◄*Dyne rd.*
301 Webersladt R. E. an Co., drapers
303 Sheath Sydney, cab net maker
   Davies & Evans, oi men
307 Lansdell W. H., frui erer and greengroce
309 Davis Mrs. E., dinin rooms
311 Dormer Henry, chees monger
313 *Victoria Wine Co.*
315 Broughton J. D., fisl monger
317 Birkett Mrs.
317 Ginger Walter, btch
321 Hortin Richard
   North London Railwa Station
325 Kitchen W. T., butch
327 *French and Vienn Bakery;* H. Everit manager ; post offic
329 Warriner Alfd., tbcns
331 White Wm., dining rm
◄*Cavendish rd.*

HIGH STREET.
From Rosslyn st. to Hea street.
E 6
   TRINITY PRESBYT RIAN CHURCH
3 Pearse John G., bake
4 Kerrison Edwin, build
4 Cornick Jesse, iro monger
5 Walford Wm., drape
6 Sharpe Henry, brus and comb warehous Rainbow Hy. J., uphc sterer (Elizabeth hc Hetherington F., se vants' registry
7 Franklin J. A., M.I surgeon
8 Rabbits & Sons, bo makers
9 Miles J. J., draper
9a MURE, WARNER CO., brewers (Ham stead brewery)

10 *The King of Bohemia.*
   Mrs. Stanier
11 & 12 Hewetson James,
   bookseller & stationer
13 *The Hampstead Liberal
   Club;* George E. Cole-
   brook & R. S. Fraser,
   hon. secretaries
13 & 14 Disney Charles,
   bootmaker
16 Bellamy Bros., poul-
   terers and game dlrs.
17 O'Hara Charles, butcher
18 James Edward, boot-
   maker
19 Burck George F., baker
━ *Gayton rd.*
22 POTTER   GEORGE
   WILLIAM, house and
   estate agent
23 Fenn Thomas, tailor
24 Keith A.A., ironmonger
25 & 26 Wakeford Henry,
   draper
27 Clowser Thos., builder
28a Keys Thomas R., florist
28 *London & South West-
   ern Bank, Limited;*
   J. Butterfield, mangr.
29 STAMP EDWARD B.,
   pharmaceutical che-
   mist (The Hampstead
   Pharmacy)
30 Wilson Thos., corn dlr.
31 *British & Foreign Boot
   Agency Association,*
   bootmakers
31 *Young Men's Christian
   Association*
32 Reed Thomas, hatter
33 Coates Jas. A., butcher
34 Jackson Walter, statnr.
35 BURFORD & SON,
   builders & decorators
   (Norway house)
36 Tanner Mrs. J., cook
   and confectioner
37 Askell Mrs., fruiterer
38 & 39 *The Bird in Hand,*
   Thos. B. Catherwood
40 Harrison Wm. Greaves,
   oilman
   Omnibus Office
41 Staines & Co., tbccnsts.
42 Ware J. & Son, grocers
   & provision merchnts.
━ *Flask walk*

43 Body Philip S., baker
44 King W. & H., brush
   warehouse
45 & 56 King W. & H.,
   grocers and wine mer-
   chants
46 & 47 Evans Thomas A.,
   draper
48 *Hampstead   Branch
   Post and Telegraph
   Office*
━ *Minerva pl.*
49 Pettinger E., chemist
50 Raymond Geo., watch-
   maker
━ *Heath st.*
━ *Holly hill*
51 Potter John, corn dlr.
52 Moy George, grocer
52 Ralph J., dairyman
53 KING CHARLES B.,
   builder and decorator
54a Elliott & Co., cheesemongers
55 Evans Edwin H., hosier
56a Emerson Robt., butcher
54 *The Black Boy & Still,*
   H. J. Oxford
55 Pannell W. T., butcher
56 King W. & H., oilmen
━ *Bradley's buildings*
58 Arrowsmith Brothers,
   music sellers
59 Harris E., cheesemngr.
━ *Baker's court*
60 *The Cock & Crown,*
   Jno. Gurney Busbridge
━ *Johnson's court*
62 *The Three Horse Shoes,*
   J. Green
63 Keil Rowland, baker
64 Hayward F. H., hatter
━ *Wells buildings*
65 Rogers J., pork butcher
69 Mason T. E., butcher
70 Welch A., berlin re-
   pository, agent for
   Stevenson Brothers
   celebrated Dye Works,
   Dundee, establd. 1814
   (Berlin house)
70 Short A. A., watch-
   maker
72 Skoyles Robert, iron-
   monger
━ *Perrin's court*
73 Forster James, grocer

74 Hudson Messrs., bldrs.
75 Andrew Jesse, saddler
76 Sell Mrs.
76 *New River Co.* (office);
   W. H. Hayes, collector
━ *Church lane*
77 *William the Fourth,*
   Thomas Smith
77 Phipps William, job-
   master
78 Fitzgerald   William,
   coachbuilder
79 Paveley F.E., provision
   merchant
80 Chinnery George, boot-
   maker
81 *London Parcels Deli-
   very Company
   Hampstead & Highgate
   Express Office*
82 Dolman George, per-
   fumer
82 Acret J. T., artist
   (studio)
83 & 84 Willis & Humphrey,
   ironmongers

High Street,
Child's Hill,
see Child's hill.

HILGROVE ROAD,
St. John's Wood.
*From Finchley rd. to
Belsize rd.*

G 6   **3**

RIGHT SIDE.
1 Crake Walter
3 Morton Miss
5 Baldwin Miss
7 Fox Hubert
9 Cobb Thomas
11 Crickmay Cecil
13 Norton Frederick
15 Wood Sidney
17 Miéville Charles
19 Meaden W. J.
21 Fooks W. Cracroft,
   LL.B.
23 Johnson Mrs.
LEFT SIDE.
2 Warne Frederick
4 Henderson William
6 Williams John C.
10 Clatworthy Wm. Hy.
12 Greig John Borthwick
14 Archer Thomas

HILGROVE RD.—*contd.*
16 Schleifer Mrs. Amelia
20 Allison Mrs.
22 Senior Chas., surgeon
24 Frazer Miss, ladies'
     school (Douro house)

Hill Side,
see Cricklewood.

HILLFIELD ROAD,
West Hampstead.
From Fortune green lane.
E 4   4
LEFT SIDE.
1 Welch J. B.
2 Cordeaux John Henry
3 Hughes James
4 Read Edmund
     Smith W.H. (Boscobel)
     Helm William H.(Mo-
     gador)
     Archer James (Nether-
     side)
     Knight Richard Alfred
     (Belmont house)
     ClarkeGeorgeB.(Chud-
     leigh)
     H e m m i n g Joseph
     (Hampden)
     Townshend A r t h u r
     (Penlee)
     Green Charles Thorpe
     (Ambleside)
     Edwards Herbt.(Fern-
     hurst)
15 Attwood Thomas
16 Bright John H. R.
17 Wibberley Frederick
18 Bond Henry
19 Cooper Charles
20 Spink Thomas
21 Boys Isaiah
22 LynchWilliam(Lynch-
     field)
24 Manning W. H.
25 Parvin R. J.
26 Connell William Kerr
27 Allen Richard Ash
     Hannaford
28 Barrett Francis C.
     StoneWilliamE.(Lynd-
     hurst)
     Seddon H. C. (St.
     Winifred's)
     Johnson Alfred (May-
     field)

     Wastnage Percy (Cla-
     rence house)
34 Boyd Richard
     PerryJohn(Linton ho.)
RIGHT SIDE.
     Mack Arthur J. (Fair-
     mount)
     Fowle John A. (The
     Nest)
     ThwaitesJames(Netley
     villa)
     Stuckey W. A. (Mona
     villa)
     Turner Nicholas (Flor-
     ence villa)
     Balkwill Mrs. W. H.
     (Cambridge villa)
     Dolleymore A r t h u r
     (Banavie)
     Moreton Thomas (Hill-
     field lodge)
     Brothers George (Ox-
     ford villa)
     Wadlow Henry George
     (Albion villa)
     Cosway Edward Chas.
     (Elm lodge)
     Shepherd Mark (Stam-
     ford villa)
74 Mager Thomas
     Drayson S. Herbert
     (Brooklyn)
     Poole Mrs.(Sunnyside)
     Whiddington J o h n
     Chilvers (Tickenhall)
     Field Lane Boys' Cer-
     tified Industrial Schl.;
     George Thomas Peall,
     superintendent

HILLTOP ROAD,
Kilburn.
From 8 Sheriff rd.
F 5   4
LEFT SIDE.
1 Bingermann Alfred E.
     (Glenholme)
3 List Arthur (Fern-
     dale)
5 Little Robert (Bid-
     destone)
RIGHT SIDE.
2 Wither Charles (Bar-
     more)
4 Scroggie John (Apna
     Chur)

HOLFORD ROAD.
From Christ Church to
East Heath.
D 6   *1*
     Thornely Wm. (High
     close)
     Palmer John, jun.(Bel-
     ton grange)
2 TempleSir Richd.,bart.
3 Holford Geo., barrister
4 Hügel Baron Friedrich
     von
     Inman R. J. (The
     Knoll)
     East heath rd.

HOLLY HILL.
From High st.
E 6   *1*
     Grant Mrs., dress and
     mantle maker (Holly
     hill cottage)
     PotterG.& Son,builders
     Norton Miss Ann,
     ladies' school
1 Beckett Robert
2 Roch Joseph John
3 Hipwell W.. bootmkr.
4 Clements John
5 Bashford Thomas
6 Evans Mrs.

HOLLY MOUNT.
From Holly bush hill to
Heath st.
D 6   *1*
1 Hough Wm. Barthw.
2 Gibbs Henry
3 *Gas Light & Coke Co.;*
     Charles Hoyle, gas
     inspector
4 Paine Henry
5 Warren Charles
6 Juffs James
7 Nash Henry
8 Earl Samuel
9 Osborn George John
10 Tibberth Richard M.
11 Gray William
12 Henley James
13 Farr William
14 Toye William Thomas
     Keith Miss (Percy ho.)
     Windebank William
     (Alma cottage)
     Provost & Co., printers
     Bowen G.

Hudson James (Holly
  bush house)
The Holly Bush Hotel,
  C. M. Froud
Norris Charles
Warren John

HOLLY PLACE.
*From the Parish Church
to Mount Vernon.*
E 6   **1**
2 Shepherd Thomas
2 Tracey Rev. M. G., M.A.
3 Day Henry
4 *St. Vincent's Orphan-
  age;* Canon Purcell,
  superior
4 *St. Mary's Catholic
  School;* Miss Plummer,
  mistress
  ST. MARY'S CATHOLIC
  CHURCH
5 Purcell Canon A. Dillon
6 McDonald J. Allen
7 Bishop Albert
8 Bolt John
9 Attoe John (Hollyberry
  house)

HOLLY BUSH HILL
*From Holly mount to
Windmill hill.*
D 6   **1**
  Swift Edward (Alpine
  cottage)
2 & 3 Slater Mrs.
  Constance Samuel

HOLLY BUSH VALE
From 51 High st.
E 6   **1**
4 Neill Josiah, chimney
  sweep

HOLMDALE ROAD,
West Hampstead.
F 5
From Denington park.
  RIGHT SIDE.
1 Saxby James Samuel
3 Robins Charles
9 Morten Alexander Geo.

HOLTHAM ROAD.
From 101 Abbey rd.
G 5   **4**
  RIGHT SIDE.
2 Douglas Alexander

4 Klaftenberger William
  Heinrich Hubert
6 Brown E.
10 Rosenstein Rev. M.
12 Davies F.
16 Milne John Vine
  LEFT SIDE.
1 Mulford Mrs.
3 Sanders Wm. Henry
5 Garvey Mrs.
7 Muston Mrs. Fanny
9 Doel Edwin
11 Fisher Mrs. Anne
13 Rowe Alfred John
15 Paxton Mrs., ladies'
  school
17 Eccles Thomas J.

IVERSON ROAD,
Kilburn.
*From Cricklewood to West
end lane.*
F 4   **4**
  LEFT SIDE.
1 Crook & Sons, jobmstrs.
3 Smith Alfred J.
5 Preston George Prior,
  coachbuilder (Bea-
  consfield house)
7 Walton G., auctioneer
  & house agent (Glad-
  stone house)
9 & 11 *Brondesbury Hall
  and Sunday School*
13 Elliott Miss
15 Alaway Chas., builder
17 Shurley William
35 Edwards Thomas, boot-
  maker
37 Howard William
  Everett C. H., contrac-
  tor (Iverson works)
43 Trill Peter
45 Holt William
71 Marshall George (Wa-
  verly cottage)
73 Beach William (Ararat
  house)
  ⸺*Ariel st.*
75 Thornicroft Thomas
77 Baker H. J.
79 Bolton Major William
81 Heylin Joseph George
83 Allen Rev. Bevill
85 Jarvis Mrs.
87 Sims Mrs. Annie
89 Harris Edward

93 Millen George John
95 Hooper Charles
97 Greene Charles John
  (Cambridge house)
99 Larkin Thomas Joseph
103 Blaikley David James
105 New George Beasley,
  architect
107 Harris John (Mizpah
  villa)
109 Fussey William
111 Smyth Hy. (Trent vil.)
113 Gittens Mrs. (Tamar
  villa)
115 Wall Miss
117 Fancourt Mrs. M. A.
119 Banks Francis
121 Bolton Chris., engineer
123 Stair George
125 Moxey Wm. Thomas
127 Hilder Wm., phtgrphr.
129 Peters John
131 Hawkings Geo. Fredk.
133 Sowden Robert, tailor
135 Miller George
137 Wyatt William Thos.
139 Edmead George
141 Pole Mrs.
143 O'Connor Francis
145 Howell Edward James
  ⸺*Maygrove rd.*
  Warren F. & Co., coal
  merchants
  Booth Brothers, coal
  merchants
  Macpherson R. & Co.,
  coal merchants
  Corston H. B. & Co.,
  coal merchants
  Walter C. A. & Co.,
  coal merchants
  Ellis & Everard, coal
  merchants
  Adams & Co., lime,
  cement, &c., merchants
  Bacon & Co., cement
  merchant
  *Midland   Railway,
  West End Station*
  Gillespie John (Cum-
  berland house)
  Cutler Mrs. (Chester-
  field house)
  RIGHT SIDE.
2 Oaker Alfred William
4 Foot Frank
6 Cliff Thomas

IVERSON RD.—*continued*
8 Butler William
10 Watson Mrs. H.
10 Watson Hy., plasterer
12 De la Camp Isidor S.
14 Fennell Henry Thomas
18 Beattie J. H.
20 Hyndman Thomas
22 Gent Frank
24 Butler Walter,gasfitter
36 Groves J. B.
36 Groves Mrs., ladies' school
38 Julian Richard
40 Blower Mrs. (Girton villa)
42 Deveson Daniel (Kent lodge)
44 Rodrick Mrs. (Alton lodge)
    Felton George, contractor(Iverson yard)
86 Kissack Thos., architect
88 Jackson Miss
92 Stock William
94 Kemmler Charles
96 Chester Thomas Wm.
98 Millis Percy A.
100 Russell J. E.
102 Palmer William
104 Dixon Mrs. E.
104 Dixon Wm., decorator
106 Taylor Thomas
108 Cable William Drew
112 Tibbals Miss
114 Nicholls Mrs. Sarah
116 Wallace Mrs.
118 Tucker Francis L.
120 Eldridge Miss E.
122 Hamlen Charles
124 Adams Henry
126 Goss George Dean
130 Day Mrs. and Misses, dressmakers
134 Bucknell J.G.,bldr.&c.
136 Harrison Mrs.(Kelvin lodge)
138 Wakerley Mrs.
140 Morgan Mrs.
142 Jones Mrs. C.
144 Hawkings Robert Jno., teacher of music
146 Wallace Miss A., kindergarten
148 Reeseg John F.
150 Taylor Frank
152 York Robert

154 Maclean Mrs.
156 Madden Edward
158 Crichton William, draper(Dalmuir ho.)
160 Hope James
162 Hayles William(Lyon house)
164 Green Charles,undertaker
    ——*Medley rd.*
166 Hall Charles
170 Clunn John
172 Russell William
174 Steger Mrs.
176 Macpherson Robert & Co., coal merchants
176 Lewis T. H.
180 Collier Charles (Lissoy house)
182 King Mrs. (Nocton house)
184 Bull Mrs. L. (Iverson dairy)

JOHN STREET.
From Downshire hill.
E 7   **1**
    Woof Henry (St. Alban's villa)
    Phillips Thomas (Adelaide house)
3 Luard Miss
4 Frazer John James
    Dryhurst Arthur Geo.
    Britannia Villas.
1 Bowman John M.
2 Carlisle Captain John
    John Street.
    Maddox Misses, ladies' school (The Cottage)
    Goodwin Alfred (Kent lodge)
    Temple Robert Scott (Lawn bank)
    Hudson Thos. (Wentworth house)
    Asquith Herbert H. (Eton house)
    Bird Henry L. J. (Scarr cottage)
14 Douglas Mrs.
    Maddox George (Milford house)
    Bellamy Wm. Fredk. (Wycliffe cottage)
    Homfray Miss (Byron cottage)

    Haynes John (Campbell cottage)
21 Hobbs William Henry
    Cracknell Wm. Edwd., surveyor (Brentwood cottage)
    Barlow Charles (Surry cottage)
    Gellibrand Dunscombe Bradford(Albion cot)

KEIL'S COTTAGES,
see Back lane.

KELSON STREET,
Kilburn.
From Palmerston rd.
F 4   **4**
    LEFT SIDE.
2 Cutler F., oilman
4 Robbins John, baker
6 Edwards G., provision dealer
8 Cayford W. W., wardrobe dealer
10 Grey Hy., beer retailer
12 Warwick Geo., grngrcr.
26 Clark Walter William, insurance agent
28 Youngman George
34 Belcher Benjamin,bootmaker
    RIGHT SIDE.
9 Plant Mrs. Rose
    Board School

KEMPLAY ROAD,
Rosslyn Hill.
From Willoughby rd.
E 7   **1**
    LEFT SIDE.
    CONGREGATIONAL CH.
    Gray Nutter (Plevna house)
    Brady Patrick L. O. H. (Avoca)
1 Jervis Thomas
2 Schmeisser William
3 Towell Mrs.
4 White William
5 Mestayer Mrs.
6 Haig General F. T.
7 Nutting H. W. W.
8 Latreille Ulysses
9 Caspersz Charles Peter
10 Dobbin Charles
11 Smith J.Orton,solicitor

Page J. (The Cottage)
RIGHT SIDE.
Perrins   John   Hill
(Chaddesley villa)
Henrici Olaus (Meldorf cottage)
Glen Thomas (Carlisle house)
Welsh Miss J. (Egremont house)

KILBURN PRIORY,
Maida Vale.
I 5   **4**
RIGHT SIDE.
2 Pedlar William (Ontario lodge)
4 Harris C. J.
6 Kerr George
8 Lucas E. W.
10 Merton J. S.
12 Rochfort Mrs. Benj. (Howard lodge)
14 Redhouse James W.
16 Ullmann E.
18 Roberts Mrs.
20 Levi Mrs. Joseph
22 Hunter H. T.
24 Williams Miss, ladies' college (York house and Belmont house)
LEFT SIDE.
17 Corsbie Dennis
19 Wood Henry
21 Sturgis Mrs.
23 Hitchin Mrs.
25 Barnett Joseph Alfred (Ferndale)
25 Barnett Miss Emma (Ferndale)
27 Goldby Miss
29 & 31 Hall Charles
33 Sparks Frank, photographic artist
35 Stride H. Phillips
⌐*Alexandra rd.*
⌐*Mortimer rd.*

KILBURN VALE.
From 10 West end lane.
G 5   **4**
1a Garnham Robert
1b Hood Albert
1 Gandy Mrs., laundress
2 Chappell Edwin, crpntr
3 Mitchell Matthew
4 Daniel Mrs., laundry
5 Hobbs John

6 Osborn Charles
7 Shore John
8 Gardner George
9 Turner John
10 Brooks William
11 Carter James
12 House S.
Vale Cottages.
1 Parker Job
Kilburn Vale.
EBENEZER CHAPEL
Chinery Philip John (Ebenezer cottage)
Howe James (Providence cottage)

KINGDON ROAD.
From Denington park.
F 5   **4**
RIGHT SIDE.
1 Ell George P.
3 Parker Mrs.
5 Scott Arthur
7 Crundell Arthur
9 Sullivan Mrs. (Fernleigh)
11 Womack   Frederick, M.B., B.SC. LOND.
13 Dare George Julius
15 Platt Peregrine
17 Blackbec Frnk. Hayden
19 Machion Harry
21 Simmons John
23 Simmons William
LEFT SIDE.
2 Woollan Miss
4 Roberts Mrs.
6 Van   Camp   Marie Antoinetta
8 Leftwich Robert V.
18 Simmons Charles
20 Merington Miss Emily
22 Ellis Henry
24 Davison Mrs.
26 Millington Thomas
28 Pritchard F. Phelps
30 Spence Ernest

KING HENRY'S RD.
From Regent's park rd.
to Adelaide rd.
G 7   **3**
LEFT SIDE.
5 Thorpe Thomas
7 Schirges Henry
9 Comber Miss Amelia
11 Haviland Mrs.

13 Butcher William Hy.
17 Badock T. C.
19 Boys J. C.
23 Dunphie Charles J.
25 Winterbon E.
27 Myers Mrs. Elizabeth
29 Flamank Mrs.
⌐*Ainger rd.*
31 Thomas Richard
33 Shepherd Dr. Fredk.
35 Marshall Henry
37 Campbell Charles
39 Gomersall Wm., M.C.P. OXON (S. Bernard's school)
41 Green Frank
43 Gwyther Fredk. Geo.
45 Nash William
47 Davis David J.
49 Solomon Philip
51 Whyte Robert
53 Mason Henry Watts, artist
55 Davis Edward John
55 Isaacson Judah
57 Beavis Charles
59 Gill Charles John
61 Tape Arthur Stanley
63 Jansson E.
65 Berghmann Hugo
67 Butler Mrs.
69 Mannooch Chas. Henry
71 Gibson William T.
73 Eassie William, C.E.
79 Dowling Edmund
79 Colls E.
81 Dent Garwood
83 Allum John
85 Bartlett Mrs.
87 & 89 Buss Miss
⌐*Primrose hill rd.*
CHURCH OF ST. MARY THE VIRGIN
Thomson Hugh (Elleray)
93 Milne John
97 Blumenthal Julius
99 Hyams David
101 Baily William H.
103 Wyman Chas. Wm. Hy.
105 Smith Mrs. Thomas
107 Parsons Mrs. James
109 Scarth Robert Gilyard
111 Nore Mrs.
113 Baynes F., timber mer.
⌐*Merton rd.*
115 Hilder John

KING HENRY'S RD.—*cntd*
117 Bacharach Carl M.
119 Stephenson John William J.
121 Frewer Charles
123 Smith Arthur Clifford
125 Compton Edward
127 Ayers Mrs.
129 Matthew James E.
131 Palmer Alfred
133 Davis Oliver Henry
135 Galloway Wm. Chas.
137 Bassett Misses
139 Bingham Reuben
141 Williams Wm. Powell
143 Drewry Henry R.
143 Drewry Miss Louisa
143 Drewry Miss Ellen B.
145 Warne John
147 Robertson Struan
149 Bowden Edward
151 Watts Henry
   Eton and Middlesex Cricket Ground
155 & 157 Locket Misses, school
159 Whitaker Thomas (Sandford house)
   RIGHT SIDE.
10 Ackermann Misses
14 Cambell Miss
18 Tegetmeier Miss, kindergarten and school
20 Guilding Randolph
24 Wilman Mrs.
26 Nelson Mrs.
28 Turner Godfrey W.
30 Acurbach Mrs.
32 Seligmann Soloman
34 Schloss Joseph
36 Johnston Alexander
38 Pinchin Edwin S.
40 Guyatt Thomas
42 Sollas William Henry
44 Findlay John Adamson
46 Avarne Augustus
48 Milligan Mrs.
50 Bowser Henry
52 Mason Mrs.
54 Jolliffe E. Y.
56 Baddeley Edward
58 Haywood Walter Robt.
   Primrose hill rd.
80 Hall Newman Vine
82 Cancellor Francis
84 Joachim E. B.
84 Oesterreicher W.

86 Edwards Alfred
90 Ralston William
92 Whitham Mrs.
94 Gill W. G.
96 Dawson Philip William
98 Fuller Rev. C. Jas., M.A.
   Eton pl.
100 Fritsch Herman
102 Harvey Mrs.
104 Grant Miss
106 Procter C. W. C.
108 Behrens Sydney Lucas
112 Kneustub F. J.
114 Adams Mrs. Francis
   Merton rd.
116 Gretton George Le Mesurier
118 Dyer Mrs. This'leton
120 Hippesley Geo. Wyld
122 Snow Mrs. Fanny
124 Humble Mrs.
126 Ratcliff Sidney Geo.
128 Daft Mrs.
130 Steet G. Carrick, F.R.C.S.
132 Smith Francis
134 Collison William
136 Boyes Frederick
140 Daniell Mrs. Spencer
144 Mathew Miss
146 Shewin Robert
148 Thompson Neale
150 Powles Evelyn
   King's college rd.
152 Welsh Mrs. E. Kirkley
156 Riviere Mrs.
156 Cancellor Miss
158 Wallace Colonel W.H.
160 Richardson Misses
162 Bingham William

King's Cottages,
see West end lane.

KING'S COLLEGE MEWS.
From 9 King's college rd.
G 7   **3**
   Jinks Wm., jobmaster
17 Penn James, sweep
5 Holman Thos., builder and decorator
6 Day H., gasfitter
18 Holman Thos., builder and decorator
   Bridge Isaac, jobmstr.

KING'S COLLEGE ROAD.
From 199 Adelaide rd.
G 7   **3**
   LEFT SIDE.
1 Pipe W., chemist; post office
3 Frank Joseph, grocer
7 Hemming Miss, dressmaker
9 *The Prince Consort*, Mrs. Grace Grose
   King's college mews
11 Golding William, coffee and dining rooms
13 Sheer John, draper
13 Higgs John, verger of St. Paul's Church
15 Topps Francis, watchmaker
17 Beddeson Frncs., fruitr.
19 Page Jas., fishmonger
21 & 23 Stubbs & Son, grcrs.
   RIGHT SIDE.
2 Bailey James, cnfctnr.
4 Houghton F., cheesemonger
6 Elliott Bros., fruiterers and greengrocers
8 Cooper James, butcher
10 Browning Thos., china and brush warehouse
12 Pitcairn David, bookseller and stationer
14 Cutler William, dairy
16 Sapsford Geo., plumber
18 Moore Joseph, surveyor
20 Lloyd Edward, tailor
22 Bridge Isaac, corn dlr. and jobmaster
24 Reeves Rchd., bootmkr.
26 Stiles Mrs., bootmaker
28 STUBBS C., tailor and family outfitter

KINGSFORD ST.
From Southampton rd.
E 8   **2**
1 Stacey Thomas
2 Beman Edward
3 Beard A. E.
4 Dix Frank
5 Franklin William
6 Janes Joseph
7 Franklin Henry
8 Smith J. S., carpet grounds

KINGSGATE ROAD,
Kilburn.
From Quex rd. to Hemstall rd.

G 5   **4**

RIGHT SIDE.

7 Mark Frederick
9 Foulger Miss
11 Dyer Miss
11 Bell Thomas
13 Hill James
15 Wright George
17 Pryor H. L.
19 O'Connor Joseph
21 Leitch Mrs.
23 Corbyn James
25 Holmes Arthur John
27 Wilson John
29 Robinson Miss C.
31 Ward Ernest
33 White Mrs. Caroline
35 Freegard George
39 Moore Edward
41 Jeffery John
43 Allen Joseph
45 Redding H.
47 Mortimer W. H.
49 Gray Alfred
51 Wilkins Henry
53 West G.
55 Allen J.
57 Manley W. B.
⎯*Smyrna rd.*
  Moir J., upholsterer
  Mitchell A. R. (Covent garden stores)
  Gater R., provision dlr.
  Lenny H., baker and confectioner
  Roe H.
  Duckett D. (Hampshire farm dairy)
  Hoare J., ironmonger
⎯*Gascony avenue*
⎯*Messina avenue*
⎯*Cotleigh rd.*
⎯*Dynham rd.*
LEFT SIDE.

2 Spackman Isaac T.
4 Wade Alfred
6 Carr Mrs. Jane
8 Quarry Charles
10 Moss C. W.
⎯*Kingsgate mews*
12 Nathan Charles
14 Kelly Mrs.
16 Yates William

18 Andrews Robert
20 Hills Harold
22 Britnell L.
24 Denny Thomas
26 Scott George
28 Knights James
30 Cayford Saml. Everett
32 Barton Chas. William
34 Bryan J. T.
36 Leonhardt William
38 Feakes H.
40 Cecil Henry
42 Isaac Arscott John
44 Lowman Henry
46 Dettmer W. J., pianoforte tuner
48 Blencowe Alfred
50 Watson Alfred
52 Rogers David
⎯*Eresby rd.*
⎯*Gascony avenue*
63 Savage T., fruiterer and greengrocer
65 White James, bootmkr.
67 Wilkins H. C., grocer and general stores
⎯*Messina avenue*

LAMBOLLE ROAD.
From 13 Belsize sq.

F 7   **2**

LEFT SIDE.

1 Bullen Edward, barrister-at-law
2 Levy Hy. (Holland ho.)
RIGHT SIDE.

3 Hibbert Horace
5 Bamberger Stanley
  Hardy T. B. (Danesmere)
9 Rosenheim William
  Galloway John, builder (Forres)
  Landsberg Edward (Stony Cliff)
  Hirschhorn L. (Holmwood)
⎯*Lancaster rd.*

LANCASTER PLACE
From Belsize sq.

F 7   **2**

RIGHT SIDE.

1 Davis Alfred, verger & collector of St. Peter's
LEFT SIDE.

2 Firnberg Max

6 Watson E.
8 Forbes Thos. Lawrence
12a Bunn Robert T.

LANCASTER ROAD.
From Belsize park.

F 7   **2**

1 Hudson Edwin
2 Schuster Ernest
3 Darley J. J.
4 Jarvis Mrs.
5 Watson Edward
6 Arnholz Adolph
7 Radermacher John
8 Ward Nelson
9 Marcus John
10 Mackintosh Donld., M.D.
11 Limebeer John
12 Herbert Wm. Hawkins
13 Chandler B. W.
14 Matthews John Henry
15 Chattock Richard S.
16 Meissner William Hy.
18 Hibbert Mrs.
⎯*Lancaster pl.*
  Geddes A.C. (Thornton)
25 Jackson Edward E. (Southcotte)
26 Landauer D.
28 Faehse Robert
  Bowlby Charles C. (Wilton lodge)
20 Cobb Mrs.
21 Motherwell Captain Charles W.
22 Henderson John
23 Dixon Mrs. E.
24 Cohn Maurice
⎯*Eton avenue*
  Edwards & Thomas, jobmasters (Lancaster stables)
  Edwards Charles (Rowton house)
  Thomas John (Rowton house)

Lansdowne Terrace,
see Hemstall rd.

LAWN ROAD,
Haverstock Hill.

F 8   **2**

1 Green George Robert
2 Staines Henry T.
3 Nutt Edward Henry
4 Lermit G. Henry
5 Cornick Mrs. Henry

LAWN RD.—*continued*
6 Powell Mrs.
7 Rowe John Kingdon
8 Smith J. Walter
9 Marsden R. J.
10 Druce Samuel B. L.
11 Watts Mrs.
12 Eisenlohr Ferdinand
15 Stanfield Herbert
16 Dickinson Charles J.
17 Carden James M.
18 Bagshawe F. G.

LICHFIELD ROAD,
Kilburn.
From Cricklewood lane.
D 4
1 Farr Joseph
2 Groves A.
3 Taylor Edwin
4 Lovell Mrs.
5 Mather Mrs.
6 Mills John
7 Pearce George
8 Parkes Elliott
8 Cheshir William
    Scholfield John Howorth
10 Pettet Thomas
11 Warburg Herman
12 Marsh E. T., B.A.
13 McClintock Edwin
14 Bannister Charles
15 Bateman Alfred Horace
16 Cory Henry Albert
17 Meugens Mrs.
18 Gent Alfred
19 Lomax Major James
20 West W. T.
21 Stamper Henry
22 Simmons Charles
23 Rawson John
24 Cheshir Charles, builder
25 Booth Walter Scott
26 Allen Mrs.
27 Pryke John A.
28 Rudall George
29 Chinery John
30 Millar Rev. A.
31 Debnam Mrs. L.
32 Callow Henry William

LINSTEAD STREET,
Kilburn.
From Palmerston rd.
F 4
1a Cain Miss, general shop
1 Allen George, plumber
2 Foreigner James

3 Hawkins William Alley, joiner
4 Moore Noah
5 Cundle John
7 Sisley George
8 Bingham W.
9 MacVitie Miss
10 Saxby George
11 Jacob Thomas
13 Atkins Rowland
14 Bean Henry
15 Brewer John

LITHOS ROAD.
From Finchley new rd.
F 6
LEFT SIDE.
1 Alaway Robert
3 Davey Henry
5 Potter Ebenezer
7 Bethell Henry
9 Briggs Charles
11 Andrews Robert
13 Etkins George
15 Willis William
19 Hughes J. V.
21 Mayer J.
23 Sinclair Mrs.
RIGHT SIDE.
2 Higgins Alfred
4 Woodthorpe Enos
6 Hazzard Miss
8 Burdett Dixon
10 Almond Thomas
12 Simmonds Henry
14 Borrett Mrs.
16 Adcock William

LITTLE CHURCH ROW.
From Church row.
E 6
3 Shepherd T. & B., plmbrs
2 Martin Edward
1 Walker & Son, marine store dealers
    Hately J., general smith
    PRIMITIVE METHODIST CHAPEL
6 Hill Henry, genl. shop
7 Seymour Walter Jas., general shop
    Baker's row
8 Morris Geo. William, greengrocer
    Roberts J.
    Bradley's buildings

LOUDOUN ROAD,
St. John's Wood.
From Springfield rd. to Belsize rd.
G 6
LEFT SIDE.
27 Dadge Frederick Wm.
29 Schnieder Montague
31 Martin Mrs.
33 Norton Edward
35 Simpson Mrs.
37 Rivers Mrs.
    Boundary rd.
41 Hackworth Alf., builder
    Loudoun road mews
43 Brusey T., coffee rooms
45 Webster Ernest, watch and clock maker and jeweller
47 *The Alexandra Hotel*, C. J. Coles
    Alexandra rd.
    Cox Geo. J. (Zelinda vl.)
RIGHT SIDE.
56 Chaplin Joseph (Aberdour house)
58 Lemesurier A.
60 Dodd John Theodore, barrister
62 Kent Charles Alston
64 Tanner William
66 Greatorex Henry
68 Hemming Miss
    Boundary rd.
    ALL SOULS' CHURCH
    Alexandra rd.
    L. & N. W. Railway Station
    Hilgrove rd.
    Belsize rd.

LOUDOUN ROAD MEWS.
From 41 Loudoun rd.
G 6
1 Runciman —, carman and contractor
2 Palmer George, farrier
3 Callingham Geo., chimney cleaner
8 Stancombe G.W., coach builder & wheelwright
15 & 16 James Edward, jobmaster; livery stables

LOVERIDGE ROAD,
Kilburn.
From Cricklewood.

F 4   **4**

LEFT SIDE.
157 HarndenE.,confectnr.
159 Harriss A., builder
161 Bates Joseph, beer retailer
163 Davenport Mrs. laundry
165 Edgar James
170 Hanwell N., decorator
172 Nicholson H. Walker, tailor
173 Stone Thos. Midgley, gun maker
174 Dibb Wm., carpenter
175 Brown Thomas
176 Johnson H. W.
177 Pulley JosephWilliam
178 Long Charles
179 Jamison Mrs. E.
181 Rogers William
182 Keates Mrs., dressmaker
183 Soper George
184 Witham Mrs. M. A., preparatory school
188 Milton John, grocer
190 Brightwell Richard, tailor
191 Chad Thomas
192 Perks Charles
193 Knight Alfd.Augustus
194 Roberts William
195 Pledger J. J.
196 Campbell John
197 Jelpke John Ludwig
198 Brown Miss
200 Barnes Alfred
201 Brade Robert J.
202 BristerWilliam(Loveridge house)
203 Jones Alfred
204 Bowman Bernard
205 Notley ThomasGeorge
206 Germain William
RIGHT SIDE.
1aLavers Fredk., oilman
2aRaseyHy.,glass wareho
31 Berry James
30 Keats Frederick
29 Newland W. G., commission agent
28 Powell Nugent
27 Sutherland Mrs.

26 Ball Francis
25 Gladman Charles
24 Neale Peter
23 Buckoke Solomon
21 Simpson Alfred
20 Burt Richd., carpenter
18 Hendy John
17 Tully George
16 Smith David
15 Mallett Thomas
14 Lomas Charles
13 Leyton William
12 Morton Miss, teacher of music
12 King Henry, pianoforte tuner
11 Ward William
10 Finch Geo. W., gardnr.
9 Walden Mrs.
8 Avant William
7 Bailey James S.
6 Birch Thomas
5 Elton Mrs. A.
4 Baker Edward
3 Archell Thomas John
2 Leonard Xavier
1 Whythe Mrs.

LOWER TERRACE.
From Branch hill.

D 6   **1**
1 Burnett Mrs. (Frognal hill)
2 Tupman Charles J. T., surveyor and estate agent
3 Street George
4 Webb Horatio (West hill lodge)

LOWER CROSS RD.,
Haverstock Hill.
From 57 Park rd.

F 8   **2**
2 Jones Arthur
3 Jenkins John

Lower Heath Cotts.,
see Willow rd.

LOWER LAWN RD.
From Fleet rd.

E 7   **9**
1 Marriott John
2 Vigurs John
3 Medhurst Mrs.
4 Wallis Richard
5 Andrews William

6 Barnden Frederick
7 Maidlow Miss
8 Pavier John, contrctr.
9 Fox Frederick
— *Lawn rd.*
15 Jeffery John
16 Nichols William
17 Maidlow Miss Emma
18 Pepper Archibald
19 Shenton Edward
20 Sexton William

LOWFIELD ROAD,
Kilburn.
From Hemstall rd. to Sheriff rd.

F 5   **4**
LEFT SIDE.
2 Keith James
6 Robson Mrs.
8 Jenkins Charles
10 Gordon William, artificial flower maker
12 Holmes Benjmn.,tailor
14 Sargeant Charles
16 Palmer Thomas
18 Harris John
20 Greaves Charles
22 Forsberry Charles
24 Brend J.
28 Harding George
32 LewingtonMrs., lndrss.
38 Cameron Kenneth
40 Passmore Robert
RIGHT SIDE.
1 Davis Richard, beer retailer
3 Green Joseph
3 Green Mrs ,dressmaker
9 Ford Samuel
11 Jarrett Mrs., laundress
11 Calvert James, tailor
19 Ostick James, plumber
23 Day Joseph William
27 Willes Harry, turncock
29 Lewis W., laundry
33 Mortlock Ernest, accountant
39 Harding Jesse
47 Delve William
49 Miggand Alexander
51 Howitt John
53 Benfield Charles

LUTTON TERRACE.
From 49 Flask walk.

E 6
2 McLean George

LUTTON TER.—*continued*
3 Roche James
Bland Edward (Fernley cottage)
CHRIST CHURCH MISSION ROOMS
Model Lodging Houses

LYNDHURST GARDENS.
F 7
From Belsize cres.
Wood D. P. (Elim)

LYNDHURST RD.
From Rosslyn hill.
E 7   *1*
1 Holford Miss
2 Innes F. W., M.D., C.B.
3 Dart Frederick G.
5 Pattison Samuel
6 Craigie Patrick George
7 Haag Carl, R.W.S.
8 James W. M.
11 Jordan William
Eldon rd.
Huggins J.(Rosslyn lo.)
13 Nevinson Mrs.
14 Stenhouse Mrs.
14 Stenhouse Frank
15 Lake Ernest E.
16 Tatham J. Perceval
17 Douglas John S.
18 Schofield Mrs. Joseph
Woodd Charles H. Lardner (Rosslyn house)

Maitland Park Road and Villas,
see our " Camden & Kentish Towns Directory."

MANCHESTER MEWS,
Kilburn.
From 1 Springfield villas.
G 5   *4*
Entwistle W., upholstr.

MANSFIELD PLACE
From 11 Heath st.
E 6   *1*
1 Morris Mrs. Ann
2 Pratt G.
3 Powley Arthur
4 Hill James R.

5 Hall Alexander
6 Watts Charles
7 Denneford Peter
8 Matthews Augustus
9 Bunyan Charles
10 Gregory James
11 Jarvis Joseph, carpenter and joiner
12 Ilbery Hubert
13 Searle Henry

MANSFIELD VILLS
From Lyndhurst rd. to Rosslyn ter.
E 7   *1*
1 Dawkins Mrs. Rose
2 Smith Mrs.
3 Howell William I.
4 Coe Augustus F.
5 Beckley Col. T., R.E.
6 Groom Robert
7 Harvey Mrs.
Day Hon. Sir John Charles (Green bank)
10 Evershed Dr. Arthur, physician
11 Osler Timothy Smith (The Limes)
12 FitzGerald Misses, ladies' school
13 Drummond Rev. J., LL.D.
14 Downing Miss
15 Cooke John
16 Wells Josiah (Mansfield house)

MARESFIELD GARDENS.
From Fitzjohns' avenue to Netherhall ter.
F 6   *1*
RIGHT SIDE.
1 Cawkwell Wm. (Fernacre)
2 and 3 Maynard Miss (Westfield)
4 Dowling Thomas
5 Cockle Miss
6 Stow Montague H., slctr.
7 Miley John (Kenmore)
8 Voigt S. E. (Maresfield house)
10 Wilson Julius
11 Stevens G. W.
12 Daniell Cyrus
Nutley ter.

Devitt Andrew (Ethelstane)
LEFT SIDE.
Williams John Haynes (Wridhern)
Girls' Public Day School Co., Limited
Nutley ter.
Griffin Colonel James T. (Oneóta)
De Pass Daniel (Oaklands)
Reid Geo.(Dalkeith)

MAYGROVE ROAD,
Kilburn.
From Cricklewood.
F 4   *4*
RIGHT SIDE.
2 Fordham John
4 Graham Mrs.
6 Nailard Thomas
8 Sweet Wm., gasfitter
10 Stickland Charles
12 Stewart Thos., engineer
14 Pearce Mrs. R., drssmkr.
16 Vooght John
18 Hagelsieb Wilhelm
20 Chilcot W. B., tailor
22 Chappell Mrs. W.
22 Welch Saml., carpenter
24 Moss Fredk. Richard, coachbuilder
26 David David, brass finisher
28 Gyllenspetz Charles Edward, insur. agent
30 Wyburn Robert
32 Barker William
34 Piper Alexander Chas.
36 Lowmass William Hy.
38 Durham James Edward
40 Burgess George
42 Watts George, gardener
44 Gurney Charles
46 Lane James
48 Noble Frederick William, stained glass works (York house)
50 White William Henry (Cromer house)
52 Shilcock John
58 Russell Thomas
60 Carnegy Charles
62 Drake Mrs.
64 Houston Miss, ladies' school (Acacia villa)
68 Kelly Miss

72 Windle Job
76 Simmons John O.
78 Dines Mrs.
80 Mordant Frederick
82 Webb Thomas
84 Green Matthew Henry
86 Webb Charles
88 Bayne James Bane, artist in stained glass
90 Parks Samuel
92 De St. Croix Arthur J.
94 Rogers Charles George
96 Goy Joseph
98 Bendall Henry, surgeon-dentist
100 Wigley John
102 Sayers Edwin Charles, carpenter
104 Tully E.
108 Feacey James
110 Shepherd Frederick, gardener
112 Hepher Fredk., tailor
114 Wilkie Edmund
116 Slimmon Mrs.
118 Percy Isaac
—*Ariel st.*
120 Hunt Mrs.
124 Brittain William
126 Jones Edward
128 Beckington William
130 Southgate Thomas
132 Gregory A. W.
136 Brothers John A.
138 Katterns Douglas
140 Moore Arthur, wholesale ironmonger
142 Millgate George
144 Brown Francis
152 Smith Wm. Barnard, accntnt.(Suffolk ho.)
154 Lee Chas.,watchmaker
156 Toll Charles Henry
158 Vey George
160 Harper Joseph
162 Howes Wm.,carpenter
164 Buston Samuel
166 Potter Robert (Allbury house)
168 Howie Mrs.
170 Wilmot Charles(Maygrove cottage)
172 Battock John (Percy villa)
174 Carter Mrs. M. A.
176 Merry George (Oak lodge)

LEFT SIDE.
1 Blackmore Capt. J.,R.N
3 Wright Edward
5 Marrian Henry
7 Riddle Henry
9 Ratto Adolphus
11 Puente Mrs.
13 Killingback Chas. Wm.
15 Thorpe C. Stuart
17 Green W. H.
19 Stephens Benjamin
23 Smith W. Crowther
25 Petch Alfred
27 Paterson Mrs. W. R. (Clive villa)
37 Reeve Mrs. Jane
39 Pask Arthur Thomas
—*Fordwych rd.*
41 Sparks T. B.
43 Anley George
45 Bartrum Mrs.
47 Bishop Mrs.
49 Nightingale John
51 Blockley Edward
53 Goodwin John M.

MEDLEY ROAD,
Kilburn.
From Iverson rd.
F 5   **4**
1 Freeman John
2 Freer Ireson
3 Syme David John
4 Minister Mrs. F. A.
5 Webb Benjamin Wm.
6 Callaway Henry
7 Stringer Alfred Herbt.
9 James William Henry
10 Sowerby Edward Jsph.
11 Haxell James
12 Bridger Frederick Voller, registrar of births and deaths, attendance given on Tuesday and Friday evenings from 7 to 8 p.m.

MERTON ROAD.
From 165 Adelaide rd.
G 7   **8**
1a Köttgen Gustav
—*Adelaide rd.*
1 Howard Cosmo Gordon (The Grove)
2 Wilson Crawford
4 Spears Mrs.
6 Buchanan George
7 Gylby Miss

MESSINA AVENUE,
Kilburn.
From 232 High rd.
G 5   **4**
LEFT SIDE.
—*Kingsgate rd.*
15 Judson Benjamin
17 Spray Thomas
19 James Alfred
21 Cooke Mrs.
23 Daugars Mrs. & Miss
Byatt Charles A. F. (Suffolk house)
Foot Alfred Edwin (Helsdon house)
Kerr-Smith Rev. W. (The Parsonage)
Edwards Capt. Charles (North lodge)
Newton Mrs. Henry (Brendon house)
Culling James(Rutherford house)
194 Hicks E.
195 Mellor Mrs.
Goring Harry (Lindore villa)
RIGHT SIDE.
4 Jacobs Mrs.
6 Asplet G., teacher of french
8 Bridle W.
12 Duncan Mrs.
14 Yescombe Mrs.
20 Goldstein Walter
22 Lockhart Mrs.
24 Lovell Mrs.
36 Broughton A.
38 Lewis Edward
40 Wyatt Mrs.
42 Beit Mrs.
44 Davis Mrs.
46 Hayter Mrs.
48 Dean William
50 Kelly Duncan George
52 Webb Mrs.
54 Hayes J. C.
—*Kingsgate rd.*
Richmond Villas.
7 West Edward
6 Rosher Percy
5 Raggett R.
4 Saer William
4 Saer Mrs., dressmaker
3 Stewart Rev. George
2 Fueski Madame Rosalia
1 Mott William Ruffell

MESSINA AVENUE—*contd*
Messina Avenue.
Rackham Rev. H. E. (Florence villa)
Mosley Mrs. (Taunton lodge)
Nobes W. J. (Gloucester house)
Lanham Walter J. (Surrey villa)
Mogford John (Cawthorne)

Midland Cottages,
see Cricklewood & Mill lane.

MILL LANE,
Kilburn.
From Cricklewood to West end.
E 5   **4**
RIGHT SIDE.
Price Sidney (Kingsgate farm)
Midland Cottages.
10 Harms John
9 Brian David
8 Reedman Wm. Fredk.
7 Parker George
6 Harris Robert
5 Dury William
4 Mullens Arnold
3 Renshaw Charles
2 Mattock John
1 Halls John
Mill Lane.
Wythe Albert, builder (Albert house)
—*Ravenshaw st.*
20 Smith Henry (New West End dairy)
—*Broomsleigh st.*
—*Sumatra rd.*
Foster H., draper (Downshire house)
Cedar Villas.
6 Monk Albert
—*Narcissus rd.*
5 Green H. (Fernside)
4 Nobbs Charles William
3 Romanes Mrs.
2 Newman John
1 Colchester James
Mill Lane.
James Saml. (Trevlyn)
Snell Alfred Walter (Everley)
Watling David (Elm cottage)

LEFT SIDE.
Tompkins Walter (Rose cottage)
Grand Junction Water Works; Wm. Watts, reservoir keeper
Cottage Home for Destitute Orphan Girls; Miss M. A. Cole, supt.
—*Hillfield rd.*
EMMANUEL CHURCH
Watt's Cottages.
8 Abercrombie Mrs., lndrs
6 Brewer Mrs.
5 Stevens George
4 Watts Miss
3 Dawson Wm., bricklyr.
2 Spicer Robert, farrier
1 Davis Mrs.
Mill Lane.
Schofield Mrs. (Rose cottage)
Farnall Mrs. George Rooke (Burley lodge)
Emmanuel Schools

MINERVA PLACE.
From 48 High st.
E 6   **1**
Askew Samuel (Albion house)
Nixon Thomas

MORTIMER CRES.
From 12 Mortimer rd.
G 5   **4**
RIGHT SIDE.
Farmer Leopold (Severn villa)
Dickenson Chas. Henry (Isis house)
Frankenstein Saml. M. (Cherwell house)
Gowler A. (Esk villa)
Davies Mrs. (Coniston house)
LEFT SIDE.
Balfour Jno. (Mayfield)

MORTIMER ROAD,
Kilburn.
From 19 Greville rd.
G 5   **4**
RIGHT SIDE.
1 Winterton W. R.
2 Nelke Paul
3a Finlay Alexander L.
3a Macculloch Mrs.
3b Hornidge Miss

4 Allen John
5 Woodin Mrs.
6 Lett Arthur, architect
9 Turner Haswell Joseph (The Rowans)
10 Manlove Mrs.
11 Orchard Frederick
12 Thompson Frederick (Kingswood)
—*Mortimer cres.*
—*Springfield villas*
LEFT SIDE.
Boskowitz Ignatz (North hall)
Stanley Wm. Edward (Harlestone villa)
St. Peter's Home and Sisterhood
Milne J. V., B.A., F.R.G.S (Henley house school)
Milne Alexander, B.A (Henley house school)

MOUNT VERNON.
From Holly pl. to Holly hill.
E 6
North London Hospital for Consumption and Diseases of the Chest; Lionel F. Hill, M.A. sec
Miss Blaxland, mtrn
Tucker Harry (Holly terrace)
Pearce Edwd. (Mount Vernon cottage)
1 Butler Christopher, jun
2 Butler Christopher
4 Comyns Alfred
5 Ritchie Robert, landscape gardener
6 Morris Henry
Gandar W. (Abernethy house)

Munden Cottages,
G 5
West end lane.

MURRAY PLACE.
From 67 Flask walk.
E 6
1 Hodder George
2 Hill Benjamin

MURRAY TERRACE
From 67 Flask walk.
E 6
1 Rouse William

2 Warner John
3 Gardener George
  Jones George(The Cottage)

MUTRIX ROAD.
From Quex rd.

G 5   **4**

St. Dominic's School

NARCISSUS ROAD,
West Hampstead.
From Mill lane.

E 5   **4**

1 Greer John Henry
2 Sellick John George
3 Driver David
5 Ready Charles
6 Waymouth Frederick
7 Hicks William
7 Hicks Mrs.,accouchuse.
  of the female medical society
8 Webb Jsph.Jas.,builder

NASSINGTON RD.
From 22 South hill pk. rd.

E 7   **1**

3 Atkinson James
5 Topping John
6 Moody John

NETHERHALL TER.
From Fitzjohns' avenue
to Finchley new rd.

F 6   **1**

RIGHT SIDE.

1 T h o r n e l y   Charles
  (Netherhall house)
2 Parker Mrs. G. Russell
  (Netherhall lodge)
2 Parker Herbert S.
  (Netherhall lodge)
3 Howard Charles (Alton
  house)
4 Arnold Jacob
5 Cuthbertson Thomas
6 Wilson R. (St. Kilda)
7 P i c k w o r t h Rowland
  (Kenmure)
  Leckie Peter(Braemar)
  P u z e y   Frederick
  (Mount Waltham)
  Pope Thomas (Baston
  house)
  Eastlake Lewis(Home
  stead)

LEFT SIDE.

═*Maresfield gardens*
  Fall Thomas(Wensley)
  Collett Walter (Woodbrook)
═*Nutley ter.*
Fitzjohns' Mansions.
  Lush Montague
  Duff William
  Watson Johnston
  Colman Stuart
Netherhall Terrace.
  Davidson Thos., artist
  (Culloden)
  Snell H. Sexton, architect (Hillcotte)

NETHERWOOD ST.,
Kilburn.
From 316 High rd.

F 4   **4**

LEFT SIDE.

1a Neale P., bootmaker
3 Humphreys Mrs.
5 Smith W. P.
7 Smith Frederick
9 Jones Mrs.
13 White Henry,carpenter
15 Gunn Alfred
19 Fitzell Mrs.
21 Hayne Joseph
25 Skinner Richard
27 Scott Miss
29 Whorne George
31 Midson Mrs.
39 Bussey Geo.,upholstrer.
39 Bussey Mrs.,dressmakr.
41 Curtis John Charles,
   laundry
43 Gough William
51 Wingate Charles Geo.
55 Wright Thomas
57 Bentley Mrs.
67 Leitch William
75 Garlick Mrs.
77 Boddy Benjamin Smith,
   carpenter
79 Wright Robert
83 Chambers Henry
85 Owen Thomas
89 Bickel Daniel
91 Crapp William

RIGHT SIDE.

2a Bucknell John Geen,
   builder
2 Needham Francis
4 Dawkings W. E.

6 Pearce James
10 Tofield Robt., carpentr.
20 Shore Danl., beer retlr.
24 Goodchild Mrs., tobacconist and newsagent
26 Jervis H. Frncs.,grocer
28 Yates John, greengrcr.
30 Lonon John, butcher
32 Albrow Wm., fishmngr.
48 Nixon Jas., lay agent
50 Hembrow Charles Geo.
50 *Dispensary,*   Robert
   Connel, M.D.
52 Tyers William, cheesemonger
═*Kelson st.*
  St. Mary's Mission Hall ;
  Rev. W. Kerr-Smith
  M.A., minister
60 Keyworth George
  Board School

NEW END.
From Heath st.

D 6   **1**

RIGHT SIDE.

2 Collin Danl., genl.shop
3 Keys Matthias
  Hampstead Workhouse
10 Simmons George
11 Morris J., drill master
13 & 14 *Hampstead Provident Dispensary ;* J.
  Fenn, secretary
15 Flitt Mrs.Elizabeth A.,
  general shop
16 Parker John, tailor
17 Culverhouse Thomas
18 Pancutt William
19 Wilkins Henry, dairy
20 Adams Mrs., laundress
21 Fowler George, wheelwright
21 Harper Miss
22 Savage Wm.,greengrcr.
23 Watts Thomas
═*Brewhouse lane*
24 Taylor W.,beer retailer
25 Falkner J., gardener
26 Trilsbach Augt., baker
28 Martin Mrs.
29 Brunt John
30 Webb Mrs.
31 Grant Thomas, painter
32 Hern Mrs. Elizabeth,
  dressmaker
═*New end sq.*

NEW END—*continued*
Southwell Terrace.
8 Dawes Miss Mary, restaurant
6 Bourne Sydney
5 Musty Jonah
4 NaylorThos.,cartwright
3 Poole Edwin
2 Leach Mrs. Jane, china dealer
1 Aynscombe Bros.,grcrs.
White Bear lane
Well rd.
LEFT SIDE.
Willow Terrace.
1 Hayter J. G., harness maker
2 Messenger Bros., sign writers
5 Gardner Mrs., dyer
6 Stockley G., plumber
New End.
The Duke of Hamilton, F. W. Smith
Cooksley R. K. (Chestnut house)
Christchurch passage
Grove Terrace.
1 Page Joseph
2 & 3 Hill Wm., grocer
4 Hatch John
5 Lowe George
6 Wicks Mrs.
7 Perry Henry, carpenter and joiner
8 Baxter Mrs.
EBENEZER BAPTIST CHAPEL
9 Calvert Mrs.
10 Cassie Charles
11 FreemanGeo.,bootmkr.
12 Osborne Mrs.
13 Winterman Saml.,grcr.
14 Toomes Richard
Grove pl.

NEW END SQUARE.
D 6   **1**
1 Godfrey Robt.,carpntr.
Low Thomas H., forge
4 Perkins W., builder
5 Richardson Charles
6 Seymour James
Stevens Thomas Alfred (Rose lodge)
7 Fowler C., coach bldr.
PaceThos.,(Teresa cot.)
Pace Miss, dressmaker (Teresa cottage)

Moore Rechab (Heath house)
New end

New West End,
see Finchley new rd.

Norfolk Place,
see Child's hill lane.

NORTH END,
Hampstead Heath.
C 6   **1**
Ambridge Cottages.
1 Hawkins Arthur
2 Howell Allen
3 Hayter William
North End.
HolwellEdwardFredk.
Bryars John
Lay Mrs. Mary Ann, upholsteress
Sheehy Jno., tea grdns.
Fensom James
Benwell Francis, bootmaker
Weeks Mrs. Mary
Jacobs James, laundry
9 Youll Miss
10 Baker Richard
11 Argent William
12 Lloyd James
Infant School, Miss Stowell, mistress (Grove cottage)
StainesWilliamCharles (West house)
Phillips James (Percy house)
Tooley Thos.,dairyman
Durrant Mrs. Caroline, confectioner
Lay Edward, laundry
Golder's Hill Cottages.
Watts Mrs.
Chalk John
Dawters Mrs. Mary Ann, laundry
Roff Josiah, laundry
2 Lay Edward
3 Coney Mrs.
4 Furnell William
5 Lambourn Mrs.,lndry.
6 Crampton James
North End.
Borley Alfred, grocer ; post office
Wells Sir Spencer,bart. (Golder's hill)

White John L. (Ivy house)
Johnston Miss (Manor house)
Golder's Hill Terrace.
1 Reading John
2 Smith Mrs.
3 Foreman James
4 Rogers Mrs.
5 Hammon Mrs.
6 Martin Josiah
7 Kenchatt Philip
8 Ward Matthew
9 Williams W.
10 Clarke Samuel
North End.
Saunders W. P., jobmaster (Elm cottage)
Wildwood Grove.
1 Jackman James Josiah
2 Williams James
3 Johnstone George
4 Egelton Josiah
5 Frost Mrs. Louisa
6 Caplin Charles
7 Hughes Joseph
9 Norris Nehemiah
10 Gardner Thomas
11 Warner W. H.
12 Jack Mrs.
13 Dutton Thomas
Hook Samuel (The Retreat)
Wildwood Terrace.
4 Fell Mrs.
North End.
The Hare and Hounds, William Brett
Welton William (The Limes)
The Bull and Bush, Henry Humphreys
Stowe House.
1 Humphreys Henry
2 Pillans Thos. Dundas
North End.
Haynes Wm. (Wildwood house)
Chapman William (Grove cottage)
Lewin Mrs. (Woodbine cottage)
The Avenue.
Ellis Mrs. Edward
MacInnes Mrs. J. R.
Hoare Miss
North End.
Webb Conrade Elliott (Wildwood lodge)

Wenham Henry James (Wildwood)
Hartwell Mrs. Earl (Wildwood)
Hill Mrs. John Henry (North end lodge)
Jackson Frdk. (Heathside cottage)
Wilson Arthur (Wildwood farm)
Grundon George (Heath farm)

NUTLEY GRDNS.
From Fitzjohns' avenue to Daleham gardens.
F 6
Jackson Alexander (Combehurst)
Venables Mrs. (Iver)

NUTLEY TERRACE.
From Fitzjohns' avenue.
F 6   **1**
Fry S. (Sompting)

OAK GROVE,
Cricklewood.
From 4 Cricklewood lane.
E 3
1 Smith Jonas
5 Humphreys Miss Jennett

OAK HILL PARK.
From Frognal.
E 6   **1**
RIGHT SIDE.
1 Robertson David (Dunedin)
2 Macdonald Rev. W. A., M.A.
3 Henderson Misses
LEFT SIDE.
4 Lindsay T. S.
5 Smith Miss
6 Norris Colonel Henry Macfarlane
6 Norris Miss
7 Toller Charles George
9 Hopkins Manley
10 Claudet Frederic
1 Robertson James
2 Smith Mrs. Curwen
3 Gardner Thomas
Steinkopff Edwd. (Oak hill lodge)

Wigram Rev. F. E.. M.A. (Oak hill house)

Oakland Terrace,
see Cricklewood.

OPPIDANS ROAD,
Primrose Hill.
G 8   **3**
LEFT SIDE.
1 Hales John Wesley, barrister-at-law
2 Spiller Mrs.
3 Corelli Charles
4 Gorton Alfred
5 Braby Mrs.
6 Jellico John (Cromer lodge)
7 Dalziel Thomas
8 Miller Mrs.
9 Jennings Mrs.
11 Todd Charles
12 Hunt Rev. H. G.
13 Wood Richard James
14 Harwood Thomas
15 Peachey Mrs. Pearse
16 Calkin George, professor of music
17 Youatt G. H.
18 Rusby James, F.R.H.S.
19 Law Mrs.
20 Barker John, M.I.C.E.
21 Weekes William
RIGHT SIDE.
Tooth Anthony (Torbay villa)
Rojas de Ruiz Mrs. Nathalie (Aurora vil.)
Atterbury Benjamin J. (Acacia villa)
Wrightson Mrs. (Beaumont lodge)
Webb Mrs. (Park lo.)
Noble William (Hill lo.)
Riessmann Hy. (Saxony villa)
29 Low Mrs.
28 Waggett F. (The Limes)
Levy Charles (Frances villa)
Falconar Lieut.-Colonel Geo. A.H. (Falcon lo.)
Fletcher S. Howard (St. Valérie)

Oriel Cottages,
see Church pl.

ORNAN ROAD.
From Haverstock hill to Belsize lane.
E 7   **2**
Read John Walter (Brightside)
Buston John Truman (St. Ronan's)

OSBORNE TER.,
Kilburn.
From Goldsmith pl.
G 5   **4**
1 Dearing Mrs., drsmkr.
1 Powell Mrs.
2 Kilburn Baths; Alfred Ward, proprietor
Mechanics' Lecture Hall
6, 7, 8 & 9 Roper Wm., general draper

PALMERSTON RD.,
Kilburn.
From High rd.
F 4   **4**
1 Gardner Henry, builder
2 Muddyman William
3 Hargrave Thomas
4 Tole Edward
6 Pelham Frederick
7 Bingham John
8 Jeal John
9 Kersley Mrs.
10 Andrews James
11 Brazier Thomas
11 Brazier Saml., bootmkr.
12 Byrchall Edwd., lndry.
13 Clarke Thos., plumber
14 Holman Thomas
15 Trussell William
16 Cross Mrs.
18 Baker George
19 Buck Francis
21 Thatcher James
24 Buckoke Mrs.
25 Terry James
26 Carbert John Charles
27 French Mrs.
28 Osgood Charles
Garrett T., carman
Howard I. & W., lath-renders
30 Myers Mrs.
31 Perry Charles, plumber
32 Birch Edwin
33 Pye Richard, carpenter

PALMERSTON RD.—*contd.*

34 Lilley Wm.,bootmaker
36 Harris Henry
37 Parry William
38 Hessel Cornelius
39 Dawson Hy., gardener
40 Shipley Edward
41 Harris Henry
41 *Palmerston Blue Rib-*
   bon Mission Room
Linstead st.
Kelson st.
   Allen J. & Sons, bldrs.
80 Matthews Henry, gen-
   eral shop
81 Bloomer George
81 Cotton W.
Peebles mews
84 Roberts Frederick
85 Biles John
86 Whitcher John
90 Longhurst Rchd.,sweep
91 Bingham Mrs.
92 Marsh Matthew Henry,
   beer retailer
94 Loscombe Jno.,butcher
95 Harper John, provi-
   sion dealer
96 Meadow W., slater, &c
97 Hayes H.,grindery dlr
98 Maile Wm., genl. shop
99 Rudiger Mrs., baker

PARK ROAD,
Haverstock Hill.
From No. 110.

F 8   **2**

RIGHT SIDE.

2 Wilson Robert
6 Loop Harry
8 Hill H. R.
10 Collins Ernest
14 Lawrence John
18 Matthews Henry Peter
20 Shiell R. S.
22 Miles George R.
24 Hastie Peter
26 Adolph Albert Joseph
28 Powell Eyre B., C.S.I.
30 Raw John Frederick
32 Browne Charles
34 Arrowsmith Thomas J.
36 White Adolphus Chas.
38 Manly Miss
42 Bertlin Mrs.
44 Cuddon Mrs.
46 Bagshawe Mrs. C.

---

50 Walton George
52 Graham Mrs.
54 Tuck Harry
Church rd. & The Mall
58 Rotter Charles G.
60 Low Miss Marie A.,
   artist
62 Read John R.
64 Bullen Mrs.
66 Turner George William
68 Lovell William H.
70 Slater John
74 Johnston Mrs.
76 Brennan Mrs.
78 White John
80 Whitehead Miss
82 Rance Mrs.
   Clements James, florist
   (Park road nursery)
90 *The Fleet Tavern,*
   William Hy. Williams
92 Satterthwaite E.,btmkr
94 & 98 Ruck Thos.,builder
96 Evans E. & D., dairy
100 Loader R., greengrcr.
102 Maule W. P., chemist

LEFT SIDE.

1 Lee S.(Bathford lodge)
3 Munday Miss
5 Jackson Mrs. George
   (Langdale villa)
9 Barnes Misses, ladies'
   school
11 Danby Thomas, artist
13 Biddolph Mrs.
15 Hamper Henry
17 Mogford John, R.I.
19 Marks Benjamin
21 Yeld Edward
23 Wood Lewis J., artist
25 Squire Josiah
27 Joyce Mrs. Jane
29 Hansom H.
31 Ball C. J.
33 Dyke Charles
35 Robertson Mrs.
37 Horsley Miss
39 Vanlessan N.
41 Sangster James
43 Atkins Mrs.
45 Batterbury Miss
Church rd.
47 Milner William(Green-
   side villa)
49 Banner William
51 Seton Robert
53 Hose Rev. J. C.

Park Road Studios.

1 Hill J. S., artist
2 Raeburn-Macbeth —,
   artist
5 Bell J. S., artist
Lower cross rd.

Park Road.

57 Compton Mrs.Caroline,
   laundry
57 Muschamp F., furni-
   ture dealer & valuer
59 Flack Matthew, din-
   ing rooms
   London Street Tram-
   ways Company,Lmtd.
   (stables of the)

PARLIAMENT
HILL ROAD.
From South hill park.

E 7   **1**

LEFT SIDE.

1 Acton Roger
3 & 4 *Hampstead Home*
   Hospital and Nurs-
   ing Institute ; Miss
   Macnicoll, matron ;
   R. A. Owthwaite,
   honorary secretary
5 Friend Mrs. Sophia
6 Smith Miss
7 Jay Mrs. C.
8 Lucas Frederick
9 Hearn G. F.
10 Leese Mrs.
11 Smithers Frederick W.
12 Byles Mrs.
13 Lowden Thomas C.
14 Clay William James
   South Hill Park Road
   Estate Office
15 Sontaine A.
17 Atkinson George
19 Fisher Thomas
21 Smyth Luke D., M.D.
   (Dunnaweil)
23 Ward Mrs.(Maescwyn
25 Hart William
27 Osborne Thomas
29 Bakewell Robert S.
31 Spawforth Joseph
69 Lalor R. D., M.D.
71 Ham Rev. Jas. Panto
73 Ely Talfourd
75 Castle Henry James
   RIGHT SIDE.
16 Roe Mrs.
18 Baynes Herbert Morto

) Murray Oswald
2 Hill Lewin

Nassington rd.

4 *Countess of Ducie's Home for Ladies* (Evenlode house)
6 Harris Henry, survyr.
5 Harris Mrs., boarding house
8 Ellerton Alfred
0 Rhodes Mrs.
2 Mathieson F. Frewin
4 Fraser Mrs.
6 D'Ambrumeniel Benrice
8 Rolfe George
0 Elder William David
2 Cross John
2 Mellor Benjamin
6 Schleicher Otto
8 Timme Oscar
0 Forbes David (Craigforth)

Paxon's Cottages,
see Church lane.

'ERRIN'S COURT.
From 73 High st.

6   **1**

LEFT SIDE.
a LloydWm., greengrcr.
3 Littlefield Edward
a 3rd *Middlesex Volunteers(Hampstead Detachment)*; F.Lawler, sergeant-instructor
a Dare John, hairdresser

RIGHT SIDE.
* Mousley George, bootmaker
* KippinEdmond, sweep
a Bates J.
* Pull Thos.,frame makr.
5 Neal Thomas William, tobacconist
Clowser Thos., builder
* Pearce J. A.
* Wintle Mrs.

ILGRIM'S LANE.
From Rosslyn hill.

7   **1**

* Chamberlain Edmd.T., landscape gardener
Williams Thornton A.
ROSSLYN HILL UNITARIAN CHAPEL

Sadler Rev. Dr. Thomas (Rosslyn manse)
Wilkin Martin Hood (Sydney house)
Wilkin Miss (Cossey cottage)

Kemplay rd.

PILGRIM'S PLACE.
From 13 Rosslyn st.

E 7   **1**

1 Caudell Daniel,painter
2 Emery Thomas
3 Eyers Mrs. M.

PLATT'S LANE.
From Finchley rd. to Hampstead heath.

D 5   **1**

West Middlesex Water Works (Kidderpore Reservoir) ; Henry English, reservoir attendant ; John Geary, turncock
Hobbs Joseph (The Farm)

POND STREET.
From Hampstead green to South end rd.

E 7   **1**

9 Rainbow Henry J.
10 Gilchrist Mrs. Matilda
11 Hunter J. H.
12 Kennedy John
13 Smith John, carpenter
14 GoodmanEdmd.,grocer

Portland Villas,
see East Heath rd.

PRIMROSE HILL ROAD.
From Regent's park rd. to Belsize park gardens.

G 8   **2 & 3**

[*Nos. 1 to 21 Left side and 2 to 38 Right side Ward 3. The remaining Nos. in Ward 2.*]

LEFT SIDE.
1 Russell Mrs. (Garston house)
5 Clarkson Mrs. (Thirsk house)

7 Ellis Mrs. (Ely house)
9 Crump William A. (Rugby house)
11 Shaw James J. (Elsworthy house)

Elsworthy rd.
CHURCH OF ST. MARY THE VIRGIN

King Henry's rd.
13 Thornhill Edwd. Baylis
15 Cappel Mrs.
17 Wilson Mrs. J. W. (Gordon house)
19 Rea Russell

Adelaide rd.
23 Haycroft Mrs. (Trenton villa)

RIGHT SIDE.
2 Gregory Thomas (Hill View)
4 Streeter Edwin W. (The Mount)

Ainger rd.
6 Whitaker J. (Hillside)
10 DunhamMrs.Elizabeth
12 Slater Henry
14 Powell Lewis
16 Evans Edwd. Prichard
18 Maitland Frederick
22 McKee Samuel J.
24 Samuel Joseph
26 Mallalue AlbertGeorge
28 Williamson Alex. W., professor of chemistry

Oppidans rd.
32 Buzzard William
34 Gerstley Morris
36 Guiterman Sigmund
38 Harris Mrs.

Adelaide rd.
40 Rogers Thos. (Lynton house)
42 Regnart Miss, preparatory school

Fellows rd.
44 PortCharlesG.J.(Staincliffe)
46 Mitton Welbury James (Thornthwaite)
48 Buck H. O., M.D. (Buckhurst)
50 Heelas James, M.D.
50 *South Hampstead Private Hospital and Invalid Home and Nursing Institute* (Erskine lodge)

married Ellen Louisa GOSLETT

PRINCE ARTHUR MEWS.
E 6
From Church lane.
4 Chambers Miss, dressmaker (Prince Arthur's cottage)

PRINCE ARTHUR ROAD.
From Rosslyn hill to Ellerdale rd.
E 6   *1*

RIGHT SIDE.
Hampstead Public Library and Literary Institute ; A. Wilson, honorary treasurer (Stanfield house)
6 Martelli Mrs.
8 Groves F. W.
Paveley George (Vernal house)
12 Burnett George
14 De La Condamine Robert C.
Greenhill rd.
16 Topham F. W. W. (Ifield)
18 Carlill Mrs. (Fernbank villa)
LEFT SIDE.
1 Andrews Dr. James (Everleigh)
Greenhill rd.
3 Curwen Mrs. Thomas (Westridge)
5 Price Chas. (Homelea)
7 Blumfeld Louis (Brauneck)

PRINCESS MEWS.
From 2a Belsize cres.
F 7   *1*
5 Peter H., gas and hot water engineer

Princess Terrace,
now numbered in Belsize rd.

PRIORY MEWS,
Kilburn.
From 6 Abbey lane.
G 5   *4*
Palmer Thomas, cowkeeper
Barnes R.C., contractor

PRIORY ROAD,
Kilburn.
From Belsize rd.
G 5   *4*

LEFT SIDE.
1 Barnes Walter
3 Spofforth John Richard
5 Savage Nathaniel
9 Willis Walter, A.K.C., civil engineer
13 Wilson Alfred Harry
15 Nickolls George Albert
17 Bergtheil Louis M.
19 Pereda Mdme. Vicento
25 Nicholas John
29 Bergman Conrad
31 Jeffs Harry
33 Duncan Mrs.
35 Fulton Mrs. Alexander
37 Prout William
39 Bidgood Frederick
Abbott's rd.
41 Hopkins William Henry artist (St. Hubert's lodge)
43 McRae James Gilbert (Braeside)
45 Maas W. J.
47 Abrahams S. B.
49 Harting Joseph T.
51 Flower Harry T.
Abbey rd.
53 Bonas Henry
55 Hudson A. R.
57 Levi Gerald A.
Wavel mews
59 Tyssen Amherst Daniel, D.C.L., barrister-at-law
61 Marks Henry (Mayevelda)
63 Churchill John (Courcils)
65 Collinson William
Acol rd.
67 Bingham Wm. (Besthorpe)
69 Barber George L.
71 Head Chas. (Newlands)
Woodchurch rd.
73 Weldon H. (Churchill)
75 Stillwell Mrs. (Eastcote)
77 Tetley Joseph
79 Hertz Leon (Hollywood)
81 Waterlow David S. (Fairlight)

83 Stubbs William, solicitor (Woodstock)
85 Pritchett H. Talbot (Cleve court)
Cleve rd.
87 Gibbs Clement (Edgbaston)
89 Bennett Mrs. (Waldridge house)
93 Hay Mrs.
95 Stone Mrs.
99 Oakes Arthur, M.D. (Merimbula)
Chislett rd.
101 Magee Mrs.
103 Stohwasser Francis A. (Warwick lodge)
105 Adams Mrs. (Knotty wood)
107 Howard Wm. Fredk. (Arundel house)
109 Boulton Mrs. (Avondale)
111 Irvine R. J.
113 Parkyn William B.
115 Docker F. A. W., professor of music (Kingston)
117 Beasley George F. (Westward Ho)
119 Unwin George (Wisteria)
121 Hanson Oliver Henry (Astoria)
Broadhurst gardens
RIGHT SIDE.
2 Goodliffe Wm. Gimber
4 Rowan James *
6 Dixon Frederick
8 Barnes Samuel
10 Warner Robert
12 Houghton John Moor
14 Davis Shelly K.
16 Kirkwood Mrs. Eliza
18 Coulthard Rev. Ernest Newton, M.A.
18 Coulthard William
22 Davis Charles
24 Barnewall Henry Chas.
26 McBean Miss
30 Dymond Miss
30 Bowman Miss, ladies' school
32 Strickland Wm. George
34 Freeman Henry P.
36 Trickey Frank
38 Hayman Phenœus

4 Sherrat James, M.A.
 Abbey rd.
 ST. MARY'S CHURCH
0 Roberts Rev. John (St.
 Mary's vicarage)
2 Cobbett H. (Canfield
 house)
4 Baker Joshua (West-
 field)
6 Hunting R. (Holm-
 dale)
8 Allen R. W. Goldhurst
 Goldhurst rd.
0 Rumford J. K. (Oak-
 lands)
4 Tomlinson Joseph
 (Woodchurch)
6 Lotinga Mrs. Leah
 (Lotinga house)
8 Willans J.G (Westcroft)
0 Oldrey Percy
 Westcroft rd.
2 Grosvenor A. Octavius,
 M.D., surgeon (The
 Tower)
4 Hayman Henry
6 Low Robert
8 Beart Victor Oswin
0 Davis Robert (Rosedale)
2 Turner H. J. (Newton
 lodge)
4 Martin Rev. David
 (Coniston house)
6 Middleton Wm. John
 Canfield gardens
8 Hymans Henry (Nor-
 manhurst)
0 Davey Henry
2 Blair P. R.
4 Thornton W. D.
6 McGill Miss (Belair)
8 Yeo Thomas
 Fairhazel gardens
00 Tildesley Edwin
 (Ridgmount)
02 Samuel Maximilian
04 Willson Wm. (Pino)
06 Pardon Arthur (More-
 ton)
08 Batistoni E. (Linden-
 hurst)
 Broadhurst gardens

PROSPECT PLACE
 From Holly pl.
6   1
1 Beauchamp Alfred

2 McGregor Mrs.
3 Richardson William
4 Spendley George

PROSPECT ROAD.
 *From Finchley rd. Child's
 hill.*
 D 5
1 Whitchurch Edwin
2 Cook Edward
4 Maund George
5 Purks Alexander
6 Perryman Frederick
7 Moore Hayman
7 Holloway George, de-
 corator & undertaker
8 Hobbs Arthur
9 Davis David
10 Coxon David
11 Megevan Mrs. Selina
12 Russell Mrs.
13 Marshall John Arthur
14 Sumption William
15 Stubbings James
16 Toye George
17 Whitestone P. B.
18 Rhodes A., carpenter
19 Mayo William S.
20 Abel James
21 Jones Frederick
22 Jones James
23 Hutchings William
24 Johnson A.
25 Shaw Barnett
26 Gower John
27 Statham Fredk. Geo.
28 Disney George
29 Downing Arthur
30 Etheridge James
31 Walden Emanuel
32 Cash W., bootmaker
33 Marsden William
34 Kirby Henry George
35 Carter Isaac
36 Watts Charles
38 Chilcott Thomas Robert
 Prospect Villas.
1 Jones Richard
1 Rushton James, piano-
 forte tuner
2 White Charles
4 Hunter Walter Oswald
5 Mapple Alfred

Prospect Villas,
 see Prospect rd.

Providence Place,
 see West end.

PROVIDENCE PL.,
 Kilburn.
 *From Belsize rd. to
 West end lane.*
 G 5   4
1 Jackson Charles W.
2 Bird Emanuel
3 Cook Mrs. E.
4 Batchelor Jehu
5 Humphreys James
6 Brice William
7 Gillett Alfred
8 Baker Robert Henry
9 Collard Mrs.
 William Terrace.
1 Grundy Peter
2 Bonner Robert
3 Smith Frederick W.
4 Schwieso Frederick
5 Hughes Joseph, gas
 engineer
6 Barry Abel Thomas
 Edward Terrace.
1 Dennis Mrs., senior,
 monthly nurse
2 Crawford Richard
3 Dennis Edward
4 Annets Edward
5 Grover William
6 Parker Tom

Provident Place,
 see Cricklewood lane.

PROVOST ROAD.
 *From College rd. to Eton
 road.*
 F 8   2
1 Cormock Mrs.
2 Pearce W. T.
3 Lipscombe W.
4 Shute William
5 Thairlwall Mrs.
6 Roberts William F.
8 Innes Robert
8 Gower Mrs.
9 Sillars Rev. Duncan
10 Edmunds Silas
11 Daniels George Walter
13 Macgregor Alexander
14 Smith Miss
15 Howard John C.
17 Lammin Miss E.
18 Turner Mrs.
19 Maile George Charles

QUEX ROAD,
Kilburn.
From 126 High rd.
G 5   **4**

RIGHT SIDE.

1 Verey A. S. & Co., wine
  and spirit merchants
  Crook C. W., jobmaster
    (Quex mews)
  Snowball John (Fern
    villa)
  Blumenthal M. A. (Ivy
    villa)
  Baker A. (Pine villa)
  Ramus Isaac (Olive
    villa)
  Sharp John (Lime
    villa)
  Chase Misses (Haddon
    lodge)
  Posener A.(Acacia vil.)
  Cattanach Jas. (Lawn
    villa)
  *Convent of the Sisters
  of Hope for Nursing
  the Sick*(Hope house)
  Westlake N. J.(Falcon
    house)
⸺*Mutrix rd.*
  Hewitt Mrs. (Grafton
    lodge)
  Meyer Mrs. S. (Carlton
    house)
  Willey Josiah (Buck-
    land house)
  Du Pre Miss J. (Bea-
    consfield house)
  Lechmere Rev. W. L.
    (Orsett house)
LEFT SIDE.
  Howe Arbourn, gas-
    fitter (Leith house)
  Gray & Smyth Mes-
    dames, shirt & collar
    dressers
2 Turner T., hairdresser
3 Cole Richard,stationer
⸺*Kingsgate rd.*
  WESLEYAN CHAPEL
  CHURCH OF THE
  SACRED HEART
  New Priory.
  O'Donnell Very Rev.
    P., D.D.
  Cox Rev. Charles
  Ring Rev. W.

RAVENSHAW ST.,
West Hampstead.
From Mill lane.
E 5   **4**

RIGHT SIDE.

1 Davis J. W.
2 Bignell E.
3 Mills Josiah
  Tidd David(Lovedons)
7 Mustill J.
8 Waddleton J.
  Denton Charles (Oak-
    ley villa)
  Denton Mrs.,dressmkr.
    (Oakley villa)
15 Cox W. J., carpenter
  Bufton Wm. F. (Mos-
    sat villa)
  Dakers David (Isla
    villa)
  Lowe H. Reginald(Tay
    villa)
LEFT SIDE.
1*a*Bradsell T.
4 Camp A. W.

REDDINGTON RD.
From Frognal.
E 6   **1**

  Lawford Percy(Wood-
    cote)
  Pfeil A. L. A.(Wiston)
  Burnaby Rev. Sherrard
    Beaumont, M.A. (The
    Vicarage)
4 Holland Jos. Robberds
    (Wellesley house)

Regent's Park Rd.,
*see our "Camden and Ken-
tish Towns Directory."*

Richmond Villas,
see Messina avenue.

Ridge Mews.
From Cricklewood lane.

Ridge Terrace,
see Child's hill.

Rockall Terrace,
see Cricklewood.

ROSSLYN COTTS.
From 13 Rosslyn st.
E 7   **1**
5 Dickens Timothy

4 Newman Mrs.
3 SaundersMrs.,umbrell
  maker
2 Somerville Mrs.
1 Ginn William John

Rosslyn Gardens,
see Belsize lane.

ROSSLYN HILL.
*From Hampstead hill
gardens to Rosslyn st.*
E 7

  Atkinson Mrs. Beau
    mont (South grove)
  Cornford Rev. Jame
    (Grove house)
  Winter Robt., surgeo
    (Eland house)
  White Z. (York house
  Watts Mrs. (Clare ho
  Hayward James (Lau
    rel cottage)
⸺*Downshire hill*
  Smith Thomas Eustac
    (Elm cottage)
  Cowell Albrt.(St.Ann
    cottage)
  MauriceChas.Edmund
    barrister (Sydney cot
  Hood C. C. (Rossly
    hill house)
⸺*Pilgrim's lane*
  Gardner Wm.(Heddo
    house)
  Nash William
  Redfern W. G. T
    collegiate school
  Redfern Mrs. (Abe
    crombie villa)
  Police Station; Davi
    Collis, inspector
  *Soldiers' Daughter
  Home;* C.R.Lowe, sec
    Miss Bartlett, matro

ROSSLYN LANE.
From Rosslyn hill.
E 7
  CawthornJoseph (Vin
    lodge)

ROSSLYN STREE
*From Rosslyn hill to
High st.*
E 7
  Rosslyn Hill Schools
1 Davies & Evans, oilm

1 Whitehorn Thos., watch-maker
2 Banger John W., tailor
3 Day Miss E., dyer
4 Price Wm., fishmonger
5 King Mrs. L., tobccnst.
6 Brumbridge Jas., dairy
7 Haines Geo., poulterer
8 Britton Jas., bootmaker
9 Carver Miss, baby-linen warehouse
10 Lunn L., sign writer
10 Lunn Mrs., confectnr.
11 & 12 Dudman John, grcr.
Rosslyn cottages
13 Baily Wm. H., draper
14 Woodward Miss J., bookseller
15 Camp James, greengrocer
16 *The Rosslyn Arms*, Frank Raggett
17 MILLIST AND SON, grocers and provision merchants
18 MILLIST AND SON, china and glass warehouse
19 Gray W. C., hairdresser

ROSSLYN TER.
From Mansfield villas to Rosslyn hill.
E 7   **1**
1 Cooper Dr. Herbert, surgeon
2 Renton Mrs.
3 Morton Thomas Honor
4 Lang Mrs. S. T.
5 Evans Charles E., architect
   Rose Henry Cooper, M.D. (Penrose house)

RUDALL CRES.
From Willoughby rd.
E 7   **1**
LEFT SIDE
1 Shaw John, M.D.LOND. (Burlington house)
3 Boyce Mrs. (Palasmore)
7 Fuller Mrs. Frances
11 Parkinson Herbt. Wm.
13 May William Charles, sculptor (Penn house)
15 Fleming James (Hastings villa)

17 Rochford T. (Dunloe villa)
19 Kennedy Rev. John, D.D. (Cluny cottage)
21 Walker John James, M.A., F.R.S. (Canny cot)
23 Johnson Percy
RIGHT SIDE.
2 Gardner Percy, D.L.
4 Ash E. C.
6 Carwardine Thomas

St. Ann's Terrace,
see Gascony avenue.

ST. GEORGE'S RD.,
Kilburn.
From 224 Belsize rd.
G 5   **4**
LEFT SIDE.
1 Leveroni James
3 Sharp Mrs.
5 Davidson Alexander
7 Loveridge George A.
9 East Henry
13 Maurier Eugene du
15 Hunt G. W.
17 Stevens Jas. Edmund (Wilton villa)
19 Morris Jas., B.A., tutor
21 James Miss
23 Strugnell Geo. Fredk.
27 Chope Rev. Thomas
29 Hooper Wm. E. Parry
31 Leefe Octavius
33 Gilbert Mrs. Thomas W. (Carlton house)
39 Wharton Hy. Thornton, M.A., M.R.C.S., F.Z.S., surgeon
Abbey rd.
RIGHT SIDE.
2 Clarke Wellington, school (Temple lo.)
8 Boram Arthur William
10 Rishworth Walter W.
12 Haydon William
14 Reade J. H.
16 Griffiths Mrs.
18 Salter Mrs. (St. George's college)
20 Marshall Mrs.
22 Willis Mrs.
30 Watson Mrs.
32 Stapleton Miss
34 Smedley J. V., M.A.

ST. JOHN'S WOOD PARK.
From Upper Avenue rd. to Queen's rd.
G 6   **3**
RIGHT SIDE.
1 Hill Richard
2 Edmunds G. R.
3 Harris Mrs. Alicia
4 Michel L. E.
5 Pannot J.
6 Catenhusen A., MUS. DOC.
8 Faulconer Thomas, J.P.
10 Pleister Mrs., preparatory school
11 Palmer Lady
12 Dickens George
13 Davis Lewis
14 Thorne Edwin R. (The Birches)
Boundary rd.
16 Wood Mrs. (Ashbury house)
17 Brabant Wm. Frederick, solicitor
18 Luxmoore Coryndon H., F.S.A., M.R.I.
21 Robislio Frederick
22 Taylor Frederick
24 Johnson J., M.D.
LEFT SIDE.
   Gardner J. E. (Park ho.)
   Roberts Thomas Alex. (The Manor hall)
   Smithers Arthur E. (Holmefield)
31 Perrin Henry Story
32 Green Edwin
33 Smith Richard
34 Monsell John Crawford
35 Cossart William
37 Peile Mrs.
38 Bland Thomas C.
39 Heydemann Edward
40 Edwards Charles
41 Biggs George
43 Rumpff T. A. A.
44 Clark Mrs.
45 Cotton Mrs.
46 Walker Andrew Gillon
   Howden D. (Manor ho.)

Saunders Cottages
see Child's hill.

SHERRIFF ROAD,
Kilburn.
From 5 Exeter ter.
West end lane.
RIGHT SIDE.

F 5   **4**

1 Dobbs Samuel
3 Pope John Thomas (Rutland villa)
5 Patey Alfred George
7 Gittins Henry (Firbeck villa)
8 Beete A. F.
9 Webber Mrs.
11 Herbert Wilfrid V., artist
13 Hunter Andrew
15 Clayton Geo. Augustus (Brisbane house)
17 Berry Edward Unwin, M.R.C.S.
19 Thornbury Bruce
21 Humphris William H.
LEFT SIDE.
2 Lidstone Thomas (Devonia)
4 Chaplin Henry (Aldbury)
6 Inman H. B. (Heathfield)
8 Wilson Mrs. (The Laurels)
—*Hilltop rd.*
10 Millard Mrs. (Penshurst)
12 Perkins George Henri
20 AitchisonThos., builder
22 Monks Dr. F. Aubyn (Health villa)

Shoot-up Hill,
see Cricklewood.

SILVER STREET.
From Heath st.
E 6   **1**
2 Markham Alfred
3 Hawkins Joseph
4 Brown Thomas
5 Bassett Henry

SOUTH END GREEN
From Pond st. to South end rd.
E 7   **1 and 2**
Crump Miss Anne (Hereford house)

—*Fleet rd.*
Shockley R., florist
White Horse Terrace.
3 Hislop Chas., bootmkr.
2 Daniel S., tobacconist
South End Green.
The White Horse, Jos. Webster
Allen Edward (Clifton house)
Alexander Mrs., baker (Roseberry cottage)
Harrison Samuel (Elm cottage)
Mills Eli (South end house)
Jennings George
St. Stephen's Infant School
4 Humble Wm. Roger
3 Hodgkins Thomas
2 Yeomans James, gardener and florist
1 Cooper Mrs.
Pavier Mrs., dairy
Luckman Wm., marine store dealer
The Railway Tavern, Wm. John Matthews
—*South end rd.*
Parsons Mrs., confectioner(Elizabeth cot.)
Smith John, carpenter

SOUTH END ROAD.
From South end green to Willow rd.
E 7   **1**
Ambler G., florist and nurseryman
Hampstead Heath Stn. L.& N.W.& N.L.Rwy.
Nowell& Robson, stone merchants & contrctrs
Wigan Coal & Iron Co.; C. Parker and Son, agents
BINNINGTON F. T., house and land agent, opposite Hampstead Heath station
BarlowMrs.E.I.(Lower mount cottage)
Griffin James, builder (Fulbeck cot.)
—*John st.*
Aumonier Frederick (Russell house)

Oliver Mrs. (Leigh house)
Shinn Mrs. (Rose cot.)
Gardiner Thomas,landscape gardener (Aberdeen house)
Mitchener Hy. (Montrose)
Baptie Alexander Wm (Woodbine)
Barnes Henry (Southwell cottage)
Skilton Mrs. John (St John's cottage)
Callingham James (Bronté cottage)
George Edward H (Weston cottage)
Baptie John (Guernsey cottage)
Staples Charles (Bath cottage)
Alexander Frederic (Ivy cottage)
TrudgettStephen(Duncan cottage)
Barnes George Willia (Heath cottage)
Cooper Christophe
Bird, solicitor (Hartley house)
Bracken James (Jaspe house)
Brown Benjamin (Ben Lomond house)
New River Co.'sStatio.
Robinson Hercules deputy turncock

SOUTH HILL PARK
E 7

RIGHT SIDE.
1 Dottridge Alfred Ja
3 Sleep G. C., professo of caligraphy an stenography
5 Milne Miss
7 Rayner Edward
9 Hale Thomas Willia
11 Aubert Fredk. Charle artist
13 Johnson Thos.Matthe
15 Benard Mrs.
17 Hanscomb Edwar Knight
19 Alexander James
21 Rither Adolphe

3 Roberts Edward Chas.
5 Oakes Sydney
7 Sharp Thos. Stephen
9 Smith Robert
11 Hepburn James
13 Purry A. A.
15 Jones Philip
17 Buss Decimus
19 Henley Lionel Charles
21 Joseph David
23 Rance George
27 Smith Misses, ladies' school (Kenhurst)
29 Parkinson Joseph
31 Meyer Barrington
33 Crozier Rev. Richard
35 McWilliam Robt., B.A.
37 Miller Henry
39 Holmes Frederic Morell
41 Senior Charles
43 Hepburn W. Arnold
45 Gavin James Merricks
49 Arthur Rev. David
51 Clough James
53 Lyell John Ronaldson
55 Cocksedge Jno. Hogben
57 Daniels Miss
59 Long Miss Helen
63 Butlin Chas. Montague
65 Pickett Joseph
67 Leal Charles
69 Pownall R. B.
71 Sharp Charles Smithee, builder
73 Meads John
75 Moore John Alldin, barrister-at-law
77 Bennett Edward
99 Lawrence A. M.
101 Shaw Rev. William
101 Southby Edmund R.
103 Watson W. C.
105 Smith Miss
107 Faraday Charles A.
LEFT SIDE.
The Magdala Tavern, Charles Wm. Howell
2 Bird R. A. & Co., drprs.
4 Brown Chas., bootmkr.
6 Maxted Thomas, dairy
8 Rumbold Wm., baker ; post office
10 Rumbold Wm., grocer
12 Pocock G., fruiterer
14 Stringer Thos., decortr.
16 Smith Mrs. B. Sydney
18 Burton James

20 Salmon Mrs. Emily
22 Salmon James Dennis
24 Bernhardt Jules
26 Brand Mrs., professor of music
28 Smith Mrs.
30 Tombs Wm. (Holmwood house)
30 Tombs Mrs., pestalozzian kindergarten (Holmwood house)
32 Burnitt Thomas
34 Grimani Mrs.
36 Ambler George
38 Shipman Miss
40 Black Andrew L.
42 Ayres Edward, L.D.S., surgeon-dentist
44 Renton Edward
46 Hewat John Grayhurst
48 Bakewell Armytage
50 Gordon Robert M.
52 Thomson A. Forbes
54 Woodley Thomas
56 Bridge John, M.A.
60 Bakewell Herbert
62 Hacket Mrs.
64 Higgins Saml. Edwd.
66 Bridger Thomas
68 Brabner John
70 Rogers James Edward
72 Phillips Wm. Phillips
74 Jacob Mrs.
76 Woodall Frederick
78 Rothwell Mrs.
80 Taylor John
82 Ward H. L. D.
84 Johnston Alexander
86 Warner Mrs.
88 Burckhardt John Chas
90 Hudson Morris
92 Balmer James S.
94 Greenhill Chas. Pope, solicitor
96 Wrightson Leonard
98 Bourne Herbert
100 Churchill R. T.
102 Free Richard W.
104 Scammell Whitfield
106 Scammell Alfred Thos.
108 Prosser Wm. Henry
110 Welsh James Edward
112 Wale Frederick
114 Harris H.
114 Griffith Charles
116 Hilbery Francis Wm.

118 Giles Charles S., R.N.

SOUTH HILL PARK GARDENS.
From South hill park.
D 7   1
RIGHT SIDE.
1 Bloomer Caleb
3 Harris H.
5 Turnbull T. D.
7 Mitchell George A.
9 Collie Alexander, M.D.
11 Smith Frederick
13 Fraser Robert Stevens
15 Dixon Thomas
17 Owthwaite R. A.
19 Campbell C.
21 Rose Edward
23 Williams Major-Genl. H. E. T.
LEFT SIDE.
2 Baynes Carleton
4 Blelloch Rev. David
6 Davies Rev. John
10 Sheffield Mrs. Emma
12 Brown Compton Fosbrooke
14 Read Thomas Fredk.
16 Saltmarsh Edward
18 McKinlay Thomas M.
20 Copeland W.
22 Yewens John White
22 Hough Edwin
Hart George (Strad lo.)

South Hill Park Rd.,
now called Parliament hill rd.

Southwell Terrace,
see New end.

Spaniards Road,
see Hampstead heath.

Spencer Terrace,
see Ariel st.

Springfield,
see Gascony avenue.

SPRINGFIELD GARDENS,
Kilburn.
From Springfield villas.
G 5   4
4 List Jas., house decoratr

E

SPRINGFIELD GDNS.—*con*
5 Ellis William
6 Richards Levi
7 Clayden William
8 HamiltonT.,chair caner
9 Beak John, bootmaker
10 Hinton John, sweep
18 Gosling R., bottle dlr.

SPRINGFIELD RD.,

St. John's Wood.
From Abbey rd. to
Loudoun rd.

G 6   **4**

RIGHT SIDE.

1 Wallis Arthur
3 Pringle A. W.
5 Hollingworth Hy. Geo.
13 Hill Hy., prof.of music
15 Moutrie Felix
17 Abrahams Mrs. A.
19 Stevenson Gideon
21 Ring Richard
23 Barfoot E.
25 Stott David
27 Abbott George
29 Chapman James
31 Lesser Mrs.
35 Currie James. sculptor
37 Curtis Hermann
39 Barnett Miss
41 Franklin Fredk. Thos.
43 Paine Jas. H., pianist
45 Humphrey Henry J.
47 Crewe Joseph
49 Banfield Miss Eliza
51 Rayne Mrs.
53 Barrett Edward L.
59 Weal —
61 Morris Mrs.
63 Nock G. T.
65 Humphry Jsph. Alfred
67 Norton Francis
69 King Miss
71 Witt Gerard R.
73 Foulsham Geo.(Bridge house)

LEFT SIDE.
2 Herbert Mrs.
4 Ware Mrs. E.
6 Relph John
8 Shultz Mrs.
10 Maitland David
12 Hyndman Thomas
14 Smyth Mrs.
16 Fletcher Frank
18 De Nops James

20 Haynes George B.
22 Magnus Mrs.
24 Thomas Michael
26 Postlethwaite F. E.
28 Sutherland Mrs.
30 Southwood Fredk. C.
32 MorterWilliam,builder
34 Ellis Mrs. S.
40 Benham Robert Thos.
42 Kelly Miss
44 Matthews Miss Jane
46 Gibbs Thomas
48 Plomer Mrs.
48 Plomer G. D.
50 Robinson H., C.E.,F.G.S.
52 DangerfieldWm.,A.C.A.
54 Lord John
56 Moore William
58 Walker Mrs. Sydney
60 Besch John
62 Felsentein Ludwig
64 Ravenscroft Francis (Birkbeck lodge)

Springfield Villas,

now numbered in Greville
rd. and Kilburn Priory.

SQUIRE'S MOUNT.

From East heath rd.

D 6   **1**
Squire'sMountCottages.
1 Tombs Mrs.
2 Alsop Mrs.
3 Hayter Miss M.
4 Matheson Greville
5 Williams J.
Squire's Mount.
Symons William C. (Chestnut lodge)
Mortlock Miss (South lodge)
Field Mrs. E. W.
⸗*Cannon pl.*
⸗*Heathfield gardens*

STAMFORD PLACE.

From 33 Heath st.
D 6   **1**
15 Williams J., bootmkr.

STANLEY GRDNS.

From England's lane to
Belsize park gardens.
F 7   **2**
LEFT SIDE.
Simpson J., collegiate school(Stanley house)
9 Cropper James C.

15 Hall James
17 Le Cren Samuel
19 Ravenscroft Thomas
21 Nauen Charles
23 Dale Alfred
25 Rylands John Paul
27 Cayley Claude
29 Wray A. W.
31 BrightmanChas.Edwd
33 Widash Fredck. Chas.
35 Glover Mrs.
37 Steele Mrs.Sarah Blake
39 Gifford Miss
41 Hawthorn Genl. Robt
43 Metcalfe Mrs.
45 Davis Miss
47 Messenger Mrs.
49 Thorn W. T.
53 Webb F. H.
55 Wardell Miss
57 Williams Mrs.
RIGHT SIDE.
2 Monville & Co., confectioners
4 McMahonMrs.,milline
6 Greene Mrs.
16 Newton Miss
18 Stevenson Robt. Wm.
20 Russell William
22 Geare Henry Cecil
24 MacDonnell John
26 Waters Capt. Georg Alexander, R.N.
28 Gill Crandon Dawes
30 Barlow B. J.
32 Kent Walter George
34 Pearce L. A.
36 Miller A. W. K.
38 Pearce Arthur Renau
40 Michelson Leopold
42 Bowly Mrs.
44 Waugh T. W. Spense
46 Wurtzburg Edwar Albert, barrister
48 Ratcliff Thomas

Station Villas,

see Cricklewood lane.

STEELE'S MEWS

From Steele's rd.
F 8
Phipps W., jobmaste

STEELE'S ROAD

Haverstock Hill.
From Fellows rd.
F 8
2 Green Edward F.

3 Gould Misses
5 Waugh James
6 Wagner H.
7 Hecht Philip
8 Davis George Acton
9 Shuter James L.
10 Hackett A. R.
11 Grieves John
12 Crews Samuel
14 Manley Mark
——Eton villas
15 Staniland Charles
16 Johnson Miss
17 Bruce Mrs.
18 Edwards Mrs. Elizabeth
19 Gowing Thomas W.
20 Ingpen Edward T.
22 Hanhart Nicholas, LL.B.
——Steele's mews
23 Albert Hilary
24 Thorpe R. H.
25 Smithers William
26 Frankau Frederick J.
27 Boyle Augustine
28 Turner Peter
29 Gill George T. S.
30 Finch Arthur Elley
31 Hollingshead John (Springbank)
32 Allan Robert Weir
33 Morse Thomas F. (Huntley villa)
   Bishop Edward (Woodward villa)
   Linton James D. (Ettrick house)
   Johnson Chas. Edward (Morven house)
   Barnard Fredk. (Warrington house)
   Hayes Edwin (Briscoe house)
   Kilburn George Goodwin (Hawkhurst ho.)
   Kerslake Jno. (Downes Bury)
   Schumann Jno. Ludwig (Laurel bank)

Steele's Studios,
see Haverstock hill.

SUMATRA ROAD.
From Mill lane.
J 4   4
RIGHT SIDE.
1 Somerville Dvd. Hughes

3 Stewart Miss
5 Beill William
9 Chambers George
11 Gibson John K.
13 Miller Charles J.
15 Lawrence John
17 Bullen A. Henry
19 Court Francis
21 Brittain H. A.
23 Told James Albert
25 Wynyard William
LEFT SIDE.
2 Lowe Francis
189 Welsh William Henry
190 McGregor Alexander
——Glenbrook rd.
   Tillman John (Hillside)

SUNNYSIDE VILS.,
Child's Hill.
From Finchley rd.
E 3
1 Uttin Mrs.
2 Beadle Miss
4 Clarke Walpole
5 Roux Hy. Augustus
6 Meo Gaetano
——Cricklewood lane

SWISS TERRACE,
Belsize Road.
G 6   3
Swiss Cottage Railway Station
1 Houghton Herbert, chsmngr. & poulterer
2 Clingo Mrs. E., florist
——Belsize park mews
3 Solesbury G., wine and spirit merchant
4 Humphreys R., pharmaceutical chemist
4 King J. A., artist
5 Evans E., fruiterer
6 Brightwell R. & Son, butchers
7 Browning H., brush and comb warehouse
8 King James, bootmaker
9 Thoden F., watchmaker
10 Dunhill H., pianoforte warehouse
11 Weber H. & Co., cigar merchants
12 Boone Geo., stationer

13 BELCHER JOHN S., corn & flour merchant
14 Thorne Mrs., fishmngr.
15 Tomlins E., grocer
16 Boden J. W., auctneer.

TELEGRAPH HILL.
From West Heath.
D 5   1
   Schroeder William
   McNair James

THE AVENUE.
From Cricklewood lane.
D 4
   Dickers H. J. (Avenue farm)

The Avenue,
see North end.

The Chestnuts,
see Branch hill.

The Cottages,
see Cricklewood lane.

The Gables,
see Vale of Health.

The Green,
see West end.

THE GROVE.
From Windmill hill.
D 6   1
   Trewby Geo. Careless (Fenton house)
   Dawe N. F. (Old Grove house)
   Du Maurier George B. (New Grove house)
   Sharpe Mrs.
   Roche Miss (Grove lo.)
   Witty Richard James (Terrace lodge)
   Smither A. (Netley cot.)

The Mall,
see Church rd. Haverstock hill.

THE MOUNT.
From Heath st.
D 6   1
1 Boulting Wm., L.R.C.P. LOND., surgeon

THE MOUNT—*continued*
2 Alexander Joseph Hy.
  Boulting Wm., senior
   (Belmont house)
  Hudson Miss(Bentham
   house)
  Bell Edward
  Dawson Benjamin,B.A.
   (The Mount school)
  Culleton Thos. (Bath-
   ville house)
  Taylor Alfred, solicitor
   and commissioner for
   oaths & declarations
  Jackson Samuel(Bryan
   house)
  White William (Holly
   cottage)
  District Surveyor's
   Offices; H.E. Kendall,
   surveyor (Holly cot.)
  White William (Caro-
   line house)
  Osborn Charles (St.
   Helen's cottage)
  Baker D., cab propltr.

THE RIDGE,
Child's Hill.
D 4
The Dispensary; Dr.
  Biggs
Ridge mews
  Grundon John, con-
   tractor
  Turpie Joseph, builder
   (The Exchange)
  Abel William, plumber
  Harvey H. (Garfield
   villa)
  Rickard Rev. William
   (Homelea)
  Dunkley Mrs. (Clare-
   mont cottage)
Claremont Villas.
1 Packer Mrs.

The Village,
see Child's hill.

THURLOW ROAD.
From Rosslyn hill.
E 7   **1**
1 Squire Mrs.
2 Isaacson Mrs.
3 Evans, HerbertN.,M.B.,
  surgeon

4 Kirkman Rev. Joshua,
  M.A.
5 Jeremy Walter David
6 Wedmore Frederick
7 Spiller William Cook
8 MathesonRev.Jno.,M.A.
9 Leycester Mrs.
10 Ewart Miss
11 Geoghegan William J.
12 Hertz Heinrich
15 Simpson R.
15 Noel Miss
16 Hallam John B.
17 Laurence Alexander
18 Little Matthew
19 Gentle John
Windsor ter.
  Smith Arnold C.(High-
   bury house)
  Underhill Edwd. Bean,
   LL.D.(Derwent lodge)
22 Monro Frederic
23 Goodchild John
24 Wood W.(TheRowans)
25 Pollock Mrs.
26 Coghlan Mrs.
27 Hill Frederic, barrister
   (Inverleith house)
28 Preston Thomas San-
   some, solicitor
Eldon rd.
29 Neatby Dr. Thomas
30 Field Mrs. Horace

**UPPER AVENUE
ROAD.**
South Hampstead.
G 6   **2 and 4**
RIGHT SIDE.   (*Ward 2*)
  NEWCOLLEGECHAPEL
2 Dunsterville Edward
4 Field Allan
6 Chadwick Mrs. (Boston
   house)
  Schuster Francis Jsph.
   (Sunnyside)
  *London Society Blind
   School;* Mrs. Legge,
   matron
LEFT SIDE.   (*Ward 3*)
1 Archer Lewis H.,surgn.
3 Gray Samuel
5 Crampon Alfred
7 Todd Mrs.
9 Topham Charles
11 Blake Joseph William
13 Stevens Henry, F.S.A.

UPP. BELSIZE TER
South Hampstead.
F 7
1*a* Emery Thos.,ironmng
1 *The Belsize Taver*
   Mrs. E. C. Tidey
2 Camp A., greengroce
3 Barry J. W., carpent
   and upholsterer
4 Cranwell Hy.,bootmk
5 Thomas William
   fishmngr. & poultere
6 Coles W. A., butcher
7 Collins Wm., confctn
8 Dudman John, groce
9 Dudman John, oil an
   colourman
10 Baker & Son, builders
11 PETER HENRY, ga
   fitter and plumber
12 Dudman John, win
   and spirit merchant
12*a* Humphreys R., chemi

UPPER PARK RD
Haverstock Hill.
F 8
    RIGHT SIDE.
2 Wilkinson John Robt
4 Bowen Michael
6 Gowing Richard
8 Morley Henry
10 Cumming Hugh P.
12 BatterburyThomas, a
   chitect
14 Hair John
24 Haycraft W.Sydenha
28 Angus John
30 Dorrell George Edwar
36 Duncan Mrs.
Church rd.
38 Hawkins Edward Tho
40 White John Power
42 Preedy Mrs.
44 Tunley George
50 Cocke T. H.
52 Steinberg N. S. E.
56 Pyne Thomas
58 Le Brasseur Mrs. H.
60 Willing James
Fleet rd.
52 Shepston Thomas, co
   fectioner
54 Temple Thomas, boo
   maker
66 Thomas John William
   grocer

8 Odwell Richard John, decorator
0 Walker Elihu, builder
4 Smith Mrs. Jane, dressmaker
6 Elsley Robert, cnfctnr.
━*Fleet mews*
8 Webber Charles (Ivy cottage)
LEFT SIDE.
1 Corke William (Handel house)
1 Corke Mrs., ladies' school (Handel house)
3 Ewing J. (Haydn ho.)
5 Blagden George
7 Gossell Otto
9 Smith Mrs.
1 McKewan Misses
3 White Chrstphr. Ward
5 Bell Thomas
7 Low George, architect
9 Hooke H. F.
1 Shout Misses
3 Gilfillan Mrs.
5 Wike John Mellin
7 Wrentmore Isaac H., solicitor
9 Andrews W. W.
1 Pasmore John Henry
3 Davis Mrs. William
5 Ashworth Miss
7 Archer Miss
9 Cave Walter Robert
1 Saunders C. D., jun
3 Bonnor William James
5 Wilson Mrs.
7 Manley George
9 Cooper A. W., florist
1 Sheldrick Mrs.
3 Jones William
5 Told Tom
9 Pooley Josiah
9 Rowe William
1 Jackson Mrs.
3 Spring Alfred

Upper Park Terrace,
now numbered in Upper Park rd.

UPPER TERRACE.
From Branch hill to The Grove.
D 6   1
Goddard Joseph (The Priory)

Coates Miss (Upper Terrace lodge)
James Mrs. and Miss (Upper Terrace lodge)
2 Ainger Rev. A.
Squire Edmd. Burnard, solicitor
Scott Thos. (The Cott.)
9 Esterbrooke Mrs.
10 Royston Miss
Johnstone John (Upper Terrace house)

Vale Cottages,
see Kilburn vale.

VALE OF HEALTH,
Hampstead Heath.
D 6   1
Long Geo., tea gardens
Stamp Mrs., tea gardens
Powley Peter, tea gdns.
The Gables.
2 Hobrow F. W. Chant, solicitor
1 Sayer William
Vale of Health.
Bourn James (South villa)
Dearman Miss (Vale villa)
Lee Joseph (Vale house)
Louden Misses F. & J., teachers of music (Vale cottage)
Gould R. (Vale lodge)
Statham Alfred (Hawthorn cottage)
Whiting James E., head gardener (Laburnum cottage)
Browne Jas. L. (Woodbine cottage)
Bowden & Porter, swps.
Schröder William (St. Ann's cottage)
Henderson Robt. Bruce (North villa)
Villas on the Heath.
1 Jealous Geo. Samuel
2 Smith Mrs. Fanny
4 Pridham Arthur E.
5 Culverhouse Mrs. E.
6 Rodway Mrs.
Vale of Health.
Goodfellow Hy. (1 St. Ann's pl.)

Paine Benjamin (Rose cottage)
Rice William Pierce (Sydney cottage)
The Athenæum, Henry Braun
Café Restaurant, B. De Bolla & Co.
Heath Villas.
1 Hutchins Henry
2 Hurst William
3 Hart Charles
4 Baker Joseph Henry
5 Pottle Mrs.
6 Elworthy Francis, gardener
Vale of Health.
Vale of Health Tavern, Charles Peters
General Supply Stores, Charles Peters
Salvation Army Barracks
Heath Villas.
7 Willett Ansley Henry
8 Cooke William C.
11 Schroder Walter
12 Hannah Mrs. Charlotte
Vale of Health.
Foley Henry Joseph (Heatherlea)
Maitland Mrs. (Heathcote)
Gittens Thomas (Hill view)
Bishop Miss Julia, dress & mantle maker (Alfred villa)
Hare J. (Lily lodge)
Meyer William Francis (Holly cottage)
Turner Wm. (Manor lo)

Villas on the Heath,
see Vale of Health.

Watt's Cottages,
see Mill lane.

WAVEL MEWS,
Kilburn.
From 59 Priory rd. to Acol rd.
G 5   4
3 & 4 Burch W., jobmaster

WEECH ROAD.

From Finchley new rd.

E 5   4

1 Atkinson Miss Caroline
1 Bond Miss Jessie
2 Carter Charles
3 Saleeby E. J.
4 Smith Percy
6 Plowman Alfred

WELL ROAD.

From New end.

D 6   1

The White Bear, Mrs. Honora Utting
Paxton Arthur John, dining rooms
Smith Wm., coachmkr.
1 Household Benjamin
2 Roff Arthur
3 Channan Richard
4 Bowring Mrs. Elizbth.
Cook George, builder (Weatherall cottage)
—*Christchurch rd.*
Gushlow George(Holly Hedge cottage)
Maxted Charles (Providence cottage)
Pocock Noel Lewis (Lynton)
7 Blaikie William F. G.
8 Pocock Lewis (Clovelly)
9 Boot W. H. J. (Markeaton)
10 Lovitt James John
11 Garlich William
12 Gilchrist Mrs. (Keats corner)
13 Rotheram William

WELL WALK.

From Gayton rd.

D 7   1

LEFT SIDE.

Purry Mrs. E. (Rosemount)
Tait Adam (Wingfield lodge)
Grylls T. J.(Burgh ho.)
Rooth Goodwin (Weatherall house)
3 Lennard F. Barret (Lested lodge)

5 Woodroofe Mrs. G. H.
—*Christchurch rd.*
Slade John (The Limes)
Reed Eliot Pye-Smith (Holmleigh)
15 Bartrum Arthur Clement (Manaton lo.)
—*East Heath rd.*
RIGHT SIDE.

Well Walk Terrace.

7 Carpenter Henry A., joiner
6 Parish John
5 Challis George
4 Russell W. D.
4 Metcalfe C. E., professor of music
3 Gascoyne Andrew
2 Ridge Thomas
1 Durrant Mrs.

Well Walk.

2 SkinnerAlfred Earnest
4 Bockett Miss
6 Finlay Thomas
8 Coates William Henry
10 Finch George
12 Le Pla Rev. Henry
14 Gentery Frederick
—*Christchurch rd.*
16 *The Wells Tavern*, Mrs.MaryAnnNewton
18 Burns David B.
20 Peppiatt Edward
22 Morant Mrs.
26 Smith Mrs. Bruce
28 Flight Dr. W.
30 Sharpe Henry
32 Bradbee Miss
—*Gainsborough gardens*
Pooley H. F. (Scotter)

Well Walk Terrace,
see Well walk.

WELLS BUILD-INGS.

From 64 High st.

E 6   1

Model Lodging Houses ;
Michael Tobin, superintendent

West Cottages,
see West end.

WEST END,

Kilburn.

From West Hampstead Station.

E 5

RIGHT SIDE.

West Hampstead Station,   Metropolitan Railway
Owers Oscar, auctnee?
—*Blackburn rd.*
Scoles A., tile and brick depôt and office
Cannock Chase Coal Co.'s Office
Lea Thomas & Co., coal merchants
Lister A. H. (Canterbury house)
Fletcher John S. (Treherne house)
Miles Mrs. (West end house)
Winyard William, jun carpenter and builder
Kent & Co., bakers post office
Wainwright Mrs.
Chambers L. G. & Son florists
Stevens George,builder (Lawn cottage)
Bragg John Longman (Fern cottage)
Cock and Hoop, John Hall
Fishenden Geo., florist
Temperance Coffee House ; John Towers manager
Fenn William, gardener (The Cottage)
King Geo., cowkeeper (The Dairy)
LEFT SIDE.
Burgess Mrs. (Sandwell house)
—*Lauriston park rd.*
Potter Thomas (Poplar house)
Sellick Misses F. & C. milliners & drssmkrs.
Winyard William,sen. carpenter
Featherstone Samuel painter
Purcell Mrs. E. (Alpha cottage)

Chambers William R., grocer

Miles Nelson, grngrcr.

Smith W.

Smith Thomas Joseph, beer retailer

Willow Cottages.

1 Dennison Thos., fitter

2 Penn David, bootmkr.

Providence Place.

1 Moore Joseph, gardener

2 Hassell Mrs., laundry

3 Lambert Hy., carman

4 Stokes Isaac

5 Pocknee James

7 Joynes Richard

West Cottages.

1a James Charles, fitter

1 Bradshaw Wm., gardnr.

2 Moore Henry, fitter

3 Smith William, fitter

3 Smith Mrs., midwife

4 Wyer Joseph

5 Vincent James, ironmoulder

6 Harris Richard

7 Harris Alfred

8 Carroll Mrs.

9 Brindley Thomas, jun.

10 Crump Henry

11 Churchill Mrs., lndrss.

12 Brindley T., sen., ironmoulder

13 Hale Thos., ironmoulder

Potter and Sons, engineers

The Green.

1 Sherry Nathaniel

2 Slocombe Alfred

3 Tucker Arthur

West End.

Cullum O. A. (Cedars)

WEST HEATH.

D 6 **1**

Hoare Joseph (Child's hill house)

Waterhouse Thomas Greaves (Sunnyfield)

WESTCROFT RD.,
Kilburn.
From 70 Priory rd.

5 **4**

LEFT SIDE.

2 Sasse John (Sunnyside)

1 Jones John Prichard (Lorne house)

RIGHT SIDE.

Tullock G.(Chester ho.)

Westcroft Villas,
see Cricklewood lane.

WEST END LANE,
Kilburn.
From 74 High rd.
to West Hampstead Station.

G 5 **4**

RIGHT SIDE.

2 Britt Edmund

4 Hobden Joseph, engine fitter

6 Robson Mrs.

St. Mary's Schools

Providence pl.

Broadhurst A., general shop

Munden cottages

8 Drabwell Wm., paperhanger (Holton cott.)

8 Drabwell Mrs., laundress (Holton cottage)

King's Cottages.

1 Allen William

2 Shellum Albert

3 Warwick Joseph

4 Hawtree James

5 Burn C.

6 Twyford John

West End Lane.

10 Glasscock H., grocer

Kilburn vale

12 Miller G., beer retailer

14 Hamilton J., umbrella repairer

14 Bowden G. & W., lathrenders

Abbey lane

16 Reed George, carman

16 Reed Mrs., laundress

18 Eggmore Mrs. (Albany cottage)

20 Townsend Thos., gardener (Rose mount)

24 Handford Geo. (Trafford lodge)

26 Willson T. J.

28 Lefort Miss (St. Leonard's villa)

30 Marslen Mrs. A. (Sandringham villa)

32 Stewart Geo. A. (Braemar lodge)

Abbot's rd.

Abbey rd.

Hulbert Mrs. (Quex lo.)

Cooper John Robert (Queen's lodge)

Acol rd.

Willis Arthur K., surgeon (Gascony house)

Long Edwin (Glencairn)

Housley Samuel John (Crowhurst)

Davis Oliver Henry (Crowhurst)

Altman Albert Joseph (Elmira)

Woodchurch rd.

Cotton Francis, solicitor (The Knoll)

Bloomfield Richard Zadoc (The Laurels)

Smith Sidney, solicitor (Brooklands)

Pope Abraham (Taunton lodge)

Green Isaac (Lymington)

Lowe William Edward (Sunnyside)

Cleve rd.

Nelson E. M. (Cleve house)

Carr R. M. (Glengarry)

Thornton Thos. (Townley house)

Vasmer Theodore (The Homestead)

Spain Lewis (Oaklands)

Hobson Thos. Fredk. (Runnymede)

Chislett rd.

Kitchen James (Cromer lodge)

King John Thornton (Clovelly)

Van-Wyhe Mrs. (Bracknell)

Tanner Mrs. (Franklands)

Hammack Richard (Rathleigh gate)

Police Station

Exeter Terrace.

1 Evans E., greengrocer

2 Randall H. G., butcher

WEST END LANE—*cntd.*

3 Richards James, dairyman
4 Lorkin George, baker
   The Railway Hotel,
   Richard Pincham
Broadhurst gardens
West Hampstead Statn.
LEFT SIDE.
1 Williams Edward, upholsterer
3 Griffin Henry, dairy
5 Welstead Thos.,btmkr.
7 Chivers George, timber merchant (Clyst ho.)
9 Clark Edwin
11 Smith Harry
13 Thatcher William
15 Aldred James J.
19 Aldridge A. T.
21 BeecherF.T.,wood trnr
23 & 25 Beecher Arthur E.
Mutrix rd.
27 Stagg William (The Limes)
29 Marchant Miss (Belmont)
31 Lenthall Henry (Oakleigh)
35 Chipp O. (Newstead)
37 Fleming Sidney (Kendall villa)
39 Flavell C. E., jun. (Burnside)
41 Benson St. Patrick
43 Cremer John
Birchington rd.
Quex rd.
Herbert John Rogers, R.A. (The Chimes)
Smith H. (The Forge)
Bailey Edward (Ford)
Blackman C. W. (Natcott)
Thistleton-Dyer Rev. T. F. (Beckland)
Gascony avenue
Peek Francis Ansley (Messina house)
Messina avenue
Cotleigh rd.
Herman Henry (Dorchester)
Dynham rd.
Hemstall r.l.
Clark Charles William (The Beacon)

Phillips Harry B. (Northbrook)
Rogers Alfred (Glen Innis)
Matthews Hy. Leonard (Rosedale house)
Cooper Joseph (West Lynne)
Davis David Jeffreys (Waldeck)
Platt Dr. William (St. James's lodge)
Sherriff rd.

Exeter Terrace.

5 French E. & Co., grcrs.
6 Elliott Russell, cheesemonger
7 Phipps J. H., fishmngr.
8 Hyne Harry, pharmaceutical chemist
9 Jeffcoat Chas., tbccnst.
10 Pleasance Ernest, watchmaker & jewllr.
11 Dainton S.T., bldr., &c.

WEST HEATH RD.

From Finchley rd. to West heath.

D 6

Mathieson Frederic C. (Beechworth)
Price William (Saint Mary's)
Ambrose W., Q.C.(Westover)
Gotto H. G. (West Heath house)
May P. (St. Margaret's)
Bayliss Moses (St. Cuthbert)
Hopkinson James (Ardlethen)

WHITE BEAR LANE

From New end sq.

D 6   *1*

1 Cruttwell Charles H.. plumber
2 McKay Charles
3 Rowland Mrs.
4 Dennis Mrs.
Well rd.

White Horse Terrace,
see South end green.

Wildwood Grove, and Terrace,
see North end.

William Terrace,
see Providence pl. Kilburn.

WILLIAM'S MEWS.

From Belsize park ter.

F 7   *1*

1 & 2 Mildon Richard, veterinary forge

WILLOUGHBY RD.

From Rosslyn hill to Willow rd.

E 7   *1*

RIGHT SIDE.

1 Olliff William
2 Moir Mrs. Macrea
3 Young G.
4 O'Donoghue Rev. E. G.
5 Peck Henry William
6 Howard Mrs.
7 Brown Charles
Kemplay rd.
Coates C. J., collector of parochial rates (Bedford villa)
Coates Joseph, insurance agent; agent to *The Alliance* Life and Fire Offices, and to the *Norwich and London* Accident Insurance Association (Bedford villa)
Burchett Arthur (Willoughby lodge)
Carlingford rd.
Russell E. B. (Danehurst)
Bickersteth Hugh (Saxon house)
Cornick Jesse (Kingsbridge house)
13 James R. H.
Denning rd.
Berdoe Jas. (Fernlea)
Davies James Allman, verger of St.Stephen's church(Rodley house)
Lewinton Hny.(Lundy house)
LEFT SIDE.
Johnstone John(Gower house)

Friederichs Mrs. (Ru-mah)
Williams Mrs. (Kingston Lisle)
George James William (Strathearn)

Rudall cres.

Cedar Terrace.

1 Johnstone Mrs. Napier (Highfield)
2 Trufant Gilbert Carr (Boston house)
4 Yeo Alfred William (Ideside)
5 Wellings John

Rudall cres.

Willoughby Road.

Gilchrist Percy C. (Ruscombe)
Walker Charles (Silverlea)

Willow Cottages,
see West end & Willow rd.

Willow Place,
see Christchurch rd.

WILLOW ROAD.
From Well walk to South end rd.

E 7   1

1 Thwaites Geo., grocer

Gayton rd.

2 Horn J. W., statnr., &c.
3 Potter George
6 Faraday Harold
7 Duncum Joseph
8 Clack Mrs.

Willow Cottages.

9 Day John
8 King Job P.
7 Hurst Alfred
6 Watkins William
5 Cooper Mrs.
4 McQueen George
3 Price Thomas
2 Sell Walter George
1 Wood James

Willoughby rd.

Willow Road.

Granville Mrs (Bifrons)
Bell G. C. (Ferndale cottage)
Gittens William (Beaumont)
Fry Charles (Farleigh)

Angus C. J. (Lyncombe)
McKean W. Blair (Mountanvert)
Salmon Mrs. (Heath view)
Botcherby George (Heath view)
Flook Walter (Heath lea)
Watson William (Carlile villa)

Heath Rise.

11 Dalton Cornelius Neale
10 Holland P. H.
9 Owen William
8 Pritchard Urban, M.D., F.R.C.S.
7 Harris Edwin
6 With Rev. A. R., M.A. (St. Ethelbert's schl.)
5 Graham H. Howgrave
4 Davies W. H.
3 Adams William
2 Mitchel Miss Ingledean
1 Bursill C. Hy. (Holmdale)
1 Martin Miss (Holmdale)

Worsley rd.

Inman John (Daisy bank)
Clarke William (The Downs)
Chandler Dan Edwin (Brae side)

Lower Heath Cottages.

4 Johnson John
3 Webster Edward
2 Broad Mrs., laundress
1 Pickford Josiah, bath chair proprietor

Willow Terrace,
see New end.

WINCHESTER RD.,
South Hampstead.
From Adelaide rd.

G 7   2

LEFT SIDE.

1 Simpson Jas. Carrington (Winchester lo.)
3 Blind Karl
5 Twentyman Colonel Augustus
11 Wilson S.

13 Smart Miss
15 Hart Lemon
17 Brazill Miss M., tailoress
19 Titmuss Albert, berlin wool repository
21 HAWKINS J., builder and decorator
23 Wilson & Co., builders
25 Trimbee Frederick, bootmaker
27 Harwood Benj., dairy
29 Timms John, oilman
31 Stone W., greengrocer
33 Skipper Miss, dressmkr.

St. Paul's Schools

RIGHT SIDE.

2 Tollit Frederick
4 Althaus Frederick
6 Sheffield Henry
8 Bird James
12 Francis John
14 Nash William
16 Wright Mrs.
18 Hall Frederick William
20 Osborn Colonel

Fellows rd.

24 Keirf L.
30 Scudamore George
32 Chalmers Henry

WINDMILL HILL.
From Branch hill to The Grove.

D 6   1

Wood A. B. (Bolton house)
Vandervelde Emanuel (Volta house)
Gall T. (Holyrood ho.)
Allen Mrs. (Windmill hill cottage)

Windsor Cottages,
see Child's hill.

WINDSOR TER.
From Thurlow rd.

E 6   1

Bond Mrs. (Elm bank)
Gilfillan Samuel (Ashbridge)
Frankau Mrs. (Newmount lodge)
Orgill John James (Springmead)

WINDSOR TER.—*contind.*
Bell Alfd. (Bayford ho.)
Adkin Charles (The Hermitage)
Lyndhurst rd.

WOODCHURCH RD.
From Priory rd. to West end lane.
G 5   **4**
LEFT SIDE.
1 Lucas Seymour (New Place)
3 Rogers Thomas Henry Tait (Westhaven)
5 Pitzipios Stephen D. (Henley house)
7 Strickland Robert
9 Negri Misses de (Oak leigh)
11 Evans Roger (Clovelly)
13 Lawrence Basil Edwin (Arnecliffe)
15 Farmer Mrs. (Palma villa)
17 Watt Fredk. (Saltram)
19 Taylor John T. (West-court)
21 Fletcher Banister (Anglebay)
RIGHT SIDE.
2 Rous Henry
4 Cotton Mrs. (South-wood house)
6 Beckwith H. (Cheneys house)
8 Turner John (Sher-wood house)
10 Butcher Arthur A. (Roslyn house)
14 Fitzgibbon V. B. (Bruin lodge)
16 Wildy L. (Homelea)
18 Waterhouse William Dakin, B.A., LL.D., physician (Ovoca)
18 Whaley & Waterhouse, surgeons (Ovoca)

20 Short Martin (Durban lodge)
22 Henderson Henry (Woodchurch house)

WORSLEY ROAD.
From Willow rd.
E 7   **1**
RIGHT SIDE.
Havergal Mrs. & Miss (Home lodge)
Miller Miss (Field end villa)
Atkinson Mrs. (Roth-bury house)
Denning rd.
Neish Mrs. (Maurice villa)
Gordon Alfd. (Maurice villa)
Field Thomas Meagher (Kenrick villa)
LEFT SIDE.
Ashworth Howard Haughton (Crow-hurst)
Soden James (Haw-thorden)
Bradley George M. (Ec-clesbourne)
Weddell William (Fern-leigh)
Claxton William Brooks (West view)
Thomas J. (Heathcroft)
Daubeney Walter (2 The Elms)
Brown Captain Harry (The Elms)
King James (Ellers-leigh house)
6 Le Breton Mrs.
5 Fairman Frederick Dobede
3 Glyn Charles H.
2 Beeching J. P. G.
1 Claxton Miss

Wychcombe Studios,
see England's lane.

Wychcombe Villas,
see England's lane.

YEW GROVE.
From Cricklewood.
E 3
LEFT SIDE.
1 Rennie John
3 Macdona Henry
5 Humphreys William
7 Kelly Joseph P.
9 Challacombe Arthur N.
11 France Frederick A.
13 Faulkner Percy
15 Goss James P.
19 Lehmann Augustus
RIGHT SIDE.
20 Pescod J.

Yew Terrace,
see Cricklewood.

YORKSHIRE GREY YARD.
From Little Church row.
E 6   **1**
The Yorkshire Grey, Henry Hawksley
1 Fowle Mrs.
2 Williams John
3 Simpson Charles
4 Pratchett Samuel
5 Diggins James
6 Warne Charles
8 Kebbell Theodore
9 Mathews James
10 Mason Frederick
12 Heathfield Stephen
13 Francis Mrs.
14 Satterthwaite Joseph J.
15 Hately J., gasfitter
16 Welch William

[5]

INTERNATIONAL HEALTH EXHIBITION.

GOLD   MEDAL.

LONDON, 1884.

AWARDED TO

HENRY LOVIBOND & SON,

Cannon Brewery, North End, Fulham, S.W.

MESSRS. HENRY LOVIBOND & SON,

In recommending their Ales, guarantee them brewed solely from Malt and Hops of the finest quality, and free from any other ingredient.

LIST OF PRICES.

MILD ALES.

		Per 18 galls.	Per 9 galls.
XX	Mild Ale	18/	9/
XXX	Extra Strength ...	24/	12/
XXXX	Best Quality ...	30/	15/
XXXXB	A Strong Bitter Beer	36/	18/

PALE BITTER ALES.

		Per 18 galls.	Per 9 galls.
XB	Light Bitter ...	15/	7/6
VPA	VICTORIA PALE ALE, TONIC BITTER *(Strongly Recommended.)*	20/	10/
†XVPA	Extra Strength...	24/	12/
‡XXB	Best Quality ...	30/	15/

‡ *(Season-brewed in 18-gallon Casks.)*

INTERMEDIATE ALES.

		Per 18 galls.	Per 9 galls.
AK	Mild Bitter ...	19/	9/6
XAK	Extra Strength...	24/	12/
XXAK	Best Quality ...	30/	15/

STOUT AND PORTER.

		Per 18 galls.	Per 9 galls.
P	Porter	18/	9/
†SS	Single Stout	24/	12/
*S	Best Quality	27/	13/6

* *Carefully selected for Nursing, upon application by letter.*

† *These may be had in pint bottles, imperial measure, price 3/- per doz. ; also XXB Best Quality, 4/- per doz. Bottles charged 2/- extra per doz., and allowed for when returned.*

COUNTRY ORDERS DELIVERED FREE TO ALL LONDON STATIONS. DELIVERIES TO ALL PARTS WITHIN 12 MILES OF THE BREWERY, TWICE TO FOUR TIMES WEEKLY ACCORDING TO DISTANCE. CITY AND WEST END DAILY.

☞ NOTE ONLY ADDRESS:

CANNON BREWERY, NORTH END, FULHAM. S.W.

THE

HAMPSTEAD DIRECTORY.

————o————

ALPHABETICAL LIST

OF

PRIVATE INHABITANTS.

NOTE.—*The Postal District is N.W.*

Further information respecting the situation of Streets may be obtained on reference to the Streets Directory ; for instance, anyone requiring the address of George Abbott, refers to the Alphabetical List of Private Inhabitants and finds his address given 27 Springfield rd.; by turning to Springfield rd. in the Streets Directory, page 98, it is found described as Springfield rd., St. John's Wood, from Abbey rd. to Loudoun rd. **G 6**

G 6 *signifies the position of Springfield rd. on the Map.*

Abbott George 27 Springfield rd.
Abel James 20 Prospect rd.
Abrahams Hyman A. 7 Belsize park
Abrahams Mrs. A. 17 Springfield rd.
Abrahams S. B. 47 Priory rd.
Abram Edward 7 Belsize cres.
Ackermann Misses 10 King Henry's rd.
Acret C. H. J. 4 Gayton rd.
Acret J. M. 4 Gayton rd.
Acret J. T. 82 High st.
Acton Roger 1 Parliament hill rd.
Acworth Joseph W. (Sheldmont house) Cricklewood
Adam John Booth 5 Eton villas
Adams Rev. Dr. 17 Birchington rd.
Adams George 51 Ainger rd.
Adams Henry 124 Iverson rd.
Adams John 2 The Village
Adams Mrs. 3 Devonshire pl.
Adams Mrs. (Knottywood)105 Priory rd.
Adams Mrs. Francis 114 King Henry's rd.
Adams William 3 Heath rise

Adamson Mrs. Ellen 7 Downshire hill
Adcock William 16 Lithos rd.
Addison Miss 95 Alexandra rd.
Addison William 79 Belsize park gdns.
Addy Samuel John 4 Midland cottages
Addy W. F. 1 Cricklewood lane
A'Deane John 57 Belsize park
Adelmann G. (Ballin-Collig) 8 Daleham gardens
Adeney A. W. 5 Springfield
Adkin Charles (The Hermitage) Windsor ter.
Adolph Albert Joseph 26 Park rd.
Adrian Mrs. (Mayfield) 40 Elsworthy rd.
Aeurbach Mrs. 30 King Henry's rd.
Agabeg Aviet 61 Boundary rd.
Aggleton Mrs. 10 Elm grove
Agnew Major-General William 6 Belsize park gardens
Agues Edward 90 Belsize park gardens
Ainger Rev. A. 2 Upper ter.
Alaway Robert 1 Lithos rd.

Alberga Eugene 18 Avenue villas
Albert Hilary 23 Steele's rd.
Albon Mrs. 14 Devonshire pl.
Albrow Mrs. (Gateway house) Thompson's mews
Aldred James J. 15 West end lane
Aldridge A. T. 19 West end lane
Alexander Frederick (Ivy cottage) South end rd.
Alexander James 72 Adelaide rd.
Alexander James (Avening house) 12 Arkwright rd.
Alexander James 19 South hill park
Alexander John 16 Eton rd.
Alexander Joseph Henry 2 The Mount
Alexander M. 94 Belsize rd.
Alexander Mrs. 104 Abbey rd. Kilburn
Alexander Mrs. 102 Adelaide rd.
Alford Frederick Stephen S., F.R.C.S., L.A.S. 61 Haverstock hill
Alison Miss 49 Denning rd.
Allan Robert Weir 32 Steele's rd.
Allchin Sidney (Mansel cottage) 115 Haverstock hill
Allen Rev. Bevill 83 Iverson rd.
Allen Charles 4 Gascony avenue
Allen Charles John 11 Alexandra rd.
Allen Edward (Clifton house) South end green
Allen J. 55 Kingsgate rd.
Allen John 15 Midland cottages
Allen John 4 Mortimer rd.
Allen John William 13 Fairfax rd.
Allen Joseph 43 Kingsgate rd.
Allen J. E. 2 Gascony avenue
Allen Mrs. 83 Finchley rd.
Allen Mrs. 26 Lichfield rd.
Allen Mrs. (Windmill hill cottage) Windmill hill
Allen Mrs. Elizabeth (Kingsgate) Cricklewood
Allen Richard Ash Hannaford 27 Hillfield rd.
Allen R. W. (Goldhurst) 58 Priory rd.
Allen William 1 King's cottages
Allingham Theodore Frederick (Hawthorn lodge) Cricklewood
Allison Mrs. 20 Hilgrove rd.
Alliston George Thomas 41 Ainger rd.
Allum Francis Henry 13 Gascony avenue
Allum John 83 King Henry's rd.
Almond Thomas 29 Fleet rd.
Almond Thomas 10 Lithos rd.
Almore F. 63 Goldhurst rd.
Alp Robert 48 High rd.
Alsop Mrs. 2 Squire's Mount cottages
Althaus Frederick 4 Winchester rd.

Altman Albert Joseph (Elmira) West end lane
Alvey Mrs. (Myrtle cottage) Christchurch passage
Ambler George 36 South hill park
Ambrose William, Q.C. (Westover) West Heath rd.
Anchor Richard 134 Alexandra rd.
Anderson J. 72 Belsize park gardens
Anderson James (Frognal park) Frognal
Anderson J. Ford, M.D. 28 Buckland cres.
Anderson Miss 8 Elsworthy rd.
Anderson Mrs. 2 Garlinge rd.
Anderson William 33 Midland cottages
Anderson Wm. D. (The Ferns) Frognal
Andrade Saml. Da Costa 105 Abbey rd.
Andreade Victor 2a Merton rd.
Andresen Gustav Adolph 3 Carlingford rd.
Andrew John May, M.D., M.R.C S.E. 140 Haverstock hill
Andrews Dr. James (Everleigh) 1 Prince Arthur rd.
Andrews Jabez 2 Ebenezer rd.
Andrews James 10 Palmerston rd.
Andrews John 25 Broadhurst gardens
Andrews Misses 74 Alexandra rd.
Andrews Mrs. 5 College ter.
Andrews Robert 18 Kingsgate rd.
Andrews Robert 11 Lithos rd.
Andrews R.L. 2 Canfield gardens Kilburn
Andrews William 5 Lower Lawn rd.
Andrews Wm. Ward 29 Upper Park rd.
Angus C. J. (Lyncombe) Willow rd.
Angus John 103 Haverstock hill
Angus John 28 Upper Park rd.
Anley George 43 Maygrove rd.
Annets Edward 4 Edward ter.
Anson Adml. Talavera V. 7 Colleg ecres.
Anstead J. W. 167 Belsize rd. Kilburn
Anstie Mrs. F. E. 6 Broadhurst gardens
Anthony Mark (The Lawn) Hampstead heath
Applin B. A. (Canfield house) 2 Canfield gardens
Archell Thomas John 3 Loveridge rd.
Archer James (Netherside) Hillfield rd.
Archer Lewis H. 1 Upper Avenue rd.
Archer Miss 37 Upper Park rd.
Archer Reuben 153 Adelaide rd.
Archer Thomas 14 Hilgrove rd.
Argent William 11 North end
Arkel Frederick 1 Windsor cottages
Arnett Charles 32 Albion rd.
Arnholz Adolph 6 Lancaster rd.
Arnold Frederic Hudson 15 Fellows rd.
Arnold Jacob 4 Netherhall ter.

Arrowsmith Rev. William Robson, M.A. 99 Adelaide rd.
Arrowsmith Thomas J. 34 Park rd.
Arscott George 8 Gardnor rd.
Arscott William (Norfolk cottage) 37 Downshire hill
Arthur Rev. David 69 South hill park
Ash Claudius James 15 Eton rd.
Ash E. C. 4 Rudall cres.
Ashcombe James 1 Avenue villas
Ashdown Edwin 1 East Heath rd.
Ashton Jonas, M.A. (Raithby) 59 Fitzjohns' avenue
Ashworth Howard Haughton(Crowhurst) Worsley rd.
Ashworth Miss 35 Upper Park rd.
Ashworth Mrs. (Crown lodge) 148 Haverstock hill
Askew Samuel(Albion house)Minerva pl.
Askin Francis 2 Buckland cres.
Aspinall William(Woodstock)119 Haverstock hill
Aspland Mrs. 93 Fellows rd.
Asplet G. 6 Messina avenue
Asquith Herbert H. (Eton ho.) John st.
Atchison Charles 106 Belsize rd.
Atchison Wm.(Elm bank) 29 Greville rd.
Atherton Mdme.Lucquet 203 Adelaide rd.
Atkins Henry 6 Fairhazel gardens
Atkins Mrs. 3 Ariel st.
Atkins Mrs. 43 Park rd.
Atkins Rowland 13 Linstead st.
Atkins Thomas 9 Dunboyne st.
Atkinson George 17 Parliament hill rd.
Atkinson James 3 Nassington rd.
Atkinson Miss 6 Gayton cres.
Atkinson Miss Caroline 1 Weech rd.
Atkinson Mrs. 11 Belgrave rd.
Atkinson Mrs.(Rothbury ho.)Worsley rd.
Atkinson Mrs. Beaumont (South grove) Rosslyn hill
Attenborough Robert 56 Avenue rd.
Atterbury Benjamin J. (Acacia villa) Oppidans rd.
Atterbury J. H. (Melcombe house) Broadhurst gardens
Attoe John (Hollyberry ho.) 9 Holly pl.
Attwood Thomas 15 Hilfield rd.
Aubert Frederick Charles 11 South hill park
Auerbach Emil 138 Alexandra rd.
Augener George 207 Adelaide rd.
Auld Miss 6 Belsize avenue
Aumonier Frederick (Russell house) South end rd.
Aumonier J. 84 Fellows rd.
Austen Edmund 4 Cricklewood ter.

Austin John 71 Fairfax rd.
Austin J. G. 11 Daleham gardens
Austin J. V. (Swincote) Acol rd.
Austin Mrs. 8 Christchurch rd.
Autram Rev. R. (Orchardleigh house) 5 Dynham rd.
Avant William 8 Loveridge rd.
Avarne Augustus 46 King Henry's rd.
Avery J. 31 Elm grove
Ayers Mrs. 127 King Henry's rd.
Ayres Edward, L.D.S. 42 South hill park

Bacharach Carl M. 117 King Henry's rd.
Bach Julius Otto (Donanwerth) Broadhurst gardens
Back Mrs. 179 Belsize rd.
Bacon Mrs. J. L. 1 Harley rd.
Baddeley Edward 56 King Henry's rd.
Badock T. C. 17 King Henry's rd.
Bagehot Edward (Fern cottage) Hampstead heath
Bagshawe F. G. 18 Lawn rd.
Bagshawe Mrs. C. 46 Park rd.
Bagshawe W.H.G.,Q.C.182 Haverstock hl.
Bailey Edward (Ford) West end lane
Bailey Frederick 126 Belsize rd.
Bailey James S. 7 Loveridge rd.
Baily Alfred Head 10 College ter.
Baily Walter (Auchmore) 176 Haverstock hill
Baily William H. 101 King Henry's rd.
Bain George 4 Eton rd.
Baines Fredk. E. 17 Broadhurst gardens
Baird Mrs.(St.Aidans) 3 Denington park
Baird Sydney (Longwood) Acol rd.
Baker Alfred (Pine villa) Quex rd.
Baker Edward 4 Loveridge rd.
Baker Frederick John 172 Alexandra rd.
Baker George 18 Palmerston rd.
Baker H. J. 77 Iverson rd.
Baker James Wood 31 Belsize park
Baker Joseph Henry 4 Heath villas
Baker Joshua (Elm lodge) 167 High rd.
Baker Joshua (Westfield) 54 Priory rd.
Baker Miss Amy 42 Denning rd.
Baker Moses 12 Gardnor rd.
Baker Mrs. (Longleat ho.) 1 Dynham rd.
Baker Mrs. William 115 Belsize rd.
Baker Richard 10 North end
Baker Robert Henry 8 Providence pl.
Bakewell Armytage 48 South hill park
Bakewell Herbert 60 South hill park
Bakewell Robt. S. 29 Parliament hill rd.
Baldwin Christopher George 21 Broadhurst gardens
Baldwin Henry 2a Abbey cottages
Baldwin Miss 5 Hilgrove rd.

Balfour John (Mayfield) Mortimer cres.
Balkwill Mrs. W. H. (Cambridge villa) Hillfield rd.
Ball C. J. 31 Park rd.
Ball Francis 26 Loveridge rd.
Ball H. A. 155 Fellows rd.
Ball Walter Fredk. 100 Haverstock hill
Ballance Mrs. 58 Fellows rd.
Balmain James F. 17 Belsize avenue
Balmer James S. 92 South hill park
Bamberger Stanley 112 Abbey rd. Kilburn
Bamberger Stanley 5 Lambolle rd.
Banfield Miss Eliza 49 Springfield rd.
Banford James William (Cambridge villa) 67 Haverstock hill
Banford William 7 Gascony avenue
Banks Francis 119 Iverson rd.
Banks Miss 2 Gayton cres.
Banner William 49 Park rd.
Bannister Charles 14 Lichfield rd.
Baptie Alexander William (Woodbine) South end rd.
Baptie John (Guernsey cot.) South end rd.
Barber George L. 69 Priory rd.
Barber Joseph V. 7 Elsworthy ter.
Barber Mrs. (The Grange) Branch hill
Barchewitz von Josephi Hermann L. R. 49 Belsize avenue
Barclay Edgar 1 Wychcombe studios England's lane
Barfoot E. 23 Springfield rd.
Barham George (Danehurst) 112 Haverstock hill
Barker Rev. Johnson, LL.B. 3 Belsize avn.
Barker Frank William Sizer (Florence house) 37 Haverstock hill
Barker John, M.I.C.E. 20 Oppidans rd.
Barker Misses 23 Belsize park gardens
Barker B. J. 30 Stanley gardens
Barlow Chas. (Surrey cottage) John st.
Barlow Mrs. E. I. (Lower Mount cottage) South end rd.
Barnard Frederick (Warrington house) Steele's rd.
Barnard Peter 23 Broadhurst gardens
Barnden Frederick 6 Lower Lawn rd.
Barnes Alfred 200 Loveridge rd.
Barnes Edwin 109 Belsize rd.
Barnes George William (Heath cottage) South end rd.
Barnes Henry (Southwell cottage) South end rd.
Barnes Misses 9 Park rd.
Barnes Mrs. 89 Finchley rd.
Barnes Mrs. 118 Haverstock hill
Barnes Samuel 8 Priory rd.

Barnes Walter 1 Priory rd.
Barnett Rev. S. A., M.A. (Harrow lodge) Hampstead heath
Barnett Joseph Alfred 25 Kilburn priory
Barnett Miss 39 Springfield rd.
Barnett Miss Emma 25 Kilburn priory
Barnewall Henry Charles 24 Priory rd.
Barratt Samuel 10 Fairfax rd.
Barratt Thomas J., Hampstead heath
Barrett Edward L. 53 Springfield rd.
Barrett Francis C. 28 Hillfield rd.
Barrett John T. Cresswell 125 Belsize rd.
Barrett William 4 Ebenezer rd.
Barry Abel Thomas 6 William ter.
Barry Charles J. 26 Belsize park
Barry Mrs. Dykes 26 Belsize park
Barter James 4 Hampstead sq.
Bartlett Charles Thos. 173 Adelaide rd.
Bartlett Mrs. 85 King Henry's rd.
Bartlett Thomas Henry 57 Fellows rd.
Barton Chas. A. (Nutley) 44 Fitzjohns' avn.
Barton Charles William 32 Kingsgate rd.
Barton V. J. 32 Elsworthy rd.
Bartrum Arthur Clement (Manaton lodge) 15 Well walk
Bartrum Mrs. 45 Maygrove rd.
Bartrum T. 2 Grafton ter.
Bashford Thomas 5 Holly hill
Bass Alfred 6a Golden sq.
Bassett Henry 5 Silver st.
Bassett Misses 137 King Henry's rd.
Batchelor Jehu 4 Providence pl.
Batchelor John 28 Heath st.
Bate Frederick 78 Alexandra rd.
Bateman Alfred Horace 15 Lichfield rd.
Bateman E. 40 Belsize sq.
Bates J. 3a Perrin's court
Bates Mrs. (Elm lodge) Cricklewood
Bates Mrs. B. M. 3 Fellows rd.
Bates Robert (Elm lodge) Cricklewood
Bath John 2 Chalcot gardens
Batho Thomas William 1 Devonshire pl.
Batistoni E. (Lindenhurst) 108 Priory rd.
Batley Henry Gurson 34 Adelaide rd.
Batley Richard 38 Albion rd.
Batsford Bradley Thos. 55 Boundary rd.
Batten John 114 Belsize rd.
Batterbury Miss 45 Park rd.
Batterbury Thomas 12 Upper Park rd.
Battiss W. S., M.R.C.S. ENG., L.S.A. 147 High st.
Battock John (Percy villa) 172 Maygrove rd.
Batty Colonel George M. 11 College cres.
Batty Miss 14 Christchurch rd.
Bauer Victor 166 Adelaide rd.
Baumer Edward 67 Boundary rd.

Baxter Herbert Fleming (The Tower) 55 Fitzjohns' avenue
Baxter Mrs. 8 Grove ter.
BaxterWm.(Cambridge ho.)82 Abbey rd.
Bayes Alfred Walter 82 Fellows rd.
Bayliss Moses (St. Cuthbert) West Heath rd.
Baynes Carleton 2 South hill park grdns.
Baynes Herbert Morton 18 Parliament hill rd.
BaynesLister(Silverdale)Carlingford rd.
Baynes Mrs. (Mount view) Greenhill rd.
Bays Samuel 4 Claremont rd.
Bazin Mrs. 5 College cres.
Beach Benjamin 23 Gayton rd.
Beach George 170 Haverstock hill
Beach Wm. (Ararat hc.) 73 Iverson rd.
Beadle Miss 2 Sunnyside villas
Beak Miss M. 84 Belsize rd.
Beale Mrs. M. 61 Belsize avenue
Bean Henry 14 Linstead st.
Bear J. P. 2 Belsize park
Beard A. E. 3 Kingsford st.
Beard Miss C.(Mount view) Greenhill rd.
Beard Miss Maria Louisa 1 Greenhill villas Greenhill rd.
Beard Thos. (Marlow cot.) Cricklewood
Beardall Robert 4 Devonshire villas
Beart Victor Oswin 78 Priory rd.
Beasley George E. (Westward Ho) 117 Priory rd.
Beaton Mrs. 42 Gascony avenue
Beattie J. H. 18 Iverson rd.
Beauchamp Alfred 1 Prospect pl.
Beavis Charles 57 King Henry's rd.
Beck Mrs. M. A. 109 Abbey rd.
Beckett Robert 1 Holly hill
Beckington William 128 Maygrove rd.
Beckley Col. T., R.E. 5 Mansfield villas
Beckwith H. (Cheneys house) 6 Woodchurch rd.
Bedford John 92 Boundary rd.
Bedingfield J. (Richmond villa) 65 Haverstock hill
Beecham Miss 34 Ainger rd.
Beecher Arthur E. 23 & 25 West end lane
Beeching J. P. G. 2 Worsley rd.
Beedle Joseph 28 Belgrave rd.
Beer Philip 3 Alfred ter.
Beesley Misses 45 Boundary rd.
Beete A. F. 9 Sherriff rd.
Beeton Henry Coppinger 2 Adamson rd.
Beeton Henry Ramie 42 Belsize sq.
Beeton Mrs. 180 Haverstock hill
Begg David Gray 4 Buckland villas
Behrend David 19 Belsize avenue
Behrens Miss 28 Avenue rd.

Behrens Sydney Lucas 108 King Henry's rd.
Beill William 5 Sumatra rd.
Beit Mrs. 42 Messina avenue
Belford G. 4 Christchurch rd.
Bell Alfred (Bayford house) Windsor ter.
Bell Charles 40 Belsize park
Bell Edward, The Mount
Bell George (Bramerton) Hampstead hill gardens
Bell G. C. (Ferndale cottage) Willow rd.
Bell J. 5 Park road studios
Bell Thomas 11 Kingsgate rd.
Bell Thomas 15 Upper Park rd.
Bellamè Geo. T. 125 Abbey rd. Kilburn
Bellamy Thomas (Wychecombe) 99 Haverstock hill
Bellamy W. 10 Ariel st.
Bellamy William Frederick (Wycliffe cottage) John st.
Belton Bernard Joseph 27 Adamson rd.
Beman Edward 2 Kingsford st.
Benard Mrs. 15 South hill park
Bence Henry Robert 17 Crossfield rd.
Bendall Henry 98 Maygrove rd.
Benfield Charles 53 Lowfield rd.
BenhamRobertThomas 40 Springfield rd.
Benito D. 8 Albion rd.
Bennett Rev. John W. 8 Adamson rd.
Bennett Deane (Eton villa) Haverstock hill
Bennett Edward 97 South hill park
Bennett Joseph 109 Finchley rd.
Bennett Mrs. (Waldridge house) 89 Priory rd.
Bennett William 62 Boundary rd.
Bensley Surg.-Maj. E. C. 127 Fellows rd.
Benson Alfred 1 Belsize park
Benson St. Patrick 41 West end lane
Bentley Alfred 78 Avenue rd.
Bentley Mrs. 57 Netherwood st.
Bentwitch Herbert, LL.B. (The Limes) 145 Abbey rd. Kilburn
Berdoe James (Fernlea) Willoughby rd.
Berghmann Hugo 65 King Henry's rd.
Bergman Conrad 29 Priory rd.
Bergmans Mrs. 13 Buckland villas
Bergtheil Louis M. 17 Priory rd.
Berliner Isidore 104 Belsize rd.
Bernhardt Jules 24 South hill park
Berrey Miss Caroline 17 Daleham gdns.
Berridge Frederic 19 Albion rd.
BerryEdwd.UnwinM.R.C.S.17Sherriff rd.
Berry James 31 Loveridge rd.
Bertiole F. 13 Downshire hill
Bertlin Mrs. 42 Park rd.
Bertram Julius 106 Adelaide rd.

Besant Walter 12 Gayton cres.
Besch John 60 Springfield rd.
Best Mrs. (Burlington house) Broadhurst gardens
Bethel Francis 8 Church lane
Bethell Henry 7 Lithos rd.
Bickel Daniel 89 Netherwood st.
Bickersteth Hugh (Saxon house) Willoughby rd.
Biddle Arthur Cuming 75 Fellows rd.
Biddle Frank Hayward 68 Finchley new rd.
Biddle Mrs. Daniel 68 Finchley new rd.
Biddolph Mrs. 13 Park rd.
Bidgood Frederick 39 Priory rd.
Bienvenue Wm. Henry 6 Oakland ter.
Biggs George 41 St. John's wood park
Biggs J. M., L.R.C.P.L. 2 Claremont rd.
Biggs J. M., Finchley rd. Child's hill
Bignell E. 2 Ravenshaw st.
Biles John 85 Palmerston rd.
Billing Chas. Eardley 6 College villas rd.
Billing Eardley 35 Alexandra rd.
Billing E. J. 44 Bolton rd.
Bindon Mrs. 71 Alexandra rd.
Bingermann Alfred E. (Glenholme) Hilltop rd.
Bingham John 7 Palmerston rd.
Bingham Mrs. 91 Palmerston rd.
Bingham Mrs. R. 65 Flask walk
Bingham Reuben 139 King Henry's rd.
Bingham Thomas 24 Belsize park gardens
Bingham W. 8 Linstead st.
Bingham William 162 King Henry's rd.
Bingham Wm. (Besthorpe) 67 Priory rd.
Binny Wm. (Hillfield) Haverstock hill
Birch Edwin 32 Palmerston rd.
Birch John H. 7 Oakland ter.
Birch Mrs. C. F. 25 Buckland cres.
Birch Mrs. Eliza 68 Belsize rd.
Birch Thomas 174 Haverstock hill
Birch Thomas 6 Loveridge rd.
Bird Arthur 61 Belsize park gardens
Bird Charles E. (Ainger ho.) 29 Ainger rd.
Bird Emanuel 2 Providence pl.
Bird George King 65 Belsize rd.
Bird Hy. L. J. (Scarr cottage) John st.
Bird James 8 Winchester rd.
Bird Mrs. 22 Albion rd.
Bird William (Grosvenor lodge) 18 Fitzjohns' avenue
Birkett Mrs. 317 High rd.
Birley Samuel, M.D. 49 Haverstock hill
Bishop Major Luke 14 Belgrave rd.
Bishop Albert 7 Holly pl.
Bishop Edward (Woodward villa) Steele's rd.
Bishop Miss 50 Bolton rd.

Bishop Mrs. 28 Alexandra rd.
Bishop Mrs. 47 Maygrove rd.
Black Andrew L. 40 South hill park
Black Mrs. 4 Elsworthy ter.
Blackbee Frank Hayden 17 Kingdon rd.
Blackborn Edward 11 Elsworthy rd.
Blackborn Mrs. 32 Haverstock hill
Blackley C. A. 17 Haverstock hill
Blackman C. W. (Natcott) West end lane
Blackmore Captain John, R.N. 1 Maygrove rd.
Blackstone E. 147 Haverstock hill
Blagden George 5 Upper Park rd.
Blaikie William F. G. 7 Well rd.
Blaikley David James 103 Iverson rd.
Blaiklock Frank Edward 18 Elsworthy rd.
Blaiklock Reginald 6 Eton rd.
Blair P. R. 92 Priory rd.
Blake Dr. Edward 29 Daleham gardens
Blake Joseph W. 11 Upper Avenue rd.
Blanchard J. J. W. 15 Gascony avenue
Bland Edward (Fernley cot.) Lutton ter.
Bland Thos. C. 38 St. John's wood park
Blelloch Rev. David 4 South hill park gardens
Blencowe Alfred 48 Kingsgate rd.
Blind Karl 3 Winchester rd.
Blockley Edward 51 Maygrove rd.
Bloomer Caleb 1 South hill park grdns.
Bloomer George 81 Palmerston rd.
Bloomfield Richard Zadoc (The Laurels) West end lane
Blow Mrs. Emma 103 Finchley rd.
Blower Mrs. (Girton vil.) 40 Iverson rd.
Bloxam Alfred (The Corner) 2 Daleham gardens
Bloxham T. Say 1 and 2 Midland cotts.
Bluck Mrs. Mary Ann 18 Alexandra rd.
Blumenthal Julius 97 King Henry's rd.
Blumenthal M. A. (Ivy villa) Quex rd.
Blumenthal Mrs. E. 16 Fellows rd.
Blumfeld Louis (Brauneck) 7 Prince Arthur rd.
Blundell Miss 184 Alexandra rd.
Blunt A. W. 40 Downshire hill
Blyth Edmund Kell 73 Finchley new rd.
Blythe James Nisbit 110 Haverstock hill
Bockett Miss 4 Well walk
Boden Joshua Wigley 47 Finchley new rd.
Bodkin E. F. 98 Fellows rd.
Bodkin F. E. 7 Park road studios
Bodkin Peter 3 Church rd.
Bodley George Frederick 24 Church row
Boldero Mrs. 25 Belsize cres.
Bolford Alfred 4 Avenue villas
Bolt John 8 Holly pl. Hampstead
Bolton Major William 79 Iverson rd.

Bompas Henry M., Q.C. (Abingdon house) Greenhill rd.
Bonacina Ludovico 178 Haverstock hill
Bonas Henry 53 Priory rd.
Bond Edward Philip 4 Fellows rd.
Bond Henry 18 Hillfield rd.
Bond Miss Jessie 1 Weech rd.
Bond Mrs. (Elm bank) Windsor ter.
Bond R. 34 Gascony avenue
Bonifint Warren Henry 25 Ainger rd.
Bonner Robt.2 William ter. Providence pl.
Bonner William James 43 Upper Park rd.
Bonney Rev. Prof. T. G. 23 Denning rd.
Boocock Jno.(Wyldecroft)19 Denning rd.
Boodle Mrs. 79 Haverstock hill
Boon Charles Edward 4 Oakland ter.
Boot W. H. J. (Markeaton) Well rd.
Booth Allen 125 Haverstock hill
Booth Walter Scott 25 Lichfield rd.
Boram Arthur William 8 St. George's rd.
Borrajo Edward M. 13 Haverstock hill
Borrett Mrs. 14 Lithos rd.
Borrow William Henry 6 Goldhurst ter.
Borthwick Francis 3 Goldhurst ter.
Boskowitz Ignatz (North hall) Mortimer road
Botcherby Geo. (Heath view) Willow rd.
Boulting W., L.R.C.P. LOND. 1 The Mount
Boulting William, sen. (Belmont house) The Mount
Boulton Mrs. (Avondale) 109 Priory rd.
Bouman Bernard 204 Loveridge rd.
Bounford Isaac 185 High rd.
Bourn James(South villa)Vale of Health
Bourne Herbert 98 South hill park
Bourne Sydney 6 Southwell ter.
Bousfield William, M.A. 9 Station villas
Bouverie Mrs. 5 Belsize ter.
Bowden Edward 149 King Henry's rd.
Bowden Wm. John, M.D. 189 Adelaide rd.
Bowdich John 15 Fitzjohns' parade
Bowen G., Holly mount
Bowen G. D. (St. Winifred's) 28 Fitzjohns' avenue
Bowen James 53 Flask walk
Bowen Michael 4 Upper Park rd.
Bowerbank John A. 12 Fordwych rd.
Bowlby Charles C. (Wilton lodge) Lancaster rd.
Bowles G. 5 Elm grove
Bowling C. R. (Gladwyn) Shoot-up hill
Bowly Mrs. 42 Stanley gardens
Bowman John M. 1 Britannia villas
Bowman Miss 30 Priory rd.
Bowman Mrs., M.D. 24 Claremont rd.
Bowring Miss Edith A. (Norton lodge) 3 Arkwright rd.

Bowring Mrs. Elizabeth 4 Well rd.
Bowser Henry 50 King Henry's rd.
Box Joseph 106 Alexandra rd.
Boyce Mrs. (Palasmore) 3 Rudall cres.
Boyd Rev. Sydney A., M.A., B.C.L. 2 Crossfield rd.
Boyd J. P. (Woodcote) Cleve rd.
Boyd Phillip 4 Crossfield rd.
Boyd Richard 34 Hillfield rd.
Boyes Frederick 136 King Henry's rd.
Boyes John Henshall 202 Adelaide rd.
Boyle Augustine 27 Steele's rd.
Boyle William 9 Chalcot gardens
Boys Charles Octavius 107 Finchley rd.
Boys Isaiah 21 Hillfield rd.
Boys J. C. 19 King Henry's rd.
Boys Miss 107 Finchley rd.
Brabant William Frederick 17 St. John's wood park
Brabner John 68 South hill park
Braby Mrs. 5 Oppidans rd.
Brackebusch Dr. W. 97 Finchley rd.
Bracken Jas. (Jasper ho.) South end rd.
Brackenbury Captain E. F. (Lincoln house) Greenhill rd.
Bradbee Miss 32 Well walk
Bradbury J. (Shrewsbury vil.)2 Elm gro.
Bradbury John 9 Cricklewood ter.
Bradbury John 17 Gardnor rd.
Brade Robert J. 201 Loveridge rd.
Braden Henry 36 Bolton rd.
Bradford Mrs. 46 Ainger rd.
Bradford Nicholas 52 Avenue rd.
Bradley George M.(Ecclesbourne) Worsley rd.
Bradsell T. 1a Ravenshaw st.
Bradshaw Henry 33 Fellows rd.
Bradshaw Miss 7 Hampstead green
Brady Patrick L. O. H. (Avoca) Kemplay rd.
Bragg John Longman (Fern cottage) West end
Bramston Mrs. Amelia A. 27 Belsize rd.
Brand Charles(Holly lo.) 3 New West end
Brand Mrs. 26 South hill park
Brandon Miss 198 Adelaide rd.
Bratzali N. 3 Claremont rd.
Brazier Thomas 11 Palmerston rd.
Bremner Thomas, jun. (Acacia) Frognal
Brend J. 24 Lowfield rd.
Brenier George 146 Abbey rd. Kilburn
Brennan Mrs. 76 Park rd.
Breslauer Louis (Glenville) 5 Daleham gardens
Brett James 13 Dunboyne st.
Brett William 4 Arch pl.
Brewer Frederick 8 Birchington rd.

Brewer Henry 21 Crossfield rd.
Brewer John 15 Linstead st.
Brewer Mrs. 33 Belgrave rd.
Brewer Mrs. 6 Watts cottages
Brewster Edwin Fredk. 32 Fellows rd.
Brewtnall E. F. 1 The Mall
Brian David 9 Midland cottages
Brice William 6 Providence pl.
Bridge John, M.A. 56 South hill park
Bridger Thomas 66 South hill park
Bridges Frank 67 Flask walk
Bridgman Alfred Ernest 9 Avenue villas
Bridle W. 8 Messina avenue
Brient William 11 Ash grove
Briggs Amos 12 Fleet rd.
Briggs Charles 9 Lithos rd.
Bright John H. R. 16 Hillfield rd.
Brightman Chas. Edwd. 31 Stanley gdns.
Brightman F. W. 7 Denington park
Brightman Mrs. (Braine l'allend)
    Broadhurst gardens
Brindley Thomas, jun. 9 West cottages
Brinsmead Edgar Wm. 29 Adelaide rd.
Brinsmead Thomas 19 Eton villas
Brinton Mrs. Mary 7 College ter.
Brister William (Loveridge house)
    202 Loveridge rd.
Britain John 159 Adelaide rd.
Britnell L. 22 Kingsgate rd.
Britt Edmund 2 West end lane
Brittain H. A. 21 Sumatra rd.
Brittain William 124 Maygrove rd.
Broad Stephen 21 Spencer ter.
Brocheton E. (Rose bank) 25 Daleham
    gardens
Brock Rev.W.(Rose Lea) 16 Ellerdale rd.
Brockman Frederick(Canfield residence)
    6 Canfield gardens
Brodie Miss 50a Haverstock hill
Brooke Edwin 11 Station villas
Brooke W. H. 35 Bolton rd.
Brookfield John Storrs, M.D. 2 Devon
    shire villas
Brooks Arthur 6 Haverstock ter.
Brooks Benjamin 121 Haverstock hill
Brooks Charles William 58 Boundary rd.
Brooks Henry (Mount grove) Green-
    hill rd.
Brooks Henry J. 5 Hampstead hill gdns.
Brooks James 21 Devonshire pl.
Brooks William 10 Kilburn vale
Brookson Charles 59 Gayton rd.
Broom Charles 3 Baker's row
Broom William 5 Hampstead sq.
Brothers Geo. (Oxford villa)Hillfield rd.
Brothers John A. 136 Maygrove rd.
Brough William Stanley 4 Heath mount

Broughton A. 36 Messina avenue
Brown Capt.Harry(TheElms)Worsley rd.
Brown Alfred 97 Alexandra rd.
Brown Benjamin (Ben Lomond house)
    South end rd.
Brown Charles 7 Willoughby rd.
Brown Clifton(Mayfield lo.)Burgess hill
Brown Compton Fosbrooke 12 South hill
    park gardens
Brown E. 6 Holtham rd.
Brown Francis 144 Maygrove rd.
Brown George 22 Church row
Brown George 12 Devonshire pl.
Brown Gordon 96 Fellows rd.
Brown G. W. 64 Belsize park
Brown Harold (Howe-foot) 20 Fitz-
    johns' avenue
Brown Henry 21 Belgrave rd.
Brown Henry Duncan 134 Belsize rd.
Brown John 2 Grove pl.
Brown Joseph 54 Avenue rd.
Brown Miss 198 Loveridge rd.
Brown Mrs. 132 Alexandra rd.
Brown Mrs. (Canfield residence) 6 Can-
    field gardens
Brown Mrs. T. H. 7 Goldsmith pl.
Brown Oswald (Malplacquet) Broad-
    hurst gardens
Brown Samuel Simmons 36 Belsize sq.
Brown Thomas 4 Grove cottages
Brown Thomas 175 Loveridge rd.
Brown Thomas 4 Silver st.
Brown Walter H. 13 Eton villas
Browne Charles 32 Park rd.
Browne Henry Doughty 34 Avenue rd.
Browne James L. (Woodbine cottage)
    Vale of Health
Browne Miss 65 Boundary rd.
Browne Mrs. 13 Fellows rd.
Browning George 209 Adelaide rd.
Bruce George Barclay 64 Boundary rd.
Bruce Mrs. 17 Steele's rd.
Brunt John 29 New end
Bruty Wm. John 9 Belsize park gardens
Bryan Benj.(Lauder cottage)Flask walk
Bryan J. T. 34 Kingsgate rd.
Bryars John, North end
Buchanan George 6 Merton rd.
Buck Francis 19 Palmerston rd.
Buck George Henry 28 Avenue villas
Buck H. O., M.D. (Buckhurst) 48 Prim-
    rose hill rd.
Buckfield J. 21a High rd.
Buckingham Andrew 22 Midland cotts.
Buckingham Mrs. Edward 116 Belsize
    park gardens
Buckoke Mrs. 24 Palmerston rd.

Buckoke Solomon 23 Loveridge rd.
Buckton Mrs. (Leathes house) 19 Fitz-johns' avenue
Budd Miss 96 Boundary rd.
Budden Herbert (Cleveland cottage) Cricklewood lane
Bufton William F. (Mossat villa) Ravenshaw st.
Buist John 79 Adelaide rd.
Buist Robert Gray 104 Alexandra rd.
Bull Miss 46 Belsize rd.
Bull Mrs. (Iverson lo.) 184 Iverson rd.
Bullen A. Henry 17 Sumatra rd.
Bullen Edward 1 Lambolle rd.
Bullen Mrs. 64 Park rd.
Bullock Mrs. (Vernon cot.) 97 Belsize rd.
Bunce Wm. (Prospect cot.) Cricklewood
Bunn Robert T. 12a Lancaster pl.
Bunyan Charles 9 Mansfield pl.
Burchatt Thomas James 43 Alexandra rd.
Burchett Arthur (Willoughby lodge) Willoughby rd.
Burckhardt Dr. William (Burlington house) Broadhurst gardens
Burckhardt John Chas. 88 South hill park
Burd Thomas Charles 62 Fleet rd.
Burden Henry Charles 3 Cressy rd.
Burdett Dixon 8 Lithos pl.
Burdon-Sanderson Miss (Branksome) Greenhill rd.
Burfield James (The Cottage) Cricklewood lane
Burford H. T. B., M.D. 13 Greville rd.
Burgess Charles Henry 33 Ainger rd.
Burgess George 40 Maygrove rd.
Burgess Miss, Burgess hill
Burgess Miss C. E. 47 Haverstock hill
Burgess Mrs. (Sandwell ho.) West end
Burke Mrs. 85 Avenue rd.
Burleigh Joseph 140 Abbey rd. Kilburn
Burn C. 5 King's cottages
Burn Miss 10 Downshire hill
Burn Mrs. 28 Albion rd.
Burnaby Rev. Sherrard Beaumont, M.A. (The Vicarage) Reddington rd. Frognal
Burnet William Cadell 16 Eton villas
Burnett Frank (The Oaks) Frognal
Burnett George 12 Prince Arthur rd.
Burnett John R. F. 2 College villas rd.
Burnett Mrs. (Frognal hill) 1 Lower ter.
Burnett Mrs. Frances 7 Goldhurst ter.
Burnitt Thomas 32 South hill park
Burns David B. 18 Well walk
Burr Alexander 3 Wychcombe studios
Burr John (Warwick ho.) 86 Adelaide rd.
Burrell Charles E. 33 Adamson rd.
Burroughs Colman 95 Adelaide rd.

Bursill Chas. Hy. (Holmdale) 1 Heath rise
Bursill Charles John 17 Avenue villas
Burt Miss 11 Christchurch rd.
Burton Benjamin 1 Grafton ter.
Burton Fredk. Thos. 24 Buckland cres.
Burton James 18 South hill park
Burton Walter Hally 76 Adelaide rd.
Busby Mrs. 2 Golden sq.
Busby Robert 17 Fellows rd.
Bush Rev. Robert Wheler, M.A., F.R.G.S. 67 Belsize park
Bush H. J. 15 Bolton rd.
Buss Decimus 37 South hill park
Buss Miss 87 & 89 King Henry's rd.
Buston John Truman (St. Ronan's) Ornan rd.
Buston Samuel 164 Maygrove rd.
Butcher Arthur A. (Roslyn house) 10 Woodchurch rd.
Butcher Isaac 58 Fleet rd.
Butcher Wm. Henry 13 King Henry's rd.
Butler Christopher 2 Mount Vernon
Butler Christopher, jun. 1 Mount Vernon
Butler Miss 9 Park rd.
Butler Mrs. 6 Fortune green
Butler Mrs. 67 King Henry's rd.
Butler William 8 Iverson rd.
Butlin Chas. Montague 83 South hill park
Butt W. F., M.D. (The Bijou) Cricklewood
Butterfield John 5 Cricklewood ter.
Butterworth Rev. J. H. 15 Belsize sq.
Buttery John 15 Belsize avenue
Button James 3 Cricklewood ter.
Buxton Dr. David 47 Alexandra rd.
Buxton Mrs. 41 Belsize sq.
Buzzard William 32 Primrose hill rd.
Byas Edward H. 25 Belsize park
Byatt Charles A. F. (Suffolk house) Messina avenue
Byles Mrs. 12 Parliament hill rd.
Byrnard Herbert 5 The Cottages

Cable William Drew 108 Iverson rd.
Cadby Miss 29 Birchington rd.
Cadman Lieut.-Col. William E. 70 Fellows rd.
Cahn Victor 85 Fellows rd.
Calkin George 16 Oppidans rd.
Calkin J. W. A. 18 Harley rd.
Calkin Percy R. 18 Denning rd.
Callard D. J. 76 Belsize park gardens
Callard Thomas Karr 6 Hill side
Callaway Henry 6 Medley rd.
Callingham James (Bronté cottage) South end rd.
Callow Henry William 32 Lichfield rd.
Calvert Mrs. 9 Grove ter.

Cambell Miss 14 King Henry's rd.
Cameron Kenneth 38 Lowfield rd.
Camp A. W. 4 Ravenshaw st.
Campbell C. 19 South hill park gardens
Campbell Charles 37 King Henry's rd.
Campbell John 196 Loveridge rd.
Campbell R. B. 14 Ash grove
Cancellor Francis 82 King Henry's rd.
Cancellor Miss 156 King Henry's rd.
Cann Alfred Henry 41 Gayton rd.
Canney Charles R. (Camden cottage) Christchurch rd.
Canney Mrs. 14 Belsize avenue
Cannon Chas.(Tan-y-Bryn) Cricklewood
Cannon Misses (Kidderpore hall) Finchley new rd.
Cant Benjamin (Hollywell house) 74 Haverstock hill
Canti George F. 41 Belsize park
Capes Rev. J. M., M.A. (Grove house) Christchurch passage
Capes Alfred (Grove house) Christchurch passage
Capham George 10 Oakland ter.
Capleton — 54 Haverstock hill
Caplin Charles 6 Wildwood grove
Capp George 6 Devonshire pl.
Capp Joseph 42 Gayton st.
Cappel Mrs. 15 Primrose hill rd.
Capstick Mrs. 15 Elsworthy ter.
Carahee Henry 4 Golden sq.
Carbert John Charles 26 Palmerston rd.
Carden James M. 17 Lawn rd.
Carey Edward Fricker 39 Belsize avenue
Carey Miss 57 Alexandra rd.
Carisbrick Mrs. 5 Gascony avenue
Carlebach Rudolf 11 Belsize park
Carlill Mrs. (Fernbank villa) 18 Prince Arthur rd.
Carlisle Captain John 2 Britannia villas
Carlton Thomas William, M.I.M.E. 1 Canfield gardens
Carlyle A., B.A. 3 Chalcot gardens
Carlyle Mrs. Robert 182 Adelaide rd.
Carman Henry 11 Haverstock hill
Carmichael Mrs. 38 Belsize rd.
Carnegie Alexander 63 Boundary rd.
Carnegy Charles 60 Maygrove rd.
Carpenter Rev. Joseph E. 19 Fitzjohns' avenue
Carpenter Miss 3 College cres.
Carpenter Robert S. 16 Crossfield rd.
Carr Miss 38 Fairfax rd.
Carr Mrs. 16 Greville rd.
Carr Mrs. Jane 6 Kingsgate rd.
Carr R. M. (Glengarry) West end lane
Carroll Mrs. 8 West cottages

Cart Rev. H., B.A. 44 Haverstock hill
Carter Charles (St. Austin's) 9 Birchington rd.
Carter Charles 2 Weech rd.
Carter David 3 Grove pl.
Carter G. R. 9 Belsize avenue
Carter Henry 40 Denning rd.
Carter Isaac 35 Prospect rd.
Carter James 29 Belsize rd.
Carter James 11 Kilburn vale
Carter John, jun. (Oakwood house) 134 Haverstock hill
Carter Miss 11 Adelaide rd.
Carter Misses (Sandfield lo.) Branch hill
Carter Mrs., M.A. 174 Maygrove rd.
Carter Mrs. Ellen 14 Gardnor rd.
Carter Robert (Ivy house) 6 Acol rd.
Carter William 5 Devonshire villas
Carthew Mrs. 19 Birchington rd.
Carvalho R. N. (Lamorna) 32 Fitzjohns' avenue
Carwardine Thomas 6 Rudall cres.
Case Mrs. (Heath brow) Hampstead heath
Casella Louis Marino (Beauchêne) 47 Fitzjohns' avenue
Casey Daniel 5a and 6 Golden sq.
Cash Mrs. (Banks hill) East Heath rd.
Caspersz Charles Peter 9 Kemplay rd.
Cassal Charles 105 Adelaide rd.
Cassie Charles 10 Grove ter.
Castle Henry Jas. 75 Parliament hill rd.
Castle James 6 Ebenezer rd.
Castor Mrs. 44 Ainger rd.
Catenhusen A., MUS. DOC. 6 St. John's wood park
Cathcart Mrs. 117 Adelaide rd.
Cathcart Percy 117 Adelaide rd.
Cattanach James (Lawn villa) Quex rd.
Catterson John Josias (Athol house) 90 Adelaide rd.
Cave Frederick 4 Goldhurst rd.
Cave Walter Robert 39 Upper Park rd.
Cawkwell William (Fernacre) 1 Maresfield gardens
Cawthorn Joseph (Vine lo.)Rosslyn lane
Cayford Ebnzr.(Home villa)Cricklewood
Cayford Saml. Everett 30 Kingsgate rd
Cayley Claude 27 Stanley gardens
Cecil Henry 40 Kingsgate rd.
Chad Thomas 191 Loveridge rd.
Chadd Mrs. C. 15 Boundary rd.
Chadwick John Oldfield 46 Bolton rd.
Chadwick Mrs. (Boston house) 6 Upper Avenue rd.
Chadwick Richard 105 Finchley rd.
Chalk John, Golder's hill cottages

Challacombe Arthur N. 9 Yew grove
Challice George 2 Devonshire pl.
Challis George 5 Well walk ter.
Chalmers Henry 32 Winchester rd.
Chamberlain Thomas 13 Ainger rd.
Chamberlain Vincent Ind 44 Belsize rd.
Chamberlain William 4 Elm ter.
Chambers George 9 Sumatra rd.
Chambers Henry 83 Netherwood st.
Chambers John 10 College cres.
Chambers Thomas (Stratheden) Burgess hill
Champion James 37 Boundary rd.
Champion W. Smith 23 Belsize park
Champneys Basil (Manor farm) Frognal
Champneys Mrs. (Priory hill) Frognal
Chandler B. W. 13 Lancaster rd.
Chandler Dan Edwin (Brae side)Willow road
Channan Richard 3 Well rd.
Channell Arthur (Whitwell house) 64 Fitzjohns' avenue
Chant Thomas 208 Adelaide rd.
Chaplin Henry (Aldbury) 4 Sherriff rd.
Chaplin Joseph (Aberdour house) 56 Loudoun rd.
Chapman Arthur 25 Midland cottages
Chapman Henry 2 Rockhall ter.
Chapman James 29 Springfield rd.
Chapman Wm. (Grove cott.) North end
Chapman W. H. (Oakhurst) Cricklewood lane
Chappell Mrs. W. 22 Maygrove rd.
Chard George 6 Station villas
Charles Mrs. (Combe edge) Branch hill
Charles Mrs. 23 Broadhurst gardens
Chase Misses (Haddon lodge) Quex rd.
Chatfield Rowland 77 Finchley rd.
Chattock Richard S. 15 Lancaster rd.
Chaudoux Emile 128 Belsize rd.
Cherer Mrs. (Newton lodge) 72 Finchley new rd.
Cheshir Charles 12 Station villas
Cheshir William 8 Lichfield rd.
Cheshire Miss 23 Adelaide rd.
Cheshire Richard 17 Flask walk
Chester Daniel 1a Golden sq.
Chester Thomas William 96 Iverson rd.
Chesterman C. F. (Stalisfield house) 9 Acol rd.
Chesterman Mrs. Elizabeth (Finedon villa) 148 Abbey rd. Kilburn
Chettle Misses 31 Belsize sq.
Chettleborough Mrs. 7 Church lane
Chilcott Thomas Robert 38 Prospect rd.
Child James Robert 9 Oakland ter.
Child John 142 Fellows rd.

Child Robert Carlyle 7 Denning rd.
Childs A. B. (Galeton ho.) Adamson rd
Chinery John 29 Lichfield rd.
Chinery Philip John (Ebenezer cottage) Kilburn vale
Chipp Oliver (Newstead) 35 West end lane
Chisolm Mrs. 34 Denning rd.
Chittenden Charles 70 Alexandra rd.
Chitty Mrs. 75 Belsize park gardens
Chomel Mrs. 6 Christchurch rd.
Chope Rev. Thomas 27 St. George's rd.
Chrisp Joseph 15 Ariel st.
Christian Ewan (Thwaitehead) East Heath rd.
Christie Rev. George Alexander 16 Denning rd.
Christie Duncan 135 Fellows rd.
Churchill John (Councils) 63 Priory rd.
Churchill Miss 31 Belsize rd.
Churchill R. T. 100 South hill park
Clack Mrs. 8 Willow rd.
Clark Adolphus 101 Adelaide rd.
Clark Charles William (The Beacon) West end lane
Clark Edwin 9 West end lane
Clark Isaac John 12 Belsize rd.
Clark Melville 3 Harley rd.
Clark Mrs. 3 St. Ann's ter.
Clark Mrs. 44 St. John's wood park
Clark Mrs. Sarah 67 Fellows rd.
Clark William N. P. 102 Belsize rd.
Clarke Edward 20 Devonshire pl.
Clarke Eli 3 Golden sq.
Clarke F. G. B., M.D. 7 Fordwych rd.
Clarke G. 1 Elm cottages
Clarke George B.(Chudleigh)Hillfield rd.
Clarke Henry 31 Belsize avenue
Clarke John Moir, of Garthdee (Kinchyle) 37 Fitzjohns' avenue
Clarke Mrs. G. M. 94 Adelaide rd.
Clarke Mrs. W. 7 Gayton rd.
Clarke Samuel 7 Bradley's buildings
Clarke Samuel 27 Daleham gardens
Clarke Walpole 4 Sunnyside villas
Clarke Wellington (Temple lodge) 2 St. George's rd.
Clarke William (The Downs) Willow rd.
Clarke W. G. 3 Belmont
Clarkson Mrs. (Thirsk house) 5 Primrose hill rd.
Clarkson William Hill 32 Gayton rd.
Clatworthy William Henry 10 Hilgrove road
Claudet Frederic 10 Oak hill park
Claxton Alfred 4 Gascony avenue
Claxton Miss 1 Worsley rd.

Claxton William Brooks (West view) Worsley rd.

Clay Rev. J. H. (The Vicarage) Church walk

Clay William Jas. 14 Parliament hill rd.

Clayden William 9a Dunboyne st.

Clayden William 7 Springfield gardens

Clayton George Augustus (Brisbane house) 15 Sherriff rd.

Clayton James W. 182 Belsize rd.

Clayton John Essex 145 Fellows rd.

ClaytonJohn Richard(Broomfield house) 11 Fairfax rd.

Clayton William 2 Heath mount

Cleaver William 1 Cricklewood ter.

Clements John 4 Holly hill

Cliff Thomas 6 Iverson rd.

Clough James 71 South hill park

Clouser Mrs. 2 Granville ter.

Clowser Richard 3 Gayton rd.

Clulow George 51 Belsize avenue

Clunn John 170 Iverson rd.

Coates C. J. 33 High st.

Coates Herbert 5 Midland cottages

Coates Joseph 79 Avenue rd.

Coates Joseph (Victoria cottage) 35 Downshire hill

Coates Miss (Upper terrace lodge) Upper ter.

Coates William Henry 8 Well walk

Cobb Mrs. 20 Lancaster rd.

Cobb Mrs. Lucy 31 Fairfax rd.

Cobb Thomas 54 Boundary rd.

Cobb Thomas 9 Hilgrove rd.

Cobbett H. (Canfield ho.) 52 Priory rd.

Cocke T. H. 50 Upper Park rd.

Cockle Miss 5 Maresfield gardens

Cocks Robert Macfarlane (Jesmond) Greenhill rd.

Cocks Stroud Lincoln 19 Boundary rd.

CocksedgeJohn Hogben 75 South hill pk.

Coe Augustus F. 4 Mansfield villas

Coghlan Mrs. 26 Thurlow rd.

Cohen Albert 10 Adamson rd.

Cohen Edward (Stanmore house) 15 Adamson rd.

Cohen Henry 1 Devonshire villas

Cohen Miss (Bouchain) Broadhurst gardens

Cohn Martin Albert 164 Belsize rd.

Cohn Maurice 24 Lancaster rd.

Coish Frederick John 41 Adelaide rd.

Coit Mrs. 31 Gayton rd.

Coke Alfred 102 Fellows rd.

Colchester James 1 Cedar villas

Coldwell W. G. 21 Broadhurst gardens

Cole Chas. (Tregenna) 14 Fitzjohns' av.

Coleman Mrs. 20 Greville rd.

Collard Mrs. 9 Providence pl.

ColesOakley (Inglesant)19 Arkwright rd

Coller Richard(Albemarle) 25 Fitzjohns' avenue

Colles William Morris 16 Birchington rd.

Collett Mrs. (Laurifer) 7 Arkwright rd.

CollettWltr (Woodbrook)Netherhall ter.

Collie Alex., M.D. 9 South hill park gdns.

Collier Chas. (Lissoy ho.)180 Iverson rd.

Collier Mrs. V. J. 32 Belsize park gdns.

Collier T. (Etherow) Hampstead hill gardens

Colling William Bunn 71 Belsize rd.

Collins Captain John Stratford 120 Alexandra rd.

Collins Ernest 10 Park rd.

Collins George William 66 Adelaide rd.

Collins Mrs. Jane 66 Adelaide rd.

Collinson William 65 Priory rd.

Collison William 134 King Henry's rd.

Collmann L. 4 Abbott's rd.

Colls E. 79 King Henry's rd.

Colman Jeremiah (Clifton house) Shoot-up hill

Colman Miss 20 Eton villas

Colman Stuart, Fitzjohns' mansions (3rd floor)

Colnett Mrs. 49 Belsize rd.

Colt Frederick Hoare 6 Adamson rd.

Comber Miss Amelia 9 King Henry's rd.

Comins W. W. 210 Adelaide rd.

Compton Edward 125 King Henry's rd.

Compton James 17 Fordwych rd.

Comyn Miss 35 Gayton rd.

Comyns Alfred 4 Mount Vernon

Concannon Michael 13 Denning rd.

Coney Mrs. 3 Golder's hill cottages

Connell William Kerr 26 Hillfield rd.

ConnettGeorge Alfred (Bickleigh lodge) Shoot-up hill Cricklewood

Conor Captain 14 Chalcot gardens

Conquest Alfred 7 The Mall

Conrath Fredk. John 90 Boundary rd.

Constance Samuel, Holly bush hill

Cook A. H., M.R.C.S., L.R.C.P., L.S.A. 25 Denning rd.

Cook Edward 2 Prospect rd.

Cook Frederick 81 Adelaide rd.

Cook Mrs. Bickersteth (Clover-lea) Carlingford rd.

Cook Mrs. E. 3 Providence pl.

Cook Mrs. Mary Elizabeth 131 Abbey rd Kilburn

Cook William 3a Golden sq.

Cooke James 17 Greville rd.

Cooke John 136 Haverstock hill

Cooke John 15 Mansfield villas
Cooke Mrs. 21 Messina avenue
Cooke Mrs. Harriet 152 Adelaide rd.
Cooke William Christopher 8 Heath villas Vale of Health
Cooksley R. K. (Chestnut ho.) New end
Coombes Charles 8 Gayton rd.
Cooper Dr. Herbert 1 Rosslyn ter.
Cooper Charles 19 Hillfield rd.
Cooper Christopher Bird (Hartley house) South end rd.
Cooper Edward 45 Flask walk
Cooper Frederick (Edinburgh) Shoot-up hill Cricklewood
Cooper Fredk. Eastman 6 Alexandra rd.
Cooper Henry James 89 Fellows rd.
Cooper John Foster 94 Finchley rd.
Cooper John Robert (Queen's lodge) West end lane
Cooper Joseph 2 Provident pl.
Cooper Joseph (West Lynne) West end lane
Cooper Mrs. 1 South end green
Cooper Mrs. 4 The Village
Cooper Mrs. 5 Willow cottages
Cooper Mrs. E. 142 Belsize rd.
Cooper Mrs. J., M.R.C.P. 10 Gayton rd.
Cooper W. Wellington 175 Adelaide rd.
Coote F. R. 10 Ainger rd.
Coote George J. 99 Alexandra rd.
Cope Arthur 4 Fairfax rd.
Copeland J. L.R.C.P.E. 78 Alexandra rd.
Copeland W. 20 South hill park gardens
Copestick F. D. Rees (Calton house) Denning rd.
Corani H. 6 Dynham rd.
Corbett Arthur John 18 Belsize sq.
Corbyn James 23 Kingsgate rd.
Cordeaux John Henry 2 Hillfield rd.
Cordell James 2 Arch pl.
Cordery Mrs. 143 Haverstock hill
Corelli Charles 3 Oppidans rd.
Corey William 86 Avenue rd.
Corfe Mrs. 10 Rockhall ter.
Corke Mrs.(Handel house) 1 Up.Park rd.
Corke William (Handel house) 1 Upper Park rd.
Cormock Mrs. 1 Provost rd.
Corner Walter William 117 Belsize rd.
Cornford Rev. James (Grove house) Rosslyn hill
Cornick Jesse (Kingsbridge house) Willoughby rd.
Cornick Mrs. Henry 5 Lawn rd.
Cornish Henry 54 Adelaide rd.
Cornwell Mrs. 20 Goldhurst rd.
Corpe Sandenson 136 Fellows rd.

Corsbie Dennis 17 Kilburn priory
Corsbie George W. R. (Broxbourne) 4 Acol rd.
Cory Henry Albert 16 Lichfield rd.
Cory William 1 Heathfield gardens
Cossart John 42 Alexandra rd.
Cossart William 35 St. John's wood park
Cossey William (Leigh ho.) Cricklewood
Coston James 221 Belsize rd. Kilburn
Cosway Edward Charles (Elm lodge) Hillfield rd.
Cotter Miss (Park house) Gascony avn.
Cotton Francis(The Knoll)West end lane
Cotton Mrs. 194 Haverstock hill
Cotton Mrs. 45 St. John's wood park
Cotton Mrs. (Southwood house) 4 Woodchurch rd.
Cotton W. 81 Palmerston rd.
Coulthard Rev. Ernest Newton, M.A. 18 Priory rd.
Coulthard Christopher 27 Fordwych rd.
Coulthard William 18 Priory rd.
Court Francis 19 Sumatra rd.
Cousins Mrs. (Elm ter. archway) Elm ter.
Coutant Madame 49 Denning rd.
Cow John (Montredon) Arkwright rd.
Cowan Walter 19 Fellows rd.
Cowderoy R. 10 Adelaide rd.
Cowell Albert (St. Ann's cottage) Rosslyn hill
Cowley Arthur 14 Denning rd.
Cowley Mrs. Catherine 14 Denning rd.
Cowper Mrs. 8 Alexandra rd.
Cox Rev. Chas. (New priory) Quex rd.
Cox Cornelius 50 Fellows rd.
Cox Edwin 12 Midland cottages
Cox E. W. 11 Gayton cres.
Cox Geo. J. (Zelinda villa) Loudoun rd.
Cox John 35 Midland cottages
Cox Leonard P. (Buckingham house) 6 Garlinge rd.
Cox Mrs. 9 Denning rd.
Coyte George 9 Fairfax rd.
Coxon David 1 Prospect rd.
Crabb William F. 117 Boundary rd.
Cracknell Hy. (Trellis cottage)Grove pl.
Cracknell Mrs. Anne 39 Belgrave rd.
Cracknell William Edward (Brentwood cottage) John st.
Craigie Patrick George 6 Lyndhurst rd.
Crake Walter 1 Hilgrove rd.
Crampon Alfred 5 Upper Avenue rd.
Crampton James 6 Golder's hill cottages
Cran John, M.D. (Netherdale) Broadhurst gardens
Crapp William 91 Netherwood st.
Crawford Richard 2 Edward ter.

Crawley Joseph 16 and 17 Gayton rd.
Cremer John 43 West end lane
Crewe Joseph 47 Springfield rd.
Crews Samuel 12 Steele's rd.
Crickmay Cecil 11 Hilgrove rd.
Crigan Captain Charles A. R. 8 Belsize park gardens
Crocker John 6 Granville ter.
Croft Adolphus 160 Alexandra rd.
Crompton William 15 Belgrave rd.
Cronin Walter D. 143 Abbey rd. Kilburn
Cropper James C. 9 Stanley gardens
Crosley Lady 47 Belsize park gardens
Cross John 5 Gayton rd.
Cross John 42 Parliament hill rd.
Cross Mrs. 16 Palmerston rd.
Crossley Charles Richard 44 Albion rd.
Crossley Mrs. A.M.147 Abbey rd.Kilburn
Crouch Charles 35 Fellows rd.
Crowson Thomas Henry 2 Paxon's cotts.
Crozier Rev. Richard 53 South hill park
Cruckshank William 2 Elsworthy ter.
Crudginton John 27 Fleet rd.
Crudginton William John 26 Fleet rd.
Crump Henry 10 West cottages
Crump Miss Anne (Hereford house) South end green
Crump William A.(Rugby house) 9 Primrose hill rd.
Crumplen Benj.(Allerton)Gascony aven.
Crundell Arthur 7 Kingdon rd.
Cuddon Mrs. 44 Park rd.
Cuff Christopher Robert (Lavant house) 36 Fitzjohns' avenue
Cuff Misses 59 Alexandra rd.
Cuff William S. 45 Belsize rd.
Culleton Thos.(Bathville ho.) The Mount
Culling James (Rutherford house) Messina avenue
Cullis William 2 Gardnor rd.
Cullum O. A. (Cedars) West end
Culverhouse Mrs. E. 5 Villas on the heath
Culverhouse Thomas 17 New end
Cumberland E. B. 42 Ainger rd.
Cuming Capt.Fredk.Geo.29 Fordwych rd.
Cuming Mrs. Elizabeth 163 Adelaide rd.
Cumming Hugh P. 10 Upper Park rd.
Cundle John 5 Linstead st.
Cunningham Percy Burdett (Beaulieu) 8 Arkwright rd.
Currie James 35 Springfield rd.
Currie Mrs. William C. 8 Carlingford rd.
Curtis George 4 Gardnor rd.
Curtis Henry 22 Avenue villas
Curtis Henry(Linden villa)Cricklewood
Curtis Hermann 37 Springfield rd.

Curtis Mrs. Mary 109 Alexandra rd.
Curtis Mrs. S. Stuart 4 Eldon rd.
Curtis Thomas 4 Alexandra rd.
Curwen Mrs.Thomas(Westridge)3 Prince Arthur rd.
Cutforth Miss 26 Belsize rd.
Cuthbertson Thomas 5 Netherhall ter.
Cutler Mrs. (Chesterfield house) Iverson rd. West end lane
Cutts Rev. Edward L., D.D.(Holy Trinity vicarage) 76 Haverstock hill

Dadge Frederick Wm. 27 Loudoun rd.
Dadson J. T. (Melrose) Shoot-up hill
Dadswell E. D. 2 Windsor cottages
Daft Mrs. 128 King Henry's rd.
Dakers David (Isla vil.) Ravenshaw st.
Dakin T. B. 60 Fitzjohns' avenue
Dale Alfred 23 Stanley gardens
Dale Hylton William 8 Chalcot gardens
Dale John (Holmside) Carlingford rd.
Dale Mrs. 3 Golden yard
Dalgleish William 103 Adelaide rd.
Dalton Cornelius Neale 11 Heath rise
Dalton John 3 Elm row
Daly Miss (Ethel house) Gascony avenue
Dalziel Edward 33 Belsize park gardens
Dalziel George (Wooler house) Greenhill rd.
Dalziel Mrs. 36 Belsize park gardens
Dalziel Thomas 7 Oppidans rd.
D'Ambrumeniel Benrice 36 Parliament hill rd.
Danby Thomas 11 Park rd.
Dane Thomas 86 Finchley rd.
Dangerfield William, A.C.A. 52 Springfield rd.
Daniell Lieut.-Col. J. Townshend 124 Adelaide rd.
Daniell Alfred Bainbridge 93 Finchley rd.
Daniell Cyrus 12 Maresfield gardens
Daniell Mrs.Spencer 140 King Henry's rd.
Daniels Baker 49 Belsize park
Daniels George Walter 11 Provost rd.
Daniels Miss 77 South hill park
Danskin David 59 Belsize rd.
Danson William 2 Eton rd.
Danvers Mrs. 25 Fairfax rd.
Dare George Julius 13 Kingdon rd.
Dare Mrs. L. A. 119 Adelaide rd.
Dare William Henry 142 Adelaide rd.
Darley J. J. 3 Lancaster rd.
Dart Frederick G. 3 Lyndhurst rd.
Dart Joseph H. 50 Alexandra rd.
Dashwood Lady 5 Gayton cres.
Daubeney Walter(2 The Elms)Worsley rd
Daugars Mrs. & Miss 23 Messina avenue

Davenport Mrs. 2 Church row
Davenport-Hill Misses 25 Belsize avenue
Davey Henry 3 Lithos rd.
Davey Henry 90 Priory rd.
Davey Horace 41 Flask walk
Davey John (Grove cot.)Christchurch rd.
Davidson Rev. Samuel, D.D., LL.D. 14 Belsize cres.
Davidson Alexander 5 St. George's rd.
Davidson Alexander Harvey 12 Carling-ford rd.
Davidson Mrs. P.(Arden lo.)Cricklewood
Davidson Thos.(Culloden)Netherhall ter.
Davidson William 14 Belsize rd.
Davies Commander Robert Watts, R.N. 45 Ainger rd.
Davies Rev. John, M.A. 16 Belsize sq.
Davies Rev. John 6 South hill park gdns.
Davies Alfred 4 Hampstaed green
Davies F. 12 Holtham rd.
Davies Frederick 183 Adelaide rd.
Davies Herbert, M.D. (Vale mount) Hampstead heath
Davies James Allman (Rodley house) Willoughby rd.
Davies John 6 Ariel st.
Davies Mark 12 Alexandra rd.
Davies Mrs.(Coniston ho.) Mortimer rd.
Davies Richard 8 Station villas
Davies Robt. Fredk. 162 Alexandra rd.
Davies W. G. 181 High rd.
Davies W. H. 4 Heath rise
Davis Benn 38 Avenue rd.
Davis Charles 22 Priory rd.
Davis David 9 Prospect rd.
Davis David J. 47 King Henry's rd.
Davis David Jeffreys (Waldeck) West end lane
Davis Edward John 55 King Henry's rd.
Davis George 118 Alexandra rd.
Davis George Acton 8 Steele's rd.
Davis J. W. 1 Ravenshaw st.
Davis Lewis 13 St. John's wood park
Davis Miss 45 Stanley gardens
Davis Mrs. 44 Messina avenue
Davis Mrs. 1 Watts cottages
Davis Mrs. William 33 Upper Park rd.
Davis N. Newnham 19 Greville rd.
Davis Oliver Henry 133 King Henry's rd.
Davis Oliver Henry (Crowhurst) West end lane
Davis P. D. R. 12 Ash grove
Davis Robert (Rosedale) 80 Priory rd.
Davis Shelly Kennard 14 Priory rd.
Davis Simon 42 Birchington rd.
Davison Mrs. 11 Chalcot gardens
Davison Mrs. 24 Kingdon rd.

Davison Robert 2 Eton villas
Davy Edward Montague, M.R.C.V.S.L. 95 Abbey rd.
Davys Rev. E., Denington park
Daw John M. 9 Belgrave rd.
Dawe N. F. (Old Grove house)The Grove
Dawes Henry 21 Midland cottages
Dawkings W. E. 4 Netherwood st.
Dawkins Mrs. Rose 1 Mansfield villas
Dawson Benjamin, B.A., The Mount
Dawson Miss Ann 6 Arkwright rd.
Dawson Miss Mary 15 Arkwright rd.
Dawson Mrs. 7 Belgrave rd.
Dawson Philip Wm. 96 King Henry's rd.
Day Hon. Sir John Charles (Green bank) Mansfield villas
Day Henry 3 Holly pl.
Day John 9 Willow cottages
Day Joseph William 23 Lowfield rd.
Day R. E. 48 Belsize sq.
Dean George Henry 29 Haverstock hill
Dean Miss 60 Belsize rd.
Dean Samuel 13 Cricklewood ter.
Dean William 48 Messina avenue
Deane Mrs. Ellen 14 Albion rd.
Deans Charles 4 Belsize avenue
Dearman Miss(Vale villa)Vale of Health
Debenham S.J.(Holmstadt)4 Garlinge rd.
De Berg Adolphus 179 Adelaide rd.
Debnam Mrs. L. 31 Lichfield rd.
Deed John S. 59 Finchley new rd.
Deed Martin 24 Fellows rd.
Defries Coleman 34 Belsize park
De Hamel Felix John 70 Avenue rd.
De La Camp Isidor S. 12 Iverson rd.
De La Condamine Robert C. 14 Prince Arthur rd.
Delve William 47 Lowfield rd.
De Martino Edouardo 2 College ter.
Denneford Peter 7 Mansfield pl.
Dennis Edward 3 Edward ter.
Dennis John(Gardnor house)Gardnor rd.
Dennis Mrs. 4 White Bear lane
Denniston Mrs. Janet 13 Birchington rd.
Denny Thomas 24 Kingsgate rd.
De Nops James 18 Springfield rd.
Dent Garwood 81 King Henry's rd.
Denton Charles (Oakley villa) Raven-shaw st.
Denton George 47 Gascony avenue
De Pass Daniel (Oaklands) Maresfield gardens
De Paula Rudolph 29 Belsize park gdns.
De Quincey Roger 76 Avenue rd.
De St. Croix Arthur J. 92 Maygrove rd.
Desaxe Morris 101 Alexandra rd.
Deschamps C. W. 9 Dalcham gardens

Despard Major W. 40 Hampstead hill gardens
Des Ruffiéres Mrs. 68 Belsize park gdns.
Dever Henry 78 Finchley rd.
Deveson Daniel (Kent lo.) 42 Iverson rd.
Devitt Andrew (Ethelstane) Maresfield gardens
Devitt Henry (Bay Tree lodge) Frognal
Dewick George 1 Granville ter.
Dey Robert 145 Adelaide rd.
Dherang Geo. (Espérance) Gascony avn.
Dibb Mrs. Ashton 26 Gayton rd.
Dibdin Lewis Tona 14 Gayton cres.
Dick Allan B. 47 Belsize park
Dickens George 12 St. John's wood park
Dickens H. P. T. 6 Harley rd.
Dickens Timothy 5 Rosslyn cottages
Dickenson Charles Henry (Isis house) Mortimer cres.
Dickers H. J. (Avenue farm) The Avenue
Dickinson Dr. 1 Bridge rd.
Dickinson Charles J. 16 Lawn rd.
Diggins James 5 Yorkshire Grey rd.
Dines Mrs. 78 Maygrove rd.
Dinham C. (Louvain) Broadhurst gdns.
Diplock Albert 9 Midland cottages
Disney George 28 Prospect rd.
Disney Mrs. E. 19 Downshire hill
Dix Frank 4 Kingsford st.
Dixon ArthurWm.122 Abbey rd. Kilburn
Dixon Frederick 6 Priory rd.
Dixon J. M. (Canfield house) 2 Canfield gardens
Dixon Mrs. 1 Albion rd.
Dixon Mrs. 11 Denning rd.
Dixon Mrs. E. 104 Iverson rd.
Dixon Mrs. E. 23 Lancaster rd.
Dixon Thomas 15 South hill park gdns.
Dobbin Charles 10 Kemplay rd.
Dobbs Samuel 1 Sherriff rd.
Dobree George 81 Fellows rd.
Dobson Mrs. Mary 113 Abbey rd.
Dobson Thos.Wm.149 Abbey rd. Kilburn
Docker F.A.W. (Kingston) 115Priory rd.
Dockrell William R. (The Conduit lodge) 68 Fitzjohns' avenue
Dodd Rev. F. W. (Ramilles) Broadhurst gardens
Dodd John Theodore 60 Loudoun rd.
Dodd Thomas 6 Grove pl.
Doel Edwin 9 Holtham rd.
Doggett Richard 180 Adelaide rd.
DolleymoreArthur(Banavie)Hillfield rd.
DolleymoreEdwin183Belsize rd. Kilburn
Dolleymore John, sen. 6 Abbey cottages
Donagan Richard 182 Alexandra rd.

Donaldson Andrew B. (Devereux house) 6 Daleham gardens
Donelan James 61 Flask walk
Donnoven Miss 14 Gayton rd.
Dorrell George Edwd. 30 Upper Park rd.
Dottridge Alfred James 1 South hill park
Doucet Mrs. 23 Albion rd.
Douglas Alexander 2 Holtham rd.
Douglas John S. 17 Lyndhurst rd.
Douglas Mrs. 14 John st.
Douglas-Hamilton Major-Genl. (Langdale house) 1 Denington park
Douthwaite Mrs. 7 Crossfield rd.
Dow Alexander 12 Belgrave rd.
Dow Mrs. (Aberfeldie) Finchley new rd.
Dowling Edmund 75 King Henry's rd.
Dowling Mrs. S. E. 83 Adelaide rd.
Dowling Thomas 4 Maresfield gardens
Downing Arthur 29 Prospect rd.
Downing Miss 14 Mansfield villas
Downton Frederick 9 Ariel st.
Dowse John 39 Flask walk
Drake Mrs. 62 Maygrove rd.
Draper David 11 Midland cottages
Drayson S. Herbert (Brooklyn) Hillfield road
Drewry Henry R. 143 King Henry's rd.
DrewryMissEllenB.143King Henry's rd.
Drewry Miss Louisa 143 KingHenry's rd.
Drewry Mrs. H. Stewart 25 Gayton rd.
Drinkwater Edward F. 43 Fleet rd.
Driver David 3 Narcissus rd.
Druce Samuel B. L. 10 Lawn rd.
Drucker Charles 45 Belsize park
DrummondCapt.Alf.M.54Fitzjohns' avn.
Drummond Rev. James, LL.D. 13 Mansfield villas
Dryhurst Arthur George 5 John st.
Drysdale Mrs. (Kingston) 7 Acol rd.
Drysdale Mrs. A. D. 39 Belsize park
Du Bois Misses 44 Belsize park gardens
Duff William, Fitzjohns' mansions
Dulcken Henry, PH.D. (Arundel house) 79 Boundary rd.
Du Maurier George B. (New Grove house) The Grove
Dumbleton E. C. 50 Primrose hill rd.
Dun Alex. Campbell 19 Christchurch rd.
Duncan Dr. Hy. Montague 98 Abbey rd.
Duncan Rev. Henry 2 Carlingford rd.
Duncan — 1 Haverstock ter.
Duncan George F. 2 Abbott's rd.
Duncan J. H. (Briarlea) 24 Ellerdale rd.
Duncan Miss (Dunelm) 22 Ellerdale rd.
Duncan Mrs. 12 Messina avenue
Duncan Mrs. 33 Priory rd.
Duncan Mrs. 36 Upper Park rd.

wife Eliza: Sister to Ann 2nd wife of William WHARTON

Duncan William Wallace (Fern bank) 9 Ellerdale rd.
Duncum Joseph 7 Willow rd.
Dunham Miss Maria 1 Rockhall ter.
Dunham Mrs.Elizbth.10Primrose hill rd.
Dünkelsbühler Anton 36 Belsize park
DunkleyMrs.(Claremont cott.)TheRidge
Dunn George 34 Belgrave rd.
Dunn Richard 88 Adelaide rd.
Dunphie Charles J. 23 King Henry's rd.
Dunsterville Edward 2 Upper Avenue rd.
DuplantierEmile 187 Belsize rd. Kilburn
Duppuy Mrs. Eliza 8 Avenue villas
Du Pre Miss J. (Beaconsfield house) Quex rd.
Durham C. 81 Belsize rd.
Durham James Edward 38 Maygrove rd.
Durrant Mrs. 19 Belgrave rd.
Durrant Mrs. (Sunny bank) Christ church rd.
Durrant Mrs. 1 Well walk ter.
Dury William 5 Midland cottages
Dutton Thomas 13 Wildwood grove
Dyer Miss 9 Kingsgate pl.
Dyer Mrs. Henry 48 Ainger rd.
Dyer Mrs. Thisleton 118 KingHenry's rd.
Dyke Charles 33 Park rd.
Dymond Mrs 30 Priory rd.
Dyson William 25 Belsize park gardens
Dyter John 1 Flask cottages

Eadie Hy. Alexander 70 Boundary rd.
Earl Alfred William (Denning house) 2 Denning rd.
Earl Samuel 8 Holly mount
Earl Thomas H. 34 Fellows rd.
Eassie Wm., C.E. 73 King Henry's rd.
East Alfred 14 Adamson rd.
East Henry 9 St. George's rd.
East Thomas 10 The Village
Eastlake Lewis (Homestead) Netherhall road
Easton Mrs. M. A. 107 Abbey rd.
Eberhart Charles Leopold (Thuringia house) 13 Fitzjohns' avenue
Ebsworth Robert M. 23 Fordwych rd.
Eccles Thomas J. 17 Holtham rd.
Eddowes John 21 Ainger rd.
Edgar James 165 Loveridge rd.
Edgar Mrs. 9 Rockhall ter.
Edis Robert 2 Portland villas East Heath rd.
Edmead George 139 Iverson rd.
Edmondson Thomas (Boundary house) 2 Boundary rd.
Edmunds Alfred Sayres 1 Fairfax rd.
Edmunds G. R. 2 St. John's wood park

Edmunds Silas 10 Provost rd.
Edwards Captain Charles (North lodge) Messina avenue
Edwards Alfred 86 King Henry's rd.
Edwards Charles (Rowton house) Lancaster rd.
Edwards Chas. 40 St. John's wood park
Edwards Charles Hy. 196 Adelaide rd.
Edwards Edwin Thomas, M.R.C.S. 103 Abbey rd.
Edwards Francis 5 Church row
Edwards Frederic Yeats (Cromwell ho.) 42 Hampstead hill gardens
Edwards Frederick 31 Midland cottages
Edwards Henry (Norma cottage) 33 Broadhurst gardens
Edwards Henry Edward 56 Fellows rd.
EdwardsHerbert(Fernhurst)Hillfield rd
Edwards Mrs. 26 Daleham gardens
Edwards Mrs. Elizabeth 18 Steele's rd.
Edwards Mrs. Hannah 9 Fellows rd.
Edwards Robert Clarke 1 Buckland cres.
Edwards W. S. (Ardenlea) 5 Garlinge rd.
Egelton Josiah 4 Wildwood grove
Eggmore Mrs. (Albany cottage) 18 West end lane
Eisdell J. A. 6 Carlingford rd.
Eisenlohr Ferdinand 12 Lawn rd.
Elder Wm. David 40 Parliament hill rd.
Eldridge Miss E. 120 Iverson rd.
Eley Mrs. 211 Adelaide rd.
Elgood George J. (Branksome) 4 Fitzjohns' avenue
Elisha James 13 Avenue villas
Ell George P. 1 Kingdon rd.
Ellaby Thomas (The Elms) Cricklewood
Ellerton Alfred 28 Parliament hill rd.
Elliot Frederick 43 Belsize rd.
Elliott Alfred Harraden (Warwick house) 12 Downshire hill
Elliott Edward 31 Fordwych rd.
Elliott Ernest B. 26 Birchington rd.
Elliott James Wm. & Mrs. 160 Belsize rd.
Elliott Miss 13 Iverson rd.
Elliott Mrs. 48 Alexandra rd.
Elliott Wm. Timbrell 113 Adelaide rd.
Elliott W. W. 34 Birchington rd.
Ellis Alexander H. B. 1 Gardnor rd.
Ellis George 8 Bolton rd.
Ellis Henry 7 Chalcot gardens
Ellis Henry 22 Kingdon rd.
Ellis Mrs. (Ely house) 7 Primrose hill rd.
Ellis Mrs.Edward,The Avenue North end
Ellis Mrs. S. 34 Springfield rd.
Ellis Ralph Arthur Frederick William 7 Abbott's rd.
Ellis William 5 Springfield gardens

Elton Mrs. A. 5 Loveridge rd.
Ely Talfourd 73 Parliament hill rd.
Embury Arthur 27 Avenue villas
Emery Thomas 2 Pilgrim's pl.
Emes Miss 206 Adelaide rd.
Emmanuel — 15 Fitzjohns' parade
England George 12 Gayton rd.
Englefield Mrs. (Homeleigh) Crickle-wood lane
English John 25 The Village
English Walter 64 Adelaide rd.
Ernsthausen Oscar Von 54 Belsize park gardens
Escott Mrs. 4 Ash grove
Essex Alfred (Dinas) 4 Arkwright rd.
Esterbrooke Mrs. 9 Upper ter.
Etheridge Henry 3 Ebenezer rd.
Etheridge James 30 Prospect rd.
Etkins George 13 Lithos rd.
Evans Charles E. 5 Rosslyn ter.
Evans Edwd. Prichard 16 Primrose hill rd.
Evans Frederick 72 Abbey rd.
Evans George 2 Ash grove
Evans Herbert N., M.B. 3 Thurlow rd.
Evans John Edward 12 Albion rd.
Evans John Henry (Fairlight villa) Elsworthy rd.
Evans John Houghton 12 Claremont rd.
Evans John Lane 3 Downshire hill
Evans John Meredith 95 Belsize rd.
Evans M. H. 2 Hampstead sq.
Evans Mrs. 63 Fellows rd.
Evans Mrs. 6 Holly hill
Evans Richard H. 3 Hampstead hill gdns.
Evans Roger 11 Woodchurch rd.
Evans W. H. 90 Finchley rd.
Eveleigh Miss 59 Fairfax rd.
Evens Richard Underhay (Clyde house) Broadhurst gardens
Everard Miss 40 Belsize park gardens
Everett John 1 Christchurch rd.
Evershed Dr. Arthur 10 Mansfield villas
Evill Edward 6 Greville rd.
Ewart Miss 10 Thurlow rd.
Ewell Miss Louisa 38 Downshire hill
Ewing James (Haydn house) 3 Upper Park rd.
Eyers Mrs. M. 3 Pilgrim's pl.

Faber Louis C. 59 Fellows rd.
Fabian Henry 108 Adelaide rd.
Faehse Robert 28 Lancaster rd.
Fairer Alfred Richard 13 Ariel st.
Fairfax Mrs. Charles (Mayfield) 12 Fitzjohns' avenue
Fairman Frederick Dobede 5 Worsley rd.
Faithorn George 3 Avenue villas

Falcke B. 70 Finchley rd.
Falcke Philip 70 Finchley rd.
Falconar Lieut.-Colonel George A. H. (Falcon lodge) Oppidans rd.
Falconer Mrs. 11 Belsize park gardens
Falkenburg Louis 114 Adelaide rd.
Fall Thomas (Wensley) Netherhall ter.
Fancourt Mrs. M. A. 117 Iverson rd.
Faraday Charles A. 107 South hill park
Faraday Harold 6 Willow rd.
Farjeon B. L. 13 Adelaide rd.
Farmer John S. (Heath lodge) Hampstead heath
Farmer Leopold, Mortimer cres.
Farmer Mrs. (Palma villa) 15 Woodchurch rd.
Farmer Mrs. Mary 49 Fleet rd.
Farmery Mrs. 141 Adelaide rd.
Farmiloe G., jun. (Campbell house) 14 College ter.
Farmiloe J. (Montrose) 38 Fitzjohns' avn
Farnall Mrs. George Rooke (Burley lodge) Mill lane
Farniloe Thomas M. 21 Arkwright rd.
Farr Joseph 1 Lichfield rd.
Farr William 13 Holly mount
Farrer Rev. William, LL.B. (Oakleigh) Arkwright rd.
Farrer Miss 36 Belsize rd.
Farrer Thomas Charles (Queen Anne house) Elsworthy rd.
Fase Berkeley William 10 Harley rd.
Faulconer Thos., J.P. 8 St. John's wood pk
Faulding A. J. (Burlington house) Broadhurst gardens
Faulkner E. 11 Gardnor rd.
Faulkner Percy 13 Yew grove
Feacey James 108 Maygrove rd.
Feakes H. 38 Kingsgate rd.
Feis Jacob 69 Avenue rd.
Feldenheimer Ferdinand (Eudora house) 11 Fitzjohns' avenue
Fell John Corry 6 Denning rd.
Fell Miss (St. Hilda's college) 111 Abbey road
Fell Mrs. 4 Wildwood ter.
Fellowes Mrs. 16 Elsworthy rd.
Fellows Frank P. 8 Hampstead green
Felsenstein Ludwig 62 Springfield rd.
Fenn J. 13 and 14 New end
Fennell Henry Thomas 14 Iverson rd.
Fensom James, North end
Ferguson Donald 9 Alexandra rd.
Ferguson Robert 57 Ainger rd.
Ferguson Thomas 16 Belsize cres.
Fernan George 63 Belsize park gardens
Fidler William 5 Buckland cres.

'ield Abraham 8 Buckland villas
'ield Allan 4 Upper Avenue rd.
'ield Edward 85 Alexandra rd.
'ield Mrs. (Burlington house) Broad-
    hurst gardens
'ield Mrs. E. W., Squire's mount
'ield Mrs. Horace 30 Thurlow rd.
'ield Thomas Meagher (Kenrick villa)
    Worsley rd.
'ield Walter (The Pryors) East Heath rd.
'ife Mrs. 52 Adelaide rd.
'inch Alfred (Rockhall cottage) Crickle-
    wood lane
'inch Arthur Elley 30 Steele's rd.
'inch Arthur John 87 Fellows rd.
'inch George 10 Well walk
'indlay John Adamson 44 King Henry's
    road
'indlay William L. 42 Belsize rd.
'inlay Alexander L. 3a Mortimer rd.
'inlay Thomas 6 Well walk
'irnberg Max 2 Lancaster pl.
'ischel Leopold 55 Belsize park gardens
'ishburn Miss 1 Station villas
'isher Mrs. 13 Albion rd.
'isher Mrs. Anne 11 Holtham rd.
'isher Thomas 19 Parliament hill rd.
'isher William 10 Belsize rd.
'itton Walter 10 Greville rd.
'itzell Mrs. 19 Netherwood st.
'itzGerald Misses 12 Mansfield villas
'itzgerald Mrs. Samuel 42 Avenue rd.
'itzGerald William 17 Carlingford rd.
'itzgibbon V. B. (Bruin lodge) 14
    Woodchurch rd.
'lachfeld Julius 11 Buckland villas
'lamank Mrs. 29 King Henry's rd.
'lavell C.E., jun. (Burnside) 39 West end
    lane
'lavell Mrs. 17 Buckland cres.
'leming Jas. (Hastings vl.) 15 Rudall cres.
'leming John 111 Belsize rd.
'leming Sydney (Kendall villa) 37 West
    end lane
'letcher Banister (Anglebay) 21 Wood-
    church rd.
'letcher Frank 16 Springfield rd.
'letcher George A. B. 15 Belsize rd.
'letcher Henry 13 Midland cottages
'letcher John S. (Treherne house) West
    end
'letcher Mrs. 4 Church lane
'letcher Mrs. 14 Eton rd.
'letcher Mrs. Robert (St. Nicholas)
    Frognal
'letcher Richard 11 Devonshire pl.
'letcher S. 25 Adelaide rd.

Fletcher Sidney Howard (St. Valérie)
    Oppidans rd.
Fletcher Thomas 4 Springfield
Flight Dr. W. 28 Well walk
Flint Frederick 2 Station villas
Flint James 24 Avenue villas
Flook Walter (Heath Lea) Willow rd.
Flower Harry T. 51 Priory rd.
Flugel Adolph 31 Adelaide rd.
Foley Henry Joseph (Heatherlea) Vale
    of Health
Folkard Misses (Chigwell house) Broad-
    hurst gardens
Folkard Richard 4 Rockhall ter.
Fooks W. Cracroft, LL.B. 21 Hilgrove
    road
Foot Alfred Edwin (Helsdon house)
    Messina avenue
Foot Frank 4 Iverson rd.
Forbes David (Craigforth) 70 Parliament
    hill rd.
Forbes Thomas Lawrence 8 Lancaster pl.
Ford Colonel Arthur 18 Crossfield rd.
Ford Rev. Joseph 6 College ter.
Ford Edward 164 Adelaide rd.
Ford Everard Allen 2 Eldon rd.
Ford James 42 Bolton rd.
Ford Samuel 9 Lowfield rd.
Ford Wharton 49 Fellows rd.
Fordham John 2 Maygrove rd.
Foreigner James 2 Linstead st.
Foreman James 3 Golder's hill ter.
Forman Arthur 16 Claremont rd.
Forsberry Charles 22 Lowfield rd.
Forster Mrs. 11 Goldhurst rd.
Forsyth James (Ednam ho.) Finchley rd.
Foskett George 54 Gayton rd.
Foster Major Kingsley 11 Belsize rd.
Foster Andrew 15 Claremont rd.
Foster G. Carey 18 Daleham gardens
Foster John (Dean's cottage) 34 Down-
    shire hill
Foster Joseph 21 Boundary rd.
Foulger Miss 9 Kingsgate pl.
Foulsham George (Bridge house)
    73 Springfield rd.
Fouracres Mrs. 15 Elm grove
Fowke Francis 8 College ter.
Fowle John A. (The Nest) Hillfield rd.
Fowle Mrs. 1 Yorkshire Grey yard
Fowler Mrs. Helen 15 Ash grove
Fox Dr. William Smith 29 Adamson rd.
Fox Frederick 9 Lower Lawn rd.
Fox George 1 Belsize rd.
Fox Hubert 7 Hilgrove rd.
Fox Miss 29 Goldhurst ter.
Fox Mrs. Mary 46 Boundary rd.

Fox Mrs. Tilbury (The Hermitage) Child's hill lane
France Frederick A. 11 Yew grove
France Miss (Westhaven) Cricklewood
Francis George Bishop 41 Boundary rd.
Francis John 12 Winchester rd.
Francis Mrs. 13 Yorkshire Grey yard
Francis Mrs. I. C. 45 Fellows rd.
Francis Reginald 23 Goldhurst ter.
Franck Mrs. 44 Boundary rd.
Frank Gustav 9 Haverstock hill
Frankau Frederick Joseph 26 Steele's rd.
Frankau Mrs. (Newmount lodge) Windsor rd.
Frankel Sigismund 7 Adamson rd.
Frankenstein Samuel Manuel (Cherwell house) Mortimer cres.
Franklin Frederick T. 41 Springfield rd.
Franklin Henry 7 Benham's pl.
Franklin Henry 7 Kingsford st.
Franklin J. A., M.D. 7 High st.
Franklin William 1 Back lane
Franklin William 10 Belgrave rd.
Franklin William 5 Kingsford st.
Franks Mrs. (St. Aubyn's) 1 Daleham gardens
Fraser Robert Stevens 13 South hill park gardens
Fraser William John 121 Adelaide rd.
Frazer John James 4 John st.
Frazer Miss (Douro ho.) 24 Hilgrove rd.
Frazer Mrs. 34 Parliament hill rd.
Frazer Thomas Henry 62 Abbey rd.
Free Richard W. 102 South hill park
Freegard George 35 Kingsgate rd.
Freeland Mrs. 128 Alexandra rd.
Freeman Rev. Frederick John, M.A. 53 Alexandra rd.
Freeman Charles H. (Abbeyfield) 152 Abbey rd. Kilburn
Freeman Francis T. (Abbeyfield) 152 Abbey rd. Kilburn
Freeman Hy. Golding 68 Alexandra rd.
Freeman H. P. 34 Priory rd.
Freeman John (Higham house) 35 Haverstock hill
Freeman John 1 Medley rd.
Freeman Mrs. 36 Fellows rd.
Freer Ireson 2 Medley rd.
Freeth Colonel William 3 Buckland crescent
Freeth Charles 4 Buckland cres.
French Mrs. 27 Palmerston rd.
Frenché Andrew 22 Bolton rd.
Frewer Charles 121 King Henry's rd.
Friederichs Mrs. (Rumah) Willoughby rd.
Friend Mrs. Sophia 5 Parliament hill rd.

Fripp Alfred D. 43a Hampstead hi gardens
Fripp George Arthur 23 Fairfax rd.
Frisby Robert, jun. 47 Flask walk
Fritsch Herman 100 King Henry's rd.
Frodsham J. 47 Ainger rd.
Frost George 1 Goldsmith's gardens
Frost Mrs. Hannah 42 Adelaide rd.
Frost Mrs. Louisa 5 Wildwood grove
Frost R. 16 Ainger rd.
Frost William Henry 11 Spencer ter.
Fry Charles (Farleigh) Willow rd.
Fry Danby Palmer 138 Haverstock hill
Fry Robert 36 Belgrave rd.
Fry Thomas 9 Devonshire pl.
Fryer Christopher 139 Fellows rd.
Fryer George Henry 107 Belsize rd.
Fryer Miss 2 Springfield
Fueski Madame Rosalia 2 Richmond vil
Fuller Rev. C. J., M.A. 98 King Henry's rd
Fuller Alfred 31 Belsize park gardens
Fuller Miss Mary 7 College villas rd.
Fuller Mrs. A. C. 48 Belsize rd.
Fuller Mrs. Frances 7 Rudall cres.
Fuller Mrs. H. H. 19 Fairfax rd.
Fuller Thomas 9 Spencer ter.
Fulton Mrs. Alexander 35 Priory rd.
Furnell William 4 Golder's hill cottage
Fussey William 109 Iverson rd.
Fyfe Fames 48 Fellows rd.

Gahagan Edwin C. 193 Adelaide rd.
Gairdner James 5 Carlingford rd.
Gairdner Mrs. 15 Broadhurst gardens
Galbraith William R. 91 Finchley rd.
Gale Miss 57 Boundary rd.
Gale Mrs. Sarah 57 Fleet rd.
Gall Thomas (Holyrood house) Wind mill hill
Galloway Wm. Chas. 135 King Henry's rd
Gammie John 38 Belgrave rd.
Gandar William (Abernethy house Mount Vernon
Garcia Rodriguez (Mon Abri) Shoot-up hill
Gard W. Garrad Snowdon, LL.B. 13 Adelaide rd.
Gardener Geo. 3 Murray ter. Flask walk
Gardiner J. T. 7 Buckland villas
Gardner Charles 173 Belsize rd. Kilbur
Gardner George 8 Kilburn vale
Gardner J. E. (Park house) St. John' wood park
Gardner Miss 76 Alexandra rd.
Gardner Percy, D.LITT. 2 Rudall cres.
Gardner Robert 10 Broadhurst gardens
Gardner Thomas 13 Oak hill park

ardner Thomas 10 Wildwood grove North end
ardner Wm. (Heddon ho.) Rosslyn hill
arle Acton (Elmstead) Cricklewood
arle Mrs. (Winterdyne) Cricklewood
arlich William 11 Well rd.
arlick Mrs. 75 Netherwood st.
arner Thomas 20 Church row
arnham Robert 1a Kilburn vale
arrett James 66 Belsize park
arvey Mrs. 5 Holtham rd.
ascoine William (Melton house) Burgess hill
ascoyne Andrew 3 Well walk ter.
askell William 53 Adelaide rd.
ass Mrs. (Ravenscourt) 17 Denning rd.
atliff Charles 12 Hampstead hill gdns.
avan Alexander 1 Fitzjohns' avenue
avin James Merricks 65 South hill park
ay John 51 Belsize park
ay John 4 The Village
eare Henry Cecil 22 Stanley gardens
eare William A. (Southbrook) 4 Daleham gardens
eary Thomas 27 Goldhurst ter.
eddes A. C. (Thornton) Lancaster rd.
eesin Mrs. 100 Alexandra rd.
ellibrand Dunscombe Bradford (Albion cottage) John st.
ent Alfred 18 Lichfield rd.
ent Frank 22 Iverson rd.
entery Frederick 14 Well walk
entle John 19 Thurlow rd.
eoghegan William J. 11 Thurlow rd.
eorge Edward H. (Weston cottage) South end rd.
eorge Edwin Herbert 91 Fellows rd.
eorge James William (Stratbearn) Willoughby rd.
erbert R. 31 Gascony avenue
erds C. 15 Fordwych rd.
ermain William 206 Loveridge rd.
erman George 28 Fleet rd.
erstley Morris 34 Primrose hill rd.
ervis Frederick H. 1 Fellows rd.
ibbon Mrs. 98 Adelaide rd.
ibbons Charles 8 Fortune green
ibbons John 11 Ariel st.
ibbsClement (Edgbaston) 87 Priory rd.
ibbs Henry 2 Holly mount
ibbs Jas. (Howard lodge) 35 Greville rd.
ibbs Joseph Melton 139 Alexandra rd.
ibbs Miss 30 Belsize rd.
ibbs Nathaniel B. 74 Abbey rd.
ibbs Thomas 46 Springfield rd.
ibsonRev.Dr.John Monroe 15 Cleve rd.
ibson Rev. R. B., M.A. 4 Adamson rd.

Gibson Alfred (Clyde house) Broadhurst gardens
Gibson Jaspar (Stonecroft) Cleve rd.
Gibson John K. 11 Sumatra rd.
Gibson Mrs. 43 Fellows rd.
Gibson William T. 71 King Henry's rd.
Gieseler Misses 9 Crossfield rd.
Gifford Miss 39 Stanley gardens
Gilbert Alfred 68 Finchley rd.
Gilbert George 7 Golden sq.
Gilbert George Henry 2 Cricklewood lane
Gilbert Mrs. Thomas W. (Carlton house) 33 St. George's rd.
Gilbert William 8 Alfred ter. Back lane
Gilbey Daniel 10 Cricklewood ter.
Gilchrist Mrs. (Keat's corner) 12 Well rd.
Gilchrist Mrs. Matilda 10 Pond st.
Gilchrist Percy C. (Ruscombe) Willoughby rd.
Giles Charles S., R.N. 118 South hill park
Gilfillan Mrs. 23 Upper Park rd.
Gilfillan Samuel (Ashbridge) Windsor terrace
Gill Charles John 59 King Henry's rd.
Gill Crandon Dawes 28 Stanley gardens
Gill Francis 25 Haverstock hill
Gill George T. S. 29 Steele's rd.
Gill W. G. 94 King Henry's rd.
Gillespie John (Cumberland house) Iverson rd.
Gillett Alfred 7 Providence pl.
Gillies Miss Margaret 25 Church row
Gillingham John 8 Goldhurst ter.
Gillott John Robert 46 Adelaide rd.
Ginn William John 1 Rosslyn cottages
Giovana Madame Marie 155 Fellows rd.
GittensMrs.(Tamar villa)113 Iverson rd.
Gittens Thomas (Hill view) Vale of Health
Gittens William (Beaumont) Willow rd.
Gittins Hy. (Firbeck villa) 7 Sherriff rd.
Gladman Charles 25 Loveridge rd.
Gladman George (Ivy lo.) Cricklewood
Glandt Reynold 4 Spencer ter.
Glen Thomas (Carlisle ho.) Kemplay rd.
Gloag J. R. 128 Haverstock hill
Glover Miss C. 30 Haverstock hill
Glover Mrs. 35 Stanley gardens
Glover W. B. 4 College villas rd.
Glyn Charles H. 3 Worsley rd.
Glyn Richard H. 2 Hill side
Goddard John L. 9 Buckland villas
Goddard Joseph (The Priory) Upper ter.
Goddard Philip 96 Abbey rd.
Godwin Rev. J. H. 1 Belsize ter.
Godwin Henry 162 Belsize rd.
Goldby Miss 27 Kilburn priory

Goldsmith Alfred (Richmond villa) Cricklewood
Goldsmidt Edward 23 Adamson rd.
Goldsmith Walter Charles 45 Belsize sq.
Goldstein Henry (Carisbrook) 17 Elsworthy rd.
Goldstein Walter 20 Messina avenue
Gole Russell (The Ferns) 65 Finchley new rd.
Gomersall William, M.C.P. OXON. 39 King Henry's rd.
Gonner Peter 57 Finchley new rd.
Gooch Walter 46 Avenue rd.
Goodall Frederick (Rosenstead) 62 Avenue rd.
Goodchild Edwd. 145 Belsize rd. Kilburn
Goodchild John 23 Thurlow rd.
Goodchild Miss 6 Eaton villas
Goodfellow Henry 1 St. Ann's pl. Vale of Health
Goodliffe William Gimber 2 Priory rd.
Goodman Thomas Warner 155 Haverstock hill
Goodwin Alfred (Kent lodge) 9 John st.
Goodwin John M. 53 Maygrove rd.
Goodwyn Charles 23 Boundary rd.
Gordon Rev. John B., M.A. 21 Fairfax rd.
Gordon Alex. 4 Hampstead hill gardens
Gordon Alfred(Maurice vil.) Worsley rd.
Gordon Mrs. (Aboyne ho.) 29 Fellows rd.
Gordon Robert M. 50 South hill park
Goring Harry (Lindore vil.)Messina avn.
Gorton Alfred 4 Oppidans rd.
Gorton J. E. 18 Belsize cres.
Goslett William Maynard 66 Fellows rd.
Goss George Dean 126 Iverson rd.
Goss James P. 15 Yew grove
Gossell Otto 7 Upper Park rd.
Gotch Thomas 86 Fellows rd.
Gotto Edward (The Logs) East Heath rd.
Gotto H. G. (West Heath house) West Heath rd.
Gottschalk Gustave 20 Adamson rd.
Gough C. H. 19 Adamson rd.
Gough William 43 Netherwood st.
Gould Abraham,F.R.G.S.(Somerset lodge) 111 Adelaide rd.
Gould Misses 3 Steele's rd.
Gould R. (Vale lodge) Vale of Health
Gow Charles 27 Birchington rd.
Gow Mrs. Mary Owen 5 Haverstock ter.
Gower John 26 Prospect rd.
Gower Mrs. 8 Provost rd.
Gowing Richard 6 Upper Park rd.
Gowing Thomas W. 19 Steele's rd.
Gowler A. (Esk villa) Mortimer cres.
Goy Joseph 96 Maygrove rd.

Graham H. Howgrave 5 Heath rise
Graham Mrs. 4 Maygrove rd.
Graham Mrs. 52 Park rd.
Graham Robert 7 Park rd.
Grant Miss 104 King Henry's rd.
Granville Mrs. (Bifrons) Willow rd.
Grasemann Carl 150 Belsize rd
Grave Miss 141 Abbey rd. Kilburn
Gray Alfred 49 Kingsgate rd.
Gray John Selby (Stoneleigh) Acol rd.
Gray Mrs. 25 Alexandra rd.
Gray Nutter (Plevna house) Kemplay rd
Gray Samuel 3 Upper Avenue rd.
Gray S. O. 71 Belsize park gardens
Gray William 11 Holly mount
Greatorex Henry 66 Loudoun rd.
Greaves Charles 20 Lowfield rd.
Greaves Charles Haslehurst 55 Belsiz park
Greaves William 48 Downshire hill
Green Aveling 2 Steele's studios
Green Charles (Charlecote) Hampstea hill gardens
Green Charles Thorpe (Ambleside) Hil field rd.
Green David 8 Grafton ter.
Green Edward F. 2 Steele's rd.
Green Edwin 32 St. John's park rd.
Green Frank 41 King Henry's rd.
Green George Robert 1 Lawn rd.
Green George Sangster (Stafford house 26 Fitzjohns' avenue
Green H. 5 Cedar villas
Green Henry 161 Belsize rd. Kilburn
Green Isaac (Lymington) West end lan
Green Joseph 3 Lowfield rd.
Green Matthew Henry 84 Maygrove r
Green Miss 136 Alexandra rd.
Green Mrs. 73 Alexandra rd.
Green Theodore(Leyland)1 Arkwright r
Green Thomas Allen 21 Belsize sq.
Green W. H. 17 Maygrove rd.
Greenaway Alfred John 50 Frognal
Greene Charles John (Cambridge house 97 Iverson rd.
Greene Mrs. 6 Stanley gardens
Greenfield Harvey 79 Finchley rd.
Greenhill Chas. Pope 94 South hill pa
Greenway W. (The Firs) Cricklewood
Greenwood Mrs. 56 Ainger rd.
Greenwood Wm. (The Beeches)Acol r
Greenwood W. O. 6 Hermitage villas
Greer John Henry 1 Narcissus rd.
Gregory A. W. 132 Maygrove rd.
Gregory Henry 22 Crossfield rd.
Gregory James 10 Mansfield pl.
Gregory Miss Teresa 41 Gascony aven

regory Thomas (Hill view) 2 Primrose hill rd.

reig John Borthwick 12 Hilgrove rd.

reig William James (Blenheim cottage) 39 Downshire hill

retton George Le Mesurier 116 King Henry's rd.

ribble William 15 Belsize park

rieves John 11 Steele's rd.

riffin Colonel James T. (Oneóta)Maresfield gardens

riffin Frederick 64 Abbey rd.

riffin Richard B. 27 Midland cottages

riffith Charles 114 South hill park

riffith D. C. 10 Heathfield gardens

riffiths George 18 Albion rd.

riffiths Henry J. (Belmont) Greenhill

riffiths Mrs. 16 St. George's rd.

rimaldi Madame 8 Adelaide rd.

rimani Mrs. 34 South hill park

rimes William 41 Bolton rd.

ripper F. F. 17 Elm grove

rissell Mrs. M. 71 Fellows rd.

riswood Richard 1 Oriel cottages

room George 61 Goldhurst rd.

room John 31 Heath st.

room Robert 6 Mansfield villas

rosvenor A. Octavius, M.D.(The Tower) 72 Priory rd.

rover William 5 Edward ter.

roves A. 2 Lichfield rd.

roves Edward (Walmer house)26 Goldhurst ter.

roves F. W. (Vernal house) 8 Prince Arthur rd.

roves J. B. and Mrs. 36 Iverson rd.

rundy P. 1 William ter. Providence pl.

rylls T. J. (Burgh house) Well walk

ude Joseph 23 Downshire hill

uilding Randolph 20 King Henry's rd.

uiterman Sigmund 36 Primrose hill rd.

ullick Thomas 111 Finchley rd.

unby Henry John 46 Fleet rd.

undry Joseph 108 Haverstock hill

unn Alfred 15 Netherwood st.

urden Benjamin 14 Midland cottages

urden Charles (Aspens) Hampstead hill gardens

urney Charles 44 Maygrove rd.

urney Mrs. 10 Birchington rd.

ush Mrs. William F. 41 Fellows rd.

ushlow George (Holly Hedge cottage) Well rd.

aterbock George 16 Hemstall rd.

athrie Charles I. 9 Ash grove

atteman Augustus 26 Buckland cres.

ayatt Thomas 40 King Henry's rd.

Gwyn Walter 51 Belsize rd.

Gwynn Edmund, M.D. 6 Hampstead hill gardens

Gwyther Frederick George 43 King Henry's rd.

Gylby Miss 7 Merton rd.

Haag Carl, R.W.S. 7 Lyndhurst rd.

Hacket Mrs. 62 South hill park

Hackett A. R. 10 Steele's rd.

Hackworth Richard (Brightside) Arkwright rd.

Hadenfelt Rubert 181 Adelaide rd.

Hadfield Charles Alfred 153 Fellows rd.

Hadow Miss 2 Fairfax rd.

Hadrill George, Golden yard

Hadrill Henry John 53 Belsize avenue

Hagelsieb Wilhelm 18 Maygrove rd.

Haig General F. T. 6 Kemplay rd.

Haigh Mrs. James 27 Belsize park gdns.

Hailstone Robert Henry 91 Adelaide rd.

HainesEdwardWalter 125 Alexandra rd.

Haines Frederick,F.S.A.(Boreham house) 184 Haverstock hill

Hair John 14 Upper Park rd.

Hale Miss, Branch hill

Hale Thomas William 9 South hill park

Hales John Wesley 1 Oppidans rd.

Hall Rev. Newman (The Ivy house) 1 Hampstead sq.

Hall Alexander 5 Mansfield pl.

Hall Charles 166 Iverson rd.

Hall Charles 31 Kilburn priory

HallFrederickWilliam 18 Winchester rd.

Hall George 101 Fellows rd.

Hall James 15 Stanley gardens

Hall John 7 Golden yard

Hall John Vine 66 Avenue rd.

Hall Newman Vine 80 King Henry's rd.

Hall Robert Gresly 60 Avenue rd.

Hall Walter (Clairville) Acol rd.

Hall William 3 Eton villas

Hallam John B. 16 Thurlow rd.

Halle S. B. 59 Adelaide rd.

Halliday J. (Bowerhayes) 35 Fitzjohns' avenue

Hallowes Alexander 6 Albion rd.

Halls John 1 Midland cottages

Halls Mrs. 25 Broadhurst gardens

Halpin Colonel George 54 Belsize park

Halpin Rev. R. C. 22 Belsize sq.

Halse William 4 Station villas

Ham Rev. James Panton 71 Parliament hill rd.

Hamilton Miss 9 Greville rd

Hamilton Mrs. 144 Belsize rd.

Hamilton Thomas 11 Gayton rd.

F

Hamilton William D., F.S.A. (Beaumont cottage) College rd.
Hamlen Charles 122 Iverson rd.
Hammack H. Laurence 16 Belsize park
Hammack Richard, Rathleigh gate West end lane
Hammon Mrs. 5 Golder's hill ter.
Hammond George 51 Adelaide rd.
Hammond Mrs. R. 12 Avenue villas
Hammond R. C. (Stourcliffe house) 1 Westcroft villas
Hamper Henry 15 Park rd.
Hamshaw Thomas Philip 30 Adelaide rd.
Hanbury Mrs. 64 Goldhurst rd.
Handcock Richard 5 Bolton rd.
Handford Ebenezer 27 Gascony avenue
Handford George (Trafford lodge) 24 West end lane
Hands Mrs. Jane 81 Finchley rd.
Hanes John 108 Alexandra rd.
Hanhart Nicholas 7 Eton villas
Hanhart Nicholas, LL.B. 22 Steele's rd.
Hannah Mrs. Charlotte 12 Heath villas
Hannell Henry 4 Grafton ter.
Hanscomb Edwd. Knight 17 South hl. pk.
Hansom H. 29 Park rd.
Hanson James Joseph 11 Bolton rd.
Hanson Oliver Hy. (Astoria) 121 Priory rd.
Hanson Samuel H. 1 Ariel st.
Harben Charles Henry (Highfield) 75 Finchley new rd.
Harben Hy. (Seaford lodge) 2 Fellows rd.
Harben Henry Andrade 68 Fellows rd.
Harben Miss 75 Adelaide rd.
Harcourt Robert (Stanley house) 160 Haverstock hill
Hardcastle John (Beechenden) Heathfield gardens
Harding Major Charles 91 Alexandra rd.
Harding George 28 Lowfield rd.
Harding Jesse 39 Lowfield rd.
Harding R. B. 21 Adelaide rd.
Hardwick H. 6 Belgrave gardens
Hardwicke R. R. 47 Gascony avenue
Hardy Albert (Inez villa) 13 Boundary rd.
Hardy T. B. (Danesmere) Lambolle rd.
Hare J. (Lily lodge) Vale of Health.
Hargrave Thomas 3 Palmerston rd.
Harland Leonard 77 Alexandra rd.
Harley Thomas, M.D. (The Lawn) 48 Haverstock hill
Harms John 10 Midland cottages
Harmsworth Alfred 94 Boundary rd.
Harnett Mrs. A. H. 133 Abbey rd. Kilburn
Harper Geo. Povey, M.A. 35 Adelaide rd.
Harper Joseph 160 Maygrove rd.
Harper Miss 21 New end

Harraden Samuel (Homeside) 24 Fitzjohns' avenue
Harris Alfred 7 West cottages
Harris C. J. 4 Kilburn priory
Harris Edward 89 Iverson rd.
Harris Edwin 7 Heath rise
Harris F. W. (Hill Top vil.) Cricklewood
Harris H. 3 South hill park gardens
Harris Henry (The Bandalls) 60 Belsize park gardens
Harris Henry 36 Palmerston rd.
Harris Henry 41 Palmerston rd.
Harris James 3 The Cottages Cricklewood lane
Harris John (Farley cott.) Church lane
Harris Jno. (Mizpah vil.) 107 Iverson rd.
Harris John 18 Lowfield rd.
Harris Miss 3 Belsize sq.
Harris Mrs. 2 Ariel st.
Harris Mrs. 38 Primrose hill rd.
Harris Mrs. 114 South hill park
Harris Mrs. Alicia 3 St. John's wood park
Harris Mrs. R. 84 Abbey rd.
Harris Richard 42 Fitzjohns' avenue
Harris Richard 6 West cottages
Harris Robert 6 Midland cottages
Harris Walter 29 Boundary rd.
Harris William 28 Adelaide rd.
Harrison J. 2 Goldhurst rd.
Harrison John 171 Belsize rd. Kilburn
Harrison Miss (Arrandale) 8 Canfield gardens
Harrison Miss Lucy 161 Haverstock hill
Harrison Mrs. (Kelvin lo.) 136 Iverson rd
Harrison Mrs. L. (St. Margaret's lodge) High rd.
Harrison R. W. 10 Church row
Harrison Saml. (Elm cot.) South end grn
Harrison William 4 Hill side
Harrod Mrs. 10 Fellows rd.
Hart Charles 3 Heath villas
Hart George (Strad lodge) South hill park gardens
Hart Henry 12 Birchington rd.
Hart Lemon 15 Winchester rd.
Hart Mrs. 3 Westcroft villas
Hart Robert Washington 22 Fairfax rd
Hart William 25 Parliament hill rd.
Harting Joseph T. 49 Priory rd.
Hartley Thos. P. (Uffculme) 7 Garlinge rd
Harton William Henry 4 Belsize park
Hartwell Mrs. Earl (Wildwood) North en
Harvey George 5 The Village
Harvey H. (Garfield villa) The Ridge
Harvey J. W. (Woodstock ho.) 4 Albion rd
Harvey Mrs. 102 King Henry's rd.
Harvey Mrs. 7 Mansfield villas

Harwood Thomas 14 Oppidans rd.
Haskew Edward 52 Ainger rd.
Hasloch Charles 8 Hermitage villas Child's hill lane
Hassell Henry Joseph 127 Adelaide rd.
Hastie Peter 24 Park rd.
Haswell Admiral William Henry 31 Adamson rd.
Hatch George 5 Alfred ter. Back lane
Hatch John 4 Grove ter.
Hatherley Jno.(Clifton cot.)Cricklewood
Hatton Ernest 30 Birchington rd.
Havergal Mrs. and Miss (Home lodge) Worsley rd.
Haviland Mrs. 11 King Henry's rd.
Haward Frederick 62 Fellows rd.
Hawes F. Sutton (Rawdon) 17 Arkwright rd.
Hawes George 23 Fleet rd.
Hawes James 5 Hill side
Hawes Robert 6 Elm ter.
Hawkes William Henry 140 Alexandra rd.
Hawkings Robert John 144 Iverson rd.
Hawkins Arthur 1 Ambridge cottages
Hawkins Charles 51 Flask walk
Hawkins C. Thomas 27 Fellows rd.
Hawkins Edward Thomas 38 Up. Park rd.
Hawkins Geo. Frederick 131 Iverson rd.
Hawkins James 2a Golden sq.
Hawkins John 10 Belsize park
Hawkins Joseph 3 Silver st.
Hawksley Thomas P. 97 Adelaide rd.
Hawthorn Genl. Robt. 41 Stanley grdns.
Hawtree James 4 King's cottages
Haxell James 11 Medley rd.
Hay Alexander (Nettlestone) 21 Fitzjohns' avenue
Hay Mrs. 93 Priory rd.
Haycraft W. Sydenham 24 Up. Park rd.
Haycroft Mrs. (Trenton villa) 23 Primrose hill rd.
Haydon William 12 St. George's rd.
Hayes Edwin (Briscoe ho.) Steele's rd.
Hayes Gwyn Clifford 6 Gascony avenue
Hayes H. B. (The Grange) Broadhurst gardens
Hayes J. C. 54 Messina avenue
Hayes William 10 Church lane
Hayhoe R. H. 7 Elm grove
Hayles Wm. (Lyon ho.) 162 Iverson rd.
Haylesbury Henry 10 Devonshire pl.
Hayman Henry 74 Priory rd.
Hayman Phenœus 38 Priory rd.
Hayman Mrs. 10 Chalcot gardens
Hayne Joseph 21 Netherwood st.
Haynes George(Kenmore) Greenhil rd.
Haynes George B. 20 Springfield rd.

Haynes Wm.(Hartsfield) 21 Denning rd.
Haynes William (Wildwood house) North end
Hayns John (Campbell cottage)John st.
Hays Christopher 5 Golden sq.
Haysman James (Anglo-French college) Burgess hill
Hayter Miss M. 3 Squire's mount cottages Squire's mount
Hayter Mrs. 46 Messina avenue
Hayter Wm. 3 Ambridge cotts. North end
Hayter William 36 Flask walk
Hayward James (Clayton cottage) Child's hill lane
Hayward James (Laurel cottage) Rosslyn hill
Hayward William 33 Bolton rd.
Haywood Walter Robt. 58 King Henry's rd.
Hazell Mark 3 The Village Child's hill
Hazzard Miss 6 Lithos rd.
Head Rev. George Frederick (Christ Church vicarage) Cannon pl.
Head Charles (Newlands) 71 Priory rd.
Heal Harris 6 Buckland cres.
Healy Arthur 5 Prince Arthur mews
Hearn G. F. 9 Parliament hill
Heather James 123 Abbey rd. Kilburn
Heathfield Stephen 12 Yorkshire Grey rd.
Heaverman Edwd.153 Belsize rd. Kilburn
Hecht Max 35 Belsize park gardens
Hecht Philip 7 Steele's rd.
Heddle John 94 Alexandra rd.
Hedges Francis 10 Station villas
Heelas James, M.D. 50 Primrose hill rd.
Heideman Percy Francis 19 Crossfield rd.
Heilbron Selim 9 Gascony avenue
Helffenstein Harry(Rhine villa)Cricklewood
Helffenstein Henrich Christian (Aberglaslyn) Cricklewood
Helm William H. (Mogador)Hillfield rd.
Hembrow Chas. Geo. 50 Netherwood st.
Hemming Jsph. (Hampden) Hillfield rd.
Hemming Miss 34 Fairfax rd.
Hemming Miss 68 Loudoun rd.
Hemming Mrs. 8 Belsize ter.
Henderson Arthur E. 144 Alexandra rd.
Henderson Henry 22 Woodchurch rd.
Henderson John 22 Lancaster rd.
Henderson Misses 3 Oak hill park
Henderson Mrs. James 7 Hampstead hill gardens
Henderson Richard 61 Finchley new rd.
Henderson Robert Bruce (North villa) Vale of Health
Henderson William 4 Hilgrove rd.
Hendriks Philip 25 Elm grove

william F = nephew of Sarah wife of Alfred GOSLETT

Hendy John 18 Loveridge rd.
Hengler Charles (Cambridge house) 27 Fitzjohns' avenue
Henley James 12 Holly mount
Henley Lionel Chas. 39 South hill park
Henness Mrs. 12 Dynham rd.
Hennis Captain William 53 Belsize rd.
Henrici Olaus (Meldorf cottage) Kemplay rd.
Henry Alfred, F.C.A. 21 Avenue villas
Henry Michael 9 Fordwych rd.
Henshaw John 13 Daleham gardens
Hensman Mrs. 37 Adelaide rd.
Hepburn James 31 South hill park
Hepburn Mrs. 35 Adamson rd.
Hepburn W. Arnold 63 South hill park
Herapath Edwin John (Oakhurst) Cleve rd.
Herbert John Rogers, R.A. (The Chimes) West end lane
Herbert Mrs. 35 Flask walk
Herbert Mrs. 2 Springfield rd.
Herbert Wilfrid V. 11 Sherriff rd.
Herbert Wm. Hawkins 12 Lancaster rd.
Herklots Rev. Gerard Andreas, M.A. (St. Saviour's vicarage) Eton rd.
Herman Henry (Dorchester) West end lane
Hernoux Charles 1 Alexandra rd.
Herrmann Adolphus 9 Albion rd.
Hertz Heinrich 12 Thurlow rd.
Hertz Leon (Hollywood) 79 Priory rd.
Herzberg Bernard 1 Crossfield rd.
Hess Frederick 86 Alexandra rd.
Hessel Cornelius 38 Palmerston rd.
Hester William 11 Dunboyne st.
Hetherington Ivystan 4 Steele's studios Haverstock hill
Hetley James H. (Peterborough lodge) 55 Finchley new rd.
Hett Henry (Oakhurst) Branch hill
Heuland Mrs. 71 Boundary rd.
Hewat John Grayhurst 46 South hill park
Hewat Mrs. 33 Fleet rd.
Hewitt Mrs. (Grafton lodge) Quex rd.
Hewitt William 26 Adamson rd.
Hewlett George (Buckland lodge) 1 Buckland villas
Hewlett Mrs. (Batsford ho.) Cricklewood
Hewlings Stuart 63 Belsize rd.
Hewson Mrs. (Esk haven) East Heath rd.
Heydemann Edw. 39 St. John's wood pk.
Heydemann Paul 44 Fellows rd.
Heylin Joseph 81 Iverson rd.
Hibberd H. C. 8 Fellows rd.
Hibbert Arthur 10 Hampstead hill gdns.
Hibbert Horace 3 Lamballe rd.

Hibbert Mrs. 18 Lancaster rd.
Hickman Miss 26 The Village
Hicks E. 194 Messina avenue
Hicks William 7 Narcissus rd.
Hickson Mrs. 6 Chalcot gardens
Higginbotham Misses (The Glade) Branch hill
Higgins Alfred 2 Lithos rd.
Higgins Samuel Edwd. 64 South hill pk.
Hilbery Francis Wm. 116 South hill park
Hilder John 115 King Henry's rd.
Hilderley George 31 Flask walk
Hilhouse Charles 1 Belsize park gardens
Hill Arthur 117 Abbey rd.
Hill Benjamin 2 Murray pl.
Hill Edward 11 Alfred ter.
Hill Frederic (Inverleith house) 27 Thurlow rd.
Hill Frederick A., M.D. 76 Abbey rd.
Hill Henry 10 Elsworthy ter.
Hill Henry 13 Springfield rd.
Hill H. R. 8 Park rd.
Hill James 13 Kingsgate rd.
Hill James R. 4 Mansfield pl.
Hill James S. 1 Park road studios
Hill John 58 Belsize park
Hill Lewin 22 Parliament hill rd.
Hill Mrs. 200 Adelaide rd.
Hill Mrs. 13 Belsize park gardens
Hill Mrs. 114 Haverstock hill
Hill Mrs. Charles (Ivy bank) Haverstock hill and Belsize lane
Hill Mrs. John Henry (North end lodge) North end
Hill Richard 1 St. John's wood park
Hill Thomas 47 Belsize avenue
Hillhouse Mrs. 37 Belsize sq.
Hillier William 4 Belgrave gardens
Hillman Samuel 32 Ainger rd.
Hills Charles 23 Gascony avenue
Hills Harold 20 Kingsgate rd.
Hills Walter 39 Ainger rd.
Hillyard Rev. George 5 Christchurch rd.
Hilton Robert (Clyde house) Broadhurst gardens
Hilton Miss 57 Belsize avenue
Hine R. G., Arkwright rd.
Hinton Henry 3 Garfield ter.
Hippesley George Wyld 120 King Henry's rd.
Hipwood Mrs. 18 Christchurch rd.
Hirsch Adolph 37 Fellows rd.
Hirsch Bernhard Charles 72 Fellows rd.
Hirschel Arthur F. 20 Belsize avenue
Hirschhorn L. (Holmwood) Lambolle rd.
Hitchcock Charles 96 Adelaide rd.
Hitchcock William 39 Belsize park gdns.

Hitchcox Matthew Hy. 33 Adelaide rd.
Hitchin Mrs. 23 Kilburn priory
Hoare Fras. (The Hill) Hampstead heath
Hoare Jsph. (Child's hill ho.) West heath
Hoare Miss (The Avenue) North end
Hobbs Arthur 8 Prospect rd.
Hobbs John 5 Kilburn vale
Hobbs Joseph (The Farm) Platt's lane
Hobbs William Henry 21 John st.
Hobrow F. W. Chant 2 The Gables Vale of Health
Hobson Ernest E. 27 Ainger rd.
Hobson Thomas Frederick (Runnymede) West end lane
Hockley Anthony 9 Goldhurst rd.
Hodder George 1 Murray pl.
Hodge James 140 Adelaide rd.
Hodge Onslow 38 Fleet rd.
Hodge Thomas R. 11 Elm grove
Hodge William F. 79 Fellows rd
Hodges H. V. 146 Belsize rd.
Hodgkins Thomas 3 South end green
Hodgkinson William 14 Birchington rd.
Hodgskin Mrs. 19 Daleham gardens
Hodgson Arthur (Greville lodge) 33 Greville rd.
Hodgson Charles (Glyndhurst) Shoot-up hill
Hodgson James 116 Abbey rd. Kilburn
Hodgson Mrs. 26 Bolton rd.
Hodgson Mrs. (The Elms) Spaniards rd.
Hoets John William Van Rees 150 Adelaide rd.
Hogg Robert Thomas 5 Fairfax rd.
Holborn Robert 178 Adelaide rd.
Holcombe Joseph 69 Haverstock hill
Holcombe W. (Canfield house) 2 Canfield gardens
Holden A. E. 13 Elm grove
Holden A. W. 19 Goldhurst rd.
Holder John 42 Flask walk
Holdman Mrs. 6 The Village
Holdsworth J. 110 Belsize rd.
Holford George 3 Holford rd.
Holford Miss 1 Lyndhurst rd.
Holford Mrs. J. H. 3 Gayton cres.
Holiday Henry (Oak tree house) Branch hill park
Holl Frank, R.A. (The Three Gables) 6 Fitzjohns' avenue
Holland Edward 156 Belsize rd.
Holland Joseph Robberds (Wellesley ho.) 4 Reddington rd.
Holland P. H. 10 Heath rise
Holland Sidney 5 Adelaide rd.
Holland Thomas 2 Heath cottages
Hollebone Henry 82 Boundary rd.

Hollick Frank 47 Belsize rd.
Hollingshead John (Spring bank) 31 Steele's rd.
Hollingworth Henry Geo. 5 Springfield rd.
Hollobon Mrs. (Belgrave house) 14 Downshire hill
Holman Thomas 14 Palmerston rd.
Holman Wm. Hy., M.B. 68 Adelaide rd.
Holme Charles (Hill side) Hampstead hill gardens
Holmes Arthur John 25 Kingsgate rd.
Holmes Frederic Morell 59 South hill park
Holmes Henry 51 Gayton rd.
Holmes Miss 21 Haverstock hill
Holmes Misses (Bellefield house) 39 Haverstock hill
Holmes William 156 Alexandra rd.
Holt Frederick 125 Adelaide rd.
Holt William 45 Iverson rd.
Holwell Edward Frederick, North end
Home George 12 Goldhurst rd.
Homfray Miss (Byron cottage) John st.
Hood Albert 1b Kilburn vale
Hood C. C. (Rosslyn hill house) Rosslyn hill
Hook Saml. (The Retreat) Wildwood gro.
Hook William 45 and 47 Fleet rd.
Hooke H. F, 19 Upper Park rd.
Hooper Charles 95 Iverson rd.
Hooper George (Hartlands) Frognal
Hooper Miss 1 Eton villas
Hooper Wm. E. Parry 29 St. George's rd.
Hooton Richard 7 Gardnor rd.
Hope James 160 Iverson rd.
Hopkins Arthur 80 Finchley rd.
Hopkins David 7 Midland cottages
Hopkins Manley 9 Oak hill park
Hopkins William Henry (St. Hubert's lodge) 41 Priory rd.
Hopkinson James (Ardlethen) West Heath rd.
Hopkinson Mrs. 11 Belsize cres.
Hopton Captain Charles (Rosland) Arkwright rd.
Horn Benjamin 2 Elm ter.
Hornblower Jethro 21 Fellows rd.
Horne James 63 Flask walk
Hornibrook William (Mount Vernon house) Mount Vernon
Hornidge Miss 3b Mortimer rd.
Hornor Allan M. 40 Fitzjohns' avenue
Horrocks F. J. 17 Goldhurst rd.
Horsley Miss 37 Park rd.
Hort Mrs. Mary 38 Adelaide rd.
Hortin John Henry 19 Alexandra rd.
Hortin Richard 321 High rd.
Hose Rev. J. C. 53 Park rd.

Hosking Robert 22 Granville ter.
Hoskyn Mrs. (Withnoe cottage) 1 Birchington rd.
Hough Edwin 22 South hill park gdns.
Hough William B. 1 Holly mount
Houghton George (Selborne house) 102 Haverstock hill
Houghton John Moore 12 Priory rd.
House S. 12 Kilburn vale
Household Benjamin 1 Well rd.
Housley Samuel John (Crowhurst) West end lane
Houston Miss (Acacia villa) 64 Maygrove road
Howard Charles (Alton house) 3 Netherhall ter.
Howard Cosmo Gordon (The Grove) 1 Merton grove
Howard Daniel 60 Belsize park
Howard Geo. (Oaklands) Cricklewood
Howard John C. 15 Provost rd.
Howard John Henry 10 Gardnor rd.
Howard Mrs. 6 Willoughby rd.
Howard William 38 Belsize park gardens
Howard William 37 Iverson rd.
Howard William (Bloomfield cottage) 20 The Village
Howard William Frederick (Arundel house) 107 Priory rd.
Howden D. (Manor house) St. John's wood park
Howden Henry James 176 Belsize rd.
Howe Jas. (Providence cot.) Kilburn vale
Howell Allen 2 Ambridge cottages
Howell Edward James 145 Iverson rd.
Howell Horace Sydney, M.D., F.R.C.S. 18 Boundary rd.
Howell Joshua 1 Hemstall rd.
Howell William I. 3 Mansfield villas
Howie Mrs. 168 Maygrove rd.
Howitt John 51 Lowfield rd.
Howlett Samuel P. 76 Belsize rd.
Howse Gerald 19 Church row
Hoyte William S. 68 Boundary rd.
Hudson Alfred 35 Belsize rd.
Hudson A. R. 55 Priory rd.
Hudson Edwin 1 Lancaster rd.
Hudson James (Holly Bush house) Holly mount
Hudson J. W. 76 Fellows rd.
Hudson Miss (Bentham ho.) The Mount
Hudson Miss M. A. 21 Belsize rd.
Hudson Misses 39 & 40 Gayton rd.
Hudson Morris 90 South hill park
Hudson Mrs. (Delmar ho.) 39 Gayton rd.
Hudson Thos. (Wentworth ho.) John st.
Hügel Baron Fredrich von 4 Holford rd.

Huggins John (Rosslyn lodge) Lyndhurst rd.
Huggins John Frederick 32 Belsize pk.
Huggins Mrs. 7 Belsize sq.
Hughes Henry Clifford (Heath side) East Heath rd.
Hughes James 3 Hillfield rd.
Hughes Jsph. 7 Wildwood gro. North end
Hughes J. V. 19 Lithos rd.
Hughes Reginald 74 Boundary rd.
Hughes T. J. 2 Elm row
Hughes William 89 Alexandra rd.
Hughes William 30 Elsworthy rd.
Hulbert Mrs. (Quex lodge) West end lane
Humble Mrs. 124 King Henry's rd.
Humble Wm. Roger 4 South end green
Hume Major Alexander 42 Boundary rd.
Hume Rev. Charles 14 Ainger rd.
Hume John 39 Fellows rd.
Humphrey Henry J. 45 Springfield rd.
Humphrey Mrs. 24 Downshire hill
Humphreys Frederick 1 Heath cottages
Humphreys Hy. (1 Stowe ho.) North end
Humphreys James 5 Providence pl.
Humphreys Miss Jennett 5 Oak grove
Humphreys Mrs. 3 Netherwood st.
Humphreys Richard 1 Belsize avenue
Humphreys William 5 Yew grove
Humphreyson John 5 Haverstock hill
Humphris William H. 21 Sherriff rd.
Humphry Jsph. Alfrd. 65 Springfield rd.
Hunt Rev. H. G. 12 Oppidans rd.
Hunt — 32 Fleet rd.
Hunt — 18 Gascony avenue
Hunt G. W. 15 St. George's rd.
Hunt Mrs. 120 Maygrove rd.
Hunt William 2 Golden sq.
Hunter Andrew 13 Sherriff rd.
Hunter H. J. 22 Kilburn priory
Hunter J. H. 11 Pond st.
Hunter Leslie 16 Alexandra rd.
Hunter Mrs. 73 Belsize park gardens
Hunter Mrs. Jane 91 Belsize rd.
Hunter Peter 113 Belsize rd.
Hunter Walter Oswald 4 Prospect villas
Hunting Richard (Holmdale) 56 Priory rd.
Huntington Francis Henry (Abbeville house) 10 Arkwright rd.
Hurditch Chas. Russell 164 Alexandra rd.
Hurlock Edward 5 Benham's pl.
Hurlstone Mrs. Ann H. 2 Adelaide rd.
Hurst Alfred 7 Willow cottages
Hurst J. B. 5 Station villas
Hurst Mrs. 3 Gardnor rd.
Hurst William 2 Heath villas
Husband Mrs. T. (Manor ho.) Frognal
Hutchings William 23 Prospect rd.

Hutchins Henry 1 Heath villas
Hutchinson R. M. 22 Lansdowne ter.
Hutchinson Wm. Hunter 43 Fordwych rd.
Hutton J. Edward 7 Heathfield gardens
Hyams David 99 King Henry's rd.
Hyams Henry Hart 36 Birchington rd.
Hyde Arthur 48 Adelaide rd.
Hymans Henry (Normanhurst) 88 Priory rd.
Hyndman Mrs. 5 Denning rd.
Hyndman Thomas 20 Iverson rd.
Hyndman Thomas 12 Springfield rd.
Hyslop W. J. 7 Gayton cres.

I'Anson Charles 19 Adelaide rd.
I'Anson Charles 4 The Mall
Ilbery Hubert 12 Mansfield pl.
Imbert Eugene Louis 152 Belsize rd.
Imperiali W. G. 174 Alexandra rd.
Ince Edward B. 42 Albion rd.
Ince Francis (St. Fagan's) 17 Fitzjohns' avenue
Inglis Thomas Stewart 53 Ainger rd.
Ingpen Edward T. 20 Steele's rd.
Inman H. B. (Heathfield) 6 Sherriff rd.
Inman John (Daisy bank) Willow rd.
Inman Mrs. (Frognal rise) Frognal
Inman R. J. (The Knoll) Holford rd.
Innes F. W., M.D., C.B. 2 Lyndhurst rd.
Innes Miss 2 Gayton rd.
Innes Robert 8 Provost rd.
Irvine R. J. 111 Priory rd.
Isaac Arscott John 42 Kingsgate rd.
Isaac Arthur B. (Osborne ho.) 8 Garlinge rd
Isaac R. C. 90 Belsize rd.
Isaacs Henry A. 27 Belsize park
Isaacs Joseph 21 Belsize park
Isaacson Judah 55 King Henry's rd.
Isaacson Mrs. 2 Thurlow rd.
Isaacson Wotton Ward 5 Branch hill side Branch hill
Isitt Frederick Thomas 80 Adelaide rd.
Ives James T. B. 1 Elm villas

Jack Mrs. 12 Wildwood grove
Jackman James J. 1 Wildwood grove
Jackson Alexander (Combehurst) Nutley gardens
Jackson Charles W. 1 Providence pl.
Jackson Edward E. (Southcotte) Lancaster rd.
Jackson Frederick (Heathside cottage) North end
Jackson J. 39 Heath st.
Jackson John 3 Belsize park
Jackson Miss 88 Iverson rd.
Jackson Mrs. E. J. 65 Adelaide rd.

Jackson Mrs. Geo. (Langdale vil.) 5 Park rd
Jackson Mrs. Maria 61 Upper Park rd.
Jackson Samuel (Bryan ho.) The Mount
Jacob Misses 92 Belsize park gardens
Jacob Mrs. 70 Abbey rd.
Jacob Mrs. 74 South hill park
Jacob Samuel 13 Goldhurst rd.
Jacob Thomas 11 Linstead st.
Jacobs Angelo 75 Alexandra rd.
Jacobs Harry 18 Greville rd.
Jacobs Henry 4 Belmont
Jacobs Mrs. 4 Messina avenue
Jaggars Henry Edwin 38 Elsworthy rd.
James Alfred 19 Messina avenue
James Christopher 133 Fellows rd.
James David 9 Hermitage villas
James Edwin (Grosvenor ho.) Acol rd.
James Miss 7 Buckland villas
James Miss 33 Gayton rd.
James Miss 21 St. George's rd.
James Mrs. 19 Belsize park gardens
James Mrs. 11 Boundary rd.
James Mrs. and Miss (Upper terrace lodge) Upper ter.
James R. H. 13 Willoughby rd.
James Samuel (Trevlyn) Mill lane
James Thomas 7 Elm ter.
James William 87 Finchley rd.
James William Henry 9 Medley rd.
James W. M. 8 Lyndhurst rd.
Jamieson Hy. 41 Hampstead hill gdns.
Jamieson Miss J. S. 151 Fellows rd.
Jamison Mrs. E. 179 Loveridge rd.
Janes Joseph 6 Kingsford st.
Jansson E. 63 King Henry's rd.
Jarvis Miss A. M. 58 Alexandra rd.
Jarvis Mrs. 13 Christchurch rd.
Jarvis Mrs. 85 Iverson rd.
Jarvis Mrs. 4 Lancaster rd.
Jarvis Thomas 114 Abbey rd. Kilburn
Jay Mrs. C. 7 Parliament hill rd.
Jeal John 8 Palmerston rd.
Jealous George Samuel 1 Villas on the Heath, Vale of Health
Jeanes John 15 Buckland cres.
Jeffery John 41 Kingsgate rd.
Jeffery John 15 Lower Lawn rd.
Jeffs Harry 31 Priory rd.
Jeffs Mrs. 122 Belsize rd.
Jelley Miss Marion (Summerfield) Carlingford rd.
Jellico John (Cromer lo.) 6 Oppidans rd.
Jelliman Miss 1 Church row
Jelpke John L. 197 Loveridge rd.
Jenkins Charles 5 & 6 Grafton ter.
Jenkins Charles 8 Lowfield rd.
Jenkins George Thomas 63 Avenue rd.

Jenkinson Daniel 37 Flask walk
Jennings Rev. Nathaniel, M.A. 8 Broadhurst gardens
Jennings Charles Henry 48 Flask walk
Jennings F. T., Hampstead green
Jennings George, South end green
Jennings Mrs. 5 Abbott's rd.
Jennings Mrs. 9 Oppidans rd.
Jennings W. 10 Dynham rd.
Jenour Harry James 23 Belsize sq.
Jeremy Walter David 5 Thurlow rd.
Jervis Mrs. 49 Ainger rd.
Jervis Thomas 1 Kemplay rd.
Jetley Victor 17 Boundary rd.
Jevons Mrs. W. Stanley 2 The Chestnuts
Joachim E. B. 84 King Henry's rd.
Jobson William W. 64 Finchley rd.
John Hillary (Gloucester cottage) 1 Boundary rd.
Johns Chas. Frederick 212 Adelaide rd.
Johnson Rev. E., M.A. 28 Ainger rd.
Johnson A. 24 Prospect rd.
Johnson Alfred (Mayfield) Hillfield rd.
Johnson Charles Edward (Morven house) Steele's rd.
Johnson David (Cremona) 52 Fitzjohns' av
Johnson H. N. 176 Loveridge rd.
Johnson J., M.D. 24 St. John's wood park
Johnson James 8 Elm grove
Johnson John 4 Lower Heath cottages
Johnson Miss 16 Steele's rd.
Johnson Miss Kate, R.A.M. 11 Spencer ter.
Johnson Mrs. 24 Avenue rd.
Johnson Mrs. 39 Belsize rd.
Johnson Mrs. 1 Chalcot gardens
Johnson Mrs. 23 Hilgrove rd.
Johnson Mrs. E. R. 190 Adelaide rd.
Johnson Mrs. H. H. 25 Adamson rd.
Johnson Percy 23 Rudall cres.
Johnson Stephen 6 Prince Arthur mews
Johnson Thos. Matthew 13 South hill pk.
Johnston Rev. Robert 4 Eton rd.
Johnston Alexander 1 College villas rd.
Johnston Alexander 84 South hill park
Johnston Chas. (West view) Greenhill rd.
Johnston Miss (Manor house) North end
Johnston Mrs. (Verona) Acol rd.
Johnston Mrs. 74 Park rd.
Johnstone Alexr. 36 King Henry's rd.
Johnstone George 3 Wildwood grove
Johnstone John (Upper terrace house) Upper ter.
Johnstone John (Gower house) Willoughby rd.
Johnstone Mrs. 25 Belsize sq.
Johnstone Mrs. Napier (Highfield) 1 Cedar ter.

Jolliffe E. Y. 54 King Henry's rd.
Jolly Charles 13a Gardnor rd.
Jones Alfred 203 Loveridge rd.
Jones Arthur 2 Lower Cross rd.
Jones Edward 126 Maygrove rd.
Jones Edward Chester 13 Belsize rd.
Jones Frederick 21 Prospect rd.
Jones George 28 Flask walk
Jones George (The Cottage) Murray ter.
Jones G. F. 12 Elsworthy rd.
Jones James 22 Prospect rd.
Jones John Prichard (Lorne house) 1 Westcroft rd.
Jones Mrs. 20 Christchurch rd.
Jones Mrs. (Northcote house) Heath st.
Jones Mrs. 9 Netherwood st.
Jones Mrs. C. 142 Iverson rd.
Jones Philip 35 South hill park
Jones Richard 1 Prospect villas
Jones Samuel 35 Fleet rd.
Jones W. 53 Upper Park rd.
Jones William 119 Broadhurst gardens
Jordan William 11 Lyndhurst rd.
Joseph David 41 South hill park
Joshua Philip 45 Belsize avenue
Joslin Arthur 8a Dunboyne st.
Jourdain Neville 51 Fellows rd.
Jourdan F. (Avenue house) Belsize park gardens
Joyce Henry 45 Alexandra rd.
Joyce Mrs. Jane 27 Park rd.
Joynes Richard 7 Providence pl.
Judd Bertram George S. 52 Fellows rd.
Judge John 9 Fortune green
Judson Benjamin 15 Messina avenue
Juffs James 6 Holly mount
Jukes Miles P. 38 Belsize park
Julian Richard 38 Iverson rd.

Kahn Benedict 43 Belsize park
Kalterthaler Julius 170 Belsize rd.
Karberg Peter 42 Belsize park gardens
Karney Rev. Gilbert, M.A. 12 Belsize avn.
Katterns Douglas 138 Maygrove rd.
Kay Allan William 25 Downshire hill
Kay Thomas (Newlands) 2 Elsworthy rd.
Kearney J. Esmonde 9 Ainger rd.
Keats Frederick 30 Loveridge rd.
Kebbell Theodore 8 Yorkshire Grey yard
Keele Charles 4 Hemstall rd.
Keele Chas. F. (Clumber ho.) Shoot-up hl.
Keele C. F. 130 High rd.
Keele Edward Rushworth 30 Albion rd.
Keep Charles 10 Alfred ter. Back lane
Keighley Edwin Holmes (Hope villa) Cricklewood
Keirf L. 24 Winchester rd.

Keith James 2 Lowfield rd.
Keith Miss (Percy house) Holly mount
Kellond Charles A. 1 Goldhurst ter.
Kellow Frank 77 Belsize rd.
Kellow Frederick C. 51 Alexandra rd.
Kellow W. (Woodbrook house) Cricklewood
Kelly Duncan George 50 Messina avenue
Kelly Edward 26 Avenue rd.
Kelly Henry 35 Belsize sq.
Kelly John 4 Haverstock ter.
Kelly Joseph P. 7 Yew grove
Kelly Miss 68 Maygrove rd.
Kelly Miss 42 Springfield rd.
Kelly Mrs. 14 Kingsgate rd.
Kemmler Charles 94 Iverson rd.
Kemp Geo. (Sudley house) Cricklewood
Kenchatt Philip 7 Golder's hill ter. North end
Kenchington Mrs. 4 Ariel st.
Kennedy Rev. John, D.D. (Cluny cottage) 19 Rudall cres.
Kennedy John 8 Eton rd.
Kennedy John 12 Pond st.
Kennedy Alexander B. W. (Lawn house) Hampstead sq.
Kennedy C. N. 192 Alexandra rd.
Kennedy Edward 14 Avenue villas
Kent Charles Alston 62 Loudoun rd.
Kent Walter George 32 Stanley gardens
Kent William 157 Haverstock hill
Kerr George 6 Kilburn priory
Kerr-Smith Rev. W. (The Parsonage) Messina avenue
Kerslake John 41 Haverstock hill
Kerslake John (Downes Bury) Steele's rd.
Kersley Mrs. 9 Palmerston rd.
Kerswell Fredk. Bartlett, New West end
Kett Rev. C. W., M.A. 2 Haverstock ter.
Keys Matthias 3 New end
Keysell Miss 151 Abbey rd. Kilburn
Keyworth George 60 Netherwood st.
Kilburn Chas (Alvaston) 5 Arkwright rd.
Kilburn George Goodwin (Hawkhurst house) Steele's rd.
Kilburn Henry Ward 3 Cannon pl.
Killingback Charles William 13 Maygrove rd.
Kilpatrick W. (Closeburn) 28 Daleham gardens
Kimber Thomas 152 Alexandra rd.
Kinder Charles 11 Carlingford rd.
King Rev. Richard, M.A. 65 Goldhurst rd.
King David 29 Alexandra rd.
King H. 169 Belsize rd.
King H. (Leverton house) 3 Hampstead green

King Haynes (The Ingle) Broadhurst gardens
King Jas. (Ellersleigh house) Worsley rd.
King Job P. 8 Willow cottages
King John Thornton (Clovelly) West end lane
King John Webb (Chesils) Christchurch road
King Joseph (Welford house) 13 Arkwright rd.
King J. A. 4 Swiss ter.
King Miss 69 Springfield rd.
King Mrs. (Nocton house) 182 Iverson rd
King Mrs. A. 13 Eton rd.
King William 11 Belsize avenue
King W. H. 37 Fordwych rd.
Kingdon Miss 1 Dynham rd.
Kingston William Biddy 53 Finchley new rd.
Kinnaird Hon. Miss O. 50 Avenue rd.
Kinsey Mrs. 114 Alexandra rd.
Kirby Henry George 34 Prospect rd.
Kirkman Rev. Joshua, M.A. 4 Thurlow rd.
Kirkman Misses 116 Alexandra rd.
Kirkpatrick Mrs. 33 Fairfax rd.
Kirkwood Mrs. Eliza 16 Priory rd.
Kirman F. 10 Ash grove
Kissack Thomas 86 Iverson rd.
Kitchen James (Cromer lodge) West end lane
Kitchener Miss 28 Boundary rd.
Kitchin Rev. James George, M.A. 4 Heathfield gardens
Klaftenberger Alexander Augustus 13 Belsize park
Klaftenberger William Heinrich Hubert 4 Holtham rd.
Klein William 24 Belsize park
Klug Oscar 3 Belsize rd.
Klugh Arthur G. 61 Alexandra rd.
Kneller G. H. 11 Greville rd.
Kneustub F. J. 112 King Henry's rd.
Knight Alf. Augustus 193 Loveridge rd.
Knight Alfred H. 17 Claremont rd.
Knight Henry 26 Claremont rd.
Knight John 24 Goldhurst ter.
Knight Mrs. E. 7 Ariel st.
Knight Richard Alfred (Belmont house) Hillfield st.
Knights James 28 Kingsgate rd.
Knox G. Walter 132 Fellows rd.
Knox Miss 53 Belsize park gardens
Knox Mrs. 201 Adelaide rd.
Kottgen Gustav 1a Merton rd.
Kottgen Walther 65 Belsize park gardens
Krohm William 28 Belsize park gardens
Krohn Nicholas 13 Belsize sq.

Lacy Charles James 28 Belsize park
Laing Misses 170 Adelaide rd.
Laing Mrs. David 57 Haverstock hill
Lake Ernest E. 15 Lyndhurst rd.
Lake Frederick 8 Midland cottages
Lalor Miss 2 Gayton cres.
Lalor R. D., M.D. 69 Parliament hill rd.
Lamb Alfred 22 Belsize park
Lamb Jacob 30 Midland cottages
Lamb Robert 89 Belsize cres.
Lambden Edward 22a Haverstock hill
Lammas Randal 7 Devonshire pl.
Lammin Miss E. 17 Provost rd.
Lancaster John 1 Gascony avenue
Landau Max 4 Broadhurst gardens
Landauer D. 26 Lancaster rd.
Landeshut S. M. 12 Belsize park
Landsberg Edward (Stony cliff) Lambolle rd.
Lane Gilbert (Hollington) 45 Fordwych road
Lane James 46 Maygrove rd.
Lane John (Birchington cottage) 2 Birchington rd.
Lane Samuel A.(Vine ho.) Hampstead sq.
Lang Mrs. S. T. 4 Rosslyn ter.
Langley Miss 1 Belmont
Langmead Miss 3 Church row
Lanham Walter J. (Surrey villa) Messina avenue
Lankester Frederick William 15 Belsize park gardens
Lanza Madame Laura 18 Goldhurst rd.
Lardelli Thomas Francis 20 Denning rd.
Larkin Thomas Joseph 99 Iverson rd.
Larkworthy Falconer 35 Belsize avenue
Larner John 1 Ebenezer rd.
Laspee Arthur de 49 Flask walk
Latham Mrs. 47 Downshire st.
Latreille Ulysses 8 Kemplay rd.
Laubach Alfred & Walter 192 Belsize rd.
Laurence Alexander 17 Thurlow rd.
Lavender Mrs. (Heath view) Hampstead heath
Lavington Ferres W. (Belgrave cottage) Hampstead green
Law Mrs. 19 Oppidans rd.
Lawford John Lindsay 35 Denning rd.
Lawford Percy (Woodcote) Reddington road
Lawford Rowland 65 Fitzjohns' avenue
Lawless Albert Anthony 23 Haverstock hill
Lawrence A. M. 99 South hill park
Lawrence Basil Edwin (Arnecliffe) 13 Woodchurch rd.
Lawrence Geo.Washington 88 Belsize rd.

Lawrence John 14 Park rd.
Lawrence John 15 Sumatra rd.
Lawrence J. E. 36 Haverstock hill
Lawrence J. M. 37 Belsize avenue
Lawrence Mrs. 23 Devonshire pl.
Lawrence Mrs. E. 166 Haverstock hill
Lawry William 12 Buckland cres.
Laws James 11 Fellows rd.
Laws Mrs. J. 11 Fellows rd.
Lawson Archibald Scott 93 Abbey rd.
Lawson Mrs. Ellen 15 Alexandra rd.
Lawton Mrs. Sarah 124 Belsize rd.
Lay Edward 2 Golder's hill cottages
Layland H. 2 Belmont
Lazenby Rev. Albert 5 Hermitage villas
Lea G. H. 1 Claremont ter.
Lea G. Harris (Montagu grove) Frognal
Lea John 1 Claremont ter.
Leach Rev.Wm. JamesJohn 24Belsize sq.
Leach Miss 1 Gayton cres.
Leach N. (Florence cottage) Frognal
Leach William 6 Alfred ter.
Leakey James 9 Denington park
Leal Charles 87 South hill park
Learwood George 141Belsize rd. Kilburn
Leatham Charles 14 Daleham gardens
Le Brasseur Mrs. Helen F. 58 Upper Park rd.
Le Breton Mrs. 6 Worsley rd.
Lechmere Rev.W.L.(Orsett ho.) Quex rd.
Leckie Peter(Braemar) 8 Netherhall ter.
Le Cren Samuel 17 Stanley gardens
Lee Henry B. (Sunycote) Hampstead hill gardens
Ledsam Mrs. M. V. 12 Boundary rd.
Lee Joseph (Vale house) Vale of Health
Lee J. M. 17 Belsize park gardens
Lee S. (Bathford lodge) 1 Park rd.
Leefe Octavius 31 St. George's rd.
Leek Henry 2 The Cottages
Leese Mrs. 10 Parliament hill rd.
Lefort Miss(St. Leonard's villa) 28 West end lane
Leftwich Robert V. 8 Kingdon rd.
Legg Charles 4 Denning rd.
Legg Henry Simpson 80 Alexandra rd.
Lehmann A. 19 Yew grove
Leitch Mrs. 21 Kingsgate rd.
Leitch William 67 Netherwood st.
Le Jeune Henry 144 Adelaide rd.
Lemesurier A. 58 Loudoun rd.
Lennard F. Barrett (Lested lodge) 3 Well walk
LenthallHy.(Oakleigh)31West end lane
Lenton James 93 Belsize rd.
Leon Leonard (Hazel house) 15 Fairhazel gardens

Leonard John Wm.142 Abbey rd.Kilburn
Leonard Xavier 2 Loveridge rd.
Leonhardt William 36 Kingsgate rd.
Leonie Bernhardt 31 Fellows rd.
Le Pla Rev. Henry 12 Well walk
Le Riche Edward William (Ormesby house) 162 Haverstock hill
Lermit G. Henry 4 Lawn rd.
Lescher F. Harwood (Oak lodge) 149 Haverstock hill
Leslie Hy. John (Homelea)12 College ter.
Lesser Mrs. 31 Springfield rd.
Lett Arthur 6 Mortimer rd.
Leutner Albert 28 Fellows rd.
Leveroni James 1 St. George's rd.
Levi Gerald A. 57 Priory rd.
Levi Mrs. Joseph 20 Kilburn priory
Levis Julius 58 Belsize park gardens
Levy Charles (Frances vil.) Oppidans rd.
Levy David 14 Greville rd.
Levy Hy.(Heath Fern lo.) East Heath rd.
Levy Hy. (Holland ho.) 2 Lambolle rd.
Levy Lionel 72 Avenue rd.
Lewell William 20 Crossfield rd.
Lewenz Iwan 33 Belsize avenue
Lewes Mrs. 8 Downshire hill
Lewin Mrs. (Woodbine cot.) North end
Lewinton Hy.(Lundy ho.)Willoughby rd.
Lewis Edward 38 Messina avenue
Lewis I.(Hyme house)3 Fitzjohns' avenue
Lewis James 147 Adelaide rd.
Lewis Jno.(The Turrets)63 Fitzjohns' avn.
Lewis M. H. 141 Alexandra rd.
Lewis Mrs.(Oudenarde)Broadhurst gdns.
Lewis Robert (Heathcote) 56 Fitzjohns' avenue
Lewis T. H. 176 Iverson rd.
Lewis W. 29 Lowfield rd.
Leycester Mrs. 9 Thurlow rd.
Leyton William 13 Loveridge rd.
Liberty John Barnes 27 Albion rd.
Lidstone Thomas (Devonia) 2 Sherriff rd.
Liggins Henry Joseph 33 Belsize rd.
Light Charles 29 Belsize avenue
Light Mrs. F. 49 Downshire hill
Lilley Thomas A. 43 Flask walk
Limebeer John 11 Lancaster rd.
Lindoe Captain 20 Adelaide rd.
Lindsay Mrs. 10 Lansdowne ter.
Lindsay T. S. 4 Oak hill park
Lindsay William Henry 25 Greville rd.
Linsell Alfred William 146 Adelaide rd.
Linton Jas. D.(Ettrick house)Steele's rd.
Lipscombe W. 3 Provost rd.
List Arthur (Ferndale) 3 Hilltop rd.
List William (Eversfield) Shoot-up hill
Lister A. H. (Canterbury ho.) West end

Lister Henry 11 Eldon rd.
Lister Miss, Hampstead heath
Lister Mrs. Daniel 66 Finchley rd.
Little Matthew 18 Thurlow rd.
Little Robert (Biddestone) 5 Hilltop rd.
Littlefield Edward 3 Perrin's court
Llewellyn Mrs. 59 Belsize park gardens
Lloyd Edmund 5 Fellows rd.
Lloyd James 12 North end
Loader R. C. 18 Buckland cres.
Loch Mrs. Geo. 77 Belsize park gardens
Locket Misses 155 & 157 King Henry's rd.
Lockett Anthony Joseph F. (Ethandene) Acol rd.
Lockhart Miss 83 Belsize rd.
Lockhart Mrs. 22 Messina avenue
Lockwood Francis Day 31 Boundary rd.
Lockwood John Maitland 13 Carlingford rd.
Loewenthal Adolph Ferdinand 205 Adelaide rd.
Lomas Charles 14 Loveridge rd.
Lomax Major James 19 Lichfield rd.
Long Charles 178 Loveridge rd.
Long Edwin, R.A. (Kelston) 61 Fitzjohns' avenue
Long Edwin (Glencairn) West end lane
Long Miss Helen 79 South hill park
Longman Henry 30 Ainger rd.
Longman Miss 35 Belgrave rd.
Loop Harry 6 Park rd.
Lord John 54 Springfield rd.
Lotinga Mrs. Leah (Lotinga house) 66 Priory rd.
Lott Frederick Tully 119 Alexandra rd.
Louden Misses F. & J. (Vale cottage) Vale of Health
Louis S. 125 Fellows rd.
Loveland Mrs. 18 Belsize park
Lovell Miss (Fernlea) 10 Ellerdale rd.
Lovell Mrs. 4 Lichfield rd.
Lovell Mrs. 24 Messina avenue
Lovell Mrs. Peter 69 Flask walk
Lovell William H. 68 Park rd.
Lovely G. M. 2 Westcroft villas
Loveridge George A. 7 St. George's rd.
Lovitt James John 10 Well rd.
Low George 17 Upper Park rd.
Low Miss Marie A. 60 Park rd.
Low Mrs. 29 Oppidans rd.
Low Robert 76 Priory rd.
Low Thomas Henry (Wellmount) Christ Church rd.
Lowden Thomas C. 13 Parliament hill rd.
Lowe Charles H. 18 Fairfax rd.
Lowe Francis 2 Sumatra rd.
Lowe George 5 Grove ter.

Lowe George 36 Midland cottages
Lowe H. Reginald (Tay villa) Ravenshaw st.
Lowe Thomas 23 Flask walk
Lowe William Edward(Sunnyside)West end lane
Lowman Henry 44 Kingsgate rd.
Lowmass Wm. Henry 36 Maygrove rd.
Lowrie Mrs.W.(Maisonette)Gascony avn.
Lowther Mrs. 22 Adelaide rd.
Luard Miss 3 John st.
Lucas E. W. 8 Kilburn priory
Lucas Frederick 8 Parliament hill rd.
Lucas Misses 17 Adelaide rd.
Lucas Mrs. Emily 54 Alexandra rd.
Lucas Seymour (New place) 1 Woodchurch rd.
Lucas Stanley 112 Alexandra rd.
Luck Michael 8 Fairfax rd.
Luckhurst D. J. 1 Elm grove
Ludgate James 8 Ebenezer rd.
Lumley Henry Robert 81 Avenue rd.
Lund Wm. Thos. B. 172 Haverstock hill
Lunn Henry C. 67 Adelaide rd.
Lunnon William 4 Castle ter.
Lupton Thos. (Woodside) Arkwright rd.
Lush Montague, Fitzjohns' mansions
Luxmoore Coryndon H., F.S.A., M.R.I. 18 St. John's wood park
Luxton Mrs. 7 Devonshire villas
Lyell J. R. 73 South hill park
Lynch Wm. (Lynchfield) 22 Hillfield rd.
Lyndon Mrs. Elizabeth 186 Adelaide rd.
Lyon Benjamin Abbott(Uplands)Greenhill rd.
Lyon George 164 Haverstock hill

Maas E.(Kenmore ho.)Hampstead green
Maas H. 78 Fellows rd.
Maas Hugh Max. 38 Ainger rd.
Maas W. J. 45 Priory rd.
McBean Miss 26 Priory rd.
McClintock Edwin 13 Lichfield rd.
McCoy Frederick 22 Ainger rd.
McDonald John 2 & 3 Elm cottages
McDonald J. Allen 6 Holly pl.
McDowell Henry 157 Fellows rd.
McEntee W. C. 14 Crossfield rd.
McGennes Francis 13 Gardnor rd.
McGill Miss (Belair) 96 Priory rd.
McGregor Alexander 190 Sumatra rd.
McGregor Mrs. 2 Prospect pl.
McGregor William 7 Ebenezer rd.
McInnes Miss 2 Gayton st.
McKay Charles 2 White Bear lane
McKean W. Blair(Montanvert)Willow rd
McKee Samuel J. 22 Primrose hill rd.

McKewan Misses 11 Upper Park rd.
McKinlay Thos.M.18South hill park gdns
McLaren James 73 Avenue rd.
McLaughlin Henry 2 Child's hill cotts.
McLean George 2 Lutton ter.
McLean T. M. 61 Belsize park
McLeod Maj. Wm. Sim 28 Adamson rd.
McLeod Hugh Eneva(Morville) Acol rd.
McMillan John 161 Adelaide rd.
McNair Jas., Telegraph hill West heath
McOscar Mrs. John 12 Denning rd.
McQueen George 4 Willow cottages
McRae Jas.Gilbert(Braeside)43 Priory rd
McWilliam Robt., B.A. 55 South hill pk.
Macarthur Robert John (Glenlyon) Carlingford rd.
Macculloch Mrs. 3a Mortimer rd.
Macdona Henry 3 Yew grove
Macdonald Rev.W.A.,M.A.2Oak hill park
Macdonald Murdoch 5 Belsize park
Macdonald William 33 Belsize sq.
MacDonnell John 24 Stanley gardens
MacDonnell J. R. 19 Belsize sq.
Macgregor Alexander 13 Provost rd.
Machion Harry 19 Kingdon rd.
MacInnes Miss (Fern lodge)Hampstead heath
MacInnes Mrs. J. R., The Avenue
Macirone Geo. Augustus 126 Adelaide rd.
Mack Arthur J.(Fairmount) Hillfield rd.
Mackay James H. 36 Ainger rd.
Mackenzie Mrs. Sarah 32 Adelaide rd.
Mackenzie William Ord, M.D. 37 Belsize park gardens
Mackeson Charles 53 Fellows rd.
Mackie Edward 14 Alexandra rd.
Mackintosh Donald,M.D.10Lancaster rd.
Mackley Robert 3 Ash grove
Mackway Richard Wm. 60 Alexandra rd.
Maclean Charles 9 Elsworthy ter.
Maclean Mrs. 154 Iverson rd.
Macmin John 56 Adelaide rd.
Macpherson Rbt(Thorncliff)Cricklewood
MacVitie Miss 9 Linstead st.
Madden Edward 156 Iverson rd.
Maddox George (Milford ho.) John st.
Maddox Misses (The Cottage) John st.
Magee Mrs. 101 Priory rd.
Mager Thomas 74 Hillfield rd.
Magnus Mrs. 22 Springfield rd.
Magnus Samuel 72 Finchley rd.
Mahler Adolph (Berkelhurst) Acol rd.
Maidlow Miss 7 Lower Lawn rd.
Maidlow Miss Emma 17 Lower Lawn rd.
Maile George Charles 19 Provost rd.
Main Rev. Thomas John, M.A. 15 Elsworthy rd.

Maitland David 10 Springfield rd.
Maitland Frederick 18 Primrose hill rd.
Maitland Mrs.(Heathcote)Vale of Health
Makie Mrs. 7 Goldhurst rd.
Malcolm William (Birnam house) 15 Fitzjohns' avenue
Malden Mrs. 39 Belsize sq.
Malden Mrs. 6 Crossfield rd.
Malkin Miss, R.A.M. 138 Belsize rd.
Mallalue Albert Geo. 26 Primrose hill rd.
Mallard Alexander 18 Downshire hill
MalletRev.Henry F.,M.A.(Thanet house) 158 Haverstock hill
Mallett Thomas 15 Loveridge rd.
Manley George 47 Upper Park rd.
Manley Mark 14 Steele's rd.
Manley W. B. 57 Kingsgate rd.
Manlove Mrs. 10 Mortimer rd.
Manly Miss 38 Park rd.
Mann Frederick William 2 Spencer ter.
Mannering Edward Hill (Hill side) 11 Arkwright rd.
Mannering Walter 61 Fellows rd.
Manning Edward Thos. 14 Boundary rd.
Manning Thomas 8 Benham's pl.
Manning W. H. 24 Hillfield rd.
Mannooch Alfred 88 Fellows rd.
Mannooch Chas. Hy. 69 King Henry's rd.
Mansbridge Josiah 32 Birchington rd.
Mansergh James (Lune Lea) 51 Fitzjohns' avenue
Mantell Henry 32 Midland cottages
Maple J. (Bedford lodge) 151 Haverstock hill
Maples — 10 Avenue villas
Mapleson Col. Henry (Hawthorne lodge) 66 Finchley new rd.
Mapple Alfred 5 Prospect villas
March William 69 Adelaide rd.
Marchant Miss(Belmont)29 West end ln.
Marcus C. (Blenheim) Broadhurst gdns.
Marcus John 9 Lancaster rd.
Marcus Moses 37 Belsize park
Marcus Richard 27 Belsize sq.
Mark Frederick 7 Kingsgate rd.
Markham Alfred 2 Silver st.
Marks Alfred 155 Adelaide rd.
Marks Benjamin 19 Park rd.
Marks C. S. 18 Birchington rd.
Marks George Samuel 150 Alexandra rd.
Marks Henry (Mayevelda) 61 Priory rd.
Marlow Henry 29 Fairfax rd.
Marrian Henry 5 Maygrove rd.
Marrian Miss (Blakemore house) Shoot-up hill
Marriott Frederick 77 Fellows rd.
Marriott John 1 Lower Lawn rd.

Marsden Montague M. 43 Belsize avenue
Marsden Percy Montague 8 Belsize sq.
Marsden R. 11 Adamson rd.
Marsden R. J. 9 Lawn rd.
Marsden William 33 Prospect rd.
Marsh E. T., B.A. 12 Lichfield rd.
Marsh Wm. (Ravensthorpe) Cricklewood
Marshall Rev. James 138 Fellows rd.
Marshall Charles E. 2 Harley rd.
Marshall George (Waverley cottage) 71 Iverson rd.
Marshall Henry 35 King Henry's rd.
Marshall Jas. (Cannon hall) Cannon pl.
Marshall John Arthur 13 Prospect rd.
Marshall John T. (Hurst lodge) Hampstead heath
Marshall Julian 13 Belsize avenue
Marshall Mrs. 20 St. George's rd.
Marshall Wm. Henry 56 Boundary rd.
Marshall William Wier 41 Alexandra rd.
Marshall W. R. (Crescent house) 21 and 22 Gayton rd.
Marslen Mrs. A. (Sandringham villa) 30 West end lane
Martelli Mrs. 6 Prince Arthur rd.
Martin Rev. David (Coniston house) 84 Priory rd.
Martin A. 48a Finchley new rd.
Martin Edward 2 Little Church row
Martin Edward 37 Midland cottages
Martin George 17 Albion rd.
Martin Josiah 6 Golder's hill ter.
Martin Miss 148 Belsize rd.
Martin Miss (Holmdale) 1 Heath rise
Martin Mrs. 105 Haverstock hill
Martin Mrs. 31 Loudoun rd.
Martin Mrs. 28 New end
Martin William (Grove cottage) Christchurch passage
Martineau Basil 3 Eldon rd.
Martineau Russell 5 Eldon rd.
Marx Hermann 3 Buckland villas
Maslen Mrs. and Misses 14 Belsize park gardens
Mason Frederick 10 Yorkshire Grey yard
Mason George H.(St. Dunstan's) 9 Fitzjohns' avenue
Mason Henry 61 Belsize rd.
Mason Henry Watts 53 King Henry's rd.
Mason John 28 Midland cottages
Mason J. W. 20 Albion rd.
Mason Mrs. 52 King Henry's rd.
Mason Mrs. Sarah (Denmark house) 148 Alexandra rd.
Massingham William 52 Haverstock hill
Masters Mrs. Jane M. 40 Adelaide rd.
Mather Miss 7 Belsize rd.

Mather Mrs. 5 Lichfield rd.
Matheson Rev. John, M.A. 8 Thurlow rd.
Matheson Ewing 21 Church row
MathesonGreville 4Squire's mount cotts.
Matheson H. (Heathlands) Hampstead heath
Matheson Miss Isabella (Reay lodge) 7 Ellerdale rd.
Matheson Thomas 6 Heathfield gardens
Mathew Miss 144 King Henry's rd.
Mathews Frncs.Claughton8Boundary rd.
Mathews James 9 Yorkshire Grey yard
Mathieson Frederic C. (Beechworth) West Heath rd.
Mathieson Frewin 32 Parliament hill rd.
Matthew James E. 129 King Henry's rd.
Matthew John William 92 Finchley rd.
Matthew Mrs. 26 Elsworthy rd.
Matthews Augustus 8 Mansfield pl.
Matthews Henry Peter 18 Park rd.
Matthews John 3 Saunders cottages
Matthews John Henry 14 Lancaster rd.
Matthews Leonard (Rosedale) West end lane
Matthews Miss Jane 44 Springfield rd.
Matthews Philip 5 Oakland ter.
Matthews William 62 Goldhurst rd.
Mattock John 2 Midland cottages
Maund George 4 Prospect rd.
Maurice Charles Edmund (Sydney cottage) Rosslyn hill
Maurier Eugene du 13 St. George's rd.
Mawe Mrs. 2 Belsize park gardens
Maxted Chas. (Providence cot.) Well rd.
Maxton Mrs. M. 54 Fellows rd.
Maxwell Jas. Laidlaw, M.D. 26 Heath st.
May Frederick 15 Adelaide rd.
May P. (St. Margaret's) West Heath rd.
May William 32 Belgrave rd.
May William Charles 13 Rudall cres.
Mayall John 47 Adelaide rd.
Mayd Mrs. 15 Belsize cres.
Mayer J. 21 Lithos rd.
Mayer John 1 Albion ter.
Mayer John 26 Avenue villas
Maynard Miss (West lodge) Broadhurst gardens
Maynard Miss (Westfield) 2 & 3 Maresfield gardens
Mayne Robert Dawson 39 Belsize sq.
Mayo William S. 19 Prospect rd.
Mayor Miss 8 Gayton cres.
Mays J. A. 20 Daleham gardens
Meaden W. J. 19 Hilgrove rd.
Meadmore Robert 65 Alexandra rd.
Meads John 93 South hill park
Meakin Miss 6 Fairfax rd.

Mearns Misses 21 Christchurch rd.
Medhurst Mrs. 3 Lower Lawn rd.
Meeson Alfred 4 Harley rd.
Megevan Mrs. Selina 11 Prospect rd.
Meissner William Hny. 16 Lancaster rd.
Melbourn Herbert 66 Boundary rd.
Mellor Benjamin 62 Parliament hill rd.
Mellor Mrs. 195 Messina avenue
Menham John Joseph 78 Belsize rd.
Menzies Sutherland 38 Alexandra rd.
Meo Gaetano 6 Sunnyside villas
Meredith Herbert J. 143 Alexandra rd.
Merington Miss Emily 20 Kingdon rd.
Merrick William (Wycliffe) Hampstead hill gardens
Merriman T. Mark 96 Finchley rd.
Merry George (Oak lo.)176 Maygrove rd
Merton J. S. 10 Kilburn priory
Messam Thomas 5 Devonshire pl.
Messenger H. Williams 1 Downshire hill
Messenger Mrs. 47 Stanley gardens
Mestayer Mrs. 5 Kemplay rd.
Metcalfe C. E. 4 Well walk ter.
Metcalfe Mrs. 199 Adelaide rd.
Metcalfe Mrs. 43 Stanley gardens
Metzger Samuel 197 Adelaide rd.
MetzlerMrs.(Stanmore ho.)83Avenue rd.
Meugens Mrs. 17 Lichfield rd.
Meyer Barrington 51 South hill park
Meyer Hartwig (Silcote) 53 Fitzjohns' avenue
Meyer Mrs. S. (Carlton house) Quex rd.
Meyer William Francis (Holly cottage) Vale of Health
Meyers Michael 7 Greville rd.
Meyerstein Emil 25 Belsize rd
MeyrickJ.C.(Mountfield)Carlingford rd.
Michel L. E. 4 St. John's wood park
Michell Richd. C.(Oakfield) Cricklewood
Michelson Leopold 40 Stanley gardens
Middleton Francis 178 Belsize rd.
Middleton William John 86 Priory rd.
Midson Mrs. 31 Netherwood st.
Miéville Charles 17 Hilgrove rd.
Miéville Frederick 36 Albion rd.
Miggand Alexander 49 Lowfield rd.
Milde Frederick 20 Lansdowne ter.
Miles George R. 22 Park rd.
Miles J. 7 Abbey lane
Miles Mrs. (West end house) West end
Miles William 82 Belsize park gardens
Miley John (Kenmore) Maresfield gdns.
Miley Miles 21 Belsize avenue
Millar Rev. A. 30 Lichfield rd.
Millar H. E.(Heathdown) East Heath rd.
Millar Miss (South heath)East Heath rd.
Millard Mrs. (Penshurst) 10 Sherriff rd.

Millen George John 93 Iverson rd.
Miller Adam (Deanshurst)Arkwright rd.
Miller Andrew, M.D. (Blair - hyrne) 1 Hampstead hill gardens
Miller Arthur 2 Lansdowne ter.
Miller A. W. K. 36 Stanley gardens
Miller Charles J. 13 Sumatra rd.
Miller George 135 Iverson rd.
Miller Henry 57 South hill park
Miller Miss (Field End vil.) Worsley rd.
Miller Mrs. 1 Branch hill side
Miller Mrs.(St.Aidans)31Fitzjohns' avn.
Miller Mrs. 8 Oppidans rd.
Miller Mrs. Alice 43 Adelaide rd.
Millgate George 142 Maygrove rd.
Milligan Mrs. 48 King Henry's rd.
Millington Misses (St. Ambrose) Denington park
Millington R. 92 Adelaide rd.
Millington Thomas 26 Kingdon rd.
Millis Percy A. 98 Iverson rd.
Mills Eli (South end ho.) South end grn.
Mills Henry 46 Albion rd.
Mills John 6 Lichfield rd.
Mills Josiah 3 Ravenshaw st.
Mills Mrs. Sarah 9 College ter.
Milne Alexander, B.A. (Henley house) Mortimer rd.
Milne David 35 Elm grove
Milne John 93 King Henry's rd.
Milne J. V., B.A., F.R.G.S.(Henley house) Mortimer rd.
Milne John Vine 16 Holtham rd.
Milne Miss 5 South hill park
Milner Wm. (Greenside villa) 47 Park rd.
Milson Richard H., M.D. 88 Finchley rd.
Milton John 2 Fordwych rd.
Milton William 3 Saunders cottages
Minister Mrs. F. A. 4 Medley rd.
Mitchell Alexander D. (Tensleys) Hampstead green
Mitchell Geo. A. 7 South hill park gdns.
Mitchell Henry 7 Fortune green
Mitchell John G. 135 Belsize rd. Kilburn
Mitchell Matthew 3 Kilburn vale
Mitchell Miss (Ingledean) 2 Heath rise
Mitchell Robert 10 Goldhurst rd.
Mitchener Hy. (Montrose) South end rd.
Mitford Robert Hy. 153 Haverstock hill
Mitton Edgar W. 8 Eldon rd.
Mitton Welbury James (Thornthwaite) 46 Primrose hill rd.
Model Albert 11 Eton rd.
Mogford John(Cawthorne) Messina avn.
Mogford John, R.I. 17 Park rd.
Mohr Mrs.(Brightholme)28Goldhurst ter
Moir Mrs. Macrae 2 Willoughby rd.

Moir Robert Mortimer(Bank side)Christchurch rd.
Money Daniel G. 2 Benham's pl.
Monk Albert 6 Cedar villas
Monk Thomas 37 Belgrave rd.
Monk Thomas 6 Midland cottages
Monks Dr. F. Aubyn (Heath villa) Sherriff rd.
Monro Frederic 22 Thurlow rd.
Monro George 96 Haverstock hill
Monro Miss Charlotte C.2 Branch hill side
Monsell John Crawford 34 St. John's wood park
Montbard Georges 13 Chalcot gardens
Montefiore Alexander I. (Frankfort house) 1 Adamson rd.
Monti Francis 21 Birchington rd.
Moody John 6 Nassington rd.
Moody Joseph 19 Ainger rd.
Moon James 14 Buckland villas
Moon P. 8 Belgrave rd.
Moore Edward 39 Kingsgate rd.
Moore Hayman 7 Prospect rd.
Moore John Alldin 95 South hill park
Moore Mrs. 128 Abbey rd. Kilburn
Moore Mrs. 19 Gascony avenue
Moore Noah 4 Linstead st.
Moore Philip 123 Belsize rd.
Moore Rechab (Heath ho.) New end sq.
Moore Temple 6 Downshire hill
Moore Thomas 82 Alexandra rd.
Moore William 56 Springfield rd.
Moore William B. 62 Belsize park gdns.
Morant Mrs. 22 Well walk
Mordant Frederick 80 Maygrove rd.
Morel-Ladeuil L. 67 Alexandra rd.
Morell Dr. (Clevelands) 10 Fitzjohns' avenue
Moreton Thomas (Hillfield lodge) Hillfield rd.
Morgan Charles Henry 13c Garden rd.
Morgan Henry 1 Paxon's cottages
Morgan Mrs. 191 Adelaide rd.
Morgan Mrs. 140 Iverson rd.
Morgan Robert 11 Buckland cres.
Morgan Walter 2 The Mall
Morison Jas. Cotter (Clairvaux) 30 Fitzjohns' avenue
Morison Mrs. 34 Alexandra rd.
Morley Henry 8 Upper Park rd.
Morley Robert (Studio) Haverstock hill
Morley William 23 Avenue villas
Morris Frederick Chas. 24 Midland cots.
Morris Henry 6 Mount Vernon
Morris James, B.A. 19 St. George's rd.
Morris James A. 16 Adamson rd.
Morris Mrs. 61 Springfield rd.

Morris Mrs. Ann 1 Mansfield pl.
Morris William Bright 3 The Mall
Morse John (Somerville house) Finchley rd. Child's hill
Morse Thomas F. (Huntley villa) 33 Steele's rd.
Morson Thomas Pierre 35 Ainger rd.
MortenAlexander George 9 Holmdale rd.
Mortimer W. H. 47 Kingsgate rd.
Mortlock Ernest 33 Lowfield rd.
Mortlock Miss (South lodge) Squire's mount
Morton Miss 3 Hilgrove rd.
Morton Miss 12 Loveridge rd.
Morton Thomas, M.D. 15 Greville rd.
Morton Thomas Honor 3 Rosslyn ter.
Moseley Abraham 40 Boundary rd.
Moses Mrs. 16 Bolton rd.
Mosley Mrs. (Taunton lodge) Messina avenue
Moss C. W. 10 Kingsgate rd.
Moss Miles 43 Gascony avenue
Mossman David 8 Belsize rd.
Motherwell Captain Charles W. 21 Lancaster rd.
Mott Alfred 16 Fairfax rd.
Mott William 9 Fleet rd.
Mott William Ruffell 1 Richmond villas
Moule George 51 Fleet rd.
Moulin — 29 Broadhurst gardens
Mount George 5 Belsize park gardens
Mourant John 38 Bolton rd.
Mousley John Parkes 44 Adelaide rd.
Moutrie Felix 15 Springfield rd.
Moutrie Mrs. Frederick 135 Abbey rd. Kilburn
Moxey William Thomas 125 Iverson rd.
Moxon Henry 29 Gascony avenue
Moysey Mrs. 8 Ash grove
Muddyman William 2 Palmerston rd.
Mulford Mrs. 1 Holtham rd.
Mulholland William (Glenside) 26 Ellerdale rd.
Mullens Arnold 4 Midland cottages
Muller John(Manor ho.)9 Downshire hill
Mummery Rev. Isaac Vale 16 Christchurch rd.
Mummery Mrs. (Newton villa)74 Finchley new rd.
Muncey Luke 71 Avenue rd.
Munday Miss 3 Park rd.
Murch P. 9 Goldsmith pl.
Mure Arthur (Hill house) Greenhill rd.
Muriel Robert (Waratah ho.) 2 Acol rd.
Murray Andrew, M.D. 34 Gayton rd.
Murray Oswald 20 Parliament hill rd.
Murtagh Mrs. Emma 4 College cres.

Mustill J. 7 Ravenshaw st.
Muston Mrs. Fanny 7 Holtham rd.
Musty Jonah 5 Southwell ter.
Myers George H. 5 Hampstead green
Myers Mrs. 30 Palmerston rd.
MyersMrs.Elizabeth 27 King Henry'srd
Myson John 15 Gardnor rd.

Nailard Thomas 6 Maygrove rd.
Nallorie William 13 Ash grove
Nash C. 26 Greville rd.
Nash Fredk. (Beechcroft) East Heath rd
Nash Henry 7 Holly mount
Nash William 45 King Henry's rd.
Nash William, Rosslyn hill
Nash William 14 Winchester rd.
Nathan Charles 12 Kingsgate rd.
Nathan Lewis 39 Gascony avenue
Nauen Charles 21 Stanley gardens
NaylorThos. Cartwright 4 Southwell ter
Neal Joseph 2 Church lane
Neale Peter 24 Loveridge rd.
Neale Richard, M.D. 60 Boundary rd.
Neame Norman 151 Adelaide rd.
Neatby Dr. Thomas 29 Thurlow rd.
Neate George 19 Avenue villas
Neate John 53 Belsize park
Neck Charles (The Elms) Avenue rd.
Needham Francis 2 Netherwood st.
Neele George Potter (Sunny bank) 2 Elsworthy rd.
Negretti Henry Paul Joseph (Dovedale 6 New West end
Negretti Mrs., Shoot-up hill Cricklewoo
Negri Misses de (Oakleigh) 9 Wood church rd.
Neighbour Henry 96 Alexandra rd.
Neish Mrs. (Maurice villa) Worsley rd.
Neison F. G. P. 93 Adelaide rd.
Nelke Paul 2 Mortimer rd.
NelsonE.M.(Cleve house)West end lan
Nelson Miss, M.C.P. 3 Eton rd.
Nelson Mrs. 26 King Henry's rd.
Ness Alexander 9 College cres.
Neuman Jacob Elias 34 Albion rd.
Nevill Henry 12 Fairfax rd.
Nevill Miss 11 Ainger rd.
Nevinson Mrs. 13 Lyndhurst rd.
New George Beasley 105 Iverson rd.
New Miss 32 Belsize rd.
Newbery W. H. 159 Belsize rd. Kilburr
Newby Mrs. 87 Adelaide rd.
Newman J. 8 Goldsmith pl.
Newman John 2 Cedar villas
Newman Mrs. 4 Rosslyn cottages
Newport George 5 Spencer ter.
Newson George 26 Flask walk

ewth Rev. Prof. Samuel, M.A., D.D· (New College) Finchley new rd.
ewtonArthur(Belsize court)Belsize ln.
ewton H. Cecil 50 Belsize park
ewton Miss 16 Stanley gardens
ewton Mrs. Henry (Brendon house) Messina avenue
ewton William 63 Haverstock hill
ibblett Frederick(Longthorpe)Cricklewood
ichol Donald 14 Buckland cres.
icholas John 25 Priory rd.
icholl William 28 Belsize rd.
icholls Mrs. Sarah 114 Iverson rd.
ichols William 16 Lower Lawn rd.
icholson Daniel 76 Finchley rd.
icholson J. C. 15 Cricklewood ter.
icholson Mrs. 162 Adelaide rd.
ickolls George Albert 15 Priory rd.
iemann F. G. B. 124 Haverstock hill
ightingale John 49 Maygrove rd.
isbet James 5 Goldhurst rd.
ixon Thomas, Minerva pl.
obbs Charles William 4 Cedar villas
obes W. J. (Gloucester house) Messina avenue
oble William (Hill lodge) Oppidans rd.
ock G. T. 63 Springfield rd.
oel Miss 15 Thurlow rd.
olloth Mrs. H. C. 17 Belsize rd.
ore Mrs. 111 King Henry's rd.
orman John 12 Adelaide rd.
orman John Henry 4 Cannon pl.
orman Miss 120 Belsize rd
orris Col. Hy. Macfarlane 6 Oak hill pk.
orris Charles, Holly mount
orris E. 24 Flask walk
orris Miss 6 Oak hill park
orris Nehemiah 9 Wildwood grove North end
orth J. W. 4 Wychcombe studios
orton Edward 33 Loudoun rd.
orton Francis 67 Springfield rd.
orton Frederick 13 Hilgrove rd.
orton Miss Ann, Holly hill
otley Thomas George 205 Loveridge rd.
otman Captain Henry W. (Cholmley lodge) Fortune green
ott Alfred 54 Ainger rd.
owersJ.E.L.(NessBank)4Elsworthy rd.
ugent Charles Edmund (Ludlow cottage) Hampstead heath
ugent James Spencer 3 Fordwych rd.
utt Edward Henry 3 Lawn rd.
utt W. R. 14 Goldhurst rd.
utting H. W. W. 7 Kemplay rd.
yren Mrs. 9 Church row

Oaker Alfred William 2 Iverson rd.
Oakes Arthur, M.D. (Merimbula) 99 Priory rd.
Oakes Mrs. 6 Bolton rd.
Oakes Sydney 25 South hill park
Obermayer A. J. 8 Harley rd.
Obicini George Wm. 109 Adelaide rd.
Ochs Sigismund 82 Avenue rd.
O'Connor Francis 143 Iverson rd.
O'Connor Joseph 19 Kingsgate rd.
Odgers W. Blake (Savile house) 71 Fitzjohns' avenue
O'Donnell VeryRev.P.,D.D.(New Priory) Quex rd.
O'Donoghue Rev. E. G. 4 Willoughby rd.
Oesterlie Emil 50 Belsize park gardens
Oesterracher W. 88 King Henry's rd.
Oetzmann John 104 Haverstock hill
Offord Joseph 6 Boundary rd.
Ogbourne Frank 92 Belsize rd.
Ogbourne Mrs. 92 Belsize rd.
O'Keefe Mrs. 16 Adelaide rd.
Oldaker Miss 12 Ainger rd.
Oldershaw Augustus Piggott 80 Boundary rd.
Oldrey Edmund Page 192 Adelaide rd.
Oldrey Percy 70 Priory rd.
Oliver David 107 Alexandra rd.
Oliver David (Fernbank) Cricklewood
Oliver John 100 Belsize rd.
Oliver Mrs. 64 Belsize rd.
Oliver Mrs. (Leigh house) South end rd.
Oliver William 8 Cricklewood lane
Olliff William 1 Willoughby rd.
Olney Allen Mrs. 3 Belsize ter.
O'Neill William 2 Church rd.
Orchard F. 11 Mortimer rd.
Orchard John (Sandringham house) 139a Alexandra rd.
Orgill J. J. (Springmead) Windsor ter.
Orrin Herbert 15 Christchurch rd.
Orrinsmith Harvey(Sunny Bank)Christchurch rd.
Orton William 196 Haverstock hill
Osbaldeston Mrs. Martha 45 Denning rd.
Osborn Colonel 20 Winchester rd.
Osborn Charles 6 Kilburn vale
Osborn Charles (St. Helen's cottage) The Mount
Osborn George 24 Gayton rd.
Osborn George John 9 Holly mount
OsbornMrs.(Holly lo.)34 Haverstock hill
Osborne Captain 12 College cres.
Osborne Mrs. 4 Belsize park gardens
Osborne Mrs. 12 Grove ter.
Osborne Thomas 27 Parliament hill rd.
Osgood Charles 28 Palmerston rd.

Osler Timothy Smith (The Limes) 11 Mansfield villas
Osmaston F. P. 18 Church row
Osmond George (Berkeley cottage) 20 Downshire hill
Ovenden Mrs. 149 Belsize rd. Kilburn
Overend W. H. 2 Wychcombe studios
Owen Thomas 85 Netherwood st.
Owen Thomas 5 Westcroft villas
Owen William 9 Heath rise
Owen-Jones Mrs. (Northcote house) Hampstead heath
Owthwaite R. A.17 South hill park gdns.
Oxley Robert 1 Eton rd.

Pace Thomas (Teresa cott.) New end sq.
Packer Mrs. 1 Claremont villas
Page J. (The Cottage) Kemplay rd.
Page Joseph 1 Grove ter.
Page Robert 26 Downshire hill
Page William Augustus 3 Rockhall ter.
Paiba John P. 12 Belsize park gardens
Paiba Samuel 121 Belsize rd.
Paine Benjamin (Rose cottage) Vale of Health
Paine Henry 4 Holly mount
Paine James H. 43 Springfield rd.
Painter William 6 Ash grove
Palfreman F. H. 22 Buckland cres.
Palmer Lady 11 St. John's wood park
Palmer Alfred 131 King Henry's rd.
Palmer John, jun. (Belton grange) Holford rd.
Palmer John Ogilvie 129 Adelaide rd.
Palmer Miss 75 Avenue rd.
Palmer Miss (Somerset villa) 4 Birchington rd.
Palmer Saml.(Northcourt)College vils.rd
Palmer Thomas 16 Lowfield rd.
Palmer William(Alhambra villa)9 Boundary rd.
Palmer William 102 Iverson rd.
Palmer W. J. (Caerluel) Carlingford rd.
Pancutt William 18 New end
Pannot J. 5 St. John's wood park
Pardon Arthur (Moreton) 106 Priory rd.
Paris Thomas Ruffle 116 Haverstock hill
Parish John 6 Well walk ter.
Park D. F. 112 Fellows rd.
Parker Rev. Dr. Joseph, D.D.(l'ynehome) 21 Daleham gardens
Parker Frank Rowley 69 Fellows rd.
Parker George 7 Midland cottages
Parker Henry Watson 2 Hampstead hill gardens
Parker Herbert S. (Netherhall lodge) 2 Netherhall ter.

Parker Job 1 Vale cottages
Parker Mrs. 3 Kingdon rd.
Parker Mrs. G. R. (Netherhall lodge 2 Netherhall ter.
Parker Reginald Amphlett 43 Haver stock hill
Parker Tom 6 Edward ter., Providenc pl. Kilburn
Parkins William 43 Boundary rd.
Parkinson Herbert Wm. 11 Rudall cres
Parkinson Joseph 49 South hill park
Parks Samuel 90 Maygrove rd.
Parkyn William B. 113 Priory rd.
Parnell William (Spencer villa) 12 Haverstock hill
Parry Miss 51 Boundary rd.
Parry Mrs. D. 57 Belsize rd.
Parry William 37 Palmerston rd.
Parsons Mrs.James 107 King Henry's rd
Parvin R. J. 25 Hillfield rd.
Pash Mrs. 12 Elm grove
Pask Arthur Thomas 39 Maygrove rd.
Pasmore John Henry 31 Upper Park rd
Passmore Robert 40 Lowfield rd.
Paterson Edwd.Alexander 55 Fellows rd
Paterson Mrs. A. H. 18 Gayton rd.
Paterson Mrs. W. R. (Clive villa) 2 Maygrove rd.
Patey Alfred George 5 Sherriff rd.
Patrick Arthur 3 Midland cottages
Patten R. J. 122 Alexandra rd.
Patterson Mountain (Marsden villa) 6 Haverstock hill
Pattison John (Stamford lo.) Heath st
Pattison Samuel 5 Lyndhurst rd.
Paul Thomas 13 Devonshire pl.
Paveley George (Vernal house) 8 Princ Arthur rd.
Pavitt Mrs. 6 Gascony avenue
Paxton Mrs. 15 Holtham rd.
Payne Septimus,F.R.G.S.,M.S.A.(Wellin ton house) Eton rd.
Peabody Thomas 23 Church row
Peache Rev. Alfred (The Firs)Heath en
Peachey Mrs. Pearse 15 Oppidans rd.
Peake George 188 Alexandra rd.
Peall John 57 Flask walk
Pearce Arthur Renau 38 Stanley garde
Pearce Edward (Mount Vernon co tage) Mount Vernon
Pearce George 5 Gardnor rd.
Pearce Geo. Parkes Elliott 7 Lichfield r
Pearce Henry 40 Midland cottages
Pearce Henry 1 Willow pl. Chris church rd.
Pearce James 54 Fleet rd.
Pearce James 6 Netherwood st.

earce James Horne 21 Albion rd.
earce J. A. 2 Perrin's court
earceJohn 3Willow pl.Christchurch rd.
earce L. A. 34 Stanley gardens
earceMrs. 2 Willow pl.Christchurch rd.
earce William 53 Boundary rd.
earce William 58 Gayton rd.
earce W. T. 2 Provost rd.
earpoint Alfred H. 8 Eton villas
earse Alfd.(Thanehurst)Denington pk.
earsonGeo.(Lincoln ho.)39Boundary rd
ease William 45 Gayton rd.
eck Henry William 5 Willoughby rd.
eddar S. H. 4 Foley avenue
edder Henry 21 Granville ter.
ede Thomas(Belgrave house) 51 Haverstock hill
edlar Mrs. 1 Abbott's rd.
edlar William (Ontario lodge) 2 Kilburn priory
edley William 39 Midland cottages
eek Francis Ansley (Messina house)
  West end lane
eile James Kenyon 174 Adelaide rd.
eile Miss 114 Alexandra rd.
eile Mrs. 37 St. John's wood park
elham Frederick 6 Palmerston rd.
enny J. S. 166 Alexandra rd.
epler Mrs. 3 Albion ter.
epper Archibald 18 Lower Lawn rd.
eppiatt Edward 20 Well walk
ercy Isaac 118 Maygrove rd.
ereda Madame Vicento 19 Priory rd.
erino Joseph 20 Harley rd.
erkins George Henri 12 Sherriff rd.
erkins Mrs. M. A. 29 Downshire hill
erks Charles 192 Loveridge rd.
erram Rev. G. J. 128 Fellows rd.
errin Hy. Story 31 St. John's wood pk.
errin Rowland Neate 55 Alexandra rd.
errins John Hill (Chaddesley villa)
  Kemplay rd.
errins Mrs. T. H. 8 Crossfield rd.
erry Rt. Rev. Bishop,D.D.32 Avenue rd.
erry George 4 Devonshire pl.
erry John (Linton house) Hillfield rd.
erry Joseph J. (Silverholme) 186 Haverstock hill
erry Mrs. 96 Belsize rd.
erryman Frederick 6 Prospect rd.
escod J. 20 Yew grove
etch Alfred 25 Maygrove rd.
eters John 129 Iverson rd.
eters Joseph (Prospect cott.) Heath st.
eters Mrs. (The Grange) 234 High rd.
eters Simon 5 Ebenezer rd.
ettet Thomas 10 Lichfield rd.

Pettie Jno.(The Lothians)2Fitzjohns' av.
Pettitt Henry 33 Haverstock hill
Pfeiffer R. W. 4 Cricklewood lane
Pfeil A. L. A. (Wiston) Reddington rd.
Pfeil Frdk. John (Priory lodge) Frognal
Phillips — (Belgrave cottage) Belgrave
  gardens
Phillips Arthur 59 Haverstock hill
Phillips Francis Medland 2 Cannon pl.
Phillips George 10 Buckland villas
Phillips Harry B. (Northbrook) West
  end lane
Phillips Henry 84 Alexandra rd.
Phillips James (Percy house) North end
Phillips John 13 Gayton cres.
Phillips John W. 10 Christchurch rd.
Phillips Mrs. 2 New West end
Phillips Philip 6 Belgrave rd.
Phillips Saml. (Glenhurst)Elsworthy rd.
Phillips Thos. (Adelaide house) John st.
Phillips Walter 51 Finchley new rd.
Phillips Wm. Phillips 72 South hill park
Phipps Mrs. (Surrey house) Cricklewood
Pickett George J. 268 High rd.
Pickett Joseph 85 South hill park
Pickworth George 169 Adelaide rd.
Pickworth Rowland(Kenmure)7Nether-
  hall ter.
Pidcock G. Douglas, M.A., M.D. 52 Down-
  shire hill
Pierres Paul 79 Belsize rd.
Pigeon Henry, jun. 46 Belsize park
Pile C. H. 14 Elsworthy rd.
Pile J. 58 Adelaide rd.
Pillans Thomas Dundas (2 Stowe house)
  North end
Pinchin Edwin S. 38 King Henry's rd.
Pinto-LeiteMadame74Belsize park gdns.
Piper Alexander Chas. 34 Maygrove rd.
Piper Misses (Norton lodge) 3 Ark-
  wright rd.
Piper Mrs. 8 Gascony avenue
Pitcher Major D. J. 8 Rockhall ter.
Pitt John Wolley 13 Crossfield rd.
Pittman Miss 11 Crossfield rd.
Pitzipias Stephen D. (Henley house)
  5 Woodchurch rd.
Pitzschke Mrs. 23 Alexandra rd.
Plant Mrs. Rose 9 Kelson st.
Plaster Mrs. Emma 47 Gayton rd.
Platt Dr. William (St. James's lodge)
  West end lane
Platt James (Rookwood) Greenhill
Platt Mrs. 40 Alexandra rd.
Platt Peregrine 15 Kingdon rd.
Playne Mrs. 6 Buckland villas
Pledger J. J. 195 Loveridge rd.

Pleister Mrs. 10 St. John's wood park
Plomer G. D. 48 Springfield rd.
Plomer I. D. (Chesterton) Acol rd.
Plomer Mrs. 48 Springfield rd.
Plowman Alfred 6 Weech rd.
Plum Charles 13b Gardnor rd.
Plumer Mrs. 98 Belsize rd.
Plumer William 56 Fleet rd.
Plumpton Robert 36 Adelaide rd.
Pocknee James 5 Providence pl.
Pocock George 10a Elm ter.
Pocock Lewis (Clovelly) Well rd.
Pocock Noel Lewis (Lynton) Well rd.
Pohler Miss M. 89 Avenue rd.
Pole Mrs. 141 Iverson rd.
Pollak Hermann 27 Belsize avenue
Pollard Lieut. George Northmore A.,
  R.N. 5 Belsize cres.
Pollock Mrs. 25 Thurlow rd.
Pontis W. J. 38 Fairfax rd.
Poole Daniel George 2 Claremont rd.
Poole Edwin 3 Southwell ter.
Poole Frederick 6 Church row
Poole Miss 48 Avenue rd.
Poole Mrs. (Sunnyside) Hillfield rd.
Pooley H. F. (Scotter) Well walk
Pooley Josiah 57 Upper Park rd.
Pope Abraham (Taunton lo.) West end ln.
Pope John Thomas 3 Sherriff rd.
Pope Joseph 59 Flask walk
Pope Thomas (Baston ho.) Netherhall ter.
Port Charles G. J. (Staincliffe) 44 Prim-
  rose hill rd.
Port Charles Thomas 137 Adelaide rd.
Porteous Lieut.-Col. Charles A. 83 Fel-
  lows rd.
Porter E. R. (Hesket) 16 Daleham gdns.
Posener A. (Acacia villa) Quex rd.
Postlethwaite F. E. 26 Springfield rd.
Pott Charles 6 Fordwych rd.
Potter Abraham 17 Devonshire pl.
Potter Ebenezer 5 Lithos rd.
Potter George 27 Gayton rd.
Potter George 3 Willow rd.
Potter Henry (Little Dene) 5 Dening-
  ton park
Potter Robert (Allbury house) 166 May-
  grove rd.
Potter Thomas (Poplar house) West end
Pottle Mrs. 5 Heath vils. Vale of Health
Poulett Earl 30 Belsize park gardens
Poulter Rev. Jas., M.A. 165 Adelaide rd.
Poulter Reginald Clifford, B.A. 165
  Adelaide rd.
Poulter Thomas (Clifton lodge) East
  Heath rd.
Powell Eyre B., C.S.I. 28 Park rd.

Powell George Holt (Cedar lawn)
  Hampstead heath
Powell Jas. (Cromer lea) 1 Ellerdale rd.
Powell Lewis 14 Primrose hill rd.
Powell Mrs. 6 Lawn rd.
Powell Mrs. 1 Osborne ter.
Powell Nugent 28 Loveridge rd.
Powell R. L. (Heylands) East Heath rd.
Powell Thomas Edmund (Priory end)
  Frognal
Powell William Henry W. 5 Albion rd.
Powles Evelyn 150 King Henry's rd.
Powley Arthur 3 Mansfield pl.
Pownall R. B. 89 South hill park
Pownceby Saml. (Fern bank) Branch hill
Prance Reginald Heber, Frognal
Prance Robert Rooke, M.D. (Rookeslea)
  Greenhill rd.
Pratchett Samuel 4 Yorkshire Grey yard
Pratt G. 2 Mansfield pl.
Pratt James 44 Fleet rd.
Pratt Misses (Lorne ho.) 111 Alexandra rd
Pratt Mrs. 85 Adelaide rd.
Pratt Mrs. (Clarence ho.) 12 Garlinge rd
Preedy Mrs. 42 Upper Park rd.
Prendergast Edwin (Strathmore) Crickle
  wood
Prentice Ridley 11 Hampstead hill gdns
Preston Alfred 26 Fellows rd.
Preston Alfred Charles 158 Belsize rd.
Preston S. W. 7 Eldon rd.
Preston Thos. Sansome 28 Thurlow rd.
Price Chas. (Homelea) 5 Prince Arthur rd
Price Harry (Uplands) Cleve rd.
Price Miss 29 Belgrave rd.
Price Ramsden 5 Ellerdale rd.
Price Thomas 3 Willow cottages
Price Wm. (Saint Mary's) West Heath rd
Price-Williams Mrs. (Northbrow) Els
  worthy rd.
Prichard Richard R. 17 Gascony avenu
Priddle William 7 Church row
Pridham Arthur E. 4 Villas on the Heat
Prince Julius 101 Finchley rd.
Pringle A. W. 3 Springfield rd.
Pritchard Andrew Goring 8 Hampstea
  hill gardens
Pritchard F. Philps 28 Kingdon rd.
Pritchard Stephen 3 Hermitage villas
Pritchard Urban, M.D., F.R.C.S. 8 Heat
  rise
Pritchard William 45 Haverstock hill
Pritchett H. Talbot 85 Priory rd.
Procter C. W. C. 106 King Henry's rd.
Profaze George 49 Adelaide rd.
Prosser William Hy. 108 South hill par
Prout William 37 Priory rd.

'ryke John A. 27 Lichfield rd.
'ryor H. L. 17 Kingsgate rd.
'ryor William 40 Fleet rd.
'uddifoot Mrs. 11 Church row
'uente Mrs. 11 Maygrove rd.
'ugh H. 128 High rd.
'ugh John O. (Vincent villa) 56 Haverstock hill
'ugh Mrs. 14 Belsize park
'ulley Joseph William 177 Loveridge rd.
'unch John 66 Abbey rd.
'unnett John 4 New West end
'urcell Canon Arthur Dillon 5 Holly pl.
'urcell Mrs. E.(Alpha cottage)West end
'urks Alexander 5 Prospect rd.
'urney Henry 30 Alexandra rd.
'urry A. A. 33 South hill park
'urry Mrs. E. (Rosemont) Well walk
'utney Samuel 59 Belsize avenue
'uzey Frederick (Mount Waltham) 9
  Netherhall ter.
'uzey Mrs. 8 Belsize park
'utz Joseph Francis 14 Fairfax rd.
'ye W. A. 24 Daleham gardens
'yne Thomas 56 Upper Park rd.

Quaritch Bernard 3 Haverstock ter.
Quarry Charles 8 Kingsgate rd.
Quick Mrs. 2 Bridge rd.
Quin George 44 Belsize sq.
Quincey Miss 74 Avenue rd.
Quinton James 5 Golden yard

Rackham Rev. H. E. (Florence villa)
  Messina avenue
Radbourne Mrs. 4 Fairhazel gardens
Radermacher Charles John 23 Birching-
  ton rd.
Radermacher John 7 Lancaster rd.
Radford John Emanuel 48 Boundary rd.
Raeburn Macbeth — 2 Park road studios
Raffles Wm.Winter 34 Belsize park gdns.
Raggett R. 5 Richmond villas
Raikes Mrs. 63 Belsize park
Rainbow Henry J. 9 Pond st.
Rainsford John McLeod (The Retreat)
  7 Avenue villas
Rait Logan (Gloucester house) 13a
  Downshire hill
Ralph James 270 High rd.
Ralston William 90 King Henry's rd.
Ramsbotham James 24 Ainger rd.
Ramsbotham P. B. 43 Ainger rd.
Ramus Isaac (Olive villa) Quex rd.
Rance George 43 South hill park
Rance Mrs. 82 Park rd.
Randall G. H. 41 Fleet rd.

Randall John, M.D. 204 Adelaide rd.
Randegger Guiseppe 74 Adelaide rd.
Randell Richard 19 Midland cottages
Ransley Alfred 12 Dunboyne st.
Raphael Alfred 87 Alexandra rd.
Raphael Charles 22 Belsize park gardens
Rapp Eugene 6 Eldon rd.
Rasey Henry 3 Belgrave gardens
RatcliffSidney Geo. 126 KingHenry's rd.
Ratcliff Thomas 48 Stanley gardens
Rathbone Mrs. 120 Abbey rd. Kilburn
Ratto Adolphus 9 Maygrove rd.
Raven Miss J. A. (Grove cot.) Frognal
Ravenscroft Francis (Birkbeck lodge)
  64 Springfield rd.
Ravenscroft Horatio 38 Haverstock hill
Ravenscroft Thomas 19 Stanley gardens
Raw John Frederick 30 Park rd.
Rawlings Mrs. James 184 Belsize rd.
Rawson John 23 Lichfield rd.
Ray Miss(Mount cottage) 71 Flask walk
Rayment Edward 29 Park rd.
Rayne Mrs. 51 Springfield rd.
Rayner Edward 7 South hill park
Rayner W. S. G. 24 Birchington rd.
Rayson James B. 10 Eldon rd.
Rea Russell 19 Primrose hill rd.
Read Charles A. (Roselands) 4 West-
  croft villas
Read Edmund 4 Hillfield rd.
Read John R. 62 Park rd.
Read John Walter 122 Haverstock hill
Read John Wltr. (Brightside) Ornan rd.
Read Miss 4 Eton villas
Read Mrs. 167 Belsize rd. Kilburn
Read Thomas Frederick 14 South hill
  park gardens
Read W. de Courtney 28 Haverstock hill
Read William T. (Holly bank) Frognal
Reade J. H. 14 St. George's rd.
Reade Mrs. 1 Rosslyn gardens
Reading Jno.1Golder's hill ter.North end
Reading Miss 31 Haverstock hill
Readman Joseph (Ormond house) Crick-
  lewood
Ready Charles 5 Narcissus rd.
Redding H. 45 Kingsgate rd.
Redfern Mrs. (Abercrombie villa)
  Rosslyn hill
Redfern W. G. T., Rosslyn hill
Redford George, F.R.C.S. 6 Rockhall ter.
Redhead Alfred 1 Springfield
Redhouse James W. 14 Kilburn priory
Redman Mrs. J. 6 Belsize park
Redmond Francis 137 Abbey rd. Kilburn
Reece J. (Westhaven) Cricklewood
Reed Rev. A. (Ellenslea) 141 Fellows rd.

Reed Eliot Pye-Smith (Holmleigh) Well walk
Reed Frank 18 Belsize rd.
Reedman Wm. Frederick 8 Midland cotts.
Reeman Alfred 24 Devonshire pl.
Rees John 84 Finchley rd.
Rees Miss Ellen Elcum 9 Carlingford rd.
Reeseg John F. 148 Iverson rd.
Reeve E. J. 1 Hill side
Reeve Mrs. Jane 37 Maygrove rd.
Reeve Samuel 8 Spencer ter.
Regnart Miss 42 Primrose hill rd.
Reid Charles T. (Twyfordbury) 12 Ellerdale rd.
Reid George (Dalkeith) Maresfield gdns.
Reid Miss 27 Heath st.
Reid Mrs. 63 Adelaide rd.
Reid Mrs. 56 Alexandra rd.
Reid Mrs. 25 Goldhurst ter.
Reid Thomas (Plas Gwyn) Frognal
Reinganum Victor 37 Gascony avenue
Reinhold Henry 69 Finchley new rd.
Relph John 6 Springfield rd.
Render Frederick 172 Belsize rd.
Rennie John 1 Yew grove
Renshaw Charles 3 Midland cottages
Renton Edward 44 South hill park
Renton Mrs. 2 Rosslyn ter.
Revell Colonel Blackett (Shirland lodge) Goldhurst rd.
Rex C. W. 9 Elm grove
Reynolds Miss 10 Belsize avenue
Reynolds Mrs. (Providence cottage) Cricklewood lane
Reynolds Mrs. Fanny 74 Finchley rd.
Reynolds William Patrick 105 Belsize rd.
Rhind James 5 Birchington rd.
Rhodes Mrs. 30 Parliament hill rd.
Rice Henry John 20 Gayton rd.
Rice William Pierce (Sydney cottage) Vale of Health
Richards Charles 20 Birchington rd.
Richards George Chas. 24 Granville ter.
Richards John William 26 Ainger rd.
Richards Levi 6 Springfield gardens
Richards Mrs. 3 Ainger rd.
Richards Mrs. (Grange villa) 7 Claremont rd.
Richards Percy 97 Abbey rd.
Richardson Charles 5 New end sq.
Richardson James 129 Belsize rd.
Richardson Misses 160 King Henry's rd.
Richardson Wm. 64 Belsize park gardens
Richardson William 3 Prospect pl.
Rickard Rev. Wm. (Homelea) The Ridge
Ricks James 120 Adelaide rd.
Riddell R. Alfred 137 Alexandra rd.

Riddle Henry 7 Maygrove rd.
Rider Wm. (Kenwyn) 29 Fitzjohns' avn.
Rider W. R. 60 Gayton rd.
Ridge Thomas 2 Well walk ter.
Ridgway Mrs. (Dyke ho.) 34 Elsworthy rd.
Ridley John 19 Belsize park
Ridpath Edward 67 Finchley new rd.
Ries Louis (Tirlemont) Broadhurst gdns.
Riess Mrs. H. 112 Adelaide rd.
Riessmann Henry (Saxony villa) Oppidans rd.
Riethmuller Christopher J. (Fairleigh house) 9 Adamson rd.
Riley Edwd. (South Heath) East Heath rd.
Ring Rev. W. (New priory) Quex rd.
Ring Max 88 Alexandra rd.
Ring Richard 21 Springfield rd.
Ringe Charles 44 Flask walk
Ringe F. 3 Arch pl.
Risdon Misses 72 Alexandra rd.
Rishworth Walter W. 10 St. George's rd.
Risk Bouverie 3 Heathfield gardens
Ritchie Miss 116 Belsize rd.
Ritson Hugh Daniel 21 Fordwych rd.
Ritter Adolphe 21 South hill park
Rivers Mrs. 37 Loudoun rd.
Riviere Briton 82 Finchley rd.
Riviere Mrs. 156 King Henry's rd.
Roach William 4 Grove pl.
Robert John, Little Church row
Roberts Rev. John 50 Priory rd.
Roberts Arthur 66 Belsize rd.
Roberts Charles Lewis 3 Hill side
Roberts Edward Charles 23 South hill pk
Roberts F. B. 67 Fitzjohns' avenue
Roberts Frederick 84 Palmerston rd.
Roberts Henry 17 Belsize sq.
Roberts John 170 Alexandra rd.
Roberts John H., F.R.C.S. (Hill crest) Greenhill rd.
Roberts John Robinson 146 Fellows rd.
Roberts Miss 126 Belsize rd.
Roberts Mrs. 118 Abbey rd. Kilburn
Roberts Mrs. (Cricklewood lodge) Cricklewood
Roberts Mrs. (The Cottage) Cricklewood
Roberts Mrs. 7 Cricklewood ter.
Roberts Mrs. 18 Kilburn priory
Roberts Mrs. 4 Kingdon rd.
Roberts Mrs. 7 Rockhall ter.
Roberts Thomas Alexander (The Manor hall) St. John's wood park
Roberts William 194 Loveridge rd.
Roberts William F. 6 Provost rd.
Roberts W. George, 3 Back lane
Robertson Rev. John, LL.D. 123 Adelaide rd.
Robertson David (Dunedin) 1 Oak hill pk

Married Ellen Louisa GOSLETT

obertson Henry R. 1 Steele's studios

obertson James (Haughton lodge) 20 Ellerdale rd.

obertson James 11 Oak hill park

obertson John 5 Heathfield gardens

obertson Mrs. 35 Park rd.

obertson Struan 147 King Henry's rd.

obins Charles 3 Holmdale rd.

obins Charles H. 19 Devonshire pl.

obins Edmund 79 Alexandra rd.

obins Julian 17 Alexandra rd.

obinson Major-General Charles Gilbert, R.A. 3 Denning rd.

obinson Henry, C.E., F.G.S. 50 Springfield rd.

obinson James 27 Boundary rd.

obinson John R. 9 Claremont rd.

obinson Josiah 7 Fellows rd.

obinson Miss C. 29 Kingsgate rd.

obinson Mrs. Louisa 5 Belsize rd.

obislio Frederick 21 St. John's wood pk.

obson Miss 7 Alexandra rd.

obson Mrs. 6 Lowfield rd.

obson Mrs. 6 West end lane

obson Thomas (Uphill house) Finchley new rd.

oche James 3 Lutton ter.

oche Joseph John 2 Holly hill

oche Miss 9 Belsize cres.

oche Miss (Grove lodge) The Grove

ochfordT.(Dunloe villa)17 Rudall cres.

ochfort Mrs. Benjamin (Howard lodge) 12 Kilburn priory

ock E. G. 47 Denning rd.

oden Miss 7 Carlingford rd.

odick Miss Janet P. (Gangmoor) 44 Hampstead heath

odrick Mrs. (Alton lo.) 44 Iverson rd.

odway Mrs. 6 Villas on the Heath

oe H., Kingsgate rd.

oe Misses 100 Adelaide rd.

oe Mrs. 16 Parliament hill rd.

oe Mrs. Freeman 100 Adelaide rd.

off Arthur 2 Well rd.

off Walter William 22 Downshire hill

ojas de Ruiz Mrs. Nathalie (Aurora villa) Oppidans rd.

ogers Alfred (Glen Innis)West end lane

ogers Charles George 94 Maygrove rd.

ogers David 52 Kingsgate rd.

ogers Henry 90 Alexandra rd.

ogers James 8 Denning rd.

ogers Jas. Edward 70 South hill park

ogers John 21 Gascony avenue

ogers Louis 24 Adelaide rd.

ogers Miss 10 Belsize park gardens

ogers Mrs. 11 Gascony avenue

Rogers Mrs. 4 Golder's hill ter.

Rogers Mrs. Ann 188 Belsize rd.

Rogers Thomas (Lynton house) 40 Primrose hill rd.

Rogers Thomas Henry Tait (West Haven) 3 Woodchurch rd.

Rogers William 181 Loveridge rd.

Rolfe George 38 Parliament hill rd.

Rolfe H. 45 Gascony avenue

Rollason Mrs. 37 Alexandra rd.

Romanes Mrs. 3 Cedar villas

Rooth Goodwin (Wetherall house) Well walk

Roper Frank, Hampstead green

Roper John 16 Midland cottages

Roper W.(Cricklewood ho.) Cricklewood

Roscoe William 36 Avenue rd.

Rose Charles 136 Adelaide rd.

Rose Edward 21 South hill park grdns.

Rose Henry Cooper,M.D. (Penrose house) Rosslyn ter.

Rosenbaum Martin 80 Fellows rd.

Rosenheim H.(Highfield house) 62 Fitzjohns' avenue

Rosenheim Max 184 Adelaide rd.

Rosenheim Thordor 176 Adelaide rd.

Rosenheim William 195 Adelaide rd.

Rosenheim William 9 Lambolle rd.

Rosenstein Rev. M. 10 Holtham rd.

Rosenwald Edward 20 Belsize park

Rosher Percy 6 Richmond villas

Ross D. A. McBean 9 Eton rd.

Ross Edward 50 Boundary rd.

Ross Hamilton 13 Buckland cres.

Ross Miss H. R. 11 College ter.

Rossi Alexander M. 177 Adelaide rd.

Rossner Henry 69 Boundary rd.

Rost Dr. R.,PH.D., LL.D. 1 Elsworthy ter.

Rotheram William 13 Well rd.

Rotter Charles G. 58 Park rd.

Rothwell Mrs. 78 South hill park

Rous Henry 2 Woodchurch rd.

Rouse William 1 Murray ter.

Routledge Lieut.-Col. Robert 52 Belsize park gardens

Roux Henry Augustus 5 Sunnyside vils.

Row Rev. Prebendary C. A., M.A. 22 Harley rd.

Rowan James 4 Priory rd.

Rowe Alfred John 13 Hotham rd.

Rowe John Kingdon 7 Lawn rd.

Rowe Mrs. (Frognal house) Frognal

Rowe William 59 Upper Park rd.

Rowland Mrs. 3 White Bear lane

Rowlands William Bowen, Q.C., J.P. 33 Belsize park

Rowsell H. 35 Gascony avenue

Roy James W. 20 Belsize cres.
Royle Henry William (The Mount) Cricklewood
Royston Miss 10 Upper ter.
Rudall George 28 Lichfield rd.
Ruddick David 26 Fairfax rd.
Rumbold Richard 16 Gardnor rd.
Rumford J. K. (Oaklands) 60 Priory rd.
Rumpff T. A. A. 43 St. John's wood park
Rumsey A. A. 28 Claremont rd.
Rusby James, F.R. HIST. SOC. 18 Oppidans rd.
Rush Arthur 18 Lansdowne ter.
Russell Charles 30 Gayton rd.
Russell E. B. (Danehurst) Willoughby rd.
Russell John 10 Dunboyne st.
Russell Joseph 13 College ter.
Russell J. E. 100 Iverson rd.
Russell Miss 37 Greville rd.
Russell Mrs. (Garston house) 1 Primrose hill rd.
Russell Mrs. 12 Prospect rd.
Russell Mrs. Edwin 7 Haverstock hill
Russell Mrs. J. M. (Lyndale) Finchley rd. Child's hill
Russell Robert 4 Hermitage villas
Russell Thomas 1 Child's hill cottages
Russell Thomas 58 Maygrove rd.
Russell William 149 Adelaide rd.
Russell William 3 Child's hill cottages
Russell William 172 Iverson rd.
Russell William 20 Stanley gardens
Russell W. D. 4 Well walk ter.
Russell W. J. 3 Claremont ter.
Rutland Alfred 50 Ainger rd.
Rutland Joseph 1 Alfred ter. Back lane
Rutt Henry 66 Finchley rd.
Rylands John Paul 25 Stanley gardens

Sadler Rev. Dr. Thomas (Rosslyn manse) Pilgrim's lane
Saer William 4 Richmond villas
Saggs Frederick 2 Flask cottages
St. John Lieutenant St. Andrew, R.N. 4 Canfield gardens
St. Stephens Ragnar 25 Fordwych rd.
Saleeby E. J. 3 Weech rd.
Salmon James Dennis 22 South hill pk.
Salmon Mrs. 13 Fordwych rd.
Salmon Mrs. (Heath view) Willow rd.
Salmon Mrs. Emily 20 South hill park
Salter Mrs. (St. George's college) 18 St. George's rd.
Salter Richard 1 Benham's pl.
Saltmarsh Edwd. 16 South hill pk. gdns.
Sampson Samuel 127 Alexandra rd.
Samuel Joseph 24 Primrose hill rd.

Samuel Maximilian 102 Priory rd.
Sanders Miss (Westbury) Broadhurst gdn
Sanders William Henry 3 Holtham rd.
Sanderson James 9 Eldon rd.
Sandilands George M. 55 Belsize avenue
Sandilands Mrs. 56 Belsize park
Sands Richard 21 The Village
Sangster James 41 Park rd.
Sargant Mrs. Henry 56 Belsize pk. gdns
Sargeant Charles 14 Lowfield rd.
Sasse John (Sunnyside) 2 Westcroft rd
Satchell Thomas (Downshire hill house 50 Downshire hill
Satterthwaite Joseph J. 14 Yorkshir Grey yard
Satterthwaite Mrs. 3 Church lane
Sauerbrey Herr E. 37 Belsize rd.
Saunders C. D. 1 Portland villas East Heath rd.
Saunders C. D., jun. 41 Upper Park rd.
Saunders Henry 66 Alexandra rd.
Saunders William 10 Bolton rd.
Savage Nathaniel 5 Priory rd.
Savill Alfred 103 Alexandra rd.
Savory Richard 6 Adelaide rd.
Sawyer James 8 Cricklewood ter.
Saxby George 10 Linstead st.
Saxby James Samuel 1 Holmdale rd.
Sayer William 1 The Gables
Sayers William (Clyde houes) Broad hurst gardens
Scaife John 126 Alexandra rd.
Scammell Alfred Thos. 106 South hill pk
Scammell Whitfield 104 South hill par
Scarlett John 33 Birchington rd.
Scarsbrook F. 133 Belsize rd. Kilburn
Scarth Robt. Gilyard 109 King Henry's rd
Schirges Henry 7 King Henry's rd.
Schleasser Ernest 12 Daleham gardens
Schleicher Otto 66 Parliament hill rd.
Schleifer Mrs. Amelia 16 Hilgrove rd.
Schloss Joseph 34 King Henry's rd.
Schmedes Otto 80 Belsize park gardens
Schmeisser William 2 Kemplay rd.
Schmitz Leonard, LL.D., F.R.S.E. 26 Bel size park gardens
Schnegelsberg Herr W. 33 Alexandra rd
Schnieder Montague 29 Loudoun rd.
Schoell Rev. Carl, PH.D. 3 Elsworthy ter Primrose hill
Schoell Carl (Homeside) England's lan
Schofield Mrs. (Rose cottage) Mill lane
Schofield Mrs. Joseph 18 Lyndhurst rd.
Scholfield John Howorth 9 Lichfield rd
Schöller William F. P. 22 Belsize cres.
Schönberg D. Louis 47 Fellows rd.
Schroder Walter 11 Heath villas

chröder William (St. Ann's cottage) Vale of Health
chroeder Alfred 2 Albion ter.
chroederWm.,Telegraph hillWest heath
chuler Mrs. Leon 10 Gascony avenue
chultz Mrs. 8 Springfield rd.
chumann John Ludwig (Laurel bank) Steele's rd.
chuster Ernest 2 Lancaster rd.
chuster F.J.(Sunnyside)Up. Avenue rd.
chuster Felix Otto 50 Belsize sq.
chwann Frederick Sigismund (West Heath lodge) Branch hill
chwieso Frederick 4 William ter.
cott Alexander 1 Acol rd.
cott Arthur 5 Kingdon rd.
cott Frank (Woodville house) Burgess hill
cott George 26 Kingsgate rd.
cott Geo. Gilbert, F.S.A. 26 Church row
cott James 166 Belsize rd.
cott James 1 Gascony avenue
cott John 5 The Mall
cott Matthew Richard 76 Boundary rd.
cott Miss 140 Fellows rd.
cott Miss 27 Netherwood rd.
cott Mrs. 156 Haverstock hill
cottRussell 1The Chestnuts Branch hill
cott Thomas (The Cottage) Upper ter.
cott William Booth 16 Church row
cott William R. 51 Belsize pk. gardens
cratchley Arthur 4 College ter.
cripps Mrs. (Frognal cottage) Frognal
croggie J. (Apna Chur) 4 Hilltop rd.
cudamore George 30 Winchester rd.
earle Henry 13 Mansfield pl.
earle Miss (Glastonbury house) Gascony avenue
eaton Frederick (Garlinge house) Cricklewood
eddonH.C.(St. Winifred's) Hillfield rd.
elfe Thomas Vanderhorst(Thistleboon) Hampstead hill gardens
eligmann Soloman 32 King Henry's rd.
ell Mrs. 76 High st.
ell Walter George 2 Willow cottages
ellick John George 2 Narcissus rd.
elous Edric, M.D. 133 Adelaide rd.
enior Charles 22 Hilgrove rd.
enior Charles 61 South hill park
ercombe Mrs. Louisa 23 Daleham gdns.
eton Robert 51 Park rd.
evenoaks Mrs. 11 St. George's rd.
evier James Henry (Clyde house) Broadhurst gardens
ewell Charles John (Birnam villa) Greenhill rd.

Sexton R. 3 Devonshire villas
Sexton William 20 Lower Lawn rd.
Seymour James 6 New end sq.
Shaffuer — 2 Thompson's mews
Shapley Edwin 4 Adelaide rd.
Sharman Mrs. Eric R. (Ellel house) 14 Ellerdale rd.
Sharp John (Lime villa) Quex rd.
Sharp John William 35 Boundary rd.
Sharp Mrs. 3 St. George's rd.
SharpThomas Stephen 27 South hill park
Sharpe Rev. Henry (Trinity lodge) Finchley new rd.
Sharpe Arthur 87 Belsize rd.
Sharpe Charles 29 The Village
Sharpe Henry 30 Well walk
Sharpe Mrs., The Grove
Sharples R. H. 11 Ainger rd.
Shave E. S. 2 Elm villas
Shaw Rev. William 101 South hill park
Shaw Alexander 136 Abbey rd. Kilburn
Shaw Barnett 25 Prospect rd.
Shaw Charles 29 Belsize cres.
ShawHenry Scott 106 Abbey rd. Kilburn
Shaw Henry Wright 27 Alexandra rd.
Shaw James J. (Elsworthy house) 11 Primrose hill rd.
Shaw John, M.D. LOND. (Burlington house) 1 Rudall cres.
Shaw Mrs. Elizabeth 16 Albion rd.
Shaw Mrs. R. H. 30 Fellows rd.
Shaw Richd. Norman,R.A. 6 Ellerdale rd.
Sheffield Frank (Palaspai) 15 Daleham gardens
Sheffield Henry 6 Winchester rd.
Sheffield Mrs. E. 10 South hill park gdns.
Sheldrick David 51 Upper Park rd.
Shellum Albert 2 King's cottages
Shelton John 16 Ash grove
Shenton Edward 19 Lower Lawn rd.
Shephard Mark (Stamford villa) Hillfield rd.
Shepherd Dr. Fredk. 33 King Henry's rd.
Shepherd Charles 2 Alexandra rd.
Shepherd F. W. 138 Adelaide rd.
Shepherd Mrs. (Burfield)Carlingford rd.
Shepherd Thomas 2 Holly pl.
Shepherd Wm. Robert 30 Downshire hill
Sheppard Vincent (Chesnut lodge) 109 Haverstock hill
Sherbrooke W. 2 Dynham rd.
Sherman R. Tatham (St. John's) Greenhill rd.
Sherrat James, M.A. 44 Priory rd.
Sherratt Thomas 28 Gayton rd.
Sherry Nathaniel 1 The Green
Shewin Robert 146 King Henry's rd.

Shiell R. S. 20 Park rd.
Shilcock John 52 Maygrove rd.
Shine J. L. (Belsize cottage) Belsize ln.
Shinn Mrs. (Rose cottage) South end rd.
Shipley Edward 40 Palmerston rd.
Shipman Miss 38 South hill park
Shipway Major Robert William (Eversholt) Cricklewood
Shipwright Thomas 5 Elsworthy rd.
Shirreff William Moore 42 Belsize park
Shone William 151 Belsize rd. Kilburn
Shore John 7 Kilburn vale
Short Fredk. George 9 Heathfield gdns.
Short Martin 20 Woodchurch rd.
Shortis Miss 8 Claremont rd.
Shout Misses 21 Upper Park rd.
Shurley William 17 Iverson rd.
Shute William 4 Provost rd.
Shuter James L. 9 Steele's rd.
Shuter Miss 126 Abbey rd. Kilburn
Shuter William 66 Belsize park gardens
Sichel Gustave 153 Abbey rd. Kilburn
Silk William 17 Church row
Sillars Rev. Duncan 9 Provost rd.
Sillett Mrs. 129 Abbey rd. Kilburn
Silver Mrs. 24 Albion rd.
Simmonds Henry 12 Lithos rd.
Simmonds Mrs., Heath mount
Simmonds Mrs. Ann 44 Gayton rd.
Simmons Charles 18 Kingdon rd.
Simmons Charles 22 Lichfield rd.
Simmons George 10 New end
Simmons John 21 Kingdon rd.
Simmons John O. 76 Maygrove rd.
Simmons William 23 Kingdon rd.
Simon Charles M. 13 Belsize cres.
Simon Herman 46 Belsize sq.
Simons Wm. Thomas John 61 Fleet rd.
Simper George 16 Devonshire pl.
Simpson Alfred 21 Loveridge rd.
Simpson Charles 3 Yorkshire Grey yard
Simpson G. P. 49 Belsize sq.
Simpson J. (Stanley ho.) Stanley gdns.
Simpson James Carrington (Winchester lodge) 1 Winchester rd.
Simpson John 120 Belsize park gardens
Simpson Mrs. 35 Loudoun rd.
Simpson R. 13 Thurlow rd.
Simpson Thomas 36 Gayton rd.
Sims Mrs. 27 Broadhurst gardens
Sims Mrs. Annie 87 Iverson rd.
Sims William John 4 Elm grove
Sinclair Frederick 99 Finchley rd.
Sinclair Joseph 7 Belsize avenue
Sinclair Misses 25 Bolton st.
Sinclair Mrs. 23 Lithos rd.
Sinfield Joseph 3 Granville ter.

Sisley George 7 Linstead st.
Sitford William John 14 Gascony avenue
Sjolander C. V. 19 Claremont rd.
Skeel William 45 Downshire hill
Skeels Thomas 22 Greville rd.
Skilbeck John 16 Buckland cres.
Skilton Mrs. John (St. John's cottage) South end rd.
Skinner Alfred Earnest 2 Well walk
Skinner Arthur 27 Elm grove
Skinner Mrs. 4 The Cottages
Skinner Richard 25 Netherwood st.
Slade George Penkivel (Kanimbla) 33 Fitzjohns' avenue
Slade John 93 Alexandra rd.
Slade John (The Limes) Well walk
Slater Henry 12 Primrose hill rd.
Slater John 70 Park rd.
Slater Mrs. 2 and 3 Holly bush hill
Slaughter W. E. 5 Acol rd.
Sleep G. C. 3 South hill park
Slight Mrs. 27 Flask walk
Slimmon Mrs. 116 Maygrove rd.
Slocombe Alfred 2 The Green
Smallfield Frederick 52 Boundary rd.
Smallman J. T. Bruce 189 Belsize rd. Kilburn
Smart Miss 13 Winchester rd.
Smedley J. V., M.A. 34 St. George's rd.
Smith Alexander 14 Ariel st.
Smith Alfred (Belle vue) Cricklewood
Smith Alfred 15 Goldhurst rd.
Smith Alfred J. 3 Iverson rd.
Smith Arnold C. (Highbury house) Thurlow rd.
Smith Arthur Clifford 123 King Henry's rd
Smith Basil Woodd (Branch hill lodge) Branch hill
Smith Benjamin Franklin (Holme house) Hampstead hill gardens
Smith Charles 70 Belsize park gardens
Smith Charles 1 Bolton rd.
Smith Charles 22 Flask walk
Smith Charles Lacey 55 Belsize rd.
Smith David 16 Loveridge rd.
Smith E. T. Aydon, L.S.A. 10 Alexandra rd
Smith Francis 132 King Henry's rd.
Smith Frederick 7 Netherwood st.
Smith Frederick 11 South hill park gdn
Smith Frederick W. 3 William ter.
Smith Fullarton (Fern lea) 8 Fordwych rd.
Smith G. 55 Ainger rd.
Smith George Albert (Lennyfield) Callingford rd.
Smith George Edward 21 Downshire hi
Smith George William 5 Claremont r

Smith Harry 11 West end lane

Smith Harry (The Forge) West end lane

Smith James (Manor cottage) Frognal

Smith James 1 Oak grove

Smith John 12 Ariel st.

Smith John 62 Belsize park

Smith John Charles 2 Gascony avenue

Smith Joseph 52 Gayton rd.

Smith J. Orton 11 Kemplay rd.

Smith J. Walter 8 Lawn rd.

Smith Miss 1 Cannon pl.

Smith Miss 8 Church row

Smith Miss 5 Oak hill park

Smith Miss 6 Parliament hill rd.

Smith Miss 14 Provost rd.

Smith Miss 105 South hill park

Smith Misses 3 College ter.

Smith Misses (Kenhurst) 47 South hill pk.

Smith Mrs. 2 Golder's hill ter.

Smith Mrs. 20 Goldhurst ter.

Smith Mrs. 2 Mansfield villas

Smith Mrs. 28 South hill park

Smith Mrs. 9 Upper Park rd.

Smith Mrs. Bruce 26 Well walk

Smith Mrs. B. Sydney 16 South hill pk.

Smith Mrs. Curwen 12 Oak hill park

Smith Mrs. Edward (Fairfield house) 43 Hampstead hill gardens

Smith Mrs. Fanny 2 Villas on the Heath

Smith Mrs. George 103 Belsize rd.

Smith Mrs. Jane 58 Belsize rd.

Smith Mrs. Thos. 105 King Henry's rd.

Smith Percy 4 Weech rd.

Smith Richard 2 Avenue villas

Smith Richard 33 St. John's wood park

Smith Richd. T., M.D. 53 Haverstock hill

Smith Robert 29 South hill park

Smith Sidney (Brooklands) West end ln.

Smith Sydney (Dorchester house) 28 Birchington rd.

Smith T. 17 Midland cottages

Smith Thomas 10 Midland cottages

Smith Thomas Elliot 67 Belsize pk. gdns.

Smith Thomas Eustace (Elm cottage) Rosslyn hill

Smith Vernon 12 Fellows rd.

Smith W., West end

Smith William 5 Elm ter.

Smith William Barnard (Suffolk house) 153 Maygrove rd.

Smith W. Crowther 23 Maygrove rd.

Smith W. H. (Boscobel) Hillfield rd.

Smith W. P. 5 Netherwood st.

Smither A. (Netley cottage) The Grove

Smithers Arthur E. (Holmefield) St. John's wood park

Smithers F. A. 171 Adelaide rd.

Smithers Fredk. W. 11 Parliament hill rd.

Smithers William 25 Steele's rd.

Smyth Archibald J. 9 Elsworthy rd.

Smyth Henry (Trent villa) 111 Iverson rd.

Smyth Luke D., M.D. (Dunnaweil) 21 Parliament hill rd.

Smyth Mrs. & Miss 39 Alexandra rd.

Smyth Mrs. 14 Springfield rd.

Snell Alfred Walter (Everley) Mill lane

Snell H. Sexton (Hillcotte) Netherhall ter.

Snellgrove Frederick 12 Buckland villas

Snow Harry (Fernleigh) 8 Fitzjohns' avn.

Snow Mrs. Fanny 122 King Henry's rd.

Snowball John (Fern villa) Quex rd.

Snowden Joseph (Abbotsford) 22 Fitzjohns' avenue

Snudden William L. 6 Elsworthy ter.

Soden James (Hawthorden) Worsley rd.

Sollas Wm. Henry 42 King Henry's rd.

Solomon Aaron 158 Alexandra rd.

Solomon Philip 49 King Henry's rd.

Solomons N. 73 Belsize rd.

Somers John B. S. 59 Belsize park

Somervail Mrs. C. R. 12 Greville rd.

Somerville David Hughes 1 Sumatra rd.

Somerville Mrs. 2 Rosslyn cottages

Sonnenberg Charles (Ovingdean) Cricklewood

Sonnenthal George 88 Boundary rd.

Sonnenthal Richard 123 Alexandra rd.

Sontaine A. 15 Parliament hill rd.

Soper George 183 Loveridge rd.

Soulby Anthony Morland (Winton lodge) Cricklewood

Southby Edmund R. 101 South hill park

Southey Mrs. Lucy 47 Boundary rd.

Southgate Mrs. Sarah 31 Birchington rd.

Southgate Thomas 130 Maygrove rd.

Southwell Charles (Gurrey lodge) Finchley rd. Child's hill

Southwood F. C. 30 Springfield rd.

Sowerby Edward Joseph 10 Medley rd.

Spackman Isaac T. 2 Kingsgate rd.

Spain John 4 Prince Arthur mews

Spain Lewis (Oaklands) West end lane

Spalding Henry, A.R.I.B.A. (Meadow bank) 8 Ellerdale rd.

Sparkes William 4 Church row

Sparks T. B. 41 Maygrove rd.

Spawforth Joseph 31 Parliament hill rd.

Spears Mrs. 4 Merton st.

Speer Dr. Stanhope Templeman 13 Alexandra rd.

Speer Charlton Templeman 13 Alexandra rd.

Speight William 9 Benham's pl.

Spence Ernest 30 Kingdon rd.

Spence James 8 Acol rd.
Spence Miss 11 Birchington rd.
Spencer Mrs. 8 Dynham rd.
Spencer Sydney (Chalcots) England ln.
Spencer William 105 Alexandra rd.
Spendley George 4 Prospect pl.
Speyer S. (Belsize lodge) 3 Garlinge rd.
Spicer Misses 63 Finchley new rd.
Spiers Edward(West view house)Christ-
   church passage
Spiller Mrs. 2 Oppidans rd.
Spiller William 66 Fitzjohns' avenue
Spiller William Cook 7 Thurlow rd.
Spiller William Hutchinson (Fairlight)
   Hampstead hill gardens
Spink John 11 Albion rd.
Spink Peter 30 Belsize sq.
Spink Thomas 20 Hillfield rd.
Spiring William Sainsbury 18 Gardnor
   road
Spofforth John Richard 3 Priory rd.
Spooner Mrs. (Sunnyside) Elsworthy rd.
Spratt Mrs. (Castelnau lodge) 10 Ford-
   wych rd.
Spray Thomas 17 Messina avenue
Spreat John Henry 47 Belsize sq.
Spring Alfred 63 Upper Park rd.
Spurrell Mrs. S. 3 Station villas
Spyers Arthur 11 Fordwych rd.
Squire Edmund Burnard, Upper ter.
Squire Josiah 25 Park rd.
Squire Mrs. 1 Thurlow rd.
Squire Peter Wyatt 40 Avenue rd.
Stacey Albert 14 Cricklewood ter.
Stacey Bartholomew 2 Cricklewood ter.
   Cricklewood lane
Stacey Thomas 1 Kingsford st.
Stacey W. S. (Hillcote) Heathfield
   gardens
Stagg William (The Limes) 27 West
   end lane
Stainer Alfred 4 Fordwych rd.
Staines Edward 36 Fairfax rd.
Staines Henry T. 2 Lawn rd.
Staines Mrs. 49 Alexandra rd.
Staines William Charles (West house)
   North end
Stainton Mrs. Sarah Sophia 186 Belsize rd.
Stair George 123 Iverson rd.
Stalder Thomas 52 Fleet rd.
Stammers Rev. F. H., M.A. (Wellesley
   house) Finchley new rd.
Stamp Miss 2 Christchurch rd.
Stamper Henry 21 Lichfield rd.
Stanfield Herbert 15 Lawn rd.
Staniland Charles 15 Steele's rd.
Stanlake Robert 6 Gardnor rd.

Stanley William Edward (Harlestone
   villa) Mortimer rd.
Stanley Miss 116 Adelaide rd.
Staples Chas. (Bath cott.) South end rd.
Staples Henry 2 Buckland villas
Staples John, F.S.A. 87 Avenue rd.
Staples John 16 Belsize rd.
Stapleton Miss 32 St. George's rd.
Starkey William John 72 Boundary rd.
Starling Frederick 34 Flask walk
Starling Matthew Hy. 146 Alexandra rd.
Starling Robert Barker 37 Adamson rd.
Startin Charles(Fairlight)3 Ellerdale rd.
Statham Alfred (Hawthorn cottage)
   Vale of Health
Statham Frederick George 27 Prospect rd.
Stedall Henry 25 Devonshire pl.
Stedall Henry (Heath end) Heath end
Stedall Thomas 25 Flask walk
Steel Thomas 44 Belsize park
Steele Mrs. Sarah Blake 37 Stanley gdns.
Steet G. Carrick, F.R.C.S. 130 King
   Henry's rd.
Steger Mrs. 174 Iverson rd.
Steinberg Nicholas 5 Avenue villas
Steinberg N. S. E. 52 Upper Park rd.
Steinkopff Edward (Oak hill lodge) Oak
   hill park
Stengel Charles 37 Bolton rd.
Stenhouse Frank 14 Lyndhurst rd.
Stenhouse Mrs. 14 Lyndhurst rd.
Stephens Alexander 20 Buckland cres.
Stephens Benjamin 19 Maygrove rd.
Stephens Charles Viret 180 Alexandra rd.
Stephens William 20 Belsize rd.
Stephenson George 16 Belsize avenue
Stephenson John William J. 119 King
   Henry's rd.
Stern Ferdinand 8 Buckland cres.
Stevens George 1 Fortune green
Stevens George 5 Watt's cottages
Stevens G. W. 11 Maresfield gardens
Stevens Henry, F.S.A. 13 Up. Avenue rd
Stevens James Edmund (Wilton villa
   17 St. George's rd.
Stevens John 147 Belsize rd. Kilburn
Stevens Thomas 17 Ash grove
Stevens Thomas Alfred (Rose lodge)
   New end sq.
Stevenson Edmond 43 Downshire hill
Stevenson Frederick 24 Fairfax rd.
Stevenson Gideon 19 Springfield rd.
Stevenson Robert Wm. 18 Stanley gdns
Steward Miss 3 Sumatra rd.
Stewart Rev. George 3 Richmond villa
Stewart George A. (Braemar lodge) 3
   West end lane

Stewart Horatio 30 Belsize park
Stewart John 10 Gayton cres.
Stewart Miss Susan 89 Adelaide rd.
Stickland Charles 10 Maygrove rd.
Stiffe J. G. 154 Alexandra rd.
Stillwell Mrs. (East cote) 75 Priory rd.
Stock Eugene 130 Haverstock hill
Stock William 92 Iverson rd.
Stoddart Charles (Dettingen) Broadhurst gardens
Stohwasser Francis J. (Warwick lodge) 103 Priory rd.
Stokes Isaac 4 Providence pl.
Stone C. W. 291 High rd.
Stone Mrs. 95 Priory rd.
Stone Simeon (The Hollies) 7 Haverstock ter.
Stone Thomas 173 Loveridge rd.
Stone William E.(Lyndhurst)Hillfield rd.
Storey George Adolphus (Hougoumont) Broadhurst gardens
Story Henry John 83 Alexandra rd.
Stott David 25 Springfield rd.
Stott John, F.I.A., F.S.S. 7 Buckland cres
Stott Mrs. 4 Goldhurst ter.
Stovell Frederick 40 Belsize rd.
Stow Montague H. 6 Maresfield gardens
Strafford Miss 132 Adelaide rd.
Strange W. Heath, M.D. 2 Belsize avenue
Straube Albert(Fern bank)East Heath rd.
Strauss Max 18 Fellows rd.
Strauss Mrs. Seigfried 23 Fellows rd.
Strauss Otto 23 Buckland cres.
Street George 3 Lower ter.
Streeter Edwin W. (The Mount) 4 Primrose hill rd.
Stretch Matthew 3 Steele's studios
Strickland Alfred 110 Abbey rd. Kilburn
Strickland Robert 7 Woodchurch rd.
Strickland Wm. Chas. 44 Alexandra rd.
Strickland William George 32 Priory rd.
Stride H. Phillips 35 Kilburn priory
Stringer Alfred Herbert 7 Medley rd.
Stroh Augustus 98 Haverstock hill
Strong Leonard Ernest 108 Belsize rd.
Strong William 15 Avenue villas
Strudwick W. 5 Belgrave gardens
Strugnell George F. 23 St. George's rd.
Stuart Charles (Hermitage) Cleve rd.
Stuart Jno. E. (Fairview)2 Arkwright rd.
Stubbings Frederick (Catherine cottage) Flask walk
Stubbings James 15 Prospect rd.
Stubbs Wm. (Woodstock) 83 Priory rd.
Stuckey W. A. (Mona villa) Hillfield rd.
Sturgess John 118 Adelaide rd.
Sturgis Mrs. 21 Kilburn priory

Stutely Miss 65 Belsize park
Stutfield Wm. 57 Belsize park gardens
Styche Miss E. 30 Flask walk
Styer Walter 12 Eton rd.
Styer William 25 Fellows rd.
Suarez F. 1 Fairhazel gardens
Such Edwin C., MUS. BAC. CANTAB. 23 Ainger rd.
Sugden Mrs.(Roxford ho.)13 Adamson rd
Sulivan Miss (The Mansion) Frognal
Sulley Joseph 57 Adelaide rd.
Sullivan John 12 Harley rd.
Sullivan Mrs. (Fernleigh) 9 Kingdon rd.
Summerfield William 16 Church lane
Sumner Miss 62 Adelaide rd.
Sumpter G. J. 29 Elm grove
Sumption William 14 Prospect rd.
Surtees Robert W. (Campvale) 3 Daleham gardens
Sutcliffe John 3 Christchurch rd.
Sutherland Mrs. 27 Loveridge rd.
Sutherland Mrs. 28 Springfield rd.
Sutton Mrs. Sarah 22 Belsize rd.
Svendson Olaf 6 Belsize ter.
Swan Robert 2 Belsize ter.
Swann Henry Thomas 41 Belsize avenue
Swears James Fredk. 113 Finchley rd.
Sweeting Mrs. 3 Abbott's rd.
Swift Edward (Alpine cottage) Holly bush hill
Swinburn F. 4 Carlingford rd.
Swords Thomas (Jasmine ho.) Frognal
Syer John (Atherstone ho.)74 Fellows rd.
Syme David John 3 Medley rd.
Symmons Miss 1 Claremont ter.
Symonds Mrs. 4 Boundary rd.
Symons William C. (Chestnut lodge) Squire's mount

Tagart Misses (Manor lodge) Frognal
Tagert Miss 43 Belsize park gardens
Tait Adam (Wingfield lodge) Well walk
Talbot Chas.(Alton lo.)40 Haverstockhill
Tanner Mrs.(Franklands) West end lane
Tanner Nathaniel 133 Belsize rd. Kilburn
Tanner William 64 Loudoun rd.
Tansley George 167 Adelaide rd.
Tape Arthur Stanley 61 King Henry's rd.
Taplin Mrs. 7 Gascony avenue
Tapson Robt. (Montem) 13 Elsworthy rd.
Tarbox Edward 8 College cres.
Tasker Francis (Hedge Bank) Finchley new rd.
Tate Edwin (Frognal priory) Frognal
Tatham J. Perceval 16 Lyndhurst rd.
Tatham Miss (Arleux) Broadhurst gdns.
Tawse George 193 Belsize rd. Kilburn

Tayler Edward 3 Alexandra rd.
Taylor Alfred, The Mount
Taylor Charles 10 Albion rd.
Taylor C. L. 5 Belsize avenue
Taylor Edwin 3 Lichfield rd.
Taylor Enoch 25 Albion rd.
Taylor Frank 150 Iverson rd.
Taylor Frederick, Cricklewood
Taylor Frederick 22 St. John's wood pk.
Taylor George 5 Grove cottages
Taylor John 80 South hill park
✳ Taylor John Mann (Norheads) 5 Fitz-
    johns' avenue ←
Taylor John T. (Westcourt) 19 Wood-
    church rd.
Taylor Mrs. 143 Belsize rd. Kilburn
Taylor Mrs. A. M. 72 Belsize rd.
Taylor Mrs. Sarah 4 Alfred ter.
Taylor Richard 27 Belsize cres.
Taylor Thomas 106 Iverson rd.
Taylor William George 34 Belsize sq.
Tebbut Mrs. 19 Belsize rd.
Tegetmeier Miss 18 King Henry's rd.
Telfer Mrs. 24 Harley rd.
Temple Sir Richard, bart. 2 Holford rd.
Temple Robt. Scott (Lawn bank)John st.
Terrero Maximo 88 Belsize pk. gardens
Terry E. (Norfolk villa) Cricklewood
Terry James 25 Palmerston rd.
Tetley Joseph 77 Priory rd.
Thairlwall Mrs. 5 Provost rd.
Thatcher James 21 Palmerston rd.
Thatcher Thomas 43 Fairfax rd.
Thatcher William 13 West end lane
Theakstone Fawdington 39 Fordwych rd.
Thick H. G. 266 High rd.
Thies Conrad 6 Goldhurst ter.
Thistleton-Dyer Rev. T. F. (Beckland)
    West end lane
Thistlewaite Frederick (The Cottage)
    Fortune green
Thomas Rev. J. Davies (Ingleside) 15
    Denning rd.
Thomas Frank 7 Boundary rd.
Thomas John (Rowton ho.)Lancaster rd.
Thomas John (Heathcroft) Worsley rd.
Thomas Michael 24 Springfield rd.
Thomas Miss 17 Christchurch rd.
Thomas Richard 31 King Henry's rd.
Thompson Rev. John Chas. 3 Gascony av.
Thompson Francis 25 Heath st.
Thompson Frederick (Kingswood) 12
    Mortimer rd.
Thompson Henry 9 Hampstead hill gdns.
Thompson James 27 Church row
Thompson John 66 Goldhurst rd.
Thompson Mrs. 27 Haverstock hill

Thompson Neale 148 King Henry's rd.
Thompson William 56 Gayton rd.
Thomson A. Forbes 52 South hill park
Thomson Hugh (Elleray) King Henry's rd
Thorn W. T. 49 Stanley gardens
Thornbury Bruce 19 Sherriff rd.
Thorne Arnold 1 Thompson's mews
Thorne Edwin R. (The Birches) 14 St
    John's wood park
Thorne William 3 Saunders cottages
Thornely Charles (Netherhall house)
    1 Netherhall ter.
Thornely Wm. (High Close) Holford rd
Thornhill Edward B. 13 Primrose hill rd
Thornicroft Thomas 75 Iverson rd.
Thornton G. (Sedgemoor) Arkwright rd
Thornton Thomas (Townley house) West
    end lane
Thornton W. D. 94 Priory rd.
Thorpe C. Stuart 15 Maygrove rd.
Thorpe Edward 4 Benham's pl.
Thorpe R. H. 24 Steel's rd.
Thorpe Thomas 5 King Henry's rd.
Threadgale R. E., M.D. 74 High rd.
Thunder C. 7 Station villas
Thwaites Jas. (Netley villa) Hillfield rd
Thwaites Otho 45 Adelaide rd.
Tibbals Miss 112 Iverson rd.
Tibberth Richard M. 10 Holly mount
Tice Mrs. 8 Gascony avenue
Tidd David (Lovedons) Ravenshaw st.
Tildesley David 6 Devonshire villas
Tildesley Edwin (Ridgmount)100 Priory
    road
Tilley Samuel 203 High rd.
Tillman John (Hillside) Sumatra rd.
Tilly A., L.S.A. (Marlborough house)
    10 Garlinge rd.
Timewell Hy.(Borne)Gainsborough gdn
Timme Oscar 68 Parliament hill rd.
Timms John and Mrs. 36 Downshire hil
Timms W. R. 4 Ainger rd.
Tink James 5 Golden yard
Titcombe — 6 The Mall
Tod Charles 11 Oppidans rd.
Todd Mrs. 7 Upper Avenue rd.
Tofts Rev. Francis 16 Gascony avenue
Told James Albert 23 Sumatra rd.
Told Tom 55 Upper Park rd.
Tole Edward 4 Palmerston rd.
Toll Charles Henry 156 Maygrove rd.
Toller Charles George 7 Oak hill park
Toller Mrs. C., East Heath rd.
Tollit Frederick 2 Winchester rd.
Tombs Mrs. (Holmwood house) 30 South
    hill park
Tombs Mrs. 1 Squire's mount cottages

Tombs William (Holmwood house) 30 South hill park

Tomlinson Joseph (Woodchurch) 64 Priory rd.

Tompkins Henry, C.E. 130 Alexandra rd.

Tompkins Mrs. E. 10 Claremont rd.

Tompkins Walter (Rose cottage) Mill lane

Toms Edmund 4 Chalcot gardens

Tongue Mrs. A. 1 Church rd.

Tongue William 6 Benham's pl.

Tonneau Joseph (Roucourt) Broadhurst gardens

Toombs Joseph 226 Belsize rd. Kilburn

Toomes Richard 14 Grove ter.

Tooth Anthony (Torbay vil.) Oppidans rd.

Topham Charles 9 Upper Avenue rd.

Topham F. W. W. (Ifield) 16 Prince Arthur rd.

Toplis Thomas James 4 Downshire hill

Topping John 5 Nassington rd.

Towell Mrs. 3 Kemplay rd.

Towers George 77 Adelaide rd.

Towle Edward 185 Adelaide rd.

Towler Charles 112 Belsize rd.

Townshend Arthur (Penlee) Hillfield rd.

Toye George 16 Prospect rd.

Toye William Thomas 14 Holly mount

Trail Mrs. 8 Belsize avenue

Treffry Miss 130 Belsize rd.

Trehern C. M. (Goodlands) Acol rd.

Tremellen John 5 Belsize sq.

Tremlett Rev. F. W., D.C.L. (The Parsonage) Belsize sq.

Tremlett T. D. (Stanmore villa) 6 Birchington rd.

Trewby George Careless (Fenton house) The Grove

Trickey Frank 36 Priory rd.

Triems Miss 3 Haverstock hill

Trier Moritz (Tredegar ho.) 3 Adamson rd.

Trill Peter 43 Iverson rd.

Trim William 127 Abbey rd. Kilburn

Trimmer Mrs. William 104 Adelaide rd.

Trinks Carl Heinrich 40 Ainger rd.

Trobridge Lewis 62 Belsize rd.

Trotter James Charles (Kimcote) 185 Belsize rd. Kilburn

Trudgett Stephen (Duncan cottage) South end rd.

Trufant Gilbert Carr (Boston house) 2 Cedar ter.

Trussell William 15 Palmerston rd.

Tuchmann Dr. Maro 148 Adelaide rd.

Tuchmann L. 120 Haverstock hill

Tuck Harry 54 Park rd.

Tucker Arthur 3 The Green

Tucker Francis L. 118 Iverson rd.

Tucker George 3 College villas rd.

Tucker Harry, Holly ter. Mount Vernon

Tucker Joseph 42 Fleet rd.

Tucker Mrs. 3 College villas rd.

Tuckman Charles 29 Belsize park

Tulloch James (Stambridge house) 7 Fitzjohns' avenue

Tullock G. (Chester house) Westcroft rd.

Tully E. 104 Maygrove rd.

Tully George 17 Loveridge rd.

Tunley George 44 Upper Park rd.

Tupman Charles 2 Lower ter.

Turnbull Alexander 118 Belsize park gardens

Turnbull Charles (Cotswold) 23 Fitzjohns' avenue

Turnbull Edward 9 Belsize park

Turnbull George C. 5 Fordwych rd.

Turnbull T. D. 5 South hill park gardens

Turner Rev. Frederick Storrs 8 Heathfield gardens

Turner Barrow 78 Abbey rd.

Turner George William 66 Park rd.

Turner Godfrey W. 28 King Henry's rd.

Turner Haswell Joseph (The Rowans) 9 Mortimer rd.

Turner Henry (Blenheim lodge) 71 Finchley new rd.

Turner H. J. (Newton lodge) 82 Priory rd.

Turner John 9 Kilburn vale

Turner John (Beech Holme) Shoot-up hill

Turner John (Sherwood house) 8 Woodchurch rd.

Turner Miss (Belsize college) 43 Belsize park gardens

Turner Mrs. 27 Greville rd.

Turner Mrs. 18 Provost rd.

Turner Nicholas (Florence villa) Hillfield rd.

Turner Peter 28 Steele's rd.

Turner Robert Drysdale, F.G.S. 64 Alexandra rd.

Turner William 35 Broadhurst gardens

Turner Wm. (Manor lo.) Vale of Health

Turner William Coham 41 Belsize rd.

Tuteur Max 110 Alexandra rd.

Tutton William 4 Granville ter.

Tweddell Mrs. 20 Fairfax rd.

Tweddle Linton Stewart 52 Belsize rd.

Tweedie Robert 124 Abbey rd. Kilburn

Twentyman Colonel Augustus 5 Winchester rd.

Twinberrow James Kimberley (Madresfield) Acol rd. Abbey rd.

Twyford John 6 King's cottages

Tyer Edwd. (Horneck) 16 Fitzjohns' avn.

Tyler Henry 19 Gardnor rd.

Tyson Mrs. 9 Gayton cres.
TyssenAmhurst Dnl., D.C.L. 59 Priory rd.

Ullmann E. 16 Kilburn priory
Underhill Edward Bean, LL D. (Derwent lodge) Thurlow rd.
Underwood Mrs. 26 Albion rd.
Unwin George (Wisteria) 119 Priory rd.
Unwin Thos. (Geneva ho.) Cricklewood
Urwick Rev Wm.49 Belsize park gardens
Uttin Mrs. 1 Sunnyside villas
Uubelen M. (Percy cottage) College rd.
Uzielli Theodore (Hillside) 49 Fitzjohns' avenue

Vaile Thomas H. (Meadow ville) Acol rd.
Van CampMarieAntoinetta 6 Kingdon rd.
Vandervelde Emanuel (Volta house) Windmill hill
Vander Weyde Henry (Hawthorne lodge) 2 Albion rd.
Vanlessan N. 39 Park rd.
Van Praagh Isaac 64 Fellows rd.
Vansittart-Neale Edward 12 Church row
Vant Frederick Augustus 5 Ariel st.
Van-Wyhe Mrs.(Bracknell)West end ln.
Van Wyk W. 25 Claremont rd.
Vasmer Theodor (The Homestead) West end
Vassie Mrs. 265 High rd. Kilburn
Vaughan-Jones Maj. 11 Devonshire hill
Venables Mrs. (Iver) Nutley gardens
VenningWalterC.45 Belsize park gardens
Verey George (Holmby grange) Shoot-up hill
Verity George Hamilton 7 Fairfax rd.
Vernon Arthur 20 Belgrave rd.
Vernon Mrs. Annie 168 Adelaide rd.
Vert Narciso 28 Elsworthy rd.
Very John 84 Boundary rd.
Vey George 158 Maygrove rd.
Videcoq A. 60 Fellows rd.
Vigurs John 2 Lower Lawn rd.
Vincent Dr. Charles 19 Gayton rd.
Vincent Mrs. 8 Oakland ter.
Vincent William 39 Fleet rd.
Vine Thomas William 55 Flask walk
Viner Lewis (Springfield) Elsworthy rd.
Viret Benjamin Pope 115 Alexandra rd.
Vizard Philip Edward (Fernlea) 10 Ellerdale rd.
Voight L. R. 65 Fellows rd.
Voigt S. E. (Maresfield house) 8 Maresfield gardens
Vokins Mrs. Mary (Hereford villa) 94 Abbey rd.
Vooght John 16 Maygrove rd.

Wadd H. C. 8 Lansdown ter.
Waddelow J.R.,B.A. OXON. 21Greville rd.
Waddelow W. 21 Greville rd.
Waddleton J. 8 Ravenshaw st.
Wade Alfred 4 Kingsgate rd.
Wadlow Henry George (Albion villa) Hillfield rd.
Wadmore Rev. Henry Robinson, M.A. 15 Fairfax rd.
Waggett F. (The Limes) 28 Oppidans rd.
Wagner H. 6 Steele's rd.
Wainewright Robert A. 58 Avenue rd.
Wainwright Mrs. 9 The Village
Wainwright Mrs., West end
Wainwright Richard 168 Belsize rd
Wakefield John 44 Downshire hill
Wakerley Mrs. 138 Iverson rd.
Walden Emanuel 31 Prospect rd.
Walden Mrs. 9 Loveridge rd.
Wale Frederick 112 South hill park
Walford Cornelius 86 Belsize park gdns.
Walford Walter Gilson, M.D. 49 Finchley new rd.
Walker Rev.Clement Frank, M.A. OXON. (Heath mount) Heath mount
Walker A. C. 8 Belsize cres.
Walker Andrew Gillon 46 St. John's wood park
Walker Chas. (Silverlea) Willoughby rd.
Walker Francis (Wychcombe villa) England's lane
Walker George S. (Cavendish house) Cricklewood
Walker James 11 Elsworthy ter.
Walker John George 90 Abbey rd.
Walker John James, M.A., F.R.S. (Cannycot) 21 Rudall cres.
Walker Miss 36 Elsworthy rd.
Walker Mrs. 6 Elsworthy rd.
Walker Mrs. (Ravensdowne) 7 Elsworthy rd.
Walker Mrs. (Ashleigh) Gascony avenue
Walker Mrs. 44 Gascony avenue
Walker Mrs. G. F. 5 Carlingford rd.
Walker Mrs. Sydney 58 Springfield rd.
Walker R. W. 18 Claremont rd.
Walker W. J. R. 9 Buckland cres.
Wall Miss 115 Iverson rd.
Wallace Col. W. H. 158 King Henry's rd.
Wallace Alexander 15 Eton villas
Wallace Miss A. 146 Iverson rd.
Wallace Mrs. 116 Iverson rd.
Walliker E. H. J. 3 Elm grove
Wallington Isaac 1 Castle ter.
Wallis Arthur 1 Springfield rd.
Wallis Richard 4 Lower Lawn rd.
Wallman Charles 2 Bolton rd.

Walls Mrs. 10 Daleham gardens
Walter Charles 248 Belsize rd. Kilburn
Walter Jacob (Mablethorpe) Cleve rd.
Walters George S. 134 Adelaide rd.
Walters William 11 Cricklewood ter.
Walther Philip 67 Avenue rd.
Walton George 50 Park rd.
Walton Miss 1 Goldhurst rd.
Walton R. 5 Elsworthy ter.
Walton Thomas 14 Elsworthy ter.
Walton W. G. 3 Springfield
Warburg Edward (Elling lodge) Arkwright rd.
Warburg Herman 11 Lichfield rd.
Ward Charles A. 159 Haverstock hill
Ward Ernest 31 Kingsgate rd.
Ward H. L. D. 82 South hill park
Ward John Charles (The Retreat) 24 Haverstock hill
Ward John Inett 18 Belsize park grdns.
Ward Matthew 8 Golder's hill ter.
Ward Mrs. (Maescwyn) 23 Parliament hill rd.
Ward Nelson 8 Lancaster rd.
Ward William 1 & 2 Belgrave gardens
Ward William 11 Loveridge rd.
Wardell Miss 55 Stanley gardens
Wardle John 18 Bolton rd.
Wardle Robert (The Lodge) Cricklewood lane
Wardroper Frederick 139 Abbey rd. Kilburn
Wardroper Henry 85 Belsize rd.
Ware Richard 2 Claremont ter. Heath st.
Ware Mrs. E. 4 Springfield rd.
Ware Mrs. Robert 15 Gayton rd.
Warmuth Edmund 44 Avenue rd.
Warne Charles 6 Yorkshire Grey rd.
Warne Frederick 2 Hilgrove rd.
Warne John 145 King Henry's rd.
Warne Mrs. 2 Golden yard
Warner John 2 Murray ter.
Warner Miss M. A. 28 Downshire hill
Warner Mrs. 86 South hill park
Warner Robert 10 Priory rd.
Warner Sydney Gates 4 Belsize ter.
Warner W. H. 11 Wildwood grove
Warr Mrs. 4 The Village
Warren Charles 5 Holly mount
Warren James Thomas 26 Midland cotts.
Warren John, Holly mount
Wartenberg S. (Montague house) Cricklewood
Warwick Joseph 3 King's cottages
Wash Henry 41 Downshire hill
Wason Eugene 63 Belsize avenue
Wass Mrs. S. E. 26 Adelaide rd.

Wastnage Percy (Clarence house) Hillfield rd.
Waterhouse Thomas Greaves (Sunnyfield) West heath
Waterhouse William Dakin, B.A., LL.D. (Ovoca) 18 Woodchurch rd.
Waterlow Charles 20 Elsworthy rd.
Waterlow David S. (Fairlight) 81 Priory rd.
Waters Captain George Alexander, R.N. 26 Stanley gardens
Watkins Rev. W. J. 19 Fordwych rd.
Watkins Chs. A. (Rosemont) Greenhill rd.
Watkins William 6 Willow cottages
Watling David (Elm cottage) Mill lane
Watson Alfred 50 Kingsgate rd.
Watson E. 6 Lancaster pl.
Watson Edward 18 Carlingford rd.
Watson Edward 5 Lancaster rd.
Watson George 34 Fleet rd.
Watson George 5 Harley rd.
Watson Henry (Redholme) Broadhurst gardens
Watson Isaac 20 Avenue villas
Watson John 78 Adelaide rd.
Watson Johnston, Fitzjohns' mansions (2nd floor)
Watson Mrs. 108 Abbey rd. Kilburn
Watson Mrs. 30 St. George's rd.
Watson Mrs. G. 5 Gascony avenue
Watson Mrs. H. 10 Iverson rd.
Watson Napoleon Frederick 172 Adelaide rd.
Watson Wm. (Carlile villa) Willow rd.
Watson W. C. 103 South hill park
Watt Alexander 20 Flask walk
Watt Alexander Pollock 117 Alexandra rd.
Watt Fredk. (Saltram) 17 Woodchurch rd.
Watts Charles 6 Mansfield pl.
Watts Charles 36 Prospect rd.
Watts Henry 151 King Henry's rd.
Watts Henry Wm. 12 Broadhurst gdns.
Watts Hus in Wm. (The Hive) Greenhill rd
Watts Miss 4 Watt's cottages
Watts Mrs. 50 Adelaide rd.
Watts Mrs., Golder's hill cottages
Watts Mrs. 1 Heath mount
Watts Mrs. 11 Lawn rd.
Watts Mrs. (Clare house) Rosslyn hill
Watts Thomas 23 New end
Watts William M. 35 Belsize park
Waugh Edgar Weller 15 Ainger rd.
Waugh James 5 Steele's rd.
Waugh T. W. Spenser 44 Stanley gardns.
Way Mrs. 127 Belsize rd.
Way Thomas (Benthall house) 2 Hampstead green
Waymouth Frederick 6 Narcissus rd.

Weal — 59 Springfield rd.
Weanhausen David 17 Eton villas
Wear Jonathan (Swanscombe) Carling-
  ford rd.
Weatherall Henry 21 Belsize park gdns.
Webb Alfred 6 Avenue villas
Webb Benjamin William 5 Medley rd.
Webb Charles 86 Maygrove rd.
Webb Conrade Elliott (Wildwood lodge)
  North end
Webb F. H. 53 Stanley gardens
Webb Horatio (West hill lo.) 4 Lower ter
Webb James 26 Belsize sq.
Webb Mrs. 52 Messina avenue
Webb Mrs. 30 New end
Webb Mrs. (Park lodge) Oppidans rd.
Webb Thomas 43 Gayton rd.
Webb Thomas 82 Maygrove rd.
Webb William Robert 7 Grafton ter.
Webber Chas. (Ivy cott.) 78 Upper Park rd
Webber John 16 Belgrave rd.
Webber Mrs. 9 Sherriff rd.
Weber Otto 24 Greville rd.
Webster Edward 3 Lower Heath cotts.
Weddell Wm. (Fernleigh) Worsley rd.
Wedderburn Mrs. 19 Haverstock hill
Wedmore Fred 6 Thurlow rd.
Weedon Misses 181 Belsize rd. Kilburn
Weedon W. T. 3 Benham's pl.
Weekes Mrs. 24 Belsize rd.
Weekes William 21 Oppidans rd.
Weeks Mrs. Mary, North end
Weight James 168 Haverstock hill
Weir James 3 Heath mount
Weir John Alexander 7 Daleham gdns.
Weir Mrs. (Up. Frognal lodge) Frognal
Weiss Mrs. (Birch Bank) Christchurch rd.
Welch Amos 1 Oakland ter.
Welch J. B. 1 Hillfield rd.
Welch William 16 Yorkshire Grey yard
Weldon H. (Churchill) 73 Priory rd.
Weldon Mrs. 70 Belsize rd.
Weller Daniel 23 Granville ter.
Wellings John 5 Willoughby rd.
Wellington James 38 Fellows rd.
Wells Sir Spencer, bart. (Golder's hill)
  North end
Wells Rev. Edward 21 Buckland cres.
Wells Charles, M.D. 13 College cres.
Wells John 7 Albion rd.
Wells Josiah (Mansfield house) 16
  Mansfield villas
Welsh James Edward 110 South hill park
W lsh Miss J. (Egremont house) Kem-
  play rd.
Welsh Mrs. Elizabeth Kirkley 152 King
  Henry's rd.

Welsh William 189 Sumatra rd.
Welton Charles 27 Downshire hill
Wenham Henry James (Wildwood)
  North end
Wessels Mrs. (Bremen ho.) Gascony avn.
West Edward 7 Richmond villas
West G. 53 Kingsgate rd.
West John Thomas H. 9 Eton villas
West Mrs. (Maythorne) 1 Denning rd.
West Mrs. Clifton 78 Boundary rd.
West W. T. 20 Lichfield rd.
Westbury Mrs. Ruth 122 Adelaide rd.
Westlake Mrs. 73 Adelaide rd.
Westlake Mrs. 12 Lansdowne ter.
Westlake N. J. (Falcon house) Quex rd.
Westland Albert, M.D. 17 Belsize park
Weston Alfred 3 Grafton ter.
Wetherbee G. F. 12 Chalcot gardens
Wettenhall — 3 Thompson's mews
Weygang William 7 Hermitage villas
Whalley Adolphus J. 1a Steele's studios
  Haverstock hill
Wharton Henry Thornton, M.A., M.R.C.S.,
  F.Z.S. 39 St. George's rd.
Wharton James 10 Buckland cres.
Wheatley Frederick 23 Midland cotts.
Wheeler Charles Molard (St. Mary's
  lodge) 134 Abbey rd. Kilburn
Wheeler Edward 4 Thompson's mews
Whetham Charles Langley 40 Albion rd.
Whiddington John Chilvers (Tickenhall)
  Hillfield rd.
Whitaker J. (Hillside) 6 Primrose hill rd.
Whitaker John L. 18 Belgrave rd.
Whitaker Thomas (Sandford house)
  159 King Henry's rd.
Whitaker Thomas 7 Spencer ter.
Whitaker William 2 Belsize rd.
Whitcher John, F.S.S. 5 Chalcot gardens
Whitcher John 86 Palmerston rd.
Whitchurch Edwin 1 Prospect rd.
White Adolphus Charles 36 Park rd.
White Charles 2 Prospect villas
White Charles Stewart 85 Finchley rd.
White Christopher W. 13 Up. Park rd.
White John 78 Park rd.
White John L. (Ivy house) North end
White John Power 40 Upper Park rd.
White Miss 12 Christchurch rd.
White Miss 2 East Heath rd.
White Mrs. Caroline 33 Kingsgate rd.
White Robert 43 Belsize sq.
White Thomas Jennings 17 Fairfax rd.
White William 4 Kemplay rd.
White Wm. (Caroline house) The Mount
White William (Holly cottage) The
  Mount

White William Henry (Cromer house) 50 Maygrove rd.
White Zachariah (York ho.) Rosslyn hill
Whitehead Miss 80 Park rd.
Whitehead Thos. Jas. 92 Alexandra rd.
Whitestone P. B. 17 Prospect rd.
Whitfield Miss 97 Fellows rd.
Whitfield Thos.(Essex lo.) 3 Boundary rd.
Whitham Mrs. 92 King Henry's rd.
Whiting William 18 Midland cottages
Whitmore William 34 Midland cottages
Whittle Mrs. Sarah 30 Fleet rd.
Whitworth Benj., M.P. 22 Daleham gdns.
Whitworth Mrs. 80 Belsize rd.
Whorne George 29 Netherwood st.
Whyte Robert 51 King Henry's rd.
Whythe Mrs. 1 Loveridge rd.
Wibberley Frederick 17 Hillfield rd.
Wich Frederick G. 18 Eton villas
Wicks Mrs. 6 Grove ter.
Wigley John 100 Maygrove rd.
Wigley Mrs. 102 Abbey rd. Kilburn
Wigram Rev. F. E., M.A. (Oak hill house) Oak hill park
Wike John Mellin 25 Upper Park rd.
Wilcox John 2 Oakland ter.
Wild C. Kemp (Thornlea) 69 Fitzjohns' avenue
Wildash Fredk. Charles 33 Stanley gdns.
Wildy Arthur 48 Albion rd.
Wildy L. (Homelea) 16 Woodchurch rd.
Wilkes John Staley (Staley house) 1 Claremont rd.
Wilkey Charles Edward 144 Abbey rd. Kilburn
Wilkie Edmund 114 Maygrove rd.
Wilkin Martin Hood (Sydney house) Pilgrim's lane
Wilkin Miss (Cossey cot.) Pilgrim's lane
Wilkins Henry 51 Kingsgate rd.
Wilkinson Alexander 31 Belgrave rd.
Wilkinson G. 3 Oakland ter.
Wilkinson John Robt. 2 Upper Park rd.
Wilkinson Joseph 2 Foley avenue
Wilkinson Miss 61 Adelaide rd.
Willans J. G. (Westcroft) 68 Priory rd.
Willett Ansley Henry 7 Heath villas
Willett Hy. Jasper 31 Broadhurst gdns.
Willey Josiah (Buckland house) Quex rd.
Willey Mrs. 8 Greville rd.
Williams Major-General H. E. T. 23 South hill park gardens
Williams Charles 163 Belsize rd. Kilburn
Williams Charles 170 High rd.
Williams Charles 20 Midland cottages
Williams George 8 Fairhazel gardens
Williams George L. 31 Fleet rd.

Williams J. 5 Squire's Mount cottages
Williams Jas. 2 Wildwood gro. North end
Williams John 86 Abbey rd.
Williams John 2 Yorkshire Grey yard
Williams John C. 6 Hilgrove rd.
Williams John Haynes (Wridhern) Maresfield gardens
Williams Joseph Crew 30 Goldhurst ter.
Williams Miss (Belmont house and York house) 24 Kilburn priory
Williams Mrs. 57 Stanley gardens
Williams Mrs. (Kingston Lisle) Willoughby rd.
Williams Mrs. Hannah 154 Adelaide rd.
Williams Thos. (Yarth ho.) Greenhill rd.
Williams Thornton Arthur 2 Pilgrim's ln.
Williams W. 9 Golder's hill ter.
Williams W. H. 12 Belsize cres.
Williams Wm. P. 141 King Henry's rd.
Williamson A. W. 28 Primrose hill rd.
Willing Jas., jun.(Rock hall) Cricklewood
Willing James 60 Upper Park rd.
Willis A. K. 15 Greville rd.
Willis Arthur K.(Gascony ho)West end ln
Willis James 1 Gayton rd.
Willis Mrs. 6 Hampstead green
Willis Mrs. 22 St. George's rd.
Willis Mrs. Eleanor 3 Albion rd.
Willis Walter, A.K.C. 9 Priory rd.
Willis William 15 Lithos rd.
Willmott William 42 Downshire hill
Wills Charles, M.D. (Broadhurst house) Broadhurst gardens
Wills C. A. 13 Fitzjohns' parade
Wills Peter 5 Greville rd.
Wills William 29 Gayton rd.
Willson T. J. 26 West end lane
Willson William (Pino) 104 Priory rd.
Wilman Mrs. 24 King Henry's rd.
Wilmer Miss C. (Elm tree house) Hampstead green
Wilmot Charles (Maygrove cottage) 170 Maygrove rd.
Wilson Alfred Harry 13 Priory rd.
Wilson Crawford 2 Merton rd.
Wilson Edward James 135 Adelaide rd.
Wilson Fredk. 165 Belsize rd. Kilburn
Wilson F. F. 7 Birchington rd.
Wilson George 1 The Mall
Wilson John 27 Kingsgate rd.
Wilson Julius 10 Maresfield gardens
Wilson Miss 23 Belsize avenue
Wilson Miss 16 Boundary rd.
Wilson Miss (Gilling lo.) Haverstock ter.
Wilson Mrs. 3 Bolton rd.
Wilson Mrs. (The Laurels) 8 Sherriff rd.
Wilson Mrs. 45 Upper Park rd.

Wilson Mrs. J. W. (Gordon house) 17 Primrose hill rd.

Wilson R. (St. Kilda) 6 Netherhall ter.

Wilson Robert 2 Park rd.

Wilson Stephen Barton 25 Boundary rd.

Wilson Sydney 11 Winchester rd.

Wiltshire George 1 Golden sq.

Winchester William (Durham villa) 3 Birchington rd. Kilburn

Windebank William (Alma cottage) Holly mount

Windle Job 72 Maygrove rd.

Windsor James 5 Child's hill cottages

Wingate Charles Geo. 51 Netherwood st.

Winn James Michell, M.D. 21 Goldhurst ter.

Winter Emil 5 Buckland villas

Winter Ernest 14 Bolton rd.

Winter Robert (Eland ho.) Rosslyn hill

Winterbon E. 25 King Henry's rd.

Winterton W. R. 1 Mortimer rd.

Wintle Mrs. 5 Perrins court

Winyard William, sen., West end

With Rev. A. R., M.A. 6 Heath rise

Witham Mrs. M. A. 184 Loveridge rd.

Wither Charles (Barmore) 2 Hilltop rd.

Withers Alfred 31 Greville rd.

Witt G. R. 71 Springfield rd.

Witty Richard James (Terrace lodge) The Grove

Woern Lieut. Carl 132 Haverstock hill

Wolff Rudolph 7 Eton rd.

Wolff S. 69 Belsize park gardens

Womack Frederick, M.B., B.SC., LOND. 11 Kingdon rd.

Womack James 68 Abbey rd.

Womack John (Sutherland house) 101 Abbey rd. S.J.W.

Wood A. B. (Bolton ho.) Windmill hill

Wood Charles William 80 Avenue rd.

Wood David P. (Elim) Lyndhurst gdns.

Wood Henry 19 Kilburn priory

Wood H. K. 21 Belsize cres.

Wood James 1 Willow cottages

Wood John 30 Bolton rd.

Wood John 95 Fellows rd.

Wood Lewis J. 23 Park rd.

Wood Mrs. (Ashbury house) 16 St. John's wood park

Wood R. J. 117 Haverstock hill

Wood Richard James 13 Oppidans rd.

Wood Sidney 15 Hilgrove rd.

Wood Thomas 15 Crossfield rd.

Wood Wm.(The Rowans) 24 Thurlow rd.

Wood W. G. 35 Fordwych rd.

Woodall Corbet, C.E. 50 Fitzjohns' avenue

Woodall Frederick 76 South hill park

Woodcock Mrs. 2 Goldhurst ter.

Woodd Charles Henry Lardner (Rosslyn house) Lyndhurst rd.

Woodd Robert Ballard (Woodlands) Haverstock hill

Woodin Mrs. 5 Mortimer rd.

Woodley John 119 Abbey rd. Kilburn

Woodley Thomas 29 Midland cottages

Woodley Thomas 54 South hill park

Woodman Cornelius 16&17 Downshire hl.

Woodman Miss 28 Fairfax rd.

Woodrooffe Mrs. G. H. 5 Well walk

Woods Arthur 19 Flask walk

Woodthorpe Enos 4 Lithos rd.

Woodthorpe Mrs. 71 Haverstock hill

Woodward J. 32 Flask walk

Woodward Robert 6 Claremont rd.

Woodyear Samuel 11 The Village

Woof Henry (St. Alban's villa) John st.

Woolf Mortimer 3 Acol rd.

Woolford Thomas 22 Devonshire pl.

Woollams Mrs. Elizabeth 84 Avenue rd.

Woollan Miss (Beaufort) 2 Kingdon rd.

Woollcombe Richard 5 Eton rd.

Wordley James 117a Haverstock hill

Wornum George Porter 20 Belsize sq.

Wornum Mrs. 20 Belsize sq.

Worsop Mrs. Louisa 54 Belsize rd.

Wortham Frederick 50 Belsize rd.

Wray A. W. 29 Stanley gardens

Wrentmore Isaac H. 27 Upper Park rd.

Wright Chas. Edward 33 Fordwych rd.

Wright Edward 180 Belsize rd.

Wright Edward 3 Maygrove rd.

Wright George 15 Kingsgate rd.

Wright James 16 Belsize park gardens

Wright John Lawrence 190 Belsize rd.

Wright Mrs. (Blythswood house) Belsize park

Wright Mrs. 38 Boundary rd.

Wright Mrs. 16 Winchester rd.

Wright Mrs. H. (The Heath) Hampstead heath

Wright Robert 79 Netherwood st.

Wright Thomas 55 Netherwood st.

Wright T. H. (Blythswood house) Belsize park

Wright W. J. (Augusta villa) 60 Haverstock hill

Wrightson Leonard 96 South hill park

Wrightson Mrs.(Beaumont lodge) Oppidans rd.

Wrottesley Rev. Francis John, B.A. 3 Goldhurst rd.

Wroughton Mrs. General 3 Greville rd.

Wulfson Miss Johana 158 Adelaide rd.

Wurtzburg Edwd. Albert 46 Stanley gdns.

Wyatt Mrs. 40 Messina avenue
Wyatt Vitruvius (Ivor) Goldhurst rd.
Wyatt William Thomas 137 Iverson rd.
Wyburn Robert 30 Maygrove rd.
Wyer Joseph 4 West cottages
Wyman Charles William Henry 103 King Henry's rd.
Wynn Mrs. M. A. (Coleby lodge) 150 Abbey rd. Kilburn
Wynne Henry Lifton 69 Alexandra rd.
Wynyard William 25 Sumatra rd.
Wyon Allan 14 Broadhurst gardens
Wyon Mrs. 23 Belsize rd.

Yates George 38 Midland cottages
Yates William 16 Kingsgate rd.
Yeatman Miss 27 Claremont rd.
Yeld Edward 21 Park rd.
Yeo Alfred William (Ideside) 4 Cedar ter.
Yeo Thomas 98 Priory rd.
Yerbury Francis William 7 Ash grove

Yescombe Mrs. 14 Messina avenue
Yewens John White 22 South hill park gardens
York Robert 152 Iverson rd.
Youatt G. H. 17 Oppidans rd.
Youll Miss 9 North end
Young Major-General Ralph 70 Finchley new rd.
Young Colin 7 Adelaide rd.
Young David 25 Avenue villas
Young David 143 Fellows rd.
Young G. 3 Willoughby rd.
Young George 2 Canal ter.
Young Jas. (Venetian vil.) 30 Avenue rd.
Young Mrs. 9 Christchurch rd.
Young Mrs. 5 Downshire hill
Young Morgan Henry 15 Birchington rd.
Young Robt. (Thornbank) Shoot-up hill
Youngman George 28 Kelson st.

Zingler Maximilian 19 Buckland cres.

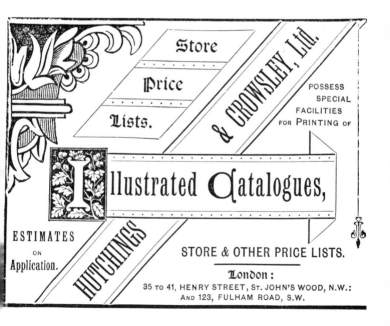

COUNTY COURT FEES.

For Plaint for Sum not exceeding.				Judgment by Consent or Default.			Hearing.			On Judgment Summons.			Second Hearing.			Execution or Commitment.		
£				£	s.	d.	£	s.	d.	£	s.	d.	£	s.	d.	£	s.	d.
1	....			0	1	0	0	2	0	0	0	9	0	0	6	0	1	6
2	....			0	2	0	0	4	0	0	1	6	0	1	0	0	3	0
3	....			0	3	0	0	6	0	0	1	9	0	1	6	0	4	6
4	....			0	4	0	0	8	0	0	2	0	0	2	0	0	6	0
5	....			0	5	0	0	10	0	0	2	3	0	2	6	0	7	6
6	....			0	6	0	0	12	0	0	2	6	0	3	0	0	9	0
7	....			0	7	0	0	14	0	0	2	9	0	3	6	0	10	6
8	....			0	8	0	0	16	0	0	3	0	0	4	0	0	12	0
9	....			0	9	0	0	18	0	0	3	3	0	4	6	0	13	6
10				0	10	0	1	0	0	0	3	6	0	5	0	0	15	0
11				0	11	0	1	2	0	0	3	9	0	5	6	0	16	6
12				0	12	0	1	4	0	0	4	0	0	6	0	0	18	0
13				0	13	0	1	6	0	0	4	3	0	6	6	0	19	6
14				0	14	0	1	8	0	0	4	6	0	7	0	1	1	0
15				0	15	0	1	10	0	0	4	9	0	7	6	1	2	6
16				0	16	0	1	12	0	0	5	0	0	8	0	1	4	0
17				0	17	0	1	14	0	0	5	3	0	8	6	1	5	6
18				0	18	0	1	16	0	0	5	6	0	9	0	1	7	0
19	....			0	19	0	1	18	0	0	5	9	0	9	6	1	8	6
20				1	0	0	2	0	0	0	6	0	0	10	0	1	10	0
50	....			1	0	0	2	0	0	0	6	0	0	10	0	1	10	0

When the plaint is for £5 or upwards, either party can claim a jury three clear days before hearing, paying 5s.

Defendants cannot be committed for non-appearance, nor unless the plaintiff prove that the defendant obtained credit by false pretence or fraud, that he had not, at the time of obtaining the credit, a reasonable expectation of being able to pay;—that he has transferred or removed his property; or that he has had, since the judgment, the means of paying it.

No charge for paying money into or out of Court. No mileage for serving summonses or executing process, with the exception of serving subpœnas. In plaints for recovering possession, the fees are to be calculated on the amount of rent for the letting—that is, by the week, month, or year. Arrears of rent to the extent of £50 calculated to the day of hearing, may be included in the same plaint.

When a debt is admitted as to part, such part may be paid into Court, with the proportionate fees. When a less sum than the amount sued for is recovered, the defendant is only to pay the costs on the sum found to be owing.

One-half of the hearing-fees will be saved by admitting the debt before the Registrar or any Clerk of the Court, or if the defendant and plaintiff arrange and sign a memorandum of the conditions of payment at the Registrar's Office, or in presence of an attorney, before the cause is called on.

ALLOWANCES TO WITNESSES IN THE COUNTY COURTS.

For attendance and expense, per day—Surgeons, Surveyors, and Attorneys, 7s. 6d.; Tradesmen, Yeomen, and Farmers, 5s.; Journeymen, Mechanics, &c., 2s. Travelling expenses, 6d. per mile.

ESTABLISHED 1845.

W. DENSHAM & SONS,

UNDERTAKERS

AND

FUNERAL FURNISHERS,

17, CIRCUS ROAD,

AND

45, COCHRANE STREET.

Office—17, Circus Road.

FUNERALS PERFORMED

With respectability and economy, in any of the Metropolitan
Cemeteries, and in all parts of the Country.

 ## OAK AND LEAD COFFINS

SUPPLIED ON THE SHORTEST NOTICE.

TOMBS AND MONUMENTS

OF EVERY DESCRIPTION ERECTED.

[10]

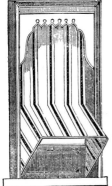

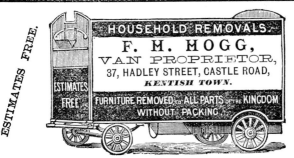

◁ H. RIEGER, ▷

Pastrycook, Confectioner,

FANCY BREAD & BISCUIT BAKER,

20, ELIZABETH TERRACE,

ENGLAND'S LANE, BELSIZE PARK, N.W.

All kinds of Wedding, Christening, and other Cakes made to order.

FAMILIES WAITED UPON DAILY.

GERMAN BREAD MADE ON THE PREMISES.

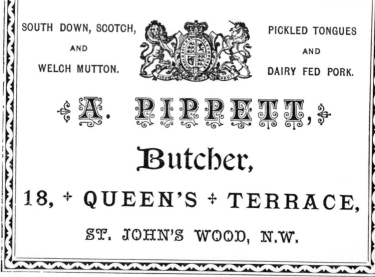

THE

HAMPSTEAD DIRECTORY.

——o——

ALPHABETICAL LIST

OF

TRADESMEN AND OTHERS.

NOTE.—*The Postal District for Hampstead is N.W.*

Further information respecting the situation of Streets may be obtained on reference to the Streets Directory : for instance, anyone requiring the address of William Abercrombie, bootmaker, refers to the Alphabetical List of Tradesmen and Others, and finds his address given 71, Fairfax rd.; by turning to Fairfax rd. in the Streets Directory, page 58, it is found described as Fairfax rd., from 72 Finchley new rd. to Belsize rd. **G 6.**

G 6 *signifies the position of Fairfax rd. on the Map.*

Abel J., carpenter 7 Willow pl.

Abel Matthew, laundry 4 Willow pl.

Abel William, plumber, The Ridge

Abercrombie Mrs., lndrss. 8 Watt's cotts.

Abercrombie Wm., btmkr. 71 Fairfax rd.

Adams Hy., cheesemonger 120 High rd.

Adams H. H., stationer 119 Broadhurst gardens

Adams J. & Co., lime and cement merchants, Iverson rd.

Adams Mrs., laundress 20 New end

Adams Thos., undertaker 60 Gayton rd.

Adams W. J. N., carpenter 40 Flask walk

ADDISON T., milliner 16 High st. Kilburn

Aedy William, cab propr. 4 Colla's mews

Aërated Bread Co., Limited 59 High rd.

Aitchison Thomas, builder 20 Sherriff rd.

Alaway Charles, builder 15 Iverson rd.

Albrow Wm., fishmngr. 32 Netherwood st.

Alderson M., chimney sweep 15 Belsize park ter.

Aldridge A. C., draper 47 Fairfax rd.

Alexander Mrs., baker (Roseberry cottage) South end green

Allchin Alfred, pharmaceutical chemist 1a Elizabeth ter.

Allen Charles B., pharmaceutical chemist 20 High rd.

Allen George, plumber 1 Linstead st.

Allen J. & Sons, builders, Palmerston rd.

Allen J., builder (The Limes) Hemstall rd.

Allen J. W., chemist 19 Elizabeth ter.

Ambler G., florist and nurseryman, South end rd.

Ambrose Charles, painter 10a Elm ter.

Anchor Coffee Tavern 63 High rd. Kilburn

Anderson Charles Frederick, hairdresser 15 Flask walk

Anderson John E., nurseryman, Belsize park gardens and 38 Gayton rd.

Andover & Weyhill Horse Company, Cricklewood lane ; Henry Newman, manager

Andrew J., harness maker 1a Belsize cres.

Andrew Jesse, saddler 75 High st.

Andrews G. N., draper 63 Fairfax rd.

Andrews James, bootmaker 9 Church ln.

Andrews Jas., bootmaker 20 Gardnor rd.

Anstead Mrs., dressmaker 167 Belsize rd. Kilburn

Anthony Bros., cheesemongers 334 High road

Archer James, baker 30 Heath st.

Arnold George, pawnbroker 228 High rd.

Arnold James J., newsagent 44 Heath st.

Arrowsmith Bros., music sellers 58 High st.

Ascott Lewis, *The North Star*, Finchley new rd.

Askell Mrs., fruiterer 37 High st.

Astrope John Chas., oilman 65 Fleet rd.

Atkins Miss, dressmkr. 6 Fairhazel gdns.

Atkinson George, gas and hot water engineer 195 & 271 Belsize rd. Kilburn

Atkinson John George, pharmaceutical chemist 196 Belsize rd. Kilburn

Atlas Sewing Machine Company 14 High rd.

Auger Matthew, bootmaker 3 Ash ter.

August Mrs., Eton nursery, Eton rd.

Austin A. F., *The Earl Derby* 155 High rd.

Aynscombe Bros., grocers 25 Fleet rd. and 1 Southwell ter.

Babidge Richard, wheelwright (Cricket cottage) Haverstock hill

Back Walter H., builder 131 Belsize rd. Kilburn

Bacon & Co., lime, cement & brick merchants (Midland railway depôt) Finchley new rd. and Iverson rd.

Bacon E., umbrella mkr. 14 Haverstock hill

Badger William, artists' colourman 97 Boundary rd.

Bailey Daniel, butcher 199 High rd.

Bailey J., baker & confectioner 2 King's college rd.

Baily William H., draper 13 Rosslyn st.

Baines Thomas, printer 14 to 18 Fairfax mews

Baker & Son, builders 10 Upper Belsize ter.

Baker D., cab proprietor, The Mount

Baker D., jobmaster, Heath st.

Baker Joshua & Wilkinson (late Baker and Sons, of Kilburn) auctioneers 106 High rd. Kilburn and St. Stephen's chambers Telegraph st. E.C.

Balfour James, baker 91 Abbey rd.

Ballinger William, builder 3 Adelaide rd.

Banger John W., tailor 2 Rosslyn st.

Barber Wm., plasterer 3 Fortune green

Bardill H., oil and colorman 16 Elizabeth ter.

Barker Alfred, *The Eton Hotel* 143 Adelaide rd.

Barnden Cornelius, greengrocer 1 Bartram ter.

Barnes Isaac, builder 252 High rd.

Barnes R. C., furniture and van office 199 Belsize rd. Kilburn (Town hall chambers) Belsize rd. Kilburn and Priory mews

Barnett Mrs. George, professor of dancing 27 Belgrave rd.

Barrat T., dyer 211 Belsize rd. Kilburn

Barratt William, butcher 78 and 184 High rd.

Barrett Fredk., butcher 18 Elizabeth ter.

Barrett Frederick George, nurseryman (Belsize nursery) 67 Belsize rd.

Barrett Jas., confectnr. 34 Boundary rd.

Barrett Thos. A., corn mer. 41 Fairfax rd.

Barron H., sanitary engineer 70 High rd.

Barry James W., carpenter 3 Upper Belsize ter.

Barter William, stationer 134 High rd.

Bartlett and Hawkins, builders 38a Boundary rd.

Bartlett William, bootmaker 25 High rd.

Barton Mrs., fancy repository 79 Haverstock hill

Basham T., genl. shop 1 Coleridge gdns.

Basham Thos., bootmkr., Fairhazel gdns.

Batchelor R., locksmith 1 Grove cottages

Bate & Walter, tea dealers 246 & 248 Belsize rd. Kilburn

Bate John, agent 46 High rd.

BATE THOMAS & CO., auctioneers 54 High rd. Kilburn

Bate Thomas, Falcon works, Broadhurst gardens

Bate Walter, grocer 58 High rd.

Bateman & Mead, greengrocers 60 Fleet rd.

Bateman T. H., pharmaceutical chemist 342 High rd.

Bates Jsph., beer retlr. 161 Loveridge rd.

Bates R. & A., *Kilburn Flour Mills*, Shoot-up hill Cricklewood

Batho T. A. & Sons, builders 5 Ardwick ter.

Baxter Benj. A., carpenter, Church lane

Baxter Jas., grocer 106 & 108 Boundary rd.

Baxter John Richard, sweep 9 Elm ter.

Baynes Frederick, timber merchant 113 King Henry's rd.

Beahan M., dairy 13 Fitzjohns' parade

Beak John, bootmaker 9 Springfield gdns.

Beckensall Miss Emily S., milliner 4 Ash ter.

Beckensall R. W., insurance agent 4 Ash ter.

Beckington W., Brondesbury nursery, Cricklewood

Beddeson Francis, fruiterer 17 King's college rd.

Beecher F. T., wood turner 21 West end lane

Belcher Benjn., bootmaker 34 Kelson st.

Belcher John S., corn & flour merchant 13 Swiss ter. Belsize rd. and 5 Broadhurst gardens

Bell Frederick, blacksmith 2 Norfolk pl.

Bellamy Bros., poulterers 16 High st.

Belsize Park Laundry Co., Limited 13 Fairhazel gardens

Bennett J., draper 150 High rd.

Benwell Francis, bootmaker, North end

Bevan William, chemist 195 High rd.

Biggs Dr., dispensary, The Ridge

Billingham Mrs.,dressmaker2Abbey lane

Binnington F., house agent (Hilldrop house) 10 Denning rd.

Binnington F. F., house and land agent, South end rd.

Birch Thomas, bricklayer 7 Alfred ter.

Bird R. A. & Co., drapers 2 South hill pk.

Birkett A., dyer & cleaner 3 Dawson ter.

Bishop Miss Julia, dress and mantle maker (Alfred villa) Vale of Health

Blackmore A., *The Haverstock Hotel* 154 Haverstock hill

Blake & Co., grocers 222 High rd.

Blake Thomas, laundry 3 Castle ter.

Bloxam Alfred, dairy 9 Albion ter. and 8 Clock ter.

Boam Thomas & Co., coal merchants, Finchley new rd.

Boddy Benjamin Smith, carpenter 77 Netherwood st.

Boden Joshua W., auctioneer and estate agent 16 Swiss ter.

Body Philip S., baker 43 High st.

Boggis E., greengrocer 8 Belsize park ter.

Bohlich Adam, tailor 46 Heath st.

BoltonChrstphr.,engineer 121Iverson rd.

Bond & Son, corn mers. 203 High rd.

Boone George, stationer 12 Swiss ter.

Booth Bros., coal merchts.,Midland Railway station, Finchley new rd., and Iverson rd.

Borasch H., hairdresser 172 High rd.

Borley Alfred, grocer 34 Heath st. and North end

Bourne & Co., booksellers and stationers 67 Abbey rd.

Bowden & Porter,sweeps, Vale of Health

Bowden Bros., lathrenders, Abbey lane

BowdenG.&W.,lathrenders,West end lane

Bowen Alfred Walter, photographer 48 Heath st.

Bowen J., photographer 161 High rd.

Bowen John T., chemist 238 Belsize rd. Kilburn

Bowles George, baker 139 High rd.

Bowling & Thomas, drapers 288 and 300 High rd.

Bowman George, beer retlr. 53 Fleet rd.

Brace J., nurseryman, Adelaide rd.

Brackley John, carpenter 8 The Village

Bradberry Joseph,cheesemgr.63 Fleet rd.

Bradbury Geo.,zinc worker 16 Flask walk

Braddish Angelo,bootmaker112High rd.

Bradley Guss Alfred, ladder maker 277 High rd.

Bradman R.,fruiterer10aFairhazel gdns.

Bradshaw Wm., gardener 1 West cotts.

Brandon J., Swiss cottage dairy, Finchley rd.

Braun Henry, *The Athenæum*, Vale of Health

Braun Henry C., dentist 119 High rd.

BrazierSaml,bootmaker11Palmerston rd.

BrazillMissM.,tailoress17 Winchester rd.

Brett R., greengrocer 340 High rd.

Brett William, *The Hare & Hounds*, North end

Bridge Isaac, corn dealer and jobmaster 22 King's college rd.

BridgeIsaac,jbmstr.,King's college mews

BridgelandMrs.M., laundress 12 Cricklewood ter.

Bridger Frederick Voller, registrar of births and deaths 12 Medley rd.

Bridges Mrs., tobacconist 143 High rd.

BridgmanEdward,bootmkr. 21 Heath st.

Briggs Mrs., hairdresser 5 Flask walk

BrightwellR. & Son, butchers 6 Swiss ter.

BrightwellRichd.,tailor190Loveridge rd.

Brindley T., sen., iron moulder 12 West cottages

British & Foreign Boot Agency Association, bootmakers 31 High st.

Brithnell Geo.,cheesemonger 29 High rd.

Britton James, bootmaker 8 Rosslyn st.

BroadMrs.,laundress2 LowerHeath cotts.

Broadhurst A.,genl. shop, West end lane

Brooking &Co.,fancy rpstry.298 High rd.

Broughton J. D., fishmonger 176 and 315 High rd.

Broughton James D., cheesemonger 230 High rd.

BrownCharles,bootmaker4South hill pk.

Brown Charles, mineral water manufacturer 1b Church pl.

Brown Charles, undertaker 81 High rd.

Brown J. A., draper 14 Elizabeth ter.

Brown J. A., milliner 5 Elizabeth ter.

Brown Miss Emma, tbcnst. 11 Granville ter

Browning H., brush and comb warehouse 7 Swiss ter. Belsize rd.

Browning Thomas, china and brush warehouse 10 King's college rd.

Brumbridge James, dairyman 47 Hampstead hill gardens and 6 Rosslyn st.

Brumby Geo., coal dlr. 3 Flask cottages

Brusey T., coffee rooms 43 Loudoun rd.

Bryant Chas., chimny. sweep 2 Cranfield pl

Buckingham James, dairy 2 Fairfax mews

Buckingham James, dairy 91 Fairfax rd.

Buckle George, fruiterer 68 Heath st.

Bucknell J. G., builder 134 Iverson rd. and 2a Netherwood st.

Bulford T., oilman 32 Boundary rd.

Bull Mrs. L., Iverson dairy, Iverson rd.

Burbidge Bros., wine & spirit merchants 117 High rd.

Burbidge William, china & glass warehouse 12 Belsize park ter.

Burch W., jobmaster 3 & 4 Wavel mews

Burck George F., baker 19 High st.

Burdett William, jobmaster and livery stables 1 Belsize cres., Finchley rd., and 27 Fairfax mews

BURFORD & SON, builders and decorators (Norway house) 35 High st. and (Crown cot.) 150 Haverstock hill

Burkett Thomas, butcher 220 High rd.

Burr Mrs. Sarah Ann, tbcnst. 63 Heath st.

Burrage Tompkins & Co., timber merchants, Cricklewood

Burt Richard, carpenter 20 Loveridge rd.

Busbridge John Gurney, *The Cock & Crown* 60 High st.

Bussey Geo., upholsterer 39 Netherwood st

Bussey Mrs., drssmkr. 39 Netherwood st.

BUTCHER W. H., builder, house agent and undertaker 10 Fitzjohns' parade Finchley new rd. ; works, Cochrane st. St. John's wood

Butler Cornelius, smith 8 Devonshire pl.

Butler Jas., turncock 1 Belsize road mews

Butler Walter, gasfitter 24 Iverson rd.

Byrchall Edwd., laundry 12 Palmerston rd.

Cain Miss, general shop 1a Linstead st.

Cale W., florist 121 Finchley rd.

Cale William, florist 214 Adelaide rd.

Callingham George, chimney cleaner 3 Loudoun road mews

Callon J., jun., hairdresser 240 High rd.

Calvert James, tailor 11 Lowfield rd.

Camp A., greengrocer 2 Upper Belsize ter.

Camp James, greengrocer 19 Broadhurst gardens and 15 Rosslyn st.

Cannock Chase Coal Co., West end

Carpenter Hy. A., joiner 7 Well walk ter.

Carpenter Thomas Wood, baker and confectioner 41 High rd.

Carter A. W., watchmaker 21 High rd.

Carter Ernest, fancy repository 206 Haverstock hill

Cartridge James, statnr. 83 Boundary rd.

Carver Miss, ladies' outfitter 9 Rosslyn st.

Cash W., bootmaker 32 Prospect pl.

Catesby E., furniture dlr. 187 High rd.

Catherwood Thomas Burn, *The Bird in Hand* 38 & 39 High st.

Caudell Daniel, painter 1 Pilgrim's pl.

Cayford Walter W., wardrobe dealer 3 and 5 Bell ter. and 8 Kelson st.

Chadd Mrs., laundress 2 Grove cottages

Challenger M.C., statnr. 132 Boundary rd.

Challis Mrs., confectioner 1a Church pl.

Challis Thomas, gardener 7 Albion ter.

Chamberlain E., nurseryman and florist 188 and 192 Haverstock hill and Fitzjohns' avenue

Chamberlain Edmund T., landscape gardener 1 Pilgrim's lane

Chambers L. G. & Son, florists, West end

Chambers M. & E., dyers 76 High rd.

Chambers Miss, dressmaker (Prince Arthur's cott.) 4 Prince Arthur's mews

Chambers Mrs., laundry 15 The Village

Chambers Wm. R., tea dlr., &c., West end

Chapman Edward, baker 24 Fleet rd.

Chapman Joseph John, pharmaceutical chemist 20 Boundary rd.

Chappell David, baker 132 High rd.

Chappell Edwin, carpntr. 2 Kilburn vale

Charsley John, plumber and gasfitter 1 Grove pl.

Cheshir Charles, builder 24 Lichfield rd.

Chilcot W. B., tailor 20 Maygrove rd.

Chinnery George, bootmaker 80 High st.

Chivers George, timber merchant (Clyst house) 7 West end lane

Church of England Temperance Society Coffee Hut ; Robert Rogers, hut keeper, Cricklewood lane

Churchill E. A., butcher 49 & 168 High rd.

Churchill Mrs., laundress 11 West cottages

Clark James, baker 2 Ardwick ter.

Clark John, insurance agent 48 Fleet rd.

Clark Walter William, insurance agent 26 Kelson st.

Clark Herbert, grocer 6 Clock ter.

Clarke J. M., baker 20 Granville ter.

Clarke Thomas, plumber 13 Palmerston road

Clegg Mrs. Mary Ann, *The Prince Arthur* 36 Boundary rd.

Clements James, florist (Park road nursery) Park rd.

Clements J. E., fancy draper 154 High rd. Kilburn

Clifford Henry, *The Sir Richard Steele* 97 Haverstock hill

Clingo Mrs. E., florist 2 Swiss ter.

Clisby John, fishmonger 30 Boundary rd.

Clowser Thomas, builder 27 High st. and Perrin's court

Coates C. J., collector of parochial rates (Bedford villa) Willoughby rd.

Coates James A., butcher 33 High st.

Coates Joseph, insurance agent (Bedford villa) Willoughby rd.

Coffin Henry, *The Stag*, Fleet rd.

Cohen & Co., fruiterers 302 High rd.

Cole Hy., coffee rooms 17 Cricklewood ter.

Cole Richard, stationer 3 Quex rd.

Coles Alexander, butcher 87 Fairfax rd.

Coles Charles J., *The Alexandra Hotel* 21 Alexandra rd.

Coles John, *The Prince of Wales* 4 Fortune green

Coles W. A., butcher 6 Upper Belsize ter.

Collin Daniel, general shop 2 New end

Collins William, confectioner 7 Upper Belsize ter. and 10 Belsize park ter.

Collis David, inspector, Police station, Rosslyn hill

Compton Mrs. Caroline, laundry 57 Park rd.

Connell F. H., watchmaker 83 High rd.

Cook Edward, upholsterer 6 Albion ter.

Cook George, builder (Weatherall cottage) Well rd. and Flask walk

Cook James, carpenter 7 Colla's mews

Cook Mrs.. laundry 27 The Village

Coomber Mrs., dressmaker 155 Belsize rd. Kilburn

Coombes M., harness maker 75 High rd.

Cooper & Co., dairy 6 Belsize park ter.

Cooper A. W., florist 49 Upper Park rd.

Cooper Bros., oilmen 93 High rd.

Cooper Jas., butcher 8 King's college rd.

Cooper W. J., butcher 24 High rd.

Cork W. J., fruiterer 16 Haverstock hill

Cornick Henry, ironmonger 1 and 3 Broadhurst gardens

Cornick Jesse, ironmonger 4 High st.

Cornwell C. & E., grocers 126 Boundary rd.

Corston H. B. & Co., coal merchants, Iverson rd.

Cosser Mason, toy warehouse 206 High rd.

Cosway & Rutter, chemists 109 High rd

Cotterell Henry L., coffee rooms 6 Haverstock hill

Coulter Mrs. Ann, general shop 16 Ariel st.

Coulton H. H., corn merchant 3 High rd.

Courtney Geo. H., bootmaker 1 Heath st.

Coward Mrs., chair-caner 16 Belsize pk. ter.

Cowie David, bootmkr. 3 Fairhazel gdns.

Cox Charles, fruiterer 17 Elizabeth ter.

Cox Jas., tbccnst., Finchley rd. Child's hill

Cox John, confectioner 19 High rd.

Cox W. J., carpenter 15 Ravenshaw st.

Cracknell Mrs. E., drsmkr. 31 Alexandra rd.

Cranwell Henry, bootmaker 4 Upper Belsize ter.

Crease William, butcher 19 Granville ter.

Cremer George, ladies' outfitter 159a High rd.

Cresswell William, cutler 2 Keil's cottages

Crichton William, draper (Dalmuir house) 158 Iverson rd.

Cridlan Thomas, butcher 75 Abbey rd.

Cripps Mrs. A., laundress, Fleet mews

Crockett Thomas William, stationer 312 High rd.

Cronk George, baker 98 Boundary rd.

Cronk Thomas, builder 34 Bolton rd.

Crook & Sons, jobmasters 1 Iverson rd.

Crook Charles William, jobmaster 273 High rd. Kilburn and (Quex mews) Quex rd.

Crook James, undertaker 263 High rd. Kilburn

Crowe John, undertaker 71 Heath st. and 4 Ridge ter. Child's hill

Crowe Miss, confectioner 4 Ridge ter.

Cruttwell Charles H., plumber 1 White Bear lane

Cuffley A., carver & gilder 115 Finchley rd.

Culverhouse Geo., jobmaster 2 Church pl.

Culverhouse John, laundry 4 Saunders cottages

Curram J., baker 212 High rd.

Curryer Wm. B., jeweller 61b Abbey rd.

Curtis John Charles, laundry 41 Netherwood st.

Curtis Mrs., laundress 50 Flask walk

Cutler F., oilman 2 Kelson st.

Cutler William, dairy 14 King's college rd.

Dainton S. J., builder 11 Exeter ter.

Dainton Samuel Joseph, builder and decorator 234 Belsize rd. Kilburn

Dalley John, carver & gilder 62 Heath st.

Daniel Mrs., laundry 4 Kilburn vale

Daniel S., tobacconist 2 White Horse ter.

Dare John, hairdresser 4a Perrin's court

Darling Alfred, police inspector 21 Flask walk

Davenport Mrs., laundry 163 Loveridge rd.

Davey F., sweets dealer 43 Heath st.

Davey R. A. & Co., tobacconists 330 High rd.

David David, brass finshr. 26 Maygrove rd.

Davidge Thomas, *Horse and Groom* 13 Heath st.

Davies and Evans, oil and colourmen 1 Rosslyn st. and 141 and 305 High rd. Kilburn

Davies Arthur, watchmaker and jeweller 3 Fitzjohns' parade

Davies G. & J., bakers 58a Heath st.

Davies James Allman, verger of St. Stephen's Church (Rodley house) Willoughby rd.

Davies Stephen, baker 10 Flask walk

Davis Alfred, verger and collector of St. Peter's Church 1 Lancaster pl.

Davis Edward, greengrocer 1 High st.

Davis Mrs. E., dining rooms 309 High rd.

Davis Richd., beer retailer 1 Lowfield rd.

Davy Edward Montague, M.R.C.V.S.L., veterinary infirmary 8 & 9 Alexandra mews

Dawes Miss Mary, coffee bar 8 Southwell ter.

Dawson Hy., gardener 39 Palmerston rd.

Dawson Wm., bricklayer 3 Watt's cotts.

Dawters Mrs. Mary Ann, laundry, Golder's hill cottages North end

Day H., gasfitter, King's college mews

Day Miss E., dyer 3 Rosslyn st.

Day Mrs. & Misses, drsmkrs. 130 Iverson rd.

Day William Henry, fancy draper 8 Haverstock hill

Dean George Henry, court dressmaker 56a Haverstock hill

Deans R. G., ham and beef dealer 92 High rd.

Dearing Mrs., dressmaker 1 Osborne ter.

Dearlove Mrs., fancy repository 200 Belsize rd. Kilburn

Death S. S., *The Priory Tavern* 250 Belsize rd. Kilburn

Debenham William E., photographer (Massingham house) 46 Haverstock hill

De Bolla B. & Co., café restaurant, Vale of Health

De Coster & Co., drapers 114 Boundary rd.

Dennis Mrs., sen., monthly nurse 1 Edward ter.

Dennison Thomas, fitter 1 Willow cotts.

Denton Mrs., dressmaker (Oakley villa) Ravenshaw st.

Dettmer G. F., *The Roebuck Hotel* 49 Hampstead hill gardens

Dettmer W. J., pianoforte tuner 46 Kingsgate rd.

Dibb Wm., carpenter 174 Loveridge rd.

Dickens Mrs., laundress 6 Grove cotts.

Dickson & Son, butchers, Haverstock hill

Dickson D. M. & Sons, butchers 1 Adelaide rd. Haverstock hill

Dimond William, cheesemonger 11 Fairhazel gardens

Dimond Wm., oilman 9 Fairhazel gdns.

Disney Chas., bootmaker 13 & 14 High st.

Dixon Wm., decorator 104 Iverson rd.

Dolman & Pearce, auctioneers 62 Haverstock hill

Dolman George, perfumer 82 High st.

Donner Joseph, draper 62 High rd.

Dormer Henry, cheesemonger 311 High rd. Kilburn

Drabwell Mrs., laundress (Holton cottage) West end lane

Drabwell William, paperhanger (Holton cottage) West end lane

Draper Arthur S., ironmonger 95 Boundary rd.

Duckett D., Hampshire farm dairy, Kingsgate rd.

Duckett Farm Dairy Co.; John Saunders, manager 3a Fleet rd.

Dudley Mrs., laundress 5 Albion ter.

Dudman John, grocer 11 & 12 Rosslyn st., Upper Belsize ter., and 5 Belsize park ter.

DUGGIN J. F. & CO., dyers to H.M. the Queen & H.R.H. the Prince of Wales 42 Duke st. Manchester sq. and 37 Craven rd. Lancaster gate

Dunham William Henry, china and glass dealer 130 Boundary rd.

Dunhill H., pianoforte warehouse 10 Swiss ter. Belsize rd.

Dunn George, grocer 5 Ridge ter.

Durrant Mrs. Caroline, confectioner, North end

Eaton Mrs., laundry 8 Golden sq.

Eddy G., builder 4a Fleet rd.

Edge Frank, tobacconist 15 Heath st.

Edwards and Coxwell, corn merchants 88 Haverstock hill

Edwards & Thomas, jobmasters (Lancaster stables) Lancaster rd.

Edwards Geo., prov. dealer 6 Kelson st.

Edwards H., servants' registry 7a Elizabeth ter.

Edwards Hy., corn dealer 7a Elizabeth ter.

Edwards Peter, florist 121 High rd.
EdwardsThomas,bootmkr. 35 Iverson rd.
EedeS.,hairdrssr.270aBelsize rd Kilburn
Egan J. G., builder 163 High rd.
Elliott & Co.,cheesemongers 54a High st.
Elliott Bros., greengrocers 6 King's college rd.
Elliott Edward, grocer 1 Ardwick ter.
Elliott Russell, cheesemngr. 6 Exeter ter.
Ellis & Everard, coal mers., Iverson rd.
Ellis C. & Son, estate agnts., 366 High rd.
Ellis John, *The Red Lion* 34 High rd.
ElsleyRobert,confctnr.76Upper Park rd.
Elworthy Francis, gardener 6 Heath villas Vale of Health
Emerson Robert, butcher 56a High st.
Emery Thomas, ironmonger 1a Upper Belsize ter.
Endean Miss, dress and mantle maker 138 Belsize rd.
ENDERSON & BROMLEY, decorators 275 High rd.
Entwistle W., uphlstr.,Manchester mews
Escott C., builder 1 Ainger rd.
Estate Office, Parliament hill rd.
Estcourt Ernest,builder 8 Canfield gdns.
Etheridge Timothy, blacksmith 11 Elm terrace
Evangelistic Mission, Office of (The) 190 Alexandra rd.; C.Russell Hurditch
Evans Chas., turncock 1 Belsize rd. mews
Evans E. & D., dairy 96 Park rd.
Evans E., fruiterer 5 Swiss ter.
Evans E., greengrocer 1 Exeter ter.
Evans Edwin H., hosier 55 High st.
Evans Frederick, tailor 5 Ainger rd.
Evans Thomas, draper 68 High rd.
Evans Thomas Andrews, draper 46 & 47 High st.
Eveleigh Geo. Hy.,builder 59 Fairfax rd.
Everett C. H.,contractor (Iverson works) Iverson rd.
Express Dairy Co., Limited, Heath st.

Fairchild George, grocer 1 Fleet rd.
Falkner J., gardener 25 New end
Farebrother, Ellis, Clark & Co., auctioneers 14 Fitzjohns' parade
Farley H. A., statnr. 6 Fitzjohns' parade
Farley James, grocer 1b Fleet rd.
Farmer Leopold, auctnr., &c. 12 High rd.
Faulkner Mrs.,laundress 8 Hampstead sq.
Fazan William Slater, butcher 242 Belsize rd. Kilburn
Featherstone Samuel, painter, West end
Fehrenbach E., watchmaker 29a High road

Felton George, contractor(Iverson yard) Iverson rd.
Fenn Thomas, tailor 23 High st.
Fenn William, gardener (The Cottage) West end
Ferris Edward C.,watchmaker & jeweller 2a Elizabeth ter.
Field Miss R., draper 28 Boundary rd.
Figden J. F., corn merchant 236 High rd.
Finch George W., gardener 10 Loveridge rd.
Findlay James, confectioner 125 Finchley rd. and 1 Fitzjohns' parade
Fine Art Emporium, K.Moss53Fairfax rd.
Fire Fly Coffee Tavern 66 Fleet rd.
FirmingerAmos,builder124Boundary rd.
First Clothing Hall Co., The, merchant tailors & boys' outfitters 128 High rd.
Fishenden George, florist, West end
Fisher Charles, draper 10 High rd.
Fisk W. J. & E. C., dentists 183 High rd.
FitzgeraldWm.,coachbuilder 78 High st.
FlackMatthew,dining rooms 59 Park rd.
Flitt Mrs. E. A., general shop 15 New end
Flower Clare, carver & gilder 32 High rd.
FooksGeo.Harris,bandmaster7Ainger rd.
Ford & Sons, printers 5 High rd.
Ford William, ham and beef warehouse 35 High rd.
Forster F.A.,A.P.S.,chemist 4 Dawson ter.
Forster James, grocer 73 High st.
Forster James, oilman 59 Heath st.
ForsythJ.,monumental sculptor (Ednam house) Finchley new rd.
Foster George, chemist 29 Heath st.
Foster George, gentleman's outfitter (Cromer house) 84 High rd.
Foster H., draper (Downshire house) Mill lane
Foster J. O., water rate clctr. 12 High rd.
Found Nathaniel,carpenter 9Gardnor rd.
Fowler & Son, genl. wheelwrights, Alfred terrace mews
Fowler Bros., statnrs. 92 Haverstock hill
Fowler C., coach builder 7 New end sq.
Fowler George, wheelwright 21 New end
Fox Alfred, labourer 2 Fortune green
Fox Hy.,butcher46Hampstead hill gdns.
FramptonWm.,greengrocer 9 Flask walk
Francis James, sweep (The Cottage) Cricklewood lane
Frank Joseph, grocer 3 King's college rd.
Fraser A., saddler and harness maker 267 High rd. Kilburn
Freeman Geo., bootmaker 11 Grove ter.
Freeman James Joseph, *The Flask Tavern*, Flask walk

French and Vienna Bakery 327 High rd. Kilburn ; H. Everitt, manager

French E. & Co., grocers 5 Exeter ter.

French Joseph, confectioner 86 Haverstock hill

Frost D. W., tailor 23a High rd.

Frost Miss, dressmaker 11 Spencer ter.

Frost William, stationer 1 Norfolk pl.

Froud C. M., *The Holly Bush Hotel*, Holly mount

Fry E. A., oilman 18a Haverstock hill

Funnell John, bootmaker 219 Belsize rd

Gaillard Frank & Co., wine merchants 84 Haverstock hill

Galer Miss, servants' registry 5 Dawson ter.

Galloway John, builder (Forres) Lambolte rd.

Gandy Mrs., laundress 1 Kilburn vale

Gardiner Miss, dressmaker 53 Gayton rd.

Gardiner Thomas, landscape gardener (Aberdeen house) South end rd.

Gardner Alfred, draper 8 Albion ter.

Gardner George, tailor 14 Heath st.

Gardner Hy., builder 1 Palmerston rd.

Gardner Mrs., dyer 5 Willow ter.

Garfield Coffee Palace 1 Garfield ter.

Garrett T., carman, Palmerston rd.

Garwood William, oilman 1 High st.

Gas Light and Coke Company, Office for Hampstead 3 Holly mount; Chas. Hoyle, inspector

Gater R., provision dealer, Kingsgate rd.

Gearing H. W., confectioner 39a High rd.

General Supply Stores, Charles Peters, Vale of Health

George A. L., glass wareho. 2 Abbey lane

GEORGES L. A. & CO., plate, sheet and flint glass warehouse, Abbey lane Kilburn (close to Town hall)

Gervis & Alford, surgeons 1 Fellows rd. and 61 Haverstock hill

Gianella Joseph, café 99 High rd. Kilburn

Gibson Thomas, painter 16 The Village

Gidden W. & H., saddlers 8 Elizabeth ter.

Giles W., greengrcr. 207 Belsize rd. Kil.

Gill John, plumber 120 Boundary rd.

Gilling William, fruiterer 220 Belsize rd.

Ginder W. C., *The Albert Edward* 31 Bolton rd.

Ginger Alfd., pork butcher 296 High rd.

Ginger Walter, butcher, High rd. Kilburn

Girls' Public Day School Co., Limited, Maresfield gardens

Glasscock H., grocer 10 West end lane

Godfrey Robert, carpenter, &c. 1 New end square

Godsel H. P., *The George* 210 Haverstock hill

Golding William, coffee rooms 11 King's college rd.

Goodchild Mrs., tobacconist 24 Netherwood st.

Goodenough Thos., dairy 111 Boundary rd.

Goodman Charles, grocer 45 High rd.

Goodman Edmund, grocer 14 Pond st.

Goord C. W., fancy repstry. 65 Heath st.

Gordon William, artificial flower maker 10 Lowfield rd.

Gosling R., bottle dealer 18 Springfield gardens

Goss George, confectioner 238 High rd.

Goubert J. B., nurseryman 2 High rd. Kilburn

Graham & Graham, tea dlrs. 152 High rd.

Granaries Company 4 High rd.

Grand Junction Water Works; William Watts, reservoir keeper, Mill lane

Grant Mrs., dress and mantle maker (Holly hill cottage) Holly hill

Grant Thomas, painter 31 New end

Gray & Smyth Mesdames, shirt and collar dressers, Quex rd.

Gray W. C., hairdresser 19 Rosslyn st.

Green & Co., blind mkrs. 165 High rd.

Green Chas., undertaker 164 Iverson st.

Green Edwin, accountant 21 Fleet rd.

Green George, bricklayer 5 Hemstall rd.

Green J., *The Three Horse Shoes* 62 High st.

Green Joseph, wood turner 13 Fleet rd.

Green Mrs., dressmaker 3 Lowfield rd.

Grey Henry, beer retailer 10 Kelson st.

Grey Henry, builder 33 Flask walk

Griffin Henry, dairy, West end lane

Griffin James, builder (Fulbeck cottage) South end rd.

Griffiths Thomas, dairy 218 High rd.

Griggs John, tobacconist 91 Boundary rd.

Grose Mrs. Grace, *The Prince Consort* 9 King's college rd.

Gross Mrs., certified nurse 135 Belsize rd. Kilburn

Grover James, coffee and dining rooms 116 High rd.

Grundon George, Heath farm, North end

Grundon John, contractor, The Ridge

Gudgeon Robert, fancy draper 87 Haverstock hill

Guy George, turncock 5 Grove pl.

Gwynn Francis, laundry 17 and 18 The Village

Gyllenspetz Charles Edward, insurance agent 28 Maygrove rd.

Hackworth A., builder 41 Loudoun rd.

Haines George, poulterer 7 Rosslyn st.

Hale Thomas, ironmoulder 13 West cotts.

Hall Charles, plasterer 16 Fleet rd.

Hall C. H., jeweller 13 Belsize park ter.

Hall John, *The Cock & Hoop*, West end

Hall Mrs., dressmaker 202 Belsize rd. Kilburn

Halls W. H., fruiterer 174 High rd.

Hamilton J., umbrella repairer 14 West end lane

Hamilton T., chair caner 8 Springfield gardens

Hamilton William, baker 64 Fleet rd.

Hammond Edgar, butcher 32 Heath st.

Hammond Miss H., fancy draper 33 Heath st.

Hampstead & Highgate Express Office, High st.

Hampstead Life, Fire and Accident Insurance Offices 66 Fleet rd.; J. Burman Rosevear, manager

Hampstead Model Steam Laundry, Limited, Cressy rd.

Hampstead Public Library and Literary Institute ; A. Wilson, hon. treasurer (Stanfield house) Prince Arthur rd.

Hampstead Trading Bank, Limited 66 Fleet rd.; J. Burman Rosevear, secretary

Hankin C., builder 46 Downshire hill

Hannett A.H.& Sons, dyers69 Fairfax rd.

Hannington Mrs.,greengrcr. 4 Church pl.

Hanwell N., decorator 170 Loveridge rd.

Harding Edwd., upholsterer 108 High rd.

Harding Richard, builder and decorator 20 Haverstock hill

Hardyment Archibald F., china & glass warehouse 114 High rd.

Harland Bros., grocers and wine merchants 77 Abbey rd.

Harnden E.,confectnr. 157 Loveridge rd.

Harper Edwin H., music warehouse 75 Haverstock hill

Harper John, provision dealer 95 Palmerston rd.

Harrington W. E., bootmaker 13 Broadhurst gardens

Harris E., cheesemonger 59 High st.

Harris Fredk.Wltr.,bootmkr.58Heath st.

HarrisHy.,surveyor 26Parliament hill rd.

Harris Mrs., boarding house 26 Parliament hill rd.

Harrison Charles, turner 2 Hemstall rd.

Harrison Joseph, butcher 2 Flask walk

Harrison William G.,oilman 40 High st.

Harriss A., builder 159 Loveridge rd.

HARROW MUSIC SCHOOL; Misses Fox and Frost, principals 15 Fitzjohns' parade

Hart Frederick, coffee and dining rooms 1 Canfield pl. Canfield gardens

Hartley T. H. P., *The Queen's Arms* 1 High rd.

Hartstone Thos., hairdrssr. 67 Fairfax rd.

Harvey Wm., School house, Church walk

Harwood Benj., dairy 27 Winchester rd.

Harwood William, *The Bell* 38 High rd.

Hassall Mrs., laundry 2 Providence pl.

Hately J.,gasfitter 15 Yorkshire Grey yd.

Hately J., genl. smith,Little Church row

Hatton Francis, stationer 104 High rd.

Hawker Alfred Christopher, decorator 29 Flask walk

Hawkins Hy., confectioner 28a Heath st.

Hawkins J., builder 21 Winchester rd.

Hawkins John, *The Nag's Head* 61 Heath st.

Hawkins William Alley, joiner 3 Linstead st.

Hawkins W. M., draper 91 High rd.

Hawksley Henry, *The Yorkshire Grey*, Yorkshire Grey yard

Hayden Benjamin,*The Princess of Wales* 121 Abbey rd. Kilburn

Hayes H., grindery dlr.97 Palmerston rd.

Haynes Samuel & Sons, ironmongers' smiths 73 High rd.

Hayslep Mrs. M.,tobacconist 1a Fleet rd.

Hayter John,bath chair prop.Heath mnt.

Hayter J. G., harness mkr. 1 Willow ter.

Hayward F. H., hatter 64 High st.

Hazell Miss, dressmaker 6 Ainger rd.

HEALEY E. J., ale stores 125a High rd.

HEATH HENRY, hat manufacturer 105, 107 & 109 (late No. 393) Oxford st. W. Ladies' show room. Awarded gold and silver medals at Health Exhibition

Heels W., greengrcr. 20 Belsize park ter.

Heighton Bros., ironmongers 18 High rd.

Hemming Miss, dressmaker 7 King's college rd.

Hendrick Chas., baker 4 Elizabeth ter.

Hepburn David, bootmkr. 38 Flask walk

Hepher Fredk., tailor 112 Maygrove rd.

Herbert G. &[Co.,bootmakers 64 High rd.

Herbstritt Geo.,watchmaker 159High rd.

*Herington'sServants'Registry*39High rd

Hern Mrs. E., dressmaker 32 New end

Hetherington F., servants' registry, High st.

Hetherington J., jobmaster (The Slade) Cricklewood

HEWETSON JAMES, bookseller and stationer 1] and 12 High st.

Hewett Chas., butcher 26 Boundary rd.

Hewett George, lime and brick merchant, Finchley new rd.

Hewing Wm., beer retailer 254 High rd.

HickleyT.H.,statnr.125Broadhurst gdns.

Hicks Mrs., accoucheuse 7 Narcissus rd.

Higgs John, verger of St. Paul's Church 13 King's college rd.

High School for Boys 97 Finchley rd. ; Dr. W. Brackebusch, head master

Hilder Mrs., laundress 13 The Village

HilderWm.,photographer 127 Iverson rd.

Hill Hy., genl. shop 6 Little Church row

Hill Rowland, *The Freemasons' Arms*, Downshire hill

Hill William, carriage proprietor, Downshire hill

Hill William, grocer 2 and 3 Grove ter.

Hindley & Son,cabinetmkrs.,Erskine rd.

Hinton John, sweep 10 Springfield gdns.

Hinton Mrs., ladies and children's outfitter 3 Garfield ter.

Hipwell Mrs., laundress 1 The Village

Hipwell W., bootmaker 3 Holly hill

Hislop Charles, bootmaker 3 White Horse ter.

Hoare H. A., bootmaker 276 High rd.

Hoare J., ironmonger, Kingsgate rd.

Hobbs Wm. Hy., estate agent 8 Fleet rd.

Hobden Jsph.,engine fitter 4 West end ln.

Hoggett Mrs., servants' registry office 12 Abbey lane

Holgate William, mineral water manufacturer 8 Ainger rd.

Hollidge J. E., tobacconist 46 High rd.

Holliman Hopton, *The Vistoria Tavern* 205 High rd.

Holloway George, decorator and undertaker 7 Prospect rd.

Holloway Wm., decorator 4 Albion ter.

Holman John, tailor 98 High rd.

Holman Thomas, builder 5 & 18 King's college mews

Holmes Benjamin, tailor 12 Lowfield rd.

Holmes Henry, fishmonger 7 Flask walk

Holmes Mrs., laundress 3 Grove cottages

Hook William, coffee rooms 4 Fleet rd.

Hopkins G., *Jersey Farm Dairy*, Broadhurst gardens

Hopcroft Henry, grocer 9 & 10 Granville terrace

Horn F.,baker & confectioner 79 High rd.

Horn J. W., stationer 2 Willow rd.

Houghton F. & Son, cheesemongers 61 High rd.

Houghton Frank, cheesemonger 81 Boundary rd. and 4 King's college rd.

Houghton Herbert, cheesemonger and poulterer 1 Swiss ter.

HowardI.&W.,lath rendrs.,Palmerston rd

Howe Arbourn, gasfitter (Leith house) Quex rd.

Howell Charles William, *The Magdala Tavern*, South hill park

Howell Mrs., laundress 1 Hemstall rd.

Howes Wm.,carpenter 162 Maygrove rd.

Howlett Robt.,gardener 5 Fortune green

Hows T. & Co., corn dlrs. 85 Abbey rd.

Hudson Messrs., builders 74 High st.

Hudson W. J., *The Spaniard's Hotel*, Heath end

HughesH.,boot&shoe'mkr.40Belgrave rd.

Hughes Joseph, gas engineer 5 William terrace

Hughes W. H., bootmaker 45 Hampstead hill lane

HumphreysC.E.,wardrobe dlr.2Heath st.

Humphreys Fredk., corn dlr. 9 Heath st.

Humphreys Henry, *The Bull & Bush*, North end

Humphreys R., pharmaceutical chemist 4 Swiss ter. and 12a Upper Belsize ter.

Hunt Mrs., shirt and collar dresser 1 Goldsmith pl.

Hunt Richard, provision dlr. 10 Elm ter.

Hutchings T. P., bootmaker (Forres house) 82 Haverstock hill

Hutchins L. & Co., dyers and cleaners 4 Belsize park ter.

Hyde George,cheesemngr.61a Abbey rd.

Hyne Harry, pharmaceutical chemist 8 Exeter ter.

Ingram Algernon M., glass and china warehouse 22 High rd.

Ingram Mrs., plumber 2 Eton pl.

Isaac E. J.,bldr. & decortr. 85 Fairfax rd.

Isitt Levi, wardrobe dealer 250 High rd.

Ivens W., hairdresser 205 Belsize rd. Kilburn

Jackson Walter, stationer 34 High st.

Jacobs Asher, *Kilburn Supply Stores* 8 High rd.

Jacobs James, laundry, North end

Jacoby Frederick, oilman 218 Belsize rd. Kilburn and 118 Boundary rd.

James Charles, fitter 1a West cottages

James Edward, bootmaker 18 High st.

James Edward, jobmaster and livery stables 15 and 16 Loudoun rd. mews Loudoun rd.

James John G., draper 4 & 5 Heath st.
Jarrett Mrs., laundress 11 Lowfield rd.
Jarvis Joseph, carpenter 11 Mansfield pl.
Jarvis William, tailor 73 Fairfax rd.
JeffcoatCharles,tobacconist 9 Exeter ter.
Jervis Hy. F., grocer 26 Netherwood st.
Jinks William, jobmaster, King's college
  mews
Joel C., portmanteau mkr. 180 High rd.
Johnson J., tailor 2 Belsize park ter.
Johnson John, oilman 1 Flask walk
Johnson Walter, dentist 50 Belsize rd.
Joiner Joseph, bottle mer. 1 Church lane
Jolly George, builder 54 Belsize rd.
Jolly Mrs., dressmkr. 33 Gascony avenue
Jones Albert, fishmonger 36 Fleet rd.
Jones Albert, ironmonger 11 Heath st.
Jones Bros., drapers 71 Abbey rd.
Jones James, builder 256 High rd.
Jones John P., gardener (Mansfield
  cottage) Heath st.
Jones Misses, dressmakers 50 Gayton rd.
Jones Saml., watchmaker 212 Belsize rd.
  Kilburn
Jones W. Joseph,btmkr. 13 Granville ter.
Jordan Edwd.,tobacconist 12 Flask walk

Kay Miss, stationer 62 Gayton rd.
Keates Mrs.,dressmkr. 182 Loveridge rd.
Keele & Co., chemists 130 High rd.
Keil Rowland, baker 63 High st.
Keith A. A., ironmonger 24 High st.
Kelly H. & E.,estate office, Fitzjohns' av.
Kelly R., bazaar 101 High rd.
Kemp J., draper 214 & 216 High rd.
KempW.,King Henry's nursery,Eton pl.
Kendall H. E., district surveyor (Holly
  cottage) The Mount
Kent & Co., bakers, West end
Kent R. Howard, draper and outfitter
  215 Belsize rd. Kilburn
Kerrison Edwin, builder 4 High st.
Kessels Frncs., dining rooms 38 Heath st.
Kettelwell Mrs., fancy draper 352 High
  road
Keys Thomas R., florist 28a High st.
Kilburn Baths 2 Osborne ter. ; Alfred
  Ward, proprietor
Kilburn House, Land, and Investment
  Co., Limited, Belsize rd. Kilburn
Kilburn Town Hall Co., Limited,
  Belsize rd. Kilburn ; Arthur H.
  Ayres, secretary
King Charles B., builder and decorator
  53 High st.
King George, cowkeeper (The Dairy)
  West end

King Henry, pianoforte tuner 12 Love-
  ridge rd.
King James, bootmaker 8 Swiss ter.
King Mrs. E. J., beer retlr.164 High rd.
King Mrs. E.J., cheesemgr. 166 High rd.
King Mrs. H., milliner and dressmaker
  113 Boundary rd.
King Mrs. L., tobacconist 5 Rosslyn st.
King W. & H.. brush wareho. 44 High st.
KING W. & H., grocers and wine mer-
  chants 45 and 56 High st.
Kippin Edmond, sweep 2 Perrin's court
Kirby F., bootmaker 4 Erskine rd.
Kitchen WilliamT.,butcher 325 High rd.
  Kilburn
Kite S., ironmonger 81 Fairfax rd.
Klosz & Clarke, grocers 89 Fairfax rd.
Knowles James, builder 240 Belsize rd.
  Kilburn
Knowles John, lime and cement mer-
  chant, Cricklewood lane

Ladbury Mrs.. milliner 208 High rd.
Lamb J. M., ironmonger 119 Finchley rd.
Lambert Hy.Jas.,carman 3 Providence pl.
Lambert James, grocer 197 High rd.
Lambert James, oil and colourman
  189 High rd.
Lambourn Mrs., laundry 5 Golder's hill
  cottages, North end
Landrebe Adam, dairy 128 Boundary rd.
Lane John, Jack Straw's Castle, Hamp-
  stead heath
Lane J. A., builder 3 Clock ter.
Lang John, bazaar 39 Fairfax rd.
Langridge George,builder 10a Bolton rd.
LangtonJ.,chimney cleaner 2 Erskine rd.
Lansdell W. H., fruiterer and green-
  grocer 307 High rd. Kilburn
Lansdown Benjn., fruiterer 40 Heath st.
Lauezzari F., tobacconist 7 Heath st.
Lavers Fredk., oilman 1a Loveridge rd.
Lay Edward, laundry, North end
Lay Mrs. Mary Ann, upholsteress, North
  end
Laycock John S., builder 2 Boundary
  mews Boundary rd.
LeaEdward,greengrocer 17Granville ter.
Lea Thomas & Co., coal mers., West end
Leach Fredk., watchmaker 210 High rd.
Leach Mrs. Jane, china dealer 2 South-
  well ter.
Leake Miss, draper 324 High rd.
Leake T. W., pharmaceutical chemist
  44 Hampstead hill gardens
LeDongHenri,hairdrssr.101Boundary rd.
Lee&Son,oyster bar 126 High rd.Kilburn

Lee Chas., watchmkr. 154 Maygrove rd.
Lee Henry W., fruiterer 7 Elizabeth ter.
Lee Jacob, tailor 26 Belgrave rd.
Lee Nelson J., surveyor of taxes 79 Haverstock hill
Le Franc Arthur, builder and decorator 10 Abbey lane and 4 Abbey cottages
Lenny H., baker&confctnr., Kingsgate rd.
Lenny William, tailor 16 Granville ter.
Lewington Mrs., lndrss. 32 Lowfield rd.
Lewis H. J., chemist 2 Fitzjohns' parade
Lewis W., laundry 29 Lowfield rd.
Lilley Wm., bootmaker 34 Palmerston rd.
Lindsay Bros., genl. salesmen 142 High rd.
Lines A. & E., livery stables (Albert yard) Belsize rd. Kilburn
Lines Edward, stationer 79 Fairfax rd.
Lisney T., farrier, Cricklewood
List James, decorator 4 Springfield gdns.
Littlewood William, ironmonger 5a Elizabeth ter.
Lloyd Edwd., tailor 20 King's college rd.
Lloyd Wm., greengrocer 1a Perrin's court
Loader Richard, greengrocer 100 Park rd.
Lockhart & Co., coal merchants, Cricklewood station, Cricklewood lane
London & South Western Bank, Limited (*Hampstead Branch*) 28 High st. ; John Butterfield, manager ; *Kilburn Branch* 42 High rd. ; W. H. Williams, manager and 48 Finchley new rd.
London Parcels Delivery Co. 81 High st.
Long George, tea gardens, Vale of Health
Longhurst Richard, chimney sweep 90 Palmerston rd.
Longland Thomas, butcher 7 Clock ter.
Lonon John, butcher 30 Netherwood st.
Lopez G. & Co., wine merchants 121 Broadhurst gardens
Lorkin George, baker 4 Exeter ter.
Loscombe John, butcher 94 Palmerston rd.
Lougher Edwin, laundry, Cricklewood
Lougher Mrs., genl. shop, Cricklewood
Love Mrs., dressmaker 165 Belsize rd. Kilburn
Low Thomas H., forge, New end sq.
Lowmass Hy., confectioner 157 High rd.
Luckman William, marine store dealer, South end green
Lunn L., sign writer 10 Rosslyn st.
Lunn Mrs., confectioner 10 Rosslyn st.
Lush S. B. & Co., Limited, dyers 9a Bolton rd.
Lynch Richard, gasfitter 11 Fleet rd.

Mable & Co., furniture dealers 278 High rd
McCullum Geo., fishmonger 6 Ridge ter.

McGowan H., builder 1 Garlinge rd.
McMahon Mrs., milliner 4 Stanley gardens
Machell L., bootmaker 36 Gascony avn.
Macpherson Robert & Co., coal merchants 176 Iverson rd.
Maile Wm., general shop 98 Palmerston road
Maitland David, baker 93 Fairfax rd.
Mallett Henry, window blind manufacturer 1 Canfield pl. Canfield gardens
Manning G. J., builder 9 High rd.
Mansfield J., florist 216 Belsize rd.
Manvell T. W., butcher 12 Fairhazel gdns.
Marchant William, cab proprietor 5 Alexandra mews
Marden Henry, draper 6 High rd.
Marks & Co., dyers 77 Haverstock hill
Marks John, fruiterer 24 Boundary rd.
Marks L. & Co., fruiterers 60 High rd.
Marks Mrs., registry for servants, Boundary rd.
Marsh Henry, greengrocer 326 High rd.
Marsh Matthew Henry, beer retailer 92 Palmerston rd.
Marsh Miss, grocer 1a Goldsmith pl.
Marsh William Thomas, *The Load of Hay* 94 Haverstock hill
Martin B., ironmonger 65 Abbey rd.
Martin Edward, greengrocer 19 Cricklewood ter.
Martin F., coiffeur 1 Dawson ter.
Martin G. J., cheesemngr. 6 & 8 Flask walk
Martin Hy., bootmaker 104 Boundary rd.
Martin Thos., leather seller 3 Flask walk
Mash G., greengrocer 55 High rd.
Mason Henry W., general draughtsman 6 Elm grove
Mason Mrs. F.C., berlin fancy repository 65 Fairfax rd.
Mason T. E., butcher 69 High st.
Masters Rchd., coffee rms. 115 Boundary rd
Matthews E. & C., hosiers and hatters 66 High rd.
Matthews E., tobacconist 282 High rd.
Matthews Hy., genl. shop 80 Palmerston rd
Matthews William John, *The Railway Tavern*, South end green
Matthews W. A., blindmaker 170 High road
Maule W. P., chemist 102 Park rd.
Maxted Thomas, dairy 6 South hill park
May George, bookseller 69 High rd.
May Henry, fruiterer 3 Heath st.
May Joshua, beer retailer 22 The Village
Mayes George, hosier and outfitter 3 Belsize park ter.
Meadow W., slater 96 Palmerston rd.

Meager Wm., *The Windmill*, Cricklewood

Melleney Miss, dressmaker 49 Fleet rd.

Mercer A., upholsterer 116 Boundary rd.

Meredith John F., stationer 193 High rd.

Messenger Bros., sign writers 2 Willow ter.

Messinger J. H., writer (Prospect house) Heath st.

Michell & Phillips, brewers & maltsters (Kilburn brewery) 289 and 291 High rd. Kilburn

Mildenhall Jsph., bootmaker 11 Abbey ln.

Mildon Richard, veterinary forge 16 Belsize park mews & 102 William's mews

Miles J. J., draper 9 High st.

Miles Nelson, greengrocer, West end

Millard James, grocer 271 High rd. Kilburn

Miller Geo., beer retailer 12 West end lane

Miller Henry, bottle dealer 13 Abbey lane

Millist & Son, china & glass warehouse 18 Rosslyn st.

Millist & Son, grocers & provision merchants 17 Rosslyn st.

Mills Josiah, coal merchant, London & N.W. Railway station, Finchley new rd.

Millson S., draper 11 Broadhurst grdns.

Milton John, grocer 188 Loveridge rd.

Minter Geo., wardrobe dlr. 89 Abbey rd.

Mitchell A. R., *Covent Garden Stores*, Kingsgate rd.

Mitchell George, veterinary forge, Fleet mews

Mitchell John, upholsterer 1 The Cottages

Mizen Robert Henry, baker and confectioner 55 Fairfax rd.

Model Lodging House, Wells buildings ; Michael Tobin, superintendent

Moir J., upholsterer 59 Kingsgate rd.

Mole Alfred, tobacconist 4 High st. Child's hill

Monville & Co., confectnrs. 2 Stanley gdns.

Moore & Sons, house, land and estate agents 11 Belsize park ter.

Moore Arthur, wholesale ironmonger 140 Maygrove rd.

Moore Edwin, bootmaker 6 Fleet rd.

Moore G. Willis, china and glass warehouse 10 Elizabeth ter.

Moore Henry, coffee and dining rooms 203 Belsize rd. Kilburn

Moore Henry, fitter 2 West cottages

Moore Joseph, gardener 1 Providence pl.

Moore Jsph., surveyor 18 King's college rd.

Morris George William, greengrocer 8 Little Church row

Morris J., drill master 11 New end

Morris O., stationer 2 Ash ter.

Morter Wm., builder 32 Springfield rd.

Morton & Willis, surgeons 15 Greville rd.

Moseley Wm., upholsterer 66a Heath st.

Moss Chas. W., coachbuilder (Clarence house) 160 High rd. and Priory mews

Moss Frederick Richard, coachbuilder 24 Maygrove rd.

Mott J. & Co., dairy 336 High rd.

Mousley Geo., bootmaker 1 Perrin's court

Moy & Arnold, farriers 7 Fairfax mews

Moy George, grocer 52 High st.

Mudie Peter, fishmonger 33 High rd.

Mulley Searles, shoemaker 8 Elm ter.

Munday Mrs., milliner 11 Fitzjohns' parade

Murch Mrs., wardrobe dealer 9 Goldsmith pl.

Murden Mrs., laundry 1 Elm ter.

Murdoch M. J., stationer 7 Belsize park terrace

Mure, Warner & Co., brewers (Hampstead brewery) 9a High st.

Muschamp F., furniture dealer and valuer 57 Park rd.

Myring Jacob, builder 69 Abbey rd.

Neal Alfred, wardrobe dlr. 8 Abbey lane

Neal James, marine store dealer 2 Coleridge gardens

Neal Thomas William, tobacconist 5 Perrin's court

Neale P., bootmaker 1a Netherwood st.

Neame N., grocer, italian warehouseman and wine merchant 81 Haverstock hill

Neill Josiah, chimney sweep 4 Holly bush vale

New Eton & Middlesex Cricket Ground, Harley rd.; J. H. Hanson, proprietor

New River Company (office) 76 High st.; W. H. Hayes, collector

New River Company's Station, South end rd.

Newland W. G., commission agent 29 Loveridge rd.

Newman T., sweep 16 Alexandra mews

Newstead J., sweep 1 Fairhazel gardens

Newton Mrs. Mary Ann, *The Wells Tavern* 16 Well walk

Nicholls Henry, plumber 48 Hampstead hill gardens

Nicholson H. Walker, tailor 172 Loveridge rd.

Nixon James, lay agent 48 Netherwood st.

Noah Mrs. Mary, laundress 3 Elm ter.

Noble Frederick William, stained glass works (York house) 48 Maygrove rd.

Nockels W., fishmonger 6 Heath st.

NODES JOHN 3 Chelmsford ter. Willesden High rd.

Noolfrey A., coffee rooms 14 Belsize park ter.

Norley George, bootmaker 17 High rd.

Norman John, bootmaker 23 High rd.

Norman Henry, laundry 12 The Village

Norman Wm., coffee house 280 High rd.

North Western Gazette Office 84 Haverstock hill; P. J. Smyth

Nowell & Robson, stone merchants and contractors, South end rd.

Nurse H., statnr. 206 Belsize rd. Kilburn

Oakley G., painter 3 Paxon's cottages

Odwell Richard John, decorator 68 Upper Park rd.

O'Hara Charles, butcher 17 High st.

Oldrey H. B., builder 52 High rd.

Oliver Wm., *The Crown*, Cricklewood

Osborne O.H., cheesemngr. 43 Fairfax rd.

Ostick James, plumber 19 Lowfield rd.

Owen R. & Co., wine & spirit merchants 12 Elizabeth ter.

Owers Oscar, auctioneer, West end

Oxford E. W., fishmonger 12 Heath st.

Oxford H. J., *The Black Boy & Still* 54 High st.

Pace Miss, dressmaker (Teresa cottage) New end sq.

Page Jas., fishmngr. 19 King's college rd.

Page Joseph, bootmaker 240 High rd.

Palmer Geo., farrier 2 Loudoun rd. mews

Palmer Thomas, cowkeeper 5 Abbey cottages and Priory mews

Palmer Wm., dairy 230 Belsize rd. Kilburn

Pannell W. T., butcher 55 High st.

Pardoe & Sons, ironmongers 90 High rd. and 12 Colla's mews

Parker G., gardener 4 Oriel cottages Church pl.

Parker John, tailor 16 New end

Parnell Joshua, builder 41 Fordwych rd.

Parnell William, grocer 3 Elizabeth ter.

Parsons Mrs., confectioner (Elizabeth cottage) South end green

Parsons Mrs., paper costumier 15 High rd.

Patent Pyramid Night Light Works, Cricklewood ln.; Saml. Clarke, patentee

Paul William, sweep, Fleet mews

Paveley F. E., cheesemonger (Dorset house) 152 Haverstock hill

Paveley F. E., provision merchant 79 High st.

Pavier John, contractor 8 Lower Lawn rd.

Pavier Mrs., dairy, South end green

Paxton Arthur John, dining rms., Well rd.

Payne James Bane, artist in stained glass 88 Maygrove rd.

Payne Miss, dressmaker 55 Gayton rd.

Payne Thomas, baker and confectioner 81 Abbey rd.

Pearce Mrs., dressmaker 86 Belsize rd.

Pearce Mrs. R., dressmakr. 14 Maygrove rd.

Pearn Fred, saddler 122a Belsize park gardens

Pearse John G., baker 3 High st.

Pegler Enoch, oil & colourman 209 Belsize rd.

Penhey Robert, fancy draper (Swiss cottage) 117 Finchley rd.

Penn David, bookmaker 2 Willow cotts.

Penn Jas., sweep 17 King's college mews

Peover George, dealer in curiosities 2 Garfield ter.

Pepper A., sweep and carpet beater 2 Goldsmith's gardens

Percival Richard, *Metropolitan Fire Brigade Station*, Adelaide rd.

Perkins W., builder 4 New end sq.

Perraton A., tobccnst. 71 High rd. Kilburn

Perry & Co., jobmasters 39 Greville rd.

Perry Chas., plumber 31 Palmerston rd.

Perry Hy., crpntr. & joiner 7 Grove ter.

Perry Thomas, dairyman 15 Church lane

Peter H., gas and hot water engineer 5 Princess mews

Peter Henry, gasfitter and plumber 1 Upper Belsize ter.

Peters Charles, general supply stores, Vale of Health

Peters Charles, *Vale of Health Tavern*, Vale of Health

Pettinger E., chemist 49 High st.

Phillips Acton, *The Cock Tavern* 125 High rd.

Phillips Alfred, music seller 43 High rd.

Phillips H., auctioneer and estate agent 123 Finchley rd.

Philpott Thomas, butcher 2 High st. Child's hill

Phipps J. H., fishmonger 7 Exeter ter.

Phipps T. J., watchmaker 161 High rd.

Phipps W., fishmonger 95 Haverstock hill

Phipps W., jobmaster, Steele's mews

Phipps William, jobmaster 77 High st.

Pickford Josiah, bath chair proprietor 1 Lower heath cottages

Pierce B. S., fishmonger 290 High rd.

Piggott George, fruiterer 204 Belsize rd Kilburn

Pincham Richard, *Railway Hotel*, West end lane

Pincham Seymour, fruitr. 57 Fairfax rd.

Pinn J., *The Volunteer Hotel* 77 High rd.

Pipe W., chemist 1 King's college rd.

Pippett Stephen, wardrobe dlr. 4 Bell ter.

Pitcairn David, stationer 12 King's college rd.

Pleasance Ernest, watchmaker & jeweller 10 Exeter ter.

Pocock G., fruiterer 12 South hill park

Pollard Hy. John, grocer 310 High rd.

Pook George, bootmaker 44 High rd.

Poole Chas., cheesemonger 73 Abbey rd.

Poole Frederick, furniture warehouse 66 Heath st.

Poole J., hairdresser 115 High rd.

Potter G. & Sons, builders, Holly hill

Potter George William, house and estate agent 22 High st.

Potter Henry, china and glass dealer 23 Elizabeth ter.

Potter & Sons, engineers, West end

Potter John, corn dealer 51 High st.

Potter T. & Sons, engineers, West end

Pottle Miss, dressmaker 69 Heath st.

Powley P., tea gardens, Vale of Health

Preston Fredk., hairdresser 50 Fleet rd.

Preston George P., coachbuilder (Beaconsfield house) 5 Iverson rd.

Price F. H., *The Washington Hotel*, Belsize park gardens

Price S., Kingsgate farm, Mill lane

Price Sidney, dairy 162 High st.

Price William, fishmonger 4 Rosslyn st.

Priest Mrs. Frances, laundress 5 Upper Park ter.

Prior Misses H. & C., fancy repository 22 Elizabeth ter.

Prior Samuel, rustic works (Laurel cottage) Cricklewood

Pritchard George, builder 16 Heath st.

Pritchard J., dairyman 24 Heath st.

Prockter & Son, wine mers. 47 High st.

Provost & Co., printers, Holly mount

Provost Eugène, hairdresser 15 Broadhurst gardens

Pugh John, builder 4a Elizabeth ter.

Pull Thos., frame maker 4 Perrin's court

Purchas James, grocer 26 High rd.

Purchas Mrs. M. A., grocer 85 High rd.

Purry F., gas inspector 3 Holly mount

Putt Mrs., grocer 56 Flask walk

Pye Richard, carpenter 33 Palmerston rd.

Rabbits & Sons, bootmakers 8 High st.

Raby Edmund, confectioner 2 Fleet rd.

Raggett Frank, *The Rosslyn Arms* 16 Rosslyn st.

Rainbow Henry J., upholsterer (Elizabeth house) High st.

Ralph J., dairyman 52 High st.

Randall Fredk., fruiterer 89 Boundary rd.

Randall H. G., butcher 2 Exeter ter.

Randall Thomas G., butcher 6 Elizabeth ter. and 93 Haverstock hill

Randle Mrs., *The Castle*, Finchley rd. Child's hill

Randle Thomas, bootmaker 5 High st. Child's hill

Rasey Hy., baker 202 Belsize rd. Kilburn

Rasey Hy., glass wareho. 2a Loveridge rd.

Ravenhill W. J., stationer 224 High rd. Kilburn

Rawlins G. T., gasfitter 264 High rd.

Raymond Geo., watchmaker 50 High st.

Rayner W. M., tobacconist 124 High rd.

Redding Frederick Chas., cheesemonger 232 Belsize rd. Kilburn

Redge Mrs., feather cleaner 163 Belsize rd. Kilburn

Reed George, carman 16 West end lane

Reed J., tailor 269 High rd. Kilburn

Reed Mrs., laundry 16 West end lane

Reed Thomas, hatter 32 High st.

Reeves R., bootmaker 24 King's college rd.

Reynolds Joseph, beer retailer 2 Haverstock hill

Rhodes A., carpenter 18 Prospect rd.

Richards G., marine store dealer 3 Erskine rd.

Richards James, dairy 8a Elizabeth ter. and 3 Exeter ter.

Richardson J. T., manufacturing ironmonger 61 Gayton rd.

Rickett J. C., coal and coke merchant Cricklewood lane

Rieger H., baker and confectioner 20 Elizabeth ter.

Ritchie Mrs. H., milliner 19 Heath st.

Ritchie Robert, landscape gardener 5 Mount Vernon

Rix Misses, dress and mantle makers 16 Cricklewood ter.

Robbins John, baker 4 Kelson st.

Roberts Bros., butchers 244 High rd.

Roberts Arthur, veterinary surgeon 66 Belsize rd.

Robertson Bros., boot and shoe makers 96 High rd.

Robertson Henry S., ladies' & children's outfitter 116 Finchley rd.

Robinson Hercules, deputy-turncock, South end rd.

Roff & Son, builders 57 & 70 Heath st.

Roff Josiah, laundry, Golder's hill cotts.

Rogers Alexander, greengrocer 2 Granville houses

Rogers J., pork butcher 65 High st.

Rogers John, laundry 14 The Village

Rogers R., tinplate wrkr. 12 Colla's mews

Rogers T. H., bootmaker 133 High rd.

Rogers William, bootmaker 138 High rd. Kilburn

Rolfe William, grocer 2a Hemstall rd.

Roper William, draper 1 & 2 Bell terrace and 36, 36a and 40 High rd.

Rosbrook John, bootmaker 4 Flask walk

Ross Miss., haberdasher 208 Haverstock hill

Rowe Joseph, baker and confectioner 7 Fairhazel gardens

Ruck Thomas, builder 94 & 98 Park rd.

Rudderham Mrs., laundrss. 6 Hemstall rd.

Rudiger Mrs., baker 99 Palmerston rd.

Rudkin Henry, builder 3 Fleet rd.

Rudkin Mrs. F.M., tobacconist 3 Fleet rd.

Ruegenn Henry J., fruiterer 2 Ainger rd.

Ruff George, bootmaker 1 Arch pl.

Rumbold Wm., baker 8 South hill park

Rumbold Wm., grocer 10 South hill park

Runcieman—, carman 1 Loudoun rd. mews

Rushton James, pianoforte tuner 1 Prospect villas

Russell John, nursery 133 Haverstock hill

Russell Joseph, laundry 28 The Village

Russell Mrs., laundrss. 4 Child's hill cots.

Ruth E., watchmaker 60 Heath st.

Saers Mrs., dressmaker 4 Richmond villas

Saich H., carpenter 1 Eton pl.

Salter Henry William, watchmaker 18 Haverstock hill

Salter Mrs. Emma, dressmkr. 10 Fleet rd.

Sangster A., chmst. 48a Finchley new rd.

Sapsford George, plumber 16 King's college rd.

Sargeant William D., draper 194 Belsize rd. Kilburn

Sargent Mrs., dressmaker 163 Belsize rd. Kilburn

Satterley W. J., butcher 4 Yew ter.

Satterthwaite E., bootmaker 92 Park rd.

Satterthwaite Robert, bootmaker 5 & 5a Arch pl.

Saunders Mrs., umbrella maker 3 Rosslyn cottages

Saunders William, stationer and newsagent 236 Belsize rd. Kilburn

Saunders W.P., jobmaster (Elm cottage) North end &(stables) 1 East Heath rd.

Savage & Son, dyers 85 Boundary rd.

Savage T., fruiterer 63 Kingsgate rd.

Savage William, greengrocer 22 New end

Savigear Alfred & Son, *The Swiss Cottage* Finchley rd.

Saward Henry, umbrella maker 121a Finchley rd.

Sayers Edwin Charles, carpenter 102 Maygrove rd.

Schaper John, hairdrsr. 1a Belsize pk. ter

Scoles A., tile and brick depôt, West end

Scoles Albert, lime and brick merchant Finchley new rd.

Searle Wm., cheesmngr. 2 Elizabeth ter

Sears Hy. W., general draper 111 High rd

Segar & Co., ironmongers 226 High rd.

Sellick Mrs. F. & C., milliners and dress makers, West end

Selway H.J., fishmonger 9 Elizabeth ter.

Sercombe Edward, cabinetmaker 2 Belgrave rd.

Setterington Jsph., florist 103 Boundary rd

Seymour James, florist, Bridge rd.

Seymour Walter James, general shop 7 Little Church row

Sharp Benjamin, fruiterer 89 Haverstock hill

Sharp Charles Smithee, builder 91 South hill park

Sharpe C. & J., furniture dealers 11 and 13 Flask walk

Sharpe Hy., brush warehouse 6 High st

Shave E.H., veterinary surg. 69a Heath st

Sheath Sydney, cabinetmaker 303 High rd. Kilburn

Sheehy John, tea gardens, North end

Sheer John, draper 13 King's college rd

Sheffield John, carpenter 46 Flask wal

Shepherd Frederick, gardener 110 Maygrove rd.

Shepherd T. & B., plumbers 3 Little Church row

Shepston Thos., cnfctnr. 62 Upper Park rd

Shield George, *The Palmerston Hote* 308 High rd.

Shilston William George, cheesemonge 112 Boundary rd.

Shirley Mrs. Caroline, *Cricklewoo Tavern* 20 Cricklewood ter.

Shockley Richd., florist, South end gree

Shore Danl., beer retlr. 20 Netherwood s

Short A. A., watchmaker 70 High st.

Shropp John, watchmaker and jewelle 272 Belsize rd. Kilburn

Simmonds Alfd., laundry 1 Saunders cott

Simmonds W., chair caner 6 Church lan

Simmons G., grocer 5 Yew ter.

Simms James & Co., milk contracto 5 Thompson's mews

Simpkins A., bootmaker 2 Colla's mew

Simpson W., cheesemonger 83 Fairfax rd.

Skipper Miss, dressmkr. 33 Winchester rd.

Skoyles Robert, ironmonger 72 High st.

Slack Jas., contractor, Christchurch rd.

Slann Francis John, plumber 5 Church ln.

Sleven James P., watchmaker and jeweller 2a Fleet rd.

Slight George, bootmaker 2 Alfred ter.

Slow Benjamin, oilman 110 High rd.

Smalley J., *The Black Lion* 272 High rd.

Smart Frederick, engineer, Fire brigade station 73 Heath st.

Smith A., grocer 37 Heath st.

Smith A. J. & Co., wine merchants 178 High rd.

Smith Edward, cheesemonger 91 Haverstock hill

Smith Frederick, florist 148 High rd.

Smith F. W., *The Duke of Hamilton,* New end

Smith Henry, New West end dairy 20 Mill lane

Smith James, baker 90 Haverstock hill

Smith John, carpenter 13 Pond st. and South end green

Smith J.S., carpet grounds 8 Kingsford st.

Smith Mrs., midwife, 3 West cottages

Smith Mrs. Jane, dressmaker 74 Upper Park rd.

Smith Reuben, builder 1 Ash grove

Smith Thomas, *William the Fourth* 77 High st.

Smith Thomas J., beer retailer, West end

Smith William, coach maker, Well rd.

Smith William, confectioner 94 High rd.

Smith William, fitter 3 West cottages

Smyth Misses E. & S., dressmakers 134 High rd.

Snodgrass Misses E. & F., dressmakers 57 Gayton rd.

Snow & Collins, confectioners 55 Fleet rd.

Snow G., builder 17 Belsize park ter.

Snowball Joseph, draper 18 Granville ter.

Snoxall W. W., corn dealer 320 High rd.

Solesbury G., wine and spirit merchant 3 Swiss ter.

" South Hampstead Observer " Office, Fairfax rd.

Southcott R., draper 332 High rd.

Southon W., clothier 131 High rd.

Sowden Mrs. A. M., baker 228 Belsize rd. Kilburn

Sowden Robert, tailor 133 Iverson rd.

Sparks Francis, tobacconist 27 High rd.

Sparks Frank, photographic artist 33 Kilburn priory

Spells W. E., draper 103 High rd.

Spenser Whatley and Underhill, coal merchants 46 High rd.

Spicer Robert, farrier, 2 Watts cottages

Staines & Co., tobacconists 41 High st.

Staines & Son, china and glass dealers 64 Heath st.

Stamp Chas., cheesemonger 80 High rd.

STAMP EDWARD B., pharmaceutical chemist, *The Hampstead Pharmacy* 29 High st.

Stamp Mrs., milliner 82 High rd.

Stamp Mrs., tea gardens, Vale of Health

Stancombe G. W., coach builder and wheelwright 8 Loudoun road mews

Stanfield R., turncock 7 High rd.

Stanier Mrs., *The King of Bohemia* 10 High st.

Staniforth Benjamin, slater 10 Fleet rd.

Stanley W., confectioner 69 Heath st.

Stansfield R., M.P.S., chemist 85 Haverstock hill

Staples Arthur H., carver and gilder 201 High rd.

Staples George Richard, draper 83 Haverstock hill

Star & Co., mantle warehouse 102 High rd.

Stedman John, corn merchant 210 Belsize rd. Kilburn

Steeden Daniel, greengrocer 102 Boundary rd.

Steer Charles, upholsterer 37 Fairfax rd.

Stephens Mrs., dressmaker 314 High rd.

Stephens P., bedding manufacturer 153 High rd.

Stephenson J. P., confectioner 354 High road

Stevens George, builder (Lawn cottage) West end

Stevens Henry, boot & shoe warehouse 107 High rd.

Stevens Walter G., auctioneer, Finchley new rd.

Stewart & Sons, booksellers & stationers 3 Fleet rd.

STEWART JAMES, silk mercer and outfitter 53 High rd.

Stewart Thomas, engineer 12 Maygrove rd.

Stiff Edward, draper 191 High rd.

Stiles Mrs., bootmkr. 26 King's college rd.

Stimson S., greengrocer 2 Yew ter.

Stockley G., plumber 6 Willow ter.

Stokes John, *The Britannia* 95 Fairfax rd.

Stone Alfred, pawnbroker and furniture dealer 95 & 97 High rd.

Stone Richard, stationer 22 Boundary rd.

Stone Thomas Midgley, gun maker 173 Loveridge rd.

Stone Walter, grngrcr. 31 Winchester rd.

Storey John, fruiterer 61a Abbey rd.

Stout Henry John, carpenter 9a Elm ter.

Stracey R. G., coffee rooms 285 High rd.

Stray & Sons, bootmakers 232 High rd.

Street George, cowkeeper 17 Heath st.

Streeter H., writer & grainer 3 Abbey cotts.

Streeter S. A., oilman 93 Boundary rd.

Stringer Thos., decorator 14 South hill pk.

Stubbs & Son, grocers 21 & 23 King's college rd.

STUBBS C., tailor 28 King's college rd.

Stubbs John, stationer 11 Elizabeth ter.

Summerbell E., dairy 214 Belsize rd. Kilburn

Summerfield Mrs., drssmkr. 37 Fairfax rd.

Sweet & Co., tobacconists 140 High rd.

Sweet William, plumber 8 Maygrove rd.

Swinney Chas., gasfitter 24 The Village

Swiss Cottage Coffee Stall ; Mrs. Pitts, manageress, Finchley new rd.

Swiss Cottage Skating Rink, Finchley new rd. ; J. Freeman, manager

Symes William, boot maker 9 Alfred ter.

Symes Wm. G., bootmaker 4 Garfield ter.

Symonds John, harness maker 37 High rd.

Szezepkowski G., dressmaker 1a Belsize crescent

Taggett C. M., dairyman 3 Yew ter.

Tailby George, butcher 5 Fleet rd.

Tanner Charles, carpenter 139 Belsize rd. Kilburn

Tanner Mrs. J., cook and confectioner 36 High st.

Taplin Thos., toy dealer 87 Boundary rd.

Tasker Elijah, stone merchant (St. Mary's cottage) 15 Downshire hill

Taylor Alfred, solicitor & commissioner for oaths and declarations, The Mount Heath st.

Taylor Charles, cheesemonger 292 High rd.

Taylor Edward, herbalist 144 High rd.

Taylor Mrs. E., dairy 202 Haverstock hill

Taylor Thomas Bennett, cigar stores 6 Canfield gardens

Taylor W., beer retailer 24 New end

Taylor William, sweets shop 2 Castle ter.

Tebboth William, zinc worker 137 High rd.

Tebbutt Edwin, chemist 316 High rd.

Tegetmeier Miss, kindergarten & school 18 King Henry's rd.

Temperance Coffee House; John Towers, manager, West end

Temple Thos., bootmaker 64 Up. Park rd.

Thoden F., watchmaker 9 Swiss ter. Belsize rd.

Thomas Charles, greengrocer 4 Ardwick ter.

Thomas John William, grocer 66 Upper Park rd.

Thomas Joseph, boot and clothing stores 3 High st. Child's hill

Thomas Joseph, waiter 9 Bolton rd.

Thomas W. I., dairy 2 Church pl.

Thomas William I., fishmonger and poulterer 5 Upper Belsize ter.

Thompson Arthur G., fancy draper 136 High rd.

Thompson E.W., pawnbroker 51 High rd.

Thorne & Co., fancy drapers 100 High rd.

Thorne Mrs., fishmonger 14 Swiss ter.

Thwaites George, grocer 1 Willow rd.

Thwaites George, oilman 87 Abbey rd.

Ticehurst A., baby linen warehouse 146 High rd.

Tidey Mrs. E. C., *The Belsize Tavern* 1 Upper Belsize ter.

Till William, builder 9 Gayton rd.

Timms Henry, bootmkr. 105 Boundary rd

Timms John, oilman 29 Winchester rd.

Timms William Richard, bootmaker 2 Fairhazel gardens

Titchener Joseph, grocer 18 Flask walk

Titmuss Albert, berlin wool repository 19 Winchester rd.

Tofield Robt., carpenter 10 Netherwood st.

Tolhurst Mrs., dressmaker 6a Elizabeth terrace

Tomlins E., grocer 15 Swiss ter.

Tompson Bros., fancy drapers and milliners 28 and 30 High rd.

Tooley Thomas, dairyman, North end

Tooley Thomas, jobmaster 8 Heath st.

Topps Francis, watchmaker 15 King's college rd.

Townsend Thos., gardener (Rose mount) 20 West end lane

Treasure H. I. and Co., house agents 344 High rd.

Tremari & Camoccio, confectioners 1 Haverstock hill

TREVERS TREVERS, auctioneer and estate agent 4 Canfield gardens

Trevillian Miss, laundress 6 Cricklewood ter.

Trilsbach Augustus, baker 26 New end

Trimbee Fredk., bootmkr 25 Winchester re

Trinder Thomas, riding master 2 Downshire hill

Troughton E. A., ladies' and children' outfitter 4 Fitzjohns' parade

Trudgett Henry William, jobmaster 13 and 210 Haverstock hill

Trussell William, baker, Hemstall rd.

TUGWELL T. B. & SON, builders 4 Belsize cres.

Tupman Charles J. T., surveyor and estate agent 2 Lower ter.

Turner & Co.,dressmakers41Belgrave rd.

Turner & Wharton, boot factors 304 High rd.

Turner Charles,provision stores 350 High road

Turner J., tobacconist 1 Ash ter.

Turner T., hairdresser 2 Quex rd.

Turpie Joseph, builder (The Exchange) The Ridge

TyersWm.,cheesmngr. 52 Netherwood st.

Tyne Main Coal Company 71 High rd.

Tyrrell Walter, gardener 1 Provident pl.

Underwood & Sons, cemetery masons & monumental sculptors, Fortune grn.

Upton K., W. & M., milliners and fancy drapers 2 Dawson ter.

Utting Mrs. Honora, *The White Bear*, Well rd.

Vallis George, fruiterer 122 High rd.

Van Camp E., builder 314 High rd.

Van Praag Alex., tbccnst. 294 High rd.

Van Praag A. & Son, novelty stores 294 High rd.

Vanse F., tailor 11 Ariel st.

Vere William, builder 70 and 72 High rd.

Verey A. S. & Co., wine and spirit merchants 1 Quex rd.

Vickers MissA.,dressmaker 75 Fairfax rd.

Vickers V., music library 75 Fairfax rd.

Victoria Wine Co. 213 Belsize rd. Kilburn, 122 Boundary rd., 13 Elizabeth ter., 12 Fitzjohns' parade and 313 High rd. Kilburn

Vinall Frederick, *The Adelaide Tavern* 1 Adelaide rd.

Vinall Mrs. Elizabeth, Fleet laundry 20 Fleet rd.

VincentJames, iron moulder 5West cotts.

Vine Wm., gardener 7 Hampstead sq.

Vooght William J.,chemist 51 Fairfax rd.

Wain James J. & Co., grocers and wine merchants 45 & 49 Fairfax rd.

Wakeford Hy., draper 25 & 26 High st.

Walden Edward,provision dealer (Kingsgate house) Hemstall rd.

Walford Wm.,general draper 5 High st.

Walker and Son, marine store dealers 1 Little Church row

Walker Elihu, builder 70 Upper Park rd.

Walker George P., gardener 6 Gayton rd.

Walker Thos., builder 11 Claremont rd.

Walker W., rag and metal merchant 17 Belsize park mews

Walker Wm., animal doctor 87Abbey rd.

Walker William, coffee rooms 1 Yew ter.

Wallas & Jesser, wholesale ironmongers 258 Belsize rd. Kilburn

Wallman Mrs., dressmaker 2 Bolton rd.

Walter C. A. & Co.,coal mers., Iverson rd.

Walton, Hassell & Port, italian warehousemen 306 High rd.

Walton G., auctioneer and house agent (Gladstone house) 7 Iverson rd.

Walton Geo., greengrocer 113 High rd.

Walton Thomas, analytical chemist 204 Haverstock hill

Ward L.,dining rms.123Broadhurst gdns.

Ward Mrs. R., nurse 16 Cricklewood ter.

Ward Wm., tobacconist 8 Elizabeth ter.

Warden R., jobbing grdnr. 2 Abbey cots.

WardleJas,.house decorator 12 Bolton rd.

Wardle Mrs., dressmaker 18 Bolton rd.

Wardle Thomas,decorator 137 Belsize rd. Kilburn

Wardley Alfred, provision dealer 1 Granville houses, ironmonger 2 Ridge ter., and draper 3 Ridge ter.

Ware J. & Son, grocers and provision merchants 42 High st.

Ware R. P., *The Coach and Horses* 45 Heath st.

Warr & Son, tailors 182 High rd.

Warren F. & Co., coal mers., Iverson rd.

Warren George Robert, chemist 79 Abbey rd.

Warriner Alfred, tobacconist 329 High rd. Kilburn

Warwick Geo., greengrocer 12 Kelson st.

Watkins D., veterinary forge 127 and 274 High rd.

Watkins James George, coffee and dining rooms 274 Belsize rd. Kilburn

Watson A. J., chemist 2 High st.

Watson Henry, plasterer 10 Iverson rd.

Watts George, gardener 42 Maygrove rd.

Watts Saml., dairyman 14 Granville ter.

Watts W. H., builder and contractor, Church lane

Weaver Geo.,tobccnst.12 Haverstock hill

Webb Charles, horse dealer (Wyndham house) Cricklewood

Webb Jsph. Jas., builder 8 Narcissus rd.

Webb Thomas.gardener(Belgrave lodge) Belgrave gardens

Weber H. & Co., cigar merchants 11 Swiss ter. Belsize rd.

WeberstadtR.E.&Co.,drapers301High rd.
Webster Ernest, watch and clock maker and jeweller 45 Loudoun rd.
Webster Joseph, *The White Horse*, South end green
Welch & Thorpe, *Blue Ribbon Coffee Palace* 67 Heath st.
Welch A., berlin repository ; agent for Stevenson Brothers celebrated dye works, Dundee, N.B. Established 1814 (Berlin house) 70 High st.
Welch Saml., carpenter 22 Maygrove rd.
Weldon Miss, dress and mantle maker 70 Belsize rd.
Weller D.,veternry.forge18Granville ter.
Wells William, portmanteau maker 4 Haverstock hill
Welsted Thos., bootmkr. 5 West end lane
Werren & Trowbridge, grocers 287 High rd. Kilburn
West&Boreham,buildrs.50Haverstock hl.
West Henry, stationer, Finchley rd.
West London Dairy Society 31 High rd.; Robert Hornby, managing director
West Middlesex Water Works (Kidderpore reservoir) ; Henry English, reservoir attendant ; John Geary, turncock, Platt's lane
West Middlesex Water Works Co. 1 Fordwych rd. ; Cornelius Robert Cleverly, inspector
Whale George, gardener 7 The Village
Whaley & Waterhouse, surgeons (Ovoca) 18 Woodchurch rd.
Wharton & Turner, boot manufacturers 5 Fitzjohns' parade
Whatley Thomas, dairyman 31 Downshire hill
Wheeler G., dairy 4 Upper Park ter.
Wheeler Mrs. M. E., *The Belgrave Hotel* 63 Abbey rd.
White Miss A. E., *The Victoria Tavern* 83 Abbey rd.
White Gordon A.,baker and confectioner 318 High rd.
White Hy., carpenter 13 Netherwood st.
WhiteJames,bootmaker 65 Kingsgate rd.
White William, dining rooms 331 High rd. Kilburn
White Wm., fruiterer 3a Elizabeth ter.
White Wm., grocer 18 Cricklewood ter.
Whitehorn Thomas, watchmaker 18 Heath st. and 1 Rosslyn st.
WHITELEY WILLIAM, Westbourne grove
  31 hatter, sticks, whips, &c.
  33 tailor and woollen draper, liveries

WHITELEY WILLIAM, Westbourne grove
  35 & 37 gentlemen's hosier, glover, and complete outfitter
  39 counting house
  39 silks, dress materials, banking : railway and theatre ticket office
  41 haberdashery, trimmings, gloves, and hosiery
  43 lace, millinery, outfitting, furs, &c.
  45 shawls, mantles, costumes, general dressmaking, &c.
  47 jewellery, plate, drugs, and foreign fancy goods
  49 boots,shoes,india-rubber and waterproof goods
  51 ribbons, flowers, feathers
  51 costume showroom
  53 prints, calicoes, muslins, general drapery
  53 costume showroom
  53 hairdressing saloon
  55 printing, stationery, engraving, bookbinding, die sinking, &c.
  55aberlin wool and fancy needlework
  61 wines and spirits, tobaccos and cigars
WHITELEY WILLIAM, Kensington gardens sq.
  50 to 53 toys and games,confectionery and restaurant, refreshment and cloak rooms, wedding breakfasts, ball suppers, &c.
WHITELEY WILLIAM, Queen's rd.
  147 household furniture, bedding, furniture removal and warehousing depôt
  149 carpets, oilcloths, blinds, and furnishing drapery
  151 family and household linen, curtains, blankets, trunks, and travelling equipages
  153 china,glass,earthenware,and lamps
  155 ironmongery, tin ware, brushes, turnery, ball and rout furnishing and general hire department
  157 building,decorating,paperhanging, house & estate agency, auctioneering,coals,forage,shipping,cleaning and dyeing ; pianos, pictures, and general fine art depôt. Fruit floral hall,aviary,poultry, pigeons, and domestic pets
  159 meat, poultry, game, fish, grocery wine, spirits, and beer, mineral waters, and general provision warehouse

Whiting James E., head gardener (Laburnum cottage) Vale of Health
Whitley Miss, School house, Church walk
Whittlesey William C., butcher 110 Boundary rd.
Wickes T. H., engineer 15 Albion rd.
Wiffen George, livery stables, Eton pl.
Wigan Coal and Iron Co., South end rd. ; C. Parker & Son, agents
Wiggins Fred., builder 198 Belsize rd. Kilburn
Wiggins W.,confectnr. 62a Haverstock hl.
Wildy Geo., builder 18a Belsize park ter.
Wilkins C., bootmaker 1 Church pl.
Wilkins Henry, dairy 19 New end
Wilkins H. C., grocer 67 Kingsgate rd.
Wilkins W., gardener 17 Church lane
Willes Harry, turncock 27 Lowfield rd.
Williams Ambrose, timber merchant (Elm tree yard) 279 & 281 High rd.
Williams Edwerd, upholsterer 1 West end lane
Williams John, bootmaker 5 Stamford pl.
Williams Thomas, umbrella maker 256 High rd.
Williams William, mantle warehouse 186 High rd. Kilburn
Williams William Henry, *The Fleet Tavern* 90 Park rd.
Williamson C.,cheesemonger 248 High rd.
Willis & Humphrey, ironmongers 83 & 84 High st.
Wilson & Co., builders 23 Winchester rd.
Wilson & Dickens, sweeps 14a Belsize park ter.
Wilson Arthur, Wildwood farm, North end
Wilson H., bootmaker 175 Belsize rd. Kilburn
Wilson Henry, stores 18 Belsize park ter.
Wilson Joseph, fishmonger 107 Boundary rd.
Wilson J. P., chemist 15 Granville ter.
Wilson Misses, booksellers and stationers 89 High rd.
Wilson Robert, grocer 118 High rd.
Wilson Thomas, corn dealer 30 High st.
Wiltshire Richard, carpenter 9 Hampstead sq.
Wiltshire William, builder 47 Heath st.

Wiltshire William, house decorator 9 Hampstead sq.
Winbolt Mrs., dressmaker 136 Belsize rd.
Windsor J., dairy 12 Granville ter.
Windsor Richd., *The Red Lion*, The Village
Windsor Thomas, florist 19 The Village
Winterman Samuel, grocer 13 Grove ter.
Winyard William, jun., carpenter and builder, West end
Wise Samuel, laundry 30 & 31 The Village
Withers Frdk., furniture dlr. 87 High rd.
Withers H. R., draper 9 Belsize park ter. and 2 and 2a Belsize cres.
Wood Richard J., nurseryman (Haverstock hill nursery) 113 Haverstock hill & (Bedford nursery) 126 Haverstock hill
Wood Thomas, florist and seedsman 3 Belsize cres.
Woodland John, general shop 5 Goldsmith pl.
Woodrow Miss M., dressmaker 171 Belsize rd. Kilburn
Woods E., grocer 322 High rd.
Woodward J., farrier 20 Heath st.
Woodward Miss J., booksllr. 14 Rosslyn st.
Woodward Mrs., ladies' nurse 61 Fairfax rd
Woolfe B. J., grocer 57 High rd.
Wreford William, butcher 3 Ardwick ter.
Wright A., dentist (Ravena lodge) Shootup hill
Wright E. K., confectioner 348 High rd.
Wright Mrs., ladies' and children's outfitter 73 Haverstock hill
Wythe Albert, builder (Albert ho.) Mill ln.

Yates John, greengrocer 28 Netherwood st.
Yates Robert, butcher 258 High rd.
Yeo John, fishmonger 61 Fairfax rd.
Yeo Robert, estate office 35 Fairfax rd.
Yeomans Jas., gardener 2 South end green
Yerbury F. W., builder, Birchington rd.
Yerbury F. W., tailor 144 High rd.
Yerbury R. A., bookseller and stationer 156 High rd.
Yerbury R. A., builder 158 High rd.
Young Henry Tom, builder 6 Ariel st.

Zahringer P., watchmaker and jeweller 1 Belsize park ter.

STAMP DUTIES.

RECEIPTS.

	s.	d.
Receipt or discharge given for the payment of £2 or upwards............	0	1

Penalty for giving a receipt without a stamp......... £10

DRAFTS, BILLS, &c.

	s.	d.
Draft or Order for the payment of any sum of money to the bearer, or to order, on demand, including bankers' cheques	0	1

Inland Bill of Exchange, Promissory Note, Draft, or Order, payable otherwise than on demand.

	Duty.	
Not above £5	0	1
Above £5 & not above 10.	0	2
,, 10 ,, 25.	0	3
,, 25 ,, 50.	0	6
,, 50 ,, 75.	0	9
,, 75 ,, 100.	1	0
,, 100 ,, 200.	2	0
,, 200 ,, 300.	3	0
,, 300 ,, 400.	4	0
,, 400 ,, 500.	5	0

And 1s. for every additional £100 or part of £100.

AGREEMENTS.

Agreement, or any Memorandum of an Agreement, made in England or Ireland under hand only, or made in Scotland without any clause of registration, and not otherwise specifically charged with any duty, whether the same be only evidence of a contract, or obligatory upon the parties from its being a written instrument ......6d.

DUTIES & LICENCES.

	£	s.	d.
HOUSE DUTY—For every Inhabited House rented at not less than £20 per year, if used for trade purposes, or occupied as a farmhouse, for every 20s. of such annual value	0	0	6
If occupied in any other manner ...	0	0	9

DUTIES ON MALE SERVANTS, CARRIAGES, HORSES, AND ARMORIAL BEARINGS. — For every male domestic servant of any kind............ 0 15 0

For every carriage— If such carriage shall have four or more wheels, and shall be of the weight of four hundredweight or upwards............	2	2	0
If such carriage shall have less than four wheels, or, having four or more wheels, and shall be of a less weight than four hundredweight.......	0	15	0
For armorial bearings, if such armorial bearings shall be painted, marked or affixed on or to any carriage	2	2	0
If such armorial bearings shall not be so painted, marked, or affixed, but shall be otherwise worn or used	1	1	0

LICENCES.

	Per ann.		
	£	s.	d.
Appraisers............	2	0	0
Auctioneers	10	0	0
Attorneys, &c., London (or within 10 miles) Edinburgh, and Dublin.........	9	0	0
Non-residents	6	0	0
Conveyancers, Special Pleaders, London and Dublin ...	9	0	0
Dogs (each)	0	7	6
Gun	0	10	0
Game	3	0	0
Pedlar	0	5	0
Hawker with 1 Horse	4	4	0
House-agents.........	2	0	0
Makers of Playing-cards or Dice......	1	0	0
Medicine vendors...	0	5	0
Pawnbrokers.........	7	10	0
For Marriages	2	2	6

INCOME TAX.

1. Property, profits and gains, salaries and funds. Where the yearly income from every source amounts to £150 and upwards, 6d. in the pound.

Incomes under £150 exempt.

From incomes amounting to £150, and under £400, a deduction is allowed of £120 : for example, an income of £150 will be charged as £30 and £200 as £80

Elementary & Middle Class Training Schools,
(ESTABLISHED 1864,)
WILKIN STREET, KENTISH · TOWN.

*(Approached from Prince of Wales Road, by Dalby Street, adjoining the North London||Railway Station.
The Schools are three minutes' walk from this Station.
|Children's Return Tickets from Hampstead, 1d.; Second Class, 2d.)*

The Schools are recommended by Thos. Twining, Esq., Vice-President of the Society of Arts, and Founder of the Educational Museum, South Kensington; Rev. Joseph Angus, LL.D., Principal of Regent's Park College; and Robert Dunning, Esq., late Lecturer on Education to the Home and Colonial School Society's Training College.

FEES :—Infants' School, 6d. per week¦; Junior and Upper, 8d. and 9d.

The Classes not being too large, every child receives individual attention from adult and duly qualified teachers, and special care is taken to avoid all over-pressure, while giving a thoroughly good elementary education, with Needlework, Drawing, and Singing.

Parents are supplied with monthly reports of their children's progress and conduct at School, and certificates are awarded annually for passing the Government Standards.

Victoria Higher School (for Girls only).
(ESTABLISHED 1875.)

This School is held in premises adjoining the Training Schools, and is under the same Director, but entirely distinct from them. The hours of entering and leaving are different, also the staff of teachers. The Head Mistress is College trained and of long experience in the management and teaching of girls, and the Principal Teacher holds a full University Certificate.

FEES :—Four to Six Guineas per annum, according to age, including French, German, and Drawing.

WITH PREPARATION FOR THE CAMBRIDGE UNIVERSITY EXAMINATIONS.

Girls are received from Seven to Seventeen years of age, and can enter at any time, the first term being charged from date of entry. Hours :—9.30 till 2, with half-hour interval for luncheon and the recreation grounds.

Entrance Fee, 5s. Deposit, 10s. 6d. (which is returned if a term's notice is given in writing to the Director previous to the removal of the pupil).

For Prospectus and Admission Forms, apply to the Director,
Miss WILKIN, Cossey Cottage, Hampstead.

High=Class School for Girls,
CHIPPENHAM HOUSE,
51, CHIPPENHAM ROAD,
ST. PETER'S PARK, LONDON, W.
ESTABLISHED 1852.

Conducted by the Misses DELAY.

THE course of study includes English, comprehending Grammar and Analysis, English History, Literature, Composition, &c., especially adapted for the Oxford and Cambridge Local Examinations; French, Drawing, Dancing, Music, and Singing.

The Scholastic Year is divided into Three Terms.

FEES, ⎰ Pupils, £2 5s. to 4 Guineas.
per Term :— ⎱ Boarders, 10 to 12 Guineas.
Prospectuses on application.

COURS DE DANSE.

MRS. GEORGE BARNETT

Has the honour to announce that her Academies for

Dancing, Deportment & Calisthenic Exercises

ARE HELD AT HER RESIDENCE,

27, BELGRAVE ROAD, ABBEY ROAD, ST. JOHN'S WOOD, N.W.
(Opposite Greville Place Church);

AND AT BAYSWATER.

Schools and Families attended.　Private Lessons given.

[15]

Public (Endowed) Schools.

EMANUEL SCHOOL, WANDSWORTH COMMON,
S.W. (NEAR CLAPHAM JUNCTION.)

For 300 Boys.

Opened January, 1883.

English, Latin, French, German, Science, Drawing, Singing, Drill.

LIBERAL DIETARY.

Inclusive Fee, £30 a year.
Pianoforte, £4 4s. extra.
Day Boys, £9 a year.

Cricket & Football Grounds.
Gravel subsoil.
Gymnasium. Swimming Bath.
Detached Infirmary.

240 Boys already entered.

GOVERNORS.
Sir S. H. Waterlow, Bart., M.P., Chairman.
Right Hon. Lord Mayor.
Sir J. C. Lawrence, Bart., M.P.
D. H. Stone, Esq., Alderman.
Sir W. McArthur, K.C.M.G., M.P.
Sir J. Whittaker Ellis, Bart., M.P.
Sir T. Chambers, M.P., Recorder.
Sir Reg. Hanson, M.A., F.S.A.
J. Staples, Esq., F.S.A., Alderman.
Very Rev. Dean of Westminster.
Henry Arthur Hunt, Esq.
Geo. A. Spottiswoode, Esq.
Chas. Edward Mudie, Esq.
John C. Thynne, Esq.
Hon. Edward P. Thesiger.
George Potter, Esq.
W. E. M. Tomlinson, Esq., M.P.
Rev. Canon Furse.
Frederick Rose, Esq.
George N. Hooper, Esq.
James Ross, Esq.

HEAD MASTER AND CHAPLAIN.
Rev. A. TOWSEY, M.A. Camb.

ASSISTANT MASTERS.
Arthur R. Gridley, M.A. Oxford.
A. Macrae, B.A. London.
W. J. Butcher, B.Sc. London.
W. D. Shepperd, B.A. Oxford.
J. Wheater, Inter. B.A. London.
W. F. Bradshaw, R.A.M. (Music.)
W. B. Hughes, London University.

OTHER MASTERS AS REQUIRED.

MEDICAL OFFICER.
C. St. A. Hawken, Esq., M.R.C.S.

UNITED WESTMINSTER SCHOOLS,
* Day School for 750 Boys,
PALACE STREET, VICTORIA STREET (NEAR VICTORIA STATION).
Head Master: Mr. ROBT. E. H. GOFFIN, F.C.S., Honoursman, Gold Medallist, &c.
Assisted by a large Staff of fully qualified Assistants.

A thoroughly sound and practical education is given, and the Course includes the usual English subjects, Latin, French, and German, Drawing (including Machine and Building), Mathematics, Mechanics, Physics, Chemistry, and other branches of Science. Inclusive Tuition Fee, £4 and £5 5s. Each Class has a separate Room and Master, and there are also two Laboratories, Drawing School, Lecture Rooms, Dining Rooms, and extensive Playgrounds. Scholarships in the School and on leaving. Preparation for University and Public Examinations.

THE GREY COAT HOSPITAL,
* Day School for 330 Girls,
GREY COAT PLACE, NEAR VICTORIA STREET,
Head Mistress: Miss DAY, 1st Class Honours, Cambridge University.
Fifteen qualified Assistant Mistresses.

This School offers a sound and comprehensive education (including the doctrines and discipline of the Church of England, subject, however, to the conscience clause). Tuition Fee, £4 a year. Pianoforte Music, £4 a year extra. The School is annually Examined under the Cambridge Syndicate.

N.B.—*A Boarding School for Girls will be established in due course.*

* THESE SCHOOLS ARE FULL; APPLY EARLY FOR NEXT VACANCIES.

PROSPECTUSES FREE.

C. SPENCER SMITH, *Clerk and Receiver*, Palace Street, Victoria Street, S.W.

THE HIGHGATE
STREETS DIRECTORY.

NOTE.—*The Postal District for Highgate is N.*

Albert Villas,
see Archway rd.

Alpha Villas,
see Archway rd.

ANATOLA ROAD,
Highgate Hill.
From Girdlestone rd.
D 9
RIGHT SIDE.
1 Irvin Henry, carman
1 Irvin Mrs., sweets dlr.
2 Penson Richard
4 Dorey Mrs. M.
6 Dumayne Oliver
8 Twyford Frank
10 Seabrook Jas., gardnr.
14 Davidson E. G.
16 Bennis John, wood turner
18 Burke Thomas
METHODIST CHAPEL
LEFT SIDE.
1 Jewell Henry
3 Hales James
5 Hurst W.
7 Baylis W., plasterer
9 Edwards Alfred E.
11 Merrill Frederick
13 Douglas James, french polisher
15 Taylor John
19 Stacy W., bootmaker
21 Wadham Richard
23 Wiltshire Mrs.
25 Churchill Henry, french polisher
27 Schwanzer John
29 Swift Thomas
31 Perring William James

33 Foster George
ST. PETER'S CHURCH

ANNESLEY ROAD,
Highgate Hill.
From Brunswick rd.
D 10
LEFT SIDE.
Fraser John (Manor cottage)
Concannon M. (Fern cottage)
2 Benham Mrs.
4 Linford Wm., carpenter
6 Jordan James
8 Goding George
10 Dinner John
12 Davies William James
14 Collyer Mrs.
16 Clack John
18 Elliott John
20 Abbott John
22 Dewbury Benjamin
24 Fernley John
26 Bird Jabez
RIGHT SIDE.
Plant John, plumber (Homer cottage)
1 Jolliffe E. Anthony, bootmaker
7 Blake Alfred
9 Moon George
11 Webster Geo., carman
13 Cole Thos., sweets dlr.
15 Moy Francis
17 Barker George Henry
19 Wheatley James Chas.
23 Ling John, genl. shop

Archway Place,
see Highgate hill.

ARCHWAY ROAD.
From Junction rd. to North hill.
C 10
LEFT SIDE.
The Archway Tavern,
Mrs. C. Wass
Parry Henry Joseph, veterinary forge
The Holborn Union Infirmary
⸺*Bismarck rd.*
11 Coates William Henry
⸺*Winchester rd.*
13 Thatcher John Wells
15 Miles Mrs.
21 Carter Samuel S.
23 Columbine B. F.
25 Archer George
27 Wells Mrs.
29 Cooper William
31 Roberts William
33 Eadie Miss
35 Easterling Arthur Wm., solicitor
37 Ward Alfred Thomas Adolphus
41 Thompson Wm. Daniel
43 White William
45 Dawson John
49 Taylor Matthew
51 Curnow Miss, drssmkr.
53 Wheeler Edmund Wm.
55 Cheffins Alfred
57 Vanner William Thos.
⸺*Cromwell avenue*
59 Mercer J. C., tea dealer
61 Goodwin A., prvsn. mer.
63 Graham George F., organ builder

ARCHWAY RD.—*continued*
63 Graham George F., music seller

━ *Cromwell avenue*

Cholmeley Villas.

9 Lethbridge George
8 Shaw Frederick A.
7 Soper Francis L., F.L.S.
6 White Henry Brandon
5 Hoyle Mrs. C.
3 McSheehan Michael
1 Bennett Thomas John Wesley (Romanhurst)

Archway Road.

Haydon Hillyard (Cholmeley house)
Rooth Mrs. John (Greenfield lodge)
Dixon Allen

━ *Jackson's lane*

━ *Southwood lane*

Norman Villas.

1 Seed George, builder and decorator
2 Willcox Mrs. Margaret
3 Harris Mrs.
4 Dixon John

Holly Cottages.

Davis William
Root William

Park Terrace.

1 Golden Chas., coff. rms.
2 Jackson John, grocer
3 Anderson Mrs., draper
4 Hawkins S. J., fine art repository
5 Whale Joseph, tbccnst.
6 Bell George, dairyman
7 Tatton Charles Thomas
9 Warr Alfred
10 Lewis Mrs. Amelia
11 Markham Thomas T., plumber

━ *Bishop's rd.*

━ *Church rd.*

Albert Villas.

1 Barber Alfred
2 Harvey Henry
3 Hicks Robert
4 Winch Frederick
Tonge John Wilding (Rutland villa)
Row Mrs. L. R. (Hardwick villa)

Woodview Villas.

1 Kirtland Wm. Thomas
2 Watkins Robert

Woodview Terrace.

1 Percival William
2 Clarke George
3 Stone Henry
4 Crane D. B.
5 Gill Robert
6 Mathews Frank
7 Vassie William
8 Brampton Charles Hy.
9 Dean Charles, sanitary inspector
9 Dean Misses, tobccnsts.

━ *Baker's lane*

Beaconsfield Terrace.

2 Reynoldson H. B.
3 Story Thomas
4 Rogers William
The Wellington, S. Graddage

RIGHT SIDE.

WESLEYAN CHAPEL

1 Trickett H., coffee rms
2 Owen A., wardrobe dlr.
3 Feloj Joseph, confctnr.
4 Chipp James, tobaccnst.
5 Buteux E., fruiterer
6 Rowe A., hairdresser

━ *Flowers mews*

Whittington College, Rev. R. A. Currey, M.A. chaplain ; Miss Mackenzie, matron

Mercer Terrace.

1 Anceaux Mrs. Mary
2 Collier Henry
3 Skinner Mrs. Emily

━ *Thomas st.*

Archway Road.

Waple Thos. Fearnley (Claringdon villa)
Hunt William (Woodbine villa)
Holland Thomas (Whitehall lodge)

Archway Villas.

1 Emerson Robert
1 Holland Miss, drsmkr.
2 Sterne Frederick

Alpha Villas.

6 Arthur Miss (Bank vl.)
5 Chapman William
4 Wallington Charles
3 Marsh Alfred
2 Wright Mrs.

Archway Road.

16 Pattinson Richd. John, surgeon-dentist

18 Malley Joseph
22 Timewell Alfred
30 Garstin Arthur
32 Hill John C., builder
34 McCabe Thomas
36 Turner Miss, A.C.P., high class school for girls
38 Laskey Leonard (St. Leonards)
40 Jones Dr. George T.
54 Faux Edward, estate agent, &c.
St. Augustine's Temporary Church

━ *Langdon park rd.*

60 Wilkins Henry Thomas, bootmaker
62 Crocker H. H., dairy
64 Burland A. Edwin, grocer
66 Pendred, Applebee & Co., wine stores
68 Mixer Wm. J., draper
70 Beer William, stationer; post office
72 Shirtliff F., chemist
74 Smith Henry, oilman
76 Heath William James, baker
78 Walker John, butcher

━ *Wembury rd.*

94 *The Winchester Hall Hotel*, James Newton

━ *Northwood rd.*

96 Bilson C.F. & Co., grocrs.
98 *Archway Hardware Stores*
104 Davies G., dairy
106 LeCren L. H., tobccnst.
116 O'Reilly Dr. G. J. (Rathmoore)
118 Beviss Mrs.
Tibbitts Herbert, M.D. (Burfield house)
Craig J., jobmaster
Wills Thomas Hayden (Priestwood)

━ *Holmesdale rd.*

The Birbeck Tavern, William Atkins
Coleridge Buildings, Model Dwellings

━ *Shepherd's hill rd.*

Highgate Railway Stn.
The Woodman, Charles Ramsway

Wood lane
Muswell hill rd.
Victoria Cottages.
1 Cuthbert John (Con-
ingsby house)
2 Smith Henry Thomas
3 Norman Mrs.
4 Beckett Mrs. Amelia
5 McEwen Oliver
6 Sheen Fredk. Thomas,
nurseryman
7 Parker William
8 Norris Samuel
9 Grove Joseph
10 Fowke Thomas
11 Press Thomas
12 Holdom William
13 Beall Thomas
14 Farrell J. W.
15 Mott James
17 Buckland John
18 Eason Henry James
19 Coward John
Archway Road.
Twinn Mrs. Mary Ann,
laundry
Railway Cottages.
4 Roffe Frederick
3 Taylor Thomas
2 Rawlings William
1 Knight James
Archway Road.
Lawford & Sons, build-
ing material mers.
Lea & Co., coal depôt
Brooks & Co., coal
merchants

Archway Villas,
see Archway rd.

BAKER'S LANE.
From 1 Mansfield cottages
North hill.
B 8
Temperance Cottages.
1 Hooper John
2 Carter Henry
Archway rd.

Bartholomew Ter.,
see North hill.

Beaconsfield Terrace,
see Archway rd.

Bedford Place and
Cottages,
see Highgate hill.

BERTRAM STREET,
Highgate New Town.
From Chester rd.
D 9
RIGHT SIDE.
7 Clark Hy. J., plasterer
LEFT SIDE.
2aTue Wm., general shop
6 Claridge George,stone-
mason
St. Ann's National
School

BICKERTON ROAD,
Upper Holloway.
From Junction rd. to
Dartmouth park hill.
D 10
RIGHT SIDE.
2 Sheehy Michael
4 Whitehouse Henry
6 Ekin Samuel Proby
(Eben villa)
8 Biggin Edward Henry,
solicitor (Beechville
villa)
10 Birdseye Thomas
12 Crane Horace Tarbox
(Melrose villa)
14 Thompson Miss
16 Carr Ralph (Clutha
villa)
18 Woodcock Daniel(Con-
way villa)
20 Barnet-Smith George
(Cuba villa)
22 Cooke-Smith Henry
24 Morgan Mrs.
26 Hunt Thomas
28 Clarke Courtenay
30 Grimwood Robert
32 Atchley William H.
(Carlton cottage)
36 Edington George Thos.
(Rosetta villa)
38 Cox George William
(Bletsoe cottage)
40 Carroll Charles
42 Stevens Frederick
44 Meager George
46 Lee Thomas
48 Drewett Fredk. Wm.
50 Watson John
52 Appleton George
52 Frischling Mrs.
54 Berger Frank
56 Bullock Richard Steel

58 Pettigrew Robert
60 Wesley John
62 Happe Otto
64 Collins Joseph Henry
66 Furge Edward
68 Phillipps Mrs. H.
70 Reeves Robert
72 Melhuish John H.
76 Haymen W.
LEFT SIDE.
1 Hill W. (Bickerton lo.)
3 Hands Thomas L. (Oak
lodge)
5 & 7 Holdstock Miss,
school
11 Lester Louis George
13 Fuller Frederick Usher
15 Ashdown George
Tremlett grove
17 Rogers Edward
19 Stephens George
23aFowler Henry (Lynton
villa)
23 Allen John
25 Hooton Charles (Sun-
ningdale house)
27 Devenny Wm. Foster
(Talbot lodge)
29 Baker Mrs.
31 Wills Miss
33 Chapman Alfred
37 Hunt Charles
39 Child Trayton P.
41 Bankart Howard

BISHAM GARDENS.
From High st.
C 9
19 Sully William
21 Imber Alfred
Swain's lane

BISHOP'S ROAD,
The Park.
From Park house rd. to
Archway rd.
B 9
Beaumont Henry (Gor-
don villa)
Colwell Hector (Percy
villa)
GoldsEdwd.(Clyde vl.)
Gaye Gerrard (Clair-
ville)
Lovelock James Fredk.
(Rokeby house)

BISHOP'S RD.—*continued*
Askey F. D., solicitor (Beech villa)
Tattersall Mrs. (Portalta lodge)
Scoones Ernest (Wycombe)
Good Arthur M. (Clovelly)
Church W. M. H. (St. Wilfrid's)
Child Henry (Hurstly)
WebsterWilliamJustus (Tregenna)
15 Wright Henry (Parkfield)
16 Overton Peter Raven

BISHOP WOOD RD.

From Hampstead lane.
C 8
King Edwin (Inglehome)
BlanfordThomas(Field house)
McDowall Rev. Prebendary, D.D. (The School house)
Carr Miss (Earlham)
Mason Major-Gen. C.C (Whitley house)
5 Maude Thomas James
Oakley Henry (Northlands)
Filer Alexr. J. Duff (Holmwood lodge)
—*Hampstead lane*
Green Wm. (Bishopwood house)
Simpson Shepherd (Blenheim)
Harvey Alfred (Hurstbourne)
Lyle Abram. (Dunvar)
Ellis William (Brooklands)
Simmonds John (Oaklands)
Flux Edwd. Hitchings, solicitor (Cotswold)
Shepheard Alfred J. (Mayfield)
Walker Major William Thomas (Lilleshall)
Tupling Misses (Sussex house)

BLANDFORD PL.

From 2 Fortess rd.
E 9
1 Edmonds James
2 Howkins Mrs. Harriet
3 Tackley Mrs.
4 Senior John
5 Macduff David James
—*Manor cottages*
—*Falkland rd.*
—*Leverton cottages*

Blenheim Place,
see Highgate hill.

BLOOMFIELD RD.,
The Park.
From Park house rd. to Bishop's rd.
B 9
RIGHT SIDE.
Hayes Mrs. (Mendip house)
Davenport Misses (Silverhill)
Goode John (Hillside)
Goodman Albert (Witton house)
Tod John (Sans Souci)
StaggRobert(Alfriston house)
—*Bishop's rd.*
LEFT SIDE.
Tod James (Reidsdale)
WenhamMrs.(Ivyside)
—*Park villas*
—*Bishop's rd.*

Bridge Place,
see Hornsey lane.

Broadbent Yard,
see High st.

BROADLANDS RD.
From North hill to Bishop wood rd.
B 8
RIGHT SIDE.
Catling Charles(Inglethorpe)
4 Sharpe W. A.
—*Grange rd.*
Wade Israel Mark (Bracondale)
Edward G. S. (West bank)
Sargant T. J. W. (Talbot house)

Carter John (Baveno)
Carritt Frdk. Blasson, solctr. (Bishopsfield)
Birks Harry William (Enderleigh)
TurnbullReginald(Byculla)
Morley William (Denewood)
Moxon Walter, M.D. (Northolme)
LEFT SIDE.
1 Ford Arthur Ranken
Hetherington William Lonsdale,M.A.(Northcroft)

Brookfield Mews,
From Colva st.

BRUNSWICK RD.
From Highgate hill.
D 10
LEFT SIDE.
2 Newton George
4 Pope Henry
6 Paley Joseph
8 Horburn Mrs.
10 Cox Charles, carman
12 Webb Mrs. Mary
14 Haldane George
16 Kerry Misses, school
18 Haswell George
20 Thompson Geo., bricklayer
24 BarrettG.W.,carpenter
26 Bawden Mrs.
30 West W.,chmny. sweep
44 Dawson Saml.,plumber
—*Vorley rd.*
The Brunswick Arms, WalterJohnWoodwell
46 George E., genl. shop
50 Childs James
52 Hatherill William
54 Jones Thomas
56 Norris Mrs.
58 Oxford Chas., plasterer
58 Bennett Alfred
60 Grupel Mrs., marine stores
62 Dean Albert, stationer and confectioner
64 Modena Mrs., grocer and cheesemonger
RIGHT SIDE.
1a Bates James

1 Webley John Roach
3 Claus Henry
5 Hankins John
7 Stiles Mrs.
9 Gardner George
11 Greatrex James
13 Perry Walter
15 Gillam Charles
15 Field Mrs., laundress
17 Pratt Mrs.
19 Bailey Alfrd., wtchmkr.
21 Grou T., clock-wheel
      cutter
23 Hearn Mrs. S. S.
25 Newbold William
27 Grou George
⎯ *Vorley rd.*
29 Simpson Mrs.
31 Backshall Mrs.
33 King John
      St. Peter's Middle Class
      School for Girls; Miss
      Goble, mistress

BURGHLEY ROAD.
From 42 Highgate rd.
E 9
RIGHT SIDE.
2 Abbott William J. A.
4 Graves Mrs.
6 Hutchison William
8 Warren Mrs.
10 Parmley Mrs.
12 Brooks Mrs.
14 O'Kelly Owen
      Cowd Rev. J. C., M.A.
      (Kentish Town Vicar-
      age)
18 Drage William
20 Clark Charles
22 Boxsins P. F. B.
24 Clues Mrs. E.
26 Brabant George W.
28 Key Mrs.
30 Goodman Edwin
32 Dyer James Andrew
34 Billington John
36 Tomlinson Herbert
40 Praill Edward, jun
46 Stratton M s. E.
⎯ *Lady Somerset rd.*
⎯ *Oakford rd.*
      Hancock G. E.
LEFT SIDE.
1 Drummond Mrs.
3 Hodges Robert S.
5 Greene William Robert

7 Pascoe Joseph
7a Brown William
⎯ *St. John the Evange-*
      list's rd.
9 Bailey Henry
11 Bailey H.
13 Richardson Mrs.
15 Godfrey Alfred
17 Clark William Philip
19 Backshell Mrs.
21 Black George, B.A., sol.
23 Clarke Arthur Leslie
25 Kitson Mrs.
27 Lyte Mrs.
31 Hill James France
33 Hill Miss
37 Drake John
39 Evard Victor
⎯ *Lady Somerset rd.*
41 Clare Charles Henry
43 Kain Francis
45 Hopwell Miss
47 Stuart Rev. F. C.
49 Boullangier C.
51 Walmsley F. E.
53 Spencer John
55 Wickham Chas. Thos.
57 Begbie Jas. Hamilton
59 Copsey Charles Edwd.
61 Klaftenberger Mrs.
63 Haining Mrs.
65 Sutton Frederick Wm.
67 Garnett Mrs.
69 Newport W. W.
71 Jackson E.
73 Cox W. N.
      Board School
93 Saunders John Charles
95 Speary Alfred Horace
97 Godden Henry
99 Smith William
101 Burgess John
103 Cansick W. N., builder

Caen Terrace,
see Hampstead lane.

Cambridge Cottages,
see College lane.

CARROL ROAD.
From Highgate rd. to
York rise.
E 9
LEFT SIDE.
1 Hatt Charles George
5 Cox George, coal mer.
7 Bartley R. B.

9 Solomon A.
11 Browne Charles
13 Bacon William
15 Reeks Henry
17 Stanton Joseph J.,
      pianoforte tuner
19 Thomson R.
21 Stevens Joseph
23 Weavers Harry
25 Westbrook William
27 Ewings William H.
29 White Walter Wakefield
29 Campbell W. F., phy-
      sician and surgeon
31 Rose Joseph Henry
33 Marshall Mrs.
35 McIntyre Robert
37 Hatt John
39 Scott Robert
41 Mathews Francis Rchd.
43 Dyer Richard
47 Lawes John James H.
49 Sim Alexander
55 Bailey Thomas
59 Walker James Brown,
      staircase maker
61 *The Carrol Dairy,*
      Edward Deinchfield
63 Holmes W. R., grocer
65 Smith Mrs. Mary Ann,
      boot warehouse
67 Green W. J., chemist
RIGHT SIDE.
2 Mayer Edward (Rou-
      mania cottage)
⎯ *Twisden rd.*
4 Colclough William
6 Ronald John Stuart
8 Barrett Mrs.
10 Brakel Theodor
14 Cockerell James
16 Easun Wm., decorator
18 Jude George
20 Chisman John N.
22 Hopper Edwin
24 Craines Philip
26 Sabin Joseph Henry
28 Hickman Walter
30 Ross William Thomas
32 Copp Henry
34 Ginelack Frederick
36 Smith Mrs. F.
38 Whitley Oliver Clark
40 Jefferies Mrs.
42 Pearce F.
44 Bridgman S.
46 Lomes Thomas

H

CARROL RD.—*continued*
52 Vines Benjamin
54 Hirst John, builder
   ⊏*Twisden rd.*
56 Ling James, green-grocer
58 Bartley Reily Bloxam, bookseller & stationer
60 Wilson James, baker
62 Herbert R. J., oilman

CASTLE YARD.
From 58 North rd.
B 9
1 Ballard Geo., cabinet-maker
2 Baldwin George
3 Pemberton Joseph
4 Leaman Joseph
5 Truine Mrs.
6 Thomas Joseph
7 Kelly Mrs.
8 Howard Thomas
9 Allen Matthew
10 Truine Joseph, chimney sweep
11 Halsey James
   ⊏*Southwood lane*

CATHCART HILL.
From Junction rd. to Dartmouth park hill.
D 10
1 Wheeler Mrs.
2 Bacon John
3 Badrow Edward
5 Bailey Henry
6 Muirhead David
7 Wells Algernon
9 Miall Charles
10 Hayward Samuel
11 Fevez J.
12 Davis Alfred
13 Rushbrooke W. G.
14 Sargeant Joseph F.
15 Keen Henry
   Sutton Miss, collegiate school (Stella house)

CHESTER ROAD,
Highgate New Town.
From Dartmouth park hill to Swain's lane.
D 9
LEFT SIDE.
1 Cox William
2 Dewberry James

3 Blank Frederick Wm.
   ⊏*Winscombe st.*
4 Cope Frederick
5 Hicks Henry
6 Vine Joseph
7 Matthews John
8 *The Totnes Castle,* T. J. Boalch
   ⊏*Bertram st.*
10 Witty John H.
11 Mills George P., monumental mason
   ⊏*Holly village*
RIGHT SIDE.
Cornwall Villas.
1 Stott John
2 Cooke James
4 Flexman William
5 Rand Henry
Chester Villas.
3 Evans Edward
5 Inch Thomas Alfred
   Perham John (Plevna villa)
Chester Terrace.
1 Lamerton Thomas, monumental mason (Ebenezer house)
2 Michel Philip
3 Wright J. M.
4 McKiernin William
5 Thomas Mrs.
6 Wetherly W.
7 Hill Edwin John
8 Harding Robert
9 Twaits Thomas W.
10 Hicks William
11 Walton Peter
12 Eggins William
13 McKiernin W.
14 Holbrook Thomas
15 Nelson John Faux
16 Buckthorpe James
17 Cole Richd., decorator
18 Winter George
19 Hatt Charles
20 Bye Joseph William, stonemason
Chester Road.
47 Martin George
49 Coles Joseph
51 Farrow William
53 Linnett Alexander F.
55 Young John, pianoforte tuner and repairer
57 Hine Alfred, mason
   ⊏*Raydon st.*

   Daniels Henry & Co., cemetery masons
   Monks Thomas (Chester lodge)

Chester Terrace and Villas,
see Chester rd.

CHETWYND ROAD.
From York rise.
D 9
LEFT SIDE.
3 Cowlishaw George
5 Kitchener Freeman S.
7 Warner J.
11 Bridges Isaac (Ivy cottage)
15 *Chetwynd College for Girls;* Miss A. E. Ramell, P.C.P.
15 Ramell Thos. George
17 Meyer John
19 Sinnock Mrs. (Abberley cottage)
25 Hickman Andrew Wm.
27 Cresswell Alfred John
29 Tompkins Henry
41 Wolfe Henry John
43 Burgon Miss
45 Symonds Hy. Lambert
47 Shaw Mrs.
49 Sulman Thomas
51 Kershaw Burroughs D., C.E.
53 Raban Ebenezer Thos.
RIGHT SIDE.
2 Acres B. G., grocer and wine merchant
4 Robertson John
6 Morley Henry
8 Christmas Thomas Jos.
12 Bowels William
14 Elgar Mrs.
16 Bailey Richard
18 Plowman Samuel
20 May William Oliver
22 Nash Mrs.
24 Sturgess James M.
26 Robinson Frederic
30 Thompson Frederick
32 Lambert Charles C (Talbot house)
34 Taylor J. Scott, B.A. CANTAB.
36 Rimers H. F.

38 Williams Miss
40 Harvey F. M.
42 Edwards Robert
44 Simson Robert Erskine
46 Twemlow-Cooke Rev. Daniel
48 Butler Mrs. E.
50 Potter John (Hanway cottage)

CHOLMELEY PARK
From High st. to Archway rd.
C 10
Horton L.(The Lodge)
Beauchamp John(Newtownards)
Reed Talbot Baines (Tweed house)
Crossley Mrs. (Copley Dene)
Heriot George (Lilford house)

Cholmeley Villas,
see Archway rd.

CHURCH ROAD.
From Archway rd. to North hill.
B 9
Smith Rev. Edgar,B.A. (The Vicarage)
ALL SAINTS' CHURCH
All Saints' Mission House
⸺*North hill*

CHURCHILL ROAD.
From Dartmouth park hill
E 9
1 Edwards Mrs. J.
2 Whitrow Mrs.Charlotte
3 Sheppard John
4 Courtier Mrs.
5 Thornton W.
6 Horne Mrs.
7 Gillbanks T. J.
8 Ryan Edmund
9 Wilson Joseph
10 Cooper Robert
11 Andrews Alex.Harding
12 Moggridge James H., solicitor
13 Griffith George
14 Beard G.
15 Parker Charles

16 Orton Benjamin
17 Collinson Edwin Chas., pianoforte tuner
18 Bennett Mrs. J.
19 Edwards Miss
20 Daley Henry
21 Bradley Henry
23 Howell Mrs.
24 Atchley H. M.
25 Lumley H.
26 Westhall Thomas
27 Hayes Cornelius
28 Maund Robert
28 Brown W. H.
29 Brown Mrs., laundress

Clifton Villas,
see Highgate hill.

Coal Bays,
see Mortimer ter.

COLLEGE LANE.
From 78 Lady Somerset rd. to Little Green st.
D 9
Meadow Cottages.
1 Beeby James
2 Kent John
Vine Cottages.
1 Brown W., chimney sweep
2 Cobb William
3 & 4 Leader Mrs., laundress
5 Gibbard James
6 Ball John
8 Pontin Edmund
9 Smith John
10 Holt D.
11 Saville C.
12 Flood F.
Hope Cottages.
1 Hill Henry
2 Matton Thomas, carman and contractor
College Lane.
Kent Henry (Prospect cottage)
Pleasant Cottages.
1 Milton William
2 Shaw William
College Lane.
Mullins Mrs. (College house laundry)
Cambridge Cottages.
1 Butts G.
2 Selley Charles

COLVA STREET.
From Dartmouth park hill
D 9
LEFT SIDE.
Lamerton Thos., genl. mason
North London Dental Surgery, John S. Armitage, L.D.S., R.C.S.
⸺*Raydon st.*

Cornwall Villas,
see Chester rd.

CROFTDOWN RD.
From Highgate rd. near St. Alban's rd.
D 9
RIGHT SIDE.
2 Polak Miss Flora
4 Manners William
6 Priddle James Charles
8 Catley J. H.
10 Delmar Miss
12 Wackerbath Mrs.
18 Hodge James Clark
20 Kell F. W.
22 Essex Mrs. Fanny
24 Glover Richard Thos.
⸺*Grove rd.*
26 Vezin Mrs.
28 Pearson George
30 Patten Henry
32 Couper Frederick
34 Wright James
36 Williams John
LEFT SIDE.
11 Souter - Robertson Stewart
13 Leighton Jeffrey

CROMWELL AVN.
From Archway rd. to High st. Highgate.
C 9
RIGHT SIDE.
2 Mercer J. C.
4 Clare Mrs.
6 Whyte J. F.
10 Wormald Percy C.
12 Walton J. H.
14 Eason Alexander
16 Watkins Albert
18 Shadbolt Mrs.
20 Sabine Mrs. (Shirley villa)

CROMWELL AVN.—contd.

22 Vincent Alfred
24 Greenwood Mrs.
26 Morris Joseph (Melbey villa)
28 Constable Mrs. (Exmouth villa)
30 Willis W.
32 Langsford John
34 Hobden Henry Fuller
36 Collier Edward
38 Dredge Robert
40 Cherry James (Endsleigh)
42 Faulkner Arthur
44 Sherlock A. J. B.
46 Burton John William
48 Paice Miss
50 Day R. C.
52 Keltie John S.
54 Mullins Mrs.
56 Morgan Wm. Simeon (The Hawthorns)
58 Goulding Edward (Beverley house)
60 Chard Charles
62 Cowley Alexander, M.B., surgeon
⌐ Winchester pl.
64 Nicol Mrs. Agnes
66 Hutchinson Hrbrt.Jno.
68 Copin Mdme.Josephine school
70 Horsley William
72 Newth Frederick
74 Lyons James
76 Drew Saml. Summers
78 Dell Henry
80 Poole Mrs.
82 Francis Thomas
84 Redaway William
86 Talbot Charles Henry
88 Whibley Ambrose
90 Farrance Geo. (Coomrith)
92 Brewer W., solicitor
94 Ludwig William
96 Doherty Charles

LEFT SIDE.

1 Yarnold Charles
1 Yarnold Miss Ellen, pianist
3 Rooff William B.
5 Woodgate William
7 Hartung Charles Wm.
9 Roques Frank A.
11 Graham Geo. Lowther

13 Taplin Mrs. L.
15 Smith Miss
17 Hibbert Alfred Wellesley
19 Duncan Jas. Marriott
21 Gough Hugh
23 Bosito Madame, professor of music
25 Sherwin Gerald
27 Eldred Mrs. Mary
29 Horner E.
31 Raynham Walter
33 Silvester Mrs. M. A.
35 Barnes Edwin Charles
37 Cohen M. L.
39 Morra Henry
41 Amsden Sidney
⌐ Winchester rd.
43 D'Arcy James (Beaumont)
45 Oakeshott Mrs. (Wasdale)
47 Peace Richard Henry (Hazlehurst)
49 Beaumont Lewis(Hillside)
51 Bennett George (Folingsby)
53 Fox John Arthur
55 Atchley W. W. (Worcester)
57 Jennings W.
59 Guy Thos. (Edendale)
61 Skinner Henry (Hill view)
63 Noble William
⌐ Cromwell pl.
65 Upward Walter
67 Osborne William Hy.
69 Brown William
71 Gutteridge Joseph
73 Maude Edmund
75 Ross-Murphy John

CROMWELL PL.

From 63 Cromwell avenue.
C 9

1 Hyde Thomas
3 Fisher G.
5 Davis Walter David, solicitor
7 Room Charles Turner
9 Longhurst William
11 Richmond Arthur Guinness
13 Kerry James
15 Lee Charles

17 Passmore Augustus Andrew

Cromwell Road,
now called Winchester rd.

Crown Cottages,
see Highgate hill.

DARTMOUTH RD.
D 9
From the top of Dartmouth park avenue to
51 Dartmouth park rd.

LEFT SIDE.

3 Longman V. (Stafford house)
5 Finden E. (Church hill lodge)
7 House Miss (Fernbank)
9 Gray Parker (Hollyview)
13 Wade John (Brooklyn)
15 Taylor W. S. (Glen Orkney)

DARTMOUTH PARK AVENUE.
Dartmouth park hill.
D 9
RIGHT SIDE.
⌐ Dartmouth rd.
Carr John Dale (West Lea)
Pratt & Young, florists (Somerset cottage)
4 Dimsey David Griffiths
6 Birch Walter de Gray, F.R.S.
Beckwith Arthur (Chamley villa)
Booth James Wilson (Redland villa)
Bell Mathw. (Hillside)
Woolmer Alfred J. (The Limes)

LEFT SIDE.
Philcox Henry J. (Northover)
1 Bayne Henry
3 Howe Thomas
Harman Walter John (Balcombe house)
7 Nunn Mrs. Thomas (Hartland house)
9 Schilbacher Mrs.
11 Wright Alfred George
13 Jones Alfred Wilkinson

15 Nalder Frederick
Harris L. (Linden lo.)
Keen Edwin Henry
(Birkdale)
Gouly Edward James
(St. John's lodge)
Pearson Geo.(Leighton
villa)
Jaques C. A., architect
(Ferndale)
Pratt J. A. (Lonsdale
house)
Ferris O. A. (Fairview)
Ball Geo. (The Elms)
Mills Mrs. (Dartmouth
park lodge)

DARTMOUTH PARK HILL.

*From 133 Fortess rd. and
Junction rd. to High
st. Highgate.*

D 9

LEFT SIDE.

(St. Pancras Parish.)

1 Tasker Thomas, corn
merchant
3 Fowler T. N., fishmngr.
5 Norris Wm., fruiterer
and greengrocer
7 Bryant Joseph, butcher
9 *St. Benet and All
Saints' Mission Room*
11 Xazer Geiger Franz,
ivory carver
⸻*Ingestre rd.*
⸻*Churchill rd.*
13 BretnallWilliam Henry
15 Smith Samuel
17 Caralli G. N.
⸻*Spencer rd.*
21 Tambling John
23 Pitman William
25 Hind Charles
29 Jaques Edward
⸻*Chetwynd rd.*
The Lord Palmerston,
John Beveridge
35 Boby Robert
37 Huthwaite Henry
39 Garsehen Philip
41 Mills George, builder
43 Willson John E.
ST. MARY BROOK-
FIELD CHURCH
⸻*Dartmouth rd.*

⸻*Dartmouth park avn.*
47 Hollis George
49 Cheesman Frederick I.
51 Wake Edward George,
M.D.
53 Bartlett F. H.
55 Hayton Joseph
57 Stephens Rev.Jas.,M.A.
59 Blair Mrs.
63 SuttonMatthew Bailey
65 Charles F. R.
67 Pearce Alfred
69 Hamer John
71 Edwards George
73 May Rev. Robert Cos-
tall, M.A.
75 Cornish J.
77 Laybourn Robert G.
79 Hollick Ebenezer
⸻*Dartmouth pk. avenue*
Chatto Andrew (Dart-
mouth tower)
⸻*Chester rd.*
85 Lalor John
87 Corrick Mrs.
91 Maidment George
93 Aldridge Edwd., dairy
95 Pietrowicz Wladyslaw,
hairdresser
97 CrockerPeter,bootmkr.
99 Pim H., jeweller
101 Reavley Frank, brush
dealer
101 Reavley Mrs., dress-
maker
103 Neal Edwin, grngrcr.
⸻*Colva st.*
107 Tue J. W., grocer
109 King Mrs., marine
stores
111 Stevens Robt., oilman
113 Thornton Frederick
115 Nix Charles, dairy
117 Howes Wm., tobccnst.
119 *TheBrookfieldTavern*,
John Etheridge
⸻*Doynton st.*
121 Baumberger J., baker
123 Edwards James
125 Williams J., marine
stores
127 Ryan George, butcher
129 Dettmer Jas., general
shop
131Rowell P., stationer
Shoeing Forge, G. W.
Bennett

*Harmonium &Ameri-
can Organ Factory,*
H. Carlon & Co.
133 French J. W., con-
fectioner
135 Stacey William, boot-
maker
135 Bray Mrs., nurse
137 Carter C. A., dairy;
post office
139 Bower Thos.L.,draper
141 Hanna Francis, livery
stables
143 Christmas Peter, beer
retailer
145 N o r m a n Ebenezer,
fruiterer &greengrcr.
147 Chapman John
147 Chapman M., draper
149 Willis Thos., butcher
151 Edgerton John, baker
⸻*Raydon st.*
153 Fudge R. C. and Co.,
grocers
155 English Thomas, beer
and wine retailer
159 HuskissonF.,plumber
161 Blondell Robert
163 McCall Edward Wm.,
umbrella maker
163 Harman and Preston,
dressmakers
165 Brinkworth Robert,
shoemaker
167 Perrin William
169 Havant John
171 Wood Joseph
173 Best Ebenezer
175 Barrett Paul
177 Morris E. Brudenell
179 Sawyer John, com-
mission agent
*St. Pancras Infir-
mary;* Dr. McCann,
medical supertdnt.
Reeve Thos., gardener
(Lauderdale lodge)

RIGHT SIDE.

(Islington Parish.)
The Boston Hotel,
Edwd. Herbert Blunt
4 Mallett William, cabi-
netmaker
6 Dunn James, zinc
worker
8 Enoch Thomas, dairy
10 Aris Arthur, bootmkr.

DARTMOUTH PK. HILL—
continued
12 Milton Henry, grocer
14 Floyd Wm., stationer
16 Cookson Frederick, tobacconist
16 Cookson George, cab proprietor
20 Kernot Richard
26 Goodchap William
26 Coleman Mrs. Irene
28 Brown Mrs.
30 Allen William
— *Wyndham cres.*
32 Fletcher Misses, school (York house)
34 Shenton Edward
36 Harris Albert
38 Buckland Mrs.
42 Emmett John T.
— *Cathcart hill*
    Smith S. (Reservoir cottage)
72 .Engert Adam Cyrus (The Perseverance)
74 Clitheroe Mrs.
76 Harrower Frank W.
— *Bickerton rd.*
80 McClune S., stationer
82 Whatley George
84 Price Miss
86 Winter William
88 Batty John Higgs
90 Cooper Mrs.
92 Edgar Mrs. Jane
94 Browning Henry
98 Cox Henry
100 Smith J. A., uphlstrer.
102 Bacon Walter George
104 Jordan James
— *Hargrave park rd.*
106 Oldham Fredk. Ernest
108 Carew Joseph
110 Couzens Mrs.
114 Stone Charles
122 Baker —., oilman
— *Langdon rd.*
    ST. PETER'S CHURCH
— *Anatola rd.*
    Fordham Isaac, rustic worker (Gladstone villa)
    Shipham William (Hartington villa)
— *Magdala rd.*
    K e m p t o n William (Stonefield house)

Coxall George (Cornwall house)
Small Pox Hospital

DARTMOUTH PARK ROAD.
From Highgate rd. to York rise.
D 9
RIGHT SIDE.
1 Flower Frank
3 Townshend W., legal architect
5 Gouda Arnold
7 Spain Vice-Admiral D.
9 Amery G. W.
11 Lakeman Henry B.
13 Payne Robert
15 Nichol Mrs.
17 Cox James Abraham
21 Foxall Samuel
23 Fynn Herbert
27 Crassweller Henry V.
29 Stephenson Jas., artist
31 George Augustin
33 James William
35 Jarvis Edward
37 Goodwin Frederick
39 Bray Charles
41 Charles John
43 Mudie Alfred
45 Maxfield John
47 Turner W.
— *York rise*
51 Frisby James
LEFT SIDE.
2 Carte Richard
4 Smith Richard
6 Cox George John
8 Taylor John
10 Boby William
— *Grove rd.*
12 Williams Mrs. Charles
14 Hearn R. John
16 Hadley Joseph
18 Hertslet Mrs.
20 Legg William
22 Taylor John
24 Barnes Theodore
26 Boxsius James Joseph
28 Fea Mme., ladies' schl.
30 Barnard William
32 Turner William
34 Hearn A. W.
38 Kurz William John
40 Abercrombie Arthur
42 Whiffen Frederick

— *York rise*
44 Stephens James

Dorothy Cottages,
see Southwood lane.

DOYNTON STREET,
Highgate New Town.
From Dartmouth park hill
D 9
1 McCarthy C.
3 Watchorn Francis
5 Robinson James
7 Horne Frederick
9 Boyden John
11 Platten Henry
13 Hayter Ambrose
15 Yates Wm. Joseph H.
17 Maynard Thomas
19 Bradish Michael
21 Hunns Jabez
23 Seed Rchd., decorator
25 Whitaker Frederick
27 Lloyd Thomas
29 Diggins George, painter
31 Hyde Henry
33 Vaughan Wm., bookbinder
35 Higgs Joseph
— *Raydon st.*

FITZROY PARK.
From The Grove to Millfield lane.
C 8
    Piper W. (Beechwood)
    Gössell Otto (Elm lo.)
    Lea Thos. (The Limes)
    Lewis Charles Lee (Hillside)
    Wilkinson Col. Josiah (Southampton lodge)

Florence Villas,
see Wood lane.

FORTESS ROAD.
From 2 Highgate rd. to Dartmouth park hill.
E 9
LEFT SIDE.
1 Cooper George, pork butcher
3 Milton I., fishmonger
7 Keane Thomas, mason
7 Keane Mrs., greengrcr.

9 Chaffe John Frederick, sweep
9 Chaffe Mrs., general shop
11 Green Wm., plumber
13 *The Tally Ho!* Thomas Lovelock
⎬ *Willow walk*
15 Knowles Sam.,bootmkr
17 Brown Wm., tobccnst.
21 Hudson E. T.
23 Hermon Richard
25 Durrant Henry
27 Miles Arthur, artist
29 BromleyF.,L.D.S.,R.C.S. EDIN.
31 Lambert J., builder
33 Elliott G. B.
35 Fraser & Heigh, auctioneers
35 RaeEdmund Chadwick
37 Bennett Thomas
39 Daniel A. B., M.R.C.V.S. CHURCH OF OURLADY HELP OF CHRISTIANS
41 ConnollyRev.Jas.,M.A.
55 MarshallThos,M.B.,C.M.
57 Webb George
59 Kitto Mrs.
61 *The Junction Tavern*, Benjamin Acres
⎬ *Lady Somerset rd.*
63 Silvani Alexander
65 Lawes Mrs. Amelia J.
69 Smith Harry
71 Brühling W., private tutor
73 Witt William B.
75 Jackson William
75 JacksonMrs.,dressmkr.
79 Mayer S., watchmaker
81 Brilliant Joseph
83 Semmens Edward
85 Arrowsmith William, wood engraver
87 Harrison Joseph B., preparatory school
89 Holland Charles Major
89 Holland and Walter, dressmakers
89 Walter Miss M.
91 Smerdon Robert John
93 Page Henry William, slate merchant
97 Trinnick John
99 Oliver James, colliery agent

101 Partridge Mrs. P.
103 Greaves Philip H.,diamond jeweller
105 Opie Bennett, cheesemonger
107 Beeston E.J., milliner
109aPanzer & Co.,cnfctnrs.
109 Panzer & Co., tbcnsts.
111 Simonds S., butcher
113 Weight C., fruiterer
115 Jones E., draper
117 Baker Wm., bootmkr.
119 BarkerWilliam,music warehouse
121 Rogers & Co., grocers
123 WoodsG.W.,gen.drpr.
125 WilliamsT. H., chmst.
127 Salmon Jos., oilman
129 Draper T., dairy
129 Howard E. S., sweets dealer
131 Peacock T. P., ham and beef warehouse
133 Heal B., furniture dlr.
⎬ *Burghley rd.*
     RIGHT SIDE.
2 Engall H. M., bootmkr.
2 Engall Mrs., toy dealer
4 Munday Wm., tailor
6 Dunbar Miss H., stationer ; post office
10 Everson E., hairdresser
12&14SalmonJsph.,oilman
16 Flint William, brass finisher
   ElliottB.G.,timber mer.
⎬ *Fortess grove*
36 Dyer Charles
38 Wing William
40 Thwaites Geo. Henry
42 James George
44 Deane Hugh
48 Rex William
50 KentishCharles,builder and decorator
52 Thorne Mrs.
54 Lamb Mrs.
56 Wilson William
60 Greatbatch William
62 Beadle Arthur
64 Hoare P., pianoforte manufacturer
66 Holmes Mrs. Mary
68 Holdgate Mrs.
70 Williams Mrs.
74 Williams Robert John
76 Hildersley James J.

78 MacDowell Mrs. R. C.
82 Wolfenden R. S.,pianoforte tuner
84 Ball Frederick
90 Tiffin Miss (Ivy porch house)
92 Dettmer Henry
92 Callow Geo. William, artist
94 Conway John C.
96 Baldwin Richard
98 Brighouse George
106 Boam Mitchell
108 Banks E. G., artist
110 Tweddle James
   Boys' Public Day School, Co.,Limited ; Alfred Allen, B.A. TRINITY COLL. DUBLIN, head master ; R. Parry, B.A., & G. H. N. Ingle, TRINITY COLL. DUBLIN, assistant masters.; Edwd. Johnson, sec. (Paddock lodge)
⎬ *Ravely rd.*
152 Skinner & Co., grocers
154 *St. George'sDistillery*, Pendred Applebee & Co.
156 StückWltr.C.,jeweller
158aWatmore John, baker
158 Doggrell Stanley, tobacconist

Francis Terrace,
see our " Hornsey, Upper Holloway, and Finsbury Park Directory."

Girdlestone Cotts.,
see Girdlestone rd.

GIRDLESTONE RD
From Langdon rd.
     D 10
     RIGHT SIDE.
1 Barratt George
2 Killip Mrs.
9 Hines Mrs.
10 Lofthouse Henry
11 King Edwin J.
12 Farrow John
13 Hickmott Stephen
14 Bennett George
⎬ *Brunswick rd.*

GIRDLESTONE RD.—*cntd.*
15 Hensby Samuel, builder
16 Barnett George
16½ Hensby Mrs., laundress
21 Aldridge James, fishmonger
Girdlestone Cottages.
1 Sims Mrs.
2 Wilson Mrs.
3 Trollope D.
⌐*Salisbury rd.*
LEFT SIDE.
Girdlestone Road.
⌐*Magdala rd.*
7a Dickeson W., ale stores
6a Coles Joseph Thomas
4 Colson Arthur E.
4 Colson Thornton E., undertaker
3 Holman Mrs.
1a Whyman John, greengrocer and goods remover
⌐*Anatola rd.*
8a Hiscott Mrs., genl. shop
9a Curlewis Harry
10a Sheppard William
11a Osborne William
13a Cowie Mrs.
14 Tebbutt Geo., grngrcr.
15 Upton Charles, baker
⌐*Annesley rd.*
41 Auld Alston (Hope cottage)
42 Sullivan Mrs.
43 Reeve Henry
44 Cook E.
45 Clark James
46 Parlby Josiah, artist
47 Concannon Michael
48 Bedwell James, bootmaker
49 Stanford Edward

GORDON HOUSE ROAD.
From 157 Highgate rd.
E 8
CATHOLIC APOSTOLIC CHURCH
Bretnall W. H. & Co., tracing paper manufacturers
1 Read Samuel
3 Rochford James A.
7 Cloran Michael
8 Mahoney Rev. P. R.

9 Clements Charles
10 Bodgener William
11 Phillips Mrs.
13 Bradbury John
14 Valentine Miss
15 Peppys Mrs.
18 Cullen John
19 Carstairs Andrew

GOSPEL OAK STATION.
In Gordon house rd.
E 8
Gamman, Son & Carter, coal merchants
New F. A. & Co., coal merchants
New Co-operative Coal Company; William Owen, secretary
The Lilleshall Co.; John Jefferys, wharf manager
Shenton Edward, slate merchant and slater
Fenn Henry & Co., coal merchants

GRANGE ROAD.
From Broadlands rd.
B 8
King Mark William (The Grange)
McCormick William & Son, builders (Hillside)
⌐*North hill*

Grove Cottages,
see West hill.

GROVE PLACE.
From High st.
C 9
1 *Police Station*
2 Wheeler William
3 Barber John
4 Lewis Mrs.
5 Shuttleworth Harry Stanley
6 Lowe Charles
7 Weston George
⌐*Pond sq.*
⌐*South grove*

GROVE ROAD.
From Dartmouth park rd. to Woodsome rd.
D 9
LEFT SIDE.
3 Dawson John
5 Easton Mrs.
9 Mizon John
11 Wood William John
13 Rayner Thos. James
15 Hale John
17 Sinclair Bland Gardner
19 Gilmour Henry F.
21 Stansfeld George
23 Grant Alexander
25 Collins John H.
27 Orhly Theodore D.
29 Cockman Chas. Roadnight, B.A.
31 Biggers John Robert
33 Hughes Arthur Edwin
RIGHT SIDE.
2 Metherell John K.
4 Palmer John
⌐*Lewisham rd.*
8 Papworth Mrs. S.
8 Papworth Harry J.
12 Lawford Miss
14 Heild J.
22 Bodmer Richard, F.C.S., analytical chemist

Grove Terrace,
see Highgate rd.

HAMPSTEAD LANE
From High st. Highgate to Hampstead heath.
C 8
LEFT SIDE.
⌐*South grove*
1 Harris Wm. Redford
2 Hayward Miss
3 De Beaumont A. R.
4 Sime John
6 Henderson Alexander Milne, M.D.
7 Church Henry G.
Lea Mrs. (Park villa)
Caen Terrace.
1 Box William Braund
2 Pitt William R.
3 Nash Thomas Russ
4 Jackson Mrs.
Hampstead Lane.
Eastwick Jas. (Coombe house)

Park Terrace.
2 Adams Frederick
3 Butler Samuel Thorpe

Hampstead Lane.
Evans Mrs. Robert L (Mansfield villa)
RickettsF.(Caen Wood towers)
Mansfield Rt. Hon.The Earl (Kenwood)

RIGHT SIDE.
Parkinson Rawlinson (Grove lodge)
North grove
Trinder Rev. Daniel, M.A. (The Vicarage)
Binney Mrs.
Forman Mrs. (Cintra)
Grant Wilfred Dryden
Church Chas. (Cotham)
Cooper James Davis (Lynton house)
Bishop wood rd.

Hargrave Road,

see our " Hornsey, Upper Holloway, and Finsbury Park Directory."

HARGRAVE PARK ROAD.

From Junction rd. to Dartmouth park hill.

D 10

RIGHT SIDE.
2 Tucker E. K.
4 Stevens Frederick
6 Lack Mrs.
8 Burt Charles M.
10 Leipold John
12 Parvin Mrs.
14 Spain John
16 King Thomas Isaac
18 Davies Thomas
20 Wade William
22 Edwards Mrs.
24 Petford Alfred
26 Stephenson Miss
28 Osborne Rev. John Francis, M.A.
30 Hutt Charles
32 Burtt Miss, ladies' schl.
34 Hanford Mrs. W.
36 BruceGeorgeFrederick
38 Funke Otto, school
40 Brocklesby William

42 & 44 Lorimer & Co., manufctrng. chemists
46 Dawkins James T.
48 Shoppee Miss
50 Shirley John
54 Murison John
56 Atkins Henry
58 Smith Alfred R.
60 Piears Frederick
62 Lawson Thomas
64 Obery John H.
66 Crockett John
68 Crooke James
70 Broden William
Board Schools
72 Pincott E.
74 Honour Francis, gas & hot water engineer

LEFT SIDE.
1 Hewitt Joseph
3 Pringle Thomas
5 Slatford William
7 Rogers John R., C.E.
9 Bent Robert
11 Bird Mrs.
13 Robinson Henry
17 Cansick Fredk.Teague, F.R.H.S.
19 Jeffries John
21 Cruickshank Mrs. E.
25 Dawson CharlesJoseph
27 McCarthy Henry
29 Montanari Mrs.
31 Hawes Robert V.
33 Pilcher Charles Henry
35 Morris W. G.
37 Turpin Henry William
39 Stagg James George
43 Wills Alfred
45 Mulford John C.

York Villas.
1 Lye Alfred
2 Cole George
3 Dodd Frederick
4 Smith James
5 Hodges Walter
7 Pryke William
8 Osborne Thomas
9 Lee David
10 Frampton Henry Wm.
11 Peach Arthur Henry
12 Nicholls Francis
13 Fernie D. S.

Hermitage Villas,

see West hill.

HIGH STREET.

From Hornsey lane to Southwood lane.

C 9

RIGHT SIDE.
The Bank.
Rogers Mrs. (Bryanston)
Bellord James,sen.(Edburga house)
Bellord Edmund Jsph., solictr. (Edburga ho.)
Ponsford Arthur, solicitor (Ranmore)
Hughes ThomasArthur (Mount Melleray)
Hospital for Sick Children (Cromwell house) ; S. Whitford, secretary
9 WilliamsonMrs.Emma, little boys' day school and girls' boarding school
Lockhart William S. (Lyndale house)
7 Hardy Samuel
6 Pearson Arthur(Betchworth house)
4 Towgood Mrs. John
3 Carr Robert
Wood Wm.(West view)
High School for Girls; Miss Matilda Sharpe, manager (Channing house)

High Street.
Cholmeley park
Shipstone Mrs. John (Cholmeley lodge)
Spears Rev.R.(Ivy ho.)
2 Crawford R. Dawson (Elgin house)
6 *The Highgate,Hornsey, and Stoke Newington Benefit Building Soc.;* E. Mote, secretary
8 *Steep Grade Tramways and Works Co., Limited;* ClaudScott, managing director (George Dirs Mertens, secretary)
10 Holmes &Sons,builders (White house)
12 Martin John (Oxford house)

HIGH ST.—*continued*
14 *London & South Western Bank, Limited*, High-gate Branch (Hornsey ho.); W.T.Snell,mngr.
16 *The Duke's Head*, Mrs. M. A. Belton
18 Cole C., stationer and librarian (Llama ho.)
20 James Mrs., dress and mantle maker
20 James Thos.,coachbldr.
Broadbent Yard.
Collins John
Palmer James
High Street.
22 Horwood W., decorator
24 Beck Carl, watchmkr.
26 Lipscombe Owen, hair-dresser
28 Newman Misses M. E. and F., milliners
30 Wade George, boot and shoe maker
32 Prickett, Venables & Co., auctioneers, &c.
32 & 34 BRYCE GEORGE, wine merchant
36 Walker W. R.,irnmngr.
38 Chitty Edwin, florist
40 *The Highgate Emporium*
42 Ellis Arthur
Townshend Yard.
1 Pringle Mrs., professed cook
2 Ling George James
3 West John W.
4 McMullin John
5 West Geo.,chmny.clnr.
6 Friend Wm., rag dealer
7 Searle Zebulun
8 Fowler George
9 Tuck William
10 Bradshaw Benjamin
11 Rockhall Charles
12 Lowen Robert
13 Warr John
14 Sanders James, jun.
15 Sanders James, sen.
16 Mead Alfred
High Street.
44 Rogers Robert, hatter
46 Freeman Robert, baker
48 *The Coopers' Arms*, Mrs. Emma Lupton
50 Lowe Wm. F.,bootmkr.

52 & 54 WHITTARD A. H., hosier, hatter & tailor
56 Davies Jas. C., grocer
58 Marriott Mrs. Alfred John, corn dealer
60 Weaver Fred, cigar merchant
Kent's Cottages.
1 Andrews Joseph
2 Baker Matthew
3 Storey Mrs.
4 Perry Mrs.
5 Andrews Joseph, sen.
6 Phippen Simeon
High Street.
62 Garrett Hy., butcher
64 Corder G. A., mineral water manufacturer
64 Wilkins RobertElliott, chemist
66 Martin & Co., drapers
68 Rogers G., cook and confectioner
70 May, Burck & May, printers
72 Dyble Robert & Son, bootmakers
74 Abbott Wm., grocer
76 Kelly William, statnr.
78 ClarkeThos., greengrcr
80 Tattersall John, draper
82 Randall J. G., butcher
84 Lunnon Jas., bootmkr.
86 *The Rose and Crown*, Chas.Kaye Maishman
88 & 90 Burrows W. E. and Son, grocers; post office
⊐*North rd.*
LEFT SIDE.
⊐*Bisham gardens*
Filler Richard Henry, turncock
Harding Mrs.,uphlstrss
Southgate Mrs. Henry, dressmaker (Victoria house)
Cork Charles George
5 Williams H. R., china warehouse
5 Mitton Wm., hairdrssr.
BushellW.,confectioner (Alexandra house)
3 Wolstenholme Mrs., corset maker
2 Constable T., fish-monger and poulterer

Angel Inn,David Bond
⊐*Angel row and South grove*
Dodd William, farrier
Broadbent T., plumber and decorator
Judge Thomas, watch-maker and jeweller
Rawlings Wm., dyer, cleaner, and bleacher
Attkins J., fishmonger
7 EarlLancelot,bootmkr.
8 Mizen Robert George, beer retailer
Attkins Mrs. E., pork btchr. & sausage mkr.
Cutbush W., stationer
Holmes Benjamin,hair-dresser
Kerry Edward & Son, builders & contractors
Watson Thos.,grngrcr.

HIGHGATE HILL.
From Holloway rd. to High st.
C 10
LEFT SIDE.
Sutton Place.
1 Lee Joseph, oilman
1 Baldry & Co., auctnrs.
2 Currey Wm., tobccnst.
3 Smith Mrs. E.A.,draper
4 Orton Charles, grocer
5 *The Dick Whittington Coffee Tavern*
Sundial Row.
1 Williams Benjamin S. (Victoria & Paradise nurseries)
2 Williams Henry
Highgate Hill.
3 Silk J. F. W., M.D. (Victoria house)
Dawson George, horti-cultural builder (Acacia house)
Whittington Place.
1 Beer William, coffee & dining rooms
2 RobinsFredk.,stationer
3 Webber Geo., butcher
4 Welford J., cowkeeper
5 Brown E. W. & Co., chemists
6 Kurz A., baker
⊐*Brunswick rd.*

7 Drinkwater R.W.,coffee and dining rooms
8 Barnes James Thomas, builder
9 Green George Fredk., tobacconist
10 Harris Fredk.,fruiterer

Whittington Terrace.
1 Woodham R., wardrobe and furntr. dlr.
2 Hayes John, leather and grindery stores
3 Rushton S.,cheesemngr.
4 Cole John, grocer
5 Flack & Sons, oil and colourmen
6 Hofmann Frederick, confectioner
7 Kelly William & Son, builders & decorators
⌐*Salisbury rd.*
  The Whittington Stone, William Law

Whittington Place.
15 Sindell Thomas, wardrobe dealer
16 Sindell Thos.,bootmkr.
17 Coles Jno.,furniture dlr.
18 Williams Mrs., catholic repository
19 Brown Arthr.,stationer

Upper Whittington Pl.
1 Jentle Reuben & Sons (Whittington nursery)
2 Jefferys Wm., confctnr.
2 Trenemen & Co.,photos.
3 Price James
4 Aris Chas., bootmaker
5 Stevens Joseph,gardnr.
6 Ferrett —
7 Kerry & Hollidge,bldrs.
  Smallpox Hospital ; Dr. Goude, superintendent; Miss Crockett, matron
11 Lunniss W., hairdrssr.
12 Walker John, butcher
13 Westerby F. M., collar dresser
14 Waller A.,general shop
  Gordon Place Lodging Houses
  The Whittington & Cat, Alexander Shaw
15½ Meakin G. R., grngrcr.
16 Mead George

17 Payne George,gardener and florist
18 Freeman Thomas
19 Howe Thomas
  St. Joseph's Catholic Schools ; Patrick O'Loughlin, master ; Madame Alban, mistress
  St. Joseph's Retreat ; Rev. Father Gregory O'Callagan, rector
⌐*Dartmouth park hill*
  RIGHT SIDE.
  Archway Place.
1 Jones Fredk., hairdrssr.
2 George Charles William, cigar stores
3 Small William, baker
4 King Joseph, fishmngr.
5 Smith Wm., confctnr. and general dealer
6 Esom Morris W.,marine store dealer
7 Tindley James, dealer in horseflesh
8 Pitcher Henry, tailor
9 Went Robert,carpenter
10 Hinkley James
11 Macdonald Jas., greengrocer
12 Rolingson Chas.,gasfttr.
12½ Fleury Felix,genl. shop
13 Rolls Mrs.
14 Groom Chas., plumber
15 Rutherford William, paperhanger
16 Parsons J., beer retailer
17 Fleming Wm., decortr.
18 Ray Mrs. E.,newsagent
19 Rogers Geo., coal mer.
20 Harris John, bootmkr.
21 Smith William
22 Davis Samuel
23 Mortiboy William
24 Elkins W.H.,watchmkr.
25 Woodward and Son, smiths
  Esom M. W., wheelwright
26 Metherell Richard
27 Colson T.E.,undertaker
  Bedford Cottages.
1 Jones Robert
2 Eldridge Richard
  Bedford Place.
1 Freeman Daniel

2 Green George
3 Collins William
4 Freeman Jonathan
5 Simpson Mrs.
6 Potter John
7 Davis Mrs.
8 Carey Alexander
9 Hare Mrs.
10 Hare James
  Blenheim Place.
1 Richards William
2 Harrison William
3 Davis Joseph, sweep
4 Hillier William
4a Simpson Thomas
5 King Mrs.
  Board School
⌐*Despard rd.*
⌐*Bismarck rd.*
  Clifton Villas.
2 Spring Mrs. M.
1 Satur E.Byrne de,artist
  Crown Cottages
8 Buckey John
7 Pepper James
6 Harris Reuben
5 Roots George
4 Snellgrove Mrs.
3 Arnold Mrs.
2 Darken Thomas
1 La Gyoury John, musical instrument maker
  The Old Crown, Mrs. C. Griffiths
⌐*Hornsey lane*
⌐*Cromwell avenue*

HIGHGATE RISE.
From Swain's lane to Millfield lane.
D S
Barrs Henry Hollier Hood (Aller cottage)
1 Webster W. (Brookfield)
2 Ford William Wilbraham (The Hawthorns)
3 Fennell Mrs.
4 Comyns William
5 Sumond Mdme., ladies' school (Brookfield vil.)
6 Jones William
7 Smith Thomas
8 Bunting Mrs.
9 Sadler Samuel
  Ackland Rev. Charles Tabor (The Vicarage)
  St. Ann's Church

HIGHGATE ROAD.

From 289 Kentish town rd. to West hill Highgate.

E 9

RIGHT SIDE.

2 Hall W. T., undertaker
4 Cooper George
6 Fletcher S., dairy
10 Westerby Mrs., collar dresser
12 Pleaden Robert, tailor
14 Taylor Henry, greengrocer
16 Perry Z., umbrella mkr.
18 Heming J., grocer
— *Willow walk*
20 Angell Jno., cabntmkr.
22 Gibbons William
24 Wilson Joseph, plmbr.
24 Wilson A., stationer
26 Oliver F., umbrella mkr
28 Maybin Samuel
28 Maybin Mrs., shirt and collar dresser
30 Briggs Miss, servants' registry office
32 Selleck Edward
34 Atkins Mrs.
36 McKewan Wm. Mawley
38 Smith Misses
40 Nicholls Mrs. E.
42 Holmes Thomas John, solicitor
— *Burghley rd.*
44 Mahon John
46 Potter Edwd. Octavius
50 Paull H. J., architect
52 Lamble S. R.
58 Boardman John
58 Boardman Mrs., lndry.
— *College lane*
60 Morgan T., greengrcr.
60 Morgan R., carpets beaten and re-laid
62 West Francis, saddler and harness maker
62 Dean Homer, bootmkr.
62 Sims Alfred & Co., carriage builders
64 Cansick Nathan, bldr.
66 Rush John, bootmaker
68 Waller Thos., carman
70 Farren John
72 Arlett William Henry
— *Lady Somerset rd.*
74 Easun Thomas, builder
76 Page Frederick, farrier

78 Porter & Sons, artists' colourmen
80 Hazlewood Henry, beer retailer
82 & 84 Johnson E., jobmstr. (The Vine Stbls.)
86 *The Vine,* Fredk. Preece
88 Turner Mrs.
88a Douglas David
90 *The Jasmine Laundry*
92 Adney Jas., bootmaker
94 Ruth Engelbert, watch and clock maker
96 *Cornwall & Devonshire Dairy Farm Produce Co.;* Edward William Small, manager
98 Ellis William, carriage builder
100 Welchman Edward
102 Rowson Thomas
104 Waller George
106 Saunders John
108 Leiros J. de, pianoforte tuner
112 Gatenby Wm. Thos.
114 Secker Thomas, builder
120 *Society for Organising Charitable Relief & Reprsng. Mendicity;* George Harris, agent
124 Main Thomas, smith
126 Pearson Robert
— *Little Green st.*
128 Cox and Thornton, coal merchants
134 Rush John, bootmaker
St. John's Park House Ladies' School, Mdlles.
Kœune & Mrs. Watson
Smith Tom (Grove end lodge)
BAPTIST CHAPEL
— *Carrol rd.*
Burlison John (Grove end house)
Hepburn Duncan (Cumberland villa)
Glover John George (Lynton villa)
— *Dartmouth park rd.*

Grove Terrace.

1 Frazer John Gordon
2 Smith Mrs.
3 Wilks James Smith
4 Booker Mrs.
5 Beves Jonas Edward

6 Strange Mrs.
7 Walker Mrs.
8 Nokes Thomas
9 Marshall Francis
11 Smith William A.
12 Green Samuel Walter
13 Dixon Thomas Parker, solicitor
14 Cook Mrs.
15 Hartridge James Hills
16 Castle George, solicitor
17 Eve Charles
18 Bayne Charles
20 Webb Richard Mallam
21 Hill Henry J. (Riversdale house)
22 Furniss Robert
23 Handyside Mrs.
25 Tucker John
26 Ambrose Edwin
29 Earnshaw Mrs. E.
30 Bovill Alfred, district surveyor
32 France H. & Son, undertakers
— *Woodsome rd.*
Highgate Road.
Bull & Last, Charles Thomas Bevan
— *Croftdown rd.*
Gotto H. (Croft lodge)
Convent of La Sainte Union Des Sacrés Cœurs; Madame Copin, lady superior
Pensionnat for Young Ladies
St. Alban's Villas.
1 Eddington George
3 Marshall Miss
4 Noakes Miss Jessie
5 Callow Edward
6 Arnold George
7 Huggins Arthur Erat
8 Williams Robert B.
9 Wood Mrs. C. P.
— *St. Alban's rd.*
10 Burchett James R.
11 Moore James
12 Buchanan Hy. Bryan
13 Hogerzeal Cornelius
14 Lamb Mrs.
Highgate Road.
The Duke of St. Alban's, William Maskell
Oliver & Smith, cemetery masons

LEFT SIDE.

1 Stott Thos. S., M.R.C.S.E.
3 Job William Henry
5 Sanders Mrs., dressmkr.
7 Giles H. P., boys' school
9 Goodchild N., M.D., surg.
11 Baker Henry West
13 Furber Alfred William, dentist
15 Try Thomas
17 Greenwood Charles
⊏ *Prospect pl.*
    KENTISH TOWN
    PARISH CHURCH
19 Philcox Mrs.
21 Hull Mrs.
23 Taylor Jas., organ bldr.
25 Lockhart James Chas.
27 Crowe Daniel, builder
29 Baker Charles
31 Watts Frdk., M.D., surg.
35 Wilkinson Mrs., dressmaker
37 Warn Reuben Thomas, M.R.C.S.E., L.S.A.
⊏ *Prospect pl.*
39 Earl Thomas, artist
41 Butt Arthur N., F.R. HIST. S.
41 Butt Mrs.
43 Preston Mrs. Elizabeth
45 Strugnell F.W., L.R.C.P., M.R.C.S., L.S.A.
47 Pain Henry, architectural modeller
49 Dyke Richard J.
51 Earnshaw Miss
53 Dyke and Son, marble and stone works
55 Grosse W. F., fishmngr.
57 Grosse Chas., greengrcr.
59 Chamberlain A. H., bootmaker
61 Cruice Wm., coffee ho.
63 Churchill A., baker
65 Leach Henry, draper
67 Wills John K.
67 *Sanitary Laundry Co.*
69 Brown Theodore, cigarette manufacturer
71 Williams F. & Co., grcrs. and provision merchants (The Stores)
75 & 77 O'Hara Wm., butcher
79 Porter D., oilman
    Arlett & Co., horticultural builders

Turner G. R., engineer and railway waggon builder
Binley & Co., railway waggon builders
Ashwell J., contractor
81 Seager Geo., cheesemgr.
83 Wale & Co., grocers
85 James William, dispensing chemist
87 & 89 Capel L. & E., bootmakers
91 Harran Mrs.
93 Hanbury John James
95 Ashwell J., contractor
97 Smith Henry and E., drapers
99 Dainton Solomon, furniture dealer
101 Parmenter T., fruiterer and greengrocer
103 Hatten W. S., cowkeeper and dairyman
105 Leaver H.. china and glass dealer
107 Thompson C. H., newsagent & stationer
109 Engall T. N., gas and sanitary engineer
111 Nerney William
113 Harris Francis
113 Rickett Smith & Co., coal merchants
115 Mitchell Joseph H. & Co., coal merchants
117 Cox & Thornton, coal merchants
119 Miles Wm., cheesemgr.
121 Williams John, oil & lamp depôt
⊏ *Pleasant row & Mortimer ter.*
123 Burleigh S., upholsterer
125 Vincent Thos., grocer
125 Scanes & Son, plmbrs.
    Railway Station
137 Keast James, builder
139 Atkin Mrs., beer retlr.
141 Paterson Frncs., baker & cnfctnr.; post office
⊏ *Wesleyan pl.*
143 Shirtliff F., chemist & dentist
145 Upton Richard John, oilman
147 Hunt Montague William, tobacconist

149 Rawlings Wm., dyer
151 Mortimer J., fruiterer and greengrocer
153 Maisey Thos., chsmngr.
155 Hinch James, grocery store
157 Mixer W. J., draper
⊏ *Gordon house rd. to Mansfield rd.*
    The Grove.
    Rawlins W. P., M.D. (Gordon house)
    Hall Henry (Gordon house)
1 Goodall J. M. (Linden house)
2 Latham Henry
3 Moon Theophilus
4 Coxeter James (Bathurst house)
5 Huggins William H. (Clifton lodge)
6 Spence Mrs. (Ivy ho.)
7 Lane John (Grove ho.)
8 Osmond Frederick S. (Clevedon house)
9 Tillotson Mrs.
10 Lyell Frederick
11 Parker Richard (The Limes)
    Chalmers John Binny (The Elms)
    Highgate Road.
    Papworth Harry James (Grove Farm house)
    Glover Mrs. Thomas (The Gothic)
    Gray Nathaniel (Grove Farm cottage)
    Boucher Wm., farmer & grazier (Grove farm)
    Smith Edwd., fly prprtr.
    Ansell Thomas (Grove nursery)
    Polding Marcella (Meadow cottage)

    Holly Cottages,
    see Archway rd.

    Holly Terrace,
    see West hill.

    HOLLY VILLAGE.
    From Swain's lane to Highgate rd.
    D 9
1 Agar T. J.

HOLLY VILLAGE—*contd.*
2 Payne John Orlebar
3 Basnett Thomas
4 Whitley Edward
6 Essex C.
7 Thomson David C.
8 McCandlish Richard D.
9 Garrett R. H.
10 Elliot Robert
11 Dixon W. A.
12 Burnie Alfred

Holly Lodge Villas,
see Swain's lane.

HOLMESDALE RD.
*From 11 Northwood rd.
to Archway rd.*
B 9
RIGHT SIDE.
2 McLay James
4 Gates William
6 Pollard Frederick
8 Foreman William
10 Hughes Robert Henry
12 Eagle John George
14 Giles William Henry
16 Brown William
18a Herapath John
20 Raker Slater T.
22 Robb Robert
24 Bullimore John
26 Jamieson Andrew
⌐Orchard rd.
28 Brooks Robert
30 Barnes Alfred
32 Crabtree Robert
34 Herapath Mrs. Sarah,
   laundry (Spring cott.)
36 Barber Plant, builder
38 Barber D., builder
40 Burtt Henry Miller
42 Brees Mrs. A.
LEFT SIDE.
1 Hopewell Alfred
3 Blackmore Miss Marian
5 Smith Miss
7 Billings James
9 Bishop W.
19 Bandy William
21 Routledge Henry
23 Morey George
25 Davey Winslow Harry
29 Pointon George Wm.
23 Goodliffe —
35 Lyon Thomas
37 Hornsey Thomas

39 Burke George
41 Batson Charles
43 McGougan Eugene
47 Stone Mrs. M. (Nether-
   aven cottage)
49 Gray John
51 Porter George
53 Warren Edward
55 Hawes Henry Peck
57 Thompson Wm. Henry
59 Eastman Mrs., grocer
   and cheesemonger
61 Milborn Wm., florist
   Bourlet James (Home-
   dale villa)

Hope Cottages,
see College lane.

HORNSEY LANE.
*From High st. to Archway
road.*
C 10
LEFT SIDE.
Loutit Sinclair (Nor-
   man house)
Wallace James J.(Win-
   chester house)
Hickson Mrs. (Linden
   house)
⌐Tile Kiln lane
New River Co.'s Station
⌐Archway rd.
Lea George(Hill brow)
Burt Henry (Gwynfa)
Wright Cory (North-
   wood)
RIGHT SIDE.
1 Chapman C. C. H.,
   architect
1 Chapman Chas. Waller
   Thomas John (Bal-
   main house)
4 Jones Alexander(Neth-
   erleigh house)
   Edmunds John (Thorn-
   bury)
   Harrison Rev. J. J.
   (Underwood house)
   O'Callaghan Hon. Mrs.
   Rosina (Loretto ho.)
6 Grainger Mrs.
7 Mattinson Joseph
9 Clayton John
10 Charles John
   De Vos Desiderius
   (St. Aloysius school)

⌐Archway rd.
Ambler Miss (Harber-
   ton)
Ambler Edward (Har-
   berton)
Pratt Newton (Har-
   berton)
Wills Geo. (Whitehall)

INGESTRE ROAD,
Dartmouth Park.
From Dartmouth pk. hill
E 9
1 Geiger F. X.
2 Mills Mrs. James
   ladies' school
3 Rendell William
4 Swan William
5 O'Connor John
6 Robinson William
7 Mann William
8 Cope William
9 Squires Henry
11 Thompson Robert
12 King Frederick
13 Vincer Daniel
14 Bowyer George
   Mansfield George Wm
   (Mansfield house)
   Imperial Sanitary
   Steam Laundry ; M
   A. Baldwin & Co
   (Eagle house)

JACKSON'S LANE.
*From Archway rd. to
Southwood lane.*
B 9
Williams Henry Reade
   (Oak lodge)
Tuckett Philip D
   F.G.S., F.R.G S., M.R.
   (Southwood lawn)
Lloyd John H. (Hill
   side)
Cook Miss
Toyne William (Ban
   Point cottage)

Judd Cottages,
see North hill.

JUNCTION ROAD,
Upper Holloway,
*From Highgate hill t
Dartmouth park hill.*
D 10
RIGHT SIDE.
2 Lott Bros., cheesemngrs

4 HazellAlfd.,corn dealr.
6 Hazell Joseph, livery stables
8 Bezant S. H., pawnbrk.
10 Rushton Saml., cheesemonger
12 Barltrop Albert T., bootmaker
14 Baker & Baker, drapers
16 Rowe W., bldr. & dcrtr.
18 Stephens E., house and estate agent
24 Silverthorne William Harper
28 Foster Michael E.
Victoria Nursery, Benjamin S. Williams
30 Tasker John G., dentist
32 Burton William
34 Salkeld John (St.John's villa)
Vorley rd.
36 Goodman Charles
36 Codling Wm.S.,archtct.
38 Sanders James Lewis
40 Whittle Edward
42 Baxter Mrs. S. J.
44 Durnford Hy., builder
46 Spilling Henry
48 Rogers John, photophr.
50 Greaves Frank, M.R.C.S.E.
Langdon rd.
52 Ross William John
54 Hoffman J.
56 Wood George
58 Lloyd John James
60 Ledwidge Francis
62 Rees William, cabinetmaker
64 Galloway Mrs.
66 Courteney Richd. John
68 Ford Walter, plumber
70 Beckett W. J., furnishing undertaker
Hargrave park rd.
72 Stephenson C. S.
74 Brede Alfred Robert, architect
74 Hargraue WilliamHy., solicitor
78 Bucknall Edwd.,school
80 Jones S.,carver & gilder
82 Brown JamesH.,wholesale paper hangings
84 London Mrs. S. A., china & glass wareho.

86 *The Junction Arms,* Henry Howson
Bickerton rd.
88 Campbell W. F., M.D., M.R.C.S.
92 Puzey Anthony
94 Lockyer George
96 Kindell James
98 Parkinson Robert
100 Heaton Mrs. E.
102 Batho William Smith
CONGREGATIONAL CHURCH
Tremlett grove
104 Cresswell E., baker
106 Cunnington John, cheesemonger
108 Farr J. E., corn dlr.
110 Rickard John, grnger.
112 Lower F. J., oilman
London Street Tramway Company's Depôt
114 Murthwaite E. S., coffee house
116 *Economical Boot Repairing Company*
118 Lambert W.,stationer
120 Randal Henry, tailor
122 Muir Edward, draper
Poynings rd.
124 Hards James, auctnr.
126 LunchHy.,hairdresser
128 Inwood Thomas,china and glass dealer
130c Koblich & Son, tailors
130b Pursey G. F., picture dealer
130a Read Thomas, dairy
130a Baldwin F., collar dresser
Cathcart hill
132 Barton Benjamin (Grosvenor lodge)
134 Rowe William E.
138 Ball Francis W. (Ivy lodge)
140 Pridmore Thomas W. (Grosvenor villa)
142 Knight Joseph (Suffolk villa)
144 Giblett Mrs.
146 Cooke Mordecai C., M.A.
148 Adams George (Grosvenor house)
150 Reid Geo. W. (Bridge house)

Wyndham cres.
158 Coat Jacob & Co.,genl. & cemetery masons
160 Tew F. W.
162 Lawrence John
164 Roberson Miss Jane
166 Player Mrs., ladies' school
168 Latimer John
170 Baker Edward
172 Knight William
174 TrowbridgeWilliam H
176 Blunt Walter
176 Price Mrs.
Stanley Hall & Baths; E. H. Blunt, proptr.
The Boston Hotel, Edward H. Blunt
LEFT SIDE.
1 *The Lion Tavern,* Isaac Simpson
3 Morton William James, fishmonger
5 *International Tea Co.*
7 Gardiner Robt., baker
9 Philp Wm., butcher
11 Edwards Wm., greengrocer
13 Herring George, hairdresser and hatter
15 Fenn John, coffee rms.
17 Cox Edward, oil and italian warehouse
19 Bickerton Richard, grocer and tea dealer
21 Bond B.R.,fancy draper
23 Blake Mrs., china and glass warehouse
25 Nix Charles, dairyman
27 Hiller William, pork butcher
29 Frost A.,fancy repstry.
31 *Lion Cigar Stores*
33 Tuckey Henry, greengrocer
35 Applegate Edwin, chemist
Hargrave rd.
37 Bassett George, corn dealer
39 Gregory Wm., grocer
41 Colebrook Stephen, butcher
43 Lascelles Jonathan T., cheesemonger
45 & 47 LyddonWilliam H., boot & shoe wareho.

JUNCTION RD.—*contind.*

49 Parkins Geo. H., wine merchant
51 Parker J. W., piano and music warehouse
53 *Victoria Wine Compy.*
55 Windsor S., draper
57 Hurrell Jas.,pork btchr.
59 Erbach Bros., bakers
61 Hobbs A. I., dairyman
63 Manlove Joseph Hy., ironmonger
65 Watkins William B., hairdresser
67 Cowper Wm.,carpenter
67 Evans H., bootmaker
69 Ovens Edward, tailor
71 Thorn Wm., tripe drsr.
73 Lingwood Geo., bookseller and stationer
75 Andrew S.,confectioner
77 Wright Mrs., milliner
77 Lamb J.,coal merchant
79 Smith B. W., butcher
81 Brass John, baker
83 Shilton George, grocer
85 Salmon Joseph, oil and colourman
87 Bunting John, greengrocer
89 Greenfield J., tobccnst.
⌐*Brook rd.*
91 *St. John's Tavern*, Jas. John Winter
⌐*St. John's park*
93 *London General Provision Stores*
95 Usher Albert & Co., coal office
95 Hurwood W., tailor
97 Safe Misses E. & A., baby linen warehouse
99 Smith Fredk,watchmkr
101 Parr John, bootmaker
101 &103 Hughes Hy.,brush maker ; post office
107 Bloice John, draper
⌐*Pemberton gardens & Pemberton ter.*
109 Bevan W., tea dealer
111 Gray Francis Henry, watchmaker
113 Wheeler R.,coffee and dining rooms
115 Hodgson William, bootmaker
117 Potter A., fishmonger

119 Dunmill Joseph C., printer
121 Burnard W. J., dairy utensil maker
123 Honour William, tobacconist.
125 Osborn Mrs.
127 Palmer Frederick
129 Barber Miss
131 French Joseph Stephen
135 Baylis Charles
137 Smith Thomas
139 Fleming John
141 Stockley Mrs., wardrobe dealer
143 Lee Frederick, tobacconist
145 Martin Wm.,stationer
147 Young Henry, florist and gardener
149 Moon M. J., chemist
⌐*Francis ter.*
151 *Prince of Denmark*, Chas. Albt. Hartland
153 Young Thomas
155 Jenkin Geo., artists' brush maker
157 Whiteley Henry
159 Harrison Edward
161 Sale Charles
163 Evans William
165 Faircloth Robert N.
179 Warde Danl., solicitor
181 Rumsey William
183 Fisher Edward, glover, &c.
185 Browne Henry
187 Cornwell Mrs.
189 Aulburn George
191 Emsley George, servants' registry
193 Phippard Samuel
193 Buck Mrs.
195 Monk William
197 Wilkinson Miss
199 Laver James
201 *La Sainte Union des Sacrés Cœurs*
205 Taylor T.
207 Hills James
Junction Road Railway Station, M.R.
215 Norton Nathaniel, photographer
217 Gibbons Mrs.
⌐*Ward rd.*
219 Hedgecoe Walter

221 Clarke & Co.,dyers,&c
221 Rowley Frederick, estate agent
223 Lawrence Henry
225 Denham Thomas
227 Henderson Alexander
229 Poltz Heinrich
233 Walker William
⌐*Fulbrook rd.*
237 Stone J. H., butcher
237a King Bros.,tobaccnsts
239 Skelton Saml., baker
241 Roylance Charles shirt & collar dresser
243 Routledge J.,cabinet maker
243 Strong J. C., saddler
245 Scott John, sen., gasfitter
247 Slater Miss Sarah grocer ; post office
249 Brightman Benjamin coffee & dining rms.
251 Chubb J. R.,dairyman
253 Scott & Co., builders and decorators
255 Phillips E. T., grocer

Kents Cottages,
see High st.

LADY SOMERSET ROAD.
From Fortess rd.
E 9
LEFT SIDE.
1 Charlier H.
3 Kelly R. W.
5 Cross Mrs. C. K.
7 Bisborne Henry
9 Pizey Henry
11 Hitchman F.
13 Wright Henry
15 Pulley Miss
21 Ward Mrs.
⌐*Burghley rd.*
25 Gilby Henry
27 Engall Thomas, M.D.
29 Andrews John Richard
31 Foskett Samuel
35 Milne Mrs.
37 Parsons John
39 Shallard James B.
⌐*St. John the Evangelist's rd.*
41 Goodworth George
43 James William Henry

47 Brice Charles
49 Mead John
51 Phillips Arthur
53 Hodge Edward
55 Down James
57 Clues Mrs.
⌐Highgate rd.
RIGHT SIDE.
2 Reeves Miss, teacher of music
4 Potter T. J.
6 Dorè Morris B.
8 Watts Edward
⌐Oakford rd.
10 Ambler Matthew
12 Dearle Miss
14 Crombet P. T.
16 Flemyng Major-Genrl. Augustus
18 Copping Edward
20 Nuth Alfred
20 Nuth Edward
22 Davis Mrs.
24 Henderson William C.
26 Cockram Henry
⌐Burghley rd.
30 Strickland Geo. Henry
32 Watling Thomas
38 Petyt Mrs.
40 Ryder H.
42 Ashwell Mrs.
44 Williams C.
46 Poley E. W., architect
48 Miles Thomas
50 Loewenstein S.
52 Howes Harmen
54 Holker Arthur
56 Hulbert Rchd. Stephen
58 Hunter W. N.
62 Noble John
64 Praill Edward
64 Borkett Frederick
66 Shotter H. B.
68 Scarnell Herbert
70 Andrews Mrs.
72 Hunt William R.
74 Boxall John
76 Easy Mrs.
⌐College lane
8 Smith Samuel

LANGDON ROAD.
From Junction rd.to Dartmouth park hill.
D 10
LEFT SIDE.
1 Clutton Miss

3 Chilman Edward
5 Wright Mrs.
7 Hutt George
9 Newman Mrs.
11 Cato Thomas R.
13 Dennis Henry A.
15 Suckling Francis Jas.
17 Elwin Edward
19 Corbett Mrs.
21 Hawkins Thomas
25 Lodge James
27 Perry William D.
29 Webb Richard
33 Mellish Frederick
39 Jones William
41 Elvins Harry
43 Maidman William
45 York Thomas
47 Gregory Percival
47aBrown T., contractor and carman
49 Young Joseph & Mrs. Margaret, wardrobe dealers
51 Mercer Edward
57 Wallace William
59 Jull Mrs.
61 Godfrey Albert Edwin
63 Hobbs Thomas
67 Avery Richard
67 Avery Mrs. (Clyde house laundry)
Board Schools
69 Botham Mrs. C. E., midwife
71 Smith William, mason
73 Boswell W. J., builder
RIGHT SIDE.
2 BrownW.T.,contractor
4 Warrell J. C.
6 Robertson Thomas
8 Little Mrs. Rebecca
10 Lakeman Mrs.
12 Kynvin Mrs.
14 Blackall John
16 Salmons Henry
18 Roffe William, artist
20 Oliver Mrs.
22 Esling George Henry
26 MurreyMiss,ladies'schl
28 Cook Henry
30 Sweeting Mrs. (Belgrave villa)
32 Coyne Joseph P.
32aBarnes Mrs., tobccnst.
32aPowell James, newsvendor

⌐Girdlestone rd.
34 Dawe Henry
36 Stirling William
38 Puttock Robt.,brcklyr.
40 Leggett G.
42 Galvin Stephen
44 Allen Charles
46 White Robert
48 Woodgate E.
50 Dent William
56 Short James
58 Bostock James
93 Harding J. W. (The Langdon oil & colour stores)
92 Price Edward, mason
91 Muir J. M.
90 Gullett James
89 Clarke James
ST. PETER'S CHURCH

LANGDON PARK ROAD.
From Archway rd. to Northwood rd.
B 9
LEFT SIDE.
1 Lee Joseph
3 Sharp William Herbert
5 Wright William Henry
7 Stevenson Robert W.
9 Gardiner Frederick
11 Weston J. B.
13 Gorham Chas. Turner
15 Cartwright James Joel
25 Lomer E.
27 Eaton E. J. Applebee
29 Moginie Daniel B.
31 Bunce William Henry
33 Wright W. T.
35 Paun Charles
37 Townsend William
39 Matthews Mrs.
⌐Wembury rd.
41 Clayton Capt. J. Pegg
43 Hulme J. A.
45 Johnson Edwd. Henry
47 Koch Herbert Sigismund, prof. of music
RIGHT SIDE.
22 Dickson Thomas
22 Dickson Mrs., professor of music
24 Norris Daniel
26 Payne Rev. W. L.
26 Payne Wm. Michael
28 Lindquist Oscar M.

LANGDON PK. RD.—*cntd.*
30 Balfour Mrs. E.
32 Meade T. de Courcy
34 White James
36 Gotobed Edward
40 Peacock T.
44 Halsey James
46 Tinsley George
50 *Mildmay Mission to the Jews' Convalescent Home;* Rev. John Wilkinson
60 Smith J. A.
62 Loutit Mrs. Sinclair
64 Edan Alfred
66 Lindsay George
68 Greenwood Charles T.

LEWISHAM ROAD.
From 14 Grove rd.
D 9
LEFT SIDE.
2 Hankins Richard
6 Brown Mrs. Isaac
8 Davis Richard
10 Newman Charles
12 Comber Mrs. Charles
16 Smith David
30 Mudie Ernest
RIGHT SIDE.
3 Samuda Miss Isabelle
7 Marshall Charles Jas. Kittermaster
11 Present F. W.
15 Mahomed Rev. J. D. K., B.A.
21 Tugman James E.
Barnes H. (Patschull house)
Trotter G. (Legge ho.)

LITTLE GREEN ST.
From 124 Highgate rd.
E 9
2 Lloyd William
3 Hughes John
4 Tumber Harry
5 Parish William
6 King David
7 Baker John
8 Wilmott William
9 Linford George
Main Thos., genl. smith

Lulot Street.
From 69 Retcar st.
D 9

MAGDALA ROAD,
Highgate Hill.
From Girdlestone rd.
D 9
1 Larcy J.
3 Heard Edward
4 Storey James
6 Hare Henry
8 Burleigh Walter
9 Reynolds Henry
10 Curtis Alfred
11 Woodham George
12 Priest Mrs.
13 Winter Richd., gardnr.
15 and 16 Dublack Mrs. Caroline
17 Boff Frank
18 Canham Mrs
19 Scuffle Edward
21 Bedmead Frederick
23 Penny John
24 Middleton W.
25 Nathan Hyam
Campbell J. (Pensee villa)
Dumenil Adolph (Park cottage)
Boxhall Henry (Fairfield house)
27 Smith William, sculptor
30 Casbold J.
31 Findlay Alexander
32 Hembrow Chas. Wm.
33 James Mrs.
34 Green George, coal and coke merchant
35 Mills John (Camelia cottage)
36 Unwin J. J.
37 Gunn William
38 Holland Christopher J.
39 Hoffman Edwin
40 Ray Frederick
41 Foxcroft James Charles
42 Dickeson William

Mansfield Cottages,
see North hill.

Meadow Cottages,
see College lane.

Mercer Terrace,
see Archway rd.

MERTON LANE.
From West hill to Millfield lane.
C 8
Scrimgeour Mrs. Isbla.
Lovell Charles Henry
Glover John (Merton lodge)

MILLFIELD LANE.
From Highgate rise.
D 8
LEFT SIDE.
Lodge Mrs. (Millfield villa)
Stock Elliot (Fern lo.)
Ford Wm. (Brookfield house)
Lyell John Skene (Millfield cottage)
Glass H. G., florist
RIGHT SIDE.
Southampton Villas.
Street Edmund
Miles Joseph J.
Lloyd Fredk. Giesler
Millfield Lane.
Rawlins Henry (The Laurels)
Tatham T. C. (Millbrook house)
Grindley Mrs. (Millfield)
Webb James E. (The Cottage)
Bowler Thomas (Millfield lodge)
Theobald William (Ivy cottage)
Hine Arthur (Fitzroy cottage)
Ward Thomas, farmer and cowkeeper (Fitzroy farm)
⌐*Fitzroy park*

Moreton Cottages,
see North hill

MORTIMER TER.
From Pleasant row to Wesleyan pl.
E 9
2 Buckerfield Thos. H.
12 Edbrook G.
13 Wise James

14 Tarry Isaac
15 Ellsmoor Brian
16 Daniel William

Coal Bays.
1, 2 & 3 Mitchell Joseph H. & Co., coal mers.
4 & 5 *Pinxton Colliery Company*
6, 7 & 8 Cox & Thornton, coal merchants

Norman Villas,
see Archway rd.

NORTH GROVE.
From Hampstead lane.
C 9
1 Marshall Arthur
2 Evans Charles
3 Smith Willoughby
4 Hammond Robert
6 Lowe Francis
7 Scott Robt. Turnbull
8 Harris William

NORTH HILL.
From North rd.
B 8
LEFT SIDE.
Park Place.
3 Sadler Miss
2 Cockburn Mrs.
1 Tatham Conway
Rowsell Edwin (Sussex house)
Baker William (Park cottage)
North Hill.
The Bull Inn, James Steventon
Bateman Wm., gardnr.
Bennett Felix, baker
Homewood S., baker
—*Broadlands rd.*
Tanner W. S., artists' repository ; post office
Johnson Miss (Lawn house)
Bartholomew Terrace.
1 Storey Allen
2 Stokes Alfred John, gardener
3 Lowen Robert, brick-layer
4 Playfoot William
4 Woollard A., gardener

Mission Hall
North Hill.
Gibbs & Imber, buildrs.
Cowdry Wm. (Noemi cottage)
Boughay David John (North cottage)
North Place.
1 Garrood Henry
2 Mackeson Henry
4 Sims J. C.
5 Windsor Peter John, stone carver
6 Bailey Mrs.
North Hill.
Challis Mrs. (North hill house)
Wray Wm., optician (Laurel house)
Model Dwellings
—*Ward's cottages*
Twinn John, grocer
Andrews Wm., btmkr.
Tilley James
Ayres Mrs.
Brindle Geo., carpenter (Francis house)
Brindle Mrs., laundress
Aldcroft Thomas Agar, laundry
Canning Geo., painter
Canning W. J., plmbr.
Richardson Edward
—*Grange rd.*
Nicholson Thomas E. (Melton house)
White's Cottages.
1 Downing George
2 Cokeham Geo., carrier
3 Heptinstall William, carpenter
North Hill Terrace.
1 Wills H. W.
2 West Frederick
3 Pettifer Arthur
4 White Miss
5 Byecroft Frederick
6 Barnard Rev. J. H.
North Hill.
Clarke Joseph, F.R.G.S. (North hill villa)
Prospect Cottages.
1 Coates William C.
2 Sharman William
3 Hill Edward Henry
4 Leaman Walter

North Hill.
Wakelin Plant (Pro-vidence cottage)
Prospect Terrace.
1 Teedon —
2 Edmondson Christphr.
3 Gale Joseph
4 Violet Albert
5 Blowers Charles
6 Searle Zebulon
Board Schools
Springfield Cottages.
Westlake J. G., contrctr.
—*Archway rd.*
RIGHT SIDE.
Toyne James, grocer
London Diocesan Peni-tentiary ; Rev. J. H. Amps, warden (Park house)
Gaskell Roger
—*Park house rd.*
Pawle R. (Gothic cot.)
Kieffin Alex. (1 Milton cottages)
Stone Mrs. (2 Milton cottages)
Massingham W.A.(The Woodlands)
Gosbell Miss, school (The Woodlands)
Baker Joseph William, farmer (Woodland cottage)
Westlake J. G., carman and contractor (Pine cottage)
Westlake John (Pine cottage)
Fernee T. F., bootmkr.
Corbett John (Myrtle cottage)
Johnston Mrs. M. A., dairy & coachbuilder
The Victoria, John Hardy
Bruce Alfred, grocer
Abrahams J. (Wood-land place)
Atkins Henry (Wood-land place)
Harris Mrs. (The Limes)
Jones Miss (North-wood cottage)
Allen Charles (Wood-side cottage)
Shorter Chas. (Oak vil.)

NORTH HILL—*continued*
Badcock Henry James
  (Woodville cottage)
*All Saints' Mission
  House;* Miss Mary
  Hughes, lady suprtnt.
Church rd.
Collinson Mrs.
Noakes Benjn. (Hope
  cottage)
Wood T. McKinnon
  (Fernwood)
Dean D.W.(South ldge)
Bell Wm. (North ldg.)
Reddall Stratford Wm.
  (Mylor cottage)
  Judd Cottages.
1 Sherlock Wm., gardnr.
2 Allcock Samuel
  North Hill.
AskewGeo.(Rose bank)
  Moreton Cottages.
Richardson Frederick
  Wellington Terrace.
1 Drake Mrs.
{ 2 Gale Joseph
3 Longman Miss, dress-
  maker
5 Outing Saml.,bootmkr.
6 Dench Alfred F.
  North Hill.
Freeland Jas.(Ivy cot.)
Dent George (Rochelle
  cottage)
  Mansfield Cottages.
Baker's lane
1 AldermanEsau,cnfctnr
2 Dickins John
3 Huntingford George
4 Stanbridge E.
5 Yeatman Edward
6 Jackson Joseph
7 Sheppard Richard
  Wellington Cottages.
2 Slight Alfred
1 Reid Christopher

**North Place & North
  Hill Terrace,**
  see North hill.

NORTH ROAD.
From High st. to North hill.
  B 9
  LEFT SIDE.
The Gate House Hotel,
  Mrs. Eliza Folkes

Fire Engine Station
Hampstead lane
1 Clothier Henry, M.D.
3 Attkins Miss H. L.
5 VandergootDouwe Jan
7 Tomlinson Charles
9 Bishop John N., F.Z.S.
11 Bennett James Robert
  Sterndale
13 RobinsonJ.(Byron ho.)
17 Taylor T. (Byron cot.)
19 Shelton Edward Lyon,
  solicitor (The Syca-
  mores)
21 Stokes James
23 Bloomfield Edward,
  wheelwright
25 *The Red Lion & Sun,*
  Arthur Silvester
27 Fleming Francis A.,
  corn dealer
29 Babb Henry, carpenter
31 *The Bell and Horns,*
  J. Phillips
33 Fleming Francis A.,
  corn dealer
35 Key Thos.,greengrocer
37 Hale Benjamin
39 Hunter Edward
41 Snowton James
45 Hayhoe T., veterinary
  forge
47 Glead George
49 Glead John
51 Cave George, A.A., preparatory school for
  the sons of gentlemen
  (Gloucester house)
53 Sulman James
57 Lashmore John
  HighgateNationalSchls.
  North Road Cottages.
West A. G., chimney
  sweep
Snow George
Bass Thomas Henry
  North Road.
Bower B. W., monu-
  mental mason
61 Woodward Mrs.
63 Bullen George
65 Goldthorpe F.
67 Johnson D.
69 Outing L.
71 Childs J.
73 Calvert Frederick W.
75 Surridge Job

77 Tuck Henry
79 Boswell F.
81 Abbey Andrew
83 Flanders D.
  Huntington H. (North-
  field drill hall)
85 Harrison Miss (The
  Cedars)
87 ReynoldsAlf.J.(North-
  field)
  RIGHT SIDE.
*Sir Roger Cholmeley's
  School,*Chs.McDowall,
  M.A.,D.D.,head master
4 & 6 Saunders Charles,
  chemist
8 Gardner Thos., jobmstr.
10 *The Green Dragon,*
  Mrs. M. Clark
12 Hunt M. & Son, green-
  grocers
14 BürckW. M.,ironmngr.
16 HarrisonWm.G.,oilmn.
18 BrownW.E.,watchmkr.
  (Cholmeley house)
20 Pringle H. & M., clthrs.
22 Gieve Thomas, um-
  brella maker
24 Eagles Mrs.
26 Attkins Mrs. (The
  Hermitage)
28 Dolley Miss, draper
30 Ballard George Henry,
  dairyman
32 White Edward, builder
  and decorator
36 Webb Reuben W.,
  upholsterer
38 Bailey Richard,builder
40 Sharpe H. U., furniture
  dealer
42 Andrew J., harness
  maker
44 Cuthbert Tom. butcher
46 Appleton Robt., baker
48 Taylor Thomas, grocer
50 Beardwell Mrs. Mary
  Ann, confectioner
52 Smith George, green-
  grocer
54 Reed J. S., draper
56 RedfernW. F.,coff.rms.
Castle yard
58 Ballard George, sen.,
  cabinetmaker
60 Oliver Hy., gardener
60 Oliver Mrs., laundress

64 Wright John, marine store dealer
68 Catlin Charles
70 Tarrier Charles
72 HAMP JOSEPH S., tailor
74 Thomas Mrs. E., general shop
76 Garrood Henry
78 Taylor W., bootmaker
78 Bennett G. W., general smith
80 Rogers James Benjamin
82 Heath William
90 Tester Thomas
92 Dodd R. H., clockmaker
94 *The Red Lion*, E. J. Norris
96 Gibbs Thomas
98 Watson Robt., F.R.G.S. (Falcutt house)
100 Roberts Alfred T., M.A. (Rosslyn house)
The Wrestlers' Tavern, Charles Taylor

NORTHWOOD RD.
From Archway rd.
C 10
LEFT SIDE.

1 Rowe & Harvey, builders (office)
3 Kemp William
5 Naghten John E. A. B., barrister-at-law
7 May John
9 Dickson Thomas Edwd.
11 Rowe William, builder
—*Holmesdale rd.*
13 Storr John (Sawley house school)
15 Davy W.
17 Ash C. J.
19 Gillow Joseph
21 Faux Edward
23 Tugwell Miss, children's home
25 Fowler Miss, middle class school
—*Orchard rd.*
RIGHT SIDE.
—*Langdon park rd.*
4 Groom & Pride Misses, dressmakers
6 Rundell Alfred Robert
8 Murray John

30 Mallett Samuel
32 Ewing John
36 Scott C. B.
38 Windsor Charles
40 Potts Joseph Ellwood
42 Engels Lawrence
44 Christon Fred
48 Kessels P. M., builder
—*Claremont rd.*

OAKFORD ROAD.
From 8 Lady Somerset rd. to Burghley rd.
RIGHT SIDE.
E 9

1 Gore F.
3 Watts John T.
5 Crowhurst W.
7 Simpson H.
9 Greenhill Wm. Smith
11 Goodacre Henry
13 Cooper Charles Henry
15 Baly James Alfred (Overdale house)
17 Wright John
19 Wyatt Joseph
21 Seadon John (St. John's house)
23 Johnson Thomas Hy. (Cambridge house)
25 Cobb C. A.
29 Venn Mrs.
31 Pringle John
33 Bird J.
33 Summers Henry
35 Jones William
37 Johnson William
39 Marchetti Joseph
41 Hall William
43 Webster Miss
45 Charlier A.
47 Innocent J.
LEFT SIDE.
18 Elgar S.
20 Shotter T. E.
22 Tavener J.
24 Langman Philip L.
26 Rollason Mrs.
28 Greenfield W. P.
30 Messenger G.
32 Chase W.
34 Smith John
36 Jones T.
38 Gamble Henry
40 Yeo Thomas
42 Jackman Paul, artist

44 Dawe Mrs.
44 Roberts Mrs.

ORCHARD ROAD.
From Northwood rd. to Holmsdale rd.
B 9
LEFT SIDE.

1 Harvey Frank
3 Smythers Alfred (The Poplars)
5 Weaver James (The Laurels)
7 Woolley Mrs. (The Yews)
9 Shoosmith Wm. Henry
11 Manly Henry
13 Dixon Henry
17 Bourlet Charles (The Hollies)
19 Hill Elles
21 Ross Archibald Robert (The Sycamores)
23 Bulmer Walter
27 Allington Samuel
31 Hateley David
RIGHT SIDE.
2 Carter Simeon, builder
8 Sibley Joseph
10 Hunt Mrs. Elizabeth
18 Thrussell James
20 Axford Mrs. Catherine
22 Cohen W. H., carver and gilder
24 Walker Thomas Christie architect
26 Booty Miss Emily
28 Gee Dennis
30 Knecht Joseph
34 Garnsey William
36 Robinson John

Park Place,
see North hill.

Park Terrace,
see Hampstead lane and Archway rd.

PARK VILLAS,
The Park.
From Bloomfield rd. to Bishop's rd.
B 9

1 Walker Edward
2 Sawday Charles B
3 Wood Mrs. Hugh

PARK HOUSE RD.,
The Park.
From Southwood lane.
B 9
Scholefield Rev.Arthur
  Fredk. (Esmonde ho.)
Low Mrs. W. H. (Clare-
  mont house)
══Bishop's rd.

Pleasant Cottages,
see College lane.

PLEASANT ROW.
From 121 Highgate rd.
E 9
1a Walker Edwd., marine
  store dealer
  Hayward G.
2 Roome Robert
3 Kent Stacey
4 Kemp George
5 Langton John
6 *The Jasmine Laundry*
══Mortimer ter.

POND SQUARE,
High Street.
C 9
1 Lowen & Sons, carmen
2 Baker Mrs.
8 Edwards Andrew
  R a w l i n g s   Charles
  (Chamelion cottage)
══Grove pl.
1 Wheeler Albert(Reser-
  voir house)
2 Mead Thomas
3 Gardener Wm.M.,tailor
3 Turner Albert, florist
  and nurseryman
4 Stark Thomas
5 Tatum Alfred S.
  B u m b e r r y   Joseph,
  builder (Rock house)
  Highgate Dispensary,
  Dr. Clothier and Dr.
  Forshall (Rock house)
══South grove

POYNINGS ROAD.
From 122 Junction rd.
D 10
RIGHT SIDE.
2 Dick Henry Page
4 Gibson John Arthur
8 Parry Mrs.

12 Lovell Edward
14 & 16 *New Pure Bever-*
  age Co., Limited ; J.
  H. W. Rumsey, sec.
20 Edsar F.
24 Body A. S.
26 Ranson W. M.
28 Young W.
30 Schirges A. R.
32 Tinsdale W.
34 Lega-Weekes Mrs.
36 Broomfield J. E.
38 Dennis G. K.
     LEFT SIDE.
1 Gaskin Frederick, pro-
  fessor of music
3 Hibberd Albert W.
5 King J.
7 Palmer Samuel
9 Parry Robert
11 Morgan C.
13 Tigwell John
15 Cooper Mrs.
17 Izod William Henry
19 Raybould William J.
21 Eastwood Mrs.
23 Freame Mrs.
25 Bromley F. S.
27 Ealand R. F.
29 Bryan Frederick
31 Gauntlett W. H.
33 Jackson James
35 Hale Thomas
37 Reed G. R.
39 Mylrea Edward
41 Groves Allen
43 Staunton F.
45 Coomber W. O.

Prospect Cottages &
Terrace,
see North hill and
Prospect pl.

PROSPECT PLACE.
From 17 Highgate rd.
E 9
1 Paxton Mrs. Maria
2 Birchall Jas., gardener
3 Woolley Mrs. E.
4 Carroll Richard Henry,
  shoemaker
5 Freeman William
  Whitelaw John George,
  builder (Prospect ho.)
Prospect Cottages.
1 Peet George, plasterer

2 Smith Wm., laundry
3 Welch Walter
4 Moody James
5 Collingridge William
6 Haynes John
7 Palmer John
8 Yonwin Henry James
9 Miller Joseph
10 Harvey James
11 Millwood Joseph
12 Stock Isaac
13 Thompson Mrs.
14 Humberstone William
15 White Andrew
16 Ells George
  Coles Thomas,cab prop.

Railway Cottages,
see Archway rd.

RAYDON STREET.
From Chester rd.
D 9
LEFT SIDE.
1 Reeve Edmund
3 Piper Joseph
5 Tyson George
7 Martin Charles
9 Strickland Robert
11 Snow James
13 Smith W.J.,monumen-
  tal mason
15 Flaxman George
17 Day Walter Henry
19 Reeve Mrs.
21 Charter George
23 Langley Henry
25 Wightwick George
27 AlexanderAlfredFredk
29 White Benjamin
31 Rogers Francis
33 Pearce Thomas
35 Millward James, ceme-
  tery mason
37 Perry Henry James
39 Crighton David
41 Watkinson James Wm.
43 Sparksman James
45 Bilby Edward
47 Deacon Mrs. Agnes
══Retcar st.
  Alexander A.F.,green-
  grocer and fishmonger
══Dartmouth park hill
RIGHT SIDE.
2 *Reading & Coffee Rooms*
4 Bunyan Alfred James

6 Salsbury Joseph
⌐*Colva st.*
*St. Anne's Mission
Room*
⌐*Doynton st.*
46 Munns George, grocer
42 Newman A., dentist
33 Barr Thomas, builder

RETCAR STREET.
From 65 Raydon st.
D 9
72 Geard A., builder, sawing and planing mills
86 Deane George Arthur,
baker
⌐*Lulot st.*

ST. ALBAN'S ROAD.
*From 9 St. Alban's villas
Highgate rd.*
D 9
RIGHT SIDE.
1 Jones Mrs.
3 Clarke Robert G.
7 Harper Thomas
9 Eyres Henry Charles
LEFT SIDE.
2 West Daniel Kemp,
C.E. (The Cedars)
4 King Edward (The
Limes)

St. Alban's Villas,
see Highgate rd.

St. John's Park,
*see our " Hornsey, Upper
Holloway, and Finsbury
Park Directory."*

ST. JOHN THE EVANGELIST'S RD.
From 9 Burghley rd.
E 9
LEFT SIDE.
1 Gamble Mrs. William,
dressmaker
3 Saunders Samuel Des-
heyes, prfssr.of music
5 Page Frederick
11 Holdernesse Charles
17 Presdee S.
RIGHT SIDE.
2 Tonge Arthur

4 Stokes William
10 Gibson E.
12 Stiles William
14 Pratt Cornelius James
16 Rawlinson Edward

SALISBURY ROAD.
From Highgate hill.
C 10
LEFT SIDE.
1 Aris Henry
3 Willis D. W.
5 Fuller George
7 Christian Edward
9 Mortiboy Henry
11 Lance William C.
13 Ingram Mrs.
15 Westall Richard
19 Hillier Henry
21 Sluce John
23 Middlemiss Mrs.
25 Taylor William
27 Giddy William
29 Roberts Charles, greengrocer
⌐*Vorley rd.*
31 Hulme Edward, baker
31a Bush Richard
37 Hopkins George
39 Cottis Mrs., genl. shop
41 Redman Alfred
43 Simms J. & Co., dairy
RIGHT SIDE.
4 Phillips Mrs.
6 Finch Mrs.
6 Anderson John
8 Davies William
10 Oliver Thomas E.
12 Wainwright George
14 Russell Richard
16 Parsons Joseph
18 Patfield Mrs. John
22 Bull Thomas W.
24 Johnston Henry
26 Garner William
28 Harrison W. L.
30 Whiting Charles D.,
solicitor
32 Chaplin Mrs.
34 Gould Mrs.
36 Brown Mrs.(Whitting-
ton villa)
38 Jenkins John, brick-
layer
40 Kerr Mrs.
42 Elbourn William

SHEPHERD'S HILL ROAD.
From Archway rd.
B 9
Stedall Colonel Robert,
J.P. (The Priory)
⌐*Crescent rd.*
⌐*Montenotte rd.*
Shorter J., statn. mstr.
Leighton G. C. (Fair-
light)
Reynolds E. R. B.,
M.R.C.S. (Highcroft)
Kenneth H. (Hurst-
leigh)
Whittington C. J.
(Broughton lodge)
Eaves William (Bolobo)
Smith Harry (Kyneton
lodge)
Smith Alfred (Shep-
herd's cot)
Geard Charles (North
view)

SOUTH GROVE.
*From West hill to
High st.*
C 9
Duval S.S.(Chesterfield
lodge)
Wooder Wm. (Alfred
cottage)
South Grove Cottages.
1 Beaumont Benjamin
2 Howard William
3 Sharp Daniel
South Grove.
The Flask Inn, Wm.
John Wooder
Wooder William John,
cab and fly proprietor
South Grove Cottages.
4 Goodwin William
5 Hitchcock John
6 Dowsett John
7 Baxter Thomas
Victoria Cottages.
1 Hunt Robert ; cabs,
broughams, and open
carriages for hire
2 Wicks James
2 Wicks Miss, dressmaker
South Grove.
1 Dixon J. W., builder
3 Cutbush H. J.
4 Durrad W. R.

SOUTH GROVE.—*continued*
5 Sharp Martin Charles
6 George Mrs.
7 Crang Edmund
8 Staniforth Thomas
  Worsley, professor of
  music
9 Randall Joseph
  Watkins John, job-
  master
  Dickinson A. E. C.
  (Grove house school)
  Crowdy F., M.B., sur-
  geon
⊏*Grove pl.*
⊏*High st.*
  Maurice Miss
  Maskell Mrs. (Wood-
  ville)
⊏*Bromwich walk*
  Horwood Mrs. (South
  grove house)
  Bloxam Miss
  ST. MICHAEL'S CH.
  Wark Mrs. (Old Hall)
  Casella Louis Pasquale
  (The Lawns)
  Bartlett Rev. Geo. D.,
  M.A.(Solsgirth house)
  Austin Joseph (More-
  ton house)
  HIGHGATE CONGRE-
  GATIONAL CHAPEL
  Dutton Mrs.
  Davies Charles, dairy
⊏*Swain's lane*
  *Literary and Scientific
  Institution;* J. H.
  Lloyd, hon. secretary
  Daniels Henry & Co.,
  cemetery masons
  (Church house)
  Marks Wm., cemetery
  foreman (Russell ho.)
6 RICHARDSON & CO.,
  general & furnishing
  ironmongers
5 Oxley Oscar
4 Lunnon James
3 Horsley Thomas, baker
2 Peachey Alfred, con
  fectioner
1 Ward James, grocer
⊏*Pond sq.*

Southampton Villas,
see Millfield lane.

**Southwood Cottages
and Terrace,**
see Southwood lane.

SOUTHWOOD LN.
*From High st. to
Archway rd.*
C 9
RIGHT SIDE.
3 Sargood Alf. Leonard,
  tailor
4 Coxhead Mrs., haber-
  dasher
5 Scott Herbert
6 Dyble Robert
7 Chapman Mrs. Thorn-
  ton
8 Forshall Frncs. H.,M.D.
  Bartholomew Mrs.
  (Cholmeley house)
10 Burrows W. E., solctr.
11 Pearse Miss Mary
12 Southcott Deagon
  HIGHGATE BAPTIST
  CHAPEL
  Browett Hy. Leonard
  (Avalon)
Southwood Terrace.
1 Taffs Joseph
2 *Girls' Friendly Society;*
  Miss Lacy, matron
3 Hill J. G.
4 Terrell Mrs.
5 Walters Robert, R.N.
6 Coombes John
7 Peel Alexander Scott
8 Atkins Mrs.
9 Pearson William Grey
10 Davies Charles
11 Cooper Mrs.
12 Kennedy ErnestEdwd.
13 Shorter George
Southwood Lane.
  Davies William (Mal-
  don house)
  Long A. (Southwood
  lodge)
  Standfast Geo. Edwin
  (2 Southwood pl.)
  Parker Frederick (Tre-
  leigh house)
  Fletcher George, M.D.
  (Soham house)
  Williams Edwd. Philip
  (Everley)
  Charles Mrs. (Hillside)

  GreenwoodHarry,M.A.,
  barrister (The Limes)
  Johnson J. G. (South-
  wood court)
⊏*Jackson's lane*
  Wells Hill.
1 Chisman Thomas
2 Green Edward
3 Pike John
4 Mattick Benjamin
5 Knowles W. A.
6 Lee Miss, dressmaker
7 Venables Miss, lndrss.
8 Stimpson H.
  Southwood Lane.
  Hughes Mrs. Walter
  (Southwood house)
  LEFT SIDE.
  Hamp George
  Southcott&Co.,builders
1 Fenn John
2 Crane William
  *Southwood Lane Alms-
  houses*
⊏*Constitution hill*
  Burton Eli (Alma cot.)
  Bulworthy G. E.,
  chimney sweep
  Bailey Richard, buil-
  der and contractor
  Barnaby Hy. (Ivy cot.)
  Smith James (2 Ivy
  cottages)
⊏*Castle yard*
  WaterhouseMrs.,lndry.
  (Holly cottage)
  Southwood Cottages.
1 Dean Alfred
3 Wright George
4 Stoker John
  Southwood Lane.
4 & 5 Baker W., gen. dlr.
  Highgate ReadingRms.
  Wright Mrs.
  Baker William Edwin
  Harris Mrs.
  Dicks Henry
  *Cholmeley School Sana-
  torium* (Cholmeley
  lodge); Mrs. Wade,
  caretaker
  Wheeler Henry (Har-
  wood house)
  Richardson Mrs.
  (Woodside)
  Hall E. D.(Myrtle cot.)

Williams R. Wheatley (Endsleigh villa)
School Board for Hornsey
Office of the Hornsey Local Board of Health
Davies Frederick(Pet's cottage)
⌐*The Park*
Kirby Wm.(Well cott.)
Sandison Rev. Alexander (Elmside)
Robertson Mrs. (Lal-Tiba)
Gibbon Rev.J.M.(Therfield)
Löwen Reinhart(Holmhurst)
Morris W. (The Ferns)
⌐*Archway rd.*
Dorothy Cottages.
1 Rogers Richard
2 Bunyan Richard
3 Beare R. H., plumber and decorator

SPENCER ROAD.
From York rise.
D 9
LEFT SIDE.
1 Freeman Henry
3 Keyes Richard
5 Hicks Thomas James
7 Phillips William
9 Holeman W.
11 Williams John, builder
13 Dickinson George
15 Miller Charles
17 Andrews Robert
19 Anderson Wm. Thomas
21 Evetts Henry
23 Holder Charles
25 Jordan Richard
27 Hooley Samuel
29 Chalk George Thomas
31 Boden Anthony
35 Ottey William
37 Hipkins Miss
39 Hickman Arthur James
41 Foster John
43 Bedford C.
45 Sheldrick William
47 Taylor William,leather worker
49 Saunders Joseph
51 Currie William
53 Sargeant Edward

57 Smee M.
59 Barnett Alfred
61 Dawe Misses(Rose cot.)
63 Price James
65 Brett John William (Vine cottage)
67 Kemp William James
RIGHT SIDE.
2 Chapple Charles,grocer
4 Stevens Charles
6 Knapton Harry
8 Lee William
10 Balaam William
12 Bloom George James
14 Quinton George
16 Saltford Geo., laundry
18 Banks William L.
18 Banks Mrs. William L., laundress
20 Shuttlewood John
22 Ridgley Mrs. Elizabeth
24 Pook W., gardener
32 Perry Charles Henry
34 Webb Stephen
36 Smith Edward
38 Massey Edward James
40 Mayo John
42 Smith Mrs.
44 Laurence H. William
46 Wood John
48 Daniels Miss, school
50 Turner Allen
52 Turner George
54 Williamson Arthur
56 Aris Chas., bootmaker
58 Sutton Charles
60 Wood John
62 Whitmore Samuel
64 Salloway George
66 Young William
68 Hancock Edwin Fredk.
70 Goss Mrs. Mary Ann
72 Irish Frank
74 Singleton Francis
76 Creswick Henry,verger of St. Mary's Brookfield

Springfield Cottages,
see North hill.

Sundial Row,
see Highgate hill.

Sutton Place,
see Highgate hill.

SWAIN'S LANE.
From Highgate rd. to South grove.
D 9
Oliver & Smith, cemetery masons
Holly Lodge Villas.
1 Baird Walter
2 Sherwood Henry (Pontefract villa)
3 Hume Alfred
4 Stratford Mrs.
⌐*Holly village*
⌐*Chester rd.*
Swain's Lane.
The London Cemetery ; F. W. Ta Bois, superintendent
12 Richardson Thomas
11 Saunders John
10 Thoroughgood William
9 Mead Benjamin
8 Audsley Mrs.
7 Richardson Joseph
6 Baker Charles
5 Philbey Thomas
4 Wallis Thomas
3 Saunders Thos.,gardnr.
2 Long George
1 Bush Samuel,carpentr.
Dunkley Thos., cemetery mason
Phippen E.,gardener & florist (Rose nursery)
Daniels Henry & Co., monumental masons
Hanchet & Co., cemetery masons

Temperance Cotts.,
see Baker's lane.

The Bank,
see High st.

The Grove,
see Highgate rd.

THE GROVE.
From West hill to Hampstead lane.
C 8
1 Wilkins Mrs., ladies' college
2 Price H. S. P.
3 Smith Hy. R. Cooper
4 Pike Mrs. Warburton

THE GROVE—*continued*
5 Fry Right Hon. Sir Edward
6 Scrimgeour Walter
7 Lodge Robert J.
8 Lodge T. B.
9 Reynolds Walter
━*Fitzroy park*
10 Morton Mrs.
11 Ellis Edward
12 Dyne John Bradley
    Gallatly Mrs., ladies' school
    Morris Rev. R. Leslie, M.A. (Fitzroy lodge)

Townshend Yard,
see High st.

TREMLETT GROVE.
From 100 Junction rd.
D 10
2 Lyon Robert H., professor of music (Tremlett lodge)
    South Mrs.
6 Beckett Mrs.
6 Poole G. S.
8 *Mrs. Giniver's Infants' Orphan Home ;* Miss Tiffin, matron
10 Woffendale J.
10 Gliddon Frederick
12 Sparrow John William
14 Horton Frederick
16 Brown Frederick
20 Morle Mrs.
22 Maddle John William
26 Wright Charles
40 Stokes Thomas Charles
41 Hale William E.
43 Vine G. F.
39 Would Mrs.
38 Williamson William
37 Fielding John
36 Snow Albert, accountnt.
35 Bond John
34 Nearly T.
33 Cox T. H. W.
32 Cornford William
31 Smith James Dunn
30 Mitchell Mrs.
29 Boss Henry
28 Searl William P.
27 Glover Frederick
25 Hill Arthur
23 Watt C. A.

21 Butler John
21 Gore Allan
19 Gawan Alfred, artist
17 Nicholls Frank
15 Rowe Wm., surg.-dntst.
13 Dorsey Martin
11 Blenkinsop Mrs.
9 MacEgan J.
7 Chappell Wm. Thomas
5 Winter Henry T.
3 Morgan Mrs.
1 Tubby James William

TWISDEN ROAD.
From Carrol rd. to Spencer rd.
E 9
RIGHT SIDE.
2 Hall Mrs. Sarah
4 Drayson Walter
6 Maistre Paul, professor of French
8 Roberts Benjamin Jas.
10 Scattergood Edward Walter
12 Kershaw Robert
14 White Charles
16 Mitchell Sugden
18 Turton William
20 Burr George
22 Brown G. R.
24 Halder Elijah James
26 Diplock Frank
28 Quarry P.
30 Seed John
32 Crockett Joseph
34 Pelerin Henry
36 Frauer Frederick
38 Hawksworth William
40 Neil James
42 Hucklesby G.
44 Jukes William
46 Woolston C.
48 Frost William Thomas
50 Sirr Harry
52 Humber Walter
54 Roberts John
56 Witherden W.
58 Cooper Miss, dressmkr.
60 Cates Alfred Tennison
62 Schnauber John
64 Rowley Alfred
66 Middleton Mrs.
68 Lee Thomas
70 Pinnock Charles
72 Bateman John
74 Lawrence Joseph

LEFT SIDE.
1 Clayton A.
5 Morgan H.
7 Flood Edward
9 Dace Gustavus Orlando, professor of music
11 Curry Thomas
13 Langford Alfred
15 Britton N.
17 Bush James
17 Bush Miss, dressmaker
21 White Nicholas
23 Earle Henry
25 Callard Samuel
27 Pinkstone Thos. Wm.
29 Sears S.
31 Wilson Frank
33 Feast Robert Allen
35 Gwinnett J.
37 Pearson Thomas
39 Tapster Henry
41 Greig Thomas
43 Dodsworth J.
45 Garrod John
47 Way John
49 Aulsebrook Henry
51 Cooper Miss C.

Upper Whittington Place,
see Highgate hill.

Victoria Cottages,
see Archway rd. & South grove.

Vine Cottages,
see College lane.

VORLEY ROAD.
From Junction rd.
D 10
LEFT SIDE.
1 Huggins Samuel
3 Hooper George
5 Barber Edgar
7 Pryke Alfred
9 Mead Charles
11 Cresswell William
13 Child James, carpenter
15 Halifax Mrs.
17 Simpson John
19 Austin John
21 Hardy Mrs. S.
23 Kendrick James, house decorator

27 Woodward Henry, gas & hot water engineer
43 Jackson William
45 Woodrow Thomas
47 Farrow Frank

⌐*Brunswick rd.*

49 *Sydney House Laundry*
51 *Mission Room*
53 Stephens G., chimney cleaner and carpet beater
55 Day George
59 Scutchings John
61 Buckingham George
63 Climpson Mrs.
65 Smith Thomas
67 Eldridge James
69 Lester H.

RIGHT SIDE.

2 Wood Henry
4 Harrison John
6 Harris John
8 Ellis William
10 Burgess Mrs.
12 Hinton Mrs.
14 James James
16 Laurence John
18 Laing Henry J., carpenter
20 Jenkins W., bricklayer
22 Thomas Henry
24 Evans Charles
24a Kindell James, bootmaker
28 Hamblin W. H.
38 Warry William K.
40 Steeper John
42 Upton Mrs.
44 Goodman James
44a Fairall James

⌐*Brunswick rd.*

46 Daines David, greengrocer
48 Clark Robert
52 Millard George
54 Clark Thomas

Wards Cottages,
see North hill.

Wellington Cottages and Terrace,
see North hill.

Wells Hill,
see Southwood lane.

Wembury Road.
B 9
From Archway rd. to Langdon park rd.

WESLEYAN PLACE.
From 141 Highgate rd.
E 9
1a Ellis James
1 Anscomb Francis
2 Lloyd Edward M., silversmith
3 Thomas Henley
4 Simpson William
5 Carr Robert William
6 Platt Mrs. Matilda (St. John's cottage)

⌐*Mortimer ter.*

WEST HILL.
From Millfield lane to South grove.
C 8
LEFT SIDE.
Hermitage Villas.
12 Tims Mrs.
9 Brain John
8 Mackay David
7 Bodkin Miss
6 Hooman James
5 Oyler David Jonathan
3 Garman Miss, preparatory school
1 Allen Charles Harris
West Hill.
Beddall Herbert (Park villa)
Gardner Mrs. (Merton cottage)
Hurst Mrs. (Mortimer cottage)
Frost John Norris (Mornington villa)
Lee John Thos. (Glenmoor lodge)
Tatham John
Goslett Alfred, J.P.
Bodkin W. P. (West hill pl.)

⌐*Merton lane*

Atkinson Mrs. (Highgate lodge)
Williamson Thomas (West hill lodge)
Lawson W.H.S.(Cintra cottage)

Bailey William (Sutton house)
The Fox & Crown, Mrs. Emma West
Block A. W. (Parkfield)
Grove Cottages.
Atkinson G. T. (Grove cottage)
2 Woodnatt William
West Hill.
Fayrer Rev. Robt.,M.A. (Grove bank)
⌐*The Grove*
RIGHT SIDE.
Burdett-Coutts Baroness (Holly lodge)
Burdett-Coutts W. L. Ashmead - Bartlett (Holly lodge)
Holly Terrace.
1 Mummery Jno.Howard
2 Knight Miss
3 Chapman Chas. Edwd.
4 King Charles Thomas
5 Locker Arthur
6 Bishop Frank
9 Baker John
10 Oldfield David
West Hill.
Curtis Robert L.(Holmwood)
Stansbury Wm. Price (Hollyside)
Cutbush Wm. & Son, nurserymen

White's Cottages,
see North hill.

Whittington Place and Terrace,
see Highgate hill.

WILLOW WALK.
From 18 Highgate rd.
E 9
LEFT SIDE.
1 Baker Henry
3 Pratt Arthur
Metropolitan Fire Brigade Station
5 New Mrs. Mordicia, coal dealer
7 Alford Andrew, baker
RIGHT SIDE.
2 Neal James
4 Goodwin H.

WILLOW WALK—*contind*
6 Simmons John
8 Morrell William

WINCHESTER PL.
From Cromwell avenue.
C 9
2 King Charles (The Hollies)
4 Collins James (Saxonhurst)
6 Matthews R. E. J. (The Hoffe)
8 Larcher G. F.
10 Helliar Mrs. Elizabeth
14 Head J.

WINCHESTER RD.
From Archway rd. to Cromwell avenue.
C 9
LEFT SIDE.
—*Tile Kiln lane*
3 Sell Clarke (Stirling)
5 Drew Edwin John (Arundel)
7 Goodwin Nathaniel (Inchkeith)
9 Treacy Martin (Cuthberts)
11 Catchpole Edward (Stoneleigh)

WINSCOMBE ST.
From Chester rd.
D 9
RIGHT SIDE.
1 Day Samuel
3 Davis Caleb, gardener
3 Davis Mrs. S. A., professional cook
5 Clangan James
7 Burgess Albert Alfred
9 Emerton Henry
11 Rand Mrs. Emma
13 Rintoul Robert
15 Martin Robt.,contractr.
LEFT SIDE.
2 Ketley Thomas, greengrocer
4 Davis William
6 Carter James Henry
8 Bertin Benjamin
10 Seed William
12 Williams Alfred
14 Wring Benjamin
16 Rice Isaac
18 James Joseph
20 Edgington Hy., crpntr.

WOOD LANE.
From Muswell hill rd.
B 9
RIGHT SIDE.
2 Pachett John,signlmn.
4 Brand Richard John
10 Skelhorn William
12 Burry Edmund Bezant (Warwick house)
18 Hutton Robt.,gardener
18 Hutton Mrs., laundress
28 Logan Mrs. Martha (Ye Hutte)
30 Smith Mrs. Toulmin, senior
32 Craig Wm. D.,engineer
34 Frank John Henry
44 Dix James (Hurstdale)
46 Ryland Joseph Edgar (Holton lodge)
48 Nutt George James (Walden lodge)
LEFT SIDE.
1 Miles Alfred
5 Dixon John, M.B., C.M. (Calverley lodge)
7 Foley J. B. (Wheatly villa)
9 Girdlestone Henry
11 Paul Mrs. Mary
13 Edis Mrs.
15 James John
17 Potter William
19 Wirths Rudolf
21 Robson Mrs. Naomi
23 McCombie Wm.Downie
25 Scott John, gardener
27 MacGregor Mrs.Martha (Glengyle)
29 Murphy Joseph(Mountfields)

WOODSOME ROAD.
From Highgate rd. to York rise.
D 9
RIGHT SIDE.
1 Courtice James Leyster
3 Dreyfus Arthur
5 Brown Jsph. Harrison
7 Cooper Thomas Walker
9 Hepburn Alexander
11 Longson Luke
13 Chapman Mrs. Ann
15 Macfarlane Jas. Laird
17 Dalliston Miss

19 Jenkin Charles Brown
21 Davis Alexander James
23 Beaumont Wm. George
—*Grove rd.*
25 Hughes James Benjn.
27 Bayley William
29 Clutton William
31 Hulland Thomas
33 Shury William
35 Bowcher John
37 Jones Joseph
39 Morrell John Turner
41 Miles L. C.
43 Anderson Robert
45 Burns George Herbert
47 Taylor Twyford
53 Farley Henry
55 Lidwell Henry Joseph
57 Allaway Robert
LEFT SIDE.
2 Taylor George
4 Hogben Miss
6 Tite Joseph
8 Sumner John
10 Butterfield James
14 Jennings Mrs. E.
14 Praill Samuel
16 Painter William
18 Pittman G. J. W.
20 Dixon Thomas
22 Rippon William
24 Fletcher William Wolfe
26 Keedle William
30 Strevens George (Laura villa)
—*Grove rd.*
34 Cronk Thomas
36 Shoosmith John
38 Silveyra Eugene
40 Andrews W.
42 Harrison George
44 Logan Richard
46 Bates John Samuel
48 Greaves William
50 Sparks Herbert
52 Binch Mrs.
56 Tucker Thomas Frost
60 Milner Robert
62 Raynes Alfred Ernest
66 Hughes George Henry
68 Darnton Charles, professor of music
70 Birkenfeld G.
72 Mitchell Henry
74 Berwick Mrs. James
76 Turner Thomas
78 Baxter Henry

WYNDHAM CRES.
From 150 Junction rd.
D 9
1 Miall Leonard Henry
2 Conder Mrs.
3 Birks H.
4 Cussans John Edwin
5 Baker Thomas
6 Nunn Philip (St. Leonards)

YORK RISE,
From Dartmouth park rd.
E 9
RIGHT SIDE.
1 Skinner John A.,baker

The Dartmouth Arms,
Robert William Dyer
Dove Wm. Lambert
(Dartmouth park nursery)
11 Butler Mrs. Emma,
general draper
⸺*Carrol rd.*
13 Jones Miss Elizabeth
14 Ebbens James
16 Routledge Augustus
17 Zegers Peter John,
builder and decorator
LEFT SIDE.
6 Oatley Mrs., laundress
6 Oatley Alfred

2 DettmerJames,general
shop
10 Kitson Richard, ironmonger
FoxfordWilliam,greengrocer
Scotchman Saml., bldr.
1aClark Benjamin, cowkeeper
⸺*Chetwynd rd.*
1aTaylor Miss A.,laundry
40 North Richard

York Villas,
see Hargrave park rd.

FOREIGN MONIES, AND THEIR EQUIVALENTS IN ENGLISH.

FRANCE, BELGIUM, ITALY, AND SWITZERLAND.

	s.	d.
1 Franc (in Italy *Lira*) = abt.	0	9½
5-Fc. piece („ 5 Lire) = abt.	4	0
20-Fc. „ („ 20 „) = abt.	16	0
10 Cntms. („ 10 Cntsimi.) = abt.	1d.	
100 „ = 1 Fc.; 100 „ = 1 Lira.		

HOLLAND.

	s.	d.
5 Cents = abt.	0	1
100 „ = 1 Florin or Guilder = abt.	1	8
1 Gold 10-Florin piece = abt.	16	8

UNITED STATES OF AMERICA.

	s.	d.
1 Cent = abt.	0	0½
100 „ = 1 Dollar = abt.	4	1½
5 Dlrs. = 1 Half-Eagle = abt.	20	6½
Eagle of 10 Dollars = abt.	41	1¼

SPAIN AND PORTUGAL.

	s.	d.
8 Cuartos = 1 Real = 25 Centimes of a Peseta = -	0	2½
8 Reals = 1 Peseta = abt.	0	10
10 „ = 2½ Pesetas = 1 Escudo = abt.	2	0
20 „ = 5 Pesetas = 1 Duro = abt.	4	2
40 „ = 4 Escudos = 10 Pesetas = abt.	8	4
100 „ = 10 Escudos = 25 Pesetas = 1 Alphonso = abt.	20	9

GERMANY.

	s.	d.
10 Pfenninge = abt.	0	1¼
50 „ = abt.	0	6
100 „ = 1 Mark = abt.	1	0
10 Marks = abt.	9	9½
20 „ = abt.	19	7

RUSSIA.

	s.	d.
100 Kopecs = 1 Silver Rouble at par, abt.	3	1
3 Roubles = 1 Ducat = abt.	9	3
1 Gold Half-Imperial = abt.	16	4

AUSTRIA.

	s.	d.
5 Kreutzers = abt.	0	1
100 „ = 1 Florin (Paper) = abt.	1	8¼
10 Florins (Paper) = abt.	16	10
8 „ (Gold) = 20 Francs = abt.	16	0

DENMARK, SWEDEN, AND NORWAY.

COPPER.	s.	d.	SILVER.	s.	d.
1 Ore =	0	0⅛	10 Ore =	0	1¼
5 „ =	0	0⅝	25 „ =	0	3⅛
10 „ =	0	1¼	50 „ =	0	6¾

GOLD.			s.	d.
5 Kronor		=	5	6¾
10 „		=	11	1½
20 „		=	22	3½

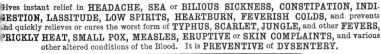

THE

HIGHGATE DIRECTORY.

———o———

ALPHABETICAL LIST

OF

PRIVATE INHABITANTS.

NOTE.—*The Postal District for Highgate is N.*

Further information respecting the situation of Streets may be obtained on reference to the Streets Directory: for instance, anyone requiring the address of Arthur Abercrombie, refers to the Alphabetical List of Private Inhabitants, and finds his address given 40 Dartmouth park rd.; by turning to Dartmouth park rd. in the Streets Directory, page 198, it is found described as Dartmouth park rd., from Highgate rd. to York rise, **D 9**

D 9 *signifies the position of Dartmouth park rd. on the Map.*

Abbott John 20 Annesley rd.
Abbott William J. A. 2 Burghley rd.
Abby Andrew 81 North rd.
Abercrombie Arthur 40 Dartmouth pk. rd.
Abrahams J., Woodland pl. North hill
Ackland Rev. C. T.(The Vicarage)Highgate rise
Adams Fredk. 2 Park ter. Hampstead ln.
Adams George (Grosvenor house) 148 Junction rd.
Agar T. J. 1 Holly village
Alexander Alfred Fredk. 27 Raydon st.
Allaway Robert 57 Woodsome rd.
Allcock Samuel 2 Judd cottages
Allen Charles 44 Langdon rd.
Allen Chas. (Woodside cottage) North hill
Allen Charles Harris 1 Hermitage villas West hill
Allen John 23 Bickerton rd.
Allen Matthew 9 Castle yard
Allen William 30 Dartmouth park hill
Allington Samuel 27 Orchard rd.
Ambler Matthew 10 Lady Somerset rd.
Ambler Edwd.(Harberton)Hornsey lane
Ambler Miss (Harberton) Hornsey lane

Ambrose Edwin 26 Highgate rd.
Amery G. W. 9 Dartmouth park rd.
Amsden Sidney 41 Cromwell avenue
Anceaux Mrs. Mary 1 Mercer ter.
Anderson John 6 Salisbury rd.
Anderson Robert 43 Woodsome rd.
Anderson Wm. Thomas 19 Spencer rd.
Andrews Alex. Harding 11 Churchill rd.
Andrews John R. 29 Lady Somerset rd.
Andrews Joseph 1 Kent's cottages
Andrews Joseph, sen. 5 Kent's cottages
Andrews Mrs. 70 Lady Somerset rd.
Andrews Robert 17 Spencer rd.
Andrews W. 40 Woodsome rd.
Anscomb Francis 1 Wesleyan pl.
Appleton George 52 Bickerton rd.
Archer George 25 Archway rd.
Aris Henry 1 Salisbury rd.
Arlett William Henry 72 Highgate rd.
Armitage John S. 1 Colva st. Dartmouth park hill
Arnold George 6 St. Alban's villas
Arnold Mrs. 3 Crown cottages
Arthur Miss (Bank villa) 6 Alpha villas
Ash C. J. 17 Northwood rd.

Ashdown George 15 Bickerton rd.
Ashwell Mrs. 42 Lady Somerset rd.
Askew George (Rose bank) North hill
Askey F. D. (Beech villa) Bishop's rd.
Atchley H. M. 24 Churchill rd.
Atchley William H. (Carlton cottage) 32 Bickerton rd.
Atchley W. W. (Worcester) 55 Cromwell avenue
Atkins Henry 56 Hargrave park rd.
Atkins Hy. (Woodland place) North hill
Atkins Mrs. 34 Highgate rd.
Atkins Mrs. 8 Southwood ter.
Atkinson G. T. (Grove cott.) West hill
Atkinson Mrs.(Highgate lodge) West hill
Attkins Miss H. L. 3 North rd.
Attkins Mrs. (The Hermitage) 26 North road
Audsley Mrs. 8 Swain's lane
Aulburn George 189 Junction rd.
Auld Alston (Hope cottage) 41 Girdlestone rd.
Aulsebrook Henry 49 Twisden rd.
Austin John 19 Vorley rd.
Austin Joseph (Moreton ho.) South gro.
Avery Richard 67 Langdon rd.
Axford Mrs. Catherine 20 Orchard rd.
Ayres Mrs., North hill

Backshall Mrs. 31 Brunswick rd.
Backshell Mrs. 19 Burghley rd.
Bacon John 2 Cathcart hill
Bacon Walter Geo.102 Dartmouth pk.hill
Bacon William 13 Carrol rd.
Badcock Henry James (Woodville cottage) North hill
Badrow Edward 3 Cathcart hill
Bailey H. 11 Burghley rd.
Bailey Henry 9 Burghley rd.
Bailey Henry 5 Cathcart hill
Bailey Mrs. 6 North pl. North hill
Bailey Richard 16 Chetwynd rd.
Bailey Thomas 55 Carrol rd.
Bailey William (Sutton house) West hill
Baird Wltr.1 Holly lodge vils.Swain's lane
Baker Charles 29 Highgate rd.
Baker Charles 6 Swain's lane
Baker Edward 170 Junction rd.
Baker Henry 1 Willow walk
Baker Henry West 11 Highgate rd.
Baker John 9 Holly ter.
Baker John 7 Little Green st.
Baker Matthew 2 Kent's cottages
Baker Mrs. 29 Bickerton rd.
Baker Mrs. 2 Pond sq.
Baker Thomas 5 Wyndham cres.
Baker Wm. (Park cottage) North hill

Baker William Edwin, Southwood lane
Balaam William 10 Spencer rd.
Baldwin George 2 Castle yard
Baldwin Richard 96 Fortess rd.
Balfour Mrs. E. 30 Langdon park rd.
Ball Francis W.(Ivy lo.)138 Junction rd.
Ball Frederick 84 Fortess rd.
Ball Geo.(The Elms)Dartmouth pk. avn.
Ball John 6 Vine cottages College lane
Baly James Alfred (Overdale house) 15 Oakford rd.
Bandy William 19 Holmesdale rd.
Bankart Howard 41 Bickerton rd.
Banks E. G. 108 Fortess rd.
Banks William L. 18 Spencer rd.
Barber Alfred 1 Albert villas Archway rd.
Barber Edgar 5 Vorley rd.
Barber John 3 Grove pl.
Barber Miss 129 Junction rd.
Barker George Henry 17 Annesley rd.
Barnaby H. (Ivy cot.) Southwood lane
Barnard Rev. John Heskins 6 North hill ter. North hill
Barnard William 30 Dartmouth park rd.
Barnes Alfred 30 Holmesdale rd.
Barnes Edwin Chas. 35 Cromwell avenue
Barnes H. (Patschull ho.) Lewisham rd.
Barnes Theodore 24 Dartmouth park rd.
Barnet-Smith George (Cuba villa) 20 Bickerton rd.
Barnett Alfred 59 Spencer rd.
Barnett George 16 Girdlestone rd.
Barratt George 1 Girdlestone rd.
Barrett Mrs. 8 Carrol rd.
Barrett Paul 175 Dartmouth park hill
Barrs Henry Hollier Hood(Aller cottage) Highgate rise
Bartholomew Mrs. (Cholmeley house) Southwood lane
Bartlett Rev. George D., M.A. (Solsgirth house) South grove
Bartlett F. H. 53 Dartmouth park hill
Bartley R. B. 7 Carrol rd.
Barton Benjamin (Grosvenor lodge) 132 Junction rd.
Bass Thomas Henry, North rd. cottages
Bateman John 72 Twisden rd.
Bates James 1a Brunswick rd.
Bates John Samuel 46 Woodsome rd.
Batho William Smith 102 Junction rd.
Batson Charles 41 Holmesdale rd.
Batty John Higgs 88 Dartmouth pk. hill
Bawden Mrs. 26 Brunswick rd.
Baxter Henry 78 Woodsome rd.
Baxter Mrs. S. J. 42 Junction rd.
Baxter Thomas 7 South grove cottages
Bayley William 27 Woodsome rd.

Baylis Charles 135 Junction rd.
Bayne Charles 18 Grove ter.
Bayne Henry 1 Dartmouth park avenue
Beadle Arthur 62 Fortess rd.
Beall Thomas 13 Victoria cottages
Beard G. 14 Churchill rd.
Beauchamp John (Newtownards) Cholmeley park
Beaumont Benjamin 1 South grove cotts.
Beaumont Henry (Gordon villa) Bishop's road
Beaumont Lewis (Hillside) 49 Cromwell avenue
Beaumont William G. 23 Woodsome rd.
Beckett Mrs. 6 Tremlett grove
Beckett Mrs. Amelia 4 Victoria cottages
Beckwith Arthur (Chamley villa) Dartmouth park avenue
Beddall Herbert (Park villa) West hill
Bedford C. 43 Spencer rd.
Bedmead Frederick 21 Magdala rd.
Beeby James 1 Meadow cottages
Begbie James Hamilton 57 Burghley rd.
Bell Matthew (Hillside) Dartmouth park avenue
Bell William (North lodge) North hill
Bellord Edmund Joseph (Edburga house) The Bank
Bellord James, sen. (Edburga house) The Bank
Benham Mrs. 2 Annesley rd.
Bennett Alfred 58 Brunswick rd.
Bennett George (Folingsby) 51 Cromwell avenue
Bennett George 14 Girdlestone rd.
Bennett James Robert Sterndale 11 North rd.
Bennett Mrs. J. 18 Churchill rd.
Bennett Thomas 37 Fortess rd.
Bennett Thomas John Wesley (Romanhurst) 1 Cholmeley villas Archway rd.
Bent Robert 9 Hargrave park rd.
Berger Frank 54 Bickerton rd.
Bertin Benjamin 8 Winscombe st.
Berwick Mrs. James 74 Woodsome rd.
Best Ebenezer 173 Dartmouth park hill
Beves Jonas Edward 5 Grove ter. Highgate rd.
Beviss Mrs. 118 Archway rd.
Biggers John Robert 31 Grove rd.
Biggin Edward Henry (Beechville villa) 8 Bickerton rd.
Bilby Edward 45 Raydon st.
Billings James 7 Holmesdale rd.
Billington John 34 Burghley rd.
Binch Mrs. 52 Woodsome rd.
Binney Mrs., Hampstead lane

Birch Walter de Gray, F.R.S. 6 Dartmouth park avenue
Bird J. 33 Oakford rd.
Bird Jabez 26 Annesley rd.
Bird Mrs. 11 Hargrave park rd.
Birdseye Thomas 10 Bickerton rd.
Birkenfeld G. 70 Woodsome rd.
Birks H. 3 Wyndham cres.
Birks Harry William (Enderleigh) Broadlands rd. North hill
Bisborne Henry 7 Lady Somerset rd.
Bishop Frank 6 Holly ter.
Bishop John N., F.Z.S. 9 North rd.
Bishop W. 9 Holmesdale rd.
Black George, B.A. 21 Burghley rd.
Blackall John 14 Langdon rd.
Blackmore Miss Marian 3 Holmesdale d
Blair Mrs. 59 Dartmouth park hill
Blake Alfred 7 Annesley rd.
Blanford Thomas (Field house) Bishop wood rd.
Blank Frederick W. 3 Chester rd.
Blenkinsop Mrs. 11 Tremlett grove
Block Allen W. (Parkfield) West hill
Blondell Robert 161 Dartmouth park hill
Bloom George James 12 Spencer rd.
Blowers Charles 5 Prospect ter.
Bloxam Miss, South grove
Blunt Walter 176 Junction rd.
Boam Mitchell 106 Fortess rd.
Boardman John 58 Highgate rd.
Boby Robert 35 Dartmouth park hill
Boby William 10 Dartmouth park rd.
Boden Anthony 31 Spencer rd.
Bodgener William 10 Gordon house rd.
Bodkin Miss 7 Hermitage villas West hill
Bodkin Wm. P. (West hill pl.) West hill
Body A. S. 24 Poynings rd.
Boff Frank 17 Magdala rd.
Bond John 35 Tremlett grove
Booker Mrs. 4 Grove ter.
Booth James Wilson (Redland villa) Dartmouth park avenue
Booty Miss Emily 26 Orchard rd.
Borkett Frederick 64 Lady Somerset rd.
Bosito Madame 23 Cromwell avenue
Boss Henry 29 Tremlett grove
Bostock James 58 Langdon rd.
Boswell F. 79 North rd.
Botham Mrs. C. E. 69 Langdon rd.
Boughay David Jno. (North cot.) North hl.
Boullangier C. 49 Burghley rd.
Bourlet Chas. (The Hollies) 17 Orchard rd.
Bourlet James (Homedale villa) Holmesdale rd.
Bovill Alfred 30 Grove ter.
Bowcher John 35 Woodsome rd.

I

Bowels William 12 Chetwynd rd.
Bowler Thomas (Millfield lodge) Millfield lane
Boyden John 9 Doynton st.
Bowyer George 14 Ingestre rd.
Box William Braund 1 Caen ter. Hampstead lane
Boxall John 74 Lady Somerset rd.
Boxhall Hy. (Fairfield ho.) Magdala rd.
Boxsins P. F. B. 22 Burghley rd.
Boxsius Jas. Jsph. 26 Dartmouth park rd.
Brabant Geo. Whitmore 26 Burghley rd.
Bradbury John 13 Gordon house rd.
Bradish Michael 19 Doynton st.
Bradley Henry 21 Churchill rd.
Bradshaw Benjamin 10 Townshend yard
Brain John 9 Hermitage villas
Brakel Theodor 10 Carrol rd.
Brampton Charles Hy. 8 Woodview ter.
Brand Richard John 4 Wood lane
Bray Charles 39 Dartmouth park rd.
Brede Alfred Robert 74 Junction rd.
Brees Mrs. A. 42 Holmesdale rd.
Bretnall Wm.Hy. 13 Dartmouth park hill
Brett John William (Vine cottage) 65 Spencer rd.
Brewer W. 92 Cromwell avenue
Brice Charles 47 Lady Somerset rd.
Bridges Isaac (Ivy cott.)11 Chetwynd rd.
Bridgman S. 44 Carrol rd.
Brighouse George 98 Fortess rd.
Brilliant Joseph 81 Fortess rd.
Britton Mrs. 15 Twisden rd.
Brocklesby Wm. 40 Hargrave park rd.
Broden William 70 Hargrave park rd.
Bromley F., L.D.C., R.C.S. EDIN. 29 Fortess rd.
Bromley F. S. 25 Poynings rd.
Brooks Mrs. (St. John's villa) 12 Burghley rd.
Brooks Robert 28 Holmesdale rd.
Broomfield J. E. 36 Poynings rd.
Browett Henry Leonard,Southwood lane
Brown Frederick 16 Tremlett grove
Brown G. R. 22 Twisden rd.
Brown Joseph Harrison 5 Woodsome rd.
Brown Mrs. 28 Dartmouth park hill
Brown Mrs. (Whittington villa) 36 Salisbury rd.
Brown Mrs. Isaac 6 Lewisham rd.
Brown William 7a Burghley rd.
Brown William 69 Cromwell avenue
Brown William 16 Holmesdale rd.
Brown W. H. 28 Churchill rd.
Browne Charles 11 Carrol rd.
Browne Henry 185 Junction rd.
Browning Henry 94 Dartmouth park hill

Bruce Geo. Fredk. 36 Hargrave park rd.
Brühling W. 71 Fortess rd.
Bryan Frederick 29 Poynings rd.
Buchanan Hy. Bryan 12 St.Alban's villas
Buck Mrs. 193 Junction rd.
Buckerfield Thomas H. 2 Mortimer ter.
Buckey John 8 Crown cottages
Buckingham George 61 Vorley rd.
Buckland John 17 Victoria cottages Archway rd.
Buckland Mrs. 38 Dartmouth park hill
Bucknall Edward 78 Junction rd.
Buckthorpe James 16 Chester ter.
Bull Thomas W. 22 Salisbury rd.
Bullen George 63 North rd.
Bullimore John 24 Holmesdale rd.
Bullock Richard Steel 56 Bickerton rd.
Bulmer Walter 23 Orchard rd.
Bunce William Hy. 31 Langdon park rd.
Bunting Mrs. 8 Highgate rise
Bunyan Alfred James 4 Raydon st.
Bunyan Richard 2 Dorothy cottages Southwood lane
Burchett James R. 10 St. Alban's villas
Burdett-Coutts Baroness (Holly lodge) West hill
Burdett-Coutts W. L. Ashmead-Bartlett (Holly lodge) West hill
Burgess Albert Alfred 7 Winscombe st.
Burgess John 101 Burghley rd.
Burgess Mrs. 10 Vorley rd.
Burgon Miss 43 Chetwynd rd.
Burke George 39 Holmesdale rd.
Burke Thomas 18 Anatola rd.
Burleigh Walter 8 Magdala rd.
Burlison John (Grove end house) Highgate rd.
Burnie Alfred 12 Holly village
Burns George Herbert 45 Woodsome rd.
Burr George 20 Twisden rd.
Burrows W. E. 10 Southwood lane
Burry Edmund Bezant (Warwick house) 12 Wood lane
Burt Charles M. 8 Hargrave park rd.
Burt Henry (Gwynfa) Hornsey lane
Burt Miss 32 Hargrave park rd.
Burton Eli (Alma cot.) Southwood lane
Burton John Wm. 46 Cromwell avenue
Burton William 32 Junction rd.
Burtt Henry Miller 40 Holmesdale rd.
Bush James 17 Twisden rd.
Bush Richard 31a Salisbury rd.
Butler John 21 Tremlett grove
Butler Mrs. E. 48 Chetwynd rd.
Butler Samuel Thorpe 3 Park ter.
Butt Arthur N., F.R. HIST. S. 41 Highgate rd.

Butt Mrs. 41 Highgate rd.
Butterfield James 10 Woodsome rd.
Butts G. 1 Cambridge cottages
Byecroft Frederick 5 North hill ter.

Callard Samuel 25 Twisden rd.
Callow Edward 5 St. Alban's villas
Callow George William 92 Fortess rd.
Calvert Frederick W. 73 North rd.
Campbell J. (Pensee villa) Magdala rd.
Campbell W. F. 29 Carrol rd.
Campbell W. F., M.D., M.R.C.S. 88 Junction rd.
Canham Mrs. 18 Magdala rd.
Cansick F. Teague, F.R.H.S. 17 Hargrave park rd.
Caralli G. N. 17 Dartmouth park hill
Carew Joseph 108 Dartmouth park hill
Carey Alexander 8 Bedford pl.
Carr John Dale (West lea) Dartmouth park avenue
Carr John L. (Somerset cottage) Dartmouth park avenue
Carr Miss(Earlham ho.) Bishop wood rd.
Carr Ralph(Clutha villa)16 Bickerton rd.
Carr Robert 3 The Bank High st.
Carr Robert William 5 Wesleyan pl.
Carritt Frederick Blasson (Bishopsfield) Broadlands rd. North hill
Carroll Charles 40 Bickerton rd.
Carstairs Andrew 19 Gordon house rd.
Carte Richard 2 Dartmouth park rd.
Carter Henry 2 Temperance cottages
Carter James H. 6 Winscombe st.
Carter John (Baveno) Broadlands rd.
Carter Samuel S. 21 Archway rd.
Cartwright Jas. Joel 15 Langdon pk. rd.
Casbold J. 30 Magdala rd.
Casella Louis Pasquale (The Lawns) South grove
Castle George 16 Grove ter.
Catchpole Edward (Stoneleigh) 11 Winchester rd.
Cates Alfred Tennison 60 Twisden rd.
Catley J. H. 8 Croftdown rd.
Catlin Charles 68 North rd.
Catling Charles (Inglethorpe) Broadlands rd. North hill
Cato Thomas R. 11 Langdon rd.
Cave George, A.A. (Gloucester house) 51 North rd.
Chalk George Thomas 29 Spencer rd.
Challis Mrs. (North hill ho.) North hill
Chalmers John Binny (The Elms) The Grove Highgate rd.
Chaplin Mrs. 32 Salisbury rd.
Chapman Alfred 33 Bickerton rd.

Chapman C. C. H. 1 Hornsey lane
Chapman Charles Edward 3 Holly ter.
Chapman Charles Waller 1 Hornsey lane
Chapman John 147 Dartmouth park hill
Chapman Mrs. Ann 13 Woodsome rd.
Chapman Mrs. Thornton 7 Southwood ln.
Chapman William 5 Alpha villas Archway rd.
Chappell William Thos. 7 Tremlett grove
Chard Charles 60 Cromwell avenue
Charles F. R. 65 Dartmouth park hill
Charles John 41 Dartmouth park rd.
Charles John 10 Hornsey lane
Charles Mrs. (Hillside) Southwood lane
Charlier A. 45 Oakford rd.
Charlier H. 1 Lady Somerset rd.
Charter George 21 Raydon st.
Chase W. 32 Oakford rd.
Chatto Andrew 81 Dartmouth park hill
Cheesman Frederick Inkersole 49 Dartmouth park hill
Cheffins Alfred 35 Archway rd.
Cherry James (Endsleigh) 40 Cromwell avenue
Child Henry (Hurstly) Bishop's rd.
Child Trayton P. 39 Bickerton rd.
Childs J. 71 North rd.
Childs James 50 Brunswick rd.
Chilman Edward 3 Langdon rd.
Chisholm Miss 2 Mercer ter.
Chisman John N. 20 Carrol rd.
Chisman Thomas 1 Wells hill Southwood lane
Christian Edward 7 Salisbury rd.
Christmas Thomas Joseph 8 Chetwynd rd.
Christon Fred 44 Northwood rd.
Church Chas. (Cotham) Hampstead lane
Church H. G. 7 Hampstead lane
Church William M. H. (St. Wilfrid's) Bishop's rd.
Clack John 16 Annesley rd.
Clangan James 5 Winscombe st.
Clare Charles Henry 41 Burghley rd.
Clare Mrs. 4 Cromwell avenue
Clark Charles 20 Burghley rd.
Clark James 45 Girdlestone rd.
Clark Robert 48 Vorley rd.
Clark Thomas 54 Vorley rd.
Clark William Philip 17 Burghley rd.
Clarke Arthur Leslie 23 Burghley rd.
Clarke Courtenay 28 Bickerton rd.
Clarke George 2 Woodview ter.
Clarke James 89 Langdon rd.
Clarke Joseph, F.R.G.S. (North hill villa) North hill
Clarke Robert G. 3 St. Alban's rd.
Claus Henry 3 Brunswick rd.

Clayton Captain J. Pegg 41 Langdon park rd.
Clayton A. 1 Twisden rd.
Clayton John 9 Hornsey lane
Clements Charles 9 Gordon house rd.
Climpson Mrs. 63 Vorley rd.
Clitheroe Mrs. 74 Dartmouth park hill
Cloran Michael 7 Gordon house rd.
Clothier Henry, M.D. 1 North rd.
Clues Mrs. 57 Lady Somerset rd.
Clues Mrs. E. 24 Burghley rd.
Clutton Miss 1 Langdon rd.
Clutton William 29 Woodsome rd.
Coates William C. 1 Prospect cottages
Coates William Henry 11 Archway rd.
Cobb C. A. 25 Oakford rd.
Cobb William 2 Vine cottages College lane
Cockburn Mrs. 2 Park pl. North hill
Cockerell James 14 Carrol rd.
Cockman Charles R., B.A. 29 Grove rd.
Cockram Henry 26 Lady Somerset rd.
Codling William S. 36 Junction rd.
Cohen M. L. 37 Cromwell avenue
Cole George 2 York villas
Coleman Mrs. 26 Dartmouth park hill
Coles Joseph 49 Chester rd.
Coles Joseph Thomas 6a Girdlestone rd.
Collier Edward 36 Cromwell avenue
Collier Henry 2 Mercer ter.
Collingridge William 5 Prospect cotts.
Collins Jas. (Saxonhurst) 4 Winchester pl.
Collins John, Broadbent yard
Collins John H. 25 Grove rd.
Collins Joseph Henry 64 Bickerton rd.
Collins William 3 Bedford pl.
Collinson Mrs., North hill
Collough William 4 Carrol rd.
Collyer Mrs. 14 Annesley rd.
Colson Arthur E. 4 Girdlestone rd.
Columbine B. F. 23 Archway rd.
Colwell Hector (Percy villa) Bishop's rd.
Comber Mrs. Charles 12 Lewisham rd.
Comyns William 4 Highgate rise
Concannon M. (Fern cot.) Annesley rd.
Concannon Michael 47 Girdlestone rd.
Conder Mrs. 2 Wyndham cres.
Connolly Rev. James, M.R. 41 Fortess rd.
Constable Mrs. 28 Cromwell avenue
Conway John C. 94 Fortess rd.
Cook E. 44 Girdlestone rd.
Cook Henry 28 Langdon rd.
Cook Miss, Jackson's lane
Cook Mrs. 14 Grove ter.
Cooke James 2 Cornwall villas
Cooke Mordecai C., M.A. 146 Junction rd.
Cooke-Smith Henry 22 Bickerton rd.
Coomber W. O. 45 Poynings rd.

Coombes John 6 Southwood ter.
Cooper Charles Henry 13 Oakford rd.
Cooper George 4 Highgate rd.
Cooper James Davis (Lynton house) Hampstead lane
Cooper Miss C. 51 Twisden rd.
Cooper Mrs. 90 Dartmouth park hill
Cooper Mrs. 15 Poynings rd.
Cooper Mrs. 11 Southwood ter.
Cooper Robert 10 Churchill rd.
Cooper Thomas W. 7 Woodsome rd.
Cooper William 29 Archway rd.
Cope Frederick 4 Chester rd.
Cope William 8 Ingestre rd.
Copin Madame J. 68 Cromwell avenue
Copp Henry 32 Carrol rd.
Copping Edward 18 Lady Somerset rd.
Copsey Charles Edward 59 Burghley rd.
Corbett John (Myrtle cott.) North hill
Corbett Mrs. 19 Langdon rd.
Cork Charles George, High st.
Cornford William 32 Tremlett grove
Cornish James 75 Dartmouth park hill
Cornwell Mrs. 187 Junction rd.
Corrick Mrs. 87 Dartmouth park hill
Couper Frederick 32 Croftdown rd.
Courteney Richard John 66 Junction rd.
Courtice James Leyster 1 Woodsome rd.
Courtier Mrs. 4 Churchill rd.
Couzens Mrs. 110 Dartmouth park hill
Coward John 19 Victoria cottages Archway rd.
Cowd Rev. J. C., M.A. (Kentish town vicarage) 16 Burghley rd.
Cowdry W. (Noemi cottage) North hill
Cowie Mrs. 13a Girdlestone rd.
Cowley Alexr., M.B. 62 Cromwell avenue
Cowlishaw George 3 Chetwynd rd.
Cox George John 6 Dartmouth park hill
Cox George William (Bletsoe cottage) 38 Bickerton rd.
Cox Henry 98 Dartmouth park hill
Cox Jas. Abraham 17 Dartmouth park rd.
Cox T. H. W. 33 Tremlett grove
Cox William 1 Chester rd.
Cox W. N. 73 Burleigh rd.
Coxall George (Cornwall house) Dartmouth park hill
Coxeter Jas. (Bathurst ho.) 4 The Grove
Coyne Joseph P. 32 Langdon rd.
Crabtree Robert 32 Holmesdale rd.
Craines Philip 24 Carrol rd.
Crane D. B. 4 Woodview ter.
Crane Horace Tarbox (Melrose villa) 12 Bickerton rd.
Crane William 2 Southwood lane
Crang Edmund 7 South grove

Crassweller Hy.V.27Dartmouth park rd.
Crawford Robert Dawson (Elgin house) 2 High st.
Cresswell Alfred John 27 Chetwynd rd.
Cresswell William 11 Vorley rd.
Crighton David 39 Raydon st.
Crockett John 66 Hargrave park rd.
Crockett Joseph 32 Twisden rd.
Crombet P. T. 14 Lady Somerset rd.
Cronk Thomas 34 Woodsome rd.
Crooke James 68 Hargrave park rd.
Cross Mrs. C. K. 5 Lady Somerset rd.
Crossley Mrs. (Copley Dene) Cholmeley park
Crowdy Fredk.Hamilton, M.B.,South gro.
Crowhurst W. 5 Oakford rd.
Cruickshank Mrs. E. 21 Hargrave pk. rd.
Cullen John 18 Gordon house rd.
Curlewis Harry 9a Girdlestone rd.
Currey Rev. R. A., M.A. (Whittington college) Archway rd.
Currie William 51 Spencer rd.
Curry Thomas 11 Twisden rd.
Curtis Alfred 10 Magdala rd.
Curtis Robert L. (Holmwood) West hill
Cussans John Edwin 4 Wyndham cres.
Cutbush H.J. 3 South grove
Cuthbert John (Coningsby house) 1 Victoria cottages Archway rd.

Daley Henry 20 Churchill rd.
Dalliston Miss 17 Woodsome rd.
Daniel A. B., M.R.C.V.S. 39 Fortess rd.
Daniel William 16 Mortimer ter.
Daniels Miss 48 Spencer rd.
D'ArcyJas.(Beaumont)43 Cromwell avn.
Darken Thomas 2 Crown cottages
Darnton Charles 68 Woodsome rd.
Davenport Misses (Silverhill) Bloomfield rd.
Davey Winslow Harry 25 Holmesdale rd.
Davidson E. G. 14 Anatola rd.
Davies Charles 10 Southwood ter.
DaviesFredk.(Pet's cot.)Southwood lane
Davies Thomas 18 Hargrave park rd.
DaviesWm.(Maldon ho)Southwood lane
Davies William 8 Salisbury rd.
Davies William James 12 Annesley rd.
Davis Alexander James 21 Woodsome rd.
Davis Alfred 12 Cathcart hill
Davis Mrs. 7 Bedford pl.
Davis Mrs. 22 Lady Somerset rd.
Davis Richard 8 Lewisham rd.
Davis Samuel 22 Archway pl.
Davis Walter David 5 Cromwell pl.
Davis Wm., Holly cottages Archway rd.
Davis William 4 Winscombe st.

Davy W. 15 Northwood rd.
Dawe Henry 34 Langdon rd.
Dawe Misses (Rose cott.) 61 Spencer rd.
Dawe Mrs. 44 Oakford rd.
Dawkins James T. 46 Hargrave park rd.
Dawson Chas.Jsph. 25 Hargrave park rd.
Dawson John 45 Archway rd.
Dawson John 3 Grove rd.
Day George 55 Vorley rd.
Day R. C. 50 Cromwell avenue
Day Samuel 1 Winscombe st.
Day Walter Henry 17 Raydon st.
Deacon Mrs. Agnes 47 Raydon st.
Dean Alfred 1 Southwood cottages
Dean David Wm. (South lo.) North hill
Deane Hugh 44 Fortess rd.
Dearle Miss 12 Lady Somerset rd.
De Beaumont A. R. 3 Hampstead lane
Dell Henry 78 Cromwell avenue
Delmar Miss 10 Croftdown rd.
Dench A. F. 6 Wellington ter. North hill
Denham Thomas 225 Junction rd.
Dennis G. R. 38 Poynings rd.
Dennis Henry A. 13 Langdon rd.
Dent Geo. (Rochelle cottage) North hill
Dent William 5 Langdon rd.
Dettmer Henry 92 Fortess rd.
Devenny William Foster (Talbot lodge) 27 Bickerton rd.
De Vos Desiderius(St. Aloysius) Hornsey lane
Dewberry James 2 Chester rd.
Dewbury Benjamin 22 Annesley rd.
Dick Henry Page 2 Poynings rd.
Dickeson William 42 Magdala rd.
Dickins John 2 Mansfield cottages
DickinsonA.E.C.(Grove ho.)South grove
Dickinson George 13 Spencer rd.
Dicks Henry, Southwood lane
DicksonThos.& Mrs. 22 Langdon pk. rd
DicksonThomasEdward9 Northwood rd
Dimsey David G. 4 Dartmouth park avn
Dinner John 10 Annesley rd.
Diplock Frank 26 Twisden rd.
Dix James (Hurstdale) 44 Wood lane
Dixon Allan, Archway rd.
Dixon Henry 13 Orchard rd.
Dixon John, M.B., C.M. (Calverley lodge) 5 Wood lane
Dixon John 4 Norman vils. Archway rd
Dixon Thomas 20 Woodsome rd.
Dixon Thomas Parker 13 Grove ter.
Dixon W. A. 11 Holly village
Dodd Frederick 3 York villas
Dodsworth J. 43 Twisden rd.
Doherty Charles 96 Cromwell avenue
Dore Morris B. 6 Lady Somerset rd.

Dorey Mrs. M. 4 Anatola rd.
Dorsey Martin 13 Tremlett grove
Douglas David 88a Highgate rd.
Down James 55 Lady Somerset rd.
Downing George 1 White's cottages
Dowsett John 6 South grove cottages
Drage William 18 Burghley rd.
Drake John 37 Burghley rd.
Drake Mrs. 1 Wellington ter. North hill
Drayson Walter 4 Twisden rd.
Dredge Robert 38 Cromwell avenue
Drew Edwin John (Arundel) Winchester rd.
Drew Samuel Summers 76 Cromwell avn.
Drewett Fredk. Wm. 48 Bickerton rd.
Dreyfus Arthur 3 Woodsome rd.
Drummond Mrs. 1 Burghley rd.
Dublack Mrs. Caroline 15 & 16 Magdala road
Dumayne Oliver 6 Anatola rd.
Dumenil Adolph (Park cottage) Magdala rd.
Duncan James Marriott 19 Cromwell avn.
Durrad W. R. 4 South grove
Durrant Henry 25 Fortess rd.
Dutton Mrs., South grove
Duval S. S.(Chesterfield lo.) South grove
Dyble Robert 6 Southwood lane
Dyer Charles 36 Fortess rd.
Dyer James Andrew 32 Burghley rd.
Dyer Richard 43 Carrol rd.
Dyke Richard J. 49 Highgate rd.
Dyne John Bradley 12 The Grove

Eadie Miss 33 Archway rd.
Eagle John George 12 Holmesdale rd.
Eagles Mrs. 24 North rd.
Ealand Richard Francis 27 Poynings rd.
Earl Thomas 39 Highgate rd.
Earle Henry 23 Twisden rd.
Earnshaw Miss 51 Highgate rd.
Earnshaw Mrs. E. 29 Grove ter.
Eason Alexander 14 Cromwell avenue
Eason Henry J. 18 Victoria cottages
Easterling Arthur William 35 Archway rd.
Easton Mrs. 5 Grove rd.
Eastwick James (Coombe house) Hampstead lane
Eastwood Mrs. 21 Poynings rd.
Easy Mrs. 76 Lady Somerset rd.
Eaton E. J. Applebee 27 Langdon pk. rd.
Eaves Wm. (Bolobo) Shepherd's hill rd.
Ebbens James 14 York rise
Edan Alfred 64 Langdon park rd.
Edbrook G. 12 Mortimer ter.
Eddington George 1 St. Alban's villas
Edgar Mrs. Jane 92 Dartmouth park hill

Edington George Thomas (Rosetta villa) 36 Bickerton rd.
Edis Mrs. 13 Wood lane
Edmonds James 1 Blandford pl.
Edmondson Christopher 2 Prospect ter.
Edmunds John (Thornbury) Hornsey ln.
Edsar F. 20 Poynings rd.
Edward G. S.(West bank) Broadlands rd.
Edwards Andrew 8 Pond sq.
Edwards A. E. 9 Anatola rd.
Edwards George 71 Dartmouth park hill
Edwards James 123 Dartmouth park hill
Edwards Miss 19 Churchill rd.
Edwards Mrs. 22 Hargrave park rd.
Edwards Mrs. J. 1 Churchill rd.
Edwards Robert 42 Chetwynd rd.
Eggins William 12 Chester ter.
Ekin Saml. P.(Eben villa) 6 Bickerton rd.
Elbourn William 42 Salisbury rd.
Eldred Mrs. Mary 27 Cromwell avenue
Eldridge James 67 Vorley rd.
Eldridge Richard 2 Bedford cottages
Elgar Mrs. 14 Chetwynd rd.
Elgar S. 18 Oakford rd.
Elliot Robert 10 Holly village
Elliott G. B. 33 Fortess rd.
Elliott John 18 Annesley rd.
Ellis Arthur 42 High st.
Ellis Edward 11 The Grove
Ellis James 1a Wesleyan pl.
Ellis Wm. (Brooklands) Bishop wood rd.
Ellis William 8 Vorley rd.
Ells George 16 Prospect cottages
Ellsmoor Brian 15 Mortimer ter.
Elvins Harry 41 Langdon rd.
Elwin Edward 17 Langdon rd.
Emerson Robert 1 Archway villas
Emerton Henry 9 Winscombe st.
Emmett John T. 42 Dartmouth park hill
Engall Thomas, M.D. 27 Lady Somerset rd.
Engels Lawrence 42 Northwood rd.
Engert Adam Cyrus (The Perseverance) 72 Dartmouth park hill
Esling George Henry 22 Langdon rd.
Essex C. 6 Holly village
Essex Mrs. Fanny 22 Croftdown rd.
Evans Charles 2 North grove
Evans Charles 24 Vorley rd.
Evans Edwd. 3 Chester villas Chester rd.
Evans Mrs. Robert L. (Mansfield villa) Hampstead lane
Evans William 163 Junction rd.
Evard Victor 39 Burghley rd.
Eve Charles 17 Grove ter.
Evetts Henry 21 Spencer rd.
Ewings William H. 27 Carrol rd.
Eyres Henry Charles 9 St. Alban's rd.

Fairall James 44a Vorley rd.
Faircloth Robert M. 165 Junction rd.
Farley Henry 53 Woodsome rd.
Farrance George (Coomrith) 90 Cromwell avenue
Farrell John Wm. 14 Victoria cottages
Farren John 70 Highgate rd.
Farrow Frank 47 Vorley rd.
Farrow John 12 Girdlestone rd.
Farrow W. 51 Chester rd.
Faulkner Arthur 42 Cromwell avenue
Faux Edward 21 Northwood rd.
Fayrer Rev. Robert, M.A. (Grove bank) West hill
Fea Madame 28 Dartmouth park rd.
Feast Robert Allen 33 Twisden rd.
Fenn John 1 Southwood lane
Fennell Mrs. 3 Highgate rise
Fernie D. S. 13 York villas
Fernley John 24 Annesley rd.
Ferrett — 6 Upper Whittington pl.
Ferris Octavius Allen (Fairview) Dartmouth park avenue
Fevez J. 11 Cathcart hill
Fielding John 37 Tremlett grove
Filer Alexander J. Duff (Holmwood lodge) Bishop wood rd.
Finch Mrs. 6 Salisbury rd.
Finden Edward (Church Hill lodge) 5 Dartmouth rd.
Findlay Alexander 31 Magdala rd.
Fisher G. 3 Cromwell pl.
Flanders D. 83 North rd.
Flaxman George 15 Raydon st.
Fleming John 139 Junction rd.
Flemyng Major-Genl.A. 16 Lady Somerset rd.
Fletcher George, M.D. (Soham house) Southwood lane
Fletcher Misses 32 Dartmouth park hill
Fletcher Wm. Wolfe 24 Woodsome rd.
Flexman William 4 Cornwall villas
Flood Edward 7 Twisden rd.
Flood F. 12 Vine cottages
Flower Frank 1 Dartmouth park rd.
Flux Edwd. Hitchings (Cotswold) Bishop wood rd.
Foley J. B. (Wheatly villa) 7 Wood lane
Ford Arthur Ranken 1 Broadlands rd.
Ford Wm.(Brookfield ho.) Millfield lane
Ford William Wilbraham (The Hawthorns) 2 Highgate rise
Foreman William 8 Holmesdale rd.
Forman Mrs. (Cintra) Hampstead lane
Forshall Francis Hyde, M.D. 8 Southwood lane
Foskett Samuel 31 Lady Somerset rd.

Foster George 33 Anatola rd.
Foster John 41 Spencer rd.
Foster Michael E. 28 Junction rd.
Fowke Thomas 10 Victoria cottages
Fowler George 8 Townshend yard
Fowler Hy.(Lynton vl.)23aBickerton rd.
Fowler Miss 25 Northwood rd.
Fox John Arthur 53 Cromwell avenue
Foxall Samuel 21 Dartmouth park rd.
Foxcroft James Charles 41 Magdala rd.
Frampton Henry William 10 York villas
Francis Thomas 82 Cromwell avenue
Frank John Henry 34 Wood lane
Fraser John (Manor cott.) Annesley rd.
Frauer Frederick 36 Twisden rd.
Frazer John Gordon 1 Grove ter.
Freame Mrs. 23 Poynings rd.
Freeland James (Ivy cottage) North hill
Freeman Daniel 1 Bedford pl.
Freeman Henry 1 Spencer rd.
Freeman Jonathan 4 Bedford pl.
Freeman Thos. 18 Upper Whittington pl.
Freeman William 5 Prospect pl.
French Joseph Stephen 131 Junction rd.
Frisby James 51 Dartmouth park rd.
Frischling Mrs. 52 Bickerton rd.
Frost John Norris (Mornington villa) West hill
Frost William Thomas 48 Twisden rd.
Fry Right Hon. Sir Edwd. 5 The Grove
Fuller Frederick U. 13 Bickerton rd.
Fuller George 5 Salisbury rd.
Funke Otto 38 Hargrave park rd.
Furge Edward 66 Bickerton rd.
Furniss Robert 22 Grove ter.
Fynn Herbert 23 Dartmouth park rd.

Gale Joseph 2 Wellington ter.
Gallatly Mrs., The Grove
Galloway Mrs. 64 Junction rd.
Galvin Stephen 42 Langdon rd.
Gamble Henry 38 Oakford rd.
Gardiner Frederick 9 Langdon park rd.
Gardner George 9 Brunswick rd.
Gardner Mrs. (Merton cott.) West hill
Garman Miss 3 Hermitage vils. West hill
Garner William 26 Salisbury rd.
Garnett Mrs. 67 Burleigh rd.
Garnsey William 34 Orchard rd.
Garrett R. H. 9 Holly village
Garrod John 45 Twisden rd.
Garrood Henry 1 North pl.
Garrood Henry 76 North rd.
Garsehen Philip 39 Dartmouth park hill
Garstin Arthur 30 Archway rd.
Gaskell Roger, North hill
Gaskin Frederick 1 Poynings rd.

Gatenby Wm. Thomas 112 Highgate rd.
Gates William 4 Holmesdale rd.
Gauntlett W. H. 31 Poynings rd.
Gaye Gerrard (Clairville) Bishop's rd.
Geard Charles (North view) Shepherd's hill rd.
Geiger F. X. 1 Ingestre rd.
George Augustin 31 Dartmouth park rd.
George Mrs. 6 South grove
Gibbard James 5 Vine cottages College lane
Gibbon Rev. J. M. (Therfield) Southwood lane
Gibbons Mrs. 217 Junction rd.
Gibbons William 22 Highgate rd.
Gibbs Thomas 11 Southwood lane
Giblett Mrs. 144 Junction rd.
Gibson E. 10 St.John the Evangelist's rd.
Gibson John Arthur 4 Poynings rd.
Giddy William 27 Salisbury rd.
Gilby Henry (Burghley house) 25 Lady Somerset rd.
Giles H. P. 7 Highgate rd.
Giles William Henry 14 Holmesdale rd.
Gill Robert 5 Woodview ter.
Gillam Charles 15 Brunswick rd.
Gillbanks T. J. 7 Churchill rd.
Gillow Joseph 19 Northwood rd.
Gilmour Henry F. 19 Grove rd.
Ginelack Frederick 34 Carrol rd.
Girdlestone Henry 9 Wood lane
Glead George 47 North rd.
Glead John 49 North rd.
Gliddon Frederick 10 Tremlett grove
Glover Frederick 27 Tremlett grove
Glover John (Merton lodge) Merton lane
Glover John George (Lynton villa) Highgate rd.
Glover Mrs. Thomas (The Gothic) Highgate rd.
GloverRichard Thomas 24 Croftdown rd.
Godden Henry 97 Burghley rd.
Godfrey Albert Edwin 61 Langdon rd.
Godfrey Alfred 15 Burghley rd.
Goding George 8 Annesley rd.
Golds Edward (Clyde villa) Bishop's rd.
Goldthorpe F. 65 North rd.
Good Arthur M. (Clovelly) Bishop's rd.
Goodacre Henry 11 Oakford rd.
Goodall J. M. (Linden house) 1 The Grove Highgate rd.
Goodchap Wm. 26 Dartmouth park hill
Goodchild N., M.D. 9 Highgate rd.
Goode John (Hillside) Bloomfield rd.
Goode John, LL.B. (Hillside) The Park Highgate
Goodliffe— 33 Holmesdale rd.

Goodman Albert (Witton house) Bloomfield rd.
Goodman Charles 36 Junction rd.
Goodman Edwin 30 Burghley rd.
Goodman James 44 Vorley rd.
Goodwin Fredk. 37 Dartmouth park rd.
Goodwin H. 4 Willow walk
Goodwin Nathaniel (Inchkeith) Cromwell rd.
Goodwin William 4 South grove cotts.
Goodworth George 41 Lady Somerset rd.
Gore Allan 21 Tremlett grove
Gore F. 1 Oakford rd.
GorhamCharlesTurner13Langdon pk.rd.
Gosbell Miss (The Woodlands)North hill
Goslett Alfred, J.P., West hill
Goss Mrs. Mary Ann 70 Spencer rd.
Gössell Otto (Elm lodge) Fitzroy park
Gotobed Edward 36 Langdon park rd.
Gotto H. (Croft lodge) Highgate rd. and (New house park farm) St. Alban's
Gouda Arnold 5 Dartmouth park rd.
Gough Hugh 21 Cromwell avenue
Gould Mrs. 34 Salisbury rd.
Goulding Edward (Beverley house) 58 Cromwell avenue
Gouly Edward James (St. John's lodge) Dartmouth park avenue
GrahamGeorgeLowther11 Cromwell avn
Grainger Mrs. 6 Hornsey lane
Grant Alexander 23 Grove rd.
Grant Wilfred Dryden, Hampstead lane
Graves Mrs. 4 Burghley rd.
Gray John 49 Holmesdale rd.
Gray Nathaniel (Grove farm cottage) Highgate rd.
Gray Parker (Hollyview) Dartmouth rd
Greatbatch William 60 Fortess rd.
Greatrex James 11 Brunswick rd.
Greaves Frank,M.R.C.S.E.50 Junction rd.
Greaves William 48 Woodsome rd.
Green Edward 2 Wells hill
Green George 2 Bedford pl.
Green Samuel Walter 12 Grove ter.
Green William (Bishop wood house) Bishop wood rd.
Greene William Robert 5 Burghley rd.
Greenfield W. P. 28 Oakford rd.
Greenhill William S. 9 Oakford rd.
Greenwood Charles 17 Highgate rd.
Greenwood Chas. T. 68 Langdon pk. rd.
Greenwood Harry, M.A. (The Limes) Southwood lane
Greenwood Mrs. 24 Cromwell avenue
Gregory Percival 47 Langdon rd.
Greig Thomas 41 Twisden rd.
Griffith George 13 Churchill rd.

Grimwood Robert 30 Bickerton rd.
Grindley Mrs. (Millfield) Millfield lane
Grou George 27 Brunswick rd.
Grove Joseph 9 Victoria cottages
Groves Allen 41 Poynings rd.
Gullett James 90 Langdon rd.
Gunn William 37 Magdala rd.
Gutteridge Joseph 71 Cromwell avenue
Guy Thomas (Edendale) 59 Cromwell av.
Gwinnett J. 35 Twisden rd.

Hadley Joseph 16 Dartmouth park rd.
Haining Mrs. 63 Burghley rd.
Haldane George 14 Brunswick rd.
Halder Elijah James 24 Twisden rd.
Hale Benjamin 37 North rd.
Hale John 15 Grove rd.
Hale Thomas 35 Poynings rd.
Hale William E. 41 Tremlett grove
Hales James 3 Anatola rd.
Halifax Mrs. 15 Vorley rd.
Hall E. D.(Myrtle cot.) Southwood lane
Hall Henry (Gordon house) The Grove
Hall Mrs. Sarah 2 Twisden rd.
Hall William 41 Oakford rd.
Halsey James 11 Castle yard
Halsey James 44 Langdon park rd.
Hamblin William Henry 28 Vorley rd.
Hamer John 69 Dartmouth park hill
Hammond Robert 4 North grove
Hamp George, Southwood lane
Hanbury John James 93 Highgate rd.
Hancock Edwin Fredk. 68 Spencer rd.
Hancock G. E., Burghley rd.
Hands Thomas L.(Oak lo.)3 Bickerton rd.
Handyside Mrs.23 Grove ter. Highgate rd.
Hanford Mrs. W. 34 Hargrave park rd.
Hankins John 5 Brunswick rd.
Hankins Richard 2 Lewisham rd.
Happe Otto 62 Bickerton rd.
Harding Robert 8 Chester ter.
Hardy Mrs. S. 21 Vorley rd.
Hardy Samuel 7 The Bank
Hare Henry 6 Magdala rd.
Hare James 10 Bedford pl.
Hare Mrs. 9 Bedford pl.
Hargraue Wm. Henry 74 Junction rd.
Harman Walter John (Balcombe house) Dartmouth park avenue
Harper Thomas 7 St. Alban's rd.
Harran Mrs. 91 Highgate rd.
Harris Albert 36 Dartmouth hill
Harris Francis 113 Highgate rd.
Harris George 120 Highgate rd.
Harris John 6 Vorley rd.
Harris Mrs. 3 Norman vils. Archway rd.
Harris Mrs. (The Limes) North hill

Harris Mrs., Southwood lane
Harris Reuben 6 Crown cottages
Harris William 8 North grove
Harris William Redford 1 Hampstead lane
Harrison Rev. J. J. (Underwood house) Hornsey lane
Harrison Edward 159 Junction rd.
Harrison George 42 Woodsome rd.
Harrison John 4 Vorley rd.
Harrison Joseph B. 87 Fortess rd.
Harrison Miss (The Cedars) 85 North rd
Harrison William 2 Blenheim pl.
Harrison W. L. 28 Salisbury rd.
Harrower Frank W. 76 Dartmouth park hill
Hartridge James Hills 15 Grove ter.
Hartung Charles William 7 Cromwell avenue
Harvey Alfred (Hurstbourne) Bishop wood rd.
Harvey Frank 1 Orchard rd.
Harvey F. M. 40 Chetwynd rd.
Harvey Henry 2 Albert villas
Harvey James 10 Prospect cottages
Haswell George 18 Brunswick rd.
Hateley David 31 Orchard rd.
Hatherill William 52 Brunswick rd.
Hatt Charles 19 Chester rd.
Hatt Charles George 1 Carrol rd.
Hatt John 37 Carrol rd.
Havant John 169 Dartmouth park hill
Hawes Henry Peck 55 Holmesdale rd.
Hawes Robert V. 31 Hargrave park rd.
Hawkins Thomas 21 Langdon rd.
Hawksworth William 38 Twisden rd.
Haydon Hillyard (Cholmeley house) Archway rd.
Hayes Cornelius 27 Churchill rd.
Hayes Mrs. (Mendip ho.) Bloomfield rd.
Haymen W. 76 Bickerton rd.
Haynes John 6 Prospect cottages
Hayter Ambrose 13 Doynton st.
Hayton Joseph 55 Dartmouth park hill
Hayward G. 1 Pleasant row
Hayward Miss 2 Hampstead lane
Hayward Samuel 10 Cathcart hill
Head J. 14 Winchester pl.
Heard Edward 3 Magdala rd.
Hearn A. W. 34 Dartmouth park rd.
Hearn Mrs. S. S. 23 Brunswick rd.
Hearn R. John 14 Dartmouth park rd.
Heath William 82 North rd.
Heaton Mrs. E. 100 Junction rd.
Hedgecoe Walter 219 Junction rd.
Helliar Mrs. Elizabeth 10 Winchester pl.
Hembrow Charles Wm. 32 Magdala rd.
Henderson Alexander 227 Junction rd.

Henderson Alexander Milne, M.D. 6 Hampstead lane
Henderson Wm. C. 24 Lady Somerset rd.
Hepburn Alexander 9 Woodsome rd.
Hepburn Duncan (Cumberland villa) Highgate rd.
Hepburn Mrs. 8 Brunswick rd.
Herapath John 18a Holmesdale rd.
Heriot George (Lilford house) Cholmeley park
Hermon Richard 23 Fortess rd.
Hertslet Mrs. 18 Dartmouth park rd.
Hetherington William Lonsdale, M.A. (Northcroft) Broadlands rd.
Hewitt Joseph 1 Hargrave park rd.
Hibberd Albert W. 3 Poynings rd.
Hibbert Albert Wellesley 17 Cromwell avenue
Hickman Andrew Wm. 25 Chetwynd rd.
Hickman Arthur J. 39 Spencer rd.
Hickman Walter 28 Carrol rd.
Hickmott Stephen 13 Girdlestone rd.
Hicks Henry 5 Chester rd.
Hicks Robert 3 Albert vils. Archway rd.
Hicks Thomas James 5 Spencer rd.
Hicks William 10 Chester ter.
Hickson Mrs.(Linden ho.) Hornsey lane
Hield J. 14 Grove rd.
Higgs Joseph 35 Doynton st.
Hildersley James J. 76 Fortess rd.
Hill Arthur 25 Tremlett grove
Hill Edward Henry 3 Prospect cottages
Hill Edwin John 7 Chester ter.
Hill Elles 19 Orchard rd.
Hill H. 1 Hope cottages College lane
Hill Henry J. (Riversdale house) 21 Grove ter.
Hill James France 31 Burghley rd.
Hill J. G. 3 Southwood ter.
Hill Miss 33 Burghley rd.
Hill Wm. (Bickerton lo.) 1 Bickerton rd.
Hillier Henry 19 Salisbury rd.
Hillier William 4 Blenheim pl.
Hills James 207 Junction rd.
Hind Charles 25 Dartmouth park hill
Hine Arthur(Fitzroy cott.)Millfield lane
Hines Mrs. 9 Girdlestone rd.
Hinkley James 10 Archway pl.
Hinton Mrs. 12 Vorley rd.
Hipkins Miss 37 Spencer rd.
Hitchcock John 5 South grove cottages
Hitchman F. 11 Lady Somerset rd.
Hobbs Thomas 63 Langdon rd.
Hobden Henry F. 34 Cromwell avenue
Hodge Edward 53 Lady Somerset rd.
Hodge James Clark 18 Croftdown rd.
Hodges Robert Saunders 3 Burghley rd.

Hodges Walter 5 York villas
Hoffman Edwin 39 Magdala rd.
Hoffman J. 54 Junction rd.
Hogben Miss 4 Woodsome rd.
Hogerzeal Cornelius 13 St. Alban's villas
Holbrook Thomas 14 Chester ter.
Holder Charles 23 Spencer rd.
Holdernesse Charles 11 St. John the Evangelist's rd.
Holdgate Mrs. 68 Fortess rd.
Holdom William 12 Victoria cottages
Holdstock Miss 5 and 7 Bickerton rd.
Holeman W. 9 Spencer rd.
Holker Arthur 54 Lady Somerset rd.
Holland Charles Major 89 Fortess rd.
Holland Christopher J. 38 Magdala rd.
Holland Thomas (Whitehall lodge) Archway rd.
Hollick Ebenezer 79 Dartmouth pk. hill
Hollis George 47 Dartmouth park hill
Holman Mrs. 3 Girdlestone rd.
Holmes Mrs. Mary 66 Fortess rd.
Holmes Thomas John 42 Highgate rd.
Holt D. 10 Vine cottages
Hooley Samuel 27 Spencer rd.
Hooman James 6 Hermitage villas
Hooper George 3 Vorley rd.
Hooper John 1 Temperance cottages
Hooton Charles (Sunningdale house) 25 Bickerton rd.
Hopewell Alfred 1 Holmesdale rd.
Hopkins George 37 Salisbury rd.
Hopper Edwin 22 Carrol rd.
Hopwell Miss 45 Burghley rd.
Horne Frederick 7 Doynton st.
Horne Mrs. 6 Churchill rd.
Horner E. 29 Cromwell avenue
Hornsey Thomas 37 Holmesdale rd.
Horsley William 70 Cromwell avenue
Horton Frederick 14 Tremlett grove
Horton L. (The Lodge) Cholmeley park
Horwood Mrs. (South grove house)South grove
House Miss (Fernbank) 7 Dartmouth rd
Howard Thomas 8 Castle yard
Howard William 2 South grove cottages
Howe Thomas 3 Dartmouth park avenue
Howe Thomas 19 Upper Whittington pl
Howell Mrs. 23 Churchill rd.
Howes Harmen (The Ferns) 52 Lady Somerset rd.
Howkins Mrs. Harriett 2 Blandford pl.
Hoyle Mrs. C. 5 Cholmeley villas
Hucklesby G. 42 Twisden rd.
Hudson E. T. 21 Fortess rd.
Huggins Arthur E. 7 St. Alban's villas
Huggins Samuel 1 Vorley rd.

Huggins William H. (Clifton lodge) 5 The Grove
Hughes Arthur Edwin 33 Grove rd.
Hughes George Henry 66 Woodsome rd.
Hughes James Benjamin 25 Woodsome rd.
Hughes John 3 Little Green st.
Hughes Mrs. Walter (Southwood house) Southwood lane
Hughes Robert Henry 10 Holmesdale rd.
Hughes Thomas Arthur (Mount Melleray) The Bank
Hulbert Richard Stephen 56 Lady Somerset rd.
Hull Mrs. 21 Highgate rd.
Hulland Thomas 31 Woodsome rd.
Hulme J. A. 43 Langdon park rd.
Humber Walter 52 Twisden rd.
Humberstone William 14 Prospect cotts.
Hume Alfred 3 Holly lodge villas
Hunns Jabez 21 Doynton st.
Hunt Charles 37 Bickerton rd.
Hunt Mrs. Elizabeth 10 Orchard rd.
Hunt Thomas 26 Bickerton rd.
Hunt Wm. (Woodbine vl.) Archway rd.
Hunt William R. 72 Lady Somerset rd.
Hunter Edward 39 North rd.
Hunter W. N. 58 Lady Somerset rd.
Huntingford George 3 Mansfield cotts.
Hurst Mrs. (Mortimer cott.) West hill
Hurst W. 5 Anatola rd.
Hutchinson Herbert John 66 Cromwell avenue
Hutchison William 6 Burghley rd.
Huthwaite Hy. 37 Dartmouth park hill
Hutt Charles 30 Hargrave park rd.
Hutt George 7 Langdon rd.
Hyde Henry 31 Doynton st.
Hyde Thomas 1 Cromwell pl.

Imber Alfred 21 Bisham gardens
Inch Thomas Alfred 5 Chester villas
Ingram Mrs. 13 Salisbury rd.
Innocent J. 47 Oakford rd.
Irish Frank 72 Spencer rd.
Izod William Henry 17 Poynings rd.

Jackman Paul 42 Oakford rd.
Jackson E. 71 Burghley rd.
Jackson James 33 Poynings rd.
Jackson Joseph 6 Mansfield cottages
Jackson Mrs. 4 Caen ter. Hampstead lane
Jackson William 75 Fortess rd.
Jackson William 43 Vorley rd.
James George 42 Fortess rd.
James James 14 Vorley rd.
James John 15 Wood lane
James Joseph 18 Winscombe st.

James Mrs. 33 Magdala rd.
James William 33 Dartmouth park rd.
James Wm. Henry 43 Lady Somerset rd.
Jamieson Andrew 26 Holmesdale rd.
Jaques Charles Alfred (Ferndale) Dartmouth park avenue
Jaques Edward 29 Dartmouth park hill
Jarvis Edward 35 Dartmouth park rd.
Jefferies Mrs. 40 Carrol rd.
Jeffries John 19 Hargrave park rd.
Jenkin Charles Brown 19 Woodsome rd.
Jennings Mrs. E. 14 Woodsome rd.
Jennings W. 57 Cromwell avenue
Jewell Henry 1 Anatola rd.
Job William Henry 3 Highgate rd.
Johnson D. 67 North rd.
Johnson Edward Henry 45 Langdon park rd.
Johnson J. G. (Southwood court) Southwood lane
Johnson Miss (Lawn house) North hill
Johnson Thomas Henry (Cambridge house) 23 Oakford rd.
Johnson William 37 Oakford rd.
Johnston Henry 24 Salisbury rd.
Jones Dr. George T. 40 Archway rd.
Jones Alexander (Netherleigh house) 4 Hornsey lane
Jones Alfred Wilkinson 13 Dartmouth park avenue
Jones Joseph 37 Woodsome rd.
Jones Miss (Northwood cott.) North hill
Jones Miss Elizabeth 13 York rise
Jones Mrs. 1 St. Alban's rd.
Jones Robert 1 Bedford cottages
Jones T. 36 Oakford rd.
Jones Thomas 54 Brunswick rd.
Jones William 6 Highgate rise
Jones William 35 Oakford rd.
Jones William 39 Langdon rd.
Jordan James 6 Annesley rd.
Jordan James 104 Dartmouth park hill
Jordan Richard 25 Spencer rd.
Jude George 18 Carrol rd.
Jukes William 44 Twisden rd.
Jull Mrs. 59 Langdon rd.

Kain Francis 43 Burghley rd.
Keedle William 26 Woodsome rd.
Keen Edwin Henry (Birkdale) Dartmouth park avenue
Keen Henry 15 Cathcart hill
Kell F. W. 20 Croftdown rd.
Kelly Mrs. 7 Castle yard
Kelly R. W. 3 Lady Somerset rd.
Keltie John S. 52 Cromwell avenue
Kemp George 4 Pleasant row

Kemp William 3 Northwood rd.

Kemp William James 67 Spencer rd.

Kempton William (Stonefield house) Dartmouth park hill

Kennedy Ernest Edward 12 Southwood terrace

Kenneth H. (Hurstleigh) Shepherd's hill rd.

Kent Geo. (Southwood) Southwood lane

Kent Henry (Prospect cot.) College lane

Kent John 2 Meadow cottages

Kent S. 3 Pleasant row

Kernot Richard 20 Dartmouth park hill

Kerr Miss 40 Salisbury rd.

Kerry James 13 Cromwell pl.

Kerry Misses 16 Brunswick rd.

Kershaw Burroughs D., C.E. 51 Chetwynd rd.

Kershaw Robert 12 Twisden rd.

Key Mrs. 28 Burghley rd.

Keyes Richard 3 Spencer rd.

Kieffin Alexander 1 Milton cottages North hill

Killip Mrs. 2 Girdlestone rd.

Kindell James 96 Junction rd.

King Chas. (The Hollies) 2 Winchester pl.

King Charles Thomas 4 Holly ter.

King David 6 Little Green st.

King Edward (The Limes) 4 St. Alban's rd.

King Edwin (Inglehome) Bishop wood rd.

King Edwin J. 11 Girdlestone rd.

King Frederick 12 Ingestre rd.

King J. 5 Poynings rd.

King John 33 Brunswick rd.

King Mark Wm. (The Grange) Grange rd.

King Mrs. 5 Blenheim pl.

King Thomas Isaac 16 Hargrave park rd.

Kirby William (Well cottage) Southwood lane

Kirtland Wm. Thomas 1 Woodview villas

Kitchener Freeman S. 5 Chetwynd rd.

Kitson Mrs. 25 Burghley rd.

Kitto Mrs. 59 Fortess rd.

Klaftenberger Mrs. 61 Burghley rd.

Knapton Harry 6 Spencer rd.

Knecht Joseph 30 Orchard rd.

Knight James 1 Railway cottages

Knight Miss 2 Holly ter.

Knight William 172 Junction rd.

Knights Joseph (Suffolk villa) 142 Junction rd.

Knowles W. A. 5 Wells hl. Southwood ln.

Koch Herbert Sigismund 47 Langdon park rd.

Koeune Mdlle. (St. John's park house) Highgate rd.

Kurz Wm. John 38 Dartmouth park rd.

Kynvin Mrs. 12 Langdon rd.

Lack Mrs. 6 Hargrave park rd.

Lakeman Henry B. 11 Dartmouth park rd

Lakeman Mrs. 10 Langdon rd.

Lalor John 85 Dartmouth park hill

Lamb Mrs. 54 Fortess rd.

Lamb Mrs. 14 St. Alban's villas

Lambert Charles C. (Talbot house) 3 Chetwynd rd.

Lamble S. R. (Norfolk villa) 52 Highgate rd.

Lance William C. 11 Salisbury rd.

Lane John (Grove house) 7 The Grove

Langford Alfred 13 Twisden rd.

Langley Henry 23 Raydon st.

Langman Philip L. 24 Oakford rd.

Langsford John 32 Cromwell avenue

Langton John 5 Pleasant row

Larcher G. F. 8 Winchester pl.

Larcy J. 1 Magdala rd.

Lashmore John 57 North rd.

Laskey Leonard (St. Leonard's) 3 Archway rd.

Latham Henry 2 The Grove

Latimer John 168 Junction rd.

Laurence H. William 44 Spencer rd.

Laurence John 16 Vorley rd.

Laver James 199 Junction rd.

Lawes John James H. 47 Carrol rd.

Lawes Mrs. Amelia J. 65 Fortess rd.

Lawford Miss 12 Grove rd.

Lawrence Henry 223 Junction rd.

Lawrence John 162 Junction rd.

Lawrence Joseph 74 Twisden rd.

Lawson Thomas 62 Hargrave park rd.

Lawson W. H. S. (Cintra cot.) West hi

Laybourn Robt. G. 77 Dartmouth pk. hi

Lea George (Hill brow) Hornsey lane

Lea Mrs. (Park villa) Hampstead lane

Lea Thomas (The Limes) Fitzroy park

Leaman Joseph 4 Castle yard

Leaman Walter 4 Prospect cottages

Ledwidge Francis 60 Junction rd.

Lee Charles 15 Cromwell pl.

Lee David 9 York vils. Hargrave pk. r

Lee John Thos. (Glenmoor lodge) West h

Lee Joseph 1 Langdon park rd.

Lee Thomas 46 Bickerton rd.

Lee Thomas 68 Twisden rd.

Lee William 8 Spencer rd.

Lega-Weekes Mrs. 34 Poynings rd.

Legg William 20 Dartmouth park rd.

Leggett G. 40 Langdon rd.

Leighton G. C. (Fairlight) Shepherd hill rd.

Leighton Jeffrey 13 Croftdown rd.

Leipold John 10 Hargrave park rd.
Lester H. 69 Vorley rd.
Lester Louis George 11 Bickerton rd.
Lethbridge George 9 Cholmeley villas
Lewis Charles Lee (Hillside) Fitzroy pk.
Lewis Mrs. 4 Grove pl.
Lewis Mrs. Amelia 10 Park ter.
Lidwell Henry Joseph 55 Woodsome rd.
Lindquist Oscar M. 28 Langdon park rd.
Lindsay George 66 Langdon park rd.
Linford George 9 Little Green st.
Ling George James 2 Townshend yard
Linnett Alexander F. 53 Chester rd.
Little Mrs. Rebecca 8 Langdon rd.
Lloyd Frederick Giesler (Southampton villa) Millfield lane
Lloyd John H. (Hill side) Jackson's lane
Lloyd John James 58 Junction rd.
Lloyd Thomas 27 Doynton st.
Lloyd William 2 Little Green st.
Locker Arthur 5 Holly ter. West hill
Lockhart James Charles 25 Highgate rd.
Lockhart W. S. (Lyndale ho.) The Bank
Lockyer George 94 Junction rd.
Lodge James 25 Langdon rd.
Lodge Mrs. (Millfield villa) Millfield lane
Lodge Robert J. 7 The Grove
Lodge T. B. 8 The Grove
Loewenstein S. 50 Lady Somerset rd.
Lofthouse Henry 10 Girdlestone rd.
Logan Mrs. Martha (Ye Hutte) 28 Wood ln.
Logan Richard 44 Woodsome rd.
Lomer E. 25 Langdon park rd.
Lomes Thomas 46 Carrol rd.
Long A. (Southwood lo.) Southwood lane
Long George 2 Swain's lane
Longhurst William 9 Cromwell pl.
Longman V. (Stafford ho.) 3 Dartmouth rd
Longson Luke 11 Woodsome rd.
Loutit Mrs. Sinclair 62 Langdon park rd.
Loutit Sinclair (Norman ho.) Hornsey ln.
Lovell Charles Henry, Merton lane
Lovell Edward 12 Poynings rd.
Lovelock James Frederick (Rokeb house) Bishop's rd.
Low Mrs. W. H. (Claremont house) Park house rd.
Lowe Charles 6 Grove pl.
Lowe Francis 6 North grove
Lowen R. (Holmhurst) Southwood lane
Lowen Robert 12 Townshend yard
Lodwig William 94 Cromwell avenue
Lumley H. 25 Churchill rd.
Lunnon James 4 South grove
Lye Alfred 1 York villas
Lyell Frederick 10 The Grove
Lyell John S. (Millfield cot.) Millfield lane

Lyle Abram (Dunvar) Bishop wood rd
Lyon Rbt. H. (Tremlett lo.) 2 Tremlett gro
Lyon T. 35 Holmesdale rd.
Lyons James 74 Cromwell avenue
Lyte Mrs. 27 Burghley rd.

McCabe Thomas 34 Archway rd.
McCandlish Richard D. 8 Holly village
McCarthy C. 1 Doynton st.
McCarthy Henry 27 Hargrave park rd.
McCombie William Downie 23 Wood lane
McDowall Rev. Prebendary, D.D. (The School house) Bishop wood rd.
McEwen Oliver 5 Victoria cottages
McGougan E. M. 43 Holmesdale rd.
McIntyre Robert 35 Carrol rd.
McKewan Wm. Mawley 36 Highgate rd.
McKiernin W. 4 & 13 Chester ter.
McLay James 2 Holmesdale rd.
McMullin John 4 Townshend yard
McSheehan Michael 3 Cholmeley villas
MacDowell Mrs. R. C. 78 Fortess rd.
Macduff J. 5 Blandford pl.
MacEgan J. 9 Tremlett grove
Macfarlane Jas. Laird 15 Woodsome rd.
MacGregor Mrs. Martha (Glengyle) 27 Wood lane
Mackay David 8 Hermitage villas
Mackeson Henry 2 North pl. North hill
Maddle John William 22 Tremlett grove
Mahomed Rev. J. D. K., B.A. 15 Lewisham rd.
Mahon John 44 Highgate rd.
Mahoney Rev. P. R. 8 Gordon house rd.
Maidman William 43 Langdon rd.
Maidment Geo. 91 Dartmouth park hill
Maistre Paul 6 Twisden rd.
Mallett Samuel 30 Northwood rd.
Malley Joseph 18 Archway rd.
Manley Henry 11 Orchard rd.
Mann William 7 Ingestre rd.
Manners William 4 Croftdown rd.
Mansfield Right Hon. The Earl (Kenwood) Hampstead lane
Mansfield George W. (Mansfield house) Ingestre rd.
Marchetti Joseph 39 Oakford rd.
Marsh Alfred 3 Alpha villas Archway rd.
Marshall Arthur 1 North grove
Marshall Charles J. K. 7 Lewisham rd.
Marshall Francis 9 Grove ter.
Marshall Miss 3 St. Alban's villas
Marshall Mrs. 33 Carrol rd.
Marshall Thomas, M.B., C.M. 55 Fortess rd.
Martin Charles 7 Raydon st.
Martin George 47 Chester rd.
Maskell Mrs. (Woodville) South grove

Mason Major-General C. C. (Whitley house) Bishop wood rd.
Massey Edward James 38 Spencer rd.
Massingham W. A. (The Woodlands) North hill
Mathews Francis Richard 41 Carrol rd.
Mathews Frank 6 Woodview ter.
Matthews John 7 Chester rd.
Matthews Mrs. 39 Langdon park rd.
Matthews R. E. J. (The Hoffe) 6 Winchester pl.
Mattick Benjm. 4 Wells hill Southwood ln.
Mattinson Joseph 7 Hornsey lane
Maude Edmund 73 Cromwell avenue
Maude Thomas James 5 Bishop wood rd.
Maund Robert 28 Churchill rd.
Maurice Miss, South grove
Maxfield John 45 Dartmouth park rd.
May Rev. Robert Costall, M.A. 73 Dartmouth park hill
May John 7 Northwood rd.
May William Oliver 20 Chetwynd rd.
Maybin Samuel 28 Highgate rd.
Mayer Edward (Roumania cottage) 2 Carrol rd.
Maynard Thomas 17 Doynton st.
Mayo John 40 Spencer rd.
Mead Alfred 16 Townshend yard
Mead Benjamin 9 Swain's lane
Mead Charles 9 Vorley rd.
Mead George 16 Upper Whittington pl.
Mead John 49 Lady Somerset rd.
Mead Thomas 2 Pond sq.
Meade T. de Courcy 32 Langdon park rd.
Meager George 44 Bickerton rd.
Melhuish John H. 72 Bickerton rd.
Mellish Frederick 33 Langdon rd.
Mercer Edward 51 Langdon rd.
Mercer J. C. 2 Cromwell avenue
Merrill Frederick 11 Anatola rd.
Messenger G. 30 Oakford rd.
Metherell John K. 2 Grove rd.
Metherell Richard 26 Archway pl.
Meyer John 17 Chetwynd rd.
Miall Charles 9 Cathcart hill
Miall L eonard Henry 1 Wyndham cres.
Michel Philip 2 Chester ter.
Middlemiss Mrs. 23 Salisbury rd.
Middleton Mrs. 66 Twisden rd.
Middleton W. 24 Magdala rd.
Miles Alfred 1 Wood lane
Miles Arthur 27 Fortess rd.
Miles Joseph J., Southampton villas Millfield lane
Miles L. C. 41 Woodsome rd.
Miles Mrs. 15 Archway rd.
Miles Thomas 48 Lady Somerset rd.

Millard George 52 Vorley rd.
Miller Charles 15 Spencer rd.
Miller Joseph 9 Prospect cottages
Mills John (Camelia cot.) 35 Magdala rd.
Mills Mrs. James 2 Ingestre rd.
Millwood Joseph 11 Prospect cottages
Milne Mrs. 35 Lady Somerset rd.
Milner Robert 60 Woodsome rd.
Milton William 1 Pleasant cottages
Mitchell Henry 72 Woodsome rd.
Mitchell Mrs. 30 Tremlett grove
Mitchell Sugden 16 Twisden rd.
Mizon John 9 Grove rd.
Moggridge James H. 12 Churchill rd.
Moginie Daniel B. 29 Langdon park rd
Monk William 195 Junction rd.
Monks Thos. (Chester lodge) Chester rd.
Montanari Mrs. 29 Hargrave park rd.
Moody James 4 Prospect cottages
Moon George 9 Annesley rd.
Moon Theophilus 3 The Grove
Moore James 11 St. Alban's villas
Morey George 23 Holmesdale rd.
Morgan C. 11 Poynings rd.
Morgan H. 5 Twisden rd.
Morgan Mrs. 24 Bickerton rd.
Morgan Mrs. 3 Tremlett grove
Morgan William Simeon (The Hawthorns) 56 Cromwell avenue
Morle Mrs. 20 Tremlett grove
Morley Henry 6 Chetwynd rd.
Morley Wm. (Denewood) Broadlands rd
Morra Henry 39 Cromwell avenue
Morrell John Turner 39 Woodsome rd.
Morrell William 8 Willow walk
Morris Rev. Robert Leslie, M.A. (Fitzroy lodge) The Grove
Morris E. Brudenell 177 Dartmouth park hill
Morris Joseph (Melbey villa) 26 Cromwell avenue
Morris Wm. (The Ferns) Southwood ln.
Morris W. G. 35 Hargrave park rd.
Mortiboy Henry 9 Salisbury rd.
Mortiboy William 23 Archway pl.
Morton Mrs. 10 The Grove
Mott James 15 Victoria cottages
Moxon Walter, M.D. (Northolme) Broadlands rd.
Moy Francis 15 Annesley rd.
Mudie Alfred 43 Dartmouth park rd.
Mudie Ernest 30 Lewisham rd.
Muir J. M. 91 Langdon rd.
Muirhead David 6 Cathcart hill
Mulford John C. 45 Hargrave park rd.
Mullins Mrs. 54 Cromwell avenue
Mummery John Howard 1 Holly ter.

Murison John 54 Hargrave park rd.
Murphy Jsph.(Mountfields)29 Wood lane
Murray John 28 Northwood rd.
Mylrea Edward 39 Poynings rd.

Naghten John E. A. B. 5 Northwood rd.
Nalder Fredk.15 Dartmouth park avenue
Nash Mrs. 22 Chetwynd rd.
Nash Thos.Russ 3Caen ter.Hampstead ln.
Nathan Hyam 25 Magdala rd.
Neal James 2 Willow walk
Keil James 40 Twisden rd.
Nearly T. 34 Tremlett grove
Nelson John Faux 15 Chester ter.
Nerney William 111 Highgate rd.
Newbold William 25 Brunswick rd.
Newman Charles 10 Lewisham rd.
Newman Mrs. 9 Langdon rd.
Newport W. W. 69 Burghley rd.
Newth Frederick 72 Cromwell avenue
Newton George 2 Brunswick rd.
Nichol Mrs. 15 Dartmouth park rd.
Nicholls Francis 12 York villas
Nicholls Frank 17 Tremlett grove
Nicholls Mrs. E. 40 Highgate rd.
Nicholson Thomas E. (Melton house)
   North hill
Nicol Mrs. Agnes 64 Cromwell avenue
Noakes Benj.(Hope cottage) North hill
Noakes Miss Jessie 4 St. Alban's villa
Noble John 62 Lady Somerset rd.
Noble William 63 Cromwell avenue
Nokes Thomas 8 Grove ter.
Norman Mrs. 3 Victoria cottages
Norris Daniel 24 Langdon park rd.
Norris Mrs. 56 Brunswick rd.
Norris Samuel 8 Victoria cottages
North Richard 40 York rise
Nunn Philip (St. Leonards) 6 Wyndham
   crescent
Nunn Mrs. Thomas (Hartland house)
   7 Dartmouth park avenue
Nuth Alfred 20 Lady Somerset rd.
Nuth Edward 20 Lady Somerset rd.
Nutt George James (Walden lodge)
   48 Wood lane

Oakeshott Mrs. (Wasdale) 45 Cromwell
   avenue
Oakley Hy.(Northlands) Bishop wood rd.
Oatley Alfred 6 York rise
Obery John H. 64 Hargrave park rd.
O'Callaghan Hon. Mrs. Rosina (Loretto
   house) Hornsey lane
O'Connor John 5 Ingestre rd.
O'Kelly Owen 14 Burghley rd.
Oldfield David 10 Holly ter.

Oldham Fredk. Ernest 106 Dartmouth
   park hill
Oliver Mrs. 20 Langdon rd.
Oliver Thomas E. 10 Salisbury rd.
O'Reilly Dr. G. J. (Rathmoore) 116
   Archway rd.
Orhly Theodore D. 27 Grove rd.
Orton Benjamin 16 Churchill rd.
Osborn Mrs. 125 Junction rd.
Osborne Rev. John Francis, M.A. 28 Har-
   grave park rd.
Osborne Thomas 8 York villas Hargrave
   park rd.
Osborne William 11a Girdlestone rd.
Osborne Wm. Henry 67 Cromwell avenue
Osmond Frederick S. 8 The Grove
Ottey William 35 Spencer rd.
Outing L. 69 North rd.
Overton Peter Raven 16 Bishop's rd.
Oxley Oscar 5 South grove
Oyler David Jonathan 5 Hermitage vils.

Page Frederick 5 St. John the Evange-
   list's rd.
Paice Miss 48 Cromwell avenue
Painter William 16 Woodsome rd.
Paley Joseph 6 Brunswick rd.
Palmer Frederick 127 Junction rd.
Palmer James, Broadbent yard
Palmer John 4 Grove rd.
Palmer John 7 Prospect cottages
Palmer Samuel 7 Poynings rd.
Papworth Harry James 8 Grove rd.
Papworth Harry James (Grove farm
   house) Highgate rd.
Papworth Mrs. S. 8 Grove rd.
Parish William 5 Little Green st.
Parker Charles 15 Churchill rd.
Parker Frederick(Treleigh house)South-
   wood lane
Parker Richard (The Limes)11The Grove
Parker Wm. 7 Victoria cotts.Archway rd.
Parkinson Rawlinson (Grove lodge)
   Hampstead lane
Parkinson Robert 98 Junction rd.
Parlby Josiah 46 Girdlestone rd.
Parmley Mrs. 10 Burghley rd.
Parry Mrs. 8 Poynings rd.
Parry Robert 9 Poynings rd.
Parsons John (Netley house) 37 Lady
   Somerset rd.
Parsons Joseph 16 Salisbury rd.
Partridge Mrs. P. 101 Fortess rd.
Parvin Mrs. 12 Hargrave park rd.
Pascoe Joseph 7 Burghley rd.
Passmore Augustus Andrew 17 Crom-
   well pl.

Patfield Mrs. John 18 Salisbury rd.
Patten Henry 30 Croftdown rd.
Pattinson Richard John 16 Archway rd.
Paul Mrs. Mary 11 Wood lane
Paull H. J. 50 Highgate rd.
Paun Charles 35 Langdon park rd.
PawleRobert (Gothic cottage) North hill
Paxton Mrs. Maria 1 Prospect pl.
Payne Rev. W. L. 26 Langdon park rd.
Payne John Orlebar 2 Holly village
Payne Robert 13 Dartmouth park rd.
Payne Wm. Michael 26 Langdon park rd.
Peace Richard Henry (Hazlehurst) 47
    Cromwell avenue
Peach Arthur Henry 11 York villas
Peacock T. 40 Langdon park rd.
Pearce Alfred 67 Dartmouth park hill
Pearce F. 42 Carrol rd.
Pearce Thomas 33 Raydon st.
Pearse Mrs. Mary 11 Southwood lane
Pearson Arthur (Betchworth house)
    6 The Bank High st.
Pearson Georg e28 Croftdown rd.
Pearson George (Leighton villa) Dart-
    mouth park avenue
Pearson Robert 126 Highgate rd.
Pearson Thomas 37 Twisden rd.
Pearson William Grey 9 Southwood ter.
Peel Alexander Scott 7 Southwood ter.
Pelerin Henry 34 Twisden rd.
Pemberton Joseph 3 Castle yard
Penny John 23 Magdala rd.
Penson Richard 2 Anatola rd.
Pepper James 7 Crown cottages
Peppys Mrs. 15 Gordon house rd.
Percival William 1 Woodview ter.
Perham John (Plevna vil.) Chester vils.
Perrin William 167 Dartmouth park hill
Perring William James 31 Anatola rd.
Perry Charles Henry 32 Spencer rd.
Perry Henry James 37 Raydon rd.
Perry Mrs. 4 Kent's cottages
Perry Walter 13 Brunswick rd.
Perry William D. 27 Langdon rd.
Petford Alfred 24 Hargrave park rd.
Pettifer Arthur 3 North hill ter.
Pettigrew Robert 58 Bickerton rd.
Petyt Mrs. 38 Lady Somerset rd.
Philbey Thomas 5 Swain's lane
Philcox Henry (Northover) Dartmouth
    park avenue
Philcox Mrs. 19 Highgate rd.
Phillips Arthur 51 Lady Somerset rd.
Phillips Mrs. 11 Gordon house rd.
Phillips Mrs. 4 Salisbury rd.
Phillips Mrs. H. 68 Bickerton rd.
Phillips William 7 Spencer rd.

Phippard Samuel 193 Junction rd.
Phippen Simeon 6 Kent's cottages
Piears Frederick 60 Hargrave park rd.
Pike John 3 Wells hill
Pilcher Chas. Hy. 33 Hargrave park rd.
Pincott E. 72 Hargrave park rd.
Pinkstone Thomas W. 27 Twisden rd.
Pinnock Charles 70 Twisden rd.
Piper Joseph 3 Raydon st.
Piper Wm. (Beechwood) Fitzroy park
Pitman William 23 Dartmouth park hill
Pitt William R. 2 Caen ter.
Pittman G. J. W. 18 Woodsome rd.
Pizey Henry 9 Lady Somerset rd.
Platt Mrs. Matilda (St. John's cottage)
    6 Wesleyan pl.
Platten Henry 11 Doynton st.
Player Mrs. 166 Junction rd.
Playfoot William 4 Bartholomew ter.
Plowman Samuel 18 Chetwynd rd.
Pointon George Wm. 29 Holmesdale rd.
Polak Miss Flora 2 Croftdown rd.
Polding Marcella (Meadow cottage)
    Highgate rd.
Poley E. W. 46 Lady Somerset rd.
Pollard Frederick 6 Holmesdale rd.
Poltz Heinrich 229 Junction rd.
Ponsford Arthur (Ranmore) The Bank
Pontin Edmund 8 Vine cottages College
    lane
Poole G. S. 6 Tremlett grove
Poole Mrs. 80 Cromwell avenue
Pope Henry 4 Brunswick rd.
Porter George 51 Holmesdale rd.
Potter Edward Octavius 46 Highgate rd
Potter John 6 Bedford pl.
Potter John (Hanway cottage) 50 Chet
    wynd rd.
Potter T. J. 4 Lady Somerset rd.
Potter William 17 Wood lane
Potts Joseph Ellwood 40 Northwood rd
Praill Edward, jun. 40 Burghley rd.
Praill Edward 64 Lady Somerset rd.
Praill Samuel 14 Woodsome rd.
Pratt Arthur 3 Willow walk
Pratt Cornelius J. 14 St. John the Evange
    list's rd.
Pratt J. A. (Lonsdale house) Dartmouth
    park avenue
Pratt Mrs. 17 Brunswick rd.
Pratt Newton (Harberton) Hornsey lane
Presdee S. 17 St. John the Evangelist's rd
Present Frederic Wm. 11 Lewisham rd.
Press Thomas 11 Victoria cottages
Preston Mrs. Elizabeth 43 Highgate rd
Price H. S. P. 2 The Grove
Price James 63 Spencer rd.

Price James 3 Upper Whittington pl.
Price Miss 84 Dartmouth park hill
Price Mrs. 176 Junction rd.
Priddle James Charles 6 Croftdown rd.
Pridmore Thomas W. (Grosvenor villa) 140 Junction rd.
Priest Mrs. 12 Magdala rd.
Pringle John 31 Oakford rd.
Pringle Thomas 3 Hargrave park rd.
Pryke Alfred 7 Vorley rd.
Pryke William 7 York villas
Pulley Miss 15 Lady Somerset rd.
Puzey Anthony 92 Junction rd.

Quarry Phillip 28 Twisden rd.
Quinton George 14 Spencer rd.

Raban Ebenezer Thos. 53 Chetwynd rd.
Rae Edmund Chadwick 35 Fortess rd.
Raker Slater T. 20 Holmesdale rd.
Ramell Thomas George 15 Chetwynd rd.
Rand Henry 5 Cornwall villas
Rand Mrs. Emma 11 Winscombe st.
Randall Joseph 9 South grove
Ransom W. M. 26 Poynings rd.
Rawlings Charles (Chamelion cottage) Pond sq.
Rawlings William 2 Railway cottages
Rawlins Hy. (The Laurels) Millfield lane
Rawlins W. P., M.D. (Gordon house) The Grove
Rawlinson Edward 16 St. John the Evangelist's rd.
Ray Frederick 40 Magdala rd.
Raybould William J. 19 Poynings rd.
Rayner Thomas James 13 Grove rd.
Raynes Alfred Ernest 62 Woodsome rd.
Raynham Walter 31 Cromwell avenue
Read Samuel 1 Gordon house rd.
Redaway William 84 Cromwell avenue
Reddall Stratford William (Mylor cottage) North hill
Redman Alfred 41 Salisbury rd.
Reed G. R. 37 Poynings rd.
Reed Talbot B. (Tweed house) Cholmeley park
Reeks Henry 15 Carrol rd.
Reeve Edmund 1 Raydon st.
Reeve Henry 43 Girdlestone rd.
Reeve Mrs. 19 Raydon st.
Reeves Miss 2 Lady Somerset rd.
Reeves Robert 70 Bickerton rd.
Reid Christopher 1 Wellington cottages
Reid George W. (Bridge house) 150 Junction rd.
Rendell William 3 Ingestre rd.
Rex William 48 Fortess rd.

Reynolds Alfred J. (Northfield) 87 North road
Reynolds E. R. B., M.R.C.S. (Highcroft) Shepherd's hill rd.
Reynolds Henry 9 Magdala rd.
Reynolds Walter 9 The Grove
Reynoldson H. B. 2 Beaconsfield ter. Archway rd.
Rice Isaac 16 Winscombe st.
Richards William 1 Blenheim pl.
Richardson Edward, North hill
Richardson Frederick, Moreton cottages
Richardson J. 7 Swain's lane
Richardson Mrs. 13 Burghley rd.
Richardson Mrs. (Woodside) Southwood lane
Richardson Thomas 12 Swain's lane
Richmond Arthr Guinness 11 Cromwell pl.
Ricketts F. (Caen wood towers) Hampstead lane
Ridgley Mrs. Elizabeth 22 Spencer rd.
Rimers H. F. 36 Chetwynd rd.
Rintoul Robert 13 Winscombe st.
Rippon William 22 Woodsome rd.
Robb Robert 42 Holmesdale rd.
Roberson Miss Jane 164 Junction rd.
Roberts Alfred T., M.A. (Rosslyn house) 100 North rd.
Roberts Benjamin James 8 Twisden rd.
Roberts John 54 Twisden rd.
Roberts Mrs. 44 Oakford rd.
Roberts William 31 Archway rd.
Robertson John 4 Chetwynd rd.
Robertson Mrs. (Lal-Tiba) Southwood ln.
Robertson Thomas 6 Langdon rd.
Robinson Frederic 26 Chetwynd rd.
Robinson Henry 13 Hargrave park rd.
Robinson James 5 Doynton st.
Robinson John (Byron ho.) 13 North rd.
Robinson John 36 Orchard rd.
Robinson William 6 Ingestre rd.
Robson Mrs. Naomi 21 Wood lane
Rochford James A. 3 Gordon house rd.
Rockhall Charles 11 Townshend yard
Roffe Frederick 4 Railway cottages
Roffe William 18 Langdon rd.
Rogers Edward 17 Bickerton rd.
Rogers Francis 31 Raydon st.
Rogers James Benjamin 8 North rd.
Rogers John R., C.E. 7 Hargrave park rd.
Rogers Mrs. (Bryanston) The Bank
Rogers Richard 1 Dorothy cottages
Rogers W. 4 Beaconsfield ter. Archway rd.
Rollason Mrs. 26 Oakford rd.
Rolls Mrs. 13 Archway pl. Highgate hill
Ronald John Stuart 6 Carrol rd.
Rooff W. B. 3 Cromwell avenue

Room Charles Turner 7 Cromwell pl.
Roome Robert 2 Pleasant row
Root Wm., Holly cottages Archway rd.
Rooth Mrs. John (Greenfield lodge) Archway rd.
Roots George 5 Crown cottages
Roques Frank A. 9 Cromwell avenue
Rose Joseph Henry 31 Carrol rd.
Ross Archibald (The Sycamores) 21 Orchard rd.
Ross William John 52 Junction rd.
Ross William Thomas 30 Carrol rd.
Ross-Murphy William 75 Cromwell avenue
Routledge Augustus 16 York rise
Routledge Henry 21 Holmesdale rd.
Row Mrs. L. R. (Hardwick villa) Archway rd.
Rowe William 15 Tremlett grove
Rowe William E. 134 Junction rd.
Rowley Alfred 64 Twisden rd.
Rowsell E. (Sussex house) North hill
Rowson Thomas 102 Highgate rd.
Rumsey William 181 Junction rd.
Rundell Alfred Robert 26 Northwood rd.
Rushbrooke W. G. 13 Cathcart hill
Russell Richard 14 Salisbury rd.
Ryan Edmund 8 Churchill rd.
Ryder H. 40 Lady Somerset rd.
Ryland Joseph Edgar (Holton lodge) 46 Wood lane

Sabin Joseph Henry 26 Carrol rd.
Sabine Mrs. (Shirley villas) 20 Cromwell avenue
Sadler Miss 3 Park pl. North hill
Sadler Samuel 9 Highgate rise
Sale Charles 161 Junction rd.
Salkeld John (St. John's villa) 34 Junction rd.
Salloway George 64 Spencer rd.
Salmons Henry 16 Langdon rd.
Salsbury Joseph 6 Raydon st.
Samuda Miss Isabelle 3 Lewisham rd.
Sanders James, jun. 14 Townshend yard
Sanders James, sen. 15 Townshend yard
Sanders James Lewis 38 Junction rd.
Sandison Rev. Alexander (Elmside) Southwood lane
Sargant T. J. W. (Talbot house) Broadlands rd. North hill
Sargeant Edward 53 Spencer rd.
Sargeant Joseph F. 14 Cathcart hill
Satur E. Byrne de 1 Clifton villas
Saunders John 106 Highgate rd.
Saunders John 11 Swain's lane
Saunders John Charles 93 Burghley rd.
Saunders Joseph 49 Spencer rd.

Saunders Samuel Desheyes 3 St. John the Evangelist's rd.
Saville C. 11 Vine cottages
Sawday Charles Burt 2 Park villas
Scarnell Herbert (Milverton house) 68 Lady Somerset rd.
Scattergood Edward Wltr. 10 Twisden rd.
Schilbacher Mrs. 9 Dartmouth park av.
Schirges A. R. 30 Poynings rd.
Schnauber John 62 Twisden rd.
Scholefield Rev. Arthur Frederick (Esmonde house) Park house rd.
Schwanzer John 27 Anatola rd.
Scoones Ernest (Wycombe) Bishop's rd.
Scott C. B. 36 Northwood rd.
Scott Herbert 5 Southwood lane
Scott Robert 39 Carrol rd.
Scott Robert Turnbull 7 North grove
Scrimgeour Mrs. Isabella, Merton lane
Scrimgeour Walter 6 The Grove
Scuffle Edward 19 Magdala rd.
Scutchings John 59 Vorley rd.
Seadon John (St. John's house) 21 Oakford rd.
Searl William P. 28 Tremlett grove
Searle Zebulun 6 Prospect ter.
Sears S. 29 Twisden rd.
Seed John 30 Twisden rd.
Seed William 10 Winscombe st.
Sell Clarke (Sterling) 3 Winchester rd.
Selleck Edward 32 Highgate rd.
Selley Charles 2 Cambridge cottages
Semmens Edward 83 Fortess rd.
Senior John 4 Blandford pl.
Shadbolt Mrs. 18 Cromwell avenue
Shallard James B. (Somerset house) 39 Lady Somerset rd.
Sharman Wm. 2 Prospect cots. North hill
Sharp Daniel 3 South Grove cottages
Sharp Martin Charles 5 South grove
Sharp Wm. Herbert 3 Langdon park rd.
Sharpe W. A. 4 Broadlands rd.
Shaw Frederick A. 8 Cholmeley villas
Shaw Mrs. 47 Chetwynd rd.
Shaw Wm. 2 Pleasant cotts. College lane
Sheehy Michael 2 Bickerton rd.
Sheldrick William 45 Spencer rd.
Shelton Edward Lyon (The Sycamores) 19 North rd.
Shenton Edward 34 Dartmouth park hill
Shepheard A.J. (Mayfield) Bishop wood rd
Shepherd Miss (Lauderdale ho.) High st.
Sheppard John 3 Churchill rd.
Sheppard Richard 7 Mansfield cottages
Sheppard William 10a Girdlestone rd.
Sherlock A. J. B. 44 Cromwell avenue
Sherwin Gerald 25 Cromwell avenue

Sherwood Henry 2 Holly lodge villas
Shipham William (Hartington villa) Dartmouth park hill
Shipstone Mrs. John (Cholmeley lodge) High st. Highgate
Shirley John 50 Hargrave park rd.
Shoosmith John 36 Woodsome rd.
Shoosmith William Henry 9 Orchard rd.
Shoppee Miss 48 Hargrave park rd.
Short James 56 Langdon rd.
Shorter Charles (Oak villa) North hill
Shorter George 13 Southwood ter.
ShotterHamilton B. 66 Lady Somerset rd.
Shotter T. E. 20 Oakford rd.
Shury William 33 Woodsome rd.
Shuttlewood John 20 Spencer rd.
Shuttleworth Harry Stanley 5 Grove pl.
Sibley Joseph 8 Orchard rd.
Silk J. F. W., M.D. (Victoria house) 3 Highgate hill
Silvani Alexander 63 Fortess rd.
Silverthorne William Harper 24 Junction rd.
Silvester Mrs.M.A. 33 Cromwell avenue
Silveyra Eugene 38 Woodsome rd.
Sim Alexander 49 Carrol rd.
Sime John 4 Hampstead lane
Simmonds J.(Oaklands)Bishop wood rd.
Simmons John 6 Willow walk
Simpson H. 7 Oakford rd.
Simpson John 17 Vorley rd.
Simpson Mrs. 5 Bedford pl.
Simpson Mrs. 29 Brunswick rd.
Simpson Shepherd (Blenheim) Bishop wood rd.
Simpson Thomas 4aBlenheim pl.
Simpson William 4 Wesleyan pl.
Sims J. C. 4 North pl. North hill
Sims Mrs. 1 Girdlestone cottages
Simson Robert Erskine 44 Chetwynd rd.
Sinclair Bland Gardner 17 Grove rd.
Singleton Francis 74 Spencer rd.
Sinnock Mrs. 19 Chetwynd rd.
Sirr Harry 50 Twisden rd.
Skelhorn William 10 Wood lane
Skinner Henry (Hill view) 61 Cromwell avenue
Skinner Mrs. Emily 3 Mercer ter.
Slatford William 5 Hargrave park rd.
Slight Alfred 2 Wellington cottages North hill
Smee M. 57 Spencer rd.
Smerdon Robert John 91 Fortess rd.
Smith Rev. Edgar, B.A. (The Vicarage) Church rd.
Smith Alfred(Shepherd's cot) Shepherd's hill rd.

Smith Alfred R. 58 Hargrave park rd.
Smith David 16 Lewisham rd.
Smith Edward 36 Spencer rd.
Smith Harry 69 Fortess rd.
Smith Harry (Kyneton lodge) Shepherd's hill rd.
Smith Hy. Richard Cooper 3 The Grove
Smith Henry Thomas 2 Victoria cottages
Smith Jas. 2 Ivy cottages Southwood ln.
Smith James 4 York villas Hargrave park rd.
Smith James Dunn 31 Tremlett grove
Smith John 34 Oakford rd.
Smith John 9 Vine cottages
Smith J. A. 60 Langdon park rd.
Smith Miss 15 Cromwell avenue
Smith Miss 5 Holmesdale rd.
Smith Misses 38 Highgate rd.
Smith Mrs. 2 Grove ter.
Smith Mrs. 42 Spencer rd.
Smith Mrs. F. 36 Carrol rd.
Smith Mrs. Toulmin, sen. 30 Wood lane
Smith Richard 4 Dartmouth park rd.
Smith S. (Reservoir cottage) Dartmouth park hill
Smith Samuel 15 Dartmouth park hill
Smith Samuel 78 Lady Somerset rd.
Smith Thomas 7 Highgate rise
Smith Thomas 137 Junction rd.
Smith Thomas 65 Vorley rd.
Smith Tom (Grove end lo.) Highgate rd.
Smith William 21 Archway pl. Highgate hill
Smith William 99 Burghley rd.
Smith William 27 Magdala rd.
Smith W. A. 11 Grove ter. Highgate rd.
Smith Willoughby 3 North grove
Smythers Alfred (The Poplars) 3 Orchard rd.
Snellgrove Mrs. 4 Crown cottages
Snow Albert 36 Tremlett grove
Snow George, North road cottages
Snow James 11 Raydon st.
Snowton James 41 North rd.
Solomon A. 9 Carrol rd.
SoperFrancis L.,F.L.S. 7 Cholmeley villas
Souter-RobertsonStwrt.11 Croftdown rd.
South Mrs. 4 Tremlett grove
Southcott Deagon 12 Southwood lane
Spain Vice-Admiral D.7 Dartmouth park road
Spain John 14 Hargrave park rd.
Sparks Herbert 50 Woodsome rd.
Sparksman James 43 Raydon st.
Sparrow John Wm. 12 Tremlett grove
Spears Rev. R. (Ivy house) High st.
Speary Alfred Horace 95 Burghley rd.

Spence Mrs. (Ivy house) 6 The Grove Highgate rd.
Spencer John 53 Burghley rd.
Spillett Miss 8 Tremlett grove
Spilling Henry 46 Junction rd.
Spring Mrs. M. 2 Clifton villas
Squires Henry 9 Ingestre rd.
Stagg James Geo. 39 Hargrave park rd.
Stagg Robert (Alfriston house) Bloomfield rd.
Stanbridge E. 4 Mansfield cottages
Standfast George Edwin 2 Southwood pl. Southwood lane
Stanford Edward 49 Girdlestone rd.
Staniforth Thomas Worsley 8 South grove
Stansfield George 21 Grove rd.
Stansbury W. Price (Hollyside) West hill
Stark Thomas 4 Pond sq.
Staunton F. 43 Poynings rd.
Stedall Colonel Robert, J.P. (The Priory) Shepherd's hill rd.
Steeper John 40 Vorley rd.
Stephens Rev. James, M.A. 57 Dartmouth park hill
Stephens George 19 Bickerton rd.
Stephens James 44 Dartmouth park rd.
Stephenson C. S. 72 Junction rd.
Stephenson James 29 Dartmouth pk. rd.
Stephenson Miss 26 Hargrave park rd.
Sterne Frederick 2 Archway villas
Stevens Charles 4 Spencer rd.
Stevens Frederick 42 Bickerton rd.
Stevens Frederick 4 Hargrave park rd.
Stevens Joseph 21 Carrol rd.
Stevenson Robert W. 7 Langdon park rd.
Stiles Mrs. 7 Brunswick rd.
Stiles William 12 St. John the Evangelist's rd.
Stimpson H. 8 Wells hill
Stirling William 36 Langdon rd.
Stock Elliot (Fern lo.) Millfield lane
Stock Isaac 12 Prospect cottages
Stoker John 4 Southwood cottages
Stokes James 21 North rd.
Stokes Thomas Chas. 40 Tremlett grove
Stokes W. 4 St. John the Evangelist's rd.
Stone Charles 114 Dartmouth park hill
Stone Henry 3 Woodview ter.
Stone Mrs. 2 Milton cottages North hill
Stone Mrs. M. (Netheraven cottage) 47 Holmesdale rd.
Storey Allen 1 Bartholomew ter.
Storey James 4 Magdala rd.
Storey Mrs. 3 Kent's cottages
Storr John (Sawley house) 13 Northwold rd.
Story Thomas 3 Beaconsfield ter.

Stott John 1 Cornwall villas
Stott Thomas S., M.R.C.S.E. 1 Highgate rd.
Strange Mrs. 6 Grove ter.
Stratford Mrs. 4 Holly lodge villas Swain's lane
Stratton Mrs. E. 46 Burghley rd.
Street Edmund, Southampton villas
Strevens Geo. (Laura vl.) 30 Woodsome rd.
Strickland Geo. Hy. 30 Lady Somerset rd.
Strickland Robert 9 Raydon st.
Strugnell F. W., L.R.C.P., M.R.C.S., L.S.A. 45 Highgate rd.
Stuart Rev. F. C. 47 Burghley rd.
Sturgess James M. 24 Chetwynd rd.
Suckling Francis James 15 Langdon rd.
Sullivan Mrs. 42 Girdlestone rd.
Sully William 19 Bisham gardens
Sulman James 53 North rd.
Sulman Thomas 49 Chetwynd rd.
Summers Henry 33 Oakford rd.
Sumner John 8 Woodsome rd.
Sumond Madame (Brookfield villa) 5 Highgate rise
Surridge Job 75 North rd.
Sutton Charles 58 Spencer rd.
Sutton F. W. 65 Burghley rd.
Sutton Matthew Bailey 63 Dartmouth park hill
Sutton Miss (Stella house) Cathcart hill
Swan William 4 Ingestre rd.
Sweeting Mrs. (Belgrave villa) 30 Langdon rd.
Swift Thomas 29 Anatola rd.
Symonds H. Lambert 45 Chetwynd rd.

Tackley Mrs. 3 Blandford pl.
Taffs Joseph 1 Southwood ter.
Talbot Charles Hy. 86 Cromwell avenue
Tambling John 21 Dartmouth park hill
Taplin Mrs. L. 13 Cromwell avenue
Tapster Henry 39 Twisden rd.
Tarrier Charles 70 North rd.
Tarry Isaac 14 Mortimer ter.
Tasker John George 30 Junction rd.
Tatham Conway 1 Park pl.
Tatham John, West hill
Tatham T.C. (Millbrook ho.) Millfield lane
Tattersall Mrs. (Portalta lo.) Bishop's rd.
Tatton Charles Thomas 7 Park ter.
Tatum Alfred S. 5 Pond sq.
Tavener J. 22 Oakford rd.
Taylor George 2 Woodsome rd.
Taylor John 15 Anatola rd.
Taylor John 8 Dartmouth park rd.
Taylor John 22 Dartmouth park rd.
Taylor J. Scott, B.A. CANTAB. 34 Chetwynd rd.

Taylor Matthew 49 Archway rd.
Taylor T. 205 Junction rd.
Taylor Thos. (Byron cott.) 17 North rd.
Taylor Thomas 3 Railway cottages
Taylor Twyford 47 Woodsome rd.
Taylor William 25 Salisbury rd.
Taylor William S. 15 Dartmouth rd.
Teedon — 1 Prospect ter.
Terrell Mrs. 4 Southwood ter.
Tester Thomas 90 North rd.
Tew F. W. 160 Junction rd.
Thatcher John Wells 13 Archway rd.
Theobald Wm.(Ivy cottage)Millfield lane
Thomas Henley 3 Wesleyan pl.
Thomas Henry 22 Vorley rd.
Thomas John (Balmain house) Hornsey
lane
Thomas Joseph 6 Castle yard
Thomas Mrs. 5 Chester ter.
Thompson Frederick 30 Chetwynd rd.
Thompson Miss 14 Bickerton rd.
Thompson Mrs. 13 Prospect cottages
Thompson Robert 11 Ingestre rd.
Thompson Wm. Daniel 41 Archway rd.
Thompson William Hy.57Holmesdale rd.
Thomson David C. 7 Holly village
Thomson George(Dartmouth park lodge)
Dartmouth park avenue
Thomson R. 19 Carrol rd.
Thorne Mrs. 52 Fortess rd.
Thornton Fredk.113Dartmouth park hill
Thornton W. 5 Churchill rd.
Thoroughgood William 10 Swain's lane
Thrussell James 18 Orchard rd.
Thwaites George Henry 40 Fortess rd.
Tibbitts Herbert, M.D. (Burfield house)
Archway rd.
Tiffin Miss (Ivy Porch ho.) 90 Fortess rd.
Tigwell John 13 Poynings rd.
Tilley James, North hill
Tillotson Mrs. 9 The Grove
Timewell Alfred 22 Archway rd.
Tims Mrs. 12 Hermitage villas West hill
Tinsdale W. 32 Poynings rd.
Tinsley George 46 Langdon park rd.
Tite Joseph 6 Woodsome rd.
Tod James (Reidsdale) Bloomfield rd.
Tod John (Sans Souci) Bloomfield rd.
Tomlinson Charles 7 North rd.
Tomlinson Herbert 36 Burghley rd.
Tompkins Henry 29 Chetwynd rd.
Tonge Arthur 2 St. John the Evange-
list's rd.
Tonge J. Wilding (Rutland villa) Arch-
way rd.
Towgood Mrs. John 4 The Bank
Townsend William 37 Langdon park rd.

Townshend .W. 3 Dartmouth park rd.
Toyne Wm.(BankPoint cot.)Jackson's ln.
Treacy Martin (Cuthbert's) 9 Winchester
road
Trinder Rev. Daniel, M.A.(The Vicarage)
Hampstead lane
Trinnick John 97 Fortess rd.
Trollope D. 3 Girdlestone cottages
Trotter G. (Legge house) Lewisham rd.
Trowbridge William H. 174 Junction rd.
Truine Mrs. 5 Castle yard
Try Thomas 15 Highgate rd.
Tubby James William 1 Tremlett grove
Tuck Henry 77 North rd.
Tuck William 9 Townshend yard
Tucker E. K. 2 Hargrave park rd.
Tucker John 25 Grove ter.
Tucker Thomas Frost 56 Woodsome rd.
Tuckett Philip D., F.G.S., F.R.G.S., M.R.I.
(Southwood lawn) Jackson's lane
Tugman James E. 21 Lewisham rd.
Tumber Harry 4 Little Green st.
Tupling Misses (Sussex house) Bishop
wood rd.
Turnbull Reginald (Byculla) Broad-
lands rd.
Turner Allen 50 Spencer rd.
Turner George 52 Spencer rd.
Turner Miss, A.C.P. 36 Archway rd.
Turner Mrs. 88 Highgate rd.
Turner Thomas 76 Woodsome rd.
Turner W. 47 Dartmouth park rd.
Turner William 32 Dartmouth park rd.
Turpin Hy. Wm. 37 Hargrave park rd.
Turton William 18 Twisden rd.
Twaits Thomas W. 9 Chester ter.
Tweddle James 110 Fortess rd.
Twemlow-Cooke Rev. Daniel 46 Chet-
wynd rd.
Twyford Frank 8 Anatola rd.
Tyson George 5 Raydon st.

Unwin J. J. 36 Magdala rd.
Upton Mrs. 42 Vorley rd.
Upward Walter 65 Cromwell avenue

Valentine Miss 14 Gordon house rd.
Vandergoot Douwe Jan 5 North rd.
Vanner William Thomas 57 Archway rd.
Vassie William 7 Woodview ter.
Venn Mrs. 29 Oakford rd.
Vezin Mrs. 26 Croftdown rd.
Vincent Alfred 22 Cromwell avenue
Vincer Daniel 13 Ingestre rd.
Vine G. F. 43 Tremlett grove
Vine Joseph 6 Chester rd.
Vines Benjamin 52 Carrol rd.

Violet Albert 4 Prospect ter.

Wackerbath Mrs. 12 Croftdown rd.
Wade Israel Mark (Bracondale) Broad-
    lands rd.
Wade John (Brooklyn)13 Dartmouth rd.
Wade William 20 Hargrave park rd.
Wadham Richard 21 Anatola rd.
Wainwright George 12 Salisbury rd.
Wake Benjamin Barry 27 Grove ter.
Wake Edward George, M.D. 51 Dart-
    mouth park hill
Wakelin Plant (Providence cottage)
    Prospect cottages
Walker Major William Thomas (Lilles-
    hall) Bishop wood rd.
Walker John 1 Park villas
Walker Mrs. 7 Grove ter.
Walker Thomas Christie 24 Orchard rd.
Walker William 233 Junction rd.
Wallace James J. (Winchester house)
    Hornsey lane
Wallace William 57 Langdon rd.
Waller George 104 Highgate rd.
Wallington Charles 4 Alpha villas Arch-
    way rd.
Wallis Thomas 4 Swain's lane
Walmsley F. E. 51 Burghley rd.
Walter Miss M. 89 Fortess rd.
Walton J. H. 12 Cromwell avenue
Walton Peter 11 Chester ter.
Waple Thomas F. (Claringdon villa)
    Archway rd.
Ward Alfred Thomas Adolphus 37
    Archway rd.
Ward Mrs. 21 Lady Somerset rd.
Warde Daniel 179 Junction rd.
Wark Mrs. (Old Hall) South grove
Warn Reuben Thomas, M.R.C.S.E., L.S.A.
    37 Highgate rd.
Warner J. 7 Chetwynd rd.
Warr Alfred 9 Park ter.
Warr John 13 Townshend yard
Warrell J. C. 4 Langdon rd.
Warren Edward 53 Holmesdale rd.
Warren Mrs. 8 Burghley rd.
Warry William K. 38 Vorley rd.
Watchorn Francis 3 Doynton st.
Watkin Albert 16 Cromwell avenue
Watkins Robert 2 Woodview villas
Watkinson James William 41 Raydon st.
Watling Thomas 32 Lady Somerset rd.
Watson John 50 Bickerton rd.
Watson Mrs. (St. John's park house)
    Highgate rd.
Watson Robert, F.R.G.S. (Falcutt house)
    98 North rd.

Watt C. A. 23 Tremlett grove
Watts Edward 8 Lady Somerset rd.
Watts Frederick, M.D. 31 Highgate rd.
Watts John T. 3 Oakford rd
Way John 47 Twisden rd.
Weaver Jas. (The Laurels) 5 Orchard rd.
Weavers Henry 23 Carrol rd.
Webb George 57 Fortess rd.
Webb Jas.E. (The Cottage)Millfield lane
Webb Mrs. Mary½12 Brunswick rd.
Webb Richard 29 Langdon rd.
Webb Richard Mallam 20 Grove ter.
Webb Stephen 34 Spencer rd.
Webley John Roach 1 Brunswick rd.
Webster Miss 43 Oakford rd.
Webster William (Brookfield) 1 High-
    gate rise
Webster William Justus (Tregenna)
    Bishop's rd.
Welch Walter 3 Prospect cottages
Welchman Edward 100 Highgate rd.
Wells Algernon 7 Cathcart hill
Wells Mrs. 27 Archway rd.
Wenham Mrs. (Ivyside) Bloomfield rd.
Wesley John 60 Bickerton rd.
West Daniel Kemp, C.E. (The Cedars)
    2 St. Alban's rd.
West Frederick 2 North hill ter.
West John W. 3 Townshend yard
Westall Richard 15 Salisbury rd.
Westbrook William 25 Carrol rd.
Westhall Thomas 26 Churchill rd.
Westlake John (Pine cot.) North hill
Weston George 7 Grove pl.
Weston J. B. 11 Langdon park rd.
Wetherly W. 6 Chester ter.
Whatley George 82 Dartmouth park hill
Wheatley James Chas. 19 Annesley rd.
Wheeler Albert (Reservoir house)
    Pond sq.
Wheeler Edmund Wm. 53 Archway rd.
WheelerHy.(Harwoodho.)Southwood ln.
Wheeler Mrs. 1 Cathcart hill
Wheeler William 2 Grove pl.
Whibley Ambrose 88 Cromwell avenue
WhiffenFrederick42 Dartmouth park rd.
Whitaker Frederick 25 Doynton st.
White Andrew 15 Prospect cottages
White Benjamin 29 Raydon st.
White Charles 14 Twisden rd.
White Henry Brandon 6 Cholmeley vils.
White James 34 Langdon park rd.
White Miss 4 North hill ter. North hill
White Nicholas 21 Twisden rd.
White Robert 46 Langdon rd.
White Walter W. 29 Carrol rd.
White William 43 Archway rd.

Whitehouse Henry 4 Bickerton rd.
Whiteley Henry 157 Junction rd.
Whiting Charles D. 30 Salisbury rd.
Whitley Edward 4 Holly village
Whitley Oliver Clark 38 Carrol rd.
Whitmore Samuel 62 Spencer rd.
Whitrow Mrs. Charlotte 2 Churchill rd.
Whittington C. J. (Broughton lodge) Shepherd's hill rd.
Whittle Edward 40 Junction rd.
Whyte J. F. 6 Cromwell avenue
Wickham Charles Thomas 55 Burghley road
Wicks James 2 Victoria cottages South grove
Wightwick George 25 Raydon st.
Wilkins Mrs. 1 The Grove
Wilkinson Colonel Josiah (Southampton lodge) Fitzroy park
Wilkinson Miss 197 Junction rd.
Wilks James Smith 3 Grove ter.
Willcox Mrs. Margaret 2 Norman villas
Williams Alfred 12 Winscombe st.
Williams C. 44 Lady Somerset rd.
Williams Edward Phillip (Everley) Southwood lane
Williams Henry 2 Sundial row
Williams Henry Reader (Oak lodge) Jackson's lane
Williams John 36 Croftdown rd.
Williams Miss 38 Chetwynd rd.
Williams Mrs. 70 Fortess rd.
Williams Mrs. Charles 12 Dartmouth park rd.
Williams Richard Wheatley (Endsleigh villa) Southwood lane
Williams Robert B. 8 St. Alban's villas Highgate rd.
Williams Robert John 74 Fortess rd.
Williamson Arthur 54 Spencer rd.
Williamson Mrs. Emma 9 The Bank
Williamson Thomas (West hill lodge) West hill
Williamson William 38 Tremlett grove
Willis D. W. 3 Salisbury rd.
Willis W. 30 Cromwell avenue
Wills Alfred 43 Hargrave park rd.
Wills George (Whitehall) Hornsey lane
Wills H. W. 1 North hill ter.
Wills John K. 67 Highgate rd.
Wills Miss 31 Bickerton rd.
Wills Thomas Hayden (Priestwood) Archway rd.
Willson John E. 43 Dartmouth park hill
Wilmott William 8 Little Green st.
Wilson Frank 31 Twisden rd.
Wilson Joseph 9 Churchill rd.

Wilson Mrs. 2 Girdlestone cottages
Wilson William 56 Fortess rd.
Wiltshire Mrs. 23 Anatola rd.
Winch Frederick 4 Albert villas Archway rd.
Windsor Charles 38 Northwood rd.
Wing William 38 Fortess rd.
Winter George 18 Chester ter.
Winter Henry T. 5 Tremlett grove
Winter William 86 Dartmouth park hill
Wirths Rudolf 19 Wood lane
Wise James 13 Mortimer ter.
Witherden W. 56 Twisden rd.
Witt William B. 73 Fortess rd.
Witty John H. 10 Chester rd.
Woffendale J. 10 Tremlett grove
Wolfe Henry John 41 Chetwynd rd.
Wood George 56 Junction rd.
Wood Henry 2 Vorley rd.
Wood John 46 Spencer rd.
Wood John 60 Spencer rd.
Wood Joseph 171 Dartmouth park hill
Wood Mrs. C. P. 9 St. Alban's villas
Wood Mrs. Hugh 3 Park villas
Wood T. McKinnon (Fernwood) North hill
Wood William (West view) The Bank, High st.
Wood William John 11 Grove rd.
Woodcock Daniel (Conway villa) 18 Bickerton rd.
Wooder William (Alfred cottage) South grove
Woodgate E. 48 Langdon rd.
Woodgate William 5 Cromwell avenue
Woodham George 11 Magdala rd.
Woodnatt William 2 Grove cottages
Woodrow Thomas 45 Vorley rd.
Woodward Mrs. 61 North rd.
Woolley Mrs. (The Yews) 7 Orchard rd.
Woolley Mrs. E. 3 Prospect pl.
Woolmer Alfred J. (The Limes) Dartmouth park avenue
Woolston C. 46 Twisden rd.
Wormald Percy C. 10 Cromwell avenue
Would Mrs. 39 Tremlett grove
Wright Alfred George 11 Dartmouth park avenue
Wright Charles 26 Tremlett grove
Wright Cory (Northwood) Hornsey lane
Wright George 3 Southwood cottages Southwood lane
Wright Henry (Parkfield) 15 Bishop's rd.
Wright Henry 13 Lady Somerset rd.
Wright James 34 Croftdown rd.
Wright John 17 Oakford rd.
Wright J. M. 3 Chester ter.

Wright Mrs. 2 Alpha villas Archway rd
Wright Mrs. 5 Langdon rd.
Wright Mrs., Southwood lane
Wright William Henry 5 Langdon
    park rd.
Wright W. T. 33 Langdon park rd.
Wring Benjamin 14 Winscombe st.
Wyatt Joseph 19 Oakford rd.

Yarnold Charles 1 Cromwell avenue

Yarnold Miss Ellen 1 Cromwell avenue
Yates William Joseph H. 15 Doynton
    street
Yeatman Edward 5 Mansfield cottages
Yeo Thomas 40 Oakford rd.
Yonwin Hy. James 8 Prospect cottages
York Thomas 45 Langdon rd.
Young Thomas 153 Junction rd.
Young W. 28 Poynings rd.
Young William 66 Spencer rd.

THE
HIGHGATE DIRECTORY.

———o———

ALPHABETICAL LIST

OF

TRADESMEN AND OTHERS.

NOTE.—*The Postal District for Highgate is N.*

Further information respecting the situation of Streets may be obtained on reference to the Streets Directory: for instance, anyone requiring the address of William Abbott, grocer, refers to the Alphabetical List of Tradesmen and Others, and finds his address given, 74 High st.; by turning to High st. in the Streets Directory, page 201, it is found described as High st., from Hornsey lane to Southwood lane **C 9**

C 9 *signifies the position of High st. on the Map.*

———

Abbott William, grocer 74 High st.

Acres Benjamin, *The Junction Tavern* 61 Fortess rd.

Acres B. G., grocer and wine merchant 2 Chetwynd rd.

Adney James, bootmaker 92 Highgate rd.

Aldcroft Thos. Agar, laundry, North hill

Alderman Esau, confectioner 1 Mansfield cottages

Aldridge Edward, dairy 93 Dartmouth park hill

Aldridge James, fishmonger 21 Girdlestone rd.

Alexander A. F., greengrocer and fishmonger, Raydon st.

Alford Andrew, baker 7 Willow walk

Anderson Mrs., draper 3 Park ter.

Andrew J., harness maker 42 North rd.

Andrew S., confectioner 75 Junction rd.

Andrews William, bootmaker, North hill

Angell John, cabinetmkr. 20 Highgate rd.

Angell Thos., Grove nursery, Highgate rd.

Applegate Edwin, chmst. 35 Junction rd.

Appleton Robert, baker 46 North rd.

Archway Hardware Stores 98 Archway road

Aris Arthur, bootmaker 10 Dartmouth park hill

Aris Charles, bootmaker 56 Spencer rd. and 4 Upper Whittington pl.

Arlett & Co., horticultural builders, Highgate rd.

Armitage John S., L.D.S., R.C.S., dental surgeon 1 Colva st.

Arrowsmith William, wood engraver 85 Fortess rd.

Ashwell J., contractor 95 Highgate rd.

Atkin Mrs., beer retlr. 139 Highgate rd.

Atkins William, *The Birkbeck Tavern*, Archway rd.

Attkins J., fishmonger, High st.

Attkins Mrs. E., pork butcher and sausage maker, High st.

Avery Mrs., Clyde house laundry 67 Langdon rd.

Babb Henry, carpenter 29 North rd.

Bailey Alfred, watchmaker 19 Brunswick rd.

Bailey Richard, builder and contractor 38 North rd. and Southwood lane

Baker —, oilman 122 Dartmouth pk. hill

Baker & Baker, drapers 14 Junction rd.

Baker Joseph William, farmer (Woodland cottage) North hill

Baker W., general dealer 4 and 5 Southwood lane

Baker Wm., bootmaker 117 Fortess rd.

Baldry & Co., auctioneers 1 Sutton pl. Highgate hill

Baldwin F.,collar drssr. 130aJunction rd.

Baldwin M. A. & Co., laundry (Eagle house) Ingestre rd.

Ballard George, sen., cabinetmaker 58 North rd. and 1 Castle yard

Ballard Geo. Hy., dairyman 30 North rd.

Banks Mrs. William L., laundress 18 Spencer rd.

Barber D., builder 38 Holmesdale rd.

Barber Plant, builder (Myrtle cottage) 36 Holmesdale rd.

Barker William, stationery and music warehouse 119 Fortess rd.

Barltrop Albert T., bootmaker 12 Junction rd.

Barnes James Thomas, builder 8 Whittington pl.

Barnes Mrs., tobccnst 32a Langdon rd.

Barr Thomas, builder 33 Raydon st.

Barrett G. W., crptnr. 24 Brunswick rd.

Bartley Reily Bloxam, bookseller and stationer 58 Carrol rd.

Bassett George,corn dlr. 37 Junction rd.

Bateman William, gardener, North hill

Baumberger J., baker 121 Dartmouth park hill

Baylis W., plasterer 7 Anatola rd.

Beardwell Mrs. Mary Ann, confectioner 50 North rd.

Beare R. H., plumber 3 Dorothy cotts.

Beck Carl, watchmaker 24 High st.

Beckett W.J.,undertaker 70 Junction rd.

Bedwell James, bootmkr. 48 Girdlestone road

Beer William, coffee and dining rooms 1 Whittington pl.

Beer William, stationer 70 Archway rd.

Beeston E. J., milliner 107 Fortess rd.

Bell George, dairyman 6 Park ter.

Belton Mrs. M. A., *The Duke's Head* 16 High st.

Bennett Felix, baker, North hill

Bennett G. W., genl. smith 78 North rd.

Bennis John, wood turner 16 Anatola rd.

Bevan Charles Thomas, *Bull and Last*, Highgate rd.

Bevan W., tea dealer 109 Junction rd.

Beveridge John, *The Lord Palmerston*, Dartmouth park hill

Bezant Samuel H., pawnbroker 8 Junction rd.

Bickerton Richard,grocer 19 Junction rd.

Bilson C. F. & Co., grcrs. 96 Archway rd.

Binley & Co., railway waggon builders, Highgate rd.

Birchall James, gardener 2 Prospect pl.

Blake Mrs., china and glass warehouse 23 Junction rd.

Bloice John, draper 107 Junction rd.

Bloomfield Edward, wheelwright 23 North rd.

Blunt Edward Herbert, *The Boston Hotel* Dartmouth park hill, corner of Junction rd.

Boalch T. J., *The Totnes Castle* 8 Chester rd.

Boardman Mrs., laundry 58 Highgate rd.

Bodmer Richard, f.c.s., analytical chmst. 22 Grove rd.

Bond B. R., fancy draper 21 Junction rd.

Bond David, *Angel Inn*, High st.

Boswell W. J., builder 73 Langdon rd.

Boucher William, farmer and grazier (Grove farm) Highgate rd.

Bower B. W., monumental mason, North road

Bower Thomas L.,draper 139 Dartmouth park hill

Boys' Public Day School Co., Limited, Edward Johnson, secretary (Paddock lodge) Fortess rd.

Brass John, baker 81 Junction rd.

Bray Mrs., nurse 135 Dartmouth park hill

Bretnall W. H. & Co., tracing paper manufacturer, Gordon house rd.

Briggs Miss, servants' registry 30 Highgate rd.

Brightman Benjamin, dining rooms 249 Junction rd.

Brindle George, carpenter (Francis house) North hill

Brindle Mrs., laundress (Francis house) North hill

Brinkworth Robert, shoemaker 165 Dartmouth park hill

Broadbent Thomas,plumber & decorator High st.

Brooks & Co., coal mers., Archway rd.

Brown Arthur,statnr. 19 Whittington pl.

Brown E. W. & Co., chemists 5 Whitting ton pl.

Brown James H., wholesale paper hangings 82 Junction rd.

Brown Mrs., laundress 29 Churchill rd

Brown Theodore, cigarette manufacture 69 Highgate rd.

Brown W., chimney sweep 1 Vine cotts.

Brown Wm., tobacconist 17 Fortess rd.

Brown W. E., watchmaker (Cholmeley house) 18 North rd.

Brown W. T., contractor and carman 2 and 47*a* Langdon rd.

Bruce Alfred, grocer, North hill

Bryant Joseph, butcher 7 Dartmouth park hill

Bryce Geo., wine mer. 32 & 34 High st.

Bulworthy G. E., sweep, Southwood lane

Bumberry Joseph, builder (Rock house) Pond sq.

Bunting J., greengrocer 87 Junction rd

Bürck W. M., ironmonger 14 North rd.

Burland A. Edwin, grocer 64 Archway rd.

Burleigh S., upholsterer 123 Highgate rd.

Burnard W. J., dairy untensil maker 121 Junction rd.

Burrows W. E., grocer; post and telegraph office 88 and 90 High st.

Bush Miss, dressmaker 17 Twisden rd.

Bush Samuel, carpenter 1 Swain's lane

Bushell W., confectioner (Alexandra house) High st.

Buteux E., fruiterer 5 Archway rd.

Butler Mrs. Emma, genl. drpr 11 York rise

Bye Joseph William, stonemason 20 Chester ter.

Canning George, painter, North hill

Canning W. J., plumber, North hill

Cansick Nathan, builder 64 Highgate rd.

Cansick W. N., builder 103 Burghley rd.

Capel L. & E., bootmakers 87 and 89 Highgate rd.

Carroll Richard Henry, shoemaker 4 Prospect pl.

Carter C. A., post office and dairy 137 Dartmouth park hill

Carter Simeon, builder 2 Orchard rd.

Chaffe John Fredk., sweep 9 Fortess rd.

Chaffe Mrs., general shop 9 Fortess rd.

Chamberlain A. H., btmkr. 59 Highgate rd.

Chapman M., drpr. 147 Dartmouth pk. hill

Chapple Charles, grocer 2 Spencer rd.

Chetwynd College for Girls ; Miss A. E. Ramell, P.C.P. 15 Chetwynd rd.

Child James, carpenter 13 Vorley rd.

Chipp James, tobacconist 4 Archway rd.

Chitty Edwin, florist 38 High st.

Cholmeley School Sanatorium (Cholmeley lodge) Southwood lane ; Mrs. Wade, caretaker

Christmas Peter, beer retailer 143 Dartmouth park hill

Chubb J. R., dairyman 251 Junction rd.

Churchill A., baker 63 Highgate rd.

Churchill Henry, french polisher 25 Anatola rd.

Claridge Geo., stonemason 6 Bertram st.

Clark Benjamin, cowkeeper 1*a* York rise

Clark Henry John, plasterer 7 Bertram st.

Clark Mrs. M., *The Green Dragon* 10 North rd.

Clarke & Co., dyers, &c. 221 Junction rd.

Clarke Thomas, greengrocer 78 High st.

Coat Jacob & Co., general and cemetery masons 158 Junction rd.

Cohen W. H., crvr. & gldr. 22 Orchard rd.

Cokeham George, carrier 2 White's cotts.

Cole C., stationer and librarian (Llama house) 18 High st.

Cole John, grocer 4 Whittington ter.

Cole Richard, decorator 17 Chester ter.

Cole Thos., sweets dlr. 13 Annesley rd.

Colebrook Stphn., butcher 41 Junction rd.

Coles John, furniture dealer 17 Whittington pl.

Coles Thomas, cab prop., Prospect cotts.

Collinson Edwin Charles, pianoforte tuner 17 Churchill rd.

Colson Thornton E., undertaker 4 Girdlestone rd.

Colson T. E., undertaker 27 Archway pl.

Constable T., fishmonger and poulterer 2 High st.

Cookson Frederick, tobacconist 16 Dartmouth park hill

Cookson George, cab proprietor 16 Dartmouth park hill

Cooper Geo., pork butcher 1 Fortess rd.

Cooper Miss, dressmaker 58 Twisden rd.

Corder G. A., mineral water manufacturer 64 High st.

Cornwall & Devonshire Dairy Farm Produce Co. 96 Highgate rd.; Edward W. Small, manager

Cottis Mrs., general shop 39 Salisbury rd.

Cowper Wm., carpenter 67 Junction rd.

Cox & Thornton, coal merchants 117 Highgate rd. and 6, 7, and 8 Coal bays Mortimer ter.

Cox Charles, carman 10 Brunswick rd.

Cox Edward, oil and italian warehouse 17 Junction rd.

Cox George, coal merchant 5 Carrol rd.

Cox Thornton, coal mer. 128 Highgate rd.

Coxhead Mrs., haberdshr. 4 Southwood ln.

Craig J., jobmaster, Archway rd.

Craig William D., engineer 32 Wood lane

Cresswell E., baker 104 Junction rd.

Creswick Henry, verger of St. Mary Brookfield 76 Spencer rd.

Crocker H. H., dairy 62 Archway rd.
Crocker Peter, bootmaker 97 Dartmouth park hill
Crowe Daniel, builder 27 Highgate rd.
Cruice William, coffee ho. 61 Highgate rd
Cunnington John, cheesemonger 106 Junction rd.
Curnow Miss, dressmkr. 51 Archway rd.
Currey William, tobacconist 2 Sutton pl.
Cutbush Wm.&Son, nurserymn., West hill
Cutbush William, stationer, High st.
Cuthbert Tom, butcher 44 North rd.

Dace Gustavus Orlando, professor of music 9 Twisden rd.
Daines David, greengrocer 46 Vorley rd.
Dainton S., furniture dlr. 99 Highgate rd.
Daniels Henry & Co., cemetery masons (Church house) South grove Swain's lane & Chester rd. Highgate New town
Davies Charles, dairyman, South grove
Davies G., dairy 104 Archway rd.
Davies James C., grocer 56 High st.
Davis Caleb, gardener 3 Winscombe st.
Davis Joseph, sweep 3 Blenheim pl.
Davis Mrs. S.A., professional cook 3 Winscombe st.
Dawson George, horticultural builder (Acacia house) Highgate hill
Dawson Samuel, plumber and decorator 44 Brunswick rd.
Dean Albert, stationer and confectioner 62 Brunswick rd.
Dean Charles, sanitary inspector 9 Woodview ter.
Dean Homer, bootmkr. 62 Highgate rd.
Dean Misses, tobacnts. 9 Woodview ter.
Deane Geo. Arthur, baker 86 Retcar st.
Dettmer James, general shop 29 Dartmouth park hill
Dettmer James, genl. shop 2 York rise
Dick Whittington Coffee Tavern 5 Sutton pl. Highgate hill
Dickeson W., ale stores 7a Girdlestone rd.
Diggins George, painter 29 Doynton rd.
Dixon J. W., builder 1 South grove
Dodd R. H., clockmaker 92 North rd.
Dodd William, farrier, High st.
Doggrell Stanley, tbccnst 158 Fortess rd
Dolley Miss, draper 28 North rd.
Douglas James, french polisher 13 Anatola rd.
Dove William L., florist (Dartmouth park nursery) York rise
Draper T., dairy 129 Fortess rd.
Drinkwater R. W., coffee & dining rooms 7 Whittington pl.

DUGGIN J. F. & CO., dyers to H.M. the Queen & H.R.H. the Prince of Wales 42 Duke st. Manchester sq. and 37 Craven rd. Lancaster gate
Dunbar Miss H., stationer 6 Fortess rd.
Dunkley Thos., cemetery mason, Swain's lane
Dunmill Joseph C., printer 119 Junction rd.
Dunn James, zinc worker 6 Dartmouth park hill
Durnford Henry, builder 44 Junction rd.
Dyble Robert and Son, bootmakers 72 High st.
Dyer Robert William, *The Dartmouth Arms*, York rise
Dyke & Son, marble and stone works 53 Highgate rd.

Earl Lancelot, bootmaker 7 High st.
Eastman Mrs., grocer and cheesemonger 59 Holmesdale rd.
Easun Thomas, builder 74 Highgate rd.
Easun Wm., decrtr.&undrtkr.16 Carrol rd.
Economical Boot Repairing Company 116 Junction rd.
Edgerton John, baker 151 Dartmouth park hill
Edgington Hy., carpntr. 20 Winscombe st.
Edwards Wm., greengrcr. 11 Junction rd.
Elkins W.H., watchmaker 24 Archway pl.
Elliott B.G., timber merchant, Fortess rd
Ellis Wm., carriage bldr. 98 Highgate rd.
Emsley George, servants' registry 19 Junction rd.
Engall H. M., bootmaker 2 Fortess rd.
Engall Mrs., toy dealer 2 Fortess rd.
Engall T. N., gas and sanitary engineer 109 Highgate rd.
English Thomas, beer and wine retailer 155 Dartmouth park hill
Enoch Thos., dairy 8 Dartmouth park hill
Erbach Bros., bakers 59 Junction rd.
Esom M. W., wheelwright, Archway pl
Esom Morris W., marine store dealer 6 Archway pl.
Etheridge John, *The Brookfield Tavern* 119 Dartmouth park hill
Evans H., bootmaker 67 Junction rd.
Everson E., hairdresser 10 Fortess rd.

Farr J. E., corn dealer 108 Junction rd.
Faux Edward, estate agent, &c. 54 Archway rd.
Feloj Joseph, confectnr. 3 Archway rd.
Fenn Henry & Co., coal merchants Gospel oak station

Fenn John, coffee rooms 15 Junction rd.

Fernee T. F., bootmaker, North hill

Field Mrs., laundress 15 Brunswick rd.

Filler Richard Henry, turncock, High st.

Fisher Edwd.,glover, &c. 183 Junction rd.

Flack and Sons, oil and colourmen 5 Whittington ter.

Fleming Francis A., corn dealer 27 and 33 North rd.

Fleming Wm., decorator 17 Archway pl.

Fletcher S., dairy 6 Highgate rd.

Fleury Felix, genl. shop 12½ Archway pl.

Flint Wm., brass finisher 16 Fortess rd.

Floyd William, stationer 14 Dartmouth park hill

Folkes Mrs. Eliza, *The Gate House Hotel*, North hill

Ford Walter, plumber 68 Junction rd.

Fordham Isaac, rustic worker (Gladstone villa) Dartmouth park hill

Fowler T. N., fishmonger 3 Dartmouth park hill

Foxford William, greengrocer, York rise

France H.& Son,undertakers 32 Grove ter.

Fraser & Heigh, auctioneers 35 Fortess rd.

Freeman Robert, baker 46 High st.

French J. W.,confectioner 133 Dartmouth park hill

Friend William, rag dealer 6 Townshend yard High st.

Frost A., fancy repository 29 Junction rd.

Fudge R. C.& Co., grocers 153 Dartmouth park hill

Furber Alfred William, dentist 13 Highgate rd.

Gamble Mrs. William, dressmaker 1 St. John the Evangelist's rd.

Gamman, Son & Carter, coal merchants, Gospel oak station

Gardener William M., tailor 3 Pond sq.

Gardiner Robert, baker 7 Junction rd.

Gardner Thomas, jobmaster 8 North rd.

Garrett Henry, butcher 62 High st.

Gawan Alfred, artist 19 Tremlett grove

Geard A., builder, sawing and planing mills 72 Retcar st.

George Charles William, cigar stores 2 Archway pl.

George E., genl. shop 46 Brunswick rd.

Gibbs & Imber, joinery works and builders, North hill

Gieve Thos., umbrella mkr. 22 North rd.

Glass H. G., florist, Millfield lane

Golden Charles, coffee rooms 1 Park ter. Archway rd.

Goodwin A.,provision mer.61 Archway rd.

Graddage Stephen J., *The Wellington Inn*, Archway rd.

Graham Geo. F., organ builder 63 Archway road

Gray Francis Henry, watchmaker 111 Junction rd.

Greaves Philip H., diamond jeweller 103 Fortess rd.

Green George, coal and coke merchant 34 Magdala rd.

Green George Frederick, tobacconist 9 Whittington pl.

Green William, plumber 11 Fortess rd.

Green W. J., chemist 67 Carrol rd.

Greenfield J., tobacconist 89 Junction rd.

Gregory William, grocer 39 Junction rd.

Griffiths Mrs. C., *The Old Crown*, Highgate hill

Groom and Pride Misses, dressmakers 24 Northwood rd.

Groom Charles, plumber 14 Archway pl.

Grupel Mrs.,marine strs.60 Brunswick rd.

Grosse Chas.,greengrocer 57 Highgate rd.

Grosse W. F., fishmngr. 55 Highgate rd.

Grou Thomas, clock-wheel cutter 21 Brunswick rd.

Hall W. T., undertaker 2 Highgate rd.

Hamp Joseph S., tailor 72 North rd.

Hanchet and Co., cemetery masons, Swain's lane

Hanna Francis, livery stables 141 Dartmouth park hill

Harding J. W., The Langdon oil and colour stores 93 Langdon rd.

Harding Mrs., upholsteress, High st.

Hards Jas., auctioneer 124 Junction rd.

Hardy John, *The Victoria*, North hill

Harman & Preston, dressmakers 163 Dartmouth park hill

Harmonium and American Organ Factory, H. Carlon & Co., Dartmouth park hill

Harris Fredk., fruitr. 10 Whittington pl.

Harris John, bootmaker 20 Archway pl.

Harrison Wm. G., oilman 16 North rd.

Hartland Charles J., *Prince of Denmark* 151 Junction rd.

Hatten William S., cowkeeper and dairyman 103 Highgate rd.

Hawkins S. J., fine art repository 4 Park ter. Archway rd.

Hayes John, leather and grindery stores 2 Whittington ter.

Hayhoe T., veterinary forge 45 North rd.

Hazell Alfred, corn dealer 4 Junction rd.

Hazell Joseph, livery stbls. 6 Junction rd.

Hazlewood Henry, beer retailer 80 Highgate rd.

Heal B., furniture dealer 133 Fortess rd.

HEATH HENRY, hat manufacturer 105, 107 & 109 (late 393) Oxford st. Ladies' show room. Awarded gold and silver medals at Health Exhibition

Heath Wm. James, baker 76 Archway rd.

Heming J., grocer 18 Highgate rd.

Hensby Mrs., laundress 16½ Girdlestone rd.

Hensby Samuel, builder 15 Girdlestone rd.

Heptinstall Wm., carpntr. 3 White's cots.

Herapath Mrs. Sarah, laundry (Spring cottage) 34 Holmesdale rd.

Herbert R. J., oilman 62 Carrol rd.

Herring George, hatter 13 Junction rd.

High School for Girls; Miss Matilda Sharpe, manager (Channing house) The Bank

Highgate Emporium (The) 40 High st.

Hill John C., builder 32 Archway rd.

Hiller Wm., pork butcher 27 Junction rd.

Hinch Jas., grocery store 155 Highgate rd.

Hine A., mason 57 Chester rd.

Hirst John, builder 54 Carrol rd.

Hiscott Mrs., genl. shop 8a Girdlestone rd.

Hoare P., pianoforte mnfctr. 64 Fortess rd.

Hobbs A. I., dairyman 61 Junction rd.

Hodgson Wm., bootmkr. 115 Junction rd.

Hofmann Frederick, confectioner 6 Whittington ter.

Holland & Walter, dressmkrs. 89 Fortess rd.

Holland Miss, dressmaker 1 Archway vils.

Holmes & Sons, builders 10 High st.

Holmes Benjamin, hairdresser, High st.

Holmes W. R., grocer 63 Carrol rd.

Homewood Spencer, baker, North hill

Honour Francis, gas and hot water engineer 74 Hargrave park rd.

Honour Wm., tbccnst. 123 Junction rd.

Horsley Thomas, baker 3 South grove

Horwood W., decorator 22 High st.

Howard E. S., sweets dlr. 129 Fortess rd.

Howes William, tobacconist 117 Dartmouth park hill

Howson Henry, *The Junction Arms* 86 Junction rd.

Hughes Henry, brushmaker 101 & 103 Junction rd.

Hulme Edward, baker 31 Salisbury rd.

Hunt M. & Sons, greengrocers 12 North rd.

Hunt Montague William, tobacconist 147 Highgate rd.

Hunt Robert, cab proprietor 1 Victoria cottages South grove

Huntington H., Northfield drill hall, North rd.

Hurrell Jas., pork butcher 57 Junction rd.

Hurwood W., tailor 95 Junction rd.

Huskisson F., plumber 159 Dartmouth park hill

Hutton Mrs., laundress 18 Wood lane

Hutton Robert, gardener 18 Wood lane

Imperial Sanitary Steam Laundry (Eagle house) Ingestre rd.

International Tea Co. 5 Junction rd.

Inwood Thomas, china and glass warehouse 128 Junction rd.

Irvin Henry, carman 1 Anatola rd.

Irvin Mrs., sweets dealer 1 Anatola rd.

Jackson John, grocer 2 Park ter.

Jackson Mrs., dressmaker 75 Fortess rd.

James Mrs., dress & mantle mkr. 20 High st.

James Thomas, coachbuilder 20 High st.

James William, dispensing chemist 85 Highgate rd.

Jasmine Laundry (The) 90 Highgate rd. and 6 Pleasant row

Jefferys Mrs., confectioner 2 Upper Whittington pl.

Jenkin George, artists' brush manufacturer 155 Junction rd.

Jenkins John, bricklyr. 38 Salisbury rd.

Jenkins W., bricklayer 20 Vorley rd.

Jentle Reuben & Sons, Whittington nursery 1 Upper Whittington pl.

Johnson E., jobmaster (The Vine Stables) 82 and 84 Highgate rd.

Johnston Mrs. Mary Ann, dairy, and coachbuilder, North hill

Jolliffe E. Anthony, btmkr. 1 Annesley rd.

Jones E., draper 115 Fortess rd.

Jones Fredk., hairdresser 1 Archway pl.

Jones S., carver and gilder 80 Junction rd.

Judge Thomas, watchmaker and jeweller, High st.

Keane Mrs., greengrocer 7 Fortess rd.

Keane Thomas, mason 7 Fortess rd.

Keast James, builder 137 Highgate rd.

Kelly William & Son, builders & decorators 7 Whittington ter. Highgate hill

Kelly William, stationer 76 High st.

Kendrick James, decorator 23 Vorley rd.

Kentish Chas., bldr. & dcrtr. 50 Fortess rd.

Kerry & Hollidge, builders 7 Upper Whittington pl.

Kerry Edward & Son, builders and contractors, High st.

Kessels P. M., builder 48 Northwood rd.

Ketley Thos., greengrcr. 2 Winscombe st.

Key Thomas, greengrocer 35 North rd.

Kindell Jas., bootmaker 24a Vorley rd.

KingBros.,tobacconists 237aJunction rd.

King Joseph, fishmonger 4 Archway pl.

King Mrs., marine stores 109 Dartmouth park hill

Kitson Richd., ironmonger 10 York rise

Knowles Samuel, bootmkr.15 Fortess rd.

Koblich & Son, tailors 130c Junction rd.

Kurz A., baker 6 Whittington pl.

La Gyoury John, musical instrument maker 1 Crown cottages

Laing Henry J., carpenter 18 Vorley rd.

Lamb J., coal merchant 77 Junction rd.

Lambert J., builder 31 Fortess rd.

Lambert W., stationer 118 Junction rd.

Lamerton Thomas, monumental mason (Ebenezer house) 1 Chester ter.

Lascelles Jonathan T.; cheesemonger 43 Junction rd.

Law William, *The Whittington Stone,* Highgate hill

Lawford & Sons, lime,brick, and cement merchants, Archway rd.

Lea & Co., coal depôt, Archway rd.

Leach Henry, draper 65 Highgate rd.

Leader Mrs., laundress 3 & 4 Vine cotts

Leaver H., china and glass dealer 105 Highgate rd.

LeCrenL.H.,tobacconist 106Archway rd.

Lee Fredk.,tobacconist 143 Junction rd.

Lee Joseph, oilman 1 Sutton pl.

Lee Miss, dressmaker 6 Wells hill

Leiros J. de, piano tuner108 Highgate rd.

Lilleshall Company (The); JohnJefferys, wharf manager, Gospel oak station

Linford Wm., carpenter 4 Annesley rd.

Ling James, greengrocer and fruiterer 56 Carrol rd.

Ling John, general shop 23 Annesley rd.

Lingwood George, bookseller and stationer 73 Junction rd.

Lion Cigar Stores 31 Junction rd.

Lipscombe Owen, hairdrssr. 26 High st.

Lloyd Edward M., silversmith 2 Wesleyan pl.

London & South Western Bank, Limited, Highgate branch (Hornsey house) 14 High st.; W. T. Snell, manager

London General Provision Stores 93 Junction rd.

London Mrs. S. A., china and glass warehouse 84 Junction rd.

London Street Tramway Company's Depôt, Junction rd.

LongmanMiss,drssmkr. 3Wellington ter.

Lorimer & Co., manufacturing chemists 42 & 44 Hargrave park rd.

Lott Bros., cheesemongers 2 Junction rd.

LovelockThos,*TheTallyHo!*13Fortess rd.

Lowe William F., bootmaker 50 High st.

Lowen & Sons, carmen 1 Pond sq.

Lowen Robt.,brcklyr. 3 Bartholomew ter.

Lower F. J., oilman 112 Junction rd.

LunchHenry,hairdresser126Junction rd.

Lunniss W., hairdresser 11 Upper Whittington pl.

Lunnon James, bootmaker 84 High st.

Lupton Mrs. Emma, *The Coopers' Arms* 48 High st.

Lyddon William H., boot and shoe warehouse 45 and 47 Junction rd.

McCall Edward W., umbrella maker 163 Dartmouth park hill

McClune S., stationer 80 Dartmouth park hill

McCormick William and Son, builders (Hillside) Grange rd.

Macdonald Jas., grngrcr. 11 Archway pl.

Main Thomas, smith 124 Highgate rd. and Little Green st.

Maisey Thomas, cheesemonger 153 Highgate rd.

Maishman Charles Kaye, *The Rose and Crown* 86 High st.

Mallett William, cabinetmaker 4 Dartmouth park hill

Manlove Joseph Henry, ironmonger 63 Junction rd.

Markham Thomas T., plumber 11 Park ter. Archway rd.

Marks William, cemetery foreman (Russell house) South grove

Marriott Mrs., corn dealer 58 High st.

Martin & Co., drapers 66 High st.

MartinRobert,contrctr. 15Winscombe st.

Martin Wm., stationer 145 Junction rd.

Maskell William, *Duke of St. Alban's,* Highgate rd.

Matton Thomas, carman and contractor 2 Hope cottages College lane

May, Burck & May, printers 70 High st.

Maybin Mrs., shirt and collar dresser 28 Highgate rd.

Mayer S., watchmaker 79 Fortess rd.

Meakin G. R., greengrocer 15½ Upper Whittington pl.

Mercer J. C., tea dealer 59 Archway rd.

Milborn Wm., florist 61 Holmesdale rd.

MilesWm.,cheesemngr. 119 Highgate rd.

Mills George, builder 41 Dartmouth park hill

Mills George P., monumental mason 11 Chester rd.

Millward James, cemetery mason 35 Raydon st.

Milton Hy., grocer 12 Dartmouth pk. hill

Milton I., fishmonger 3 Fortess rd.

Mitchell Joseph H. & Co., coal merchants 1, 2 & 3 Coal bays, Mortimer ter. and 115 Highgate rd.

Mitton William, hairdresser and wigmaker 5 High st.

Mixer William J., draper 68 Archway rd. and 157 Highgate rd.

Mizen Robt. Geo., beer retailer 8 High st.

Modena Mrs., grocer 64 Brunswick rd.

Moon M. J., chemist 149 Junction rd.

Morgan R., carpets beaten and re-laid 60 Highgate rd.

Morgan T., greengrocer 60 Highgate rd.

Mortimer J., fruiterer and greengrocer 151 Highgate rd.

Morton Wm. Jas., fishmngr. 3 Junction rd.

Muir Edward, draper 122 Junction rd.

Munday William, tailor 4 Fortess rd.

Mullins Mrs., College house laundry, College lane

Munns George, grocer 46 Raydon st.

Murrey Miss, ladies' school 26 Langdon rd.

Murthwaite E.S., coff. ho. 114 Junction rd.

Neal Edwin, greengrocer 103 Dartmouth park hill

New Co-operative Coal Co., Gospel oak station ; William Owen, secretary

New F. A. & Co., coal merchants, Gospel oak station

New Pure Beverage Company, Limited 14 & 16 Poynings rd. ; J. H. W. Rumsey, secretary

New River Co.'s Station, Hornsey lane

New Mrs. M., coal dealer 5 Willow walk

Newman A., dentist 42 Raydon st.

Newman Misses M. E. & F., milliners 28 High st.

Newton James, *The Winchester Hall Hotel* 94 Archway rd.

Nix Charles, dairy 115 Dartmouth park hill and 25 Junction rd.

Norman Ebenezer, fruiterer and greengrocer 145 Dartmouth park hill

Norris E. J., *The Red Lion* 94 North rd.

Norris William, fruiterer and greengrocer 5 Dartmouth park hill

Norton Nathaniel, photo. 215 Junction rd.

Oatley Mrs., laundress 6 York rise

O'Hara Wm., butcher 75 & 77 Highgate rd.

Oliver & Smith, cemetery masons, Swain's lane and Highgate rd.

Oliver F., umbrella maker 26 Highgate rd.

Oliver Henry, gardener 60 North rd.

Oliver Jas., colliery agent 99 Fortess rd.

Oliver Mrs., laundress 60 North rd.

Opie Bennett, cheesemngr. 105 Fortess rd.

Orton Charles, grocer 4 Sutton pl.

Outing Samuel, bootmaker 5 Wellington ter. North hill

Ovens Edward, tailor 69 Junction rd.

Owen A., wardrobe dealer 2 Archway rd.

Oxford Chas., plastr. 58 Brunswick rd.

Pachett John, signalman 2 Wood lane

Page Frederick, farrier 76 Highgate rd.

Page Hy. Wm., slate mer. 93 Fortess rd.

Pain Henry, architectural modeller 47 Highgate rd.

Panzer & Co., confctnrs. 109a Fortess rd.

Panzer & Co., tobacconists 109 Fortess rd.

Parker J. W., piano and music warehouse 51 Junction rd.

Parkins George H., wine merchant 49 Junction rd.

Parmenter T., fruiterer and greengrocer 101 Highgate rd.

Parr John, bootmaker 101 Junction rd.

Parry Henry James, veterinary forge, Archway rd.

Parsons John, beer retlr. 16 Archway pl.

Paterson Francis, baker and confectioner 141 Highgate rd.

Payne George, gardener and florist 17 Upper Whittington pl.

Peachey Alfred, confctnr. 2 South grove

Peacock T. P., ham and beef warehouse 131 Fortess rd.

Peet George, plasterer 1 Prospect cotts.

Pendred, Applebee & Co., wine stores 66 Archway rd.

Pensionnat for Young Ladies, Highgate rd.

Perry Z., china and glass mender 16 Highgate rd.

Perry Z., umbrella mkr. 16 Highgate rd.

Phillips E. T., grocer 255 Junction rd.

Phillips J., *The Bell & Horns* 31 North rd.

Philp William, butcher 9 Junction rd.

Phippen E., gardener (Rose nursery) Swain's lane

Pietrowicz Wladyslaw, hairdresser 95 Dartmouth park hill

Pim H., jeweller 99 Dartmouth pk. hill

Pinxton Colliery Co. 4 & 5 Coal bays Mortimer ter.

Pitcher Henry, tailor 8 Archway pl.

Plant John, plumber (Homer cottage) Annesley rd.

Pleaden Robert, tailor 12 Highgate rd.

Pook W., gardener 24 Spencer rd.

Porter and Sons, artists' colourmen 78 Highgate rd.

Porter D., oilman 79 Highgate rd.

Potter A., fishmonger 117 Junction rd.

Powell Jas.,newsvendor 32a Langdon rd.

Preece Fredk., *The Vine* 86 Highgate rd.

Price Edward, mason 92 Langdon rd.

PRICKETT, VENABLES & CO., auctioneers 32 High st.

Pringle H. & M., clothiers and outfitters 20 North rd.

Pringle Mrs., professed cook 1 Townshend yard

PurseyG.F.,picture dlr.130b Junction rd.

Puttock Robt.,bricklayer 38 Langdon rd.

Ramsway Charles, *The Woodman*, Archway rd.

Randall Henry, tailor 120 Junction rd.

Randall Joseph G., butcher 82 High st.

Rawlings William, dyer, High st. and 149 Highgate rd.

Ray Mrs. E., newsagent 18 Archway pl.

Read Thomas, dairy 130a Junction rd.

Reading & Coffee Rooms 2 Raydon st.

Reavley Frank, brush dealer 101 Dartmouth park hill

Reavley Mrs., dressmaker 101 Dartmouth park hill

Redfern Walter F., coff. rms. 58 North rd.

Reed J. S., draper 54 North rd.

Rees Wm., cabinetmaker 62 Junction rd.

Reeve Thomas, gardener (Lauderdale lodge) Dartmouth park hill

Richardson & Co., ironmongers 6 South grove

Rickard John,greengrcr. 110 Junction rd.

Rickett, Smith & Co., coal merchants 113 Highgate rd.

Roberts Chas.,greengrcr. 29 Salisbury rd.

RobinsFredk.,stationer2 Whittington pl.

Rogers & Co., grocers 121 Fortess rd.

RogersG.,cook & confectioner 68 High st.

Rogers George, coal mer. 19 Archway pl.

RogersJohn,photographer48 Junction rd.

Rogers Robert, hatter 44 High st.

RollingsonChas.,gasfitter 12 Archway pl.

Routledge John, cabinetmaker 243 Junction rd.

Rowe& Harvey,builders 1 Northwood rd.

Rowe Alfred, hairdresser 6 Archway rd.

Rowe W., builder & dcrtr. 16 Junction rd.

Rowe William, builder 11 Northwood rd.

Rowell P., statnr. 131 Dartmouth pk. hill

RowleyFrdk.,estate agnt.221Junction rd

Roylance Charles, shirt & collar dresser 241 Junction rd.

RushJohn,bootmkr.66&134 Highgate rd.

Rushton Samuel, cheesemonger 10 Junction rd. and 3 Whittington ter.

Ruth Engelbert, watch and clock maker 94 Highgate rd.

Rutherford William, paperhanger 15 Archway pl.

RyanGeo.,butcher 127Dartmouth pk.hill

Safe Misses E. & A., baby linen warehouse 97 Junction rd.

St. George's Distillery,P. Applebee & Co. 154 Fortess rd.

St. John's Park House Ladies' School, Mdlles. Kœune and Mrs. Watson, Highgate rd.

Salmon Joseph, oil and colourman 85 Junction rd. & 12, 14 & 127 Fortess rd.

Saltford George,laundry 16 Spencer rd. Dartmouth park hill

Sanders Mrs.,dressmaker 5 Highgate rd.

Sanitary Laundry Co. 67 Highgate rd.

Sargood Alfred Leonard, tailor 3 Southwood lane

Saunders Chas., chemist 4 & 6 North rd.

SaundersThomas,gardener 3 Swain's lane

Sawyer John, commission agent 179 Dartmouth park hill

Scanes & Son,plumbers 125 Highgate rd.

Scotchman Samuel, builder, York rise

Scott & Co., builders & decorators 253 Junction rd.

Scott John, gardener 25 Wood lane

Scott John,sen.,gasfitter 245 Junction rd.

SeabrookJames, gardener 10 Anatola rd.

Seager Geo., cheesmngr. 81 Highgate rd.

Secker Thomas, builder 114 Highgate rd.

Seed George, builder and decorator 1 Norman villas Archway rd.

Seed Richard, decorator 23 Doynton st.

Sharpe H.U.,furniture dealer40North rd.

Shaw Alexander, *The Whittington and Cat*, Highgate hill

Sheen Frederick Thomas, nurseryman 6 Victoria cottages

Shenton Edward, slate merchant and slater, Gospel oak station

SherlockWilliam,gardenr.1Judd cottages

Shilton George, grocer 83 Junction rd.

Shirtliff F., chemist and dentist 72 Archway rd. and 143 Highgate rd.

Shoeing Forge ; G. W. Bennett, Dartmouth park hill

K

Shorter J., station mstr., Shepherd's hillrd.

Silvester Arthur, *The Red Lion & Sun* 25 North rd.

Simms J. & Co., dairy 43 Salisbury rd.

Simonds S., butcher 111 Fortess rd.

Simpson Isaac, *The Lion Tavern* 1 Junction rd.

Sims Alfred & Co., carriage builders 62 Highgate rd.

Sindell Thomas, bootmaker & wardrobe dealer 15 and 16 Whittington pl.

Skelton Samuel, baker 239 Junction rd.

Skinner & Co., grocers 152 Fortess rd.

Skinner John A., baker 8 York rise

Slater Miss Sarah, grocer 247 Junction rd.

Small William, baker 3 Archway pl.

Smith B. W., butcher 79 Junction rd.

Smith Edward, fly proprietor, Highgate rd.

Smith Fredk., watchmaker 99 Junction rd.

Smith George, greengrocer 52 North rd.

Smith Henry & E., drapers 97 Highgate rd.

Smith Henry, oilman 74 Archway rd.

Smith J. A., upholsterer 100 Dartmouth park hill

Smith Mrs. E. A., draper 3 Sutton pl. Highgate hill

Smith Mrs. Mary Ann, boot warehouse 65 Carrol rd.

Smith William, confectioner and general dealer 5 Archway pl.

Smith Wm., laundry 2 Prospect cottages

Smith William, mason 71 Langdon rd.

Smith W. A., monumental mason 13 Raydon st.

Southcott & Co., bldrs., Southwood lane

Southgate Mrs. Henry, dressmaker (Victoria house) High st.

Stacey William, bootmaker 135 Dartmouth park hill

Stacy W., bootmaker 19 Anatola rd.

Stanley Hall and Baths ; E. H. Blunt, proprietor, Junction rd.

Stanton Joseph J., pianoforte tuner 17 Carrol rd.

Steep Grade Tramways and Works Co., Limited 8 High st. ; George Dirs Mertens, secretary

Stephens E., house and estate agent 18 Junction rd.

Stephens G., sweep and carpet beater 53 Vorley rd.

Stevens Joseph, gardener 5 Upper Whittington pl.

Stevens Robert, oilman 111 Dartmouth park hill

Steventon Jas., *The Bull Inn*, North hill

Stockley Mrs., wardrobe dealer 141 Junction rd.

Stokes Alfred John, gardener 2 Bartholomew ter.

Stone J. H., butcher 237 Junction rd.

Strong J. C., saddler 243 Junction rd.

Stück Walter C., jeweller 156 Fortess rd.

Sydney House Laundry 49 Vorley rd.

Tanner W. S., artists' repository, North hill

Tasker Thomas, corn merchant 1 Dartmouth park hill

Tattersall John, general & fancy draper 80 High st.

Taylor Charles, The *Wrestlers' Tavern*, North rd.

Taylor Hy., greengrocer 14 Highgate rd.

Taylor Jas., organ bldr. 23 Highgate rd.

Taylor Miss A., laundry 1a York rise

Taylor Thomas, grocer 48 North rd.

Taylor W., leather worker 47 Spencer rd.

Taylor William, bootmaker 78 North rd.

Tebbutt George, greengrocer 14 Girdlestone rd.

The Carrol Dairy, Edward Deinchfield 61 Carrol rd.

Thomas Mrs. E., general shop 74 North rd.

Thompson C. H., newsagent & stationer 107 Highgate rd.

Thompson George, bricklayer 20 Brunswick rd.

Thorn Wm., tripe dresser 71 Junction rd.

Tindley James, dealer in horse flesh 7 Archway pl.

Toyne James, grocer, North hill

Trenemen & Co., photographers 2 Upper Whittington pl.

Trickett H., coffee rooms 1 Archway rd.

Truine Joseph, chimney sweep 10 Castle yard

Tuckey Hy., greengrocer 33 Junction rd.

Tue J. W., grocer 107 Dartmouth pk. hill

Tue William, genl. shop 2a Bertram st.

Tugwell Miss, children's home 23 Northwood rd.

Turner Edward, florist and nurseryman 3 Pond sq. and North hill

Turner G. R., engineer and railway waggon builder, Highgate rd.

Twinn John, grocer, North hill

Twinn Mrs. M. A., laundry, Archway rd

Upton Charles, baker 15 Girdlestone rd.

Upton Richard John, oilman 145 Highgate rd.

Usher Albert and Co., coal office 95 Junction rd.

VaughanWm.,bookbinder 33 Doynton st.
Venables Miss, laundress 7 Wells hill Southwood lane
Victoria Wine Co. 53 Junction rd.
Vincent Thomas,grocer 125 Highgate rd.

Wade George, boot and shoe maker 30 High st.
Wale & Co., grocers 83 Highgate rd.
Walker Edward, marine store dealer 1a Pleasant row Highgate rd.
Walker J. Brown, staircase maker 59 Carrol rd.
Walker John, butcher 78 Archway rd.
Walker John, butcher 12 Upper Whittington pl.
Walker W. R., ironmonger 36 High st.
Waller A., general shop 14 Upper Whittington pl.
Waller Thomas, carman 68 Highgate rd.
Ward James, grocer 1 South grove
Ward Thomas, farmer and cowkeeper (Fitzroy farm) Millfield lane
Wass Mrs. C., *The Archway Tavern,* Archway rd.
Waterhouse Mrs., laundry (Holly cottage) Southwood lane
Watkins John, jobmaster, South grove
Watkins William B.,hairdresser 65 Junction rd.
Watmore John, baker 158a Fortess rd.
Watson Thomas, greengrocer, High st.
Weaver Fred, cigar merchant 60 High st.
Webb Reuben W., upholstr. 36 North rd.
WebberGeorge,butcher3Whittington pl.
Webster George, carman 11 Annesley rd.
Weight C., fruiterer and greengrocer 113 Fortess rd.
Welford John, cowkeeper 4 Whittington place
Went Robert, carpenter 9 Archway pl.
West A. G., chimney sweep, North road cottages North rd.
West Francis, saddler and harness maker 62 Highgate rd.
West George, chimney cleaner 5 Townshend yard High st.
West Mrs. Emma, *The Fox and Crown,* West hill
WestW.,chimney sweep30Brunswick rd.
Westerby F. M., collar dresser 13 Upper Whittington pl.
Westerby Mrs., collar dresser 10 Highgate rd.
Westlake J. G., carman and contractor, Springfield cottages North hill
Whale Joseph, tobacconist 5 Park ter.

Wheeler R., coffee and dining rooms 113 Junction rd.
White Edward, builder and decorator 32 North rd.
Whitelaw John George, builder (Prospect house) Prospect pl.
Whitman & Fox, stationers 13 Dartmouth cres.
Whittard A. H., hosier, hatter, and tailor 52 and 54 High st.
WHITELEY WILLIAM, Westbourne grove
　31 hatter, sticks, whips, &c.
　33 tailor and woollen draper, liveries
　35 & 37 gentlemen's hosier, glover, and complete outfitter
　39 silks, dress materials, banking ; railway and theatre ticket office
　39 counting house
　41 haberdashery, trimmings, gloves and hosiery
　43 lace, millinery, outfitting, furs, &c.
　45 shawls, mantles, costumes, general dressmaking, &c.
　47 jewellery, plate, drugs, and foreign fancy goods
　49 boots, shoes, india-rubber and waterproof goods
　51 ribbons, flowers, feathers
　51 costume showroom
　53 prints, calicoes, muslins, general drapery
　53 costume show room
　53 hairdressing saloon
　55 printing, stationery, engraving, bookbinding, die sinking, &c.
　55aberlin wool and fancy needlework
　61 wines & spirits, tobaccos & cigars
WHITELEY WILLIAM, Kensington gardens sq.
　50 to 53 toy and games, confectionery and restaurant, refreshment and cloak rooms, wedding breakfasts, ball suppers, &c.
WHITELEY WILLIAM, Queen's rd.
　147 household furniture and bedding, furniture removal and warehousing depôt
　149 carpets, oil-cloths, blinds and furnishing drapery
　151 family and household linen, curtains, blankets, trunks, cases and travelling equipages
　153 china, glass, earthenware & lamps
　155 ironmongery, tinware, brushes, turnery, ball and rout furnishing, and general hire department

WHITELEY WILLIAM, Queen's rd.
157 building, decorating, paperhanging, house and estate agency, auctioneering, coals, forage, shipping, cleaning & dyeing, pianos, pictures, and general fine art depôt. Fruit, floral hall, aviary, poultry, pigeons, & domestic pets
159 meat, poultry, game, fish and grocery. wines, spirits, and beer, mineral waters, and general provision warehouse

Whyman John, greengrocer 1a Girdlestone rd.

Wicks Miss, dressmaker 2 Victoria cotts.

Wilkins Henry Thomas, bootmaker 60 Archway rd.

Wilkins R. Elliott, chemist 64 High st.

Wilkinson Mrs., dressmaker 35 Highgate rd.

Williams Benjamin S., Victoria and Paradise nurseries 1 Sundial row and Junction rd.

Williams F. & Co., grocers and provision merchants, *The Stores* 71 Highgate rd.

Williams Hy. R., china wareho. 5 High st.

Williams J., marine store 125 Dartmouth park hill

Williams John, builder 11 Spencer rd.

Williams John, oil and lamp depôt 121 Highgate rd.

Williams Mrs., catholic repository 18 Whittington pl.

Williams T. H., chemist 125 Fortess rd.

Willis Thomas, butcher 149 Dartmouth park hill

Wilson A., stationer 24 Highgate rd.

Wilson James, baker 60 Carrol rd.

Wilson Joseph, plumber 24 Highgate rd.

Windsor Peter Jno., stone carver 5 North pl

Windsor S., draper 55 Junction rd.

Winter James John, *St. John's Tavern* 91 Junction rd.

Winter Richard, gardener 13 Magdala rd.

Wolfenden R. S., pianoforte tuner 82 Fortess rd.

Wolstenholme Mrs., corset maker 3 High st.

Wooder William John, cab and fly proprietor, South grove

Wooder William John, *The Flask Inn*, South grove

Woodham R., wardrobe and furniture dealer 1 Whittington ter.

Woods G. W., general draper 123 Fortess rd.

Woodward & Son, smiths 25 Archway pl.

Woodward Henry, gas and hot water engineer 27 Vorley rd.

Woodwell Walter John, *The Brunswick Arms*, Brunswick rd.

Woollard A., gardener 4 Bartholomew ter.

Wray William, optician (Laurel house) North hill

Wright John, marine stores 64 North rd.

Wright Mrs., milliner 77 Junction rd.

Xazer Geiger Franz, ivory carver 11 Dartmouth park hill

Young Henry, florist and gardener 147 Junction rd.

Young John, pianoforte tuner and repairer 55 Chester rd.

Young Joseph and Mrs. Margaret, wardrobe dealers 49 Langdon rd.

Zegers Peter J., builder 17 York rise

SCHWEITZER'S

COCOATINA,

Anti-Dyspeptic Cocoa or Chocolate Powder.

Guaranteed

Pure Soluble Cocoa,

without Admixture.

REGISTERED.

Strongly Recommended

by the Faculty

for Family use.

Cocoatina is the highest class of Soluble Cocoa or Chocolate in a concentrated form.

THE FACULTY pronounce it "the most nutritious, perfectly digestible Beverage for BREAKFAST, LUNCHEON, or SUPPER, & invaluable for Invalids & young Children."

It consists solely of the finest Cocoa Beans, the *excess* of fat being extracted **mechanically**, which not only renders it more delicate and digestible, but increases the proportion of flesh-forming and nourishing properties.

Made instantaneously with boiling water, palatable without Milk,

One tea-spoonful being sufficient for a cup of Cocoa *(the cost of which is less than a Halfpenny)*, and two or more for a cup of Chocolate.

Cocoatina will bear the strictest Chemical Test.

It is prescribed with great success for delicate Females and Children, when all other food is rejected; and is celebrated for its restorative qualities in cases of Debility and imperfect Digestion.

Highly commended by the entire Medical Press.

Being absolutely free from sugar (the *excess* of fat), or any admixture, it keeps for years in all climates, and is four times the strength of Cocoas *thickened* yet *weakened* with arrowroot, starch, &c., *and in reality cheaper than such mixtures.*

DIRECTIONS FOR USE ON THE LABEL OF EVERY PACKET.

Sold in air-tight Tin Packets only, at 1s. 6d., 3s., & 5s. 6d., by Grocers, Chemists, Confectioners, &c., &c.

SOLE PROPRIETORS:

H. SCHWEITZER & Co., 10, Adam Street, Strand, London, W.C.

[24]

THE

HAMPSTEAD AND HIGHGATE

PROFESSIONAL & TRADES

DIRECTORY.

☞ THE NAMES ARE ENTERED IN THIS SECTION OF THE DIRECTORY BY

SPECIAL ARRANGEMENT.

Professional.

——

ARCHITECT & SURVEYOR.

Bower W. G., F.R.I.B.A. 110 Great Russell st. Bedford sq. W.C. and 10 Marine ter. Margate

ART CLASSES FOR LADIES.

Subjects. Drawing and painting from models and nature : figure, landscape, flowers, and the draped living model : perspective, decorative painting, &c. Prospectus of terms, &c., on application to Misses MANLY 38 Park rd. Haverstock hill

ARTIST.

Acret J. F. (studio) 82 High st. Hampstead

PHYSICAL TRAINING.

Miss Chreiman's classes for the practice of Scientific Gymnastic Exercises, &c., are held at Kensington Town Hall; Hampstead Vestry Hall ; Westminster Town Hall (Victoria st.) ; Crystal Palace Hotel, Upper Norwood; Science and Art Rooms, Bennett park, Blackheath ; Finchley Assembly Rooms ; All Saints' Church Room, Green lanes N. ; Town Hall, West Brighton, &c.

Classes held in the gymnasia of high-class schools and private residences at a distance from the Gymnastic Halls, may occasionally be joined.

Private lessons to pupils in delicate health are given at Westminster Town Hall (Victoria st.) and Miss Chreiman's residence 20 Gwendwr rd. West Kensington.

PROFESSOR OF DANCING AND CALISTHENICS.

Aldier Edouard, dancing, calisthenics, hygienic & curative exercises, classes and private lessons, schools & families visited 23 Shirlock rd. Haverstock hill

PROFESSOR OF LANGUAGES.

Stengel Charles (Graduate of the University of France, Académie Impériale de Nancy) 37 Bolton rd. Abbey rd.

PROFESSORS OF MUSIC.

ACADEMY OF MUSIC, Alfred and Walter Laubach 192 Belsize rd.
Boatwright John (violincello and violin) 26 Rochester sq. Camden town
Dickson Mrs. 22 Langdon park rd.
Eveleigh Miss 59 Fairfax rd.
HARROW MUSIC SCHOOL 15 Fitzjohns' parade Finchley new rd. ; Misses Fox & Frost, principals
Malkin Miss, R.A.M. (pianoforte and singing) 138 Belsize rd.
Winter Ernest 14 Bolton rd. St. John's wood

SCHOLASTIC.

ALL SAINTS' HIGHGATE MIDDLE CLASS SCHOOL ; Rev. Edgar Smith, manager, Miss Fowler, head mistress 25 Northwood road
Brodie Miss (and kindergarten) 50*a* Haverstock hill
Cathcart Mrs. (ladies' school) 117 Adelaide rd.
Dickinson A. E. C., L.C.P. (Grove house school) Highgate
FELL MISS (St. Hilda's college for ladies) 111 Abbey rd.
Gardiner John Talbot (Belsize school) 7 Buckland villas
High School for Girls ; Miss M. Sharpe, manageress(Channing house)High st. Highgate
Holmes Misses (Queen's college for ladies) Bellefield house 39 Haverstock hill
Hudson Misses (Delmar house) 39 and 40 Gayton rd.
Johnson Mrs. E. R. (boys' school) 190 Adelaide rd.
Maslen Mrs. & Misses (ladies' college) 14 Belsize park gardens

SCHOLASTIC—*continued*

Nelson Miss, M.C.P. (Raffles ladies' college) 3 Eton rd.
North London High School for Boys (Wellington house) Eton rd. Haverstock hill ; Septimus Payne, F.R.G.S., M.S.A., head master. Islington Branch (Castle house) Mildmay grove N.
Sawley House Preparatory and Boarding School ; Mrs. Storr, principal, Northwood rd.
SMITH MISSES (ladies' school) Kenhurst 47 South hill park
Sutton Miss (Stella house collegiate school for girls) pupils prepared for public examinations, Cathcart hill Junction rd. N.
Timms Mrs. (ladies' school) 36 Downshire hill
Tombs Mrs. (pestalozzian and kindergarten) Holmwood house 30 South hill park
Turner Miss, A.C.P. (high class school for girls) 36 Archway rd.
VERNON G. F. C., A.C.P., A.E.S.I., King's College Lond. (Hillmartin college) 20 Hungerford rd. Holloway
Williamson Mrs. (little boys' day school) Ireton house 9 The Bank Highgate

SCULPTOR.

May William Charles (Penn house) Rudall cres.

SOLICITOR AND COMMISSIONER FOR OATHS AND DECLARATIONS.

Taylor Alfred, The Mount Heath st. Hampstead

SURGEON-DENTISTS.

Armitage John S., L.D.S., R.C.S. (North London Dental Surgery) 1 Colva st.
Eskell L. E. & C. 2 Onslow pl. South Kensington W.
Fisk Messrs. 183 High rd. Kilburn
OVEY AUGUSTUS 13 Coventry st. Piccadilly circus
Patterson Mountaine 62 Haverstock hill (2 doors off Prince of Wales rd.)
Styles Edwin (and mechanical) 41 Camden rd.
Webb J. P. 103 Lewisham High rd. and Brockley

VETERINARY SURGEON.

Davy E. M. 95 Abbey rd. and 8 and 9 Alexandra mews St. John's wood

---

Trades.

ART NEEDLEWORK AND FANCY REPOSITORY.

Brooking & Co. 298 High rd. Kilburn

ARTISTS' COLOURMAN.

Tanner W. S. (post office) North hill Highgate

ARTISTS' JOINER.

Baxter Benjamin A., Church lane

AUCTIONEERS AND ESTATE AGENTS.

Boden J. W. 47 Finchley new rd. and 16 Swiss ter.
Deverell John James 96 Camden rd.
Dolman & Pearce 62 Haverstock hill
Farmer Leopold 12 High rd. Kilburn
Owers Oscar, West Hampstead station West end lane
STEVENS WALTER G., Finchley road station Metropolitan railway
TREVERS TREVERS 4 Canfield gardens and at 44 Finsbury pavement

BAKERS & CONFECTIONERS.

Appleton Robert 46 North rd. Highgate
Archer James 30 Heath st.
Carpenter Thomas William 41 High rd. Kilburn
Cronk George 98 Boundary rd.
Hendrick Charles 4 Elizabeth ter. England's lane
Horn F. 79 High rd. Kilburn
Lorkin Geo. 4 Exeter ter. West end lane
Mizen Robert Henry 55 Fairfax rd.
Moore E. George (and contractor for wedding breakfasts, ball suppers, &c.) 38 Eversholt st. and 164 Regent's park rd.
Rasey Henry 202 Belsize rd.
Reiger H. 20 Elizabeth ter. England's ln.

BAKERS AND CONFECTIONERS—continued

Rumbold William (post office) 8 South hill park
Smith James (also pastrycook) 90 Haverstock hill
Sowden Mrs. A. M. 228 Belsize rd. Kilburn

BALL AND CONCERT FURNISHER.

Rogers G. 68 High st. Highgate

BATH CHAIR PROPRIETOR.

Pickford Josiah, invalid bath & brougham chairs, double or single (established 1885) 1 Lower Heath cottages Hampstead

BEER RETAILER.

Bates Joseph 161 Loveridge rd.

BERLIN WOOL REPOSITORIES.

Carter Ernest 206 Haverstock hill
Prior Misses H. & C. 22 Elizabeth ter. England's lane

BILL POSTERS.

England & Co. 9 & 41a Southampton rd

BIRD DEALER AND CAGE MANUFACTURER.

Sumner E. 135 Oxford st. W., and at Crystal palace Sydenham

BLIND MAKERS.

Baxter Benjamin A., Church lane
BAXTER JOSEPH 14 Park st. Camden town
Green & Co. 165 High rd. Kilburn. Cheaper than any other house in England.

BOARDING HOUSE.

Harris Mrs. 26 Parliament hill rd.

BOOKBINDERS.

Crockett Thomas W. (and stationer) 312 High rd. Kilburn. Books bound on the premises

BOOKBINDERS—*continued*

HUTCHINGS &CROWSLEY,LIMITED 35 to 41 Henry st. St. John's wood N.W., and 123 Fulham rd. South Kensington S.W.

BOOKSELLERS AND STATIONERS.

Bourne & Co. (late Chapman) 67 Abbey rd. St. John's wood
Cole C. (and librarian) 18 High st. Highgate
FOWLER BROS. 92 Haverstock hill
Kelly William (agent for Pullar's dye works) 76 High st. Highgate
Lines E. (and newsagent) 79 Fairfax rd.
Nurse H. 206 Belsize rd.
Phillips W. J. 248 High st. Camden town

BOOT AND SHOE MAKERS.

Abercrombie William 71 Fairfax rd.
Hayes Harry (and leather seller) 97 Palmerston rd.
Lunnon James 84 High st. Highgate
Martin Thomas 3 Flask walk High st.
Pressler C. 162 Malden rd.
Symes W. (and repairs) 9 Alfred ter. Heath st.

BOOT, SHOE AND CLOTHING STORES.

Thomas Joseph 3 High st. Child's hill

BOTTLE MERCHANTS.

Sharpe C. & J. (and furniture dealers) 11 & 13 Flask walk

BREWERS (Family).

MURE, WARNER & CO. (Hampstead brewery) 9a High st. Hampstead

BRUSH AND TURNERY WAREHOUSE.

Browning H. 7 Swiss ter. St. John's wood

BUILDERS & DECORATORS.

Alway Charles (and contractor) 15 Ivers n rd.
Back Walter H. 131 Belsize rd. Kilburn

BUILDERS AND DECORATORS —*continued*

Bailey Richard 38 North rd. and Southwood lane Highgate
Barnes Isaac 252 High rd. Kilburn
Bartlett & Hawkins 38 Boundary rd. St. John's wood
Boden J. W. 47 Finchley new rd. and 16 Swiss ter.
BURFORD & SON (Norway house)
Butcher W. H. 10 Fitzjohns' parade 35 High st. Hampstead and 84 Cochrane st. St John's Wood Finchley new rd.
COOK GEORGE (Weatherall cottage) Well rd.
Dainton Samuel J. 234 Belsize rd. Kilburn, and at 11 Exeter ter., opposite West Hampstead station
Edwards Edward 120 Leighton rd. (also agent to *The Queen* Insurance Offices, Fire and Life)
Firminger Amos 124 Boundary rd.
Gibbins Thomas 157 Prince of Wales rd.
Gibbs & Imber (joinery works) North hill Highgate
Grey Henry (and contractor) 33 Flask walk
Hackworth Alfred 41 Loudoun rd. St. John's wood
HARRIS ALFRED 159 Loveridge rd. Kilburn and 50 All Saints' rd. Kensington
Isaac E. J. 85 Fairfax rd.
KING C. B. 53 High st. Hampstead
Langridge George 10a Bolton rd. St. John's wood
Laycock John Spencer 2 Boundary mews Boundary rd.
MyringJacob69Abbey rd.St.John's wood
Oldrey Henry Baker 52 High rd. Kilburn
Pritchard George 16 Heath st.
Pugh John 4aElizabeth ter.England's ln
Roff & Son 57 & 70 Heath st. Hampstead
Snow George 17 Belsize park ter.
Southcott &Co.,Southwood laneHighgate
TUGWELL T. B. & SONS 4 Belsize cres
Van Camp E. 314 High rd. Kilburn
Webb Joseph J. (and contractor) 8 Narcissus rd.
Wiltshire William 47 Heath st.
Yerbury R. A. 158 High rd. Kilburn

BUILDING MATERIAL DEPÔT.

West & Boreham 50 Haverstock hill

BUTCHERS.

Brightwell R. & Son 6 Swiss ter. St. John's wood
Coles Alexander 87 Fairfax rd.
Dickson & Son, Haverstock hill
Ginger Walter 317 High rd. Kilburn
Hammond E. 32 Heath st.
Harrison Thomas 2 Flask walk
Pannell W. T. 55 High st. Hampstead
PIPPETT A. 18 Queen's ter. St. John's wood
Randall T. G. 93 Haverstock hill
Whittlesey William C. 110 Boundary rd.

CAB AND FLY PROPRIETOR.

Hunt Robert 1 Victoria cottages South grove

CARPENTERS AND JOINERS.

Barry J. W. (and upholsterer) 3 Upper Belsize ter.
Smith John 13 Pond st. and South end green
Wiltshire William 47 Heath st.
Winyard William, jun. (and builder) West end

CARPET BEATERS AND CLEANERS.

Simmons & Tullidge (steam works) Wharf rd. Latimer rd. Notting hill, Station rd. Camberwell, and Pleasant grove York rd. King's cross

CARRIAGE BUILDER.

Pickett Henry 41a Southampton rd.

CARVERS AND GILDERS.

Flower Clare 32 High rd. Kilburn
Staples Arthur H. 201 High rd. Kilburn

CAST-OFF CLOTHING.

Ladies' or gentlemen's, in good or inferior condition, wanted for the Colonies. Mr. and Mrs. H. Moss are giving the highest prices for the above. Gentlemen or ladies waited upon at their own residences by Mr. and Mrs. M., free of charge. Old uniforms, lace, boots, &c., bought. Terms cash. Please note the address. 56, 73, 75, and 77 Praed st. W. P.O.O. remitted for all parcels sent same day as parcels received

CHEESEMONGERS AND POULTERERS.

ELLIOTT RUSSELL 6 Exeter ter. West end lane
Harris E. 59 High st. Hampstead
Houghton Herbert 1 Swiss ter. St. John's wood
Searle William 2 Elizabeth ter. England's lane and 32 Victoria rd. Kentish town. Alderney fresh butter received daily.

CHEMISTS.

Allen Charles B. 20 High rd. Kilburn
Allen J. W. (pharmaceutical) 19 Elizabeth ter. England's lane
Atkinson John George (pharmaceutical) 196 Belsize rd. Kilburn
Bevan William (pharmaceutical) 195 High rd. Kilburn
Chapman Joseph John (pharmaceutical) 20 Boundary rd.
Hyne Harry (pharmaceutical) 8 Exeter ter. West end lane
LEAKE T. W. (pharmaceutical and homœopathic) 44 Hampstead hill gdns.
Ridley Edward H. (dispensing and family) 81 Chalk farm rd.
Saunders Charles 4 and 6 North rd. Highgate

CHIMNEY CLEANERS AND CARPET BEATERS.

Alderson Mrs. Maria 15 Belsize park ter.
Bowden & Porter, Vale of Health
Longhurst Richard 90 Palmerston rd.
Pepper A. (late A. Back) 2 Goldsmith gardens (opposite the old establishment 6 Bell ter.)
Truine Joseph 10 Castle yard Highgate

CHINA AND GLASS WARE-HOUSES.

Ingram Algernon 22 High rd. Kilburn
Millist & Son 18 Rosslyn st.
Moore G. Willis 10 Elizabeth ter. England's lane
Potter Henry 23 Elizabeth ter. England's lane

CIGAR DIVAN.

Bridges Mrs. 143 High rd. Kilburn

CIRCULATING LIBRARY.

Fowler Bros. (in connection with Mudie's) 92 Haverstock hill

COACH BUILDERS AND WHEELWRIGHTS.

James Thomas 20 High st. Highgate and Broadbent yard

Stancombe G. W. 8 Loudoun road mews St. John's wood

COAL & COKE MERCHANTS.

Ellis & Everard (West end wharf) Iverson rd.

COFFEE AND DINING ROOMS.

Brusey Thomas 43 Loudoun rd.

COIFFEUR (de Paris).

Martin F. 1 Dawson ter. Haverstock hill

COOK & CONFECTIONER.

Rogers G. (and rout furnisher) 68 High st. Highgate

CORN AND FLOUR MERCHANTS.

Barrett Thomas Albert 41 Fairfax rd.

Belcher John S. 13 Swiss ter. St. John's wood

Edwards & Coxwell 88 Haverstock hill

Marriott Mrs. A. J. (and coal merchant) 58 High st. Highgate

COWKEEPERS & DAIRYMEN.

Beahan M. 13 Fitzjohns' parade

Brandon J. (Swiss cottage dairy) Finchley rd.

Brumbridge James 47 Hampstead hill gardens and 6 Rosslyn st.

Bull Mrs. (Iverson dairy) 184 Iverson rd.

Goodenough Thomas (Belgrave dairy) 111 Boundary rd.

Jersey Farm Dairy, Broadhurst gardens West Hampstead ; George Hopkins, proprietor

Maxted Thomas 6 South hill park

Palmer William (Priory dairy) 230 Belsize rd. Kilburn

Perry Thomas (Church lane dairy) 15 Church lane High st.

Pritchard James (established 90 years) 24 Heath st.

COWKEEPERS AND DAIRYMEN—
continued

Smith H. (New West End dairy) 20 Mill lane

Street George 17 Heath st.

Walker E. 58 Haverstock hill

WEST LONDON DAIRY SOCIETY, LIMITED ; Robert Hornby, manager 31 High rd. and 11 Chichester rd. Kilburn

CURTAIN CLEANERS.

Simmons & Tullidge, Wharf rd. Latimer rd. Notting hill

DINING ROOMS.

White William 4 Gladstone ter. Cricklewood

DRAPERS.

Aldridge A. C. (general and fancy) 47 Fairfax rd.

Andrews G. N. (general) 63 Fairfax rd.

Brown J. A. 14 Elizabeth ter. England's lane

Penhey Robert (fancy and general) Swiss cottage Finchley rd.

DRAUGHTSMAN.

Mason Henry W. (general) Elm grove Cricklewood

DRESS & MANTLE MAKERS.

Chambers Miss, Prince Arthur's cottages Church lane

Denton Mrs. (Oakley villa) Ravenshaw st.

Endean Miss 138 Belsize rd.

Grant Mrs., Holly hill High st.

Hall Mrs. & Misses F. & C. 202 Belsize rd. Kilburn

Harper Miss 21 New end

James Mrs. 20 High st. Highgate

Longman Miss 3 Wellington ter. North hill Highgate

Newman Misses M. E. & E. 28 High st. Highgate

Pottle Miss 69 Heath st.

Sellick Misses F. & C. (and milliners) West end Hampstead

Weldon Miss 7 Belsize rd. South Hampstead

DYERS AND CLEANERS.

DUGGIN J. F. & CO. 42 Duke st. M.S. and 37 Craven rd. Lancaster gate (dyers to H.M. the Queen and H.R.H. the Prince of Wales)

Hannett A. H. & Sons 69 Fairfax rd. Works 102 High st. St. John's wood

Hutchins L. & Co. 4 Belsize park ter. and 29 Park st. Camden town

Newland & Son 74 Great College st. Camden town

NORTH-WESTERN STEAM CLEANING AND DYEING COMPANY, LIMITED, Dyne rd. Kilburn and 10 St. Ann's ter. St. John's wood

Rawlings W. (practical) High st. Highgate

Simmons & Tullidge (steam) Wharf rd. Latimer rd. Notting hill

ELECTRO-MAGNETIC BATHS.

The Royal York Baths 54 York ter. Regent's park ; V. A. Jagielski, M.D., superintending resident physician

ENGINEERS.

Caslake James (machines, locks, bells, and gas) 152 & 152a Kentish town rd.

Edwards Alfred 17 & 19 Southampton rd.

FANCY REPOSITORY.

Yerbury R. A. 156 High rd. Kilburn

FINE ART EMPORIUM.

Moss K. 53 Fairfax rd. St. John's wood

FISHMONGERS AND POUL-TERERS.

Jones Albert 11 Heath st.

Phipps W. 93 Haverstock hill

Selway H. J. 9 Elizabeth ter. England's lane

FLORISTS & NURSERYMEN.

AMBLER G., South end rd., opposite Hampstead heath station

ANDERSON JOHN E., Belsize park gardens and Hampstead nursery

Barrett Frederick George (Belsize nursery) 67 Belsize rd.

Chamberlain E. (Haverstock hill nursery) 188 and 192 Haverstock hill

FLORISTS AND NURSERYMEN—
continued

Chambers L. G. & Son, West end

Russell John (Devonshire nursery) 129 and 133 Haverstock hill

Setterington Joseph 103 Boundary rd.

WOOD RICHARD J. (Haverstock hill and Bedford nurseries) 113 Haverstock hill

Wood Thomas (Belsize nursery grounds) 3 Belsize cres.

FRUITERERS AND GREEN-GROCERS.

Buckle George 68 Heath st. Hampstead

Camp James 15 Rosslyn st.

Evans E. 1 Exeter ter. West end lane

Halls W. H. 174 High rd. Kilburn

Marks John 24 Boundary rd.

Mash G. 55 High rd. Kilburn

May Henry 3 Heath st.

Steeden Daniel 102 Boundary rd.

Vallis George 122 High rd. Kilburn

FURNITURE REMOVER.

Barnes R. C. 199 Belsize rd. Kilburn

GALVANO-ELECTRIC BATHS.

The Royal York Baths 54 York ter. Regent's park ; V. A. Jagielski, M.D., superintending resident physician

GARDENERS AND FLORISTS.

Phippen E. (Rose nursery) Swain's lane Highgate

Warden R. (jobbing) Abbey nursery, West end lane Kilburn

GAS AND HOT WATER ENGINEERS.

Caslake James (bath and water apparatus manufacturer) 152 and 152a Kentish town rd.

Hately J. 2 Yorkshire Grey yard and Little Church row

Segar & Co. 226 High rd. Kilburn

GENERAL SMITH.

Caslake James (mediæval art metal worker) 152 & 152a Kentish town rd.

GLASS WAREHOUSE.

The Kilburn Wholesale Glass Depôt ;
L. A. Georges & Co., Abbey lane
Belsize rd., close to Town hall. Plate
and sheet glass, tavern and confectionery, flint glass, best table glass,
globes, chimneys, &c.

GROCERS AND PROVISION MERCHANTS.

Aynscombe Bros. 25 Fleet rd. and
1 Southwell ter. New end
French E. & Co. 5 Exeter ter. West
end lane
Millist & Son 17 Rosslyn st.
Rumbold William 10 South hill park
Wilkins H. C. 67 Kingsgate rd.
Woolfe B. J. 57 High rd. Kilburn

HAIRDRESSER AND PERFUMER.

Le Dong Henri 101 Boundary rd.

HATTER.

HEATH HENRY 105, 107 & 109 Oxford
st. W. (late No. 393). Ladies' showroom. Awarded gold and silver medal
at Health Exhibition.

HOUSE, LAND, AND ESTATE AGENTS.

Moore & Sons 11 Belsize park ter.
Potter George William 22 High st.
Hampstead
Southcott and Co., Southwood lane
Highgate

IMPORTERS OF FOREIGN WINES AND SPIRITS.

Lopez G. & Co. 121 Broadhurst gardens;
agents for the celebrated Spanish
clarets and sole agents for De Tajada's
altar wine

INDIA RUBBER AND MACK-INTOSH WAREHOUSE.

Barker&Pechey83High st.Camden town

INSURANCE AGENT.

Coates Joseph (life, fire, accident, and
plate glass) Bedford villa, Willoughby
road

IRON AND TIN PLATE WORKER.

Rogers R. 12 Colla's mews High rd.
Kilburn

IRONMONGERS.

Kite S. 81 Fairfax rd.
Martin B. 65 Abbey rd. St. John's wood
Richardson J. T. (manufacturing) 61
Gayton rd. and Alfred terrace mews
Skoyles Robert 72 High st. Hampstead

JEWELLER.

Bond Jonas (working) 94 Great College
st. Camden town

JOBMASTERS.

Burch William 3 and 4 Wavel mews
Priory rd.
Edwards and Thomas,Lancaster stables,
Belsize park gardens
James Edward (and livery stables) 15
and 16 Loudoun road mews
Tooley T. 8 Heath st. (established 1835)

LADDER AND BARROW MAKER.

BradleyGuss Alfred 277 High rd.Kilburn

LADIES' AND CHILDREN'S OUTFITTERS.

Troughton E. A. 4 Fitzjohns' parade
Finchley new rd.
Wright Mrs. 73 Haverstock hill

LAUNDRIES.

Aldcroft Thomas Agar, North hill High-
gate
Avery Mrs. (Clyde house laundry) 67
Langdon rd. Junction rd. N.
BuckleW.(established 1865) Mulkern rd.
Eaton Mrs. 8 Golden sq. Heath st.
Gardiner Mrs. (established 1870) 24
Nicholay rd. Upper Holloway N.
Howard T. W. (St. John's laundry)
Nicholay rd. Upper Holloway N.
Vinall Mrs. Elizabeth (Fleet laundry)
20 Fleet rd.
*WILLESDEN SANITARY STEAM
LAUNDRY,* Dyne rd. Kilburn ;
William Dean, proprietor

LEATHER AND GRINDERY WAREHOUSE.

MARTIN THOMAS 3 Flask walk High street

LOOKING GLASS MANUFACTURER.

Millbank Arthur A. 24 Harmood st. Chalk farm rd. Frames re-gilt and glasses re-silvered

MASONS.

Coat Jacob & Co. (general & cemetery) 158 Junction rd. Cheapest place for butchers', &c., marble fittings

MILLINERS.

Brown J. A. (also fancy draper) 5 Elizabeth ter. England's lane
King Mrs. H. (also dressmaker) 113 Boundary rd. St. John's wood
Ritchie Mrs. H. 19 Heath st.
Thomas Misses S. & E. (and dressmakers) 65 Camden st.
Upton K. W. & M. (also fancy drapers) 2 Dawson ter. Haverstock hill

MONUMENTAL SCULPTORS.

Underwood & Sons (& cemetery masons) Fortune green

MOSAIC WORKER.

Cappello A. (from Salviati)472 King's rd. Chelsea. Imperishable Venetian enamel mosaic for wall decoration in all styles, on the same principle as Venice and Rome, also marble and Kerornic mosaics for wall decorations and for pavements of every description, at lower rate than any firm in England. Sole manufacturer in England of the Venetian enamel mosaic.

NEWSAGENTS.

Cartridge James (and stationer) 83 Boundary rd.
Cutbush William (and stationer) High st. Highgate
Jordan Edward H. (also tobacconist) 12 Flask walk

NURSERYMEN, SEEDSMEN, AND FLORISTS.

Chamberlain E. (Haverstock hill nursery) 188 and 192 Haverstock hill
CUTBUSH WILLIAM & SON, LIMTD., Highgate, Finchley, and Barnet
WOOD RICHARD J. (Haverstock and Bedford nurseries)113 Haverstock hill

NURSING INSTITUTION.

WILSON'S 96, 97, 98a Wimpole st. W.

OIL, COLOUR, AND ITALIAN WAREHOUSEMAN.

Pegler Enoch 209 Belsize rd. Kilburn

PAPER STAINERS.

WOOLLAMS WILLIAM AND CO. 110 High st., near Manchester sq., London, W. Artistic wall & ceiling papers, block printed, free from arsenic. Patent embossed flocks, raised flocks for painting over ; embossed leather papers, dado decorations ; dealers in all kinds of machine-made cheap papers. Numerous prize medals

PHOTOGRAPHER.

Bowen Alfred Walter 48 Heath st.

PIANOFORTE TUNER.

Dettmer W. J. (and repairer) 46 Kingsgate rd.

PICTURE FRAME MAKERS.

Pull T. (and gilder) 4 Perrins court High st.
Red Cap Picture Frame Manufactory ; B. Lyons 6a Camden rd.

PLUMBERS, GAS AND HOT WATER ENGINEERS.

Crutwell C. H. 1 White Bear lane
Gill John 120 Boundary rd.
Myring Jacob 69 Abbey rd. St. John's wood
Shepherd T. & B. 3 Little Church row High st.
Slann Francis John 5 Church lane

PORK BUTCHER & SAUSAGE MAKER.

Attkins Mrs. E., High st. Highgate

POULTERER AND GAME DEALER.

Searle William 2 Elizabeth ter. Eng land's lane and 32 Victoria rd. Kentish town

PRINTERS.

Gillingham & Palmer (also bookbinders and stationers) 257 Kentish town rd.

PROVISION MERCHANTS.

Millist & Son 17 Rosslyn st.
Searle W. 2 Elizabeth ter. England's lane and 32 Victoria rd. Kentish town. Alderney fresh butter received daily.

REGISTRY OFFICES FOR SERVANTS.

Edwards H. 7a England's lane
Fowler Bros. 92 Haverstock hill

SADDLER AND HARNESS MAKER.

Fraser A. 267 High rd. Kilburn

SANITARY & VENTILATING ENGINEERS.

Caslake James (general blacksmith's work) 152 & 152a Kentish town rd.
Myring Jacob 69 Abbey rd. St. John's wood

SCHOOL TEA GARDENS.

Sheehy John, North end Hampstead

SECOND-HAND BOOKSELLER.

May George 69 High rd. Kilburn

SERVANTS' AGENCY.

SOHO BAZAAR 77 Oxford st. and Soho sq. Servants of all classes are daily in attendance in large numbers, from 11 till 2, waiting to be seen and inter- viewed in the spacious rooms set apart for that purpose. Over 5,000 families suited yearly. Every accommodation for country visitors.

SEWING MACHINE MANU- FACTURERS.

The Singer Manufacturing Co. 51 High st. Camden town

SIGN BOARD AND GLASS WRITER.

Streeter H. 3 Abbey lane West end lane Kilburn

STAINED GLASS WORKS.

Noble Frederick Wm. 48 Maygrove rd.

STATIONER AND FANCY WAREHOUSE.

The Highgate Emporium 40 High st. Highgate

TAILORS.

Parker John 16 New end Hampstead
Snell Edward 9 Dyne rd. Kilburn

TOBACCONIST.

Jeffcoat Charles 9 Exeter ter. West end lane

TRUNK AND PORTMANTEAU MAKERS.

Barker & Pechey 83 High st. Camden town. *" Distance no object"*

TURKISH AND ELECTRO- TURKISH BATHS.

The Royal York Baths 54 York ter. Regent's park ; V. J. Jagielski, M.D., superintending resident physician

TURNER.

Stancombe J. H. (general) 41 Park st. Camden town

UNDERTAKERS.

Butcher W. H. 10 Fitzjohns' parade Finchley new rd. and 84 Cochrane st. St. John's Wood
Myring Jacob 69 Abbey rd. St. John's wood
NODES JOHN 3 Chelmsford ter. High rd. Willesden

UNREDEEMED PLEDGE STORES.

Lindsay Bros. 142 High rd. Kilburn

WARDROBE DEALERS.

Braunton Richard 245 Great College st. Camden town

Cayford Walter W. 3 Bell ter. High rd. Kilburn

Gerrard Mr. & Mrs. 68 Great College st. Camden town

Moss Mr. and Mrs. H. 56, 73, 75 and 77 Praed st.W. Ladies' and Gentlemen's cast-off clothing, in good or inferior condition, wanted for the Colonies. Mr. and Mrs. H. Moss are giving the highest prices for the above. Ladies and gentlemen waited upon at their own residences by Mr. or Mrs. M., free of charge. Old linen and children's things bought. Terms cash. Please note the address. P.O.O. remitted for all parcels sent same day as parcels received.

Stephenson Mrs. Emily 27 Prince of Wales rd. Kentish town

WATCHMAKERS AND JEWELLERS.

Brown W. E. (Cholmeley house) 18 North rd. Highgate

Davies Arthur (also chronometer and clock maker and optician) 3 Fitzjohns' parade Finchley new rd.

Jones Samuel 212 Belsize rd. Kilburn

Judge Thomas, High st. Highgate

Pleasance Ernest 10 Exeter ter. West end land

SHROPP JOHN 272 Belsize rd. Kilburn (late 5 Bank buildings High rd.)

Sleven James P. 2a Fleet rd.

Tubbs F. 15 King's college rd.

Webster Ernest (and clock maker) 45 Loudoun rd.

WHEELWRIGHTS.

Fowler & Son (in general) Alfred ter. mews Hampstead

WINDOW GLASS WARE-HOUSE.

Shafner W. 9 & 11 Southampton rd. Haverstock hill

WINE, SPIRIT, AND BEER MERCHANTS.

Applebee Pendred & Co., *St. George's Distillery and Wine Stores* 15 1 Fortess rd. and 66 Archway rd.

Bowman George 53 Fleet rd.

Gaillard Frank & Co. 84 Haverstock hill

Godsel H. P., *The George,* Haverstock hill

Hawkins John, *The Nag's Head* 61 Heath st.

Humphreys Henry, *The Bull and Bush,* North end Hampstead

Marsh William Thomas, *The Load of Hay* 94 Haverstock hill

OWEN R. AND CO. 12 Elizabeth ter. England's lane

Phillips Acton, *The Cock Tavern* 125 High rd. Kilburn

Purchas Mrs. M. A. 85 High rd. Kilburn

Savigear Alfred & Son, *Swiss Cottage,* Finchley rd.

Solesbury John 3 Swiss ter. St. John's wood

Stokes John, *The Britannia* 95 Fairfax rd

Vinall Frederick, *The Adelaide Hotel,* Haverstock hill

Wheeler Mrs. M. E., *The Belgrave Hotel* 63 Abbey rd. St. John's wood

White Miss A. E., *The Victoria Tavern* 83 Abbey rd. St. John's wood

THE

HAMPSTEAD AND HIGHGATE

DIRECTORY.

CALENDAR, 1885-6.

1885

	Sunday.	Monday.	Tuesday.	Wednesday.	Thursday.	Friday.	Saturday.
JULY	...	...	...	1	2	3	4
	5	6	7	8	9	10	11
	12	13	14	15	16	17	18
	19	20	21	22	23	24	25
	26	27	28	29	30	31	...
AUGUST	...	...	...	...	...	...	1
	2	3	4	5	6	7	8
	9	10	11	12	13	14	15
	16	17	18	19	20	21	22
	23	24	25	26	27	28	29
	30	31	...	...	...	...	...
SEPT.	...	...	1	2	3	4	5
	6	7	8	9	10	11	12
	13	14	15	16	17	18	19
	20	21	22	23	24	25	26
	27	28	29	30	...	...	...
OCT.	...	...	...	...	1	2	3
	4	5	6	7	8	9	10
	11	12	13	14	15	16	17
	18	19	20	21	22	23	24
	25	26	27	28	29	30	31
NOV.	1	2	3	4	5	6	7
	8	9	10	11	12	13	14
	15	16	17	18	19	20	21
	22	23	24	25	26	27	28
	29	30	...	...	...	...	...
DEC.	...	...	1	2	3	4	5
	6	7	8	9	10	11	12
	13	14	15	16	17	18	19
	20	21	22	23	24	25	26
	27	28	29	30	31	...	...
	...	...	...	...	...	...	...

1886

	Sunday.	Monday.	Tuesday.	Wednesday.	Thursday.	Friday.	Saturday.
JAN.	...	...	...	...	...	1	2
	3	4	5	6	7	8	9
	10	11	12	13	14	15	16
	17	18	19	20	21	22	23
	24	25	26	27	28	29	30
	31	...	...	...	...	...	...
FEB.	...	1	2	3	4	5	6
	7	8	9	10	11	12	13
	14	15	16	17	18	19	20
	21	22	23	24	25	26	27
	28	...	...	...	...	...	...
MARCH	...	1	2	3	4	5	6
	7	8	9	10	11	12	13
	14	15	16	17	18	19	20
	21	22	23	24	25	26	27
	28	29	30	31	...	...	...
APRIL	...	...	...	...	...	1	2	3
	4	5	6	7	8	9	10
	11	12	13	14	15	16	17
	18	19	20	21	22	23	24
	25	26	27	28	29	30	...
MAY	...	...	...	...	...	...	1
	2	3	4	5	6	7	8
	9	10	11	12	13	14	15
	16	17	18	19	20	21	22
	23	24	25	26	27	28	29
	30	31	...	...	...	...	...
JUNE	...	...	1	2	3	4	5
	6	7	8	9	10	11	12
	13	14	15	16	17	18	19
	20	21	22	23	24	25	26
	27	28	29	30	...	...	...

May.—The election of Vestrymen and Auditors, under the "Metropolis Local Management Act," takes place during this month, at a time appointed by the Vestry.

June 20.—Overseers to fix on Church doors, and other public places, notices to persons q'(d)lified to vote for counties to make claims.

July 20.—Assessed Taxes and Poor Rates, due on the 5th of January, must be paid on or before this day, by all Electors of Cities or Boroughs, or they will be disqualified from voting.

July 30.—Overseers to make out lists of County and Borough Electors, and to fix on Church and Chapel doors on two succeeding Sundays.

LOCAL POSTAL GUIDE.

———o———

POST OFFICES, PILLAR AND WALL BOXES,

WITH THE

Latest Time for Posting Letters, &c., for each Collection.

Offices marked thus (*) are Money Order Offices and Savings Banks.
Do.   do.   (†) are Telegraph Offices.
Do.   do.   (§) are closed at night and on Sundays.

HAMPSTEAD DISTRICT.

BRANCH OFFICES.	TIMES OF COLLECTION.
*†Haverstock hill (200) -	3.0, 8.20, 9.30, 10.30, 11.30, a.m.; 12.25, 1.30, 2.40, 3.30, 4.45, 5.30, 8.0, 9.0, p.m.
*†§High st. (48) - - -	8.55, 10.25, 11.0, a.m., 12.0; 1.20, 2.35, 3.5, 4.45, 5.30, 8.0, p.m.
Swiss Cottage Railway Station	3.0, 8.50, 10.0, 11.0, 12.0, a.m.; 12.55, 3.10, 4.45, 5.30, 7.50, 9.0, p.m.

RECEIVING HOUSES.

*Belsize park ter. (10) -	3.0, 9.20, 10.15, 11.15, a.m.; 12.15, 1.5, 3.20, 4.45 5.30, 8.0, 9.0, p.m.
*England's lane (1a) - -	3.0, 9.10, 10.10, 11.10, a.m.; 12.0, 1.0, 3.15, 4.45, 5.30, 8.0, 9.0, p.m.
*§Fairfax rd. (93) - -	3.0, 8.45, 10.0, 11.0, a.m.; 12.0, 12.50, 3.0, 4.45, 5.20, 8.0, 9.0, p.m.
*Fitzjohns' parade - -	2.50, 9.50, 10.50, 11.50, a.m.; 4.35, 5.15, 8.45, p.m.
*King's college rd. (1), corner Adelaide rd.	3.0, 8.55, 9.55, 10.55, 11.55, a.m.; 12.45, 2.55, 4.45, 5.20, 8.0, 9.0 p.m.
*North end- - - -	2.35, 10.20, 11.40, a.m.; 1.20, 5.10, 8.45, p.m.
*South hill park (8) - -	3.0, 9.10, 10.0, 11.0, a.m.; 12.0, 1.5, 3.0, 4.45, 5.30, 8.0, 9.0, p.m.
*Steele's rd. (81 Haverstock hill)	3.0, 8.20, 9.30, 10.30, 11.30, a.m.; 12.25, 1.30, 2.40, 3.30, 4.45, 5.30, 7.45, 9.0, p.m.

PILLAR BOXES.

Adelaide rd. (Eton rd.) -	3.0, 9.5, 10.0, 11.0, a.m., 12.0; 12.55, 3.5, 4.45, 5.25, 9.0, p.m.
Belsize park - - -	3.0, 9.15, 10.10, 11.10, a.m.; 12.15, 1.0, 3.15, 4.45, 5.30, 7.45, 9.0, p.m.
Belsize park gardens - -	3.0, 9.15, 10.15, 11.15, a.m.; 12.15, 1.5, 3.15, 4.45, 5.30, 8.0, 9.0, p.m.

HAMPSTEAD DISTRICT—*continued*.

PILLAR BOXES.	TIMES OF COLLECTION.
Belsize rd. - - - -	3.0, 8.40, 9.40, 10.40, 11.40, a.m. ; 12.45, 2.40, 4.40, 5.15, 9.0, p.m.
Belsize sq. - - - -	2.55, 9.15, 10.15, 11.15, a.m. ; 12.15, 1.10, 3.15, 4.45, 5.30, 8.0, 9.0, p.m.
Daleham gardens - -	2.40, 10.0, 11.0 a.m. ; 12.0, 3.5, 4.25, 5.5, 9.0, p.m.
Downshire hill - -	3.0, 9.15, 10.15, 11.15, a.m. ; 12.15, 1.5, 3.20, 4.45, 5.30, 8.0, 9.0, p.m.
Fleet rd. - - - -	3.0, 9.0, 10.0, 11.0, a.m. ; 12.0, 1.0, 3.10, 4.45, 5.25, 9.0, p.m.
Hampstead heath -	2.45, 8.45, 9.45, 10.45, 11.45, a.m. ; 2.50, 4.45, 5.20, 9.0, p.m.
High st. Hampstead -	3.0, 8.55, 10.0, 11.0, a.m., 12.0 ; 1.0, 3.5, 4.45, 5.30, 8.0, 8.50, p.m.
Lyndhurst rd. - -	3.0, 9.25, 10.20, 11.20, a.m. ; 12.20, 1.10, 3.20, 4.45, 5.30, 8.0, 9.0, p.m.
Oak hill park, Hampstead -	2.50, 8.50, 9.55, 10.55, 11.55, a.m. ; 3.0, 4.45, 5.30, 9.0, p.m.
Well walk - - -	2.45, 9.0, 10.0, 11.0, a.m. ; 12.0, 12.55, 3.0, 4.45, 5.20, 7.50, 9.0, p.m.
Willoughby rd. - -	2.50, 9.0, 10.10, 11.10, a.m. ; 12.10, 1.0, 3.10, 4.45, 5.20, 9.0, p.m.
Winchester rd. - -	3.0, 8.50, 9.55, 10.55, 11.55, a.m. ; 12.40, 2.55, 4.40, 5.15, 8.0, 8.55, p.m.
WALL BOXES.	
Arkwright rd. - -	3.0, 9.0, 10.0, 11.0, a.m., 12.0 ; 3.5, 4.45, 5.30, 9.0, p.m.
Belsize avenue - -	3.0, 9.15, 10.10, 11.15, a.m. ; 12.15, 1.0, 3.15, 4.45, 5.30, 7.35, 9.0, p.m.
Finchley Road Station (Midland Railway)	2.50, 9.50, 10.50, 11.50, a.m. ; 4.35, 5.15, 8.45, p.m.
Finchley rd., N. L. Railway Station	2.50, 9.45, 10.45, 11.45, a.m. ; 4.35, 5.15, 8.40, p.m.
Fitzjohns' avenue - -	2.40, 10.0, 11.0, a.m., 12.0 ; 3.5, 4.25, 5.5, 9.0, p.m.
Gospel Oak Station (N.L. Railway)	3.0, 9.45, 10.45, 11.45, a.m. ; 2.50, 4.40, 5.25, 8.45, p.m.
Hampstead Heath Railway Station	3.0, 9.10, 9.55, 10.55, 11.55, a.m. ; 1.10, 2.55, 4.45, 5.30, 8.0, 9.0, p.m.
Haverstock ter. - -	3.0, 9.20, 10.20, 11.20, a.m. ; 12.15, 1.10, 3.15, 4.45, 5.30, 9.0, p.m.
Heath end - - -	8.30, a.m. ; 12.30, 2.45, 7.30, 9.30, p.m.
Heath st. - - -	2.45, 8.40, 9.45, 10.45, 11.45, a.m. ; 12.50, 2.50 4.40, 5.15, 7.55, 9.0, p.m.
King Henry's rd. -	3.0, 9.0, 10.0, 11.0, a.m., 12.0 ; 12.50, 3.0, 4.45, 5.25, 8.0, 9.0, p.m.
Lower ter., Hampstead -	2.45, 8.45, 9.50, 10.50, 11.50, a.m. ; 12.45, 2.55 4.40, 5.25, 9.0, p.m.
Merton rd. near Fellows rd.	3.0, 8.55, 9.55, 10.55, 11.55, a.m. ; 12.35, 2.55, 4.35 5.10, 8.0, 9.0, p.m.
South hill park gardens	2.55, 10.0, 11.0, a.m. ; 12.0, 3.0, 4.45, 5.30, 9.0, p.m.
Squires' mount - -	2.45, 8.55, 9.50, 10.50, 11.50, a.m. ; 2.55, 4.45, 5.15 9.0 p.m.
Upper Park rd. - -	3.0, 9.15, 10.15, 11.15, a.m. ; 12.15, 1.5, 3.15, 4.45 5.30, 9.0, p.m.
Vale of Health - -	2.45, 8.50, 9.50, 10.50, 11.50, a.m. ; 2.55, 4.45, 5.15 8.50, p.m.

HIGHGATE DISTRICT.

RECEIVING HOUSES.	TIMES OF COLLECTION.
*｜High st. Highgate (88) -	8.15, 9.15, 10.15, a.m. ; 1.15, 3.25, 5.10, 9.0, 12.0, p.m. Sunday 9.0 p.m.
Highgate Archway rd. (5) -	8.55, 9.30, a.m. ; 12.55, 2.40, 4.50, 8.40, 12.0, p.m. Sunday 8.55 p.m.
*North hill, Highgate -	8.50, 9.50, a.m. ; 12.50, 3.0, 4.45, 8.45, 12.0, p.m. Sunday 12.0 p.m.

PILLAR BOXES.

Archway rd. (opposite Jackson's lane)	8.50, 9.50, a.m. ; 12.50, 2.45, 4.50, 8.40, 12.0 p.m. Sunday 8.50 p.m.
Bishop wood rd. - -	8.55, 9.55, a.m. ; 12.55, 3.5, 4.50, 8.50, 12.0, p.m. Sunday 12.0 p.m.
Millfield lane - - -	8.45, 9.55, a.m.; 12.40, 4.45, 8.45, 12.0, p.m. Sunday 12.0 p.m.
The Grove, Highgate - -	9.0, 10.5, a.m.; 12.50, 3.10, 5.0, 9.0, 12.0, p.m. Sunday 12.0 p.m.

WALL BOXES.

Archway rd. (near Cholmeley park)	8.55, 9.35, a.m. ; 12.55, 2.45, 4.50, 8.35, 12.0, p.m. Sunday 8.55 p.m.
Archway rd. (near Railway station)	8.50, 9.50, a.m. ; 12.50, 2.50, 4.45, 8.30, 12.0, p.m. Sunday 8.50 p.m.
Church rd., North hill -	8.45, 9.45, a.m. ; 12.45, 2.55, 4.40, 8.40, 12.0, p.m. Sunday 9.0 p.m.
Holly ter., Highgate - -	8.55, 10.0, a.m. ; 12.45, 4.55, 8.50, 12.0. p.m. Sunday 9.0 p.m.
North hill - - - -	9.0, 10.0, a.m. ; 1.0, 3.0, 4.55, 8.55, 12.0, p.m. Sunday 9.0 p.m.
North rd. - - - -	8.40, 9.40, a.m. ; 12.40, 4.35, 7.30, 12.0, p.m. Sunday 9.0 p.m.
Southwood lane - - -	8.40, 9.40, a.m. ; 12.40, 4.35, 8.20, 11.0, p.m. Sunday 8.40 p.m.

KENTISH TOWN DISTRICT.

RECEIVING HOUSES.	TIMES OF COLLECTION.
*Highgate rd. (141) - -	2.55, 9.15, 10.15, 11.15, a.m. ; 12.15, 3.15, 4.15, 5.20, 9.0, p.m.
*†Fortess rd. (6) -	3.0, 8.30, 9.30, 10.30, 11.30, a.m. ; 12.30, 1.30, 2.30, 3.30, 4.30, 5.30, 7.40, 9.0, p.m.
*York rise (67 Carroll rd.) -	2.45, 9.0, 10.0, 11.0, 12.0, a.m.; 3.0, 4.0, 5.10, 8.50, p.m.

PILLAR BOX.

Highgate rd. - - -	3.0, 9.15, 10.15, 11.15, a.m. ; 12.15, 3.15, 4.15, 5.20, 9.0, p.m.

WALL BOX.

Lady Somerset rd. -	3.0, 9.15, 10.15, 11.15, a.m.; 12.15, 3.15, 4.15, 5.20, 9.0, p.m.

KILBURN DISTRICT.

BRANCH OFFICE.	TIMES OF COLLECTION.
High rd. (56) - - -	8.25, 9.25, 10.15, 11.10, a.m.; 12.10, 1.10, 3.15, 4.45, 5.30, 8.0, 9.0, 12.0, p.m. Sunday 12.0 p.m.

RECEIVING HOUSES.

Belsize rd. (196)- - -	8.30, 9.15, 10.15, 10.55, a.m.; 12.20, 1.15, 3 30, 4.30, 5.15, 9.0, 12.0, p.m. Sunday 12.0 p.m.
*†§High rd. (222) Kilburn -	9.0, 10.0, 10.45, 11.45, a.m.; 1.0, 3.0, 4.20, 5.10, 8.40, p.m.
•†Child's hill - - -	9.15, 10.20, a.m.; 12.30, 4.40, 8.25, 11.35, p.m Sunday 11.15 p.m.
*Cricklewood (Granville terrace)	9.20, 10.15, a.m.; 12.20, 4.35, 8.0, 10.0, p.m. Sunday 11.25 p.m.
*Cricklewood (Yew ter.) -	9.30, 10.25, a.m.; 12.30, 4.45, 8.15, 11.50, p.m. Sunday 11.35 p.m.
*†Gladstone ter. - -	7.30, 9.45, 10.45, 11.40, a.m.; 12.45, 4.15, 5.0, 8.30, 12.0, p.m. Sunday 12.0 p.m.
West end - - - -	9.30, 10.30, a.m.; 12.45, 4.50, 8.40, 11.50, p.m. Sunday 11.0 p.m.
West Hampstead (5 Exeter terrace)	9.30, 10.35, a.m.; 12.45, 4.25, 4.50, 8.45, p.m.

PILLAR BOXES.

High rd. (near Victoria rd.)	7.40, 9.0, 10, 10.50, 11.50, a.m.; 1.0, 3.0, 4.20, 5.15, 8.50, 12.0, p.m. Sunday 12.0 p.m.
High rd. (near Oxford rd.) -	8.15, 9.10, 10.15, 10.55, a.m., 12.0; 1.0, 3.10, 4.45, 5.20, 9.0, 12.0, p.m. Sunday 12.0 p.m.
Shoot-up hill Cricklewood -	9.40, 10.35, a.m.; 12.40, 4.50, 8.20, 12.0, p.m. Sunday 11.50 p.m.

WALL BOXES.

Cricklewood - -	9.30, 10.30, a.m.; 12.30, 4.50, 8.15, 12.0, p.m. Sunday 11.40 p.m.
Burgess hill (Finchley rd.)-	9.15, 10.25, a.m.; 12.30, 4.45, 8.30, 11.45, p.m. Sunday 11.10 p.m.
Mortimer rd. - - -	7.45, 9.15, 10.0, 10.55, a.m.; 12.0, 1.0, 3.15, 4.45, 5.15, 9.0, 12.0, p.m. Sunday 12.0 p.m.
West end lane (near Abbott's rd.	9.45, 10.55, a.m.; 1.0, 3.10, 4.25, 5.10, 9.0, 12.0, p.m. Sunday 12.0 p.m.
West End Station (Midland Railway)	9.30, 10.30, a.m.; 12.30, 4.20, 4.45, 8.30, 11.55, p.m. Sunday 11.45 p.m.
West Hampstead Station -	9.30, 10.35, a.m.; 12.45, 4.50, 8.40, 11.55, p.m. Sunday 11.40 p.m.

ST. JOHN'S WOOD DISTRICT.

RECEIVING HOUSES.	TIMES OF COLLECTION.
*§Boundary rd. (22) - -	8.0, 8.55, 10.0, 11.0, a.m.; 12.0, 1.0, 3.15, 4.45, 5.20, 8.0, p.m.
*Boundary rd. (108) - -	3.0, 8.30, 9.15, 10.15, 10.50, a.m.; 1.15, 3.30, 4.45, 5.15, 8.0, 8.45, p.m.

ST. JOHN'S WOOD DISTRICT—*continued*.

PILLAR BOXES.	TIMES OF COLLECTION.
Alexandra rd. - - -	3.0, 9.45, 10.55, a.m.; 12.0, 3.15, 4.45, 5.15, 8.0, 8.40, p.m. Sunday 12.0 p.m.
Avenue rd. (near St. Paul's Church)	3.0, 7.45, 9.50, 10.55, 11.50, a.m. ; 12.50, 3.0, 4.45, 5.15, 8.50, p.m.
Loudoun rd. - - - -	3.0, 8.0, 8.55, 10.0, 11.0, a.m.,; 12.0, 1.0, 3.15, 4.45, 5.20, 8.0, 9.0, p.m.
St. John's wood park - -	3.0, 7.45, 9.0, 10.0, 11.10, a.m. ; 12.0, 1.0, 3.15, 4.45, 5.20, 8.45, p.m.

UPPER HOLLOWAY DISTRICT.

RECEIVING HOUSES.	TIMES OF COLLECTION.
Dartmouth park hill - -	8.50, 9.50, 11.25, a.m. ; 12.45, 2.50, 3.50, 4.45, 8.40, 12.0 p.m.
*Junction rd. (103) - -	9.10, 10.0, 11.45, a.m.; 12.50, 3.10, 4.10, 5.15, 9.0, 12.0, p.m. Sunday 12.0 p.m.
*Junction rd. (247) - -	9.5, 9.55, 11.35, a.m.; 12.40, 3.5, 4.5, 5.0, 8.55, 12.0, p.m. Sunday 12.0 p.m.
PILLAR BOXES.	
Highgate hill - - -	9.10, 10.10, 11.45, a.m.; 1.5, 3.10, 4.10, 5.0, 9.0, 12.0, p.m. Sunday 12.0 p.m.
Hornsey lane - - -	9.0, 10.0, 11.30, a.m.; 12.50, 3.0, 4.0, 4.55, 8.50, 12.0, p.m. Sunday 12.0 p.m.
WALL BOXES.	
Chester rd., Highgate New town	8.45, 9.45, 11.20, a.m.; 12.40, 2.45, 3.45, 4.40, 8.35, 12.0, p.m. Sunday 12.0 p.m.
Dartmouth park hill(Central London Sick Asylum)	8.50, 9.50, 11.25, a.m. ; 12.45, 2.50, 3.50, 4.45, 8.40, 12.0, p.m. Sunday 12.0 p.m.
Dartmouth park hill (near Reservoir)	9.0, 9.50, 11.30, a.m. ; 12.35, 3.0, 4 0, 4.55, 8.50, 12.0, p.m. Sunday 12.0 p.m.

RATES OF POSTAGE OF INLAND LETTERS.

Inland Letters are those which pass between places in the United Kingdom, including the Isle of Man, the Orkney, Shetland, Scilly, and Channel Islands.

The rates of postage to be prepaid are as follows, viz. :—

For a letter not exceeding 1 oz. - 1d.
 ,, exceeding 1 oz. but not ex. 2 oz. 1½d.
 ,,   ,,   2 oz. ,,   4 oz. 2d.
 ,,   ,,   4 oz. ,,   6 oz. 2½d.
 ,,   ,,   6 oz. ,,   8 oz. 3d.
 ,,   ,,   8 oz. ,,   10 oz. 3½d.
 ,,   ,,   10 oz. ,,   12 oz. 4d.

A letter exceeding the weight of 12 oz. is liable to a postage of 1d. for every ounce, beginning with the first ounce. A letter, for example, weighing between 14 and 15 ounces must be prepaid 1s. 3d.

POST OFFICE TELEGRAPHS.

TARIFF.—The charge for the transmission of Messages by Telegraph throughout the United Kingdom (excepting the Scilly, Orkney, and Shetland Islands), is 1s. for the first twenty words, and 3d. for each additional five words or part of five words. The names and addresses of the sender and receiver are not charged for.

The cost of a reply to a telegram may be prepaid.

INLAND BOOK POST.

The postage is one halfpenny for every 2 ozs. or fraction of that weight.

Every book-packet must be posted either without a cover or in a cover open at both ends, and in such a manner as to admit of the contents being easily withdrawn for examination ; otherwise it will be treated as a letter.

No book-packet may exceed 5 lbs. in weight, or one foot six inches in length, nine inches in width, or six inches in depth.

POST CARDS.

Post Cards, which bear a halfpenny impressed stamp, and double or reply Post Cards, impressed with a halfpenny stamp on each portion of them, are available for transmission between places in the United Kingdom only.

INLAND PARCELS POST.

Parcels are received for transmission at any Post office under the following general conditions in regard to weights, dimensions, and rates of postage, viz. :—

For an Inland Postal Parcel of a weight
not exceeding 1 lb. - - 3d.
 ,, ex. 1 lb., and not ex. 3 lbs. - 6d.
 ,,   3 lbs., ,, ,, 5 lbs. - 9d.
 ,,   5 lbs., ,, ,, 7 lbs. -1s. 0d.

The size allowed for an Inland Postal Parcel is :—
    Maximum length - - 3ft. 6in.
    Maximum length and girth
      combined - - - 6ft. 0in.

EXAMPLES :—

A parcel measuring 3ft. 6in. in its longest dimension may measure as much as 2ft. 6in. in girth, *i.e.*, around its thickest part ; or—

A shorter parcel may be thicker ; *e.g.* —if measuring no more than 3 feet in length, it may measure as much as 3 feet in girth, *i e.*—around its thickest part.

The Regulations under which certain Articles are prohibited from transmission by the Letter Post will—with a few exceptions—apply equally to the Parcels Post. For instance, Gunpowder, Lucifer Matches, anything liable to sudden combustion, bladders containing liquid, and Live Animals, will be excluded from the Parcels Post.

But Glass Bottles, Fish, Game, Meat, and all other Articles not above mentioned, now excluded from the Letter Post, will be admitted to go by Parcels Post conditionally upon their being packed and guarded in so secure a manner as to afford complete protection to the contents of the Mails and to the Officers of the Post Office.

REGISTRATION.

By the prepayment of a fee of 2d. any letter, newspaper, book, or other packet on which the postage has been prepaid in stamps, may be registered to any place in the United Kingdom, the British Colonies, the United States of America, Austria, Germany, Italy, and Switzerland (viâ Belgium). To other Foreign Countries Letters only can be registered.

MONEY ORDERS.

When application is made for a Money Order payable in London, or at any other town where there is more than one Money Order Office, the remitter should say at which of such offices he wishes it to be paid, otherwise the Order can be cashed at the head office alone. The commission on Inland Money Orders is:—

For sums under............10s. - 2d.
For sums of 10s. and under £2 - 3d.

,,	£2	,,	£3 - 4d.
,,	£3	,,	£4 - 5d.
,,	£4	,,	£5 - 6d.
,,	£5	,,	£6 - 7d.
,,	£6	,,	£7 - 8d.
,,	£7	,,	£8 - 9d.
,,	£8	,,	£9 - 10d.
,,	£9	,,	£10 - 11d.
,,	£10	-	- 1s.

No Money Order business is transacted on the Sunday, Christmas Day, or Good Friday. Every Money Order must contain in full the Surname and the initial of one Christian name both of the remitter and the payee.

POSTAL ORDERS.

Postal Orders for certain fixed sums from 1s. to £1, are now issued to the public at all Post Offices at which Money Order business is transacted.

The following are the amounts for which Postal Orders are issued, together with the poundage payable in respect of such order :—

Amount.	Poundage.	Amount.	Poundage.
s. d.	d.	s. d.	d.
1 0	½	4 6	1
1 6	½	5 0	1
2 0	1	7 6	1
2 6	1	10 0	1
3 0	1	10 6	1
3 6	1	15 0	1½
4 0	1	20 0	1½

Broken amounts may be made up by the use of postage stamps not exceeding fivepence in value affixed to the back of any one postal order.

POST OFFICE SAVINGS BANKS.

Savings Bank business is transacted during the same hours as for Money Orders. The deposit may be 1s., or any number of shillings, but not fractional parts of a shilling. The amount of deposits under one name must not exceed £30 in one year, nor £150 (exclusive of interest) in the whole; but the depositor may save a second sum in the name of his wife, or child in conjunction. When the saving, together with the interest, amounts to £200, it is capitalised and not allowed to increase beyond that sum. The interest of £2 10s. per cent. allowed on every complete pound deposited is added to the principal every 31st Dec.

COLONIAL AND FOREIGN MAILS.

The Mails are made up for—

Australia, New South Wales, New Zealand, Queensland, and Tasmania, every Friday E., via Brindisi, and June 11th and every 4th Thursday, via San Francisco, 6d. under ½oz.

Austria, twice daily, 2½d. under ½oz.

Belgium, twice daily, 2½d. under ½oz.

Canada, every Thurs. E., via United States every Tues. and Sat., 2½d. under ½oz.

Cape Coast Castle, every Friday E., 4d. under ½oz.

Cape of Good Hope, every Thursday E., 6d. under ½oz.

Ceylon, every Friday E., 5d. under ½oz.

China, every Friday E., 5d. under ½oz.

Denmark, twice daily, 2½d. under ½oz.

Egypt, Tuesday E., Wednesday M., and Friday E., 2½d. under ½oz.

France and Algeria, twice daily, 2½d under ½oz.

Germany, twice daily, 2½d. under ½oz.

Gibraltar, twice daily, 2½d. under ½oz.

Greece, every Mon., M., & Tues., Thurs. and Saturday E., 2½d. under ½oz.

Holland, twice daily, 2½d. under ½oz.

India, every Friday E., 5d. under ½oz.

Italy, twice daily, 2½d. under ½oz.

Malta, Thursday and Friday E., and Saturday M., 2½d. under ½oz.

Mexico, via New York, 4d. under ½oz.

New Brunswick, Nova Scotia, and Prince Edward's Island, *same as Canada.*

Newfoundland, June 9th and every alternate Tuesday E., 2½d. under ½oz.

Norway, via Denmark, twice daily, 2½d.

Russia and Poland, twice daily, 2½d. under ½oz.

Spain and Portugal, twice daily, 2½d. under ½oz.

Sweden, via Belgium, twice daily, 2½d.

Switzerland, twice daily, 2½d. under ½oz.

United States, Tuesday, Thursday, and Saturday E., 2½d. under ½oz.

Vancouver's Island, British Columbia, *same as Canada.*

ENGLISH WEIGHTS AND MEASURES.

MEASURES OF LENGTH.

	In.	Ft.	Ys.	Pls.	Ch.	Fs.
Foot	12	1				
Yard	36	3	1			
Rod,pole,or perch ...	198	16½	5½	1		
Chain	792	66	22	4	1	
Furlong	7,920	660	220	40	10	1
Mile............	63,360	5,280	1,760	320	80	8

Mile, Geographical, 6,082·66 feet.

SQUARE OR SURFACE MEASURE.

	In.	Ft.	Yds.	Pls.	Ch.	R.
Square foot..	144	1				
Square yard.	1,296	9	1			
Rod,pole,or perch ...	39,204	272¼	30¼	1		
Square chain	627,264	4,356	484	16	1	
Rood.........	1,568,160	10,890	1,210	40	2½	1
Acre	6,272,640	43,560	4,840	160	10	4

A square mile contains 640 acres, = 2,560 roods, 6,400 chains, 102,400 rods, poles, or perches, or 3,097,600 square yards.

APOTHECARIES' WEIGHTS AND MEASURES, BY WHICH MEDICINES ARE COMPOUNDED.

20 Grains......... =1 Scruple .... = 20 grs.
3 Scruples ...... =1 Drachm .... = 60 „
8 Drachms ... =1 Ounce .... =* 480 „
12 Ounces ...... =1 Pound .... =*5760 „

* The Avoirdupois oz. of 437½ grains and the lb. of 7,000 grains are the weights named in the London Pharmacopœia, and the drugs are purchased by Avoirdupois weight.

AVOIRDUPOIS.

27 11/32 Grains.........=1 Drachm = 27·34375 Grns.
16 Drachms......=1 Ounce = 437·5 Grns.
16 Ounces ......=1 Pound =7000 Grns.
28 Pounds ......=1 Quarter
4 Quarters ......=1 Hundredweight
20 Cwt. ....=1 Ton

Avoirdupois weight is used in almost all commercial transactions and common dealings, but in addition to the above there are special weights for various articles, the chief of which are :—

A Stone of Butcher's Meat .... = 8 lb.
A Stone, Horseman's weight ...... = 14 „
A Firkin of Butter........................ = 56 „
A Firkin of Soft Soap .... = 64 „
A Quintal or Cental .... = 100 „
A Barrel of Gunpowder .... = 100 „
A Barrel of Raisins .... = 112 „
A Seam of Glass, 24 Stones .... = 120 „
A Barrel of Butter—4 Firkins...... = 224 „
A Barrel (or pack) of Soft Soap ... = 256 „
A Fodder of Lead, London & Hull = 19½ cwt.
„ „ Derby .... = 22½ „
„ „ Newcastle ...... = 21½ „
A Sack—Potatoes, 168 lb.; Coals, 224 lb.; Flour, 280 lb.
A Ream of Paper, 20 quires.
A Printer's Ream, 516 sheets

HAY AND STRAW.

Truss of Straw, 36 lb.
Truss of Old Hay, 56 lb.
Truss of New Hay (to September 1st), 60 lb.
Load, 36 Trusses = Straw, 11 cwt. 2 qrs. 8 lb.; Old Hay, 18 cwt.; New Hay, 19 cwt. 1 qr. 4 lb.

WOOL.

		cwt.	qr.	lb.
7 Pounds..............	=1 Clove	0	0	7
2 Cloves	=1 Stone	0	0	14
2 Stones	=1 Tod	0	1	0
6½ Tods	=1 Wey	1	2	14
12 Sacks	=1 Last	39	0	0

TROY WEIGHT.

3·17 Grains .... = 1 Carat
24 Grains .... = 1 Pennyweight (dwt.)
20 Pennyweights ... = 1 Ounce... 480 grns.
12 Ounces.............. = 1 Pound... 5760 „

TROY is the weight used by goldsmiths and jewellers. The grains Troy, Apothecaries, and Avoirdupois are equal, and the same in England, France, the United States, Holland, and in most other countries, but the carat varies: in France it is 3·18 grns., in Holland 3·0 grns., and in the U.S.A. 3·2. The jewellery ounce is divided into 151½ carats and 600 pearl grains.

STANDARD gold consists of 22 parts pure gold alloyed with 2 parts of copper or other metal, and according to the quantity of alloy is called 9, 12, 15, or 18 carat, *i.e.*, that quantity of pure gold out of the twenty-four. Standard silver is invariably of one fineness, viz., 11 oz. 2 dwt. fine to 18 dwt. alloy. One lb. of silver is coined into 66 shillings.

CUBIC OR SOLID MEASURE.

1728 Cubic Inches .... =1 Cubic Foot
27 Cubic Feet .... =1 Cubic Yard
40 Do. of Rough, or ...... / 50 Do. of Hewn Timber =1 Ton or Load
42 Cubic Feet of Timber... =1 Shipping Ton
108 Cubic Feet .... =1 Stack of Wood
128 Cubic Feet .... =1 Cord of Wood
40 Cubic Feet .... =1 Ton Shipping

A TON WEIGHT OF THE FOLLOWING WILL AVERAGE IN CUBIC FEET.

Earth	21	Pit Sand	22
Clay	18	River ditto	19
Chalk	14	Marl	18
Thames Ballast ...	20	Shingle	23
Coarse Gravel	19	Night Soil............	18

DRY OR CORN MEASURE.

4 Quarts.......................... = 1 Gallon
2 Gallons .... = 1 Peck
4 Pecks .... = 1 Bushel
4 Bushels, 1 Sack, or .... = 1 Coomb
8 Bushels, or two Coombs ... = 1 Quarter
5 Quarters........................ = 1 Load
10 Quarters .... = 1 Last
Boll of Meal=140 lb.; 2 Bolls= 1 Sack

Coals were formerly sold by measure, 3 bushels = 1 sack, 12 sacks = 1 chaldron. Coke, apples, potatoes, and some other goods are still sold by the sack of three bushels.

MEASURES OF TIME.

60 Seconds .... = 1 Minute
60 Minutes .... = 1 Hour
24 Hours .... = 1 Day
7 Days .... = 1 Week
28 Days .... = 1 Lunar Month
28, 29, 30, or 31 Days .... = 1 CalendarMnth
12 Calendar Months .... = 1 Year
365 Days .... = 1 Common Year
366 Days .... = 1 Leap Year

READY RECKONER,

MARKETING, OR HOURLY WAGES TABLE.

No.	¼d.	½d.	¾d.	1d.	2d.	3d.	4d.	5d.	6d.	7d.	8d.	9d.	10d.	11d.	No.
1	0 0¼	0 0½	0 0¾	0 1	0 2	0 3	0 4	0 5	0 6	0 7	0 8	0 9	0 10	0 11	1
2	0 0½	0 1	0 1½	0 2	0 4	0 6	0 8	0 10	1 0	1 2	1 4	1 6	1 8	1 10	2
3	0 0¾	0 1½	0 2¼	0 3	0 6	0 9	1 0	1 3	1 6	1 9	2 0	2 3	2 6	2 9	3
4	0 1	0 2	0 3	0 4	0 8	1 0	1 4	1 8	2 0	2 4	2 8	3 0	3 4	3 8	4
5	0 1¼	0 2½	0 3¾	0 5	0 10	1 3	1 8	2 1	2 6	2 11	3 4	3 9	4 2	4 7	5
6	0 1½	0 3	0 4½	0 6	1 0	1 6	2 0	2 6	3 0	3 6	4 0	4 6	5 0	5 6	6
7	0 1¾	0 3½	0 5¼	0 7	1 2	1 9	2 4	2 11	3 6	4 1	4 8	5 3	5 10	6 5	7
8	0 2	0 4	0 6	0 8	1 4	2 0	2 8	3 4	4 0	4 8	5 4	6 0	6 8	7 4	8
9	0 2¼	0 4½	0 6¾	0 9	1 6	2 3	3 0	3 9	4 6	5 3	6 0	6 9	7 6	8 3	9
10	0 2½	0 5	0 7½	0 10	1 8	2 6	3 4	4 2	5 0	5 10	6 8	7 6	8 4	9 2	10
11	0 2¾	0 5½	0 8¼	0 11	1 10	2 9	3 8	4 7	5 6	6 5	7 4	8 3	9 2	10 1	11
12	0 3	0 6	0 9	1 0	2 0	3 0	4 0	5 0	6 0	7 0	8 0	9 0	10 0	11 0	12
13	0 3¼	0 6½	0 9¾	1 1	2 2	3 3	4 4	5 5	6 6	7 7	8 8	9 9	10 10	11 11	13
14	0 3½	0 7	0 10½	1 2	2 4	3 6	4 8	5 10	7 0	8 2	9 4	10 6	11 8	12 10	14
15	0 3¾	0 7½	0 11¼	1 3	2 6	3 9	5 0	6 3	7 6	8 9	10 0	11 3	12 6	13 9	15
16	0 4	0 8	1 0	1 4	2 8	4 0	5 4	6 8	8 0	9 4	10 8	12 0	13 4	14 8	16
17	0 4¼	0 8½	1 0¾	1 5	2 10	4 3	5 8	7 1	8 6	9 11	11 4	12 9	14 2	15 7	17
18	0 4½	0 9	1 1½	1 6	3 0	4 6	6 0	7 6	9 0	10 6	12 0	13 6	15 0	16 6	18
19	0 4¾	0 9½	1 2¼	1 7	3 2	4 9	6 4	7 11	9 6	11 1	12 8	14 3	15 10	17 5	19
20	0 5	0 10	1 3	1 8	3 4	5 0	6 8	8 4	10 0	11 8	13 4	15 0	16 8	18 4	20
21	0 5¼	0 10½	1 3¾	1 9	3 6	5 3	7 0	8 9	10 6	12 3	14 0	15 9	17 6	19 3	21
22	0 5½	0 11	1 4½	1 10	3 8	5 6	7 4	9 2	11 0	12 10	14 8	16 6	18 4	20 2	22
23	0 5¾	0 11½	1 5¼	1 11	3 10	5 9	7 8	9 7	11 6	13 5	15 4	17 3	19 2	21 1	23
24	0 6	1 0	1 6	2 0	4 0	6 0	8 0	10 0	12 0	14 0	16 0	18 0	20 0	22 0	24
25	0 6¼	1 0½	1 6¾	2 1	4 2	6 3	8 4	10 5	12 6	14 7	16 8	18 9	20 10	22 11	25
26	0 6½	1 1	1 7½	2 2	4 4	6 6	8 8	10 10	13 0	15 2	17 4	19 6	21 8	23 10	26
27	0 6¾	1 1½	1 8¼	2 3	4 6	6 9	9 0	11 3	13 6	15 9	18 0	20 3	22 6	24 9	27
28	0 7	1 2	1 9	2 4	4 8	7 0	9 4	11 8	14 0	16 4	18 8	21 0	23 4	25 8	28
29	0 7¼	1 2½	1 9¾	2 5	4 10	7 3	9 8	12 1	14 6	16 11	19 4	21 9	24 2	26 7	29
30	0 7½	1 3	1 10½	2 6	5 0	7 6	10 0	12 6	15 0	17 6	20 0	22 6	25 0	27 6	30
33	0 8¼	1 4½	2 0¾	2 9	5 6	8 3	11 0	13 9	16 6	19 3	22 0	24 9	27 6	30 3	33
36	0 9	1 6	2 3	3 0	6 0	9 0	12 0	15 0	18 0	21 0	24 0	27 0	30 0	33 0	36
40	0 10	1 8	2 6	3 4	6 8	10 0	13 4	16 8	20 0	23 4	26 8	30 0	33 4	36 8	40
42	0 10½	1 9	2 7½	3 6	7 0	10 6	14 0	17 6	21 0	24 6	28 0	31 6	35 0	38 6	42
45	0 11¼	1 10½	2 9¾	3 9	7 6	11 3	15 0	18 9	22 6	26 3	30 0	33 9	37 6	41 3	45
48	1 0	2 0	3 0	4 0	8 0	12 0	16 0	20 0	24 0	28 0	32 0	36 0	40 0	44 0	48
50	1 0½	2 1	3 1½	4 2	8 4	12 6	16 8	20 10	25 0	29 2	33 4	37 6	41 8	45 10	50
51	1 0¾	2 1½	3 2¼	4 3	8 6	12 9	17 0	21 3	25 6	29 9	34 0	38 3	42 6	46 9	51
52	1 1	2 2	3 3	4 4	8 8	13 0	17 4	21 8	26 0	30 4	34 8	39 0	43 4	47 8	52
53	1 1¼	2 2½	3 3¾	4 5	8 10	13 3	17 8	22 1	26 6	30 11	35 4	39 9	44 2	48 7	53
54	1 1½	2 3	3 4½	4 6	9 0	13 6	18 0	22 6	27 0	31 6	36 0	40 6	45 0	49 6	54
56	1 2	2 4	3 6	4 8	9 4	14 0	18 8	23 4	28 0	32 8	37 4	42 0	46 8	51 4	56
60	1 3	2 6	3 9	5 0	10 0	15 0	20 0	25 0	30 0	35 0	40 0	45 0	50 0	55 0	60
72	1 6	3 0	4 6	6 0	12 0	18 0	24 0	30 0	36 0	42 0	48 0	54 0	60 0	66 0	72
84	1 9	3 6	5 3	7 0	14 0	21 0	28 0	35 0	42 0	49 0	56 0	63 0	70 0	77 0	84
100	2 1	4 2	6 3	8 4	16 8	25 0	33 4	41 8	50 0	58 4	66 8	75 0	83 4	91 8	100

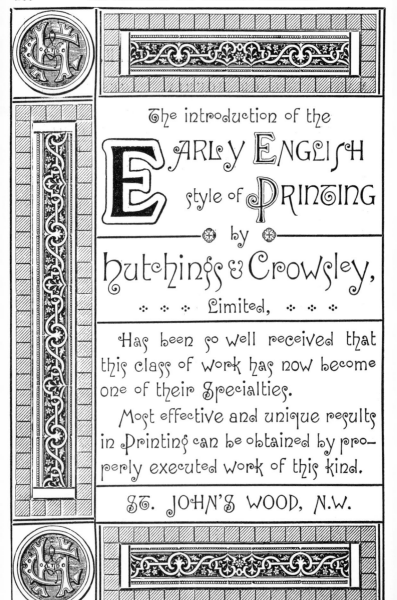

The introduction of the

EARLY ENGLISH

style of PRINTING

by

Hutchings & Crowsley,

Limited,

Has been so well received that this class of work has now become one of their Specialties.

Most effective and unique results in Printing can be obtained by properly executed work of this kind.

ST. JOHN'S WOOD, N.W.

PUBLIC MUSEUMS AND GALLERIES.

Bethnal Green Museum—Daily (except Sunday), Mon., Tues., Thurs., Fri., Sat., free; Wed., 6d.

British Museum, Great Russell st.—The Exhibition Galleries of the British Museum are open to the public free, as under :—Mon. and Sat., the whole of the galleries ; Tues. and Thurs., ditto—except the British, Mediæval, and Ethnography collections ; Wed. and Fri., ditto—except the Antiquities on the upper floor, and the rest of the department of Greek and Roman Antiquities. The hours of admission are from 10 till 4 in Jan., Feb., Nov., and Dec.; 10 till 5 in Mar., April, Sept., and Oct.; 10 till 6 in May, June, July, and Aug.; 10 till 7 on Mon. and Sat. only, from the middle of July to the end of Aug.; 10 till 8 on Mon. and Sat. only, from May 1st to the middle of July. Closed on Good Friday and Christmas Day.

College of Surgeons' Museum, Lincoln's-inn-fields (Hunterian Museum)—Mon., Tues., Wed., and Thurs., Members' Order; 11 till 5 from 1st Mar. to 31st Aug.; and from 11 till 4 from 1st Oct. till end of Feb. Histological collection is open on Thurs. from 11 till 5. Closed during Sept.

Dulwich Gallery—Every week-day from 10 to 5 in summer, and 10 to 4 in winter

Geological Museum, Jermyn st.—Mon. and Sat., 10 till 10 ; Tues., Wed., and Thurs., 10 till 5. Closed from 10th Aug. to 10th Sept., and at 4 from 1st Nov. to 1st March.

Hampton Court Palace—Every day in the year except Fridays & Christmas Day ; 1st April to 30th Sept., 10 to 6 ; 1st Oct. to 31st March 10 to 4 ; Sundays open at 2 p.m.

India Museum, Exhibition rd. South Kensington—The same regulations as the South Kensington Museum

Kew—The Botanic Gardens and pleasure grounds are open every week-day from noon till sunset (Christmas Day alone excepted) ; Sundays 1 till sunset ; and on Bank holidays, from 10 till sunset.

National Gallery—Mon., Tues., Wed., and Sat., from 10 to 6 in summer, and 10 to dusk in winter ; on Thurs. and Fri., students' days, the public are admitted after 12 o'clock on payment of 6d. Closed on Christmas Day and Good Friday.

New Palace of Westminster (Houses of Parliament); day of admission, Sat., also Mon. and Tues. in Easter and Whitsun weeks. Tickets (free) obtainable on the spot, at the Lord Chamberlain's Office.

Royal Academy of Arts, Burlington House, Piccadilly—Summer Exhibition 1st Mon. in May to 1st Mon. in Aug. ; Winter Exhibition, 1st Mon. in Jan. till 2nd Sat. in March. 1s. Gibson and Diploma Galleries, every day, 11 till 4—free.

Royal Astronomical Society's Library, Burlington House, Piccadilly—Personal introduction by a Fellow.

Royal United Service Institution Museum, Whitehall Yard—Daily (except Friday) by Members' tickets ; or by ticket obtainable from the secretary. N.B.—A stamped envelope must be forwarded.

Soane's Museum, 13 Lincoln's-inn-fields —Tues., Wed., Thurs., and Sat., in April, May, June, & Tues. and Thurs. in Feb., March, July, and Aug. ; 11 to 5—free.

Society of Arts, 18 John st., Adelphi— every day from 10 to 4, and Sat. 10 till 2—(Barry's paintings in the Lecture Theatre) ; tickets obtainable from Members or of the Secretary.

South Kensington Museum—Mon., Tues., and Sat., from 10 till 10, Free. On Wed., Thurs., and Fri., from 10 till 4, 5, or 6 according to season, 6d. each.

Tower of London, Armoury, Jewels, &c., Mon. & Sat. free; other days Armoury, 6d., Crown Jewels, 6d., 10 to 4. On free days during the months of May, June, July, Aug., and Sept. 10 to 6.

Windsor Castle State Apartments— Mon., Tues., Thurs., and Fri., April to Oct., 11 to 4; Nov. to Mar., 11 to 3, unless the Queen is in residence. Free. Albert Memorial Chapel—Wed., Thurs., Fri. and Sat. No tickets required.

Woolwich Arsenal—On Tues. and Thurs., by cards obtained by British subjects at the War Office, Pall Mall. Foreigners must apply to the representatives of their governments in this country.

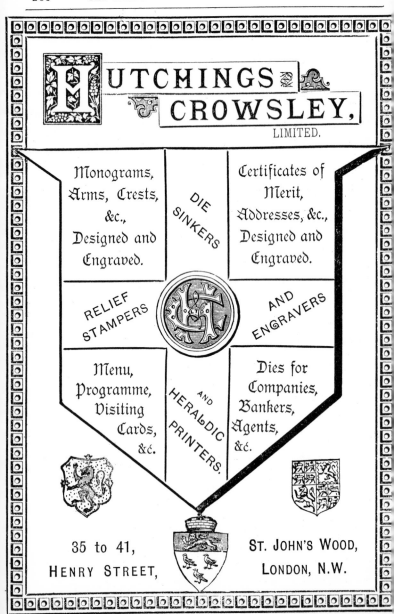

PUBLIC OFFICERS AND OFFICES.

———o———

MEMBERS OF PARLIAMENT.
County of Middlesex.

Coope Octavius E. 41 Up. Brook st. W.
Hamilton Lord George Francis 17 Montague st. Portman sq.

Borough of Finsbury.

Lusk Sir Andrew, bart. 15 Sussex sq. Hyde park
Torrens W. T. McCullagh, Brook's Club S.W.

Borough of Marylebone.

Chambers Sir Thomas, Q.C. 60 Gloucester pl. Portman sq.
Grant Daniel 12 Cleveland gardens Bayswater

SCHOOL BOARD FOR LONDON.
(Elected November, 1882)
Office—Victoria Embankment
Members for Finsbury.
Bourke W. R.
Lucraft Benjamin
Roberts Thomas
Wainwright Rev. Dr.

Webber Rev. W. Thomas Thornhill
Wilks Mark

Members for Marylebone.

Barker Rev. W., M.A.
Bond Edward
Bruce George B.
Diggle Rev. Joseph R.
Mills Arthur
Stanley Hon. E. L.
Westlake Mrs.

COUNTY COURTS.
BLOOMSBURY.

Court House—Great Portland st.
Judge—F. H. Bacon
Registrar—John Wright
High Bailiff—Robert Wright

MARYLEBONE.

Court House—179 Marylebone rd.
Judge—H. J. Stonor
Registrar—Charles Burrows
High Bailiff—Lambton Young

L

PARISH OF ST. JOHN, HAMPSTEAD.

PAROCHIAL OFFICERS.

Incumbent—Rev. Sherrard Beaumont Burnaby, M.A. (The Vicarage) Reddington rd.

Churchwardens—Alfred Bell (Bayford house) Rosslyn park, and Richard Hackworth 31 Belsize cres.

Overseers—F. J. Baker and F. W. Boden

VESTRY.

Offices—Vestry Hall, Haverstock hill.

Ex-Officio Members.

The Vicar and the Churchwardens

Elected Members.

I. will retire in 1886 ; II. will retire in 1887 ; III. will retire in 1888.

No. 1.—Town Ward.

I.

Clowser Thomas 27 High st.
Craigie Patrick George 6 Lyndhurst rd.
King Charles Bean 53 High st.
Mitton Edgar William 8 Eldon rd.
Phillips J. (Percy cottage) North end
Thompson Hy. 9 Hampstead hill gardens
Woodd Charles Henry Lardner (Rosslyn house) Lyndhurst rd.

II.

Elliot Edward 54 High st.
Hopton Charles (Rosland) Arkwright rd.
King Henry (Leverton house) Pond st.
Lake Ernest Edward 15 Lyndhurst rd.
Monro Frederic John 22 Thurlow rd.
Pritchard George 16 Heath st.
Watts Wm. Huson, The Hive, Green hill rd.

III.

Burford James (Norway house) High st.
Chamberlain Edmund Tye 192 Haverstock hill
Douglas-Hamilton Octavius (Langdale house) Denington park rd.
Hardcastle John (Beechenden) Heathfield gardens
Hewetson James 11 and 12 High st.
Pearse John Gardner 3 High st.
Williams Henry Ernest Thesiger 23 South hill park gardens
Auditor—John Griffiths James 4 and 5 Heath st.

No. 2.—Belsize Ward.

I.

Alford Fredk. Stephen 61 Haverstock hill
Baines Frdk. E., C.B. 17 Broadhurst gdns.
Bartlett Thomas Henry 57 Fellows rd.
Beckley Thomas 5 Mansfield villas
Dudman John 8 Upper Belsize ter.
Humphreys Richard 1 Belsize avenue

II.

Andrews Wm. Ward 29 Upper Park rd.
Aspinall William 119 Haverstock hill
Harben Hy. (Seaford lodge) 2 Fellows rd.
Mitton Welbury Jas. 46 Primrose hill rd.
Preston Alfred 26 Fellows rd.
Randall Thomas Gurney 6 Elizabeth ter.

III.

Alexander John 16 Eton rd.
Hanhart Nicholas 22 Steele's rd.
Harben Henry Andrade 68 Fellows rd.
Ratcliff Thomas Wm. 48 Stanley gdns.
Stone Simeon 7 Haverstock ter.
Wurtsburg Edwd. Albt. 46 Stanley gdns.
Auditor—Jno. Russell 129 Haverstock hill

No. 3.—Adelaide Ward.

I.

Belcher John Stafford 13 Swiss ter. Belsize rd.
Bridge Isaac, King's college mews
Hackworth Richard 31 Belsize cres.
Savigear Alfred, *The Swiss Cottage,* Finchley rd.
Turner William Coham 41 Belsize rd.

II.

Boden Joshua Wigley 47 Finchley new rd.
Dane Thomas 86 Finchley rd.
Fooks William Cracroft 21 Hilgrove rd.
Houghton Frank 4 King's college rd.
Russell William 20 Stanley gardens

III.

Battye Col. Geo. Money 11 College cres.
Cuff William Symes 45 Belsize rd.
Ellis Ralph Arthur Frederick William 7 Abbotts rd.
Evans John Edward 12 Albion rd.
Young Maj.-Gen. Ralph 70 Finchley new rd
Auditor—Thomas Browning 10 King's college rd.

No. 4.—Kilburn Ward.

I.

Baker Frederick John 172 Alexandra rd.
Buckingham James 91 Fairfax rd.
Nicholas John 25 Priory rd.
Robertson Josiah 96 High rd.
Roper William 36 High rd.
Shield Geo., *The Palmerston* 308 High rd.

II.

Baxter James 108 Boundary rd.
Dainton Samuel Joseph 234 Belsize rd.
Holman John 98 High rd.
Jones Samuel 212 Belsize rd.
Palmer Thomas 5 Abbey lane Kilburn
Pincham Richard, *Railway Hotel,* West end lane

III.

Aitchison Thomas 20 Sherriff rd.
Barrett Thomas Albert 41 Fairfax rd.
Farmer Leopold 12 High rd.
Hobson Thomas (Runnymeade) West
end lane
Turner Barrow 78 Abbey rd.
Wain James John 49 Fairfax rd.
Auditor—George Tawse 193 Belsize rd.
*Representative of the Vestry at the
Metropolitan Board of Works*—
Henry Harben (Seaford lo.) Fellows rd.

VESTRY OFFICERS.

Vestry Clerk—Thomas Bridger
Assistant Vestry Clerk—Alex.Wm.Baptie
Clerk—Ernest Carter
Medical Officer of Health—E.Gwynn, M.D.
Inspector of Nuisances—Geo. A. Smith
Assistant Inspector—William H. May
Surveyor—Charles Harlowe Lowe
Surveyor's Assistant—Francis Thompson
Clerks to the Surveyor—John William
Hudson, J. Williams, and H. Skipper.
Foreman of Roads—Robert Alaway
Hall Keeper—George Williamson
Messenger & Beadle—Benjamin Hill
Collectors of Parochial Rates—C. J.
Coates (Bedford villa) Willoughby rd.
Hampstead,andArthurWallis 1 Spring-
field rd.
Arrears Collector — James Culling
(Rutherford house) Messina avenue
DistrictSurveyor—KendallH.E.,Heath st.

HAMPSTEAD BURIAL BOARD.

Office—Vestry Hall, Haverstock hill.
Clerk—Alexander William Baptie
The Cemetery is at Fortune green. Notice
of burial must be given before 12 noon,
two days before the proposed interment. If for interment on Monday,
notice must be given on the preceding
Friday.
Superintendent—W. D. Cochrane.

HAMPSTEAD UNION.
GUARDIANS OF THE POOR.
EX-OFFICIO MEMBERS.

The Resident County Magistrates
ELECTED MEMBERS.
Aspinall William (Woodstock) Haver-
stock hill
Burnaby Rev. Sherrard Beaumont, M.A.
(The Vicarage) Redington rd.
Clowser Thomas 27 High st.
Ellis Ralph A. F. W. 80 Abbey rd.
Hill Frederic 27 Thurlow rd.

Mallet Rev. Henry Francis, M.A. 158
Haverstock hill
ParkerHy.Watson 2 Hampstead hill gdns.
Potter George William 22 High st.
Westlake Nathaniel H. J. (Falcon house)
Quex rd.
Wild Charles Kemp (Thornlea) Fitz-
john's avenue
YoungMaj.-Gen.Ralph 70Finchley new rd
Chairman—John Samuel Fletcher, J.P.
Vice-Chairman — Rev. Henry Francis
Mallet, M.A.

OFFICERS OF THE UNION.

Clerk to the Guardians—Thomas Bridger
Chaplain—Rev. Gerard A. Herklots, M.A.
Master of the Workhouse—J. H. Forbes
Matron—Mrs. Jane E. Rolt
Assistant to the Matron—Miss Rolt
Infirmary Superintendent—Mrs. Gold
Porter & Labour Master—Thos. Transom
Relieving Officer—Chas.Weekley,New end
*Medical Officers for the Workhouse and
the Outdoor Poor*—Dr. A. H. Cook 25
Denning rd. Hampstead, and Dr. F. A.
Hill 76 Abbey rd. St. John's wood
VACCINATION.
Public Vaccinator—A. H. Cook. At-
tends at 7 New end on the first four
Fridays in April, July, and October,
at 10 a.m. ; and at the Kilburn Provi-
dent Medical Institute, 1 Greville rd.,
on the second, third, and fourth
Fridays of the same months at noon.
Inspection is required on the Friday
following.
Vaccination Officer—Charles Weekley
BIRTHS, DEATHS, AND MARRIAGES.
SuperintendentRegistrar—Thos.Bridger,
Vestry hall Haverstock hill
Registrar of Births and Deaths—F. V.
Bridger, Vestry hall, Haverstock hill.
Office hours, 10 to 4; Saturdays 10 to
1. Attendance also at 12 Medley rd.,
Iverson rd., on Tuesdays and Fridays,
from 7 to 8 p.m.
Registrar of Marriages—Herbert E.
Bridger, Vestry hall Haverstock hill

ASSESSED INCOME & LAND TAX.
SURVEYORS.

For Wards 1 and 2—Nelson J. Lee 79
Haverstock hill Hampstead
For Wards 3 and 4—J. Dodson 159
Church st. Paddington
COLLECTORS.
Moore J. } 11 Belsize park ter.
Moore W. C. }

VOLUNTEER CORPS.

Third Middlesex Rifle Volunteer Corps,
A and B Companies' Head-Quarters
High st. Hampstead; Capt. C.G. Toller,
commandant

POLICE STATION.

Rosslyn hill, Hampstead
Inspectors—D. Collis and A. Darling

FIRE BRIGADE STATIONS.

Heath st. and Adelaide rd.

PETTY SESSIONS.

Police Station, Rosslyn hill.
A magistrate attends at the Police
Station, Rosslyn hill, every Wednesday
morning at 10 o'clock
Magistrates - Jas.Marshall,JosephHoare,
Edward Gotto, Basil Woodd Smith,
John Samuel Fletcher, Major-General
William Agnew, and E. P. Evans
Clerk to the Magistrates—Thos. Bridger

REMOVAL OF DUST.

Contractor— George Felton
Applications or complaints to be addressed (in writing) to the Superintendent of Dusting, Vestry hall, Hampstead N.W.

GAS LIGHT & COKE COMPANY.

Chief Office—Horseferry rd. Westminster
District Office—3 Holly mount
Inspector—Charles Hoyle

WATER COMPANIES.

New River Company.—Chief Office—
Clerkenwell E.C.
Secretary—Alexander Inglis
Collector—W. H. Hayes
Turncock—H. Robinson, Engine house,
Lower Heath, Hampstead

West Middlesex Water Works Company—
Chief Office—19 Marylebone rd. N.W.
Secretary--George B. Hall
Surveyor—Hamilton Rankin
District Inspector—C. R. Cleverly 1
Fordwych rd. Kilburn

PARISH OF HORNSEY.

——o——

Offices of Local Board and School Board—Southwood lane Highgate N.

PAROCHIAL OFFICERS, &c.

Rector—Rev. James Jeakes, M.A. (The Rectory) Hornsey

CHURCHWARDENS.

Reid Henry 26 Alexandra rd.
RobinsGilbert (Rathcoole)Tottenham ln

OVERSEERS.

Borley J. H. (Alpha cottage) Park rd.
Fleming F. W. 41 North rd. Highgate
Melluish C. B. 70 Mountgrove rd. South Hornsey

Poor Rate Collector—F. J. Potter, Muswell hill N.

Queen's Tax Collector—Lewis Jones 66a Ferme park rd. south

Surveyor of Taxes—N. J. Lee 79 Haverstock hill

Registrar of Births,Deaths & Marriages—Dr.Wall 75 Woodstock rd. Finsbury park. Office hours—Monday 10 a.m. to 1 p m. ; Tuesday 10 a.m. to 12 noon ; Wednesday 2 to 4 p.m. ; Thursday 10 a.m. to 1 p.m. ; Friday 6 to 7 p.m. ; Saturday 2 to 4 p.m.   At Local Board Offices, Highgate, on Fridays only 2 to 4 p.m.

LOCAL BOARD.

MEMBERS.

Chairman—H. R. Williams (Oak lodge) Jackson's lane Highgate
Bird Maj. J.W.(Woodside)Tottenham ln.
Clarke Joseph (North hill villa) Highgate N. *(deceased)*
Borley J. H. (Alpha cottage) Park rd. Crouch end
Catling C. (Inglethorpe) Broadlands rd. Highgate
Clay Major R. (Avenue ho.) Muswell hl.
Homewood S. T., North hill Highgate
Leighton G. C. (Fairlight) Shepherd's hill Highgate
Noble J. A., Eastern rd. Fortis green
Prestwich W. H. 36 Alexandra rd. Hornsey park N.
Redgrave Gilbert R. (Sunnyside) Muswell hill
Reynolds A. J. (Northfield) North rd. Highgate
Robins Gilbert (Rathcoole) Tottenham lane Hornsey
Turner C. (Stapleton hall) Stroud green
Wright Cory (Northwood) Hornsey lane Crouch end

OFFICERS.

Office hours, from 9 till 5.
Clerk—R. C. C. White
Assistant Clerk—C. F. Lawdham
Solicitor—A. C. Tatham
Surveyor—T. de C. Meade
Medical Officer—Dr. H. Clothier
Collector—W. Potter
Inspector of Nuisances—C. Dean
Building Inspector—George Poole

GUARDIANS OF THE POOR.

Hornsey (with part of Highgate) is one of the Parishes comprising the Edmonton Union, and returns eight members to the Board, viz.:

Bird John William(Woodside,)Hornsey
Clarke Joseph *(deceased)*
HarperJas.25Wilberforce rd.Finsburypk
Martin John High st. Highgate
Michell Matthew 1 High st. Stoke Newington
Pascoe William Thomas 41 Oakfield rd.
Richards Wm. Hy. 31 Stapleton hall rd.
Wickes Henry Adolphus (Ecclesfield) Seven Sisters rd. Finsbury park
Relieving Officer—W. W. Dew 4 New rd. Hornsey
Medical Officer & Public Vaccinator—Dr. Orton, Crouch end

HORNSEY SCHOOL BOARD.

MEMBERS.

Chairman—H. R. Williams (Oak lodge) Jackson's lane Highgate
Vice-Chairman—Walter Reynolds 9 The Grove Highgate
Alexander J. (Earlham) Crescent rd. Crouch end
Bird Major J. W. (Woodside) Tottenham lane Hornsey
Brand J. A. (Craigmillar) Avenue rd. Crouch end
Butler J. 1 Carlton rd. Stroud green
Catling C. (Inglethorpe) Broadlands rd. Highgate
CrossE.F.116Albion rd.StokeNewington
Jeakes Rev.J.,M.A.(TheRectory)Hornsey
Melluish C. B. 70 Mountgrove rd. Highbury N.
Tonkin T. W. T., B.A. 14 Alexandra villas Finsbury park
Clerk—R. C. C. White
Visitors—C. Battson, W. Newbold, and J. Nash

PARISH OF ST. PANCRAS.

PAROCHIAL OFFICERS.

Vicar—The Rev.Henry Donald Maurice Spence, M.A., J.P., Hon. Canon of Gloucester (The Vicarage) Gordon sq. W.C.

Churchwardens.

Dixon John William 1 South grove Highgate

Westacott Thos. Bentley 82 Camden rd.

Sidesmen.

Challen Charles 30 Oakley sq.

Whatmore William 4 Hampstead rd.

Overseers.

Davies Henry 149 Queen's cres.

Mahoney Michael 48 Clarendon sq.

All notices and applications for Licences required to be served on the Overseers must be addressed to them at the Vestry Hall

Parish Clerk.

Oliver Rev. W. E., LL.D. 22 Gordon sq., to whom notices of marriages,christenings, publication of banns, &c., for the Parish Church District only, are to be given in writing.

Verger and Beadle (St. Pancras Church) —R. Stone 5 Lancing st. Euston sq.

SPECIAL AND PETTY SESSIONAL DIVISION OF MAGISTRATES.

The Parish is a Division of the County of Middlesex. Special and Petty Sessions are held at 23 Gordon st. Gordon sq., for licensing, &c.

Clerk to the Magistrates — Walter Scadding

HIGH CONSTABLE OF
THE HUNDRED OF OSSULSTON.

Hoare Thomas 23 Gordon st. and 13 Woburn buildings Euston sq.

VESTRY.

Offices :—Vestry Hall, King's rd.

Meetings held on alternate Wednesdays at 3 p.m.

Ex-Officio Members.

The Vicar and the Churchwardens

Elected Members.

I. will retire in 1886 ; II. will retire in 1887 ; III. will retire in 1888.

Ward No. 1.

I.

Garratt George Anthony 389 Kentish town rd.

Greenwood Charles 17 Highgate rd.

Homan Reuben Alex. 8 Mansfield rd.

Jones Evan 115 Fortess rd.

Reddan Charles Peach 145 and 147 Queen's cres.

Wetenhall William James 2 Southampton rd. Maitland park

II.

Boden Anthony 34 Maitland park villas

Fox Alfred Benjamin 67 Weedington rd.

Furniss Robert 22 Grove ter.Highgate rd.

Marsh Alfred 9 Warden rd.

Sutton Matthew Bailey (Roseneath villa) Dartmouth park hill

Welch William 37 Leighton grove

III.

Beswick Benjamin 76 Carlton st.

Bolton Thomas 50 Carlton st. N.W.

Davies Henry 149 Queen's cres.

Lamble Samuel Richard (Stanley house) 52 Highgate rd.

Nash John 22a Lady Margaret rd.

Williams Thomas Howell 125 Fortess road

Ward No. 2.

I.

Bacon Oliver Batty 64 Chalk farm rd.

Fry Ernest Arthur 18a Haverstock hill

Harding Richard 20 Haverstock hill

Watkins James 36 Park st.

II.

Andrew Frederick 19 Chalk farm rd.

Beaves Thomas William 1 Lysander grove, St. John's hill Highgate hill

Johnson Job 73 Chalk farm rd.

Jones Thos. Charles 12 Chalk farm rd.

III.

Hone James 12 Wellington st.

Lucas Geo. Augustine,C.E.57 Victoria rd.

Reed Charles Henry 226 High st.

Upton Thos. Alfred 41 Kentish town rd.

Ward No. 3.
I.

Bell John, LL.D., M.A. 27 Caversham rd.

Bremner Thomas 8 Patshull rd.

Gittens Thomas William 134 High st.

Gittens William 112 & 114 High st.

Kent Richard 83 Patshull rd.

Noel Henry 182 Camden rd.

II.

Bennetts Capt.Roderick 132 Gt.College st.

Hall John Archibald 1 Camden rd.

Lyons Benjamin 6a Camden rd.

Page Henry 33 Torriano avenue

Smith Joseph 262 Camden rd.

Wilson Charles 5 Bartholomew rd.

III.

Barnes Edmund 39 Oseney cres.

Collins George 57 Pratt st.

Deverell John James 96 Camden rd.

Forsyth Dr. Anderson, 118 Gt. College st.

Guerrier William George 177 Camden rd.

Richards-Adams Rev. Edward 4 The Terrace Camden sq.

Ward No. 4.
I.

BrazierThos.10Rutland st.Hampstead rd

Harper Henry 82 Park st.

Harwood Charles 40 Delancey st.

Pearce George Henry 5 Mornington st.

Rex Charles William 1 Stanhope ter.

II.

Dart Henry 100 Park st.

Fowles Joseph 27 Delancey st.

Grantham George William 75 Park st.

Hignell Joseph Henry 125 & 167 Arlington rd.

Thornton William 164 Stanhope st.

III.

Hawes Thos. William 11 & 13 High st.

Higgs Frederick 94 Park st.

Osmond Joseph 58 Delancey st.

Smith Dr. Walter 2 Stanhope ter.

Soper Henry Charles 108 Park st.

Ward No. 5.
I.

Armstrong William 25 Edward st.

Attwater Walter 130 Drummond st.

Beere Louis Edward 23 Hampstead rd.

Snell Albion 15 Ampthill sq. N.W.

II.

Baker Frederick George 7 Hampstead rd.

Bryant William Henry 120 Albany st.

Cooper Henry 46 George st.

Cremer William Randall 7 George st.

III.

Isom Benjamin 86 Osnaburgh st.

Lancaster John Bulgin Snow 2 Osnaburgh st.

Ross Thomas 70 Hampstead rd.

Sweet Andrew 102 Hampstead rd.

Ward No. 6.
I.

Balderson Isaac 36 Chalton st. Euston rd.

Harwood Chas. William 2 and 3 Gee st.

Humphreys James 198 Seymour st.

Miles Edwin 90 Chalton st.

Purchese Frederick 45 Ossulston st.

Smith John William 14 Seymour st.

II.

Brown Alfred Dyball 16a Clarendon sq.

Ives William 175 Pancras rd.

Mahoney Michael 48 Clarendon sq.

Moore Edwin George 38 Eversholt st.

Robinson Nathan 105 and 106 Chalton st. Euston rd.

III.

Baker William 29 Eversholt st.

Brown Charles 32 Chalton st. N.W.

Perry William Thurston 53 Aldenham st.

Roberts Stephen Charles 107 Chalton st.

Wills William John 168 Euston rd.

Ward No. 7.
I.

Bower William 96 Tottenham court rd.

Buchanan John 30 Fitzroy st.

Coleing Charles 135-9 Hampstead rd.

Haine John Weeks 38 Fitzroy st.

Read Samuel 3 Howland st.

II.

Glazier Jno.Thos.193Tottenham court rd.

Kingston Thos. 11 & 12 Southampton st.

Knott George 45 Fitzroy st.

Myers Lewis Michael 19 Tottenham court rd.

Ravenhill Samuel 13 Percy st.

III.

Brown George 162 Hampstead rd.

Cooper Thomas 24 Gresse st. W.

Guy Thomas 179a Tottenham court rd.

Homer John Frederick 2 Goodge st. W.

Roberts Obed 38 Tottenham court rd.

Ward No. 8.

I.

Armstrong Henry 43 Manchester st.
Champ Robert 12 Mabledon pl.
Davison William 282 Gray's inn rd.
Eldridge Alfred 55 Euston rd.
Pratt Edward 11 Regent sq.

II.

Balfour James 77 Marchmont st.
Beauchamp John 205 Gray's inn rd.
Jackson James 83 Guilford st.
Saville John 1 Argyle sq.
Wood Daniel John 157 King's cross rd.

III.

Holman Walter 141 King's cross rd.
Matthews William Henry 276 Gray's
  inn rd.
Michael George 74 to 78 Judd st.
Perkins George 31 Liverpool st.
Sugar James 143 King's cross rd.

AUDITORS.

Abercrombie Hy. David 41 Fitzroy st. W.
Bilby Robt. Wm. 77 Caversham rd. N.W.
Lupton Geo. Edwin 32 George st. N.W.
Napier Alexander 50 & 52 Seymour st. N.W.
Wills Wm. Francis 11 Patshull rd. N.W.

MEMBERS OF THE METROPOLITAN BOARD OF WORKS.

Furniss Robt. 22 Grove ter. Highgate rd.
Wetenhall Wm. Jas. 2 Southampton rd.

ASSESSMENT COMMITTEE.

Baker Frederick George 7 Hampstead rd.
Baker William 29 Eversholt st.
Beaves Thomas William 1 Lysander
  grove St. John's hill Highgate hill
Brazier Thomas 10 Rutland st. Hamp-
  stead rd.
Gittens William 112 and 114 High st.
Hoppey James 113 Great College st.
Kent Richard 83 Patshull rd.
Lamble Samuel Richard (Stanley house)
  52 Highgate rd.
Mahoney Michael 48 Clarendon sq.
Osmond Joseph 58 Delancey st.
Thornton William 164 Stanhope st.
  Regent's park
Wilson Charles 5 Bartholomew rd.

BURIAL BOARD.

Office—Vestry Hall, Pancras rd.
Clerk to the Board and Registrar—
  Charles Greene

ST. PANCRAS CEMETERY.
Finchley, N.
(Two miles from the northern Boundary
  of the Parish.)
Superintendent—Frederick Dunsford
  The Cemetery is open to the public
on week-days from 9 a.m., & on Sundays
from half-past 1 p.m., and is closed at
7 in the evening from the 1st of April to
the 1st of May, at sunset from the
1st of September to the 31st of March,
and at 8 p.m. during the months of May,
June, July, and August.

MEMBERS OF THE BURIAL BOARD.

I. will retire in 1886 ; II. will retire in
  1887 ; III. will retire in 1888.
I.
Greenwood Charles 17 Highgate rd.
Hoppey James 113 Great College st.
Wetenhall William James 2 Southamp-
  ton rd. Maitland park
II.
Coleing Charles 135 Hampstead rd.
Kent Richard 83 Patshull rd.
Champ Robert 12 Mabledon pl.
III.
Not elected at time of going to press.

PUBLIC BATHS & WASHHOUSES.

King st. Camden town, Robert Hibbert,
  superintendent ; and Whitfield st. Tottenham court rd., William Reid,
  superintendent
Clerk—George Harrison

COMMISSIONERS FOR PUBLIC BATHS AND WASHHOUSES.

I. will retire in 1886 ; II. will retire
  in 1887 ; III. will retire in 1888.
I.
Osmond Joseph 58 Delancey st.
Thornton William 164 Stanhope st.
II.
Beaves Thomas William 1 Lysander
  grove St. John's hill Highgate hill
Welch William 37 Leighton grove
Westacott Thomas Bentley 82 Camden
  road
III.
Not elected at time of going to press.

OFFICERS OF THE VESTRY.

Vestry Clerk & Clerk to the Directors of the Poor—Thomas Eccleston Gibb
Accountant—William Frederick Bellamy
Chief Clerk—George Harrison

Collectors of Rates.

Ward 1—William Robert Green 5 Burghley rd. ; attendance on Mondays, Wednesdays, and Fridays from 10 to 4.

Ward 2—William Lawford 31 Prince of Wales rd.; attendance on Tuesdays and Thursdays from 10 to 4.

Ward 3—John Salmon 1 Oseney cres. ; attendance on Mondays, Wednesdays, and Fridays from 10 to 5.

Ward 4—Henry Fletcher 75 Arlington rd. ; attendance on Tuesdays and Thursdays from 9 to 4.

Ward 5—Walter Crane 29 Robert st. ; attendance on Mondays & Thursdays from 10 to 3.

Ward 6—William Henry Clisby 44 Charrington st. ; attendance on Mondays and Thursdays from 11 to 3.

Ward 7—Richard Westbrook 39 Fitzroy st.; attendance on Tuesdays and Thursdays from 10 to 3.

Ward 8—Charles Horatio Witt 85 Euston rd.; attendance on Tuesdays and Fridays from 10 to 3.

Inquiring and Collecting Officer.
Love Percy

Office for Stamping Weights and Measures.

Gibson John Howieson, stamper & inspector, Vestry Hall, Pancras rd., N.W. Tuesdays & Fridays from 9 to 12 at noon.

District Surveyors.

West—Frederick Wallen 106 Gower st.
North—Alfd. Bovill 24 Grove rd. Highgate rd.
East—Vincent John Grose 26 Werrington st.

DEPARTMENT OF WORKS.

Office—Vestry Hall
Chief Surveyor—Wm. Booth Scott, C.E.
Chief Clerk—Charles Worrell

Assistant Surveyors.
For Western District—Geo. Fredk. Ellis
For Central District—Chas. Isaac Booth
For Northern District—Robert Alaway
For Eastern District—Albert Nicholls Hawtrey

SANITARY DEPARTMENT.

Office—Vestry Hall
Medical Officer of Health & Examiner of Gas—
Analyst—Thomas Stevenson, M.D.
Clerk—Henry Dempsey
Sanitary Inspectors—
William Rouch 27 Wellington st.
Peter Fulton 29 Robert st.
John William Bartlett 5 Harrison st. Gray's inn rd.

Vestry Beadles—Charles Jessop and George Smith

BOARD OF GUARDIANS.

ST. PANCRAS WORKHOUSE.

The Union is at King's rd. St. Pancras, adjoining the Vestry Hall. The Board meets on alternate Thursdays at 4 p.m.
Office—Vestry Hall.

EX-OFFICIO MEMBERS.

Allen James Henry, J.P. 2 Chester ter.
Bodkin William Peter, J.P. (Merton house) West hill Highgate
Goslett Alfred, J.P., West hill Highgate
Kerr Robert Malcolm, J.P., D.L., LL.D. 7 Chester ter. Regent's park
Rashleigh Jonathan, J.P. 3 Cumberland terrace
Stilwell John Gilliam, J.P. 33 Gordon sq.
Wyatt Sir William Henry, J.P. 88 Regent's park rd.

ELECTED MEMBERS.

Adams William, F.R.C.S. (Tower lodge) Regent's park rd.
Balfour James 77 Marchmont st.
Boden Anthony 34 Maitland park villas
Bower William 96 Tottenham court rd.
Bradley William 36 Fitzroy st.
Brinsmead John 16 Albert rd.
Byrne Joseph 225 Kentish town rd.
Champ Robert 12 Mabledon pl.
Dampier Emily 8 Chester ter.
Drew George Henry 6 Cumberland ter.
Goodall Josiah Montague (Linden house) The Grove Highgate rd.
Guerrier William George 177 Camden rd.
Lancaster John B. S. 2 Osnaburgh st.
Lidgett Elizabeth S. 40 Gordon sq.
Potts William, F.R.C.S. 2 Albert ter. Albert rd.
Purchese Frederick 45 Ossulston st.
Richards-Adams Rev. Edward, M.A. (St. Paul's Vicarage) Camden rd.

Robinson Nathan 105 & 106 Chalton st.
Saville John 1 Argyle sq.
Sutton Matthew Bailey (Roseneath villa) Dartmouth park hill
Watkins James 36 Park st.

OFFICERS OF THE WORKHOUSE.
Clerk to the Guardians—Alfred A, Millward
Assistant Clerk and Collector—Vacant
Master—Captain Thomas Miller
Matron—Elizabeth Singleton
Chaplain—Rev. Francis Leedham
Medical Officer—Walter M. Dunlop
Dispenser—W. F. Barkway

Relieving Officers.
Ward No. 1. (North of the Midland Railway) Joseph Stevens 21 Carrol rd.
,, ,, 1. (South of the Midland Railway) Edward Giraud 46 Maitland park rd.
,, ,, 2. Henry Payton 155 Prince of Wales rd.
,, ,, 3. Wheatley William 14 St. Paul's rd.
,, ,, 4. Chas. Taylor 93 Albert st.
,, ,, 5. John E. Lake 20 Robert st.
,, ,, 6. George J. Moon 18 Platt st.
,, ,, 7. H. H. Woodwell 47 Fitzroy street
,, ,, 8. John Wright 19 Harrison st. or 37 Argyle sq.

RELIEF STATIONS.
For Wards 1, 2 and 3—Bower cottage Leighton grove
For Wards 4, 5, 6, 7 and 8—Clarendon sq. Somers town

District Medical Officers.
1st. Reuben Thos. Warn 37 Highgate rd.
2nd. Claremont Louis Bennett 31 Malden crescent
3rd Andrew Brown 1 Bartholomew rd.
4th. Walter Smith 2 Stanhope ter. Gloucester gate
5th. Thomas Sayer 43 Ampthill sq.
6th. John Thompson, M.D. 70 Oakley sq.
7th. Thomas C. Murphy 1 Francis st. Tottenham court rd.
8th. Sydney Lloyd Smith 32 Argyle sq.

Midwives.
Drake Mary 11 Tonbridge st. W.C.
Jones Caroline C. 284 Kentish town rd.
Wood Caroline 20 Prince of Wales cres.

Public Vaccinator.
(Appointed to vaccinate persons resident in the parish *without charge*.)
Claude Clarke Claremont, M.R.C.S. (Millbrook house) Hampstead rd.
Attends at—
Camden Hall, King st., Monday 11 a.m.
103 Euston rd., Thursday 11 a.m.
327 Kentish town rd., Tuesday 11 a.m.
36 Prince of Wales rd., Wednesday 11 a.m.
15 Winscombe st. Highgate, three first Mondays in January, April, July, and October

Vaccination Officers.
Richards John Henry, St. Pancras Vestry Hall
Webb Richard, St. Pancras Vestry Hall

REGISTRATION OF BIRTHS, DEATHS, AND MARRIAGES.
Superintendent Registrar—Alexander James Davis, Vestry Hall

Registrars of Births and Deaths.
Bradley Henry James 36 Fitzroy st. W.; attendance 6.30 to 8.30 p.m. and 8 a.m. on Tuesdays to Fridays
Greene Charles 13 Goldington cres.; attendance 9 to 11 a.m.
Hacker Edward 34 Rochester sq.; attendance 9 to 11 a.m.
Lance Martineau F. 14 Great College st.; attendance 12 noon to 4 p.m. and Saturdays 12 noon to 2 p.m.
Spong Samuel 14 Granby st.; attendance 1 to 2.30 and from 6 to 8 p.m.; Saturdays 4 to 7 p.m.
Worrell Charles 10 Argyle sq.; attendance 6.30 to 8.30 p.m. and Tuesdays to Fridays 8 a.m.

Registrars of Marriages.
Lance Martineau F. 14 Great College st.
Pierce James 8 Gaisford st.

SURVEYORS AND COLLECTORS OF LAND, ASSESSED, AND INCOME TAXES.
Surveyors.
Coles Henry 188 Euston rd.
Male W. 38 John st. Bedford row

Collectors.
Burrows Wm. George 60 Charrington st.
Hubbard Mark 333 Kentish town rd.
Rex Charles William 1 Stanhope ter.
Sherrard E. M. 8 Cromer pl.
Smith George John 82 Chalk farm rd.
Wilson Charles 130 Kentish town rd.

INLAND REVENUE OFFICES.

247 Hampstead rd.

Supervisor—W. J. Terry
Collector—W. Bradley
Chief Clerk—A. Appelbe
Clerks—S. A. Armatys, O. Marriage, H. V. Robb. and S. Evans
Officers—Michael Grace, J. W. Colville, Frank Mann, and Robert F. Jacobs

188 Euston rd.

Supervisor—John Marshall
Officers—Phillip H. M. Jamieson, James Armstrong, John Prout, and Henry Pritchard

METROPOLITAN FIRE BRIGADE.

(*Stations in and near this Parish at which there is a constant attendance of Firemen by day and night.*)

King's rd., corner of Pratt st.
Theobald's rd.
171 Great Portland st.
Willow walk, Kentish town
Essex rd. Islington
Farringdon rd., corner of Cobham rd.
Night station, Pond sq. Highgate

FIRE ESCAPE STATIONS.

(*Each attended all night by a Conductor.*)

Battle Bridge—King's Cross
Camden Road—North-west gate of Cattle Market
Camden Street—At junction of Camden st. and Kentish town rd.
Camden Town—Opposite the "Cobden Statue," High st.
Euston Road—In front of Trinity Church
Euston Square—In front of St. Pancras Church
Guildford Street—Foundling Hospital
Highgate—Pond sq.
Kentish Town—Opposite the "Moreton Arms " 65 Kentish town rd.
Tottenham Court Road—By Whitfield's Chapel

METROPOLITAN POLICE.

" Y " or Highgate Division.

Police Stations—Grove pl., Highgate ; Kentish town rd. ; Platt st. Somers town.

The Commissioner of Police of the Metropolis has appointed the under-mentioned places in the " Y " or Highgate Division, as fixed points where a Police Constable is to be permanently stationed from 9 a.m. to 1 a.m. The Police stationed at these points are at all times ready to render assistance as may be required :—

Near the *Nag's Head*, Seven Sisters' rd.
North London Railway Station, at corner of Camden rd and College st.
Corner of Malden rd., in Prince of Wales rd.
York rd., at corner of St. Paul's rd.
Pancras rd., under Railway Arch
Junction of Southampton and Circus roads, Haverstock hill
Chalton st., at junction of Churchway and Chapel st. Somers town

CORONER.

(*For Central Middlesex.*)

Danford Dr. Thomas, Coroner's office, Park lodge, Park place villas W.

DEPUTY CORONER.

Westcott Dr. Wynn, M.B. LOND. 4 Torriano avenue

CORONER'S BEADLE.

Beazley Thomas H. 61 College pl., where information relating to Coroner's Inquests is to be given

GAS COMPANY.

The Gas Light and Coke Co. Office :— Horseferry rd. Westminster ; John Orwell Phillips, secretary. District office :—9 Camden rd ; Chas. Roberts, resident inspector

WATER COMPANIES.

The New River Co. Office :—New River Head, near Sadler's Wells Clerkenwell E.C. ; James Searle, secretary

Collectors.

Barnett George J. 134 High st. ; Wednesday and Friday 12 to 1.
Disney Thomas William 130 Kentish town rd. ; Tuesday and Friday 1 to 2.
Napton Alfred H. 213 Seymour st. ; Tuesday and Friday 2 to 3.
Sage Christopher P. 27 Tavistock pl. ; Wednesday and Friday 12 to 1.
Shiers Richard 26 Great Russell st. Bloomsbury ; Tuesday and Friday 2 to 3.
Stevens Henry 82 Chalk farm rd. ; Friday 2 to 3.
Yeoman William 67 Junction rd. ; Wednesday and Friday 11 to 12.

Turncocks.

Carter James (*foreman*) 4 Raglan cottages Anglers' lane

ChildsWilliam 2 Spring row Mansfield pl.

Cumbers Henry, Camden reservoir, Clifton rd.

Filler Alfred 1 Little Drummond st. Euston sq.

Filler Henry 1 High st. Highgate

Gill Benjamin 22 Frideswide pl.

Huson James 7 Charlton King's rd. Torriano avenue

Limmer George 120 Arlington rd.

Middleton William (*foreman*) 12 Magdala rd. Dartmouth park hill

Reddick William 103 Castle rd.

Richardson Alfred 1 Wellesley st. Euston square

Searle Zebulon (Chameleon cottage) Pond sq. Highgate

Staines William 70 King st.

Wood William 57 Prince of Wales crescent

West Middlesex Water Works Co.

Office :—19 Marylebone rd. ; George Barton Hall, secretary ; Hamilton Rankin, surveyor ; G. H. Jewell, inspector

Collectors.

Davies F. C., at 19 Marylebone rd. on Tuesdays, 12.30 to 1.30 ; & at 222 Great Portland st. on Thursdays, 1 to 4

Rivers Walter, at 19 Marylebone rd. on Tuesdays, 12 to 2 ; and on Wednesdays from 11 to 4

Turncocks.

Farrell William and Ayres Stephen 65 Augustus st. Regent's park

Ladd George and Chatterley W. S. 12 Booth's pl. Wells st.

Lay John, jun. 10 Warren st.

Lay John, sen. (*foreman*) 8 Kingstown st. Princess ter. Regent's park

Willes William and Kesten John 9 Kingstown st. Regent's park